APA PUBLICATIONS L

Part of the Langenscheidt Publishing Group

☀ INSIGHT GUIDE
WESTERN EUROPE

Editorial

Project Editor
Siân Lezard
Art Director
Ian Spick
Picture Manager
Steven Lawrence
Series Manager
Rachel Fox

Distribution

UK & Ireland
GeoCenter International Ltd
Meridian House, Churchill Way West
Basingstoke, Hampshire RG21 6YR
sales@geocenter.co.uk

United States
Ingram Publisher Services
One Ingram Blvd, PO Box 3006
La Vergne, TN 37086-1986
customer.service@ingrampublisher
services.com

Australia
Universal Publishers
PO Box 307
St Leonards, NSW 1590
sales@universalpublishers.com.au

New Zealand
Hema Maps New Zealand Ltd (HNZ)
Unit 2, 10 Cryers Road
East Tamaki, Auckland 2013
sales.hema@clear.net.nz

Worldwide
**Apa Publications GmbH & Co.
Verlag KG (Singapore branch)**
7030 Ang Mo Kio Ave 5
08-65 Northstar @ AMK
Singapore 569880
apasin@signet.com.sg

Printing

CTPS – China

©2010 Apa Publications GmbH & Co.
Verlag KG (Singapore branch)
All Rights Reserved

First Edition 1984
Sixth Edition 2010
Reprinted 2011

CONTACTING THE EDITORS
We would appreciate it if readers
would alert us to errors or out-
dated information by writing to:
**Insight Guides, P.O. Box 7910,
London SE1 1WE, England.**
insight@apaguide.co.uk

ABOUT THIS BOOK

The first Insight Guide pioneered the use of creative full-colour photography in travel guides in 1970. Since then, we have expanded our range to cater for our readers' need not only for reliable information about their chosen des- tination but also for a real under- standing of the culture and workings of that destination. Now, when the internet can supply inexhaustible (but not always reliable) facts, our books marry text and pictures to provide those much more elusive qualities: knowledge and discern- ment. To achieve this, they rely heavily on the authority of locally based writers and photographers.

Insight Guide: Western Europe is structured to convey an understand- ing of the continent and its diverse countries as well as to guide readers through its myriad attractions:

◆ The **Features** section, indicated by a pink bar at the top of each page, provides a brief history of the region, followed by an illuminating A to Z of European cultural mores, from Archi- tecture to Zeitgeist via Food, Kissing and Umbrellas.
◆ The main **Places** section, indi- cated by a blue bar, is a complete guide to all the countries and sights worth visiting. Places of special interest are coordinated by number with the maps.
◆ The **Travel Tips** listings section, with a yellow bar, starts with an over- view of useful information applying to the whole of Western Europe, then provides tips for each individ- ual country; how to get there and get around, and an A to Z section of essential practical information. An easy-to-find contents list for Travel Tips is printed on the back flap, which also serves as a bookmark.

Italy specialist, **Susie Boulton**, acquired her abiding passion for the country as a student when she worked on an archaeological dig in Arezzo, and has been going back every year since then. Susie is the author of some 20 guidebooks, including titles on Venice, Milan, Sardinia and the Italian Riviera. **Marc Dubin** has been writing about Greece for more than three decades, on such diverse subjects as traditional music and back-country hiking. He currently lives on Samos.

Anthony Lambert wrote the photo feature on Europe's railways and updated the chapter on Switzerland; he has written or contributed to many travel books, including *Switzerland without a Car*, and also writes for the national press.

Travel writer **Josephine Quintero** updated Portugal. A resident of Andalusia in southern Spain, she travels frequently to neighbouring Portugal, a country which never fails to charm and surprise. The Modern Times and Europe from A to Z features were updated by **Derek Blyth**, who also wrote the Art Galleries photo feature. Currently editor-in-chief of the Belgian weekly magazine *The Bulletin*, he is uniquely placed in the capital of Europe to observe the endless diversity of European culture. **Ben Le Bas** wrote the Wildlife photo feature. **Tom Le Bas**, managing editor at Insight Guides, compiled and wrote the Best of Western Europe spreads.

The picture editors were **Tom Smyth** and **Steven Lawrence** and the designer was **Louise Boulton**. The book was proofread by **Neil Titman** and the index was created by **Helen Peters**.

The contributors

This fully revised and updated edition of the popular *Insight Guides: Continental Europe* was managed and edited by **Siân Lezard** at Insight Guides' London office. It builds on the foundations of the previous edition, overseen by **Roger Williams**, who compiled the Europe from A to Z feature with **Brian Bell**, one of Insight Guides' founding editors.

Renamed *Insight Guides: Western Europe*, this new book draws on the specialist knowledge of several writers. **Nick Inman**, a freelance travel writer specialising in France (where he lives) and Spain, updated these countries, and wrote the photo features on Europe's Festivals, Design Icons, Best Buildings and Microstates. **George McDonald**, an Insight Guide regular, updated Belgium, the Netherlands and Germany, all countries he's lived in and written about extensively. Our

Map Legend

▬ ▬ ▪ ▬	International Boundary
▬▬▬▬	Regional/Département Boundary
▬ ▬ ▬	Province Boundary
⊖	Border Crossing
▬ ▪ ▬	National Park/Reserve
▬ ▬ ▬ ▬	Ferry Route
⟨M⟩ Ⓜ	Metro
Ⓢ	S–Bahn
Ⓤ	U–Bahn
✈ ✈	Airport: International/Regional
🚌	Bus Station
❶	Tourist Information
✉	Post Office
✝ † ✝	Church/Ruins
†	Monastery
☾	Mosque
✡	Synagogue
🏰 🏚	Castle/Ruins
∴	Archaeological Site
∩	Cave
🗿	Statue/Monument
★	Place of Interest

The main places of interest in the Places section are coordinated by number with a full-colour map (e.g. ❶), and a symbol at the top of every right-hand page tells you where to find the map.

Contents

LEFT: Vaduz Castle, Lichtenstein.

Maps

Travel Tips

Inside front cover:
Western Europe: Political
Inside back cover:
Western Europe: Physical

THE BEST OF WESTERN EUROPE: TOP ATTRACTIONS

With its unmatched cultural heritage, historic sights, great cities and endless variety of scenery, deciding where to go in Western Europe can be a real challenge. Here is our summary of the best to help you plan your itinerary

△ **The Alhambra** This apogee of Moorish architecture stands high above the city of Granada. The design and attention to detail are mesmerising, while the pools and fountains provide a delightful contrast with the arid surroundings. *See pages 58, 355–6.*

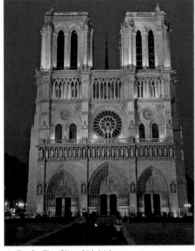

▽ **Venice** It's hard to think of any city more distinctive, or beautiful, than Venice. The absence of cars renders this watery labyrinth wonderfully peaceful – away from the crowded main thoroughfares, at least. Venture out on the canals and admire the sumptuous grandeur from a different perspective. *See pages 277–81.*

△ **Bruges** Canals thread their way around the well-preserved medieval buildings, interspersed with bars, restaurants and chocolate shops. *See pages 151–2.*

△ **Paris** The City of Light is a fixture on every tourist itinerary of Europe, an unmatched combination of sophistication, beauty, A-list sights and museums, and, of course, incomparable food. *See pages 105–13.*

▷ **Seville** Europe's hottest city (ahead of Athens) is the heart of romantic Andalucía, the Spanish deep south. On fragrant summer evenings it can seem as if the entire population is out and about, promenading the streets or crowding into the hundreds of tapas bars. *See pages 354–5.*

△ **Salzburg and the Salzkammergut** Famous for Mozart and *The Sound of Music*, Salzburg and its spectacular backyard – sheer-sided mountains reflected in quiet lakes – are the very definition of picturesque. *See pages 248–9.*

△ **Rhine cruise** With its vineyard-clad slopes and romantic castles, the middle section of the Rhine between Koblenz and Mainz is a magnificent stretch of river. The best way to appreciate it, bar none, is on board a river cruise. *See pages 200–1.*

△ **Amsterdam** City of canals and bicycles, Rembrandt and coffee houses, Amsterdam has long blazed a trail for an open-minded society and is still every bit as colourful and cosmopolitan as its reputation suggests. World-class museums vie with canal-boat cruises, markets and the distinctive brown cafés for your attention. *See pages 163–7.*

▽ **Barcelona** Gaudí's city has a great deal going for it: a wonderful climate, superb food, legendary nightlife, sandy beaches and architecture ranging from Gothic behemoths to extraordinary Modernist spectaculars. *See pages 339–43.*

△ **Berlin** The troubled recent past of Berlin lends the metropolis a fascination all its own. Battered by bombs, brutally divided into East and West during the Cold War, then regaining its status as the German capital in the 1990s, it's nothing if not resilient. *See pages 183–7.*

◁ **Tuscany**
Occasionally dubbed "Chiantishire" in reference to the enduring British love affair with its timeless scenery, this land of cypresses, vineyards and beautiful towns is a place to appreciate the finer things in life. The food and wine are part of that experience. *See pages 287–9.*

△ **Ancient Athens** The power and beauty of ancient Greece can be felt despite the muddle of modern Athens, overlooked as it is on almost every street by the majesty of the Parthenon, pinnacle of classical architecture. *See pages 305–9.*

△ **The Alps** Switzerland is dominated by the Alps. Perhaps most popular for their skiing in the colder months, these lofty mountains offer wonderful hiking and adventure sports in summer. Many of the upper slopes can be accessed via the country's superlative rail network – and the trains are always on time, too. *See pages 216, 224–5.*

△ **Greek island-hopping** From Athens's port, ferries depart for the hundreds of islands scattered across the blue waters of the Aegean. *See pages 313–19.*

◁ **Lisbon** A wonderful city of rattling old trams, grand vistas, characterful bars, intimate neighbourhoods and handsome buildings. *See pages 369–71.*

△ **Florence** With Renaissance art, architecture and heritage in abundance, from the magnificent terracotta cupola of the Duomo to the stupendous treasures of the Uffizi, Florence is always going to be at the top of the list for culture buffs. *See pages 273–5.*

△ **The Costas** Spanish beaches are hard to beat if you are looking for sun, sea and sand. The Costa Brava in the north has more in the way of rocky coves, while the Costa Blanca and Costa del Sol are known for their long stretches of pale sands. *See pages 350–2, 356–7.*

△ **Provence/Côte d'Azur** The famous sunlit landscapes and lovely old towns such as Aix and Avignon make this corner of southern France utterly entrancing. Beyond are the dazzling resorts, beaches and casinos of the Riviera. *See pages 128–31.*

△ **Châteaux of the Loire** Rising above the gentle countryside of the Loire Valley are the 15th–18th-century residences of the French aristocracy, most of them stuffed full of fine art, priceless period furniture and surrounded by glorious gardens. The ultra-decadent flamboyance of palaces such as Azay-le-Rideau, Chambord and Chenonceau has to be seen to be believed. *See pages 119–22.*

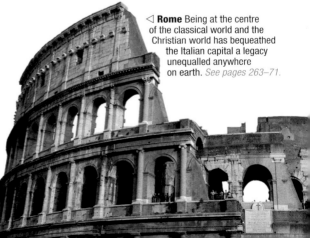

◁ **Rome** Being at the centre of the classical world and the Christian world has bequeathed the Italian capital a legacy unequalled anywhere on earth. *See pages 263–71.*

THE BEST OF WESTERN EUROPE: EDITOR'S CHOICE

Our selection of the top cultural and historical sights, the best outdoor experiences, urban highlights, family attractions, eating and drinking, amazing locations, as well as some lesser-known destinations

ART AND CULTURE

● **Louvre, Paris** Housed in a former royal palace, this is one of Europe's greatest art galleries. Highlights include the *Mona Lisa (below)* and *Venus de Milo*. *See pages 107 and 139.*

● **Uffizi, Florence** The Uffizi has been used to display art since 1581, and is the world's leading repository of Renaissance works. Botticelli, da Vinci and Michelangelo feature prominently. *See pages 138 and 274.*

● **Sistine Chapel, Vatican** Renaissance art at its finest, the ceiling is alive with Michelangelo's famous frescoes and other marvellous works adorning the walls. *See page 271.*

● **Prado, Madrid** The finest collection of 12th–19th-century Spanish art, including works by Velázquez and Goya, plus notable Italian and Flemish paintings. *See pages 138 and 335.*

● **Rijksmuseum** One of three great art galleries in Amsterdam, the Rijksmuseum showcases the incomparable Dutch Masters including Rembrandt and Vermeer. *See pages 138 and 165.*

ABOVE: the unmistakable Colosseum in Rome.

ANCIENT SITES

● **The Acropolis, Athens** A classical ensemble like no other, the 2,500-year-old Acropolis is the enduring symbol of the achievements of ancient Greece. *See page 305.*

● **Prehistoric cave art, Lascaux and Altamira** For *really* old art, head to the Dordogne region of France, or Altamira in northern Spain. *See pages 123 and 346.*

● **Colosseum, Pantheon and Forum, Rome** These remarkable remains are vivid reminders of the supreme power of Roman civilisation. *See pages 59 and 263.*

● **Greek ruins in Sicily** Highlights include a superb 2,000-year-old Greek theatre and the amazing Valley of the Temples. *See page 295.*

● **Amphitheatre, Nîmes** One of the most complete Roman ruins in Europe. *See page 128.*

● **Aqueduct, Segovia** The Roman aqueduct is just one attraction in this lovely old Castilian town. *See page 348.*

● **Pompeii** Beneath the smouldering bulk of Vesuvius, visiting this extraordinary site is an unforgettable experience. *See page 292.*

ABOVE LEFT: the Pantheon.
LEFT: the Prado.

ABOVE: Switzerland is dominated by the Alps.
BELOW MIDDLE: classic Delft pottery. **BOTTOM LEFT:**
Rhodes Old Town. **BOTTOM RIGHT:** wild Camargue horses.

PROVINCIAL CITIES

● **Avignon, France** A lively southern city bathed in luminous Provençal light. Visit the Palais des Papes and witness the street theatre. *See page 128.*

● **St-Malo, France** Small but perfectly formed, this fortified port is a delightful place to wander. Mont-St-Michel is a short drive away. *See page 118.*

● **Siena, Italy** Home to one of Europe's greatest squares and the Palio festival, the medieval centre is utterly enchanting. *See page 288.*

● **San Sebastián, Spain** This Basque city has a superb setting, a marvellous sandy beach and some of the best food anywhere in Europe. *See page 348.*

● **Coimbra, Portugal** Explore the narrow streets of this ancient university town perched above the River Mondego. *See page 374.*

● **Dresden, Germany** Few war-ravaged cities have been rebuilt as successfully as Dresden. The stunning ensemble of Baroque architecture is a highlight of a visit to Germany. *See page 191.*

● **Heidelberg, Germany** Dominated by its fabulous ruined castle, this handsome city has been a centre of learning since the 14th century. *See page 199.*

● **Delft, Netherlands** Vermeer's hometown, famed for its blue-and-white pottery, is small and relaxed, and the canals are lined with lovely old buildings. *See page 171.*

● **Rhodes town, Greece** This bustling Unesco-listed city has been in existence since the 5th century BC. Enclosed by thick walls, it is one of Europe's best-preserved ancient settlements. *See page 317.*

THE GREAT OUTDOORS

● **Picos de Europa, Spain** These soaring, craggy peaks are home to bears, wolves and some of Europe's most exciting hiking. *See page 346.*

● **Corsica** Vast tracts of virtually untrammelled mountain wilderness cover much of the interior of this Mediterranean island. *See page 130.*

● **Gorges du Tarn, France** White-water rafting and hiking amid truly majestic scenery. *See page 124.*

● **Pyrenees, France/ Spain** This long mountain chain, stretching from Atlantic to Mediterranean and marked by spectacular canyons and wild forests, marks the boundary between the Gallic and Hispanic worlds. *See pages 126 and 348.*

● **Alps** From hiking to paragliding, ice-climbing, rock-climbing and, of course, skiing, the Alps are a paradise for outdoor activities. *See also Top Attractions and pages 216, 224–5, 243 and 246.*

● **Camargue, France** Famed for its wild flamingos, horses and distinctive culture, this extensive wetland in the Rhône Delta is unlike anywhere else in Western Europe. *See page 129.*

● **Ardennes, Belgium and Luxembourg** These rolling wooded hills do not compare in drama with the mountains of the Alps further south but are very pretty nonetheless. *See page 153.*

● **Samariá Gorge, Crete** The scenery and vegetation in this dramatically sheer-sided, deep ravine resembles the Middle East or North Africa more than Europe. *See page 317.*

12

FOOD AND DRINK

● **Italy** Everyone thinks pasta and pizza, but there is more to Italian cuisine than these essential basics, with a wonderful variety of regional dishes. *See page 415.*

● **France** Fine dining for gourmets, but many people happily limit themselves to the set *menu du jour*. The cheese and, of course, wine, is superb – seek out a local market and indulge. *See page 399.*

● **Spain** Away from the well-known tapas, *calamares* and paella is a huge range of regional dishes that reward the adventurous. *See page 431.*

● **Portugal** Seafood and inventively prepared meat dishes dominate. Fresh grilled sardines with young *vinho verde* wine is a

popular standard. *See page 426.*

● **Greece** With plenty of fish, meat dishes, *mezedes* and olive oil, eating out in Greece is a pleasure. *See page 411.*

● **The Netherlands** Bucking the trend of plain food is the *rijsttafel*, an Indonesian feast that can comprise of more than 40 separate dishes. *See page 422.*

● **Belgium** Belgian cuisine is generally of a high standard, but the country is best known for its flavoured beers and the quality of its chocolate. *See page 394.*

● **Germany** Straight-forward fare is complemented by some marvellous wines and some of the world's finest beer. *See page 405.*

● **Austria** Vienna is famous for its coffee houses, with endless varieties of coffee and delectable cakes. *See page 390.*

GREAT BUILDINGS

● **Eiffel Tower, Paris** The iconic metal structure is a contender for the best-known building in Europe. *See pages 58 and 112.*

● **St Peter's Basilica, Rome** Epicentre of the Catholic faith, home to the pope and an astounding array of art, the world's largest church is an amazing sight. *See pages 270 and 271.*

● **Versailles** The palace of the Bourbon kings is the last word in divine-right decadence. Highlights include the Hall of Mirrors, fully 75 metres (246ft) in length. *See page 113.*

● **Reims Cathedral** This heavyweight of Gothic architecture can be seen from the surrounding wheatfields for miles around. *See page 137.*

● **Sagrada Família, Barcelona** Nothing can prepare you for the first encounter with this extraordinary building, still unfinished. Gaudí's singular genius emerges on a truly grand scale. *See page 343.*

● **Guggenheim, Bilbao** Gehry's unique "metal flower" flabbergasted the public when it opened in 1997 and is still astonishing over a decade later. *See page 348.*

● **St Mark's Basilica, Venice** St Mark's is a vivid testament to the wealth brought by centuries of Venetian trade and plunder. *See page 279.*

● **Duomo, Milan** This gigantic Gothic cathedral bristles with a total of 135 spires, writhing with gargoyles and statues. *See page 284.*

● **Schönbrunn Palace, Vienna** Summer retreat of the Habsburgs, with 1,440 rooms set in glorious gardens. *See page 241.*

● **Reichstag, Berlin** Symbol of the new Berlin and one of the most successful examples of modern architecture in Europe. *See page 185.*

TOP: Versailles. **ABOVE LEFT:** Belgian brew. **LEFT:** Bilbao's Guggenheim Museum. **ABOVE:** atop the Sagrada Família.

SPECTACULAR SETTINGS

● **Metéora, Greece**
Perched on a series of improbably shaped rock pillars, a remarkable sight. *See page 312.*

● **Rocamadour, France**
This ancient Christian centre seems to challenge the laws of physics as it clings to its huge cliff. *See page 124.*

● **Neuschwanstein Castle, Germany** The ultimate fairy-tale castle, high on a Bavarian hill. *See pages 58 and 196.*

● **Ronda, Spain** The largest of the *pueblos*

blancos of Andalucía is cleaved in two by the gorge El Tajo. *See page 357.*

● **Dürnstein, Austria** A romantic old town with a gorgeous setting on the Danube. *See page 249.*

● **Bellagio, Italy**
This gem on Lake Como occupies one of the most emphatically picturesque locations on the continent. *See page 285.*

● **Amalfi coast, Italy**
The dizzying coastline south of Naples is famed for its views and chic resorts. *See page 293.*

ABOVE: the Amalfi coast.

CHILDREN AND FAMILIES

● **Disneyland Paris** Since opening in 1992, Disney's first European theme park has proved to be a great success. *See page 113.*

● **Cycling in the Netherlands** Everywhere in this extremely flat land is well suited to family cycling, with facilities to match. The Zeeland area is particularly good. *See pages 173 and 420.*

● **Beaches** From Atlantic surf to the blue Aegean, there is no lack of variety to European beaches for a family holiday or day out. *See page 67.*

● **Festivals** Highlights for families include the Palio

in Siena, the Easter festivals in Spain and the Christmas markets of Germany. *See pages 250, 390, 394, 399, 405, 411, 416, 422, 426, 431, 436.*

● **Cable cars in the Alps**
Taking a cable car or chairlift up an Alpine peak is guaranteed to thrill. Swiss mountain railways are another exciting adventure. *See page 215.*

● **Leaning Tower of Pisa**
Familiar but still amazing when seen in the flesh. Arrive early to avoid queues. *See page 288.*

OFF THE BEATEN TRACK

● **Barging in Burgundy, France** Take to the water in this rich, beautiful region and enjoy the languid pace of rural France. *See page 135.*

● **Thuringian Forest, Germany** A favourite of Goethe, this is a hilly region whose landscapes will be familiar to readers of the brothers Grimm. *See page 192.*

● **Green Spain** With its forests, green pastures, rocky coast and Atlantic surf, northwest Spain is completely different from the rest of the country. *See page 346.*

● **Trás-os-Montes, Portugal** Life continues largely undisturbed by the

modern world in this remote part of northern Portugal. *See page 374.*

● **Massif Central, France** The Massif is a large, sparsely populated upland region with some fantastic scenery and endless potential for outdoor activities. *See page 122.*

● **Aeolian Islands, Italy**
A scattered archipelago off the north coast of Sicily, these islands are known for their volcanic landscapes, crystal-clear waters and rustic way of life. *See page 295.*

● **Lake Constance, Switzerland** With most visitors heading to the higher Alpine areas, the beautiful east and north of Switzerland, notably around Bodensee, can be blissfully quiet. *See page 223.*

ABOVE LEFT: Ronda. **ABOVE:** Alpine skiing.

THE HEART OF THE OLD WORLD

Europe is the heart of Western civilisation, nourishing a rich mix of cultures and providing a fertile breeding ground for human creativity in all its forms

The world's second-smallest continent, after Antarctica, has a shared history of violence and civilisation, and is as faithful and fractious as any family unit. Two thousand years after being united by the *denarii* of the Pax Romana, it is now bound by another common currency, the euro, which makes travelling around so much easier.

This is a book about the core European states that lie at the heart of the continent. It includes all six countries that joined together to form an economic union – France, Germany, Italy, Belgium, the Netherlands and Luxembourg. It also covers countries that later joined, like Spain, Portugal and Austria, as well as Switzerland, which resolutely clings to its independence and its francs. It excludes the islands at the edge – Britain and Ireland – as well as the Scandinavian countries and the 10 countries of Eastern Europe that joined in 2004 and 2006. This post-Cold War drift eastwards prompted a former US Defense Secretary – whose grandfather was originally from Bremen in Germany – to dismiss the EU's original, key members as "Old Europe".

Old Europe

Seen from the New World, what else could they be? This is the "Old World" of châteaux and champagne, La Scala and Monte Carlo, gondolas and gypsy violins. It is the home of democracy, Christianity, the Renaissance, royalty, Michelangelo, Mercedes-Benz, Beethoven, the Cannes Film Festival, pasta and tapas.

PRECEDING PAGES: the Palio, Siena; restaurant at night in Ermoupoli, on the Greek island of Syros; above the streets of Paris. **LEFT:** chatting in front of the Duomo, Florence. **RIGHT:** skateboarders in Paris.

Newer nations may carp, but even they must admit that European art is admired, its wines appreciated, its fashion copied and its languages spoken in every corner of the world.

Europeans have their own idea of themselves and their own image of Europe. To French politicians, it is a collection of well-off countries who need to get together for their own self-interest. To former Soviet republics, it is a fold that they can return to now that Communism has gone. Romantics see Paris as its centre, bureaucrats see Brussels, style-setters see Barcelona and Milan; classicists look to Athens and Rome, Catholics to the Vatican, skiers to the Alps and hedonists to the Mediterranean shore.

Wide divisions

Its countries may be physically attached, but Europe is not homogeneous, and all efforts to unite its unruly tribes have come to nothing. Charlemagne and Napoleon failed and, despite 50 years of closer union, the sense of European identity is still weak. The fact is that most Europeans, in spite of all the handshaking and treaty-signing, do not see themselves as a single unity, and voter turnout to elect members to the European Parliament can be depressingly low.

Indeed, they often don't see themselves as part of the country to which they belong. Basques, Bretons, Catalans, Flemings, Lombards and others still dream of resurrecting independent nationhood *(see Microstates, page 358)*. Mistrusts run deep, and stereotypes are still used in the nations' popular newspapers to stir up feeling.

> ❝ *I want all of Europe to have one currency. This will make trading much easier.* Napoleon Bonaparte ❞

There are epigrams to sum up every nation, every region, every city; sayings to reinforce ideas about their stubbornness or *joie de vivre*,

EUROPE'S SHARED CULTURAL HERITAGE

Today, architects move around all over the world. The work of Italy's Renzo Piano or Spain's Santiago Calatrava can crop up in any part of the globe, just as Japanese or American architects will design showcase buildings in Europe. Historically, Europe's unparalleled architecture shows that ideas have always flowed freely across the continent, regardless of borders. Builders, traders, businessmen, pilgrims and mercenaries – as well as visionaries – have constantly been on the move.

The terracotta roof tiles of the Romans colour all the Mediterranean's fashionable playground resorts. Italians built many of

Northern Europe's churches. Normans put up castles in northern Greece and southern Italy. German woodcarvers left their marks on Spanish choir stalls. Dutch Masters followed the Hansa traders to the Baltic and a visitor would be hard-pressed to tell the difference between 17th-century houses in Bremen and Amsterdam.

The great architectural movements of Romanesque, Gothic, Renaissance, Baroque and Neoclassicism touched all of Europe. In the 19th century, France's Art Nouveau was Germany and Austria's Jugendstil, Italy's Stile Liberty and Spain's Modernisme *(see Design Icons of Europe, page 204)*.

their cleverness or stupidity. Such cartoon characters are easy to sketch, from the hard-working Teutonic races of the north to the excitable Latins of the south, from boisterous Bavarians and emotional Poles to arrogant French, devious Greeks and boring Belgians. "A typical Spaniard," the Viennese psychoanalyst Sigmund Freud said of the painter Salvador Dalí. "Quite mad." His statement does not bear analysis.

The north–south divide is the most noticeable: the industrious peoples of the colder climates scorn the backward and lazy siesta-seeking peasants of sunnier parts. Typically, the strapping, healthy, fair-skinned northerner gets

the Alps and slip down into Italy. Only a love of football seems to unite Europeans, though the games themselves can seem like replays of earlier hostilities.

Roman occupation

The nearest Europe came to being united was not under one country, but under one city, ancient Rome. Pax Romana stretched all around the Mediterranean and north to the River Danube, and ruled in every country in Western Europe. Perhaps Rome's most significant bequest was a written language from which European "Romance" languages subse-

darker, lazier, louder and smaller towards the south. Even within countries there can be divisive stereotypes: Germany's northern Prussians look down on the beer-swilling Bavarians. The richer inhabitants of northern France and Italy look down on the poorer, more rural "midday" lands of the south – the Midi in France, the Mezzogiorno in Italy. In Spain the industrious northerner has no time for "lazy" flamenco-playing Andalucians. Such prejudices are put aside at holiday time as northerners head for the sun. The whoops from otherwise sober Germans are said to be audible as their cars cross

quently evolved. And then of course there is Greek, the only language in Western Europe not to use Roman script.

Teutonic tribes shaped the languages in the north, Slavs to the east. To the west, all but pushed into the sea, are the last of the Celtic-speakers, the Bretons. Trapped in pockets in between are little-used languages such as Romansch in part of Switzerland, and Basque, which shows no resemblance to other languages, spoken on the western border of France and Spain.

Language is no respecter of borders, some of which have anyway failed to remain firm. At the beginning of the 20th century modern Italy and Germany had not long been invented. Prussia had been subsumed into the German

LEFT: dancing in the streets, Mallorca. **ABOVE:** the Octoberfest is a hugely popular festival in Munich.

Empire, Austria and Hungary dramatically deflated. Since then, Germany has divided and united, Czechoslovakia united and divided, Poland re-emerged, and Yugoslavia has been pieced together and blown apart. But since the end of World War I, the heart of Europe has remained much the same.

Wider influences

Vikings came down from the north, sailing to Paris and round into the Mediterranean, scattering a little of their language on their way, often pillaging as they went but also trading. Later, both the Swedish and Russian empire-

builders came knocking at the gates. In the east the Ottoman Muslims held sway until the 19th century, when Greece and Bulgaria re-emerged as countries after many centuries of occupation. At their height, the Turkish Ottomans pushed the Austro-Hungarian Empire back to Vienna.

After the death of the Prophet Muhammad, a missionary zeal swept Arab tribes up through Spain to Poitiers, not far from Paris. It swiftly subsided back into Spain, where their caliphate produced not just an enormously rich culture and architecture in Córdoba and Granada, but affected the Spanish language to such an extent that a rousing roar of "¡Olé!" may, some historians have suggested, be a remnant of a rallying call for "Allah!"

Modern-day links

A fast and integrated road system makes communications between the countries easier than ever before. Motorways, given an "E" number in addition to their national number, glide so effortlessly across borders that there is often no sign where one country begins and one ends. It's the same with the railway system – reliable high-speed trains are in regular service between the major cities – while small airports continue to proliferate, offering inexpensive short-haul flights.

There is no difficulty in travelling the length and breadth of this small continent, whose largest country, France, at 544,000 sq km (212,900 sq miles), is smaller than both the states of Texas and New South Wales. In spite of its size, Europe has proved to be unbeatable in its ambitions. In the past 500 years it has had a good try at conquering the entire world, and residents of those former colonies and outposts return looking for their roots. Names can be traced to places. Walt Disney's family was "d'Isigny" (from Isigny in Normandy).

The French historian Fernand Braudel (1902–85) knew how to look at a family name

> The chief signs now of Europe's colonial past are its specialist restaurants: Algerian couscous in France, Indonesian rice tables in the Netherlands and Cuban salsa bars in Spain.

and point to remote European mountain valleys or city shopkeepers' alleyways as the place of its origin. This kind of non-chemical DNA can be used to excuse character or temperament. Countless millions of people scattered around the world still have a drop of "Old Europe" coursing through their veins.

But Europe is not embedded in the past; it is now a major world power that competes with the US and China in terms of global influence. It's no accident that two of the most important international events of 2009 took place on European soil – the G20 Summit in London that brought together countries representing 85 percent of global economic output, and the Copenhagen Climate Conference that convened in December to tackle global warming. ❑

LEFT: a monk from Metéora, Greece.
RIGHT: the Reichstag, Berlin.

DECISIVE DATES

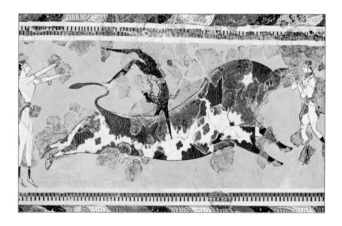

2000–1450 BC
Minoan civilisation, centred on Knossos in Crete.

1450–100 BC
Mycenaean civilisation, based at Mycenae in the Peloponnese, southern Greece.

800–500 BC
Archaic period. Athens and Sparta emerge as major city-states.

753 BC
Rome, an Etruscan trading post, said to have been founded by Romulus and Remus.

509 BC
Rome becomes a republic.

450–338 BC
Classical period. Parthenon built. Flowering of Greek literature and philosophy. Rome gradually takes over all Italy.

338–323 BC
Macedonia's Philip and Alexander the Great create unprecedented empires.

323–146 BC
Hellenistic period.

218 BC
The Carthaginians, led by Hannibal, attack Rome, unsuccessfully.

146 BC
Greece falls to Rome.

48 BC
Death of Pompey the Great in civil war with Julius Caesar.

28 BC
Pax Romana spreads through Europe and Mediterranean, but declines within 200 years.

AD 330
Constantine, the first Christian Roman emperor, establishes an eastern capital in Constantinople.

527
St Benedict founds the first monastic order, at Monte Cassino, southern Italy.

714
Spain conquered by North African Muslims.

800
In Rome, Charlemagne, a Frankish leader, is crowned Holy Roman Emperor.

11th century
Romanesque architecture evolves, characterised by simple vaulting and rounded arches. Pisa Cathedral, Italy, and Church of the Apostles, Cologne, are good examples.

1072
French Normans (descendants of the Vikings) conquer Sicily.

1096
First Crusade against Muslims in the Holy Land; 500,000 join up.

12th century
Gothic architecture, identified by pointed arches and flying buttresses, becomes prevalent. Chartres Cathedral, France, and St Stephen's Cathedral, Vienna, are prime examples.

1150–70
First universities founded.

PRECEDING PAGES: prehistoric cave painting, Lascaux, France. FAR LEFT TOP: Minoan fresco, Crete. BOTTOM LEFT: Alexander the Great. NEAR LEFT: Augustus, the first Roman emperor. TOP: 17th-century Ottoman manuscript showing map of the Crusades. ABOVE: Leonardo da Vinci. RIGHT: the Gutenberg Bible.

1283
Dante Alighieri begins writing in Florence, establishing Italian language.

1309
The papacy moves from Rome to Avignon.

1325–1495
The Renaissance is initiated by Brunelleschi, architect of Florence Duomo, and exemplified by Giotto, Michelangelo and Leonardo da Vinci.

1337–1453
Hundred Years War between France and England results in Joan of Arc's martyrdom and England losing all claims to French territory.

1346–50
Black Death sweeps the continent, killing one-third of the population.

1450
First printing press invented by Johannes Gutenberg in Germany. Bible is printed five years later.

1453
Ottoman Turks capture Constantinople and Byzantine Empire falls.

1478
The Inquisition is established in Spain.

1492
Moors driven out of Spain; Jews expelled. Christopher Columbus arrives in the Americas.

16th century
The Reformation in Northern Europe, a move against the corruption of the Church of Rome.

1503
Leonardo da Vinci paints the *Mona Lisa*.

1506–1626
St Peter's built in Rome, involving Michelangelo, da Vinci, Raphael and Bernini.

1517
Martin Luther nails his 95 points to Wittenberg church door.

1519
Portuguese navigator Fernando Magellan circumnavigates the world.

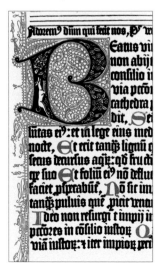

1536
John Calvin establishes Presbyterian Church in Switzerland.

1572
Protestant Huguenots purged in St Bartholomew's Day Massacre in France.

1579
United Provinces established, founding the Netherlands.

17th–18th centuries
Baroque period: its architecture is a rich style, using gold, marble and mirrors to show off wealth and power. The Palace of Versailles and Zwinger Palace in Dresden are good examples.

1618–46
Thirty Years War: initially a Protestant revolt against Catholicism.

1633
The Inquisition forces Italian scientist Galileo to renounce his Copernican belief that the earth revolves around the sun.

1643–1715
Louix XIV, creator of the Palace of Versailles in France, exemplifies a phase of absolute monarchy and the divine right of kings.

18th century
Age of Enlightenment. Tolerance is urged by French writer Voltaire and others, a practice preached by Austro-Hungarian empress Maria Theresa (1717–80), the "Mother of the Nation". Mozart plays at her court.

1755
Earthquake destroys Lisbon.

1789
The French Revolution. Louis XVI and Queen Marie Antoinette are guillotined four years later.

1796–1815
Napoleon Bonaparte of France invades Austria, Italy, Spain,

Portugal and Russia. He is defeated at Waterloo in present-day Belgium.

1830
Kingdom of Belgium is created.

Late 18th–19th centuries
Romanticism looks back to more idyllic times and inspires nationalist movements, encouraging local languages (Catalan and Provençal) and regional customs.

1822
Greece declares independence.

1848
Popular revolutions throughout Europe.

1861
Kingdom of Italy set up after Austrians ejected from the north, Spanish from the south.

1870–1
Franco-Prussian War; Paris besieged.

1874
First Impressionist exhibition held in Paris.

1914–18
World War I. War of attrition fought in northern France and Belgium results in the break-up of the Ottoman and Austro-Hungarian empires and the formation of new countries, including Yugoslavia and Czechoslovakia.

1922
Mussolini's Blackshirts march on Rome.

1933
Hitler comes to power in Germany.

1936–9
Spanish Civil War. First mobilisation of troops by air.

Nationalists win and Franco becomes dictator.

1938
Adolf Hitler annexes Austria, where he met no resistance.

1939–45 World War II

Poland, Czechoslovakia, France, the Netherlands, Belgium, Yugoslavia, Albania and Greece occupied by Germans and Italians. Allied landings in Normandy and Italy lead to end of the war. Many German cities destroyed. Europe is divided between Western and Soviet spheres of influence.

1949

Creation of NATO (North Atlantic Treaty Organization) to ensure the collective security of the US and Western Europe.

1957

Six countries sign the Treaty of Rome, setting up the European Economic Community (EEC). The founding members are France, West Germany, Italy, Belgium, the Netherlands and Luxembourg.

1961

The Berlin Wall is built by the Russians, dividing Germany into East and West.

FAR LEFT: the young Napoleon Bonaparte.
LEFT: Republican Spanish Civil War poster.
ABOVE: Germans from East and West climb onto the Berlin Wall, November 1989.
RIGHT: trading screen shows heavy selling as the financial crisis deepens.

1968

Student unrest throughout Europe. Czechoslovak "Prague Spring" crushed by USSR.

1973

Britain, Ireland and Denmark join the EEC.

1974–5

Dictatorships in Greece, Spain and Portugal end.

1978

Polish Cardinal Wojtyla becomes Pope John Paul II, first non-Italian pope for 400 years.

1981

France launches first high-speed rail link (TGV) between Paris and Lyon.

1989

Berlin Wall comes down following demonstrations across Eastern Europe.

1990

Germany is reunified.

1992

Border controls between most EEC countries end.

1993

Under the Maastricht Treaty, the European Union (EU) is created and the EEC becomes the European Community (EC).

1994

Channel Tunnel links France with Britain.

2002

The euro is adopted by all EU states apart from Denmark, Sweden and the UK.

2004

Ten new members join the EU, including eight former Communist states, to create the world's largest trading bloc, with a population of 450 million.

2006

Romania and Bulgaria join EU, bringing the total number of member states to 27.

2008

Global financial crisis brings several European banks to their knees.

2009

Europe is plunged into deep recession following the global downturn. Thousands of migrants return home. Lisbon Treaty on EU reform is accepted in an Irish referendum, paving the way for streamlining the organisation and nominating a president.

BEGINNINGS

**Centuries of domination by the Greeks
and Romans eventually gave way to the
sober morality and profound religious
sensibility of medieval Christendom**

Europa, so legend has it, was the beautiful daughter of the king of Phoenicia, who was carried away by the god Zeus to the island of Crete. There she bore him three sons, including Minos, after whom the Minoan civilisation was named. It is more likely that the name Europe comes from the Assyrian word "ereb", the land of darkness and the setting sun ("asu", or Asia, was the land of the rising sun), but it is the more romantic story which has stuck.

Early civilisations

The Minoans flourished between the Middle and Late Bronze Ages, roughly 2000–1450 BC. We take this for granted now, but it was only about 100 years ago that their civilisation was discovered and the remains of their palaces, such as the most famous one at Knossos in Crete, were excavated, their layout and wall paintings suggesting a relatively sophisticated way of life – at least for the ruling classes.

The Minoans were superseded – and no one has yet discovered how or why – by the Mycenaeans, whose civilisation on mainland Greece was also unearthed only in the late 19th century. They appear to have been dominant for some 300 years, until about 1100 BC, and again it is unclear why such a strong and wealthy civilisation should have been toppled, although outside attack and internal dissent undoubtedly played a part. Whatever the reasons, their demise plunged the Greek world into a dark age which lasted until the beginning of what historians call the Archaic period (800–500 BC).

LEFT: Greek statue from the Early Cycladic II era.
RIGHT: c.1400 BC fresco from Hagia Triada, Crete.

This was the age of the *polis* or city-state, of which Athens and Sparta emerged as the most powerful, and which gave us two words in common usage today: tyrant – a leader who seized power from the ruling nobility by means of a military coup – and oligarchy – a tightly knit group who took control or had an unduly strong influence on the government.

The Persian Empire was the greatest threat to Greek security, a threat which culminated in the Persian Wars of 490–450 BC, which are now remembered chiefly for the great Athenian victory at Marathon, and the heroic defeat at Thermopylae. Although Athens and Sparta combined forces to vanquish the Persians, during the Classical period that followed, it was Athens which became most powerful.

This was the age of the great Athenian statesman Pericles, when Plato sat at the feet of Socrates before writing the *Republic*, on which much of Western philosophy is based. It was the period when the Parthenon was built, democracy was developed, when Sophocles wrote *Oedipus Rex* and Euripides created *Medea*.

This golden age came to an end when Athens and Sparta wrestled for power during the long-drawn-out Peloponnesian War, weakening both sides and allowing Philip of Macedon to step into the breach. By 338 BC Philip had united the Greek city-states and, when he was assassinated two years later, his son Alexander the Great (356–323 BC) took over. Although only 20, he was already a seasoned soldier, as well as a pupil of the great philosopher Aristotle.

> In the 13 years of his rule Alexander the Great succeeded in conquering the entire Persian Empire, amassing an empire of unprecedented size and wealth.

Alexander's incursions into Persia were cut short when he fell ill and died in Babylon at the age of 32. Squabbling broke out among hopeful successors, and Alexander's kingdom was split into three: Egypt, Asia Minor and Macedon-Greece. In all of these, and the many smaller kingdoms, Alexander was revered as a god. This was known as the Hellenistic period, from the Greek word *Hellenistes*, meaning one who imitates the Greeks.

One thing that was imitated, or continued, was the concept of cities as political, commercial and social centres. Alexander had founded cities, named after himself, wherever he went: there were at least seven Alexandrias in the Hellenistic world, and one Bucephalia – named after his favourite horse.

Trade and agriculture flourished in this period, but competition and war between the kingdoms finally allowed the Romans to take control. Macedon was the first to go, in 167 BC, and Greece followed in 146 BC, while Egypt held out until 31 BC.

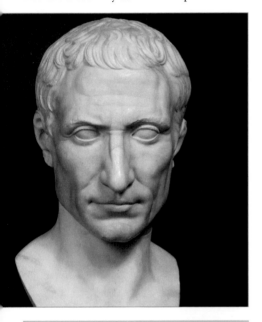

CHARLEMAGNE (742–814)

On Christmas Day in Rome, in the year 800, Charlemagne was crowned Emperor of the West by Pope Leo III. He consolidated his empire, building many palaces and churches and promoting Christianity. His court at Aix-la-Chapelle (Aachen) in Germany was an important centre of learning.

The title of "Holy Roman Emperor" was later inherited by the Austro-Hungarian Habsburgs but, as the French writer Voltaire pointed out, the empire was neither holy, nor Roman, nor indeed an empire, and was finally abolished by Napoleon.

Charlemagne's own dynasty did not survive the divisions of lands made by his heir, Louis the Pious.

Roman rule

Every Italian knows the story of Romulus and Remus, the twins abandoned on a river bank and brought up by a she-wolf; Romulus killed his brother, and founded Rome on the banks of the Tiber in 753 BC. Archaeologists agree that there was a settlement here at that time and that it grew into a flourishing city, but it is most likely that it was established as a trading post by the Etruscans, a highly civilised people who were also skilled craftsmen and metalworkers. The Etruscans ruled Rome until 509 BC, when Tarquin the Proud was ousted and a republic set up. Over the next two centuries Rome conquered the rest of the Italian peninsula and in 241 BC took Sicily from the North Africa-based

Carthaginians in the First Punic War. The Second Punic War began in 218 BC when Hannibal, a Carthaginian general, came up through Spain and France and made his famous crossing of the Alps with a huge army and a number of elephants. Hannibal was defeated, however, and after that there was no stopping the Romans: within less than a century they had conquered Carthage and Greece and were in control of the whole Mediterranean area.

During these years the rich grew richer but the poor, ousted from their menial jobs and thrown off their land to be replaced by the slaves their masters imported from conquered

death in the senate chamber on the Ides of March, 44 BC. His assassins did not long outlive him. Brutus and Cassius committed suicide after defeat in Macedonia and Mark Antony died at the side of Cleopatra, the Egyptian queen, after being decisively defeated by Octavian, Caesar's heir, at the Battle of Actium.

Octavian, who was granted the title Augustus (the revered one), was a shrewd man and a strong ruler. Handling the upper classes with tact and pleasing the masses with bread and entertainments, he presided over a period known as the Pax Romana – the Roman peace – in which trade and agriculture prospered, and

provinces, grew more discontented. Social unrest, and the volatile, factional politics of Rome's corrupt ruling class, inevitably led to civil war. Gnaeus Pompeius Magnus (Pompey the Great, 106–48 BC) restored order, forming an informal triumvirate with Marcus Crassus and Julius Caesar. But when Crassus died, civil war flared again. Pompey was killed in Egypt and Caesar returned to Rome in triumph.

It was short-lived. A group of senators conspired against him and Caesar was stabbed to

art and literature flourished, producing such great writers as Virgil and Horace.

A succession of emperors, after Augustus' death in AD 14, soon undid all his good works. Tiberius, Caligula and Nero were among the best-known and most eccentric villains; then a period of relative stability under emperors such as Trajan, Hadrian and Marcus Aurelius was followed by a series of weak or wicked rulers. Anarchy grew as the empire declined. In AD 286 Diocletian divided the unwieldy mass into two, the Eastern and Western empires. His successor Constantine, the first Christian emperor, established an eastern capital in Constantinople (Istanbul) in 330. Rome was sacked by Visigoths in 410 and the last Western Roman emperor deposed in 476,

LEFT: bust of Julius Caesar in the Museo Pio-Clementino, Vatican. **ABOVE:** Cicero asks Rome to unite against Catiline, whose conspiracy of 63 BC attempted to overthrow the senate.

but the Eastern Empire, which became known as the Byzantine Empire, was to prove much stronger, lasting for another 1,000 years.

Spread of Christianity

By the end of the 4th century Christianity had spread throughout the empire. At the end of the 6th century, Pope Gregory I sent missionaries to Northern Europe to convert the heathens, and others followed their example.

But the Western Empire was disintegrating and Germanic tribes were moving in to fill the power vacuum: the Visigoths in Spain, the Ostrogoths in Italy and the Franks (who have

bequeathed their name to France and Frankfurt), ruled over Gaul. It was the Franks who were to prove most powerful. Their leader Charlemagne conquered the lands now known as Italy, Hungary, Germany and the Lowlands.

Racial melting pot

There were huge movements of people all over Europe during these years. Lombards advanced through Italy in the 6th and 7th centuries, Slavs settled in the Balkans, Muslims from North Africa attacked Spain, conquering most of the peninsula by 714, and Arab raids on Constantinople threatened the security of the Eastern Empire. Despite this, the empire imposed Orthodox Christianity on the Russian and Bulgar peoples, and its power waned only during the 11th century, when Turks overran Asia Minor and the Normans occupied southern Italy.

The Normans were descendants of the Vikings, who had been granted land in northern France in the 10th century after repeated incursions into the Frankish kingdoms. They were soon integrated with the French nobility and strong enough to conquer England and sweep southwards, occupying southern Italy and seizing Sicily from the Arabs. Roger the Norman was crowned in Palermo in 1130 and, although Norman rule lasted barely 60 years, wonderful examples of the fusion of Arabic and Norman architecture still remain on the island.

The Crusades

At the end of the 11th century rumours spread through Christendom that the Ottoman Turks, who had held Jerusalem since the 7th century,

MEDIEVAL ECCLESIASTICAL ARCHITECTURE

During the Middle Ages styles of ecclesiastical architecture spread rapidly across Europe, partly because of the movement of pilgrims, who carried new ideas with them, and partly because some of the great monastic houses, such as Cluny in Burgundy, ruled strings of monasteries stretching right across the continent.

Byzantine architecture had spread from Constantinople in the east, and many examples of its domed churches can be seen in Greece. The Romanesque style – so called by a 19th-century French art historian because it used the rounded, classical arch and had solid grandeur

which resembled that of the architecture of Rome – appeared everywhere during the 11th and 12th centuries.

Gothic followed Romanesque, its great churches and cathedrals expressing a new airiness and grace, typified by pointed arches, vaulted ceilings, flying buttresses and numerous windows. The cathedral at Chartres, southwest of Paris, is an impressive example of early Gothic, from the middle of the 12th century.

Most of the finest examples of Gothic architecture is in Italy, such as the magnificent Doge's Palace in Venice, the Palazzo Vecchio in Florence and the Palazzo Pubblico in Siena.

were making life difficult for Christian pilgrims, and in 1096 the First Crusade set out to liberate the Holy City. Although the Crusaders were initially successful, the Muslims retained the city, and the next three centuries saw a succession of crusades, in which acts of great brutality were committed on both sides, and the Crusaders were ultimately defeated.

A huge mythology has grown up around the exploits of the Knights Templars and the Hospitallers, the members of military monastic orders founded in the early 12th century who led the Crusades; the defeat of Saladin and the capture of Richard the Lionheart are the stuff

it took another century before the Muslims were ousted from the whole peninsula, apart from the Emirate of Granada, which remained a part of Islam until 1492, when Ferdinand and Isabella, the Catholic monarchs, succeeded in uniting the country under their rule. In the same year Columbus set sail for the Americas.

> *Patronised by Ferdinand and Isabella of Spain, Christopher Columbus (1451–1506) made several sea voyages, hoping to reach India; he found the West Indies and Central America.*

of heroic legends. However, although there was genuine religious zeal at first, there was also avarice and self-interest.

The Muslim world was less successful in holding on to its lands in Spain than it was in the east, although the *reconquista*, the reconquest, was a slow process. The Christian kingdoms of Castile and Aragón gained ground during the 11th century, and the fabled hero El Cid won Valencia from the Moors in 1094. Portugal was founded as a Christian kingdom in 1139 by diverted Crusaders, but

FAR LEFT: Crusaders at Damietta, from *Le Miroir Historial de Vincent de Beauvais*, 15th century.
ABOVE: buying favours, from a 13th-century manuscript from the Bibliothèque Municipale, Tours, France.

Spread of learning

The Christian Church was the single biggest influence on the evolution of European culture and learning from late Antiquity to the Renaissance. As the religion spread across the continent, missionary communities had been founded as centres of contemplation, self-denial and learning. St Benedict had laid down the rules for monastic life at Monte Cassino in Italy in AD 527.

In the Dark Ages that followed the fall of the Western Roman Empire, the only culture that survived in any form was in the monasteries. Except in Italy, where there was always some secular education, all learning and literacy was acquired in monastic schools. The monasteries were also the recipients of gifts of land and money from the wealthy, who hoped to lay up treasure in heaven. They therefore became not only large landowners but patrons of the arts, which is why most buildings, paintings and sculptures that survive have religious themes.

During the 12th century, monasteries lost their monopoly on education, and secular schools were set up. By the century's end, universities had been established in Oxford, Paris and Bologna. By the 13th century, most members of the upper class, of both sexes, were able to read, even if they could not write.

Inspired by the 14th-century Italian poet Petrarch, scholars began to read Greek and Roman texts, and went on to question man's role in the world. These humanist ideas spread throughout Europe, and one of their most important proponents, the Dutch scholar Erasmus (1466–1536), also called for reform of the

> In 1346 an epidemic of bubonic plague arrived from the Far East and quickly spread throughout Europe. By 1350 around one-third of the population was dead.

Church. In 1450 Johannes Gutenberg had set up his printing press in Mainz and the works of Erasmus, among others, reached a wide audience.

Revolt of the masses

Most people in Europe in the 14th century were more occupied with trying to survive the arrival of the Black Death, the impact of which was enormous. Initially, land lay idle for lack of labour, food was scarce and prices rose sharply. In the long term the lack of manpower became a bargaining tool for the surviving peasants and contributed to the end of serfdom.

Under the feudal system, large landowners had received service from smaller ones, a system which spread from the monarch down to the lowliest peasant. At the top of the scale, knights would owe "knight service" to their masters and would have to fight when called upon. At the lower end, humble plot owners would have to work on their masters' land as well as on their own. After the plague this system gradually collapsed and peasants were able to take over some of the untended land.

Contributing to the unrest were royal demands for taxes to finance long-drawn-out wars, such as the Hundred Years War. This was a power struggle between the English and French kings for territory in France, which actually lasted from 1337 to 1453, interrupted by a 28-year truce. It was a war littered with famous battles and heroic deeds, most importantly the leadership and martyrdom of Joan of Arc, burnt at Rouen by the English as a heretic in 1431, and later canonised.

The Western Schism

The other great power struggle during this period was centred on the papacy. In 1309 the Pope moved the headquarters of the Catholic Church from Rome to Avignon. This upset

MEDIEVAL EPIC POETRY

During the 12th and 13th centuries a new, vernacular literature emerged to amuse the new reading public. There were tales of courtly love, in which women are served and adored by their noble knights, an art form which began with troubadours – travelling lyric poets from Provence, who would often perform their poems to music – and spread through much of Western Europe.

Perhaps the greatest work in the vernacular to emerge from the Middle Ages is Dante's *Divina Commedia* (*c.*1307), which narrates its author's redemptive spiritual journey through hell and purgatory to paradise.

many Christians, who believed that Rome and the vicar of Christ should be inseparable, The pope went back to Rome in 1377, but almost immediately the Western Schism occurred. This was a period (1378–1417) marked by the creation of antipopes, when two or three men, surrounded by ambitious followers, claimed the right to occupy the throne of St Peter.

The Church's stability was also under attack from the emergence of several heretical groupings. The Cathars, or Albigensians, in the south of France had been destroyed early in the 13th century by a combination of conversion – led by St Dominic, who founded the Dominican

The Reformation

All these ideas, and more, were to re-emerge and bring about the Reformation in the following century. The new printing presses rolled out copies of the Scriptures, and the pamphlets issued by the new movements' leaders were widely disseminated. Martin Luther, a German monk who led the attack on abuse of Church power, was excommunicated, but his ideas spread rapidly and many Lutheran churches were established.

John Calvin was the other great leader of the Reformation. His influence spread throughout the Netherlands, Hungary, Poland and parts of

I. CALVIN

order – and brute force at the hands of Crusaders, diverted from expeditions to the Holy Land, to stamp out heresy closer to home.

But during the time of the Schism, two other heresies appeared: the Lollards, inspired by the English scholar John Wyclif, rejected both the authority of the pope and the doctrine of transubstantiation; and the Hussites, led by the Czech Jan Hus, whose beliefs were similar to those of Wyclif and who flourished for another two decades after their leader was burnt at the stake in 1415.

LEFT: Joan of Arc, burnt as a heretic in Rouen in 1431.
ABOVE: portrait of Huguenot leader John Calvin.
RIGHT: Martin Luther, who led the Reformation.

Germany as well as his native France, where his followers, known as Huguenots, were involved in the 16th-century Wars of Religion. Their strength lessened after thousands of them were killed in 1572 during the St Bartholomew's Day Massacre, but they obtained toleration for their views under the Edict of Nantes in 1598.

Unsurprisingly, the Catholic Church did not take all this lying down. The Jesuit order was founded by a zealous Spaniard, Ignatius Loyola, whose name is inextricably linked with the Inquisition, the organisation responsible for investigating and stamping out heresy. Paranoia about any unorthodox beliefs led to the witch hunts which swept Europe during the 16th and 17th centuries. ❑

CONQUERORS OF THE WORLD

The collapse of Europe's great empire and the rise of
nationalism and urban prosperity led to an
unprecedented renaissance in art and architecture

From the 15th century, expansionist aims took over from religious ones. Spain resumed its ongoing war with the Netherlands, the king of Sweden invaded Germany, and France took up arms against her old enemy, the Habsburg Empire. The main conflict ended with the Peace of Westphalia (1648), which granted Protestants freedom of worship, but by this time about a third of the population of some German states had died, due to warfare, disease or famine.

An empire in decline

War between Spain and France rumbled on for another decade, but these were years of Spanish decline. Spain and Portugal had established the first great colonial empires, based on the early voyages of discovery by such explorers as Vasco da Gama and Christopher Columbus. Spanish power, consolidated by Ferdinand and Isabella's reconquest of the country, had been given a further boost when the Habsburg Charles V of Austria came to the Spanish throne and, in 1519, was elected Holy Roman Emperor, an event viewed with some alarm by the ruling House of Bourbon in France.

Charles's empire, he said, was so vast and all-encompassing that it was one over which "the sun never set". Habsburg tombstones were inscribed AEIOU, meaning *Austria est imperare orbi universo* (All the earth is subject to Austria), and there were few who would have disagreed – at least in public. When Charles abdicated he bequeathed all the Habsburg lands, except those in Austria itself, to his son Philip II of Spain,

who went on to add the Portuguese Empire to his own after the death of the king of Portugal in battle in 1578. With gold and silver flooding in from the New World to fill the national coffers, this seemed to many in Spain to be a true golden age.

Spectacular successes were followed by miserable failure. Wars with France, the continued battle for independence by the Protestant Netherlands, and the defeat of the armada by the English Navy (1588), all proved extremely expensive. When recession hit the Americas in the early 17th century and the flood of silver dwindled to a trickle, it was clear that the balmy days were over. Catalonia revolted when asked

---

LEFT: Japanese screen (*c.*1593) showing Portuguese traders. **RIGHT:** Ghirlandaio's *Columbus, c.*1520.

to shoulder some of the costs of empire, and Portugal followed suit. Although Catalonia was soon recovered, Portugal remained independent and the battle for supremacy over the Netherlands was finally lost.

The Spanish Empire was still considered a valuable prize. When the last of that branch of the Habsburgs died out and the French Bourbon monarch Philip V took the throne, Charles, Archduke of Austria, was sufficiently alarmed by growing French power to take up arms in the War of the Spanish Succession (1701–14). It was a conflict which nearly brought the Spanish and French economies to their knees, but

when it ended, with the Treaty of Utrecht in 1713, it confirmed the right of the Bourbon king to the Spanish throne.

Renaissance glory

Meanwhile, wonderful things were happening in the field of artistic endeavour during these centuries. The Renaissance began in Florence, spread to other Italian cities such as Venice and Rome, then northwards through Europe. The humanist interest in classical art forms made artists aware that Europe had a cultural past, and there were wealthy patrons prepared to finance its rebirth.

The powerful Medici banking family, who controlled so much that happened in Florence, were dominant in promoting art in the city, but it was the wool trade that financed some of the greatest paintings, sculptures and architectural gems the world has ever known. Florence had

> Cosimo de' Medici (1389–1464) and his grandson Lorenzo (1449–92) were grand dukes of Tuscany. The family also produced four popes and two queens of France.

grown rich on wool, and its wealthiest merchants, members of the Arte della Lana, or wool guild, not only provided employment for about one-third of Florence (which had made their city Europe's financial capital by the end of the 14th century), but also sponsored works of art.

The results of such patronage were spectacular. Donatello was commissioned to work on many of the city's civic projects, Giotto designed the campanile for the new cathedral and Uccello made early experiments with perspective in his painting. From Venice sprang Leonardo da Vinci, the archetypal Renaissance man – a scientist, mathematician and philosopher as well as an artist. In the north of Europe Albrecht Dürer changed the status of woodcuts and engravings from craftwork to an important art form. Hieronymus Bosch painted fantastical monsters to illustrate moral and religious themes, while Pieter Bruegel's rural scenes were a landmark in the shift from religious and allegorical themes to secular subjects.

In the late 15th and early 16th centuries the hub of the Italian Renaissance moved from Florence to Rome, as the papacy poured money into the reconstruction and embellishment of the city. Among the artistic riches this produced are Michelangelo's *Pietà* and *The Last Judgement* in the Sistine Chapel; Raphael's cartoons, also created for the Sistine Chapel; and Bramante's classical architectural designs. Later in the 16th century Palladio, who based his work on the great public buildings of ancient Rome, created a style which was emulated all over Europe.

Mannerism and Baroque art

Mannerism developed out of the Renaissance in the 16th century, producing such masters as the goldsmith Cellini, the Venetian artists

LEFT: *Cosimo I* by Vasari, Palazzo Vecchio, Florence.
RIGHT: Botticelli's *Judith*, Uffizi Gallery, Florence.

Titian and Tintoretto, as well as the dramatic paintings of El Greco in Spain, and an architectural style that was so much admired by the French king François I that he used it in the construction of his château at Fontainebleau.

The reaction to Mannerism was the florid Baroque style of the 17th century, exemplified in Italy by Guido Reni and the sculptor Bernini, in Spain by Velázquez, who won the patronage of Philip IV, but most famously of all by the Flemish painter Rubens.

The Dutch School of painting also flourished in the 17th century, stimulated by a wave of national self-confidence following the Nether-lands' deliverance from Spanish rule and its success as a trading nation. The intimate domestic scenes painted by Vermeer and the works of Rembrandt were among the most important of the School's prolific output.

Enlightened despotism

From the ideas of the Enlightenment – the late 17th- and early 18th-century intellectual movement that was based on reason and tolerance – sprang the seemingly contradictory notion of enlightened despotism. Catherine the Great of Russia was influenced by its ideas when she began her programme of reform, and Emperor

THE ABSOLUTE POWER OF LOUIS XIV

The 17th century in Europe was the age of absolute monarchy, a system under which kings dismissed any idea of consultation and held tightly to the reigns of government, believing that God had granted them a divine right to rule. Louis XIV was the most famous and flamboyant of the absolute monarchs. The concept is neatly summed up in his famous phrase, *"L'état c'est moi"*.

His ideas of personal control may have been influenced by the enormous power wielded by ministers – Cardinal Richelieu and Cardinal Mazarin – during his father's reign and his own regency. He asserted his authority over the Church and created a standing army to reinforce his secular powers, and to fight against Spain and the Holy Roman Empire. Nobles were obliged to attend the newly glorified Palace of Versailles where the king could keep an eye on them, and Louis's most able minister, Colbert, who some believe to have been the power behind the throne, created a strong navy, reorganised the tax system, set up academies of science and arts and centralised the unwieldy bureaucracy.

Although harvest failures, continuous wars and court extravagance undid many of his good works, France was still pre-eminent among European nations at the time of Louis's death in 1715.

Joseph II of Austria's attempt to abolish serfdom appears to have had a humanitarian basis,
although he may have been more strongly influenced by the ideas of his mother, Maria Theresa
(1717–80). Known as "the mother of the nation",
she opposed injustice towards her subjects.

The court of Maria Theresa had welcomed
the child prodigy Wolfgang Amadeus Mozart,
but it was not until the year after her death that
the 25-year-old musician left his home town of
Salzburg to seek his fortune in Vienna. A few
years later he was joined by Haydn – middle-
aged and already famous – and in the 1790s
the young Beethoven also arrived in the capital,
making it the musical centre of an increasingly
culture-conscious Europe.

The French Revolution

Music was not uppermost in the minds of the
French in the late 18th century. The government
was bankrupt, largely due to intervention in the
American War of Independence. The poor were
angry about the disproportionate share of taxes
they were obliged to pay. The bourgeoisie were
resentful of the privileges of the aristocracy, and
there was growing criticism of absolutism.

Louis XVI's attempt to raise taxes and reduce
privileges led to the formation of a National

THE ENLIGHTENMENT

During the reign of Louis XV a group of French thinkers known as the *Philosophes*, inspired by, among
others, the scientific discoveries of Sir Isaac Newton
and the thinking of the English empirical philosopher
John Locke, began to disseminate the ideas of the
Enlightenment.

They believed that traditional explanations of the
universe and man's place in it could no longer be taken
for granted and that truth and meaning could only be
discovered through reason and experience. Voltaire's
dictum, "I may disagree with what you say but I will
defend to the death your right to say it," encapsulates
the movement's ideals and concern for tolerance.

Assembly, the establishment of a Commune in
Paris, peasant revolts and the abolition of feu-
dalism. The Declaration of the Rights of Man
– *Liberté, Egalité, Fraternité* – was proclaimed
in 1789 and a new constitutional government
organised. Louis was eventually forced to accept
the constitution, and for a while it seemed that
a bloodless revolution had achieved its aims.

This apparent success was not welcomed
by other European powers, who feared that
revolutionary ideas would spread across their
own countries. Austria and Prussia invaded
France in 1792, while Britain entered the conflict a year later. This coalition against France
engendered an atmosphere of paranoia: conspiracy theories abounded, and 1,000 suspected

counter-revolutionaries were executed. France was declared a republic and Louis XVI and his queen, Marie Antoinette, were guillotined.

Revolts by those opposed to the Revolution broke out at home. The moderates in the new government – the Girondins – were overthrown by the Jacobins, and the Committee of Public Safety, led by Robespierre, was set up. The subsequent "Reign of Terror" left thousands dead and only ended when Robespierre himself became one of its victims. The new power group, the Directory, ended the blood-letting, but was only able to keep the peace with the aid of the army, and this increase in military influence led, in 1799, to the coup of 18 Brumaire (the Revolution had introduced a new calendar, and Brumaire was the new name for November).

Napoleon Bonaparte

The coup was led by Napoleon Bonaparte who, after serving as Consul for four years, abolished the republic and was declared emperor, heading a military dictatorship that reversed most of the reforms achieved by the Revolution. Napoleon had won his stripes at the siege of Toulon in 1793 and then fighting the Austrians in Italy. Despite subsequent defeat at the Battle of the Nile, he was still strong enough to be a hero at home, to compel Austria to accept French

> *Small in stature, grand in his designs and one of the most brilliant generals Europe has produced, Napoleon became too ambitious for his own good.*

dominance in Italy, and to emerge the apparent victor of the Peace of Amiens in 1802.

It was a fleeting peace. Britain declared war again in 1803 and defeated the emperor's fleet off Cape Trafalgar two years later. It was to be his last defeat for years: against a coalition of Britain, Austria, Russia and Naples, Napoleon seemed invincible, causing the downfall of the Holy Roman Empire and winning the support of Austria after his second marriage to an Austrian princess.

However, his disastrous defeat in the snows of Moscow in 1812, which only one-tenth of

LEFT: *Combat devant l'Hôtel de Ville de Paris le 28 Juillet 1830*, by Jean Schnetz (1787–1870).
RIGHT: Napoleon Bonaparte crosses the Alps.

his army survived, was compounded by his long-running conflict in Spain – the Peninsular War. Having handed the Spanish throne to his brother in 1808, he spent the next five years fighting aggrieved Spaniards and their British allies before his defeat by the Duke of Wellington at Vitoria and an allied army at Leipzig in 1813. When Paris subsequently fell he was exiled to the Mediterranean island of Elba. He staged a comeback the following year, but the combined forces of Prussia and Britain brought him down at Waterloo, and he was shipped off to distant St Helena, in the South Atlantic. Louis XVIII was restored to the French throne.

When the victorious allies sat round the table at the Congress of Vienna, their main aims were to stop France ever being so dominant again and, of course, to gain as much for themselves as they could. Austria kept Venice, which had previously been independent, Russia gained most of Poland, and the Netherlands became a new kingdom.

The rise of nationalism

The most dominant man around the table may well have been Metternich, Austrian prince and statesman, who spent the next three decades attempting to stem the rising tide of nationalism both in Austria and abroad. Nationalist sentiments, far from being extinguished, were strengthened by opposition, and in 1848 popular revolts broke out all over Europe.

The first revolution, in Paris in June 1848, inspired others in Italy and throughout the Austrian Empire, as Croats, Czechs and Hungarians demanded recognition as independent ethnic states. Optimism was high and initial gains were made, but the overthrow of the Orléans monarchy and proclamation of the Second Republic in France led not to democracy or liberalism but to the establishment of the Second Empire. The expulsion of Austrian rulers from northern Italy and Spanish Bourbons from the south was short-lived, and

independence in other parts of the Austro-Hungarian Empire was soon crushed.

Eastern powers

Further east, the Ottoman Empire did not remain untouched by demands for self-determination, and it was here that nationalism had one of its first successes. In 1822, a newly formed National Assembly declared Greece an independent state.

After Russian intervention in response to Turkish atrocities, Britain and France pitched in, sunk the Turkish fleet in Navarino Bay and, together with Russia, guaranteed Greek independence in 1830. Otto of Bavaria was drafted from the stock of German royalty to give the nation suitable status, a practice followed by other emergent nations.

Fear of Russian encroachment was a dominant theme in Europe in the middle of the 19th century, particularly when it involved control of the entrance to the Black Sea, the so-called "warm-water port". It did not take a great deal of political acumen to realise that the Russian doctrine of Pan-Slavism, by which Russia assumed the role of protector of smaller Slav nations who were struggling for independence, only came into play when it furthered Russia's interests.

Elsewhere, nationalist movements were quickly put down. Russia was quick to intervene in the Hungarian revolution in 1848 and this, together with her occupation of Balkan territories in 1853, contributed to the outbreak of the Crimean War, a chaotic and mismanaged affair in which half a million men died.

THE ROMANTIC MOVEMENT

Romanticism swept through the European continent, beginning at the end of the 18th century and continuing for much of the 19th. A period of cultural renaissance, it was, in part, a way of trying to make sense of the world after the enormous social dislocations and upheavals brought about by the French and American revolutions; in part, a reaction against the ugliness of the Industrial Revolution.

The Romantic movement also embodied a rejection of the rationalism which had characterised the Enlightenment. Instead, spontaneity, subjectivity and individualism came to the fore. Romantics harked back to a Golden Age: for some it was classical Greece, for others the medieval world of courtly love and chivalry. In France, Rousseau had idealised the "noble savage", the notion of man's uncorrupted, natural state, which greatly influenced Romanticism; in Germany, Goethe and Schiller extolled spritual freedom and the beauty of nature; literature and the local language were rediscovered and extolled in Catalonia and Provence. Beethoven's *Pastoral* symphony was a deeply Romantic work and composers such as Dvořák and Tchaikovsky were greatly influenced by folk music and legends.

Idealisation of the past and the search for ethnic origins blended smoothly with the political aspirations of people refusing to live under the yoke of foreign powers.

The Risorgimento

The foreign power which governed most of the Italian peninsula was that of Austro-Hungary, whose chief statesman, Metternich, once described Italy as "only a geographical expression". Although the peninsula had never been one nation, a movement known as the Risorgimento (Revival) now pressed for unification. The Carbonari were unsuccessful in uniting the 13 separate states under Italian rule, but Camillo Cavour, the prime minister of Piedmont, ejected the Austrians from northern Italy in 1859.

The following year Giuseppe Garibaldi, Italy's best-known and most colourful freedom

Austria against Denmark over the control of Schleswig and Holstein.

Bismarck then provoked a short, sharp war with his former ally, which ended with Austria's defeat at Sadowa in 1866. Finally he engineered a war with France, the Franco-Prussian War of 1870, which he won with little difficulty, enabling him to grab the border territories of Alsace and Lorraine and unite the whole Germanic area under Prussian control.

In Paris, the Prussian invasion led to the establishment of the socialist Paris Commune, modelling itself on the Jacobin-dominated Assembly of 1793. The Commune was brutally put down:

fighter, took southern Italy from the Spanish Bourbons. The new Kingdom of Italy was formed in 1861, although Vatican territory remained under French control until 1870.

Prussian supremacy

In Germany, the situation was even more complicated, and the fact that the 39 separate states became one unified country in 1871 was mainly due to the political skill of the Prussian prime minister, Otto von Bismarck. His "blood and iron" policy involved allying Prussia with

> Bismarck was well known for his ruthlessness and cunning; one of his maxims was: "Nothing should be left to an invaded people except their eyes for weeping."

the death toll was enormous, and all the revolutionary elements were subsequently imprisoned or exiled, which did great damage to hopes for socialism in France for years to come. Despite this, Karl Marx may have been right in regarding it as "the dawn of a new era", for socialist parties soon developed throughout the rest of Europe.

In the newly united Germany, the Social Democratic Party was formed in 1875, although

LEFT: *Goethe in the Roman Campagna,* by Johann Tischbein, 1787. **ABOVE:** *Garibaldi's Rout of Neapolitan Forces in Calatafimi, Sicily,* by R. Legat.

Bismarck soon forced it underground. Socialist parties of various hues were formed in Austria, Belgium, Italy and Switzerland during the 1880s and early 1890s, by which time the German party re-emerged and became dominant among European parties of the left.

Sharing the spoils

Russia, which would be the first country to embrace full state socialism, was, at this stage, still troubling the other European powers by her unwanted encroachments into the Balkans. At the Berlin Congress of 1878 Russia's possession of the Caucasus was confirmed and she was given control of Bessarabia. Bulgaria was declared an autonomous province, and Serbia, Montenegro and Romania all had their independence confirmed.

The Berlin settlement was not satisfactory however. The Ottoman Empire remained "the sick man of Europe" and complicated relations between the six Great Powers that existed now that so many disparate states had been unified. These powers – Great Britain, France, Italy, Germany, Russia and Austro-Hungary – were also rivals for overseas colonies. Between 1870 and 1914, they carved up most of Africa and the Pacific between them.

NEW MOVEMENTS IN ART

The French Impressionist movement emerged in the 1860s when, in an effort to move away from the precise draughtsmanship of earlier art and to depict the visual impression of the moment, artists began to paint straight from nature, using free, loose brushwork.

Scorned by the official Paris Salon, Monet, Renoir, Degas, Pissarro and others held their own exhibition in 1874, followed by another seven such breakaway exhibitions during the next dozen years.

The Post-Impressionists, the most celebrated of whom were Cézanne, Gauguin and van Gogh, emphasised strong colours and powerful emotions in their work. They were followed by the Fauves (literally the "Wild Beasts"), who were led by Matisse and Derain.

In Austria the Vienna Secession, led by Gustav Klimt, was another rebellion against conventional art forms. From the Secession emerged not only Klimt's erotic images, but the disturbing work of the Expressionist artists Egon Schiele and Oskar Kokoschka, and Jugendstil, the Austrian version of Art Nouveau. The fluid forms of Art Nouveau glorified European cities in the early years of the 20th century, and can be seen at their most fantastic in the work of Gaudí in Barcelona (see page 339).

Rivalries within Europe and the overseas colonies led to the alliance system. Germany, Austro-Hungary and Italy formed the Triple Alliance, while Russia, France and Great Britain became partners in the Triple Entente. This system led inexorably to World War I.

Technological age

The people of Europe, meanwhile, were having fun exploring their countries and the continent on the new railways, learning to ski in the Alps and bathing in the Mediterranean Riviera.

New developments in the visual arts were reflected in music and literature. Debussy was

and nine years before Bleriot flew an aircraft across the English Channel. German engine designer Karl Benz had produced his first petrol-engined Motorwagen in 1885, and 10 years later so many cars had appeared that the 1895 Paris–Bordeaux race was run.

Moves towards democratic forms of government had also been made in the majority of industrialised countries by the turn of the 20th century, including the rights to free speech and freedom of the press. Trade unions had been given full recognition in France by 1884 and in Germany soon after Otto von Bismarck's death in 1890.

composing prolifically and Eric Satie was creating his playful, idiosyncratic piano music. "Realist" writers such as Zola, Chekhov and Ibsen forced their readers to face sometimes unpalatable truths.

The end of the 19th and beginning of the 20th century was also a period when technology was making huge strides. Guglielmo Marconi constructed the first radio, in a Bologna attic, in 1894. The Paris–Orléans railway was electrified in 1900, the same year that Count von Zeppelin's dirigible made its first flight

LEFT: the Berlin–Potsdam railway, c.1850.
ABOVE: an early 19th-century view of wealthy Europeans at leisure in Monte Carlo.

Universal suffrage

France and Germany gave all men the right to vote in 1871, although women had to wait a lot longer – until 1918 in Germany and until the end of World War II in France. In Switzerland, women did not win the right to vote until 1971.

Immunisation and improved sanitation were improving life-expectancy rates, and slums were being cleared in most major cities. Bismarck initiated a social security system, offering insurance payments for sickness, accident and old age, and during the 1880s most other European countries introduced some or all of these benefits. All in all, unless one was very poor, life was not too bad, comparatively, in Europe in the first years of the 20th century. ❏

MODERN TIMES

Peace and prosperity followed a painful
era of war and repression in much of
Europe – but areas of conflict remain

World War I, which was sparked off by Austrian Archduke Franz Ferdinand's assassination at Sarajevo, produced carnage on a scale never before imagined. An estimated 20 million people died before the Armistice was signed on 11 November 1918. This, it was said, had been the war to end all wars, and the Fourteen Point Peace Plan put forward by US President Wilson at the Treaty of Versailles and subsequent treaties signed with Turkey and Austro-Hungary were supposed to lay the foundations for a lasting peace. In fact, they did the opposite. The old empires of Germany, Russia, Austro-Hungary and Turkey were broken up and the map of Europe completely redrawn.

New divisions

Alsace and Lorraine were returned to France, a new Polish state was created, with the Danzig Corridor giving it access, through German land, to the sea. Czechoslovakia also became an independent state and was awarded Bohemia

The division of land following World War I caused a great deal of bitterness and resentment. Even more doomed to failure were the restrictions imposed on the defeated German nation.

and Moravia, which had been part of the Austrian Empire. Hungarian-controlled land went towards the formation of Yugoslavia, while Trieste, Istria and the South Tyrol were ceded to

LEFT: Archduke Ferdinand's blood-spattered uniform.
RIGHT: an artist's impression of the assassination.

Italy. The Ottoman Empire had to relinquish much of the land it held in the Middle East, but an attempt to occupy part of Turkey itself provoked a revolt led by General Kemal Ataturk.

The Rhineland was occupied by Allied troops, the Saarland governed by an international commission, Germany's overseas colonies were controlled by the newly created League of Nations, rearmament was forbidden and the size of the army strictly limited. Most painful of all were the crippling financial reparations. They were never fully paid, but they contributed to the near collapse of the German economy and engendered huge resentment, which Adolf Hitler was able to manipulate during his rise to power.

The 1920s and 1930s were decades of harsh totalitarian regimes and a great deal of hardship caused by the severe economic recession of the Depression. At the same time, the newly created states in Eastern Europe were bedevilled by nationalist tensions.

Political instability

In Poland, a coup in 1926 left the country a virtual dictatorship under Marshal Pilsudski. In Hungary, there was a fleeting period of Communist control, and a much longer one under Romanian occupation. Ethnic arguments between Croats, Serbs and Slovenes in

Yugoslavia culminated in the murder of King Alexander by a Croat separatist in 1934. Czechoslovakia was the most successful: under the much-respected President Masaryk, democracy survived into the mid-1930s, but in the German Sudetenland a strong National Socialist Party dominated the latter part of the decade.

In Greece, the inter-war years saw constant rivalry between republicans, led by Venizelos, and royalists, loyal to King Constantine. When the monarchy was restored, in 1935, after a period of republicanism, the king could rule only with the backing of General Metaxas, a virtual dictator.

In the Iberian peninsula Portugal, a republic since the overthrow of the monarchy in 1910, came under military control in 1926, and the dictatorship of António Salazar, who was to rule for the next 36 years, began in 1932. In Spain a period of military rule by General Primo de Rivera, and the abdication of King Alfonso XIII in 1931, left a shaky republic, torn with dissent between left and right. In 1936, a military revolt led by Francisco Franco initiated a civil war that lasted for three years, with Franco's nationalists supported by Germany and Italy, the republicans by the Soviet Union and an International Brigade of volunteers.

Franco's forces defeated the Republicans in 1939. He took control of a demoralised country, its people near starvation, and ruled at the head of a Falangist (neo-Fascist) government until his death in 1975.

The rise of Fascism

The first Fascist party had arisen in Italy, where Mussolini manipulated fears of Communism to gain support and, in 1922, marched on Rome with his 25,000 Blackshirts. King Victor Emmanuel III reluctantly asked him to form a government, and four years later Mussolini declared himself Il Duce, leader of the Italian people.

Savagely repressing his opponents, he embarked on massive programmes of public works, forged links with the German Nazi Party and, in 1935, in an attempt to build an empire, invaded Abyssinia (modern Ethiopia and Eritrea). Emboldened by the fact that the League of Nations, the body formed to prevent war, simply imposed a few economic sanctions, he walked into Albania four years later.

In Germany, Adolf Hitler also exploited the people's fear of Communism, which was rife in the years following Russia's 1917 Bolshevik

---

EXPERIMENTAL ART

Despite political troubles and financial hardship in the 1920s and '30s, artistic experiment flourished in Europe. The avant-garde Surrealist movement inspired paintings by Magritte, de Chirico, Miró and Dalí. The Bauhaus School in Germany produced startlingly Modernist architectural designs, while Art Deco introduced innovative geometric forms to household objects.

Experimental plays were produced by Bertholt Brecht in Germany, Luigi Pirandello in Italy and Jean Cocteau in France. Leading proponents of the newest art form, cinema, included the German Fritz Lang and Luis Buñuel, a Spaniard working in France.

Revolution, to win widespread support for his National Socialist Party. He was also able to tap into the resentment felt by the German people over the terms of the Treaty of Versailles, the effects of which were further compounded by the economic crisis of the Depression after the 1929 Wall Street Crash.

In 1937 the town of Guernica in northern Spain entered history as the first place to be bombed from the air, an event immortalised in Picasso's painting Guernica.

he marched into Austria and proclaimed the Anschluss, the union of the two countries.

Later that year, at the Munich Conference, Britain and France capitulated to Hitler's demands and allowed him control of the Sudetenland, but the "peace in our time" that British Prime Minister Neville Chamberlain thought this ensured lasted less than a year. Hitler seized the rest of Czechoslovakia, signed a non-aggression pact with the Soviet Union, then invaded Poland. It was the end of appeasement and the beginning of World War II, in which Germany, Italy and, later, Japan, took on the world.

The weak Weimar Republic could not survive, and in 1933 Hitler became chancellor of Germany. When President von Hindenburg died the following year, Hitler established himself as Führer, banning opposition parties, giving draconian powers to the Gestapo, and initiating against Germany's Jewish population the increasingly repressive measures that would culminate in the Holocaust.

In 1936 Hitler reoccupied the Rhineland, and two year later, with the connivance of the pro-Nazi Austrian Chancellor Seyss-Inquart,

LEFT: Hitler crossing the Czech border in 1939.
ABOVE: a scene of wartime devastation in the Polish capital, Warsaw.

Aftermath of war

When the conflict finally came to an end in May 1945, Europe embarked on the long, costly process of putting itself together again. Shattered cities had to be rebuilt, particularly Cologne and Dresden, which the Allies had relentlessly bombed. Warsaw's historic streets were faithfully recreated, but in most places new buildings were erected alongside the old, changing the character of many towns but, in the process, often providing better living conditions.

In Greece, civil war between monarchists and Communists raged for four years. Spain, ostracised by the Allied powers because of her support for Hitler, suffered years of severe hardship, her *noche negra*, or black night.

In Eastern Europe, the USSR was allowed to keep within her sphere of interest all the areas occupied by the Red Army when the conflict ended. By the end of the decade, all these states had Soviet-dominated governments – although Yugoslavia and Romania soon installed their own brand of Communism.

Germany was divided in two, and the Allied powers given zones of occupation in Berlin. In 1948 tensions between the powers resulted in the Soviet Union blockading the city, and subsequent discontent in the Eastern zone, due to marked differences in living standards, led to the construction in 1961 of the Berlin

the growth of air travel and car ownership, all contributed to the birth of the mass-market holiday industry. During the 1960s sleepy fishing villages turned into bustling resorts, where bikini-clad Northern European women rubbed shoulders with black-clad Mediterranean grandmothers, and high-rise hotels overshadowed whitewashed cottages. It brought prosperity to poverty-stricken areas, along with customs and values that may have been less welcome.

Skiing, a sport for the many and not just for the rich, came a little later than sun-seeking, but soon the mountainous areas of Switzerland, Austria, Italy and France were peppered

Wall, a potent symbol of repression in post-war Europe.

Hungary also learnt the meaning of repression in 1956, when an uprising, designed to overthrow Communist rule, was brutally suppressed by the Soviet Union and its leader, Imre Nagy, executed. The Iron Curtain, as Britain's former Prime Minister Winston Churchill called it, was firmly drawn across Europe, and global conflict replaced by the Cold War.

Mass tourism

In Western Europe, the hardship and austerity of the post-war years faded and people began to enjoy more leisure and mobility. Annual paid holidays, more disposable income, and

STUDENT UNREST

An awareness of the wider world that came with developments in mass media, and in particular the daily footage showing America's involvement in the unpopular war in Vietnam, led to a questioning of values in the 1960s, especially among young people.

Student unrest swept across Europe and the US, beginning with the student protest in Paris in May 1968, which brought France to the verge of civil war. In the same spirit of defiance came the Prague Spring, when students backed the reforming leader Alexander Dubček against Czechoslovakia's Moscow-oriented regime. Their peaceful protest was crushed by Soviet tanks.

with chalets and cable cars and threatened by the ecological impact of the seasonal crowds. By the 1990s weekend city breaks in Europe were commonplace through cheap flights, high-speed trains and fast motorway links.

Closer European ties

The idea of a European identity was slowly growing during these decades. Britain, Ireland and Denmark joined the EEC in 1973, 15 years after it was created. Spain, Portugal and Greece also moved closer to Europe during the mid-seventies, after they ceased to be dictatorships. In Portugal, a left-wing military coup overthrew

The European Economic Community (which became the European Union in 1993) was born in 1957, with France, Belgium, Luxembourg, Italy, West Germany and the Netherlands as its founder members.

the heirs of Salazar, and there were democratic elections in 1976. In Greece the military junta was overthrown in 1974, and a new constitution adopted. Following the death of Franco in Spain in 1975 the monarchy was restored and a new constitution declared. Spain became a democracy and Juan Carlos a popular king. All three countries joined the EEC in the 1980s.

Democracy was also in the air in Poland in the early 1980s. *Solidarnosc* (Solidarity), an independent trade union, came to prominence in the Gdansk dockyards. The authorities imposed martial law and arrested the charismatic leader, Lech Walesa. However, after secret talks between Polish leader General Jaruzelski and the Polish-born Pope John Paul II, martial law was lifted. Walesa was awarded the Nobel Peace Prize later that year. In 1989, elections defeated the Communist Party and put a Solidarity prime minister in office.

By then, the whole face of Eastern Europe was changing. Mikhail Gorbachev's policies of *perestroika* and *glasnost* led to more openness in government in the USSR, and the end of the Brezhnev Doctrine, under which the Soviet Union had the right to intervene in the affairs of Warsaw Pact countries, opened the flood-

LEFT: student protests in the Boulevard St-Germain in Paris in May 1968. **RIGHT:** a Croatian refugee prepares to flee her village during the civil war in the Balkans.

gates throughout Eastern Europe. One by one the former satellite states renounced Communism and sought independence.

In Czechoslovakia, a new government was formed under playwright Václav Havel; and in Hungary, as in most of the other states, a democratic, multi-party government was formed. In Germany, the Berlin Wall came down, amid international rejoicing, in November 1989, and the divided country was reunited.

But poverty followed democracy in Eastern Europe, power struggles continued, and the peoples of the Balkans again suffered war and subsequent displacement. By the end of the

1990s, tempers had cooled and the millennium was celebrated amid hopes for peace and prosperity. In 2002, 12 of the 15 EU states adopted the euro (including all the countries featured in this book except Switzerland, where Swiss francs are still the currency). Two years later, 10 new members joined, and in 2007 Romania and Bulgaria brought the number to 27. Hopes for unity were high, but the new Europe is not yet the ideal many had hoped for.

Global crisis

Europe's post-war prosperity has come under intense pressure in the early 21st century as a result of several global developments. The main challenge is climate change, which threatens to bring large-scale migration of peoples from hot regions of the planet to the cooler zones in Europe. Here, the European Union has taken a leading role, introducing progressive measures to cut carbon emissions and reduce reliance on fossil fuels by 2020.

> In 2008–9, jobless figures across Europe rose dramatically, car production slumped and many small businesses struggled to find credit. For some, it seemed as if Europe was returning to the dark days of the 1930s.

they are now getting even smaller and more environmentally friendly.

Although the crisis has led many European countries to return to protectionism, most Europeans still want to work together. Moreover, many countries on the borders of the European Union have their eyes set on EU membership. Some, such as Croatia, look set to be admitted in the near future, and Iceland, which made tentative overtures following the country's recent financial collapse, could be fast-tracked into membership. But Turkey, which has been campaigning for many decades to join the union, still faces

Added to that, the banking crisis that began in 2007 in the US rapidly spread to Europe, putting enormous strains on many European countries, particularly the new democracies of Eastern Europe, where a period of explosive growth has been followed by deep recession.

The climate crisis coupled with recession have led to a dramatic shift in the European way of life, with people gradually adopting a more economical and ecological lifestyle. Many European cities have introduced measures to cut down on car use and promote public transport. City centres are often pedestrian-only zones, and some cities have even implemented car-free days or free bicycle schemes. European cars were always smaller than US models but

fierce opposition from those who argue that it is not a truly European country.

The biggest challenge now facing Europe is to implement the Lisbon Treaty, which will give Europe its own president and foreign minister, while enabling members to act more effectively. With the Irish voting in October 2009 in favour of EU reform, Europe could finally emerge as a global power with the capacity to compete on equal terms with the US and China. Only then will it be possible to talk, as Winston Churchill once did, of a United States of Europe. ❏

ABOVE: a Federalist demonstrates in Brussels in support of the Lisbon Treaty. **RIGHT:** Barcelona runs a share-a-bike scheme for residents.

BEST BUILDINGS OF EUROPE

Europe has a vast collection of interesting buildings, each with a rich story to tell. Some, however, stand out from all the rest

The landscape of Western Europe is littered with castles, cathedrals, temples, mansions, palaces and other permanent, if sometimes crumbling, landmarks, which speak to 21st-century visitors of the epochs in which they were built, and of the skills and aspirations of their architects and patrons.

These emblematic structures, recognised at a glance the world over and much imitated, were built primarily to impress. They stand, on the whole, on prominent sites where they can look down on common humanity and, more importantly, be seen. They were intended as proof of political, military or religious authority, usually combined with artistic sensibilities; to instil fear, awe or obedience in the populace; or to inspire envy of the wealth, prestige and power invested in them.

In a wider sense, they were also built simply because they could be, by civilisations anxious to reassure themselves – and others – of their success and immortality. Each building is evidence of determination (sometimes to the point of folly), technological know-how, the social organisation necessary to carry out large and complex building schemes, and, importantly, enough surplus prosperity to pay for the project over an extended period of time from start to finish.

TOP: the majestic Parthenon in Athens.

LEFT: the Eiffel Tower attracted fierce criticism when it was built in 1889. Intended to be a temporary addition to the Parisian skyline, it is still standing more than 120 years on, a world-famous icon of France.

ABOVE: the Alhambra was built in the 14th century by the Muslim rulers of Granada, and remains the most beautiful example of Islamic architecture in Spain.

LEFT: Portugal's Palácio da Pena, on a rocky peak in the Serra de Sintra, is one of the finest expressions of 19th-century Romanticism. Its orange-red clock tower dominates a collection of ornate domes, faux battlements, galleries and gateways.

GLORIES TO GOD

Early churches in Europe were built on the principles of the Roman basilica; it was not until late in the first millennium AD that a distinctly Christian architecture developed into the Romanesque style, which was characterised by thick walls pierced by small windows and roofs supported on rounded arches.

The goal of church-builders, however, was always to build higher and grander buildings to the glory of God, and their experimentation led to the breakthroughs of Gothic architecture. The ingenious use of pointed arches, rib vaults and flying buttresses meant that slender spires could be built overhead and great stained-glass windows placed in the walls to fill the interior with coloured light.

During the Renaissance, in the 15th and 16th centuries, there was a return to classical ideals of harmony and symmetry, but Baroque artists rebelled against such simplicity with an emphasis placed on drama and an exuberance of ornamentation. In modern times, architects have either drawn on earlier styles or else created churches to a stark, functional aesthetic.

ABOVE: medieval church-building reached its apogee with the daring achievements of Gothic, which included piercing the walls to make room for great areas of stained glass, as seen in this rose window in Paris's Notre-Dame cathedral.

RIGHT: Ágios Nikólaos Anapafsá is one of the Metéora group of monasteries on the plain of Thessaly, central Greece, built from the 14th century onwards on seemingly inaccessible sandstone towers, which are known as the "stone forest".

ABOVE: the Emperor Vespasian commissioned Rome's immense amphitheatre, the Colosseum, in AD 72. Spectacular and bloody gladiatorial battles, as well as fights between wild animals, were staged in it for the pleasure of the 55,000 spectators.

LEFT: Neuschwanstein Castle – literally, the New Stone Castle – was begun in 1869 by Ludwig II, in honour of his favourite composer, Richard Wagner. It is dramatically sited on the top of a hill, overlooking the Hohenschwangau Valley, Bavaria.

Son Excellence
Madame Angela MERKEL

Monsieur
le Président de la République

Son Excellence
Monsieur Gordon BROWN

EUROPE FROM A TO Z

These cultural snapshots, from Architecture to
Zeitgeist via Food, Kissing and Umbrellas, serve
as an introduction to this panoply of nations

Anyone who travels through Europe will be aware of the
many place names associated with war and destruction.
The map is dotted with tragic names like Ypres and
Auschwitz, Waterloo and Dresden, Austerlitz and Verdun. As
you notice the countless military cemeteries, it seems fair to
ask whether Europeans have ever lived together in peace.

Yet for the past 50 years, an astonishing process of recon-
ciliation has taken place, led by the oldest of enemies, the French and
Germans. Year after year, political leaders have patiently built a new
Europe founded on ideas of economic cooperation and peaceful coexist-
ence. The union has gradually expanded to embrace 27 countries with 23
different official languages.

Europe isn't perfect. It still doesn't have an inspiring
Constitution (all attempts so far have failed) or an impressive capital city (Brussels has never really risen to the challenge of its status as EU capital). But it has a population
who increasingly live and think like Europeans.

You find these new Europeans scattered all over the continent; at summer rock festivals, on high-speed trains, or
sitting on sunny café terraces overlooking restored urban
squares. They are not particularly aware of their European
identity. But it comes out in the number of languages they
speak (three is pretty common), their tolerance and understanding of
other cultures and their extended networks of friends and family members in every European country.

To many people, therefore, Europe is much more than a living museum,
a lengthy list of monuments to be ticked off as a dutiful obligation: it is
a continent whose variety and density of culture can always surprise and
often enrich the enquiring visitor. On the following pages, we focus on
some of the quirkier aspects of Europe, from kissing customs to queuing
conventions, from centres of corruption to temples of gastronomy, from
driving habits to swearing skills, which may go a little way to shedding
some light on what it means to be European. ❑

PRECEDING PAGES: European leaders at a press conference at the Elysée Palace
in Paris, to discuss the international financial crisis; Piazza Farnese, Rome.
LEFT: Lord Foster's dome on the Reichstag, Berlin. **ABOVE:** getting around
in Portofino, Italy; the peaceful Place des Vosges, Paris.

Architecture

A tourist in a new city often takes a dutiful interest in its ancient cathedrals and palaces, but Europe also has exciting and contentious modern public buildings to catch the imagination.

The starting point is the Bauhaus Museum in Dessau. The Bauhaus design school, begun by Walter Gropius, set the pace in the 1920s and 1930s. Interest was added by the Swiss architect Le Corbusier, whose designs included the modular Unité d'Habitation in Marseille using units proportional to the human figure. During the 1950s and 1960s, architectural heroes emerged,

Museums, often drear 19th-century monoliths, were brought up to date. The American Richard Meier designed the first of his "white refrigerators" in Frankfurt to house the Museum of Crafts and Allied Arts, and went on to design the Museum of Contemporary Art in Barcelona, where the 1992 Olympic Games brought a new wave of modern architecture. Among contributors were Norman Foster, who later designed the Millau Viaduct, the highest vehicular bridge in the world, spanning the River Tarn in southern France (*pictured below*).

Some of the most striking new architecture in Europe is found in former dockland areas,

such as Giovanni Ponti, who designed the radical Pirelli tower block in Milan that looks down over Ulisse Stracchini's elegant white Central Station. Josep Lluis Sert, a Spaniard who followed Gropius into the chair of architecture at Harvard University, designed the Maeght Gallery in St-Paul-de-Vence in the south of France and the Miró Foundation in Barcelona, near the rebuilt 1929 Pavilion of Mies van der Rohe, first director of the Bauhaus.

The economic upturn of the 1980s brought out new architectural stars. Paris had a head start with the 1977 Pompidou Centre, and it took the lead with such *Grands Projets* as I.M. Pei's Louvre pyramid and the French National Library, announced in 1988 and completed seven years later.

LE CORBUSIER'S MASTERPIECE

The little town of Ronchamp in Franche-Comté, France, is home to one of Europe's most famous post-war buildings: Le Corbusier's Chapel of Notre-Dame-du-Haut, which he designed to replace another church here that was destroyed during World War II. Unconstrained by a geometric framework, the design is dominated by curves, with walls and roof sloping at irregular angles, and windows of varying proportions placed haphazardly along the walls. Le Corbusier's unique vision was a deliberate gesture against the right angle and straight line, and was intended to reflect the forms of its hilltop setting and the natural features of the surrounding landscape.

where many abandoned waterfronts have become ripe for development. In Amsterdam, architects have designed astonishing new buildings in the former port area to the north of the Old City, including a new public library and music centre. Other major ports such as Antwerp, Hamburg and Rotterdam have been equally adventurous.

New projects have also sprung up in the war-damaged cities of Germany such as Berlin, where Norman Foster redesigned the Reichstag (Parliament), while Daniel Libeskind built the deeply moving Jewish Museum.

(*See also Best Buildings of Europe, page 58.*)

discourage it the European Union hands out annual Clean Beach awards.

The Atlantic's rollers are for surfing. Guincho in Portugal has a reputation among windsurfers, as does Tarifa in southwestern Spain. The cooler North Sea end of this coast, in Germany

At Mont-St-Michel in northern France, the tide is one of the fastest in the world, covering 40km (25 miles) in six hours, and the difference in height between high and low tides can be as much as 15 metres (50ft).

Beaches

Western Europe has two different shores – sea and ocean – and their characteristics are distinct. The wide stretches of Atlantic Ocean and North Sea beaches are churned up by two tides a day, which can discolour the water and shift the sand. In the more saline, tideless Mediterranean, the beaches are spread out between small rocky coves, where the water can be stunningly translucent. Of course, there is pollution and contamination, but to

LEFT: the breathtaking Millau Viaduct over the Tarn, southern France. **ABOVE:** Tsambíka Bay on the east coast of Rhodes, Greece.

and the Dutch Frisian Islands, is where German naturists bare themselves to the winds and billowing seas. But tidal waters can be a hazard, especially where the shore is flat and the twice-daily tide becomes speedy, cutting off cliffs and causeways at a frightening pace.

The Mediterranean is safe, its coves often backed with dunes and umbrella pines, but its rugged coast and unexpected winds should not be underestimated. Some resorts have half a dozen beaches with a choice of amenities and perhaps a choice of users: family, nude or gay; or they may be colonised by one nationality.

The popularity of such sandy stretches as Italy's crowded lidos around Rimini on the Adriatic, prompted some resorts to import sand. The impressive 6km (4-mile) beach at Benidorm, Spain's highly popular holiday resort, was established with sand shipped in from Morocco, and is still regularly topped up.

Cities

Europeans have been living in cities for many hundreds of years and have developed a distinctive style of urban living. They are immensely proud of their broad boulevards, grand squares, public parks and café terraces. These offer places to linger, chat to friends, stroll with children and show off your fashion sense.

The European city reached its greatest moment towards the end of the 19th century, when Paris served as the model for almost every city from Lisbon to Budapest. This was the period when architects built wide tree-lined boulevards, grand department stores and lofty museums. Many of the cities were badly damaged in World War II; some, like Dresden, were completely rebuilt, while others never recovered their old allure. Yet in recent years, led once again by France, Europe's cities have been restoring their urban quarters, installing street furniture and encouraging young families to settle in downtown areas.

CAFÉ LIFE ACROSS EUROPE

Europeans enjoy spending a lot of time in cafés drinking small cups of coffee. The habit originated in Vienna, where the first coffee house opened in 1683, and café life reached a peak in the late 19th century when grand establishments opened in capital cities across Europe, from Lisbon to Budapest.

The classic coffee house offers a place to escape from the rush of the city, sit with a strong espresso coffee served on a silver tray and read one of the newspapers on wooden poles generously provided by the establishment.

Almost every European city has its grand cafés, like Florian in Venice, the Café de la Paix in Paris, Café Central in Vienna and Café Americain in Amsterdam. The café still forms the focus of social life in most towns and villages across Europe, attracting people of all ages, from young writers and intellectuals to elderly couples. In recent years, architects have designed contemporary cafés which appeal more to younger people, like Café Costes in Paris or De Jaren in Amsterdam. Whatever the style, the emphasis is still on good coffee and quiet discussion in civilised surroundings.

Driving

Linger in the outside lane of a German *autobahn* and your rear-view mirror will soon reflect the flashing headlights of a Porsche or BMW bearing down on you at 240kph (150mph). Germany's love of speed usually triumphs over demands for a blanket speed limit on its *autobahn* system. When an accident occurs, of course, you're more likely to need a hearse than an ambulance. Germany comes just behind Poland and Italy in the league of road deaths, all with well over 5,000 a year, closely followed by France and then Spain. But of course, the size of the country counts: Luxembourg has fewer than 50 deaths a year.

Italians reflect in their driving style their anarchic attitude towards authority in general. Horns are blasted whenever traffic stops, overtaking is instinctive, and anyone foolish enough to stop as a light turns red is likely to find several drivers crashing into him. The philosophy was summed up by the reaction of some Italians when a seat-belt law was passed: such restraints being incompatible with their macho outlook, they tried to fool police by wearing T-shirts with a seat belt printed across the front. Spanish driving, it's said, reflects the culture's obsession with death. French pride interprets overtaking as insulting behaviour, while Swiss drivers are awfully proper.

Whatever the truth of such stereotypes, the first-time visitor to Europe should bear two things in mind. One is that driving styles are generally geared to getting from A to B as fast as possible. The second is that mixing driving and alcohol carries very severe penalties.

European Union

Just after World War II, which left the continent devastated, Britain's wartime leader, Winston Churchill, declared: "We must build a kind of United States of Europe." Throughout history, visionaries from Augustus and Charlemagne to Napoleon had tried to unite Europe, usually by force. In 1950 a French businessman, Jean Monnet, proposed a route dictated by economic self-interest: by pooling coal and steel resources,

Europe's industrial powers could compete in world markets more effectively.

The resulting Coal and Steel Community developed into the European Economic Community (the Common Market) in 1957. In 1993 the expanded EEC, now renamed the EC, became the European Union, with an increased degree of cooperation between member states, and most border controls removed. On 1 January 2002, a single currency, the euro, was adopted by all the EU member states apart from Denmark, Sweden and the UK, whose people remained sceptical about its benefits. In May 2004, membership of the EU expanded to 25

states, including many of the former Communist countries, and Romania and Bulgaria joined two years later. By 1 January 2009, 16 of these countries had adopted the euro, making it the common currency for 326 million people.

Unlike the US, however, the EU has no common language or culture, although English is widely regarded as the language of business and travel. When times get tough, Europe's individual members, far from uniting to solve problems, may become more nationalistic. Tariff barriers may have disappeared within the Union, but mental barriers remain. However, after centuries of war, Europeans seem determined to live together in peace. While most remain rooted in their own country and culture, a growing

---

LEFT: the Piazza San Giovanni, Florence.
RIGHT: the European Commission building in Brussels.

number move easily from one country to another and speak several languages. Young people are encouraged to study in different EU countries under the Erasmus programme, and many have mixed ethnicity. In this sense, a European identity is slowly taking shape in a continent once torn by war.

Food

European nations can be fanatical about what they eat. French restaurants often have a reverential air, Belgian gourmet gatherings are not for the light-hearted, while in Greece you are

encouraged to visit the kitchen to see what's cooking. Chefs often have celebrity status beyond their country. Paul Bocuse from foodie Lyon, voted "chef of the century" in 1989, has been eclipsed by Ferran Adrià, who every autumn closes his Costa Brava restaurant, El Bulli, for six months while he prepares his season's menus. Only 8,000 of the 300,000 who try to book a table each year are successful.

Local food is always best. Not for nothing was the Slow Food Manifesto signed in Paris in 1989, three years after its forerunner, Arcigola, was founded in Italy. And it is no surprise that farmer José Bové became a hero when he went

to jail for three months in 2002 for vandalising a McDonald's in the French town of Millau.

Regional specialities are still strong. You know what part of France or Italy you are in when you stop at a motorway service station: the produce on sale, the food, cheese and wine, invariably come from the surrounding area.

Any journey across the continent means a culinary journey, too. France extends from Normandy cider, cheese and tripe to the Provençal south of olives, wine and *bouillabaisse*, with goose farms, *cassoulet* and quiche on the way. Italy stretches from the boar and polenta of Piedmont in the north through the risotto lands of the Po Valley to the sunny south of pizza and mozzarella cheese. Iberia's Atlantic coast gives

Portuguese, Galician and Basque cookery their flavours; the Mediterranean coast brings the Arabic influence of paella. The North Sea provides herring and smoked oily fish in the Low Countries. Snack on a fish sandwich in Amsterdam; dip into a bowl of *moules* in Belgium.

> *"What's the Italian for spaghetti?" a young tourist was overheard asking her companion in a Naples restaurant. We are so familiar with a diverse range of European foods we forget where they come from.*

In Northern Europe, beer is the thing to drink. Bavarian and Czech brews are hard to beat, which perhaps in the past helped to disguise the fact that the food was not the most inventive. However, nowadays German and Austrian cooking is much more than dumplings and sauerkraut.

Then there are the pastries, notably from Belgium and Austria, where a coffee-house culture produces rich tortes and strudels. In Portugal the favourite tipple is tea – Portuguese merchants were the first to bring it to Europe from China.

LEFT: an Amsterdam cheese counter; spaghetti and clams in San Remo. **ABOVE:** at the Henri Maes Brewery, Bruges. **RIGHT:** gestures are important.

Gestures

In addition to the wide variety of languages spoken in Europe, there are a whole range of hand gestures which often vary greatly from country to country. Giving a thumbs-up sign will signify approval in most countries – but not in Greece, where it is a vulgar insult, equivalent to raising the middle finger elsewhere. Flick your ear with a forefinger in Italy and you could be suggesting someone is homosexual. Jerking your forearm up and slapping your other hand into the crook of the arm would be an insult in most of Europe – although else-

where in the world the gesture is regarded as a sign of sexual appreciation. Make a ring with your thumb or index finger and most Europeans interpret it as meaning OK, but others see it as zero or worthless, and a Greek could be referring to a bodily orifice.

A shrug can convey different things, depending on whether it is accompanied by moving the shoulders, raising the eyebrows or pursing the mouth. Is someone resigned? Indifferent? Helpless? It's sometimes hard to tell.

In France, mouth movements are important. This is partly because nine of the 16 French vowels involve rounding the lips (compared with only five in German and two in English). The French are also great gesticulators, using their hands rather than their entire arms – but their repertoire is narrower than the Italians'.

The Italians have long been regarded as Europe's most expressive people. A wide variety of hand signals are used to convey agreement, surprise, delight, disgust, and gestures familiar to ancient Greeks can still be seen today.

> *Charles V's claim that he spoke Spanish to God, Italian to women, French to men, and German to his horse sparked a tradition of jokes at other Europeans' expense.*

Immigrants

Anyone imagining they will arrive in a European country and immediately start practising their phrase-book greetings on a local may be in for a surprise, for many people in the service industry are neither native-born nor native speakers. Today you will hear Gujarati in Barcelona, Turkish in Hamburg, Russian on the Riviera, and Eastern European languages everywhere.

Migration between EU countries is reasonably fluid, but even within the EU, immigration causes problems: two years after joining, 1 million Poles left home to find work abroad,

Humour

Language plays a large part in forming humour. Thus, while French lends itself to puns, Spanish doesn't. Much French wit incorporates clever, sarcastic wordplay. On the other hand, there is a fine old tradition of slapstick in France, and the French have an earthy humour built around sex – though it's far from sexist. Belgians, by contrast, are conservative about sex, so there are few sex jokes in Belgium. Scatological humour is absent in France, but is strong in Germany, where such references appear even in children's riddles. Really, there's only one thing regarded as funny throughout Europe: other Europeans.

emptying the country of its young workforce. With the economic recession however, many have now returned home.

Europe's external borders leak like sieves, letting in hundreds of thousands illegally from Eastern Europe, Africa, Asia and elsewhere. In 2007, President Sarkozy came to power determined to deal with France's 400,000 or so illegal immigrants. But, mindful of history and the deportation of Jews, there has been support for the *sans papiers*, and a new Immigration Museum opened in Paris shortly afterwards.

Germany had Europe's most liberal immigration laws when Turkish *Gastarbeiters* ("guest-workers"), now numbering 2 million, began arriving in 1961. But attitudes hardened in

1993, after the country had been reunited, the displaced from war-torn former Yugoslavia began to arrive in large numbers and unemployment reached 6 million.

The Balkans have pushed immigrants into Greece, and Italy's Adriatic shores are constantly patrolled for Albanians in inadequate makeshift boats. North Africans regularly arrive on the shores of Sicily and southern Spain.

Attitudes to immigration are dependent on the current political and economic climates, and were particularly exaggerated following the attacks of 11 September 2001. Ultra right-wing parties gained support on a tide of racism.

Policies relating to immigration may have to change, and attitudes will need to change with them, because a whole new underclass is developing right across the continent.

Kissing

Latin has three words for "kiss", distinguishing between a kiss of friendship on the cheek, a kiss of affection on the mouth and a lover's kiss on the mouth. The Roman tradition lives on, for people around the Mediterranean are more spontaneously intimate than their northern cousins: they sit closer together, they touch more, they

The subject of immigration continues to be a political hot potato in Europe, with several far-right parties gaining seats in the European parliament in 2009, much to the alarm of the majority.

However, the populations of virtually all European countries are declining, and to compete in home and world markets, cheap immigrant labour is seen by some economists as essential.

stand closer together when talking, and everyone seems to cheek-kiss enthusiastically.

In Germany, men seldom kiss the cheeks of other men, and personal space is assiduously protected. Handshaking is more common, but usually only when meeting someone by appointment. In France, it is common to shake hands with someone each time you meet and depart, even if you meet them several times a day.

But few generalisations are reliable. The Italians are supposedly the most tactile Europeans – yet, although two men will touch frequently when talking (perhaps to deter the other person from interrupting), and even guide each other round a corner while walking, there is noticeably less touching between the sexes. Even

LEFT: drag queen at Dragshowbar Lellebel, Amsterdam. **ABOVE:** the Vasari Corridor, Florence. **RIGHT:** Italians greet with a kiss.

married couples are less likely to walk along hand in hand than they are in Denmark or Austria. Could it be possible that Italian men regard hand-holding as a sign of submissiveness?

Lavatories

Toilet amenities are a mixed bag. Modern cabins have replaced most of Paris's old *pissoirs*, which enabled a gentleman to relieve himself while continuing a conversation with his companion outside. In rural France, though, you may still find some of the old "hole in the ground" lavatories, which compel users to squat – a healthy posture, it is claimed.

It's not unusual to find restaurants with facilities used by both men and women, and many public toilets for men have female attendants. Be sure to leave a small tip, as most attendants have no other source of income. The civic pride of former Eastern European countries continues, and they tend to be scrupulously clean. Elsewhere, standards can be low.

If there is no public lavatory in sight, head for a bar or café. Some are more tolerant than others, and some keep them locked, so you have to ask for the key behind the bar; in these cases, using the loo without buying a drink or snack is frowned upon.

Monarchies

Hereditary kings and queens have shown remarkable endurance in an age so concerned with the spread of democracy. Spain even restored its monarchy in 1975 and, despite predictions that he would be known as "Juan Carlos the Brief", the popular king is still on the throne, and has successfully overseen a smooth transition from dictatorship to democracy. None of Europe's other six major crowned heads – or indeed the less weighty rulers such as Prince Albert II of Monaco or Prince Alois of Liechtenstein, whose father ceded power to him in August 2004 – looks set to lose their "job" in the near future.

The power of European monarchs is mostly symbolic. The Dutch permit their queen a great deal of influence in theory, but allow her almost none in practice. In 1990, the Belgian King Baudouin abdicated for two days so that he did not have to approve legislation legalising abortion. He died in 1993, childless, and his

younger brother, Albert, found himself king at the age of 59. The monarchy was still valued as an institution, however, because it seemed virtually the only glue holding together the Dutch and French-speaking halves of a politically divided country.

> *Most European monarchs are tolerated because they have no real power, and are valued mainly for providing a sense of tradition and continuity, and a useful focus for ceremonial events.*

European monarchies are becoming increasingly democratised as more members "marry out". In 2001 Prince Haakon, heir to the Norwegian throne, married a commoner who was a single mother. In 2004, the Spanish heir, Prince Felipe, married a former journalist, Letizia Ortiz; and Mary Donaldson became the first Australian to join European royalty when she married Crown Prince Fredrik of Denmark.

Meanwhile, deposed monarchs are patiently standing in the wings: Henri, Comte de Paris, is pretender to the French throne; Constantine would like his Greek crown back; while both Vittorio Emanuele, Prince of Naples, and Amedeo, 5th Duke of Aosta, lay claim to the Kingdom of Italy.

Monarchs have very little power in modern democracies, but they are still largely respected. The Belgian royal family can count on large crowds when they tour the country on National Day (21 July), and the Dutch were traumatised in 2009 when a man apparently tried to assassinate members of the royal family during the Queen's Birthday *(Koninginnedag)* celebrations.

Nature

Europe has some magnificent natural wonders, but these are increasingly under threat from tourism and industrialisation. From the

In France and Portugal, huntsmen dress in bright liveries, blow their bugles and give chase on horseback after foxes.

Many countries have special animals. In France, there are the long-horned black cattle of the Camargue, at the delta of the Rhône where flamingos flock. Southern Italy has water buffalo, from which mozzarella cheese is made. Switzerland has the chamois mountain goat, Spain the Iberian lynx and the Moorish gecko.

As ecological awareness grows, measures are increasingly being taken to protect landscapes and species. Many groups now campaign to protect wildernesses, forests and coastlines

eagles' eyries of the snowy Alps to the lizard sunbeds of the Spanish sierras, animal habitats are under threat. Hunting is widely permitted, and migrant birds must dodge the bullets of Italians and Spaniards who will eat anything that flaps a wing. The big-game hunters are the Germans, who like wild boar and are enthusiastic chasers of wolves and bears in the newly accessible Eastern Europe.

Boar are popular in much of Europe and in the shooting season (roughly from November to February) they are hunted, along with ducks.

from development. Yet untold damage has already been done to Europe's natural beauty, especially in the Alps and along the Mediterranean coastline.

(See also Wildlife in Europe, page 320.)

Oath-making

The Romance languages lend themselves particularly well to cursing and swearing. Italy, being a Catholic country, often combines imprecations and blasphemy: common examples are *Porco Dio!* (That pig of a God) and *Madonna puttana!* (That whore of a Virgin Mary).

Spain also embraces blasphemy. *Hostia!* (Sacramental bread) is mild enough; more extreme

LEFT: King Juan Carlos I and Queen Sofia welcome President Medvedev to Spain at El Pardo Palace.
ABOVE: chamois in Furka, Switzerland.

is *Me cago en todos los santos*, which means "I defecate on all the saints". In Germany excrement crops up readily: *Scheiss* can express frustration or be an insult. The equivalent in French *(Merde)* indicates only mild annoyance.

Punctuality

The closer you get to the Mediterranean, the slower the pace of life becomes. People even walk more slowly. Partly it's a matter of adapting to a hot climate, partly it's a reflection of the attitude that time serves people rather than the other way round. To be late for an appoint-

ment in Germany, Belgium, Austria or Switzerland would be regarded as rude, or at least inconsiderate. In Greece or Spain, by contrast, nobody is expected to show up on time. Indeed, being *very* late may even be a sign of status.

In France it is not done to discuss business at a business lunch until at least the first course has arrived; this restraint shows you know the value of friendship, not to mention food and wine, and that you are a more rounded person.

Queues

It has been said of the Englishman that, even if he is alone, he forms an orderly queue of one. This attitude is not one that is widely shared

by his continental neighbours. In affluent Switzerland, they'll form a line too, on the rational basis that this is the most efficient way for everyone to be served quickly and fairly.

In Italy, however, the free-for-all prevails: standing in an orderly line would be regarded as both an imposition and a stifling of personal initiative. Sociologists devote learned works to drawing parallels between such anarchic behaviour and attitudes towards government (especially disrespectful in Italy, France and Spain).

Robbery

Most of the world's 300 million tourists a year don't get robbed or mugged. Nevertheless, the ancient tradition of highway robbery lives on in Europe, and visitors should take precautions, especially in the cities.

Amazingly, the oldest tricks still find gullible victims. A Vespa-riding pickpocket in Rome will snatch a handbag without even slowing down. A young man in Barcelona will offer to take your photograph for you, and make off with your camera as soon as you hand it over. In Benidorm (on the southeast Spanish coast), men may pose as porters and steal tourists' luggage. In Greece, men are invited into a bar, find themselves buying drinks for a number of friendly women, and are presented with an exorbitant bill.

Importing a cunning ruse from Florida, unscrupulous French gangs steal cars and use them on a quiet stretch of *autoroute* to ram the back of a foreign-registered car, making it seem accidental. When the victim pulls over to inspect the damage, the gang relieves driver and passengers of their valuables – and maybe steals the car as well.

The French have a name for the villains: *les pirates de la route*. But their advice to potential victims is the bleak suggestion that they add a new phrase to their vocabulary: *Prenez l'argent* (Take the money).

Status

One of the significant differences between American and European social mores is the manner in which people address each other. Germans in particular put great emphasis on titles and can be seriously offended if they are not addressed properly. As the psychologist Carl

Jung once observed: "There are no ordinary human beings, you are 'Herr Professor' or 'Herr Geheimrat,' 'Herr Oberrechnungsrat' and even longer things than that."

Two colleagues with much the same job status can work in the same office for 20 years and still address each other as "Herr Vogel" and "Frau Schmidt". They would feel very uncomfortable, they will tell you, using first names. The advantage of such formality is that it distinguishes acquaintances from friends, and when a friendship is finally cemented by the adoption of first names, it is a memorable occasion, typically celebrated with a few drinks.

Such distinctions were just one of the numerous problems faced by East Germans when the country was reunited. Under Communism, they had, as comrades, been encouraged to address one another by the familiar *du*; in the capitalist West, they had to get used to using the formal term *Sie*.

> *Nothing could be further from the informal way in which Americans greet people they scarcely know than the formality that is preserved in many European countries.*

Another method by which status is delineated is in the choice of second-person pronoun. All the main European languages except English have two words for "you": the familiar form (*tu* in French, *du* in German) and the formal version (*vous* in French, *Sie* in German). Again, the move from formal to familiar is a signal that amity has become camaraderie. In a business environment, the decision to switch is usually initiated by the person with superior status. Distinctions are breaking down, particularly among young people, but they still exist.

LEFT: Bauhaus bar, popular with backpackers, in Bruges, Belgium. **ABOVE:** soldiers in the microstate of Monaco, southern France.

Telecommunications

Europe is one of the world's most sophisticated regions with excellent telecommunications. Most urban homes have a phone and internet connection, while the percentage of houses with a broadband connection is rising fast. Wireless internet is often available at airports, public libraries, on high-speed trains and in cafés, although travellers in rural areas of France and Spain will probably still have to rely on a dusty internet café with just a couple of old computers.

Mobile phone use is virtually ubiquitous and coverage extends to most of Europe. In Italy children as young as three will be sent to crèche equipped with a mobile phone with pictograms they press to keep in touch with their parents.

Television, unsurprisingly, is still the dominant media, but much of the raw material comes from America or Britain, adapted to local needs by subtitling or, more commonly, dubbing. So you may be surprised to turn on a TV in a small town in Germany and find that the locals are sitting at home watching a dubbed episode of *Friends* or *Dallas*.

Much television in Europe is state-controlled and some of it is very dull. The commercial stations are generally responsible for developing mass-appeal programmes like reality shows

and quizzes. There are, as yet, no genuinely European channels. Arte, which broadcasts in French and German, is as close as it gets.

Umbrellas

Unless you are going to the Mediterranean in high summer, you would be wise to pack an umbrella for any trip to Europe. The essence of the weather is its unpredictability: the character of winter or summer will vary wildly from one year to another, and a favourite sympathetic comment from locals as you shelter from a cloudburst is: "It's very unseasonal." The following statistics, therefore, although no guarantee of anything, may dispel a few myths.

The driest month in Berlin is March, and the wettest are July and August. In Munich, the driest is December and the wettest are June and July. Being near the Alps, southern Germany has colder, snowier winters than the north, but sharp winds from Russia can make northern Germany seem pretty arctic.

> The word umbrella comes from the Italian *ombra*, meaning shade, but in most parts of Europe an umbrella is needed for the rain rather than *para sol* – for the sun.

Confirming the wisdom of seeing Paris in the spring, rainfall is least in March and April. It's highest in August. In Marseille, July is the driest month; the wettest are October and November. The mistral wind can bring unseasonably cold weather to the south of France in spring.

In Brussels, it rains most in July (thanks partly to thunderstorms) and December, least in March and May. Winters are wetter in the south and hill fogs occur frequently. The Netherlands has a similar climate. It rains most in July and August, least in March and April.

In Italy it rains least in the extreme north of the mainland and in Sicily and Sardinia. Rome can expect least rain in July, most in November. Venice can expect least in January, with the heaviest downpours in November.

Mountainous Switzerland, affected as it is by weather both from the Atlantic and from Eastern Europe, is notoriously changeable. The driest months in Zurich are March and December, the wettest are June and July. Austria has a similar climate; most rain falls on Vienna in July, the least in January. Greece is known for its sunshine, but rainfall is heavy when it happens, notably in December. The driest months are July and August, when there is virtually no rain at all.

It's a mistake to assume that all of Spain has a Mediterranean climate; the Pyrenees give the north quite a different weather pattern. The northern region of Galicia is sometimes compared to Ireland because of the rainfall. Most rain falls on Madrid in April and December, least in July. In Palma, Majorca, hardly any rain falls in July; October is the wettest month. Coastal Portugal is at the mercy of the Atlantic. It's dry in both Lisbon and Faro in July and August, but wet in December and January.

Vendetta

Although Italy's Mafia understandably get the headlines for their acts of vengeance, most of their murders are motivated more by economic gain than personal grievance. For a cold-blooded interpretation of the biblical "eye for an eye" principle, few have been able to match the Corsicans.

The tradition began centuries ago when the islanders retaliated against their Genoese conquerors by killing a soldier for every Corsican killed by the occupiers. The Genoese would respond and the constant retaliation meant

writers, such as Balzac, Dumas and Maupassant, were also fascinated by the subject and carved a place in history for the Corsican vendetta.

Nowadays, although *vendetta corse* is still written on penknives in the island's souvenir shops, the vendetta manifests itself less in killing than in the wanton destruction of property: the supermarket that gets burnt down the day before it's due to open, for instance, because it provides unwanted competition in a seaside resort. And, as always, the perpetrators can still be sure that the ancient code of silence observed by their fellow-citizens will protect them.

that whole clans were wiped out. When France annexed the island in 1769, its rigorous penal code seemed far too weak to the passionate Corsicans, who demanded the blood of a crime's perpetrator when family honour was at stake. A man marked by the curse of a family vendetta might take refuge in the island's thorny undergrowth, but he would know that a violent death was only a matter of time.

Prosper Mérimée (1803–70), the poet who created *Carmen*, based his novella *Colomba* on a tribal drama of this kind. Other 19th-century

LEFT: taking shelter in the Englischer Garten, Munich.
ABOVE: with improved wine from New World countries, European winemakers have to be more competitive.

Winemaking

In California or Australia, the combination of an equable climate and close scientific control can ensure that wines from a particular estate vary little from year to year. In Europe, by contrast, wines are at the mercy of the continent's capricious weather: one year a wine may be classed as truly great, the next year the same slopes will produce at best a mediocre vintage. Such uncertainty adds interest.

Competition from the New World has led to greatly improved wines, especially in traditional areas forced to improve quality to compete in the market. French wine comes from eight main areas: Bordeaux, the most important;

Burgundy in the east; Touraine, including the Loire Valley, in the west; the Rhône Valley from Lyon to Avignon; the Champagne area around Reims and Epernay; Alsace, along the left bank of the Rhine; the Jura mountains; and Languedoc in the south. While Bordeaux produces a high proportion of the world's greatest wines, Burgundy whites remain fashionable (and therefore expensive).

Italy makes prodigious amounts of wine, from the Alpine valleys down to the tip of Sicily. It tends to be lighter than French, and lacks the depth, but fine wines come from Chianti, Orvieto, Soave and Valpolicella.

Spain's wines are world-class, although the best known are still Riojas from the north. Germany produces splendid wines, especially hocks; these white wines from the Rhineland can be either sweet or dry. But wherever you are, the local wine is invariably the best one to go for.

Xenophobia

Jokes can, and often are, a means of voicing inadmissable opinions. Thus the French and the Dutch make fun of the Belgians. Northern Germans mock the laziness of southern Germans, who in turn deride the stupidity of

EUROPEAN STEREOTYPES

If colonising an island, it was said in 1790, a Spaniard would first build a church, a Frenchman a fort and a Dutchman a warehouse. In 1820, Lord Byron claimed that French courage was based on vanity, German courage on phlegm, Dutch courage on obstinacy and Italian courage on anger. The modern version of the stereotype game is to define hell as a place where the Germans are the police, the Swedish are the comedians, the Italians are the defence force, the Frenchmen dig the roads, the Belgians are the pop singers, the Spanish run the railways, the Portuguese are the waiters, the Greeks run the government, and the common language is Dutch.

northerners. Both northern and southern Germans were quick to ridicule new compatriots from the former East Germany. Copenhageners will make fun of somebody from Jutland, and Belgium's Flemings and Walloons joke about each other.

Images, like fashion, are subject to change. The idea of the Germans as aggressive and authoritarian emerged only in the middle of the 19th century; previously, Machiavelli, a shrewd observer of human nature, had described them as peace-loving and rather timid.

Nicknames are subject to the whims of language and, while their origins are often quite inoffensive, their use is invariably derogatory and best avoided. In Great Britain, sauerkraut-eating Germans became known as Krauts and spaghetti-eating Italians were called Spags. How the French turned into Frogs is less obvious: the term may have derived from their eating habits, but it could equally have originated from the three leaping toads portrayed on the coat of arms of the ancient Frankish kings (later replaced by the fleur-de-lis).

The term Dago is regarded as extremely offensive by Spaniards, Portuguese and Italians, although it had innocent origins. It came from the Spanish Diego, meaning James (San Diego, or Santiago, is the patron saint of Spain), and was originally innocuous.

The preliminary diagnosis isn't too good. Confidence in business and political leaders plummeted as the global financial crisis hit Europe in 2009, leading to bank bail-outs, bankruptcies, high unemployment and student unrest. Many migrant workers who left Eastern Europe in search of better jobs in the West have returned home. As their countries plunged into deep recession, the former Communist countries began to ask serious questions about the benefits of capitalism. With economies in decline, old tensions returned and racism emerged in a new form – this time directed against Muslims where once it targeted Jews.

Zeitgeist

Zeitgeist, that popular word to define the spirit of the age, is hard to define. People used to say the 20th century was the American century. And the 21st, many argue, will belong to Asia. So where does that leave Europe? Will the world echo the words of writer F. Scott Fitzgerald, who exclaimed in 1921: "God damn the continent of Europe. It is of merely antiquarian interest"? Or will this millennium give the old world a new impetus?

LEFT: wine barrels near Lake Garda, Italy; an anxious local in Trastevere, Rome. **ABOVE:** demonstrators clash with riot police in Athens, 2007.

Yet it is not all gloomy. More people than ever are educated, affluent, in good health, living longer and able to enjoy a remarkable range of consumer goods and leisure pursuits. Better communications, with fast rail connections and cheap flights, have made "city breaks" a way of life for many. Anyone looking for the contemporary spirit of Europe will find it expressed in great cities like Paris, Berlin, Amsterdam and Athens, where exciting new architecture and progressive ideas are giving shape to the new century. In some areas, like environmental protection, social justice and urban renewal, Europe continues to lead the world. It could be, in fact, that this turns out to be Europe's century. ❑

CLASSIC RAILWAY JOURNEYS

For many travellers, trains are the easiest way to explore Europe, especially its towns and cities, and some of the routes are spectacular

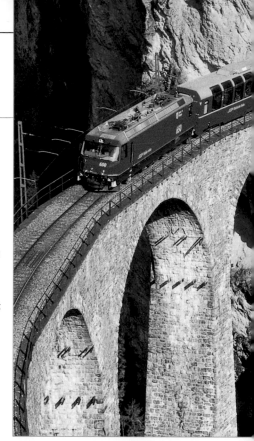

Europe has the densest railway network of any continent, complemented by tram and bus connections that make public transport an easy and pleasant way to travel. And not only is rail travel safer than driving – car crashes remain the principal cause of holiday injuries and fatalities – it is kinder to the environment than cars or planes. Most countries have maintained a high level of investment in their railway networks, so standards of comfort – and speed – are high. Stations can be an aesthetic pleasure too: besides the great cathedrals of the steam age, modern architects such as Santiago Calatrava (Lisbon, Liège, Zürich), Norman Foster (Florence, Dresden) and Nicholas Grimshaw (Amsterdam) have added new sources of civic pride.

But the most compelling reason for choosing to travel by train is that it enhances the pleasure of travel: your holiday starts when you board. It is much easier to enjoy the landscape from a train; every passenger has stories of serendipitous meetings and good conversations, but you can just as easily take the opportunity for quiet contemplation or for reading a book; and overnight sleeping-car trains are something of an adventure, as well as a good way of saving on a hotel bill. In fact, train journeys offer the kind of experiences that travel should be all about.

ABOVE: Lisbon Oriente station was designed by Santiago Calatrava to serve the Expo '98 site. One of a new generation of exciting station buildings, it adds to the legacy of great 19th- and early 20th-century stations – the cathedrals of the steam age.

LEFT: by 2020 Spain will have the longest high-speed rail network in Europe.
RIGHT: the Glacier Express links St Moritz and Zermatt in Switzerland.

HIGH-SPEED EUROPE

If time is of the essence, the continent's fast-expanding network of dedicated high-speed lines and trains is the smart way to get around. Internal flights have all but disappeared from competing routes where trains beat planes on city-centre-to-city-centre timings. The French TGV – *Train à Grande Vitesse* – was the pioneer European high-speed train, in 1981, and its astonishing success encouraged most countries to follow suit. The TGV alone serves over 200 destinations throughout France (you can travel from Lille to Marseille in just 4¾ hours), and, using conventional as well as high-speed lines, Belgium, Germany, the Netherlands and Switzerland, at speeds up to 320kmh (200mph). High-speed trains include a buffet car, and some German ICEs have a dining car with food cooked on board. Reliability is helped by having tracks clear of slower trains, and Spanish Railways is so confident about its TGV-based AVE services that passengers receive a 100 percent refund if trains are more than five minutes late. Small supplements are sometimes payable if travelling on a rail pass, and reservations are required.

ABOVE: the Landwasser Viaduct is a highlight on the Glacier Express route, and the train slows so that passengers can admire its curving masonry arches, which enhance the spectacular setting between Chur and Filisur.

ABOVE: the Orient Express has become a byword for luxury. It faithfully recreates the travel experience of the inter-war years, especially on the popular Paris–Venice route.

LEFT: the Gornergratbahn from Zermatt offers stunning views of the Matterhorn.

BELOW: the frequency of European train services makes rail-based holidays relaxing and efficient, and great value when using one of the many rail passes available.

17:25	OOSTENDE	P	10	18:02
17:31	KNOKKE	IC	8A	18:05
17:33	KORTRIJK	IC	7	18:07
17:34	BLANKENBERGE	IC	8B	18:09
17:35	BRUSSEL TONGEREN	IC	5	18:13
17:37	OOSTENDE	IC	6	18:25
17:37	GENT SINT-PIE	L	2	18:31
17:54	OOSTENDE	P	10	18:33
17:57	ANTHERPEN	IC	8	18:34
18:00	OOSTENDE	IC	10	

PLACES

A detailed guide to Europe's top destinations, with
principal sites clearly cross-referenced by
number to the maps

There is something reassuringly familiar about the continent of Europe. Its snowy mountains and beaches, its Roman remains and cathedrals, its vineyards and cafés are all places that have figured in so many books and films that we feel as if we know them. Yet there is so much architecture and art to absorb, so many miles of countryside to explore, such a lot of good food to try, so many vintage wines to taste, that nobody can know it all. What follows is a full flavour of continental Europe: 10 countries that cover the land mass from Cabo de Roca, the westernmost point of Portugal, to Greece, lingering en route in the hill towns of Tuscany, or on Germany's Romantic Road, getting caught up in the excitement of Barcelona, Paris and Rome.

Getting around the continent is no problem. Cities are linked by road and rail, and airports are busy round the clock. Theoretically the borders between most members of the European Union were removed in 1992, and although checkpoints remain in force, they often seem redundant, with uniformed officers who turn their backs on cars passing through.

There are few places that are not used to visitors all year round. Spring is the time for wild flowers, which cover the Alps and carpet the meadowlands. In summer, people flock to the playgrounds of the Mediterranean: most crowded are Rimini on the Adriatic coast, the French Riviera and Spain's Costa del Sol, but there are always empty beaches to seek out, on the Atlantic coast perhaps, or among Greece's myriad islands. In the autumn the vineyards of France, Italy, Spain and Germany's Rhineland turn red, and grape-picking is often followed by harvest celebrations. In winter the Alps attract skiers to Austria, Switzerland and France, as well as to winter sports venues in Italy and Spain. Europe has some of the world's most exciting cities, too. Gothic cathedrals and Baroque palaces overlook sleepy cobbled squares, and galleries offer breathtaking collections of art, while startling pieces of modern architecture, stylish shops and vibrant nightlife remind us that Europe is about the future as well as the past. ❏

PRECEDING PAGES: Mýrtos beach; water traffic in Venice; in the Berner Oberland, Switzerland. **LEFT:** Manueline interior of Jerónimos monastery, Lisbon. **ABOVE:** Praia da Marinha, Portugal; Louvre pyramid; the Temple of Apollo, Corinth.

Western Europe: Political

0   200 km
0   200 miles

N

NORTH SEA

DENMARK

Edinburgh

Belfast

IRELAND *Irish Sea*

Dublin

UNITED KINGDOM

Hamb
Bre

Groningen

NETHERLANDS
Amsterdam
Den Haag
(The Hague)
Rotterdam
Nijmegen
Duisburg
Essen
Düsseldorf
Köln
(Cologne)

Hannover

London

English Channel

Roubaix
Amiens

Bruxelles
(Brussels)
BELGIUM
Liège
GERM
LUXEM-
BOURG
Luxembourg
Mannheim
Fran

ATLANTIC
OCEAN

Channel
Islands

le Havre
Caen
Rouen
Reims
Metz
Strasbourg
Saarbrücken
Helc
Stut

Brest

Seine

Paris

Rennes

Orléans

Angers
Loire
Tours
Nantes

Dijon
Besançon
Basel
(Basle)
LIECHT
ST
Zürich
Vad
Bern
SWITZERLA

F R A N C E

la Rochelle

Bay of Biscay

Limoges

Clermont-Ferrand

Genève
(Geneva)

Lyon

St-Étienne

Grenoble

Milano
(Milan)

Bordeaux

Garonne

Rhône

Torino
(Turin)

Genova
(Genoa)

A Coruña
Gijón
Oviedo
Santander
Donostia
San Sebastián
Bilbao
Toulouse
Nîmes
Avignon
Nice
Monte Carlo
MONACO
Marseille
Toulon

Ourense
Vitoria-
Gasteiz
Pamplona
ANDORRA
Andorra la Vella
Perpignan

Corse
(Corsica)

Vigo

Porto
Douro
Valladolid
Salamanca
Zaragoza
(Saragossa)
Lleida
Ebro
Barcelona
Tarragona

Ajaccio

PORTUGAL

Madrid

S P A I N

Lisboa
(Lisbon)
Tajo (Tagus)

Évora
Badajoz
Albacete
Castelló
de la Plana
Valencia
Islas Baleares
Menorca
Palma
Mallorca

Sip
Macome

Sardi
(Sardi

Córdoba
Alicante
Cagliari

Murcia

Huelva
Jaén
Faro
Sevilla
Granada
Cartagena

MEDITERRANEAN SEA

Cádiz
Málaga
Algeciras
Gibraltar
(UK)
Ceuta
(Spain)
Tanger
(Tangier)
MOROCCO

Alger
(Algiers)

A L G E R I A

FRANCE

Europe's largest country draws more visitors than any other, attracted by its variety of landscapes, wealth of monuments and museums, and perhaps above all by the superb food and wine

France thinks of itself as the most essential component in Europe. Foreigners think so, too. It is the place they often think of first when they come to the continent. Its popularity is undeniable: the population of just over 63 million is far less than the number of visitors who arrive every year, making it the world's most visited country. It is Europe's largest (not counting European Russia) and one of the world's richest countries. Its population is spread thinly through a diverse landscape covering 547,000 sq km (211,200 sq miles); even on major roads, wayside towns and villages can seem deserted. But rural France is the real France. The French are proud of their agricultural heritage, and their farmers are respected as much as the food they produce.

France is also arguably Europe's oldest nation and, give or take the occasional small border shift, it has existed roughly in its present form since the 15th century. The nation's boundaries are largely natural ones, with the English Channel to the north, the Atlantic to the west, the Pyrenees and the Mediterranean to the south and the Alps, the Jura mountains and the Rhine to the east. These all contrive to make the French almost insular and, as a result, the people, who are predominantly Catholic, are

not as cosmopolitan as those in other European countries which have more openly shared borders. However, in spite of its insularity, this nation has had immense cultural influence on the rest of the world.

Among the country's riches, the châteaux of the Loire stand out, buildings whose craftsmanship could never be matched today. But French culture encompasses all the arts, especially film, and the

annual Cannes festival is the most important event in the cinema industry's year, an event that highlights the country's stunning Riviera. But most of all, when thoughts turn to France, they turn to Paris, a vibrant city of almost 10 million people, whose name has become synonymous with everything chic. ❑

PRECEDING PAGES: cycling through sunflowers in the Tour de France; time seems to stand still in rural France. **LEFT:** rue St-Jean in Lyon. **ABOVE:** playing boules is a popular pastime; the Arc de Triomphe, Paris.

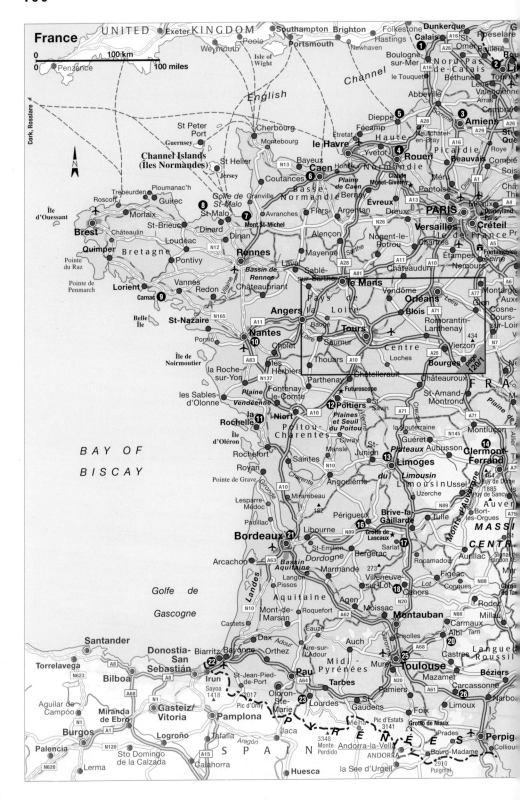

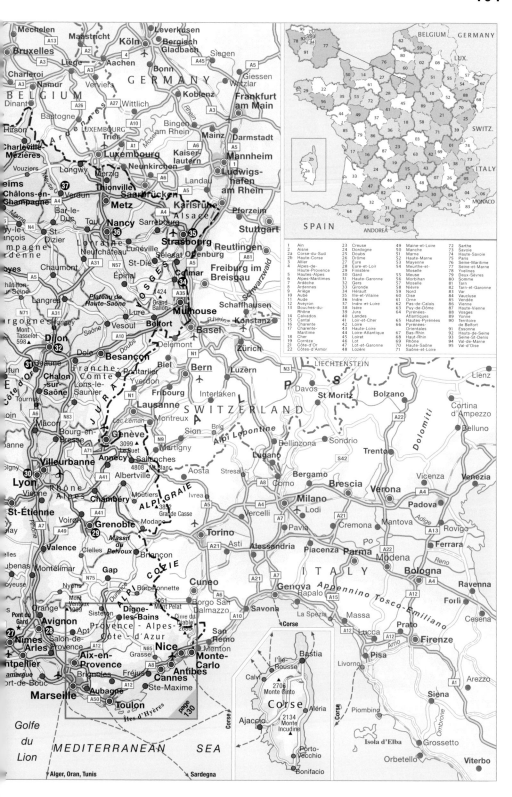

CIMETIÈRE DE MONTMARTRE

MONTMARTRE

Place de Clichy

Moulin Rouge

Rue des Abbesses

Abbesses

St-Pierre

27 Basilique du Sacré-Cœur

Barbès Rochechouart

Boulevard de la Chapelle

Paris

0   500 m

0   500 yds

Blanche

Rue Caulaincourt

Boulevard de Clichy

28

Place Pigalle

Pigalle

St-Jean

Blanche

Anvers

Boulevard de Rochechouart

Avenue Trudaine

Condorcet

Dunkerque

Poissonnière

Gare du Nord

Gare du Nord

La Fayette

Château Landon

Place du Colonel-Fabien

Colonel-Fabien

St-Georges

Rue La Bruyère

St-Georges

Rue des Martyrs

Maubeuge

Poissonnière

Magenta

Gare de l'Est

Gare de l'Est

Trinité

N.-D. de Lorette

Cadet

Fayette

Rue de Chabrol

d'Hauteville

Paradis

Strasbourg

Folies Bergères

R. des Petites Écuries

R. Richer

Château d'Eau

Jacques Bonsergent

Goncourt

Opéra Garnier **9**

Opéra

Bd des Italiens

Richelieu Drouot

Bd Montmartre

Bd Poissonnière

Bd de Bonne Nouvelle

Bonne Nouvelle

St-Denis

Bd St-Denis

République

Pl. de la République

Ste-Marie-Madeleine

7

Bd des Capucines

Grands Boulevards

Strasbourg St-Denis

Bd St-Martin

Ritz Hotel

Place Vendôme **8**

Bibliothèque Nationale-Richelieu

Bourse

Sentier

Réaumur

Musée des Arts et Métiers

Arts et Métiers

Temple

Turbigo

Oberkampf

Pyramides

R. des Petits Champs

Réaumur Sébastopol

Réaumur

St-Roch

JARDIN DU PALAIS ROYAL

Étienne-Marcel

St-Eustache

MARAIS

Nat. du de Paume

Tuileries

Comédie Française **10**

Palais Royal

Bourse de Commerce

Les Halles

Étienne Marcel

Musée d'Art et d'Histoire du Judaïsme

Filles du Calvaire

2 JARDIN DES TUILERIES

JARDIN DU CARROUSEL

Palais Royal Musée du Louvre

Forum des Halles **11**

Les Halles

Rambuteau

Centre Georges Pompidou **12**

Musée de l'Histoire de France

St-Sébastien Froissart

Musée National Picasso **13**

Musée Carnavalet

Musée d'Orsay **3**

Musée du Louvre **1**

Louvre Rivoli

St-Merri

Chemin Vert

Pont Royal

Pont Neuf

Châtelet

Hôtel de Ville

Rivoli

St-Paul

Place des Vosges **14**

Maison de Victor Hugo

Bastille

Quai de Conti

Institut de France

Conciergerie

Palais de Justice **17**

Cité

Île de la Cité

Hôtel de Ville

Hôtel d'Aumont

Rue St-Antoine

Place de la Bastille

École Nationale Supérieure des Beaux-Arts

Musée Delacroix

St-Germain-des-Prés **21**

St-Germain-des-Prés

Ste Chapelle

St-Michel

Pont Marie

Opéra National de la Bastille

Notre-Dame **16**

St-Sulpice

Odéon

Cluny-Sorbonne

Mabillon

Petit Pont

St-Michel

QUARTIER LATIN

St-Séverin

St-Julien-le-Pauvre

Île St-Louis **15**

Sully-Morland

Odéon Théâtre de l'Europe

Musée de Cluny **18**

Maubert-Mutualité

Institut du Monde Arabe

Palais du Luxembourg

La Sorbonne

St-Étienne-du-Mont

Jussieu

Panthéon **19**

Place Monge

JARDIN DES PLANTES

JARDIN DU LUXEMBOURG **20**

N.-D.-des-Champs

Muséum National d'Histoire Naturelle

Gare d'Austerlitz

Tour Montparnasse

Vavin

Cimetière du Montparnasse

Mosquée de Paris

Gare d'Austerlitz

PARIS

Its grand architecture and reputation for
high living, fine cuisine and haute couture
combine to make Paris the most glamorous
of all European capitals

Paris may at first appear a really
cosmopolitan city, but it maintains its quintessentially French
character despite the invasion of
American fast-food chains and the
proliferation of Anglicisms in the
French language, creating an idiom
called Franglais. From the *boulangeries*
(bread shops) to the *bateaux-mouches*
(glass-top boats), the crêpe-makers and
the *bouquinistes* (open-air book-sellers)
along the Seine, Paris offers a plethora
of sights, sounds and smells.

Altogether, central Paris covers an
area of 105 sq km (41 sq miles) and is
bounded by the recreational parks of
the **Bois de Vincennes** to the east and
the **Bois de Boulogne** to the west. The
city is divided into 20 districts called
arrondissements, each with its own distinct character. The lower numbers up
to nine designate the oldest districts of
the city. *La ville de Paris*, which is the
city proper (population 2.1 million), is
surrounded by a belt of communities
called the *banlieue* (suburbs) totalling
about 11½ million people.

Early settlements

The origins of Paris are concentrated on
the Ile de la Cité, the larger of the two
odd-shaped islands in the middle of the
Seine. Here, a Celtic tribe of fishermen
called the Parisii founded a village in
the 3rd century BC, which they named
Lutetia – "a place surrounded by water".
In 52 BC, during his Gallic War, Julius
Caesar conquered the settlement. More

invasions came from Germanic tribes;
the strongest of them, the Franks, made
Paris their capital in the 6th century. In
the 10th century Hugo Capet ascended
the throne as the first of the Capetian
monarchs and made Paris a medieval
centre of culture and learning.

The Renaissance monarchs were
responsible for creating what today
constitutes the classic beauty of Paris:
some of the major streets, charming squares, the Louvre Palace with
the grand Tuileries Garden and the
first stone bridge across the Seine,

LEFT: Place de
la Concorde.
BELOW: a
Montmartre café.

TIP

One of the great qualities of Paris is its compactness. You can walk almost everywhere, with just the occasional use of the metro system to save your tired feet or make an excursion to Montmartre.

the Pont Neuf. Sun King Louis XIV moved the capital to Versailles in the late 17th century but Paris continued to prosper, luxury trades adding to the prestige of the city. The overthrow of the *ancien régime* by the storming of the Bastille prison on 14 July 1789 at the start of the French Revolution was followed by the rise and fall of Napoleon Bonaparte, who left Paris the Arc de Triomphe and other great Neoclassical monuments.

The modern era

During the Second Empire, in the mid-19th century, Baron Haussmann oversaw the transformation of Paris from a medieval to a modern city, epitomised by the creation of the *grands boulevards*, wide avenues lined with harmonious buildings. Paris became a more vibrant and attractive place for the bourgeoisie to live, paving the way for the Belle Epoque at the end of the century. This period of good lving came to an end in 1914 when World War I broke out and the advancing Germans shelled Paris. However, they never entered the city as they did in World War II, when Paris was occupied for more than four years.

The post-war era again changed the face of Paris, and successive presidents have left their marks on the city. André Malraux, Minister of Culture under the presidency of Charles de Gaulle, began a large-scale programme to whitewash the facades of the capital. The **Pompidou Centre** was commissioned under President Pompidou and completed in 1977, and President Mitterrand left his mark with the **Grande Arche**, a giant rectangular office block in **La Défense** quarter to the west of the city, and the glass pyramid entranceway to the Louvre. The current president, Nicolas Sarkozy, wants to make an even bigger mark on the city than his predecessors. One plan is effectively to extend the Paris conurbation down the Seine Valley to Le Havre on the English Channel.

A city tour

The Right and Left banks of Paris grew up with separate and distinct social traditions which still prevail today. The Right Bank has retained its established role as the mercantile centre. Here are

BELOW: inside the Pompidou Centre.
BELOW RIGHT:
La Grande Arche, La Défense.

the banks, swanky department stores, posh airline and government offices and the *Bourse*, the Neoclassical stock exchange. The Left Bank, on the other hand, has been the domain of the intellectual community.

A tour of Paris may begin from any of its major landmarks. Those eager for an introductory panoramic view usually head for the Basilique du Sacré-Cœur on the heights of Montmartre or the Eiffel Tower by the river, two of the classic vantage points. Others set out for the Place de l'Opéra to explore the *grands boulevards*, the ritzy shops along the Faubourg St-Honoré or the beautifully colonnaded Rue de Rivoli. Departing from the Right Bank, it may be equally tempting to take a stroll along the Champs-Elysées. You can either walk down from the Arc de Triomphe or walk up from the Louvre, further east.

World-class museums

The **Louvre ❶** (Wed–Mon) is the largest art museum in the world, although it was originally built as a medieval fortress to protect the River Seine. I.M. Pei's dramatic glass pyramid in the forecourt has become the museum's modern symbol. The collection, ranging from European sculpture and painting to antiquities, decorative arts and objects, has been built up over hundreds of years, although Napoleon I made the greatest contribution from the spoils of his various campaigns. Spread over four vast floors, it's best to decide what you want to see and head straight for it. The *Mona Lisa* is in room 13 on the first floor of the river side of the museum.

From the Louvre to the Place de la Concorde extends the **Jardin des Tuileries ❷**, some of the best examples of typically French formal gardens where trees, plants and decorations are immaculately laid out. The small **Jeu de Paume** (Tue–Sun) has exhibitions of photography, and on the opposite (river) side of the Tuileries, the **Musée de l'Orangerie** contains Monet's "Waterlilies" series, as well as Cézannes and Renoirs (Wed–Mon).

The grand glass-and-iron Belle Epoque railway station of Quai d'Orsay, just across the river from the Louvre, has become one of the city's great art

The stunning glass pyramid of the Louvre by night.

BELOW LEFT: the Galerie d'Apollon in the Louvre. **BELOW:** admiring Renoir's dancers in the Musée d'Orsay.

A Republican Guard stands to attention outside the Elysée Palace.

BELOW: the Arc de Triomphe is at the top of the Champs-Elysées.

museums, the **Musée d'Orsay ❸** (Tue–Sun). It has a major collection of late 19th-century works, particularly by Delacroix and Ingres, as well as paintings by the Impressionists and Post-Impressionists Monet, Manet, Renoir, Cézanne and Van Gogh.

The Jardin des Tuileries opens to the **Place de la Concorde ❹**, a vast square that occupies a bloody chapter in French history. In 1793 it became the site of executions where Marie Antoinette and Louis XVI, among others, met their fate on the guillotine during the Revolution. Standing majestically in the middle of the traffic chaos, the central Obelisk of Luxor, dating from 1300 BC, was taken from the Temple of Rameses in Egypt and shipped as a gift to Paris in 1836.

Famous promenade

One of the world's most famous streets, the **Champs-Elysées ❺**, starts at the Place de la Concorde. The lower stretch to the Rond-Point is a broad avenue lined with horse chestnut and plane trees. It makes an attractive promenade and has a little park if you need to rest, north of which lies the presidential **Palais de l'Elysée**. After the Rond-Point the Champs-Elysées takes on a different character. It becomes an elegant and prestigious avenue of designer shops and fashionable bars and restaurants.

Walking up the Champs-Elysées gives a magnificent view of the monumental **Arc de Triomphe ❻**. Built between 1806 and 1836, this impressive monument stands 50 metres (165ft) high and 45 metres (148ft) wide. The Arc is noted for its frieze of hundreds of figures, each 2 metres (6ft) high, and its 10 sculptures. The names of the major victories between the Revolution and the First Empire (military defeats are omitted) are inscribed under the arch, and the Tomb of the Unknown Soldier lies beneath. The 284 steps to the top (there is a lift) give access to a spectacular view down the Champs-Elysées and up to La Défense.

The Opéra and the Marais

Directly in front of you as you walk north up Rue Royale from Place de la Concorde is the pseudo-Greek temple of **Sainte-Marie-Madeleine ❼**. Napoleon dedicated this monument to the glory of his *Grande Armée*, but it has served as a church since 1842.

A short way to the southeast from here is **Place Vendôme ❽**, the smartest of all squares in Paris. Shaped like an octagon, it is lined by 17th-century buildings which house some of the city's most exclusive stores, specialising in perfume, fashion, jewellery and watchmakers, such as Cartier and Rolex. Under the stone arches is the luxurious **Ritz Hôtel**. In the centre of the square towers a 44-metre (144ft) column with bas-reliefs of bronze cast from 1,200 cannons captured in 1805 from the Austrians at the Battle of Austerlitz, and modelled on Trajan's Column in Rome.

Up Rue de la Paix is the gloriously romantic **Opéra Garnier ❾**, designed in 1875 by Charles Garnier and enclosed by a triangle of Haussmann's

grands boulevards. Inside, the majestic staircase and rich marble decorations evoke visions of swirling gowns, tuxedos and top hats.

Follow the Avenue de l'Opéra towards the river and you come to the **Palais Royal ❿** (beside the Louvre), childhood home of Louis XIV and once an infamous den of libertines, now housing the Ministry of Culture. A few streets to the east is the **Forum des Halles ⓫**, a complex of cinema halls, boutiques, galleries and restaurants. The city market was here until 1969, and a few remaining bistros serve traditional market fare. Across the Boulevard de Sébastopol looms the giant cultural machine of the **Pompidou Centre ⓬** (the Centre National d'Art et de Culture Georges Pompidou; Wed–Mon). Built between 1971 and 1977 by the architects Renzo Piano and Richard Rogers, it is still strikingly futuristic. The galleries of the Musée National d'Art Moderne have a massive collection of early modern and contemporary art.

East of the Pompidou Centre is one of the city's most charming quarters and home to some of the finest mansions in Paris. The **Marais**, originally swampland, became a fashionable residential district in the 17th century. The **Musée National Picasso ⓭** (Wed–Mon) in the beautifully restored Hôtel Salé has paintings, drawings and sculptures from the artist's long and prolific career. **Musée Carnavalet** (Tue–Sun) is another excellent museum, occupying two mansions and giving a history of the city. In the same neighbourhood is the old Jewish quarter centred on the Rue des Rosiers, and the **Musée d'Art et d'Histoire du Judaïsme**, giving a history of Jews in Europe.

The 63 houses of **Place des Vosges ⓮**, the city's oldest square, on the edge of the Marais, have lovely symmetrical arcades. Victor Hugo (1802–85) once lived here, and his house at No. 6 is a museum (Tue–Sun).

The delightful Picasso Museum is housed in a 17th-century palace in the Marais.

Islands in the river

In the very heart of Paris, the River Seine divides to embrace two islands, the **Ile de la Cité** and **Ile St-Louis ⓯**. Traditionally a residential quarter of the Parisian gentry, Ile St-Louis has remained a patch of tranquillity in this fast-paced

BELOW: a patisserie in the Marais.

city. Neighbouring Ile de la Cité is cluttered with historic landmarks, the most celebrated being the **Cathédrale Notre-Dame de Paris** ⓰ (daily). This magnificent example of Gothic ecclesiastical architecture is simply stunning viewed from any angle. It was purportedly built on the grounds of a Gallo-Roman temple that was first replaced by a Christian basilica and a Romanesque church. The construction of the cathedral itself began in 1133 and work was only completed in 1345.

Also on Ile de la Cité is the **Conciergerie** (daily), once part of the Royal Palace where the warden of the kings used to live. This massive building is a truly beautiful sight at night when its arches are illuminated. During the French Revolution, it served as a prison for those awaiting the guillotine. Marie Antoinette was held here, and her private cell, the Chapelle des Girondins, contains her crucifix and the guillotine blade.

The **Palais de Justice**, housing the present Paris law courts, was built on the same spot that over centuries served as the administrative quarters of the ancient Roman government and the early kings. In the courtyard is **Sainte-Chapelle** ⓱ (daily), a Gothic chapel with magnificent stained-glass windows built in the 13th century by the saintly King Louis IX.

The Left Bank

From the Ile de la Cité, the **Pont St-Michel** leads to the Left Bank and straight into the **Latin Quarter**. It earned its name from the dominance of Latin-speaking students who attended the nearby Sorbonne university. East of **Boulevard St-Michel**, its main thoroughfare, the Latin Quarter is threaded with numerous narrow alleys such as **Rue de la Huchette**, a twisting lane of Greek restaurants, kebab corners, jazz spots and cinemas.

Where boulevards St-Michel and **St-Germain** meet is the **Musée de Cluny** ⓲ (Wed–Mon), housing the ruins of the Roman baths. The building also contains the exquisite tapestry of *La Dame à la Licorne* (The Lady and the Unicorn). Walking down Boulevard St-Michel and turning to the left into Rue Soufflot, you arrive at the **Panthéon** ⓳. Built as a church to fulfil Louis XV's pious vow after he recovered from an illness, the Panthéon has, since 1791, served as a shrine to France's most outstanding citizens.

On the opposite side of Boulevard St-Michel stretches the spacious **Jardin du Luxembourg** ⓴. These gardens are popular with students whiling away time between classes, and children are thrilled by the adventures of Guignol (the French equivalent of the Punch and Judy Show) which are featured in the gardens' **Théâtre des Marionettes**.

In the evening and late into the night the Left Bank becomes even more animated, as crowds of locals and visitors promenade along Boulevard St-Michel and Boulevard St-Germain, which leads from the **Pont de la Concorde** further east into the Latin Quarter. The open-air terraces of restaurants and cafés in the area are popular venues for people to sit

BELOW: sunbathing by the Seine on Ile de la Cité.

for a drink and soak in the ambience. Next to the pre-Gothic church of **St-Germain-des-Prés ㉑** are two grand cafés that have been elevated to the rank of institutions: the **Café Aux Deux Magots** and the **Café de Flore** *(see box below)*.

Heading south into **Rue de Rennes** and then changing into **Boulevard Raspail**, you pass into the **Quartier de Montparnasse**, which replaced Montmartre *(see page 112)* as the centre of bohemian life early in the 20th century. Artists, writers, poets and revolutionaries, among them Lenin and Trotsky, flocked to live here. After World War I, American expatriate writers of the "Lost Generation", such as Hemingway, F. Scott Fitzgerald and Henry Miller, joined the locals who used to congregate in famous literary cafés like Le Dôme, La Rotonde, Le Sélect or the huge dining halls of La Coupole.

All these celebrated places are now surrounded by an air of nostalgia since Montparnasse has undergone extensive urban renewal in the past two decades. Many of the quarter's artist studios and small hotels have been demolished and

the huge **Tour Montparnasse ㉒** symbolises the region's changing identity as a business centre.

Across the **Cimetière du Montparnasse** (where Jean-Paul Sartre and Simone de Beauvoir lie together) is the entrance to the **Catacombs** (Tue–Sun), where thousands of bones are stored in an old quarry. Paris does death well, and the most popular cemetery is that of **Père Lachaise**, to the east of the city centre, which contains the tombs of Oscar Wilde, Jim Morrison and Edith Piaf among hundreds of others.

Back to the Seine

The gilded **Dôme des Invalides** faces the right bank from across Pont d'Alexandre III. Immediately beneath the vast cupola rests Emperor Napoleon I, whose body was transferred here from the island of St Helena in 1840. It is encased in seven separate sarcophagi, the exterior one being made of precious red marble. The church is surrounded by the Hôtel des Invalides, built by Louis XIV as a hospital to shelter 7,000 disabled soldiers. Today the building houses the **Musée de**

A shady avenue in the Jardin du Luxembourg – the largest public park in Paris, and also the most romantic.

Left Bank Rendezvous

Paris has always been both a magnet and an inspiration for writers, aspiring and established, French and foreign, and addresses with literary associations are concentrated on the Left Bank.

The best place to start a tour with your nose in a book is the city's oldest café, **Le Procope** (13 Rue de l'Ancienne-Comédie), which was a favourite watering hole of Molière and Voltaire. Three other cafés with literary associations are located close to each other in or near the Place St-Germain-des-Prés. Existentialist philosopher and writer Jean-Paul Sartre and his lover Simone de Beauvoir consolidated the highbrow reputation of **Les Deux Magots** (6 Place St-Germain-des-Prés) in the 1950s. The café is reputed to serve the best hot chocolate in Paris. The Art Deco **Café de Flore** (172 Boulevard St-Germain) was another favourite haunt of Sartre. The other gathering place for intellectuals past and present is the Brasserie Lipp (151 Boulevard St-Germain).

A few hotels also have literary reputations. There's nothing left to see now of the "**Beat Hotel**", 9 Rue Gît-le-Cœur, where Allen Ginsberg and William Burroughs stayed in the 1950s, but in **L'Hôtel** (13 Rue des Beaux-Arts) you can reserve the room in which Oscar Wilde died in exile in 1900.

Another stop for literary types is the eccentric bookshop of **Shakespeare & Co.** just across the river from Notre-Dame at 37 Rue de la Bûcherie.

Queues for the Eiffel Tower can be up to two hours long in summer, so get there early. A lift from the second level is the only means of reaching the top.

BELOW: the lift on the way up the Eiffel Tower.

l'Armée ㉓ (daily), featuring a collection of arms, uniforms and trophies from France's military past.

Just a few steps away, at No. 77 Rue de Varenne, the former studio of sculptor Auguste Rodin (1840–1917) is now the **Musée Rodin** (closed first Mon of the month), where some of the artist's best and most famous works are on display in the house and garden.

To the west of the Invalides is the Ecole Militaire – the French Military College. It is fronted by a former parade ground, the Champ de Mars, which leads to the **Eiffel Tower** ㉔ (daily). Named after its creator, Gustave Eiffel (who had designed the structure for New York's Statue of Liberty), the tower was designed as a temporary installation, due to be dismantled in 1910, 21 years after its inauguration at the Paris World Fair. But since it proved its value as a wireless tower it remained intact, and of course it is now synonymous with Paris. The best city-gazing from the top is about an hour before sunset. A modern lighting system makes it a stunning illumination after dark.

Opposite the Eiffel Tower on the Right Bank is the **Palais de Chaillot** ㉕, dating from the International Exposition of 1937. It houses several museums and the **Cinémathèque** repertory cinema. Close by, on Avenue du Président Wilson, the Palais de Tokyo contains the underrated **Musée d'Art Moderne de la Ville de Paris** ㉖ (Tue–Sun).

Bohemian quarter

Montmartre, the haunt of writers and artists until early in the 20th century, is still one of the liveliest spots after dark. This area is often regarded as the birthplace of modern art, since Rousseau, Utrillo, Renoir, Gauguin and others spent the early part of their careers here in the late 19th century.

Known locally as *La Butte* (hill), it was once genuinely bohemian, and songs and comedies flowed from the dim cafés. Later, Montparnasse on the Left Bank took over as the artistic and literary centre. At the **Place du Tertre**, however, some of Montmartre's former reputation lives on. Street artists dominate the scene, offering tourists caricatures or Parisian townscapes. There are also plenty of bars, cafés and restaurants.

Incongruously set in Montmartre is the virginal-white **Sacré-Cœur** ㉗. Perched on a hill, its Byzantine cupolas are as much a part of the city skyline as the Eiffel Tower; when the lights are turned on at night, Sacré-Cœur resembles a lit wedding cake. It can be reached by walking up 250 steps or by taking a funicular railway.

At the foot of Sacré-Cœur, along **Boulevard de Clichy**, is **Pigalle**, the traditional entertainment quarter of Paris. It is symbolised by the neon-red windmill sails of the **Moulin Rouge** cabaret, home of cancan dancing since the days of Toulouse-Lautrec. Here, too, were the dimly lit cabarets where the legendary Edith Piaf, the "Sparrow of Paris", sang. **Place Pigalle** ㉘, a gaudy red-light district, is a popular hotspot teeming with sex shops, peep shows and strip clubs. The **Folies-Bergères**, about 2km (1¼ miles) south on Rue

Richer, is the oldest music hall in Paris and offers much the same fare as the Moulin Rouge.

Days out

The most sumptuous of all castles in France is the **Château de Versailles** (Tue–Sun; RER line C to Versailles Rive Gauche, SNCF train from Gare Montparnasse to Versailles-Chantier or Rive Droite, or bus 171). Not to be missed, it is a mere 21km (13 miles) away from the capital. Versailles was remodelled from an original manor farm by Louis XIII, who used to hunt in the surrounding woods. He had the farm converted into a rose brick-and-stone château. This was expanded by Louis XIV, the Sun King, who took 50 years to create a palace so magnificent that it was copied all over Europe.

Versailles served as capital of France on various occasions and, in its heyday, had a court population of 20,000. The palace itself, a royal residence until the Revolution of 1789, housed 5,000 people. Inside, the tour takes you through the King's Apartments and the 70-metre (233ft) Hall of Mirrors. Outside in the park, which was designed by André le Nôtre, are the smaller royal residences of the **Grand Trianon** and **Petit Trianon**, as well as Marie Antoinette's make-believe village of **Hameau**.

Slightly less touristy is the other great royal palace near Paris, the **Château de Fontainebleau** (Wed–Mon; SNCF train to Fontainebleau-Avon, then bus, or Parisvision bus from Rue de Rivoli), located in a forest 65 km (40 miles) south of the capital. A favourite royal residence from the 12th to 19th centuries, the palace is a mixture of styles, with formal gardens all around.

Chartres Cathedral (daily; SNCF train from Gare Montparnasse) is one of the greatest works of Gothic architecture in Europe. Around 90km (55 miles) southwest of Paris, it is especially famous for its collection of 172 stained-glass windows dating from the 12th and 13th centuries and the enigmatic labyrinth inset into the floor of the nave.

Of different appeal is **Disneyland Paris** (daily; RER line A to Marne-la-Vallée), 32km (20 miles) east of Paris. It is the most popular tourist attraction in Europe (*see margin note, right*). ❑

WHERE

Two- or three-day passports to Disney-land, available either at the gate or from the Disney Store or Virgin Megastore on the Champs-Elysées, are a (relatively) economical way to visit the attraction.

BELOW: art on display in the Place du Tertre, Montmartre.

AROUND FRANCE

Every region of France has something distinctive to offer; the majestic châteaux of the Loire Valley and sun-drenched beaches of the Mediterranean coast are just two of the highlights

France has an admirable network of road, rail and air transport that makes for quick and efficient travel. The *autoroute* (motorway) system runs from the north coast to the south and provides access to the southwest and the east by going round rather than through Paris. The link from Calais to Marseille via Reims makes the journey from north to south around 11 hours. The greatest asset of the French road network is the superlative quality of its clearly signposted secondary roads.

The 300kph (186mph) TGV *(Train à Grande Vitesse)* makes rail travel across much of France comfortable, quick and easy, connecting Paris with the major provincial cities.

First ports of call

Visitors coming from Britain by sea via ferry or the Channel Tunnel might like to stretch their legs in the port towns before continuing the journey inland. **Calais ❶** is distinctly shabby and soulless, but in the **Parc St Pierre** you'll find the famous bronze statue by August Rodin of the *Burghers of Calais* who, in 1346, offered their necks to Edward III, the English king, if he would spare the city. He spared both. In **Boulogne**, the 13th-century ramparts of the picturesquely cobbled upper town *(ville haute)* make an interesting walk. A good overall view of the town and harbour can be had from the top of the belfry of the town hall. A little inland, **St-Omer**'s **Basilique Notre-Dame**, begun in 1200

and completed in the 15th century, is a triumphant union of Romanesque and Gothic styles, the jewel of Flanders's ecclesiastical architecture.

Close to the Belgian border is **Lille ❷**, the capital of French Flanders, which is distinguished by its welcoming Flemish atmosphere and richly restored civic buildings, in particular the grand 17th-century **Vieille Bourse** (Old Stock Exchange) and Louis XIV's imposing citadel – a massive star-shaped construction of 60 million bricks that demanded the labour of 2,000 bricklayers.

Main attractions
D-DAY BEACHES
NORMANDY
MONT-ST-MICHEL
BRITTANY
LOIRE CHÂTEAUX
DORDOGNE
BORDEAUX VINEYARDS
THE PYRENEES
CARCASSONNE
PROVENCE AND THE CÔTE D'AZUR
THE ALPS
CHAMPAGNE

LEFT: Tour de France. **BELOW:** Place du Général de Gaulle, Lille.

TIP

Rouen Cathedral is illuminated every night during the summer until 1am. If you are staying nearby it's worth going back into town to view the spectacular silhouette.

To the south are **Arras** and **Amiens** ❸, the former famous to the English for the tapestries through which Hamlet stabbed old Polonius, and to the French as the home town of 18th-century revolutionary leader Robespierre. It is worth a visit today for its lively squares and marketplaces, most notably Place des Héros and Grand'Place. The 13th-century Gothic cathedral at Amiens is the largest in France, and even more miraculous for having survived the bombardments of two world wars. Its masterpiece is the intricate wooden carving of the 16th-century choir stalls. Back on the coast, between Boulogne and Dieppe, is the favourite seaside resort of **Le Touquet**. It was once known as "Paris-Plage", promising a touch of city sophistication at the seaside; with its air of faded gentility, it is still popular with Parisians.

Normandy

Within easy reach of Paris are the house and garden of **Giverny** (Apr–Oct Tue–Sun), created by the Impressionist painter Claude Monet, who lived there until his death in 1926. Beautifully restored, it has become a popular tourist spot, particularly the Japanese garden where the waterlilies, so famously painted by the artist, still blossom.

Downriver are the superb abbey ruins in **Jumièges** consecrated in 1067 to celebrate William's conquest of England. **Rouen** ❹, capital of upper Normandy, is cherished by the French as the place where Joan of Arc was burnt at the stake. The 11th- and 12th-century **cathedral** is only one of several splendid monuments in this great medieval city and port on the River Seine. Its solid facade was painted many times by Monet.

Dieppe ❺, located on the north Normandy coast, is the most attractive of the ports serving the Channel crossings. The **Boulevard du Maréchal Foch** offers a pleasant promenade along the extensive pebble beach. The liveliest part of town, however, is around the **Place du Puits Sale**, where you will find the renowned Café des Tribunaux. The spectacular white cliffs of **Etretat**, south of Dieppe, have earned this shoreline the epithet of the "Alabaster Coast".

BELOW RIGHT:
the splendid Gros Horloge in Rouen.

The Fatal Shore

The north of France, flat and defenceless as Belgium, has been the poignant arena for countless invasions, its place names sounding like a litany of battlefields.

Dunkirk is famous for the providential evacuation of 140,000 French and 200,000 British troops in May 1940. From the lighthouse or the Watier locks, you can see where it happened. English historians recall glorious Crécy and Henry V's Agincourt (Azincourt in French), while the French prefer to remember Bouvines, an important victory over an Anglo-German alliance in 1214.

Other battles, whether ending in victory or defeat, soaked the fields of Flanders and Picardy, the plateau of the Ardennes and the banks of the Somme and Marne in blood. There are impressive monuments to Canadian troops at Vimy (north of Arras), to the Australians at Corbie (east of Amiens) and to the Americans at Bellicourt (southwest of Le Quesnoy), while British cemeteries of World War I are found mostly in Belgium.

However, travellers in Normandy are constantly reminded of the colossal effort that went into the rebuilding of the towns and cities destroyed by fighting – Caen, Le Havre, Rouen, Avranches, Dunkirk and Boulogne have all been lovingly reconstructed from the rubble.

The most picturesque harbour towns of Normandy are further south on the Calvados coast, notably **Honfleur**. The **Musée Eugène Boudin** (Wed–Mon) attests to the town's popularity with painters – Corot, Courbet, Monet and Dufy. **Deauville**, with its casino and nightclubs, retains much of the elegance that made it a name in the Belle Epoque.

The beaches of the **D-Day landings** of 6 June 1944 – Omaha, Utah, Gold, Juno and Sword – are also to be found along the Calvados coast. The most important exhibition commemorating "Operation Overlord" is located at **Arromanches**. In the bay the remnants of the former artificial Mulberry harbour peek out of the water. The huge concrete construction, comprising a breakwater and piers, was towed across the Channel and installed off Arromanches in order to land supplies for the Allied forces.

Caen ❻ is the capital of lower Normandy and was the home of William the Conqueror before he moved to England. He and his wife Mathilde left two fine abbeys, *aux Hommes* and *aux*

Dames, west and east of the city centre. Caen was flattened in the 1944 Battle of Normandy and largely rebuilt. The impressive **Mémorial de Caen** (daily) commemorates the liberation of France and peace in general.

In the **Centre-Guillaume-le-Conquérant** (daily) at **Bayeux**, 28km (17 miles) northwest of Caen, hangs the highly celebrated and exquisite tapestry, stitched in 1067, depicting the events surrounding William of Normandy's conquest of England in 1066.

Mont-St-Michel

The most dramatic ecclesiastical building in all France, indeed one of the wonders of the Western world, is **Mont-St-Michel ❼**, in a bay at the bottom of the Cotentin peninsula. The **abbey** (daily), built between the 11th century and the 16th century, makes a strong impression when seen from a distance. It stands at the summit of an island-rock, 75 metres (250ft) above the sea, and is reached by road along a dyke.

Off the Cotentin peninsula north of Mont-St-Michel, within an easy day trip from St-Malo or Granville, are the

The 70-metre (230ft) Bayeux Tapestry is not a tapestry at all but a fine example of medieval English embroidery. It was probably made in Canterbury, southeast England.

BELOW: the dramatic bulk of Mont-St-Michel.

The menhirs (standing stones) at Carnac are 1,000 years older than the Pyramids but were aligned with extraordinary precision.

BELOW: *La Maison entre les Rochers* (the House between the Rocks) near Plougrescant, Brittany.

Channel Islands, which belong to the UK but have a character all of their own. The largest two islands are Jersey and Guernsey.

Brittany

Jacques Cartier set off from the ancient port of **St-Malo ❽** on the 16th-century voyage which led to the discovery of Canada. Much of the town was rebuilt after its almost complete destruction during World War II, but you can still walk all around the town on top of the ramparts and get a fine view aross the estuary towards **Dinard**, one of Brittany's most successful resorts.

But Brittany is appreciated most for the beauty of its craggy coastline. The pink granite rocks of the Corniche Bretonne run from **Ploumanac'h**, via **Trégastel**'s excellent swimming beach, to **Trébeurden**. The Bretons maintain their own Celtic language and customs, most notably the Pardons, religious processions by local people in their rich regional dress. Their ancient Celtic origins can be seen in the extraordinary stone circles such as those at **Carnac ❾**, where 3,000 giant stones were laid

out by their ancestors for some form of worship. The dolmens and tumuli are thought to mark burial sites.

A tour of the Loire Valley

Nantes ❿, the capital of the Loire region, is located at the point where the River Loire meets the tidal estuary that takes it to the Atlantic Ocean. The celebrated valley of the River Loire has been praised as the garden of France and has been described as a melting pot of the Celtic, Roman and Nordic civilisations. Most of all, however, it was the home of kings and princes, who have left a splendid mosaic of châteaux, recognised as among the finest in the world.

From Paris, a tour of the Loire Valley usually begins in **Orléans ❶**, an hour's drive west of the capital. The Loire proper, rising on Mont Gerbier de Joncs in the Massif Central, is, at 1,015km (634 miles), the longest river in France. The soul of Orléans, a modern city whose heart was bombed out during World War II, lives on in the cult of Joan of Arc; it was here that she successfully resisted the English army before being burnt at the stake

in Rouen. The site where she stayed in 1429 has become the **Maison Jeanne d'Arc** (Tue–Sun), where scenes from her life are recreated.

Châteaux of the Loire

Beaugency , 18km (11 miles) west of Orléans, has an 11th-century dungeon, 12th-century abbey and bridge, and Renaissance town hall. From here, the road leads on to the very heart of château country. Altogether, the Loire region has about 3,000 stately homes from various periods. The oldest ones, such as the castle of **Loches**, began life as fortified towers and served as shelters during the Middle Ages; the more recent ones, such as the opulent palace of **Cheverny**, were designed for comfort rather than for defence, serving as pleasure grounds for the aristocracy during the age of absolutism. The châteaux built between the 15th and the mid-16th centuries rank as the apogee of the Renaissance in France.

The crown of France belonged by that time to the house of Valois, so the Loire Valley consequently became known as the country of the Valois.

The first Valois to seek refuge here was Charles VII in 1418. Then Dauphin (heir to the throne) of France, he had been driven out of Paris by the Duke of Burgundy, who supported the claims of Henry IV of England to the French crown during the Hundred Years War with England. In 1429 the war took a miraculous turn when Jeanne la Pucelle, an 18-year-old peasant girl from Lorraine, appeared at the castle of Chinon, west of Tours, which was then the seat of the royal court. She revealed to the Dauphin that divine voices had told her to aid him in the reconquest of his legitimate throne. The girl became France's national heroine, Joan of Arc, and proved her divine mission by repelling the English three months later at Orléans.

The first château to be seen when entering the Loire Valley from Orléans is **Chambord** (daily), a fantasy palace that bewitched even the most blasé of the Venetian ambassadors to the court of France. The building could be described as a gigantic stairway onto which a château has been grafted. The stairway, with its double turn, is the

Joan of Arc, the Maid of Orléans, who was burnt at the stake in Rouen.

BELOW LEFT: the gardens at the château of Villandry are beautifully designed. **BELOW:** Chambord, a fantasy castle.

A depiction of medieval sailors bringing a cargo of salt down the Loire. The prosperity of the region was founded on the salt trade.

structure's pivot. It soars to the roofs, and offers an unmistakable symbol of the power of the French king. Everything about Chambord is colossal, but François I, who built it, spent only 40 days there, Henri IV never came near it and Louis XIII dropped in but once. The court stopped coming in 1684, which meant that nobody troubled to complete the enormous structure. A *son et lumière* show during the summer celebrates its past glories.

Blois D, which has France's most frequented château (daily) after Versailles, is next along the valley. Without fortifications, opening on the Louis XII wing, it has the look of a grand bourgeois dwelling offering peace, prosperity and ornament. As a vestige of its earliest years, Blois has kept its ramparts facing the Loire. Its tower of Foix provides a superb panorama over the river and suburbs.

The château at **Chaumont E** (daily), on the left bank of the Loire, lies in a setting that the Prince de Broglie transformed into a veritable pastiche of the *Arabian Nights*. Further west, on the opposite bank, is **Amboise F**, whose

château (daily), once the home of Louis XI, Charles VIII, Louis XIII, François I and Habsburg Emperor Charles V, is considered one of the finest. Much of the palace has gone, but what is left still offers a striking contrast between the "Italianate" modifications of Charles VIII and the old medieval fortress. Renaissance master Leonardo da Vinci is buried in St Hubert's Chapel.

Jewel of the Renaissance

There is no clash of style about **Chenonceau G** (daily), which achieves a perfect harmony in its Renaissance architecture. Anchored like a great ship in the middle of the River Cher, south of Amboise, and surrounded by broad fields, Chenonceau is a delicate jewel set in a green casket.

It was the preferred home of Diane de Poitiers, the "eternally beautiful" mistress of Henri II, and of cruel Marie de' Medici, bitter enemy not only of her husband Henri IV, but also her son Louis XIII. Chenonceau was famous for its festivities. One of the first was the triumphal celebration on 1 March 1560 for François II and his young

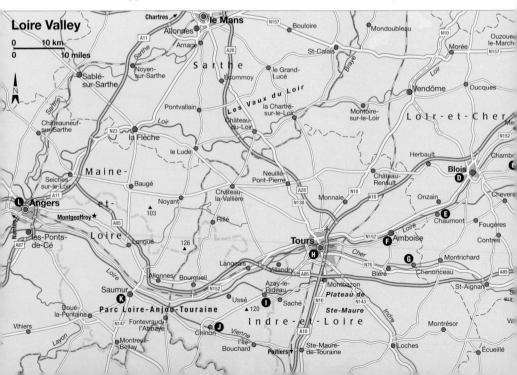

Map below

wife Mary Stuart. Today, the parties are all but forgotten, though there is still magic in the great classical gallery on a bridge of five arches creating a lovely reflection in the waters of the river.

Amboise and Chenonceau are on the eastern edge of the region called the Touraine, which has the lively university town of **Tours**  as its capital. The medieval quarter, centred on **Place Plumereau**, is a showcase of Gothic architecture. About 23km (14 miles) southwest of Tours is **Azay-le-Rideau**  (daily), a small château of exquisite proportions partly built over the River Indre. This "multi-faceted diamond… mounted on pillars, masked with flowers" as it was described by Balzac, is the quintessence of the Touraine's architecture. Not far away is the **Château de Villandry** (daily) and its famous 16th-century garden.

Ruined château fort

Chinon , 20km (12 miles) southwest of Azay, once consisted of three different fortresses. Some of the mighty fortifications as well as parts of the moat are left. A length of wall with a high

Gothic chimney-piece remains from the **Grand Logis**, the hall where the court witnessed the judgement of Joan of Arc when she recognised the Dauphin despite his disguise as a humble courtier. In the 17th century Chinon became a centre of French politics once again when Cardinal Richelieu, first minister of France, took over the castle. His family abandoned it to become the grand ruins that can be seen today.

Beyond Chinon is **Saumur** , where the surrounding woodlands are rich in mushrooms and, in this wine country where the whites are pre-eminent, the local pride is the red Champigny and sparkling Saumur. The town is dominated by its château (Wed–Mon) dating from the 12th century. Saumur is also known for the **Cadre Noir Cavalry School**; you can visit the school and its stables (Apr–Oct Mon–Sat) and watch the morning training sessions. At the end of July, the *Carrousel* festivities include impressive demonstrations of dressage and horsemanship. In Saumur itself the **Musée du Champignon** (Feb–Nov daily) offers guided visits to the underground galleries, where

This sculpture forms part of the grand entrance to the Louis XII wing at Blois, one of the most visited châteaux in France.

BELOW:
Chenonceau château, a perfect example of Renaissance architecture.

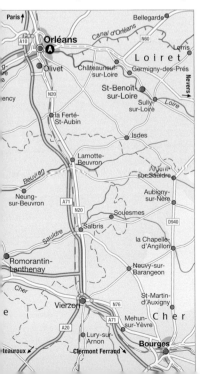

Futuroscope, just to the north of Poitiers, is great fun for children. It also attempts to teach them about clean, green technology.

BELOW: a lazy day on the water at La Venise Verte.

mushrooms are cultivated. The road from Saumur to Angers follows the riverbank, past compact white villages worth a stop for local delicacies.

At Les Ponts-de-Cé, a road leads north to **Angers ⓛ**, town of the good King René, Duke of Anjou and of Provence. In the Old Town there are fine specimens of Renaissance houses, most notably the **Logis Barrault** (housing the fine arts museum, with some noteworthy works by Watteau, Chardin and Boucher), and the **Hôtel de Pincé** (also now an art museum, devoted to Greek, Etruscan, Chinese and Japanese works). But pride of place among Angers's art treasures must go to the tapestries in the château, particularly the *Tenture de l'Apocalypse*, 70 pictures from a 14th-century work. The château itself is a splendid example of a medieval feudal fortress.

The Atlantic coast

Travelling south of Angers down the Atlantic coast brings you to the nature reserve of **Le Marais Poitevin**. Also known as La Venise Verte – Green Venice – it consists of 15,000 hectares (37,000 acres) of lush, green coun-

tryside threaded with 1,450km (900 miles) of waterways. At Coulon, 11km (7 miles) west of Niort, local boatmen await tourists with their long forked poles (*pigoulles*).

The gracious port town of **La Rochelle ⓫** is famous for Cardinal Richelieu's ruthless siege of the Protestant population in the 17th century – the Protestants are still there. Today it's a favourite port of call for yachtsmen, and the houses of the Old Town have retained their 17th- and 18th-century charm, particularly along the Rue du Palais. **Tour St-Nicolas** and **Tour de la Chaîne** face each other across the sheltered 13th-century port where a huge chain was drawn across every night to keep ships out.

Inland, the regional capital of **Poitiers ⓬** is one of the oldest cities in France. The church of **Notre-Dame-la-Grande**, in the town centre, has a magnificent, richly sculpted Romanesque facade and 12th-century frescoes in the vault of the choir. The church of St-Hilaire-le-Grand is the oldest in Poitiers, with parts dating to the 11th century. Just outside Poitiers is **Futuroscope** (daily), a theme park on technology and the future.

Into the interior: the Massif Central

France's upland heartland, the Massif Central, is relatively little visited yet holds some fine sights. Its two great cities are **Limoges ⓭**, famed for its enamel and porcelain industries, and **Clermont-Ferrand ⓮**, which surrounds a massive cathedral built of black lava. Rising above the city is the distinctive volcanic peak of the **Puy de Dôme** (1,464 metres/4,800ft), which is easily ascended on foot or by minibus for spectacular views all around. The views are even more impressive from the summit of **Puy Mary** (1,787 metres/5,863ft), reached by steps from France's highest road pass, the Pas de Peyrol, above the pretty town of **Salers**. Another high point – quite literally – of the Massif Central is the shrine of

Le Puy-en-Velay ⓯, where the Chapelle St-Michel is built on a pinnacle of tufa rock and reached by a stone staircase.

Rivers of southwest France

To the south, the Massif Central gradually gives way to a series of beautiful valleys, with rivers flowing parallel to each other westwards towards the Atlantic. The most northerly of them, and the best known, is the **Dordogne**, which is postcard-perfect as it flows past the pretty towns of **Domme**, **La Roque Gageac** and **Beynac-et-Cazenac**. The capital of the *département* is **Périgueux** ⓰, with its five-domed Byzantine-Romanesque cathedral, but the one place not to miss here is **Sarlat** ⓱, a bustling, labyrinthine market town of atmospheric streets and squares.

Between Périgueux and Sarlat, the River Vézère carves what has become known as the **Vallée de l'Homme** (the Valley of Man) because of its extraordinary number of caves and rock overhangs decorated with prehistoric art. **Lascaux** is the world's most famous painted cave, but its immense popularity threatened its conservation and it

had to be closed to visitors. A replica nearby, **Lascaux II**, is almost as good as the real thing. Further down the valley is **Les Eyzies-de-Tayac**, renowned as the "prehistoric capital of France", and home of the **Musée National de Préhistoire** (daily in July–Aug, Wed–Mon the rest of the year).

In recent decades the Dordogne has been colonised by incomers, particularly the British, drawn by the beauty of its landscapes and the promise of a bucolic lifestyle, but in reality this influx is nothing new and its innate charm has long been appreciated, as witnessed by the many exquisite châteaux that have accumulated here over the centuries. One of the most magnificent is the **Château de Hautefort** (Apr–Sept daily), built in the 17th century.

South of the Dordogne is the Lot. The highlights in its valley include the Romanesque abbey and treasury of **Conques**, the pretty perched village of **St-Cirq Lapopie**, the prehistoric cave paintings of **Pech-Merle** (daily Apr–Oct), the handsome medieval bridge over the river at **Cahors** ⓲, and an enormously deep pothole, **Gouffre de**

This cave painting at Lascaux II is from the Great Hall of Bulls.

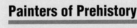

BELOW LEFT: Sarlat is one of the most atmospheric towns in the region.

Painters of Prehistory

Closed off in prehistoric times, the famous Grotte de Lascaux was not rediscovered until 12 September 1940 – during the search for a dog which had disappeared down a hole. Due to the preoccupations of World War II and ensuing hardships, crowds only started flocking to the site some years later. When an astute official learnt in 1963 that a green fungus was growing over the paintings, the cave was immediately closed to the public and a replica, Lascaux II, was built.

Most of the paintings, in black, yellow and red, are thought to date from the Aurignacian period, between 30,000–20,000 BC. The colour friezes use a range of techniques to obtain perspective, texture and movement. They cover the walls and roofs of the cave and represent a number of animals including bulls, cows, deer, bison and horses.

Outstanding as it is, Lascaux is just one of many decorated prehistoric caves in southwest France – mostly in the Dordogne but also in the foothills of the Pyrenees. Often the paintings are in inaccessible places and must have demanded great ingenuity and determination to execute. They also display extraordinary skill. Frequently the painters make use of the natural contours of the rock to produce particularly naturalistic effects. Exactly why prehistoric people went to such lengths to paint their pictures remains a mystery.

DRINK

The Bordeaux wine region covers 1,350 sq km (520 sq miles). Red wines are produced in the Médoc, St-Emilion and Pomerol vineyards to the north, while white wines such as Graves and Sauternes are made further south.

BELOW: sampling Bordeaux wine.
BELOW RIGHT: Porte des Salinières, Bordeaux.

Padirac, which is descended by stairs or lift. Above all, don't miss the ancient Christian shrine of **Rocamadour**, an accretion of crypts and chapels picturesquely clinging to a cliff.

Far to the south is the River Tarn, which flows out of the wild and beautiful schist and granite uplands of the **Parc National des Cévennes** to carve the spectacular, meandering **Gorges du Tarn ⑲** between Florac and Millau. Further downstream the landscapes become much tamer as the river passes through the handsome red-brick town of **Albi ⑳**. Next to the massive cathedral is the old bishop's palace, which is now the superb **Musée de Toulouse-Lautrec** (Apr–Sept daily, Oct–Mar Wed–Mon), in commemoration of the artist's birthplace.

Bordeaux and vineyards

These rivers join the much larger Garonne, on which stands the port of **Bordeaux ㉑**, self-styled – with good reason – as the "world's wine capital". It is a handsome, harmonious city of mainly 18th-century buildings epitomised by the **Place de la Bourse** on the riverbank, the **Palais Rohan** (now the city hall) and, above all, the **Grand-Théâtre** which stands on the Place de la Comédie, at one end of the Cours du 30 Juillet. At the other end of this street is the city's landmark, the **Monument aux Girondins**, commemorating the parliamentarians of Bordeaux who were put to death in 1793 for supposedly opposing the aims of the French Revolution. A statue of Liberty looks down from the top of a 50-metre (164ft) high column onto the **Esplanade des Quinconces** – the largest square in Europe – leading from the monument to the riverbank.

While most of the city speaks of the Enlightenment and of the age of commerce, there are some older monuments hidden in the tangle of streets and squares to the south of the Place de la Bourse. Two old gateways here, the **Porte-Cailhau** and the **Grosse Cloche**, are particularly worth seeking out.

Away from the river, you emerge from the Old Town near the **Cathédrale St-André** (11th-century but much altered) and its free-standing flamboyant Gothic belltower, the **Tour Pey-Berland**.

Nearby is the **Musée de l'Aquitaine** (Tue–Sun), a regional museum with the focus on archaeology.

No one comes to Bordeaux just to see monuments: invariably, the city is used by visitors as a starting point for a tour of the vineyards which dominate the surrounding landscape. The Bordeaux wine region is divided into more than 30 sub-regions of greater or lesser prestige and these in turn into estates, some of them surveyed by aristocratic châteaux. North of the city, on the **Médoc** peninsula, are the wine estates of **Château Margaux**, **Château Latour**, **Château Lafite Rothschild** and **Château Mouton Rothschild**. The wine and tourist information office in Pauillac is the best place to arrange visits to the various wine producers.

To the south and southeast of Bordeaux are the wine regions of **Graves** and Sauternes and to the east **Entre-Deux-Mers**, **Pomerol** and **St-Emilion**. At the heart of this last region, St-Emilion is an attractive town with an ancient underground church to visit.

The *département* of which Bordeaux forms a part, the Gironde – France's largest – has more to it than a wine industry. Its other attractions include the 12th–14th-century **Château de Roquetaillade** and the **Bassin d'Arcachon**, a lagoon open to the sea which is at once holiday resort, bird reserve and oyster farm. On the coast just south of the lagoon is Europe's highest sand dune, the **Dune du Pyla.**

French Basque Country

The extreme southwestern corner of France is the Basque Country, inhabited by a people with ancient roots and a strong sense of their own identity. **Bayonne**, its capital, stands at the confluence of the Nive and Adour rivers and is built around a large Gothic cathedral. It forms a conurbation with the elegant resort of **Biarritz** ㉒, which once attracted famous visitors, as it has done since the time of Emperor Napoleon III and his wife Eugénie. Britain's Edward VII (while still Prince of Wales) was also lured by its offer of fashion and pleasure. In the heart of the town are the **Promenades**, where steep cliffs fall to the ocean. Romantic alleys shaded by tamarisk trees lead to the **Rocher**

Colourful architecture in St-Jean-de-Luz on the Basque coast.

BELOW:
sunshades on the
beach at Biarritz.

The Basilique du Rosaire in Lourdes. Pilgrims flock here from all over the world.

BELOW: cable car to the observatory on the top of the Pic du Midi.

de la Vierge (Rock of the Virgin), from which point the Basque coast can be admired. Biarritz is famous for its huge waves, and some of Europe's most important surfing competitions are held here. Another beautiful resort on the Basque coast is **St-Jean-de-Luz**.

Inland, the Basque Country has exquisitely pretty towns, most notably **Ainhoa** and **Sare**, which stands beneath the mountain of **La Rhune**, ascended by an old cog railway.

Pilgrims from all over France converge on the historic town of **St-Jean-Pied-de-Port** to rest before crossing a pass over the Pyrenees on their long way to the shrine of Santiago de Compostela in Spain (see page 345).

Along the Pyrenees

Few international borders are as clearly marked as that between France and Spain, which follows the Pyrenees, a 400km (250-mile) mountain chain from the Bay of Biscay to the Mediterranean. The range is clearly visible from the lowlands across much of the southwest, particularly in winter when the air is clear and the peaks snow-capped. Although lower than the Alps, the Pyrenees are still a popular winter sports destination, with over 40 resorts to choose from. In summer, the mountains are busy with hikers, some of them making the trek along the GR10 footpath from coast to coast, a journey which takes a good two months. The exceptional gradients make the Pyrenees popular also with cyclists, who come to tackle the high passes (cols) – some over 2,000 metres (6,500ft) – that provide gruelling obstacles for competitors in the Tour de France.

The mountains rise in the Basque Country but reach their highest elevations due south of the cities of **Pau**, **Tarbes** and **Lourdes** ㉓, one of the most important Catholic shrines in the world, a sacred site which is overrun with pilgrims in search of miracle cures, and curious sightseers. Part of the Pyrenees is protected as a national park for its fragile flora and fauna – including brown bears. If your time in the mountains is short, make for the **Cirque de Gavarnie**, a natural rock amphitheatre formed by glaciation; the **Pont d'Espagne**, an easily acces-

Map on pages 100–1

sible beauty spot with marked walking trails; or the **Pic du Midi** (2,872 metres/9,423ft), with an observatory on top which is reached by cable car from the ski resort of La Mongie.

Moving eastwards along the range you pass through the thickly forested departement of the Ariège. In the foothills here are several impressive castles associated with the Cathars, a heretic sect persecuted to extinction by the Catholic Church in alliance with the nobles of northern France in the 13th century. They made their last stand at the castle of **Montségur**, southeast of Foix, today an atmospheric ruin. The Ariège's other major attraction is the caves at **Niaux**, with prehistoric paintings.

French Catalonia

The French part of Catalonia (which, like the Basque Country, is a self-styled nation without a state – *see page 359*) occupies the Mediterranean end of the Pyrenees and has its capital at **Perpignan**. Before the mountains finally descend to sea level, they throw up the striking silhouette of the Pic du Canigou (2,784 metres/9,134ft) above the towns of **Prades** and **Villefranche-de-Conflent**. On the slopes of the Pic is the rebuilt 11th-century monastery of **St-Martin du Canigou**, reached by an uphill slog of half an hour or more, depending on your fitness. Two choice places to visit here are **Ceret**, a cherry-producing town inland, and **Collioure ㉔** on the coast – both famous for inspiring visiting artists, including Matisse and Picasso.

Cities of the Midi

The ancient city of **Toulouse ㉕** stands on the banks of the River Garonne, geographically and culturally midway between the Atlantic and the Mediterranean. In recent decades it has grown into France's fourth-largest metropolis on the back of its aerospace industry.

Most of the older buildings are made of the local brick, earning Toulouse the epithet of the *"Ville Rose"*, or Pink City. From the central square, the **Place du**

Capitole, on which stands the 18th-century town hall, all the other sights are within an easy walk. Chief among them are the massive Romanesque pilgrimage church of **St-Sernin**, its tiered tower acting as a landmark, and the fine arts museum, **Musée des Augustins** (daily).

Contemporary attractions include the **Airbus** assembly plant beside the airport (tours by arrangement; ask at the tourist information office), and – any child's dream – the **Cité de l'Espace** (daily in summer, Sept–Mar Tue–Sun), a museum dedicated to the exploration of space.

From Toulouse, the A61 motorway towards the Mediterranean runs beside a much older channel of communication, the Canal du Midi. Built in the 17th century and kept topped up with water by an ingenious hydraulic system, it is now used as a green artery for leisure cruising, walking and cycling. An information centre is off the A61 motorway at Avignonet-Lauragais.

The motorway also passes alongside the magnificent citadel of **Carcassonne ㉖**, one of the undeniable glories of

The Cité de l'Espace, a museum dedicated to space exploration, is a treat for children.

BELOW: Carcassonne bathed in sunlight.

WHERE

The Millau Viaduct, taking the A75 motorway across the valley of the River Tarn, is the world's highest road bridge. Designed by architect Norman Foster and engineer Michel Virlogeux and opened in 2004, it has become a popular tourist attraction in its own right, with a visitor's information centre on the RD 992 going towards Albi.

France. Ringed by a double set of ramparts and guarded by myriad pepperpot towers, it is a stunning example of a self-contained medieval town. What you see today is due more to imaginative reconstruction than preservation, but it still conjures up the mood of its times, especially when seen from afar.

Two other great ancient cities of France's south – the Midi – stand on the Mediterranean coast east of the Rhône Delta. **Montpellier,** with its thriving university, including a highly regarded medical school, and its striking contemporary architecture, is considered one of the liveliest and most artistic places to live in the south. It also has an important collection of French painting in the **Musée Fabre** (Tue–Sun).

Nearby **Nîmes ㉗** is another city that strives to be up-to-date, although its greatest assets are its Roman buildings built in the 1st century AD, especially the amphitheatre of **Les Arènes** and the **Maison Carrée**, a temple which is in a superb state of conservation. One of the greatest engineering and aesthetic achievements of Roman civilisation, however, is 20km

(12 miles) north of Nîmes. The three-tiered **Pont du Gard** aqueduct (daily) is France's most visited ancient monument. It is 275 metres/yds at its longest part and almost 50 metres (164ft) high. An assembly of large heavy stones that were fitted together without mortar, it once carried water flowing at 400 litres (110 gallons) per second.

Gateways to Provence

Across the Rhône and you are in **Provence**, France's sensuous southern region, which has always attracted well-heeled foreign settlers and artists.

The lively town of **Avignon ㉘** offers a great summer theatre festival in and around its superb **Palais des Papes** (daily). This 14th-century edifice was built at a time when the popes found Rome too dangerous to stay in. Its silent cloisters, cavernous halls and imposing ramparts are a delight to explore. In contrast, the famous bridge (*"Sur le pont d'Avignon, l'on y danse, tous en rond"*) now only reaching halfway across the River Rhône, is a disappointing four-arch ruin. (In fact, the people didn't dance on it as the French song says, but underneath it.)

North of Avignon, **Orange** lies at the northern tip of Provence and was a favoured resort for the Romans when it was a colony of their empire, with a population four times the size of its present-day 25,000. The Roman theatre, graced by a statue of Emperor Augustus, is regarded as the most beautiful amphitheatre of the classical era. Surrounding Orange, the area of the **Vaucluse** is richly fertile. The fascinating ruins at **Vaison-la-Romaine** provide a glimpse of the private side of Roman life in some well-preserved houses of 2,000 years ago. **Mont Ventoux** has a view over the whole of Provence down to Marseille and the Mediterranean or clear across to the Swiss Alps. One of the great attractions of this mountain region is the **Fontaine-de-Vaucluse**, where the underground River Sorgue suddenly springs into sight in a spectacular setting of grottoes.

BELOW: street musicians perform at the Avignon festival.

The region's most picturesque site of ancient Roman life is **Arles**, which, besides its fine amphitheatre and arena, has the fascinating necropolis of Les Alyscamps in a lovely setting. The tree-shaped promenade of Les Lices creates a relaxed atmosphere for the many open-air cafés. Van Gogh famously lost his sanity here, in the sun-dappled cafés and neighbouring heat-swirled fields.

The scenic wetlands of the **Camargue**, south of Arles, are entrancing because of their birdlife – this is a good place to see flamingos in the wild – and way of life, which revolves around rearing bulls and horses. The principal town of the Camargue is Stes-Maries-de-la-Mer, and there's a visitor centre at La Capelière, to the south of Villeneuve.

Provençal life

Coming east again, **St-Rémy-de-Provence** is a delightful market town surrounded by vineyards, olive groves and almond trees. **Aix-en-Provence A**, serenest of university towns, with its wonderful arcade of plane trees across the Cours Mirabeau, is the intellectual heart of Provence. Zola grew up in the city along with his friend Paul Cézanne. One of the best ways to see Aix is by taking the Cézanne trail, following a free leaflet from the tourist office. **L'Atelier Paul Cézanne** (daily) preserves the artist's studio and house – his cape and beret hang where he left them.

South of Aix, **Marseille B** is France's oldest and second-largest city. Founded by Greek traders in 600 BC, the gateway to the Mediterranean, the Orient and beyond has been a bustling port for centuries. Today the **Vieux Port** has a colourful fish market and many seafood restaurants. The streets around **La Canebière**, Marseille's most famous thoroughfare, which leads from the port, are the liveliest in the city, especially in the evening.

Between Marseille and Toulon, the shore is distinguished by Les Calanques, steep-sided fjords carved out of cliffs, best viewed by boat from **Cassis C**. This chic resort of restored houses with a popular golden beach is known for its fragrant white wines, which tantalise the palate with hints of rosemary, gorse and myrtle – the herbs that cover these hills.

Elaborate ice creams are served in the Café de Paris, Monaco.

BELOW: a Provençal lavender field in bloom.

The port at St-Tropez is lined with boats belonging to the super-rich.

Over the sea to Corsica

Across the Ligurian Sea from the south coast of France, reached by ferry from Marseille, Toulon and Nice, is **Corsica** (*Corse* in French), the Mediterranean's fourth-largest island. Although its two *départements* are as French as all the rest, Corsica has a distinct culture and its own language. It is an extraordinary bundle of landscapes within a relatively small space, from chilly mountain summits to subtropical palm groves. Most of all, it draws holidaymakers for its unspoilt villages, lazy pace of life and beautiful beaches washed by clear waters.

The Côte d'Azur

The sun-drenched Côte d'Azur meanders lazily from **Toulon D**, home to France's Mediterranean naval fleet, to the Italian border along rocky lagoons and coves. An amphitheatre of limestone hills at Toulon screens the deep natural harbour, one of the Mediterranean's most attractive. Modern **Hyères E**, east of Toulon along the coast, is made up of a *vieille ville* and a newer area of modern villas and boulevards with date palms. This was once an ancient and medieval port, but it is now 4km (2½ miles) from the sea. Hyères was the first "climatic" resort on the Côte d'Azur, its subtropical climate encouraging sailing, scubadiving, windsurfing and waterskiing. Within the Old Town, entered via its 13th-century gate, is the **Place Massillon**, where there is a food market every day that is especially good for Arab and Provençal specialities.

The once-tiny fishing village of **St-Tropez F** is packed with visitors in summer, becoming a sort of Mediterranean extension of Paris, with all that this implies for parking and prices. French painters and writers had discovered it by the late 19th century; some of these early paintings, showing the village in its pre-touristy unspoilt state, are on display in a lovely converted chapel, the **Musée de l'Annonciade** (Wed–Mon).

The plateau town of **Fréjus G**, like Hyères, used to lie on the sea. Its name derives from *Forum Julii*; it was founded by Julius Caesar in 49 BC as a significant trading centre of Transalpine Gaul. Important Roman ruins here include the 10,000-seat arena where Picasso used to watch bullfights.

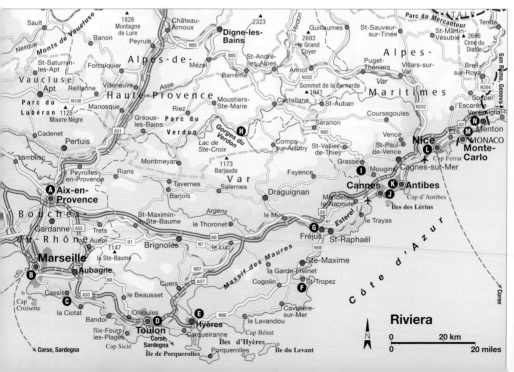

Alpine retreat

For fewer crowds, head north into the hills to the **Gorges du Verdon** , France's Grand Canyon. The Verdon cuts through limestone cliffs which plunge to the torrent 600 metres (2,000ft) below. The Norman Foster-designed museum of prehistory at Quinson is the largest of its kind. From here stretch the Alpes de Haute Provence, a wild, barren landscape leading up into the French Alps.

Heading back towards the coast, stop if you can at **Grasse** ❶, where there have been perfume distilleries since the 16th century. The **Musée International de la Parfumerie**, in an elegant 18th-century mansion, tells its history. You can also visit the commercial **Parfumerie Fragonard** (daily), opposite the **Villa-Musée Fragonard** (June–Sept daily, Oct–May Wed–Mon), where the Grasse-born artist Jean-Honoré Fragonard lived.

The International Film Festival held each May in **Cannes** ❶ is one of the highlights of an annual chain of events that attracts a set of celebrities and a media circus. Kings and queens of all kinds and persuasions, sheikhs, film stars, emperors and the fabulously wealthy are all grist for a mill that has been grinding since Lord Brougham, the Lord Chancellor of England, was stranded in Cannes in 1834 because of an outbreak of cholera in Nice, where he was headed for a winter holiday. It pleased him so much that he built a house on the side of **Mont Chevalier** and encouraged other British aristocrats to do the same. **Le Suquet** is the ancient quarter around Mont Chevalier. At dinner hour in the high season, elegant women in pearls and evening gowns and gentlemen in tuxedos emerge onto the streets, perhaps from a yacht anchored in the old harbour, and struggle up **Rue St-Antoine** to the fashionable restaurants for which Le Suquet is noted.

Dinner will be followed by a stroll along the luxurious **Boulevard de la Croisette** for the magnificent views of Le Suquet silhouetted against **La Napoule Bay**, with the chunky red hills of the Esterel in the background.

Antibes ❶ and **Cap d'Antibes** face Nice and St-Jean-Cap-Ferrat across the

An Hermès label at the Musée International de la Parfumerie in Grasse, the perfume town.

BELOW:
the spectacular
Gorges du Verdon.

The Fondation Maeght holds a glorious collection of 20th-century art.

Baie des Anges (Bay of Angels). Here the magnificent yacht harbour, lined with the playthings of the super-rich, rests at the foot of an enormous brick citadel built in the 16th century to protect the infant town from assaults by Barbary pirates. The Château Grimaldi on a terrace overlooking the sea, originally a 12th-century building but much reconstructed in the 16th, is now home to the **Musée Picasso** (Wed–Mon). It contains a remarkable collection of more than 50 works painted by Picasso during his stay here in 1946, including major works such as *La Joie de Vivre* and *Antipolis Suite*.

Artists' enclave

Matisse's **Chapelle du Rosaire** (daily) at **Vence**, northeast of Grasse by the D2210, is considered his masterpiece, a finely tuned synthesis of architectural elements, the most important being stained glass and the white walls on which their coloured light falls. The artist gave it much of his time between 1948 and 1951.

Directly south of Vence, the walled town of **St-Paul-de-Vence** was discov-

BELOW RIGHT:
Venus sculpture in the grounds of Renoir's home at Cagnes-sur-Mer.

ered by artists in the 1920s. They patronised **La Colombe d'Or** café, now an exclusive hotel and restaurant with a priceless collection of works originally donated by visiting artists. St-Paul itself is a perfectly formed hill village with a vista of villas and cypresses as far as the eye can see, but its popularity means that its narrow winding main street becomes jammed with visitors.

Just outside the village, the **Fondation Maeght** (daily) occupies a white concrete and rose-brick structure designed by the Spanish architect J.L. Sert. The collection includes paintings by Braque, Bonnard, Kandinsky and Chagall, and several outdoor sculpture areas with works by Giacometti, Calder, Miró, Arp and others.

Winter haven of the British

"The English come and pass the winter here to take the cure, soothe their chronic spleens and live out their fantasies," wrote an observer of the budding Anglo-Saxon social scene in **Nice** ❶ in 1775. They have been doing it ever since in increasing numbers, and justifiably take credit for establishing

A Legacy of Art

Painters have been especially fascinated by the Côte d'Azur because of its unique sunlight. The quality of the light is due largely to the Mistral, a cold, dry, strong wind that often blows in from the Rhône Valley, sweeping the sky to crystal clarity, enriching colours and deepening shadows. Earlier art of the south of France, such as Roman and Greek remains, also provided the inspiration for 20th-century artists.

Matisse, Picasso, Dufy and Chagall were all devoted to the region, and the products of their fidelity are displayed in museums and private collections along the Riviera.

Picasso spent 27 years on the Côte d'Azur, more than half of them at Vallauris behind Cannes, where he established a ceramics studio, the Madoura Pottery, where copies are still sold. There is also a Musée Picasso in Antibes. At the village of Biot between Nice and Cannes, the Musée Fernand Léger (Wed–Mon) houses hundreds of works by the artist, who contributed to the creation of Cubism.

Auguste Renoir spent the last 12 years of his life at Cagnes-sur-Mer, where his home, now the Musée Renoir (Wed–Mon), remains exactly as it was when he died. Nice has several important art galleries, including the Musée Chagall and the Musée Matisse. Another mecca for art-lovers is the Fondation Maeght in St-Paul-de-Vence.

this city as the centre for touring the Riviera. The **Promenade des Anglais**, the striking waterfront dual carriageway embellished with flower beds and palm trees, was originally built in 1822 by the English for easier access to the sea. Queen Victoria enjoyed her morning constitutionals along that coastal path on several occasions; in later years, she was carried along in her famous black-and-red varnished donkey cart.

Today, the promenade skirts the pebbly Mediterranean waterfront, bedecked with luxury hotels, high-rise apartment blocks and trendy cafés. A short stroll away are the narrow winding alleyways of the *vieille ville* (Old Town), where the visitor gets a salty taste of medieval Provençal lifestyles, heightened by aromas of garlic, wine and pungent North African spices emanating from a succession of couscous parlours.

A diminishing number of plain but traditional restaurants around the flower market on the **Cours Saleya** specialise in *soupe de poissons* and *bourride*, a native variation of *bouillabaisse*. *Aioli*, a rough local mayonnaise made with olive oil and crushed garlic, is traditionally served with salted codfish on Fridays.

North of the Old Town is the **Musée Chagall** (Wed–Mon), containing many of the artist's drawings and all his bronzes. The building was specially designed to house his masterpiece, *Messages Bibliques* – 17 monumental paintings depicting scenes from the Old Testament. There are also three stained-glass windows depicting *The Creation* and a 6-metre (20ft) mosaic of Elijah in his fiery chariot.

The remains of an amphitheatre, capable of seating 4,000 spectators, and three public baths dating from the Roman occupation have been uncovered at **Cimiez**, an exclusive residential quarter of Nice, located 1.6km (1 mile) northeast of the city centre. The archaeological treasures taken from the site are housed nearby in a 17th-century villa. In the same building the

Musée Matisse (Wed–Mon) has an extensive collection of paintings and other works by the artist.

Gambling and Grands Prix

East of Nice, you suddenly leave France and enter the microstate of **Monaco**  (*see also Microstates, page 358*). From the days of its early Genoese rulers, the principality of Monaco has survived as a political curiosity on the map of Europe. It exists under the protection of France but has remained a mini-monarchy of the Grimaldi family, with its own tax privileges, national licence plates and coat of arms. This tiny country of less than 1.5 sq km (1 sq mile) and a population of 32,000 has lived down its reputation as a sunny place for shady people. Today, it dotes instead on tourists – the raw material of its biggest industry. Prince Rainier III hit the headlines when he married the American film star Grace Kelly and, after her death in a car crash, lived somewhat in the shadow of his headline-grabbing daughters, the princesses Caroline and Stephanie. He worked hard to maintain Monaco's

A classic Art Nouveau depiction of the pleasures of absinthe, a drink some artists liked rather too much.

BELOW: Monaco attracts the super-wealthy.

An ornate poster advertising the Musée Océanographique in Monaco.

BELOW:
Roquebrune, one of the medieval perched villages.

year-round lustre until his death in April 2005, when he was succeeded by his 47-year-old son Albert.

If you're feeling lucky you might want to head straight for the sumptuously decorated gaming rooms of the world's most famous **Casino** in Monte-Carlo, a Belle Epoque survivor which has lost none of its style and is open to visitors as well as to its habitual clientele of social butterflies who flutter around its ornate halls and neatly trimmed gardens and terraces. The western section, the building's oldest, was built in 1878 by the same architect who designed the Paris Opéra. The centre section is a tiny 529-seat Rococo-styled theatre, the home of the Monte-Carlo Opera.

Monaco's major historic monument is the **Palais des Princes** (Apr–Oct daily) a crenellated, part-Moorish, part-Italian Renaissance castle perched on a 60-metre (200ft) rocky promontory jutting nearly 800 metres (half a mile) into the sea. Visitors can tour the state apartments and throne room, and the court of honour, which sports an arcaded and frescoed gallery. Beneath the palace is the Old Town (Monaco-

Ville), tinted with Provençal pink, orange and yellow hues, which surrounds a neo-Romanesque cathedral.

On the seashore stands the **Musée Océanographique** (daily), incorporating one of the finest and best-kept aquariums in Europe.

Perched villages

For an overview of Monaco the best place to go is the tiny village of **La Turbie**, situated behind the principality's yawning harbour. Here are the remains of one of the most impressive, yet least-known Roman monuments, the Alpine Trophy. In 6 BC Rome commemorated the final subjugation of the warriors of the Alps region by raising an enormous stone trophy where it could be seen from both directions far along the Aurelian Way (which ran from Rome to the Rhône). The impressive 35-metre (114ft) Doric colonnade is still standing and the list of conquered tribes making up the inscription to Augustus has survived.

La Turbie is one of several peasant villages which sprouted like eagles' nests on mountain peaks during and before the Middle Ages. Inaccessible and often enclosed within a protective stone barricade and fortified gate, the villages and their villagers have often shunned outsiders. But many of the more picturesque communities, such as Eze, Peille, Roquebrune and Gourdon, tolerate and even welcome tourists, as the crowds show.

Eze, the best known because it is near the sea, is easy to reach and offers a splendid panoramic overview of much of the Côte d'Azur from its 470-metre (1,550ft) elevation. It has an intriguing history of pirate assaults and Moorish massacres that can be traced back to the 1st century AD, when a colony of Phoenicians unnerved their Roman neighbours by consecrating a temple to their goddess Isis. The Romans quickly and violently replaced it with a monument more to their liking and religious persuasion. Perhaps this is what caught the imagination of

Friedrich Nietzsche, who was inspired in Eze to write *Thus Spake Zarathustra*. In addition to the crowds, Eze is noted today for the crumbling ramparts of its 14th-century castle.

Close to the Italian frontier, the 17th-century town of **Menton**  is probably the warmest winter resort on any French coast and offers one of the most typical townscapes in Provence. In the narrow, twisting, vaulted streets overhead balconies jut out over the alleyways until they almost bump balustrades.

To the Rhône Valley

A scenic highway (N85) traces Napoleon's journey after he landed on French shores in 1815 following his Elba exile, and is known as the Route Napoléon. It begins at Cannes and goes through Grasse and on to **Grenoble** . The birthplace of Stendhal, author of *The Red and the Black*, Grenoble is the undisputed capital of the French Alps. The best view of the city can be had from the **Fort de la Bastille**, which was built in the 16th century and strengthened in the 19th. In the mountains east of Grenoble are two of France's nine national parks, **Ecrins** and **Vanoise**. **Annecy**, north of Grenoble, is a lovely old town at the end of a lake. The **Palais de l'Isle** is a picturesque former prison, now a museum (daily in summer, Wed–Mon the rest of the year).

France's third-largest city, **Lyon** , is said to be the country's gastronomic capital and where southern France begins. Standing astride the rivers Sâone and Rhone, its layout can be somewhat confusing, with the city centre on a peninsula, the Presqu'Ile between the two rivers. The most interesting part is **Vieux Lyon** (Old Lyon), on the west bank of the Saône, which has some fine Renaissance houses linked by covered passages unique to Lyon, known as *traboules*. A funicular railway runs from here up the hill of Fourvière, above where there are two Roman amphitheatres and an ostentatious 19th-century basilica but, most of all, tremendous views over the city.

For centuries, Lyon was Europe's silk capital, and its history can be seen in the **Musée Historique des Tissus** (Tue–Sun). Another excellent museum, the **Musée des Beaux-Arts** (Wed–Mon), has an exceptional collection of French and other European paintings.

Burgundy wine route

Beaune has been at the heart of the Burgundian wine trade since the 18th century, and the auction of the Hospices de Beaune in **L'Hôtel-Dieu** (daily), a charity hospital historically supported by wine produced on land donated by benefactors, is still the high point in the local wine calendar. Under its splendid multicoloured roof, the long ward of the hospital contains the original sickbeds. The halls off the courtyard house a collection of artworks and tapestries, crowned by a magnificently detailed painting of *The Last Judgement* by Rogier Van der Weyden.

The undisputed capital of Burgundy is **Dijon** , and the wine country tour from Dijon down to Beaune passes through such illustrious "labels"

L'Hôtel-Dieu in Beaune still hosts a famous wine auction, as it has since the 18th century.

BELOW:
Menton lies close to the Italian border.

You will often see people playing pétanque *with enthusiasm in village squares.*

BELOW: Clos de Vougeot vineyard on the Burgundy wine route.

as **Gevrey-Chambertin**, **Nuits-St-Georges** and **Clos de Vougeot**. The monumental **Palais des Ducs**, where the 14th- and 15th-century dukes of Burgundy rest in grandiose tombs, is in Dijon's busy city centre. The oldest part of the palace houses the **Musée des Beaux-Arts** (Wed–Mon), one of the finest in France, with French, German and Italian statuary and paintings from the 14th–18th centuries.

Around 45km (28 miles) northwest of Dijon, the **Abbaye de Fontenay** (daily) makes for a welcome moment of peace in its 12th-century cloisters. Intended to be piously modest, without ornament of any kind, the bare paving stones and immaculate columns acquired, in the course of time, a look of grandeur.

West of here, set high on a hilltop, **Vézelay** ㉝ is one of Burgundy's most spectacular monuments. The majestic **Basilique Sainte-Madeleine** was founded in the 9th century as an abbey; the presence of Mary Magdalene's supposed relics in the basilica made Vézelay a place of pilgrimage.

In the Jura mountains of Franche-Comté east of Dijon, the town of

Besançon nestles in a sweeping curve of the River Doubs. The 16th-century **Palais Granville** was the aristocratic home of the Chancellor to Spanish Habsburg Emperor Charles V. This pleasant town also has an impressive 70-dial astronomical clock in the cathedral and a formidable 17th-century citadel built for Louis XIV's eastern defences.

Alsace

Lorraine and Alsace have been historic bones of contention between France and Germany. Here after World War I the French built the Maginot Line, an impressive line of fortifications along their eastern border. Unfortunately it was never used, for the Germans simply went round it.

Belfort owes its glory to its successful resistance against the Prussians in 1870, commemorated by the monumental lion designed by Auguste Bartholdi, creator of New York's Statue of Liberty. **Colmar** ㉞ has a quiet but irresistible charm; its 16th-century houses are the very essence of Alsatian tradition. Most cherished of its treasures is Mathias Grünewald's celebrated Issenheim altar painting in the **Musée d'Unterlinden** (May–Oct daily, Nov–Apr Wed–Mon).

Strasbourg ㉟ is Alsace's dignified capital and one seat of the European Parliament. The River Ill encircles the lovely Old Town where Goethe was a happy student in 1770. The graceful cathedral, with its intriguing asymmetrically erected steeple, is as inspiring as ever, particularly for its central porch and the stunning stained-glass rose window above.

On the way from Alsace to Lorraine, stop at **Ronchamp** to admire Le Corbusier's striking chapel Notre-Dame-du-Haut, a landmark of 20th-century architecture. The mountain ridge of the **Vosges** embraces a charming countryside of forests, orchards and vineyards, among which the villages of **Riquewihr** and **Kaysersberg** are true medieval gems.

Lorraine

Nancy **36** is graced by a beautifully harmonious main square, the 18th-century **Place Stanislas**, its palatial pavilions flanked by magnificent gilded wrought-iron gates. In the Old Town, the renovated houses of the Grande Rue lead to the Port de la Craffe, whose two towers and connecting bastion are impressive reminders of earlier fortifications. Along the way, the Palais Ducal contains the **Musée Lorrain** (Tue–Sun). Housed in a separate museum is the unique **Ecole de Nancy**, the epitome of Art Nouveau (Wed–Sun).

Metz, at the confluence of the Moselle and Seille rivers, is the capital of Lorraine. It has a Gothic cathedral and what is claimed to be the oldest church in France, St-Pierre-aux-Nonnains, dating from the 4th century.

To the French, the name of **Verdun** **37** symbolises heroic national resistance after one of the decisive battles of World War I was fought here between February and December 1916. A German offensive intended to end the deadlock of trench warfare on the Western Front by striking a mortal blow against French pride ended in failure, but only after huge loss of life. Verdun today receives a steady stream of visitors who come to visit the memorials and museums explaining the military events and their significance.

Champagne

Similarly of deep symbolical significance, although for difference reasons, is the city of **Reims** **38**. In 496 Clovis, first King of the Franks, was baptised in Reims, and thereafter each new monarch would make his way here to be crowned in this city's magnificent **Cathédrale Notre-Dame**, which has superb stained-glass windows ranging from the 13th-century rose window to 20th-century windows by Chagall. Administratively, modern Reims is only a sub-prefecture but more prestigiously it is the commercial centre for the production of a unique style of wine to which the *département* it belongs to has given its name: **champagne**. If you can only take one souvenir home with you it should surely be a bottle of the authentic stuff. ❑

A gilded gateway in the 18th-century Place Stanislas in Nancy.

BELOW LEFT: selling locally made *saucisson*.

Regional Foods of France

General de Gaulle is famously said to have asked: "How can you govern a country which has 246 varieties of cheese?" His figure is probably an underestimate, and as with cheese so with food in general: there is such a bewildering diversity of things to eat and drink that you could be tempted to forget about sightseeing altogether and spend your time in restaurants and bistros instead.

Many regions of France are proud producers of some particular item or other: truffles are harvested in the Dordogne; *foie gras* and garlic come from Gascony; cured ham is produced in the southwest; mustard is made in Dijon; and good fish and seafood are landed at ports almost anywhere along the coasts. And everywhere there will be a local dish to try on the menu – crêpes are a staple of Brittany; *cassoulet* is the typical meat and bean casserole of Toulouse; *bouillabaisse* the fish soup that distinguishes Marseille; and quiche the dish to order in Lorraine.

The French love not only eating but talking about what they are eating, and an interest in food on the part of the visitor is the quickest way to the heart of the country. Show curiosity about anything on your plate or on a market stall and you will be given a lecture on the geography, climate, farming and lifestyle of the region. And, of course, there is always a wine to accompany your meal, but that is another universe in itself…

EUROPE'S GREATEST ART GALLERIES

The great museums of Europe are filled with works of art from every period of history, a breathtaking display of mankind's creativity and spirit

It is almost impossible to overstate the wealth of artistic treasures awaiting the visitor to Western Europe. The great galleries of Paris, Florence, Amsterdam, Madrid and so on are as famous in their own right as the artists whose works they house.

However, while the Louvre or the Prado offer grand surroundings for the display of the greatest art, especial pleasure is offered by the intimate experience of visiting, say, El Greco's house in Toledo, where many of his greatest works are on display.

The oldest collections were founded by the church, which was the main patron of European art from late Antiquity until the Renaissance. Later on, galleries were the creation of kings and queens whose personal tastes and preferences shaped their choice of artists to patronise. As wealth spread through society, smaller collections were founded by rich merchants or bankers. The Medici, for example, amassed their wealth first as wool merchants then as bankers, and spent most of it on Florence, financing glorious new buildings and the artists to decorate them.

As one might expect, most of Europe's greatest collections have a strong national character and focus. The Rijksmuseum in Amsterdam is almost entirely filled with Dutch art of the Golden Age, while the Uffizi in Florence is a repository of Italian Renaissance art. Some, though, such as the Van Gogh Museum in Amsterdam, the Dalí Museum in Figueres and the Magritte Museum in Brussels, offer a unique insight into a single artist.

ABOVE: the Prado in Madrid provides a splendid setting for a superb collection of art amassed by the kings of Spain.

ABOVE: Rembrandt's *Isaac and Rebecca*, known as "The Jewish Bride" in the Rijksmuseum, Amsterdam. The Dutch Master won lucrative commissions to paint portraits of wealthy merchants and their wives

LEFT: Sandro Botticelli's luminous *Birth of Venus*, painted c.1480, is one of the many Renaissance masterpieces in the Uffizi gallery in Florence.

CONTEMPORARY ART

In ateliers across Europe, young artists continue to create striking and sometimes disturbing works. You will find them working in abandoned factories in former East Berlin, cramped attic rooms in Amsterdam and low-rent workshops in the outer suburbs of Paris.

The artists regularly hold exhibitions in independent galleries and also at the big events such as the Venice Biennial and Dokumenta Kassel. Collectors can also pick up works by emerging artists or established names at big art fairs such as Art Basel or the more off beat events devoted to new artists or affordable art.

Some contemporary art museums are located in striking buildings designed by modern architects, such as the Pompidou Centre in Paris and the Guggenheim in Bilbao. Other centres for contemporary art are located in converted industrial buildings, like Wiels in Brussels, which occupies a former brewery, and Berlin's contemporary art museum, which occupies the former Hamburger Bahnhof railway station.

ABOVE: in Berlin, many artists have taken to the streets. Working at night, especially in the bohemian Kreuzburg area, they adorn walls with stunning and sometimes subversive visual images.

ABOVE: Frank Gehry's Guggenheim Museum in Bilbao is one of the most striking buildings of the late 20th century.

LEFT: crowds around Leonardo da Vinci's *Mona Lisa*, Louvre, Paris.

RIGHT: Attic red-figure vase from the National Archaeological Museum in Athens.

BELGIUM

Although it's one of the smallest countries in
Europe, Belgium offers a rich and varied culture
and history, a variety of languages and, last
but not least, great food

If you don't dally, you can drive across Belgium in two
hours. Zooming along illuminated highways at night, rolling through deserted and drab industrial towns, you can
reach the far border unaware that only a few miles away, off
the beaten track, lie picturesque, medieval villages and towns
that are among the best-preserved in Europe.

This small country of 30,520 sq km (11,780 sq miles) has
a population of 10.7 million people. French-speaking
Walloons inhabit the south and Dutch-speaking Flemings
live in the north. The capital city, Brussels, lies in the centre of the
country and is officially bilingual. On the eastern border, there is a
small German-speaking community. In spite of sharing a common
history and a small territory, Walloons and Flemings are not as
neighbourly as they might be, and their rivalry has at times come
perilously close to breaking up the country.

Belgium has all the ingredients for an agreeable visit: bustling seaside
resorts, rivers and lakes, villages nestling among rugged hills and forests,
and history; the beautiful medieval towns, such as Ghent
and Bruges, with canals and cobbled streets, are easy to
explore, and Antwerp, equally venerable, is a centre of the
diamond trade. There is also an exceptional number of
good museums housing, among other things, the works
of the great Flemish painters who are a key to the story of
European art. Finally (though many would say primarily),
there is the cuisine which, Belgians will tell you, surpasses even that of
France. Thousands of bureaucrats assigned to the EU or Nato in
Brussels are especially grateful for this.

Belgium has its own royal family, acquired in
1831 with Leopold of Saxe-Coburg, who started
the dynasty, today headed by Albert II and his
Italian-born wife Paola. Belgians are good at
pageants, and some of the most colourful festivals
in Europe take place here. With luck, you will
arrive to find the flags flying high.   ❑

PRECEDING PAGES: Dinant, on the River Meuse. **LEFT:** cycling on one of Belgium's
quiet streets. **ABOVE:** *moules*, the national dish; classic gabled houses.

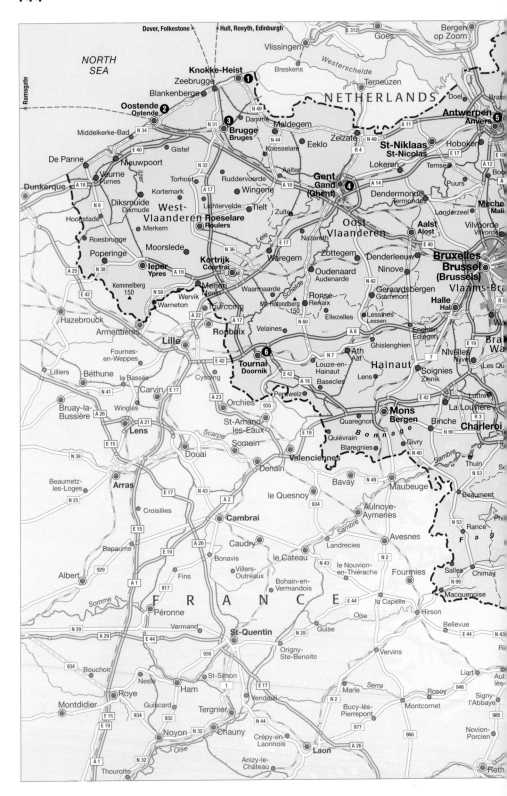

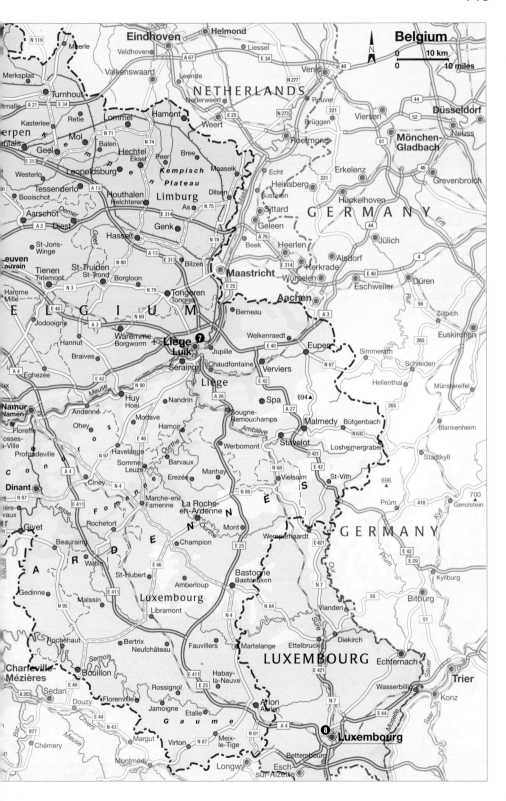

Belgium

0   10 km
0   10 miles

BRUSSELS

In the "capital of Europe", office blocks with tinted glass stand beside Gothic churches, and Art Nouveau masterpieces are wedged between concrete apartment blocks

In this city, northern and southern Europe, represented by the Dutch-speaking Fleming and the French-speaking Walloon, have been fused, more or less, into an urban hybrid, the *Bruxellois*. As befits a bilingual city, street signs are in French and Flemish. Brussels was first mentioned in 966 under the name of Bruocsella (meaning settlement in the marshes) in a chronicle of the Holy Roman Emperor Otto I. Around 979, a fortress may have been built on a little island in the River Senne, a tributary of the Scheldt. It flourished as a trading centre along the route from Bruges to Cologne and became politically important when Duke Philip the Good of Burgundy made it his capital in the 15th century.

Shortly after, the Habsburg Emperor Charles V turned it into the capital of the Low Countries, later to be dominated in turn by the Spanish, the Austrians, the French and the Dutch. The independence movement of 1830 against the Dutch finally gave the country its own identity.

The Grand'Place

The **Grand'Place ❶** is the heart of Brussels. Belgians call it the most beautiful square in the world, and many visitors agree. Here, every day except Monday and Thursday, a flower market is held, and in August in even-numbered years the square is carpeted with flowers. Seven alleys lead into the Grand'Place and its spectacle of lavishly decorated Flemish-Baroque guild houses. Dating from between 1695 and 1699, the facades appear to have been stamped from the same mould. Each one is different, however, yet blends harmoniously with the others.

Dominating the square is the magnificent Gothic **Hôtel de Ville ❷** (town hall; open for guided tours most days) with a 15th-century spire, surmounted by a statue of St Michael (the city's patron saint). Inside, fine tapestries decorate the walls. Opposite the town hall is the almost equally

Main attractions
GRAND'PLACE
HÔTEL DE VILLE
MANNEKEN-PIS
CATHÉDRAL DES
 STS-MICHEL-ET-GUDULE
PALAIS ROYAL
MUSÉES ROYAUX DES
 BEAUX-ARTS
PLACE DU GRAND SABLON

LEFT: a cheerful Brussels mural.
BELOW: the famous Manneken-Pis.

A label from one of the many varieties of Brussels beer.

The Musée Magritte (Tue–Sun), devoted to the life and work of the great Belgian Surrealist artist, opened just off Place Royale, at Rue de la Régence 3, in 2009.

magnificent neo-Gothic **Maison du Roi** (King's House; Tue–Sun), which contains the Museum of the City of Brussels, where, among other exhibits, are housed the 800 or so costumes belonging to the Manneken-Pis. Behind it begins the **Ilôt Sacré**, a labyrinth of alleys and arcades filled with restaurants. Inside the many places serving good food and fine Belgian beers, the flame of an open fireplace in winter, or a cool fan in summer, provides a warm welcome to visitors.

Legendary duke

For centuries the people of Brussels have shown a particular affection for the **Manneken-Pis ❸**, a fountain-statue of a little boy relieving himself. The sculpture, at the corner of **Rue de l'Etuve** and **Rue du Chêne**, a few blocks south of the Grand'Place, incarnates the irreverent spirit and humour of the Bruxellois.

Legend claims he represents Duke Godfrey III. In 1142, when only a few months old, the baby duke was brought to the battlefield at Ransbeke and his cradle was hung from an oak to

encourage the soldiers, dejected by his father's death. At the decisive moment, when his forces were about to retreat, the young duke rose in his cradle and made the gesture reproduced later at the fountain. This, so legend goes, encouraged his troops to victory. However, a rival legend maintains that the statuette commemorates the little boy whose action inadvertently extinguished a time bomb intended to blow up the town hall.

Going down Rue au Beurre from the Grand'Place you come to **La Bourse**, the city's Stock Exchange, a Neoclassical building dating from 1873. Here the business heart of Brussels throbs. From the end of bustling **Petite Rue des Bouchers** in the Ilôt Sacré, it is only a stone's throw to the elegant glass-roofed shopping arcades of the **Galeries Royales St-Hubert**.

The Upper City

Uphill from the Grand'Place to the east, the white stone walls of the **Cathédral des Sts-Michel-et-Gudule ❹** (daily) rise majestically on the hillside between the Upper and Lower

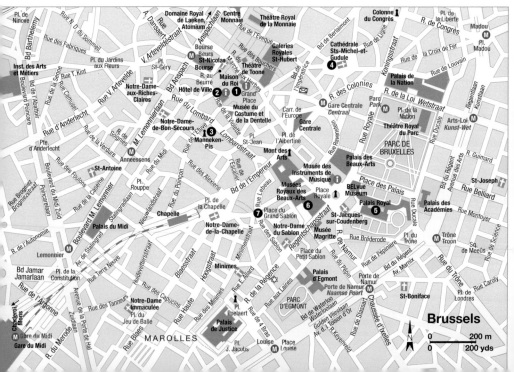

Brussels

0   200 m
0   200 yds

City, where it was built from the 13th to the 15th century. Excavations have revealed the Romanesque crypt, which can be visited. The stained glass within the cathedral is particularly fine; the West Window offers a remarkable depiction of *The Last Judgement* from 1528.

Going uphill onto Rue Royale, then passing through the elegant **Parc de Bruxelles**, brings you to graceful **Place Royale**. The square is bordered by **Saint-Jacques-sur-Coudenberg**, a Neoclassical church inspired by a Roman temple. A little way downhill on Rue Montagne de la Cour is the Art Nouveau Old England department store, now home to the **Musée des Instruments de Musique** (daily). The dignified **Palais Royal ❺**, just off Place Royale, was built in 1820, almost a century after an earlier royal household burnt down. This is where King Albert II conducts his official business.

Fine art museums

Adjoining Place Royale are the **Musées Royaux des Beaux-Arts ❻** (Tue–Sun), Belgium's finest collection of art treasures. The well-designed and interconnected collections are distributed between the **Musée d'Art Ancien** and the **Musée d'Art Moderne**. The former has a superb collection of Flemish and Dutch Masters from the 15th to the 18th centuries, including works by Rembrandt, Hals, Rubens, van Eyck and Hieronymus Bosch. The latter, with paintings and sculpture from the 19th and 20th centuries, is centred on a well of light which illuminates the eight underground floors. Highlights are masterpieces by Belgian Surrealists Magritte and Delvaux, as well as works by Ensor, Permeke and the Flemish Expressionists.

From here, Rue de la Régence leads to **Place du Grand Sablon ❼** which, with its magnificent High Gothic church of **Notre-Dame du Sablon**, marks the location of a number of antique shops. **Place du Petit Sablon**, containing a little park surrounded by 48 bronze statuettes representing traditional trades, is just across the street. Further south is the **Palais de Justice** (Law Court), its courts and 103-metre (337ft) cupola occupying an area bigger than St Peter's Square in Rome. ❑

Brussels's leading exponent of Art Nouveau was Victor Horta (1861–1947). He pioneered the concept of total design, creating furniture, carpets and wall decorations as well as the overall design of a building.

BELOW LEFT: the gigantic Atomium, a symbol of the city.

Royal Glass City

The Royal Domain lies in the outlying district of Laeken, in the north of Brussels. The magnificent botanical gardens and greenhouses have earned the domain the title of "Glass City". Although the Château de Laeken is not open to the public, the grounds of the domain are crowded with curious monuments and memorials. Leopold II extended the palace and embellished the park with two oriental follies, a Chinese pavilion, with a priceless collection of oriental porcelain, and a Japanese pagoda (Tue–Sun).

But the crowning glory of the park was the creation of the Serres Royales, the Royal Greenhouses, in 1875 (open for three weeks from mid-Apr–mid-May). Attributed to Alphonse Balat and the young Victor Horta, they present an architectural treasure comprising a huge central dome, topped by an ironwork crown and flanked by a secondary chamber, cupolas, turrets and vaulted glass tunnels.

To the northwest of the park is the Atomium (daily), a gigantic model of an iron crystal with nine atoms. The monument, which has become a symbol of Brussels, was designed for the World Exhibition in 1958. After an extensive two-year refurbishment, the Atomium reopened in 2006, shinier, better equipped and with more points of interest for visitors than before. A top-sphere restaurant offers fine food and views.

AROUND BELGIUM

A country with two main languages and two clashing cultures, Belgium is far from predictable. But its people have an infectious taste for the good things in life

Belgium's 65km (40-mile) coastline, a wide ribbon of golden sands washed by the North Sea, begins at **Knokke-Heist ❶** on the Dutch border and stretches down to **De Panne** on the French. The waters are safe but more suited to family holidays than water sports, though the spectacular hybrid known as sand-yachting has plenty of aficionados on the beach. The biggest and best known of the nine main coastal resorts is **Ostend ❷** (Oostende), with its bustling fishing and yacht harbour.

The best of the Flemish towns lie off the road from Ostend to the capital, Brussels. The route runs alongside canals, rivers and hills, past moors, heaths and lakes and through fir and pine woods. The countryside of the **Kempen**, in the north, is dotted with churches, and the peal of bells is a commonplace sound in Flanders.

Medieval Bruges

Bruges ❸ (Brugge), the *grande dame* of Flemish cities, serves as a window on Belgium's history. Miniature bridges over its delightful canals, gabled houses and verdant lawns have helped the city to retain a medieval atmosphere reminiscent of the time when it was one of Europe's greatest trade centres and held to be one of the most beautiful cities in the world. Bruges declined as the reputation of its rival, Antwerp, increased. Having never spilt over its 13th-century fortifications, the city,

with its magnificent Gothic **Stadhuis** (town hall; daily) and medieval cloth hall with an 88-metre (300ft) **bell-tower**, has become a kind of museum. By the town hall is the **Basiliek van het Heilig-Bloed** (Basilica of the Holy Blood; daily), containing a reliquary carried in a procession through the city on Ascension Day.

Bruges is also famous for its Flemish art, and some of the finest paintings of the Flemish School are exhibited at the **Groeningemuseum** (Tue–Sun), among them Jan van Eyck's portrait

Main attractions
KNOKKE-HEIST
OSTEND
BRUGES
GHENT
MECHELEN
ANTWERP
TOURNAI
LIÈGE
BASTOGNE
SPA

LEFT: Basilica of the Holy Blood, Bruges. **BELOW:** fountain in 't Zand Square, Bruges.

Rubens's Descent from the Cross *in the Cathedral of Our Lady, Antwerp.*

BELOW RIGHT: a boat tour is the best way to see Ghent.

of his wife and his *Madonna with Canon Joris van der Paele*. The **Memling in Sint-Jan/Hospitaalmuseum** (Tue–Sun) is a medieval hospice containing graceful and radiant works by the German-born Flemish Primitive artist Hans Memling. A radiant *Madonna and Child* sculpture (1504) by Michelangelo can be seen in the **Onze-Lieve-Vrouwekerk** (daily).

Five kilometres (3 miles) north of Bruges is the village of **Damme**, where a white windmill stands prettily on a green meadow. It has one of the most beautiful old marketplaces in Flanders.

Further along the road to Brussels, **Ghent** (Gent) ❹ is a city of bridges and canals. The old medieval centre is dominated by the Church of Saint Nicholas, with its Gothic belfry and 52-bell carillon. Next to the flamboyant town hall is **St-Baafskathedraal** (St Bavo's Cathedral; Mon–Sat), which houses Jan van Eyck's masterpiece, *The Adoration of the Mystic Lamb*, known as the Ghent Altarpiece.

The road from Brussels to Antwerp passes **Mechelen**, a city of belfries and carillons and home of Belgium's only school for bellringers. At the Church of Our Lady on the Dijle is Rubens's masterpiece *The Miraculous Draught of Fishes*, and at St-Janskerk is another Rubens, *The Adoration of the Magi*.

City of Diamonds

Antwerp (Antwerpen) ❺ is Europe's third-largest port and a centre for contemporary fashion. At one time, its maritime traffic surpassed even that of Venice in its heyday. But the city lost its role as a leading trade centre in the 17th century when, under Spanish rule, its wealthy merchants fled to Holland to escape the Inquisition. The home of Peter Paul Rubens (1577–1640), Antwerp has become the centre of Flemish art and culture. **Onze-Lieve-Vrouwekathedraal** (Cathedral of Our Lady; daily) is Belgium's most magnificent religious building. South of the city centre, the art collection at the **Koninklijk Museum voor Schone Kunsten** (Royal Museum of Fine Arts; daily) covers centuries of Flemish art – both classical and modern. Antwerp is known as the "City of Diamonds" for its role as a major cutting and trading

Battle of Waterloo

The road south from Brussels leads to a location where a watershed in European history took place: Waterloo. On 18 June 1815, just south of this small town, the combined British, Dutch and Prussian forces imposed the final defeat on Napoleon Bonaparte after his escape from Elba. The defeat at Waterloo put an end to Napoleon's rule as the French emperor, and marked the end of his Hundred Days of return from exile.

From the town it is about 3km (2 miles) to the site of the battle. During the nine-hour carnage, some 47,000 soldiers were killed or wounded, 25,000 of them French. The Duke of Wellington, who led the Anglo-Allied army, said the battle was "the nearest-run thing you ever saw in your life". The vast battlefield is now tranquil farmland. A prominent reminder of the battle, which changed the face of Europe, is the lofty memorial called the Butte du Lion (Lion Mound; daily). The butte rises to a height of 45 metres (147ft), and is surmounted by a 28-tonne lion. The view from the top is extensive.

Napoleon spent the night of 17 June in a farmhouse south of the battlefield at Le Caillou. The farmhouse now houses Napoleon's Last Headquarters (daily), containing mementos relating to the battle and the emperor's life. Back in the town, souvenirs and T-shirts all bear the image of Napoleon, who has been immortalised by the locals.

centre of the diamond industry. The **Antwerp Province Diamond Museum** at 19–23 Koningin Astridplein (Thur–Tue) offers a glimpse into the world of hot rocks and diamond cuts.

Southwest of Brussels is the royal residence and capital of early medieval France, **Tournai** ❻. It is famous for its five-towered Romanesque cathedral of **Notre-Dame** (daily). The **Musée des Beaux-Arts** (Wed–Mon), by architect Victor Horta, in the southern part of the Old Town, has many examples of modern art as well as paintings by Rogier van der Weyden and Rubens. **Mons**, east of Tournai, is another venerable Walloon city. The facade of the Hôtel de Ville on the handsome Grand-Place boasts the **Singe du Grand-Garde**, a little cast-iron monkey, which supposedly brings good luck when caressed.

Meuse and Ardennes

Straddling the River Meuse, **Liège** ❼ is the birthplace of one of Belgium's famous sons, Georges Simenon, creator of the Maigret detective series. This city of industry and craftsmen has established a reputation for Val-St-Lambert crystal and exquisitely designed jewellery. The **Musée d'Art Moderne et d'Art Contemporain** (daily), in the Parc de la Boverie, has an impressive collection of painting and sculpture from 1850 to the present, including works by Chagall, Ensor, Gauguin, Magritte and Picasso. North of Liège is **Tongeren**, the oldest town in the country, founded by the Romans in 15 BC.

Namur, capital of the Wallonia region, and known as the Gateway to the **Ardennes**, is dominated by a huge rocky peak which is the site of a 17th-century citadel, overlooking the Meuse. The green woods of the Ardennes, the hills where one of the great battles of World War II took place, lie east of the river. At **Bastogne**, in the east of the Ardennes, outnumbered US forces held out against a German offensive during the winter of 1944–5 that became known as the **Battle of the Bulge**. The battle cost the lives of 19,000 Ameri-

can soldiers, and their sacrifice is commemorated at the **Mardasson Liberty Memorial**, on a hill outside the town.

In the northern reaches of the Ardennes, the town of **Spa** gave its name to the tradition of "taking the waters". It has surviving examples of architecture and installations from its 19th-century heyday as an upper-crust watering hole.

Luxembourg

In the extreme southeast of Belgium is the Province of Luxembourg, a rugged region of forests and valleys whose capital, **Arlon**, an old Roman settlement, is the site of a beautiful castle and an archaeological site. The **Musée Archéologique** (daily) contains Roman remains of great importance.

This region of the Ardennes was once the western part of the Grand Duchy of Luxembourg before becoming part of Belgium. The Grand Duchy is Europe's smallest independent nation (population 462,000). The capital, **Luxembourg City** ❽, once an important fortress, is now the seat of several EU bodies and an international banking centre, thanks to its low taxes.   ❑

Bouillon, in the southern Ardennes, has a spectacular setting in the plunging valley of the River Semois, and has Belgium's finest medieval castle (daily).

BELOW: brass band concert on the Kalendenberg, Ghent.

THE NETHERLANDS

Largely reclaimed from the sea, the Netherlands owes its culture to a strong maritime tradition. The picturesque Dutch landscapes painted by the Old Masters can still be seen today

The Netherlands is a small country. Covering some 16,000 sq miles (41,500 sq km), more than half of its area lies below sea level and almost one-fifth is covered by lakes, rivers and canals. Building and maintaining dykes, barriers and dams to guard against the threat of flooding is a full-time occupation, and few other nations are so acutely aware of the dangers of global warming. While the country is flat, a lush greenness is everywhere, and the skies are sometimes filled with the silvery luminescence so distinctive in classic Dutch landscape painting. Of more than 10,000 windmills that once helped pump the land dry and featured so prominently among the favourite subjects of artists, only about 1,000 remain. They are regarded as national monuments, and many have been restored.

Most English-speakers call the country "Holland", but the Dutch know their country as *Nederland* (the Netherlands, or literally, Low Country). Strictly speaking, Holland refers only to the two western provinces of North Holland and South Holland, where the majority of the 16.5 million population lives.

The capital, Amsterdam (pop. 755,000), is in this region, along with Rotterdam, Europe's most important port, and the governmental and administrative seat of The Hague ('s-Gravenhage, or Den Haag in Dutch), where the International Court of Justice and the International Criminal Court sit. The venerable university town of Leiden is here, as well as Delft, renowned for its blue pottery, and Edam, famous for its cheese.

The 10 provinces that make up the rest of the country are surprisingly varied. Zeeland in the south is a region of former islands that have been joined together, peninsulas, sandy coastlines and bird-filled marshes which a series of huge barriers prevent from flooding. The Catholic southern provinces have flamboyant architecture and wooded hills. Heath, woodlands and orchards mark the northern provinces, and the wilder landscape in Drenthe, in the northeast, is dotted with megaliths. The one thing they have in common is the warm welcome they will offer you. ❑

PRECEDING PAGES: view from Westerkerk; Vondelpark, both in Amsterdam. **LEFT:** windmills are synonymous with the Netherlands. **ABOVE:** classic Dutch architecture.

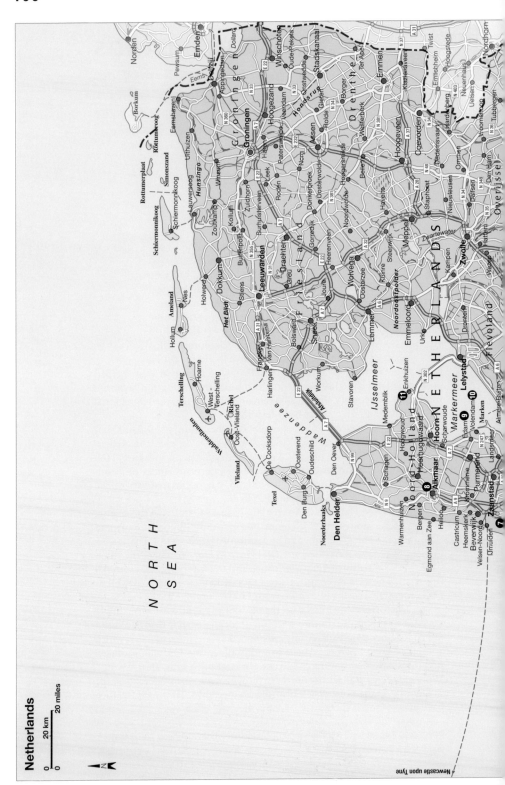

Netherlands

0 20 km
0 20 miles

NORTH SEA

Newcastle upon Tyne

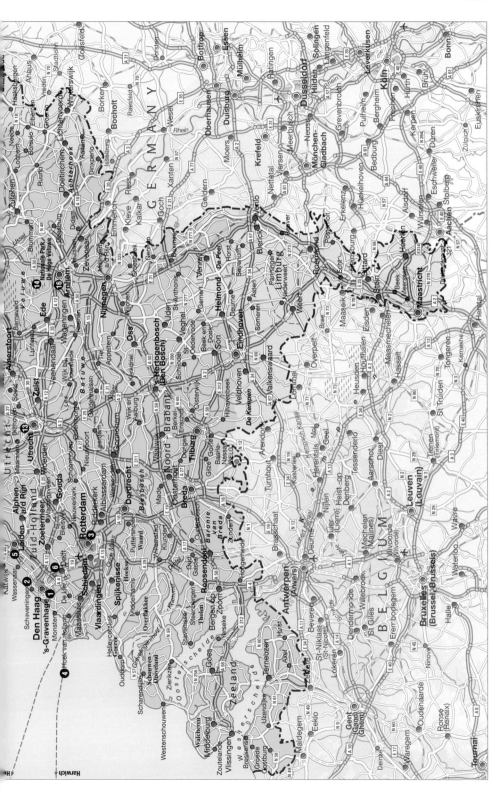

AMSTERDAM

This "city of museums" lives with one foot in its
venerable past and the other on the accelerator
of the latest social and cultural trends

The first impression of Amsterdam
may be its museum-like quality.
Indeed, 6,700 buildings in the
core of the city are protected monuments, virtually intact from the 17th-
century Golden Age, during which
time the city rose to spectacular wealth,
political power and cultural heights.
Amsterdam's prosperity depended on
ships opening trade routes to the West
and East Indies. Profits from these ventures provided funds for the growth of
a compact city built around a dam on
the River Amstel in the 13th century.
Historic models for the modern Dutch
character are common-sense merchants
and businessmen, and the city's monuments tend to be private houses rather
than imposing public buildings.

But there is nothing old-fashioned
about Amsterdam. Here you can find a
gourmet Indonesian meal, lively nightlife, a vast selection of antiques, worldfamous cheeses, great paintings from
the Golden Age (especially Rembrandt,
Vermeer and Frans Hals), and sidewalk
café-idling. To see all this requires only
a good pair of walking shoes.

Amsterdam's canal ring

Amsterdam is built on a network of
concentric horseshoe canals. A good
point to begin is at the VVV Tourist
Office at **Centraal Station** ❶ (there's
a branch inside the station and one
opposite), from where trains, trams,
buses, taxis, harbour ferries and canal
tour boats fan out to all points of the
city. From here, the main street, **Damrak**,
leads to the **Dam**, a large square that is
the hub of the canals and the site of the
stately **Royal Palace** ❷ (Koninklijk
Paleis; daily). Built in 1665, originally
as the city's town hall, the palace is
now used for diplomatic receptions.

Also in the square is the **New
Church** ❸ (Nieuwe Kerk; daily), dating from 1400, where Dutch monarchs
are crowned. It has become a cultural
centre, where temporary exhibitions are
held and concerts staged. Nearby, Warmoesstraat passes close to the late Gothic

Main attractions
CENTRAAL STATION
ROYAL PALACE
NEW CHURCH
OLD CHURCH
AMSTERDAMS
  HISTORISCH MUSEUM
BEGIJNHOF
RIJKSMUSEUM
VAN GOGH MUSEUM
REMBRANDT HOUSE MUSEUM
ANNE FRANK HOUSE

LEFT: the elegant
Zuiderkerk.
BELOW: street
entertainment.

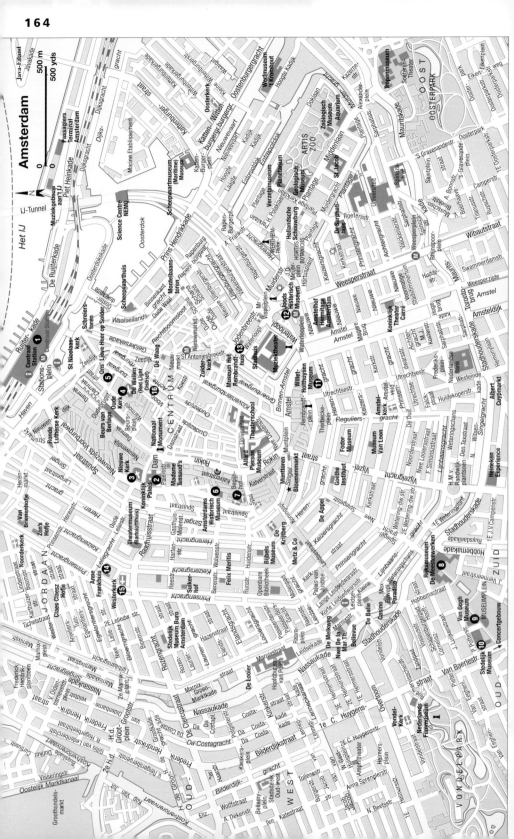

Old Church ❹ (Oude Kerk; daily), Amsterdam's oldest building and the best preserved of all its churches. The 13th-century tower is still intact, and some of the stained-glass windows date from the 16th century. Incongruously, it is all but surrounded by red-fringed prostitutes' parlours and sex clubs.

Historical museums

Also in the Red Light District (*see page 167*), **Our Lord in the Attic** ❺ (Ons' Lieve Heer op Solder; daily) is the finest of the city's "clandestine" churches, concealed within a 17th-century merchant's house. After the "Alteration", when Amsterdam became officially Protestant, Catholics were forced to worship in secret. The top floors of three gabled houses here were linked to form two galleries with space for up to 400 worshippers.

Once the city orphanage, **Amsterdams Historisch Museum** ❻ (daily) chronicles the city's history and development with paintings, furniture and cleverly juxtaposed artefacts. Highlights include *het groei carte* ("growth map"), which traces Amsterdam's development over the centuries, and the 16th-, 17th- and 18th-century group portraits of the civic guards, found in a separate outside gallery, the Schuttergalerij. The adjoining **Begijnhof** ❼ (daily) is Amsterdam's finest *béguinage*, or lay nuns' dwelling, and one of the city's most spiritual enclaves. Reached through a number of inner courtyards, it comprises a series of brick and stone gabled houses built between the 14th and 17th centuries to house the Begijnen, a lay Catholic sisterhood. Het Houten Huys, at No. 34, is the oldest house in Amsterdam, built around 1425.

An abundance of art

Walk or go by tram (lines 2 and 5) from the Dam to **Museumplein** and the **Rijksmuseum** ❽ (Philips Wing; entrance at 1 Jan Luijkenstraat, daily), the repository of much of Holland's great art from the first half of the 17th century. Until 2013 most of the vast museum is closed for renovation, but a scaled-down selection of the most outstanding works is on display under the title *The Masterpieces*. Among more than 7 million items in the museum's collections, the star attractions must be the incomparable Dutch Masters, notably Rembrandt, Jan Vermeer, Frans Hals, Jan Steen, Pieter de Hooch and Jacob van Ruisdael. Vermeer's paintings include his deeply felt and quiet works of everyday events such as *Woman Reading a Letter* and *The Milkmaid*. Rembrandt is well represented with, among many others, *The Jewish Bride*, *Syndics of the Amsterdam Drapers' Guild* and, most prominent of all, *The Nightwatch*.

From the Rijksmuseum it is a short walk to the outstanding **Van Gogh Museum** ❾ (daily). The artist's development can be traced from the haunting grittiness of his early *Potato Eaters* to the swirling hallucinogenic brilliance of his later *Sunflowers*. A modern wing (1999) by Japanese architect Kisho Kurokawa, used for changing exhibitions, has a striking design, incorporating a titanium roof and wall.

BELOW: the Rijksmuseum, a repository of great Dutch art.

The Anne Frankhuis, where Anne lived with her family and began her diary in 1942.

The **Stedelijk Museum** ⑩, due to reopen at its Museumplein home early in 2010, has the best modern art collection in the Netherlands. Artists such as Chagall, Braque, Matisse and Mondrian are represented in the collection, as are works by contemporary artists like Jan Dibbets, Ren Daniels and Stanley Brouwn.

To the west of Museumplein, **Vondelpark** is the most popular of Amsterdam's green spaces, accessible from entrances all around the perimeter. In summer there are lively concerts and dance events.

Leidseplein plunges you back into lively Amsterdam. This square is a busy tram intersection and buzzes with street performers and a plethora of bars, nightclubs and cinemas.

Along the River Amstel

A good opportunity to see behind the facades of the canal houses presents itself along **Herengracht**. At the **Willet-Holthuysen Museum** ⑪ (daily), you can see the furnishings and collections of a luxurious 17th-century house that coal magnate Pieter Holthuysen left to

his daughter Sandrina and her husband Abraham Willet in 1858.

From here, cross over the Amstel via the Blauwbrug, then take Nieuwe Amstelstraat to the **Joods Historisch Museum** ⑫ (daily), in the Ashkenazi Synagogue complex, comprising four synagogues restored after World War II damage. Extensive exhibitions trace the spread of Judaism throughout the Netherlands, culminating in the devastation of the Holocaust.

Among more than 1,000 bridges in the city, the nearby **Magere Brug** (Skinny Bridge) over the Amstel, dating from 1670, is one of the more notable, and when lit at night is one of Amsterdam's loveliest sights.

Just off Waterlooplein is the **Rembrandt House Museum** ⑬ (Museum Het Rembrandthuis; daily), where the artist lived from 1639 to 1660. The mansion contains 250 of his drawings and etchings.

Anne Frank's refuge

For an insight into life in Amsterdam during the Occupation, visit the **Anne Frank House** ⑭ (Anne Frankhuis;

Café Life

The Netherlands has a long café tradition. Some claim that the first bar opened its doors in Amsterdam in the 13th century when two men and a dog drifted ashore on the marshy banks at the mouth of the River Amstel. By the 17th century there were countless taverns in the city.

Traditional brown cafés (so called because walls and ceilings have turned brown from age and smoke) are identified by dark, cosy, wooden interiors. Coffee is generally brewed, not machine-made, and if you fancy a snack to go with your drink (alcohol is served too), there is usually a plate of olives or cheese. These cafés define the Dutch word *gezelligheid*, which means a state of cosiness or conviviality. This is where locals come for a few beers after work, to play cards, engage in political debates and tell tales. (Note that brown cafés are not the same as "coffee shops" – cafés where tokers can buy legally tolerated hashish and marijuana in small quantities.) Two of the best brown cafés are **De Tuin** (13 Tweede Tuindwarsstraat) in the Jordaan to the northwest of the city, and **'t Doktertje** (4 Rozenboomsteeg) near the Begijnhof.

The more elegant and stylish grand cafés serve lunch and desserts and tend to have high ceilings, more light, reading tables and a variety of music. If you are in search of high culture, call in at the **Café Americain** (28 Leidseplein) to luxuriate in Art Nouveau splendour.

daily) at 263 **Prinsengracht**. This is where the teenager and her family hid from the Nazis in World War II, until they were caught and Anne was sent to her death at the Bergen-Belsen concentration camp. This moving and much-visited museum includes a café.

Nearby, the **Westerkerk** ⓯ (Apr–June and Sept–Oct Mon–Fri, July–Aug Mon–Sat) dates from 1630. It is the city's finest church, a masterpiece of Dutch Renaissance, and the place when Rembrandt was buried, although his grave has never been found. From the top of the church tower, the Wester-toren (186 steps), are superb views over the canals and the Jordaan district.

Red lights and bright lights

At night the streets along the canals are lit and make engaging walking routes. The **Red Light District** ⓰, known locally as De Wallen, where prostitution is an open and government-sanctioned activity, provides an eye-opening diversion for any visitor, with semi-naked girls displaying their wares for all to see. However, this is also the oldest part of the city, with some of its finest historical architecture and prettiest canals, and not all of it has been submerged by the flesh trade.

On balmy nights the outdoor cafés along Rembrandtplein and Leidseplein throb with life. Disco, jazz and folk music flourish in small clubs. The **Melkweg** (Milky Way) entertainment complex (Lijnbaansgracht 234) is a prime location for a blend of Latin, African, reggae and rock music, alternative club nights and fringe events, as it has been since the 1960s; while **Paradiso** (Weteringschans 6), another long-running spot, provides a lively venue for rock, hip hop and world music, some by up-and-coming unknowns.

Amsterdam's music hall, the **Concertgebouw** (Concert Hall), to the south of Museumplein, has the reputation of being acoustically among the world's finest, as well as one of the most beautiful, and offers a range of excellent musical performances.

Shopping and markets

Kalverstraat is the busiest shopping street, while **P.C. Hooftstraat**, near Leidseplein, is one of the most elegant. Amsterdam is a centre of the European antiques market, and **Spiegelstraat** and **Nieuwe Spiegelstraat** (leading to the Rijksmuseum) house more than 20 antiques shops. The city is also a leading centre for cutting, polishing and mounting diamonds. **Coster Diamonds**, near the Rijksmuseum, offers a workshop tour and shop.

Amsterdam is justly famous for its markets. The most elaborate is the **Waterlooplein** market in the heart of the Jewish Quarter, selling clothing, jewellery, wood carvings and bric-a-brac. The **Albert Cuypmarkt** in the south of the city is another lively street market with a wide variety of merchandise, including fish, poultry, cheese, fruit and vegetables as well as clothes. It is an especially good place to sample a Dutch delicacy – marinated herring with chopped onion. The famous **Bloemenmarkt** on Singel, one of the best places for fresh cut flowers, also sells bulbs and tubers. ❏

EAT

Indonesian restaurants abound in Amsterdam and can offer good-value meals. The *rijsttafel* (rice table) is a tasty variant on the sweet and sour theme, consisting of a large bowl of rice and perhaps 15 condiment dishes of meat, fish, fruits, nuts and vegetables.

BELOW: Paradiso, one of Amsterdam's many nightclubs.

AROUND THE NETHERLANDS

The historic cities of the Randstad give way to
North Holland's old fishing communities and the
former royal hunting forests of Gelderland

L
ess than 100km (61 miles) from
Amsterdam is **The Hague ❶**
(formally, 's-Gravenhage; Den
Haag), home of the royal family and
seat of the Dutch Parliament and foreign embassies. In the **Vredespaleis**
(Peace Palace; guided tours Mon–Fri),
a neo-Gothic structure funded by
Scottish-American millionaire and
philanthropist Andrew Carnegie, sits
the International Court of Justice of
the United Nations and the International Criminal Court. The Hague,
with a population of 485,000, is the
third-largest city of the Netherlands,
often referred to as "Europe's largest
and most elegant village" because of its
pleasant residential character.

Core of The Hague

The historic centre was built around
the **Binnenhof**, now home of the
Dutch Parliament. This was the Inner
Court of the castle of the counts of
Holland. Its fairy-tale, 13th-century
Knights' Hall (Ridderzaal; Mon–Sat)
is now only used for ceremonial purposes. Behind the Ridderzaal a gateway leads to the classical **Mauritshuis**
(Apr–Sept daily, Oct–Mar Tue–Sun),
where the Royal Cabinet of Paintings, one of the most beautiful small
picture galleries in the world, has a
choice collection of Flemish, Dutch
and German Old Masters. Among the
treasures are such outstanding works
as Rembrandt's *The Anatomy Lesson of
Dr Tulp* and Vermeer's *View of Delft*.

Wandering through the Mauritshuis,
you have impressive views of the
Hofvijver, all that remains of the castle
moat. A pleasant walk around this lake
brings you to the **Galerij Prins Wil-
lem V** (due to reopen at the start of
2010 after a period of refurbishment;
Tue–Sun), the oldest picture gallery in
the Netherlands, with a packed collection of Dutch Old Masters.

An excellent collection of modern
painting and decorative art is on display at the **Gemeentemuseum Den
Haag** (Stadhouderslaan 41; Tue–Sun).

Main attractions
THE HAGUE
SCHEVENINGEN
ROTTERDAM
MUSEUM BOIJMANS
  VAN BEUNINGEN
LEIDEN
DELFT
HAARLEM
FRANS HALS MUSEUM
EDAM
UTRECHT
ARNHEM

LEFT: Keukenhof
with bulbs in full
bloom. **BELOW:**
Delft house.

The Erasmus Bridge on Rotterdam's dynamic modern skyline.

BELOW: the historic centre of Delft.

The museum is renowned for works by Piet Mondrian, as well as its collections of Delftware and musical instruments.

The seaboard

Holland's oldest bathing resort on the North Sea is **Scheveningen ❷**, which forms a suburb of The Hague. The promenade is dominated by a modern pier and the Belle Epoque architecture of the **Kurhaus** hotel. All year, Scheveningen offers fresh air, a choice of sports and entertainment and a fashionable casino. At **Sea Life Scheveningen** (daily) you walk through an underwater tunnel to "experience" life on the seabed without ever getting wet.

The traditional role of the Netherlands as a maritime trading nation is illustrated by **Rotterdam ❸**, its dynamic modern skyline worthy of a city that remains one of the largest and busiest ports in the world. The city centre extends into the old harbour, around the Erasmus Bridge (1998), where a bustling dockside development of shops, cafés and housing has been created. Tram and metro lines provide easy access to the area. The entire harbour can be explored by boat from a dock on the north bank of the River Nieuwe Maas, just below the Erasmus Bridge. Another vantage point is the **Euromast** (daily), an observation tower 185 metres (600ft) high that is the landmark of the modern city.

The best known of Rotterdam's many museums, the **Museum Boijmans Van Beuningen** (Tue–Sun), on the edge of **Museumpark,** just west of the city centre, houses one of the finest art collections in the Netherlands. Its permanent collection includes masterpieces by Hieronymus Bosch and Pieter Bruegel the Elder; Rembrandt's tender portrait of his son Titus; and 19th- and 20th-century canvases by Monet, Van Gogh, Kandinsky, Magritte and Dalí.

Other places worth a visit are the museum of history, **Museum Het Schielandshuis** (Tue–Sun), and the **Maritiem Museum Rotterdam** (Tue–Sun), which recounts the city's maritime history. The only surviving medieval building is the **Grote Kerk**, in front of which stands a statue of the humanist philosopher Erasmus (*c.*1466–1536). One of the most tradition-rich parts of the city is **Delfshaven** (Delft Harbour), from where the Pilgrims started out on their journey to America in 1620.

Just 26km (16 miles) west of Rotterdam lies **Hoek van Holland** (Hook of Holland) ❹, which has become part of the port of Rotterdam (ferries arrive here from Harwich and Hull in England).

Leiden, Delft and Haarlem

Leiden ❺ is a likeable university town, full of museums, cafés and student bookshops. The **Stedelijk Museum De Lakenhal** (daily), occupying a 17th-century canalside cloth hall, traces the history of the town and has a gallery of works by 17th-century local artists. An extensive collection of archaeological finds from the Netherlands, ancient Greece, Rome and Egypt is displayed in the **Rijksmuseum van Oudheden** (Tue–Sun, also Mon in school holidays). The centrepiece is the mysterious flood-

lit Temple of Taffeh, dating from the 1st century AD, and presented to the Dutch people by the Egyptian government.

The pleasant, picturesque town of **Delft** ❻, midway between The Hague and Rotterdam, has changed little over the centuries. In the Middle Ages it was a weaving and brewing centre, but an explosion of the national arsenal in 1645 destroyed much of the medieval town. The distinctive blue-and-white pottery for which the town is famous was developed from Chinese originals introduced as a result of trade in the 17th century. Tours of local factories are available, where you can also buy reasonably priced Delftware.

Lovers of classical Dutch painting should make a trip to **Haarlem** ❼, the capital of North Holland province. Here, in the **Frans Hals Museum** (daily) you can study the incisive group portraits that Hals painted of the Dutch at a time when the nation had attained the pinnacle of its economic and political power. He shows faces with a marvellous complexity of character; each is a bundle of motives, a worldly person possessed of few

illusions. The building itself, from the Dutch Renaissance, was designed as a home for elderly men. Later it became an orphanage, and in 1913 the museum was established. Artists from Hals's period are also represented, and there are temporary exhibitions.

North Holland

North of Haarlem is **Alkmaar** ❽, a pleasant old town with tree-lined canals and a traditional cheese market, held every Friday morning in summer. The town of **Edam** ❾, 22km (14 miles) northeast of Amsterdam, was once an important whaling town and is now famous for its round cheeses, which are produced by farms on the fertile Beemster and Purmer polders. Edam cheeses can be bought in the 16th-century *Waag* (weigh house) on Waagplein.

The Zuiderzee used to be an inlet of the North Sea, but a dyke built in 1932 transformed it into a freshwater lake, the **IJsselmeer**. **Volendam** ❿, on the western shore, was a Catholic village, and nearby **Marken**, a one-time island now connected to the mainland by a causeway, was its Protestant counterpart.

The distinctive blue-and-white pottery for which Delft is known.

BELOW: Holland is famous for its wheels of cheese.

Flower auctions are held every day in Aalsmeer.

BELOW: a trip on Utrecht canal.
BELOW RIGHT: the Gothic Domtoren.

Residents of both have their distinctive costumes, now worn largely (if at all) for the benefit of visitors who are drawn here by the old-world character of the two towns.

The Zuiderzee's history is vividly and entertainingly presented at the **Zuiderzeemuseum** (daily) in **Enkhuizen** ⓫. Traditional fishing boats and pleasure craft are displayed in a waterfront Dutch Renaissance building, while the outdoor museum is reached by boat. Its focus is a reconstruction of old fishing communities, made up of around 130 buildings rescued from the towns around the Zuiderzee, some of them shipped intact across the IJsselmeer.

Tulipmania

In the early 17th century, newly acquired bulbs from Turkey produced a "tulipmania" which swept the country. The tradition of bulb production and flower-growing has flourished ever since. You can enjoy this floral world by touring the flower regions west of Amsterdam in the blooming time – the 28-hectare (70-acre) **Keukenhof**

garden (late Mar–late May), outside Lisse, is one of the most spectacular.

Alternatively, you can go (early in the morning) to the flower auction held daily in **Aalsmeer** ⓬, 10km (6 miles) south of Amsterdam. From the public balcony you watch the carts of flowers being brought in and the buyers sitting below. A huge clock-like bidding wheel starts with a price higher than expected and then swirls around slowly to a lower bid.

City of churches

Utrecht ⓭ is one of the oldest cities in the Netherlands, founded by the Romans in AD 47. The **Oudegracht**, the oldest canal in the city, was dug in the 11th century to allow for sudden changes in the level of the Rhine. It is lined with brick quays and cavernous cellars that now house restaurants and bars. The **Domtoren** (cathedral tower) is one of the architectural marvels of the Gothic age. Built between 1321 and 1383, it rises to an ethereal octagonal lantern 112 metres (376ft) high. All that remains of the **Domkerk** (daily), begun in 1254, are the choir and transepts – the

nave came crashing down in a freak hurricane in 1674. The skyline of Utrecht was once a mass of spires, but many were also toppled by the hurricane. The **Centraal Museum** (Tue–Sun) has some fine pre-1850 art and an impressive collection of modern works.

The Veluwe

Bounded in the north by the former Zuiderzee coastline, the Veluwe is dominated by wild heather, pines, heathland and sand dunes. The main attraction of this popular holiday area is the **Nationale Park De Hoge Veluwe** ⓴ (daily). Once royal hunting territory, it still has mile upon mile of forests that are rich in wildlife. At the centre of the park is the exceptional **Kröller-Müller Museum** (Tue–Sun), a stunning, glass-walled structure housing a magnificent collection of 278 of Vincent Van Gogh's paintings, as well as works by other modern masters such as Mondrian, Manet, Matisse, Braque and Picasso. A fabulous sculpture park in the grounds has pieces by Rodin, Moore, Paolozzi and Hepworth, among others.

Royal hunting lodge

Just outside the town of **Apeldoorn** ⓯, to the north of the Veluwe, is the **Paleis Het Loo** (Tue–Sun), the largest and most impressive of the Dutch royal palaces. It was built by William III, Stadtholder of the Netherlands and King of England and Scotland, in 1692 as a hunting lodge, and generations of the House of Orange used it as a summer palace. The interior and the Baroque gardens, now restored to their former opulence, constitute a museum tracing the history of the House of Orange-Nassau.

In the southern part of the Veluwe, **Arnhem** ⓰, which stands on the Neder Rijn (Lower Rhine), will always be associated with the Allied paratroopers who landed here in September 1944 in a gallant but doomed attempt to secure the city's strategic road bridge across the Rhine and thereby shorten the war (dramatised in the 1977 film *A Bridge Too Far*).

At the beautifully kept **Airborne Cemetery**, in Oosterbeek, 8km (5 miles) west of Arnhem, lie the remains of 1,748 Allied troops. ❑

TIP

The best way to explore the Nationale Park De Hoge Veluwe is on one of the hundreds of white bikes that visitors can borrow for free.

BELOW LEFT: the gardens of the Paleis Het Loo, Apeldoorn.

Country Pursuits

Though the Netherlands is the most densely populated country in Europe, it has beautiful countryside. The coastline is a 290km (180-mile) stretch of sandy beaches with some 55 seaside resorts. Off the north coast is a string of five islands, called the Waddenilanden, which can be reached by boat from Den Helder in North Holland, and Harlingen, Holwerd and Lauwersoog in Friesland.

Zeeland, a cluster of former islands linked to the mainland by dykes and dams, is Holland's sunniest spot, with beaches, nature reserves and cycling trails. A fitting destination for the naturalist, the birdwatcher or the photographer is Drenthe which, after Zeeland, is the least populous Dutch province. An abundance of wild flowers and picnic areas, set amid small lakes called *vennen*, allure the traveller.

Drenthe's provincial capital, Assen, a two-hour train ride from Amsterdam, is the starting point for a day or more of driving or cycling through 300km (185 miles) of bike trails and numerous backcountry roads. The prehistoric stone burial mounds called *hunebedden* are scattered throughout this northeastern province and are worth a visit. The largest of the 51 sites is at Borger. Witnessing these large boulder burial houses (or "giant beds", as the word translates), which Stone Age or Bronze Age people built to commemorate their dead, is a memorable experience.

GERMANY

The cities are strong in culture, but it's the
picturesque villages and countryside
that linger in the memory

Germany is the financial and industrial powerhouse of Europe. But behind the skyscrapers and beyond the industrial ribbon of the Ruhr, castles and countryside remain romantic and alluring. The land the country occupies is made up of peoples of greatly differing origins and characters. Aside from the slowly fading yet still "germane" gap between east and west, at the two extremes are the Prussians of the north, sombre and upright even if they have given up their spiked helmets and monocles, and the jolly Bavarians of the south, who are represented in *lederhosen* and chamois hats, swilling foaming tankards of beer. In between is the Swabian who lives in a neat cottage and keeps his carefully washed Mercedes in a garage, the Ruhr District miner (if he still has a job) who keeps pigeons in the colliery loft, and the Lower Saxony cattle farmer who warms his damp days with glasses of schnapps.

Urban areas in the east have been substantially rebuilt, refurbished and generally prettified since the Iron Curtain and the Berlin Wall came down in 1989, just as many of those in the west also had to be substantially rebuilt after World War II. Germany's eastern cultural centres – Potsdam, Dresden and Weimar – are bustling centres of tourism once more, as are the largely unspoilt Baltic coast resorts.

The transport network is excellent. The major cities have airports, but it is just as practical and may even be quicker to travel by rail; the intercity trains generally run hourly, while the expanding network of high-speed ICE trains has reduced travel times dramatically. For a country that produces some of the world's most prestigious and expensive cars, it is not surprising that the roads are good. If the *autobahn* pace becomes a bit nerve-racking, take the secondary roads, leading from one picturesque village to another. You may find a small country festival, for Germans are good at organising their fun, not just at the explosive springtime Cologne Carnival or the Munich October Beer Festival, but at any time of year. ❏

PRECEDING PAGES: Bacharach in the Rhine Valley; enjoying Hamburg's carnival.
LEFT: flower-decked facades in Rothenburg. **ABOVE:** Schloss Sanssouci in Potsdam; girl posing for a photograph in Lustgarten, Berlin.

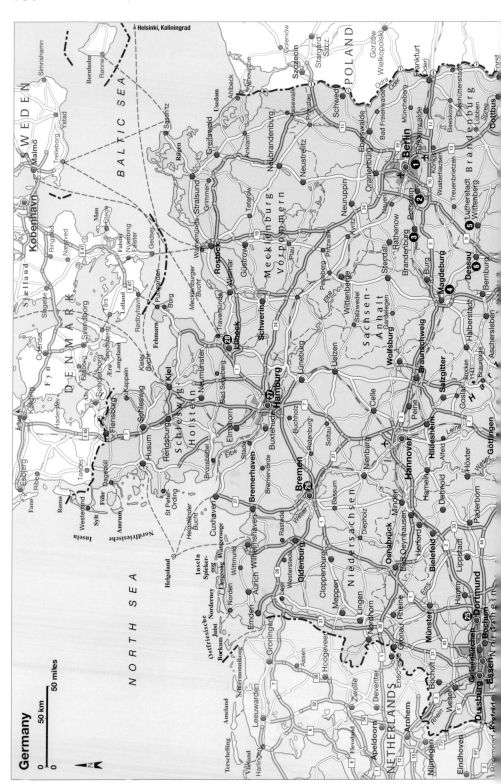

Germany

0   50 km
0   50 miles

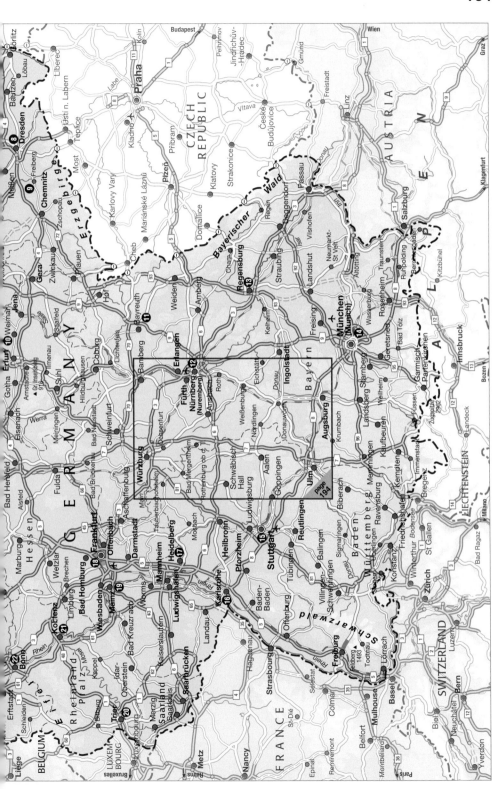

BERLIN

Twenty years and more since the Wall became history, Berlin has fully settled into its regained role as one of Europe's most adventurous and vibrant capitals

Berlin ●

Perhaps the most striking thing about modern Berlin is that it has two centres – and at least one "pretender" with a claim to be the third. On the one side, on **Alexanderplatz**, the TV tower, the city's tallest structure and once the emblem of the "capital of the GDR", marks the historical centre of Berlin – Berlin-Mitte. On the other, the blue Mercedes Star affixed to the Europa-Center marks the location of Kurfürstendamm, the bustling heart of the western part of the city. And, more or less in between, is the shiny modern architecture of the shopping and entertainment centre around Potsdamer Platz.

A decadent street

Known locally as Ku'damm, **Kurfürstendamm**, which means "The Electors' Road", used to be just a broad track leading out to the country, a bridle path for the blue-bloods who rode out from the palace towards Grunewald to go hunting. Only with Germany's rapid industrial expansion after 1871 did the street begin to take shape. Inspired by the Champs-Elysées in Paris, Bismarck decided that he wanted such a boulevard for the new capital of the Reich. Building work proceeded in "Wilhelmine" style: generous, ornate and florid; truly representative of the age.

By the 1920s, Kurfürstendamm had become the place where everything considered bohemian was on offer. The street was all but wiped from the map in World War II but, during the post-

war years, it became a symbol of Western prosperity and acquired a dazzling nightlife. On the night following the collapse of the Wall, it was to Ku'damm that most East Berliners flocked.

Shopping options

At the eastern end of Ku'damm is **Breitscheidplatz**, with the ruins of the neo-Gothic **Memorial Church ❶** (Kaiser-Wilhelm-Gedächtniskirche; daily) and its blue-glazed modern incarnation, raised in the 1960s amid the bomb-blasted ruins. A popular

---

Main attractions

ALEXANDERPLATZ
KURFÜRSTENDAMM
MEMORIAL CHURCH
TIERGARTEN
PAINTING GALLERY
REICHSTAG
BRANDENBURG GATE
MEMORIAL TO THE MURDERED
    JEWS OF EUROPE
DEUTSCHES HISTORISCHES
    MUSEUM
MUSEUM ISLAND
BERLIN CATHEDRAL
CHARLOTTENBURG PALACE

LEFT: the Reichstag.
BELOW: sculpture on Kurfürstendamm.

meeting place in summer is the **Weltkugelbrunnen** (1984), a vaguely globe-shaped fountain created by the sculptor Joachim Schmettau, next to the **Europa-Center ❷** shopping complex, one of the tallest buildings in Berlin, with a huge range of shops, restaurants, bars and a noted cabaret, the Stachelschweine. A lift goes up 20 storeys to a viewing platform, from where there is a fine view of the city. On nearby **Wittenbergplatz** is the stylish Kaufhaus des Westens (Department Store of the West), known as the **KaDeWe**, the only one of the city's great department stores to survive World War II bombing.

Close by (Ku'damm 18) is the famous **Café Kranzler**, now reduced to a small café in the traditional rotunda. Next to it is the Neues Kranzler Eck (2000), a Helmut Jahn high-rise, with offices, stores and a wide plaza housing an aviary. Behind the Zoologischer Garten station, on Jebensstrasse, the **Museum of Photography** (Museum für Fotografie; Tue–Sun; Kaisersaal closed until 2010) holds the Helmut Newton Collection, legacy of the renowned photographer who died in 2004.

In the side streets, called **Off-Ku'damm**, are some of the better restaurants, cafés and pubs – the city has more than 8,000 places to eat and drink. Close by, on Lehniner Platz, stands the avant-garde **Schaubühne**, a theatre built in the expressive style of the 1920s.

Tiergarten and museums

In the middle of the city is the 212-hectare (525-acre) **Tiergarten**, a wonderful park where many Berliners spend time at weekends. The **Zoo Berlin ❸** (daily) is just west of the Tiergarten. One of the largest zoos in the world, it is home to around 14,000 animals.

On the southern edge of the Tiergarten, close to Potsdamer Platz, the **Kulturforum** is dominated by the **Concert Hall ❹** (Philharmonie), home of the Berlin Philharmonic. Next door is the **Kammermusiksaal** for chamber-music recitals. There are a number of museums here (all Tue–Sun), among them the **Musikinstrumentenmuseum**, which contains more than 2,500 instruments; the airy **Museum of Arts and Crafts** (Kunstgewerbemuseum),

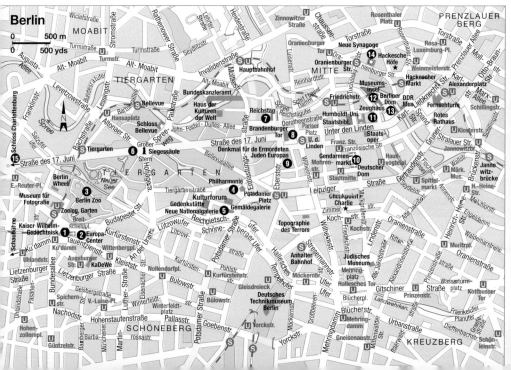

with textiles, furniture, glass and fashion; and the **Neue Nationalgalerie** ❺, Mies van der Rohe's minimalist glass-and-steel structure, which displays the work of Kokoschka, Dix, Picasso, Léger, Magritte and many others. The **Painting Gallery** (Gemäldegalerie) has one of the world's finest collections of European art from the Middle Ages to the late 18th century, including works by Dürer, Cranach, Brueghel, Vermeer and Rembrandt.

In the centre of the Tiergarten, the 67-metre (223ft) **Victory Column** (Siegessäule) ❻ was built in 1873 to commemorate Prussian victory over the Danes in 1864. From here there is a grand view down to the Brandenburg Gate. On the north side of the gate, on the park's edge, is the **Reichstag** ❼, built in the late 19th century in Italian Renaissance style, which is once more home to the national parliament, the Bundestag. Gutted by the infamous Reichstag Fire in 1933 and almost destroyed during World War II, it has been rebuilt. English architect Sir Norman Foster added the new glass dome, based on the original, containing a broad spiral ramp, enabling visitors to watch parliamentary proceedings from above, while the roof garden offers great views across the city.

Unter den Linden

Since its inauguration in 1791, the **Brandenburg Gate** ❽ (Brandenburger Tor), between the Tiergarten and central Berlin's grand boulevard, Unter den Linden, has been a symbol of the fate first of Prussia, then of Germany. Napoleon marched through it on his initially triumphant way to Russia, and sent back to Paris the gate's crowning ensemble, the *Quadriga* (the goddess Victory on her horse-drawn chariot). In 1814, the *Quadriga* was brought back in triumph by Marshal Blücher. Barricades were erected at the Brandenburg Gate during the revolution of 1848; kings and emperors paraded here; the revolutionaries of 1918 streamed through it to proclaim

the republic; and the Nazis staged their victory parades here. After the collapse of the Wall, the Gate became a symbol of the hopes and expectations of a united Germany, and is now the favoured setting for public events. New York architect Peter Eisenman's striking Holocaust memorial, a vast "field of stelae" entitled the **Memorial to the Murdered Jews of Europe** ❾ (Denkmal für die Ermordeten Juden Europas), lies to the south of the gate.

On the other side is **Pariser Platz**, rebuilt with modern touches by US architect Frank Gehry. The **Hotel Adlon**, the city's top hotel, was also rebuilt. The most Prussian of Berlin's streets, **Unter den Linden**, lined with *linden* (lime) trees, leads from here towards the heart of Old Berlin, **Berlin-Mitte**.

The imposing classical structures of Karl Friedrich Schinkel (1781–1841) testify that Berlin once ranked among the most beautiful of European cities. Strolling down this elegant boulevard today, you'll find the ambience of the old metropolis is almost tangible. Some maintain that the **Schauspielhaus** theatre on the **Gendarmenmarkt** ❿

The Brandenburg Gate was built as a symbol of peace; it now stands as an enduring testament to the reunification of East and West Berlin.

BELOW: children at the Memorial to the Murdered Jews of Europe.

Berlin Cathedral, said to be the Protestant answer to St Peter's in Rome.

BELOW: colourful remnants of the Berlin Wall. **BELOW RIGHT:** Pergamon Museum.

is the finest of Schinkel's buildings. Framed by the German Cathedral and the French Cathedral, the entire square is aesthetically perfect. Others say the **Neue Wache** near the university on Unter den Linden is Schinkel's best. This building was re-inaugurated in 1993 as the **Central Memorial of the German Federal Republic for the Victims of War and Tyranny**, and contains an enlarged version of the bronze *Pietà*, from 1937, by Käthe Kollwitz.

On the left, going east, are the monumental buildings of the **State Library** (Staatsbibliothek) and the **Humboldt University**. It was opposite the university, in the old Opern Platz, now **Bebelplatz**, that the Nazis burnt more than 20,000 books in 1933. The square, planned by Frederick the Great, is graced with splendid structures. There is the Baroque **Zeughaus** ⓫, the old arsenal, now the **Deutsches Historisches Museum** (daily), housing an exhibition on German history from the earliest times to the present. The **Opera House** (Staatsoper Unter den Linden, directed by Daniel Barenboim), the **Old Library** (Alte Bibliothek) and **St**

Hedwig's Cathedral, modelled on the Roman Pantheon, combine to create a masterpiece of urban architecture.

Museum Island

Museum Island ⓬ (Museumsinsel) ranks as one of the world's finest museum complexes, and in 2000 it was declared a Unesco World Heritage site (all museums open Tue–Sun). It came about as a result of a decree by Friedrich Wilhelm III that the royal art collections were to be made accessible to the public. The stunning diversity of displays includes everything from ancient archaeological artefacts to early 20th-century German and European art. Ongoing restoration work until 2015 means visitors might find the occasional door closed. Even so, it requires a day, at least, to visit all the museums.

The **Old Museum** (Altes Museum) is another of Schinkel's masterpieces. Following substantial wartime damage, it was reconstructed and reopened in 1966. The beautiful Neoclassical rooms house internationally renowned exhibitions and classical antiquities.

The **Pergamon Museum** contains Berlin's most highly regarded artistic treasure, a section of the Pergamon Altar (180–159 BC), taken from the ancient Hellenic city in western Turkey after excavations in 1878. The frieze describes the battle of the gods against the Titans. Under the same roof is the **Islamic Museum** and the **Near East Museum** (Vorderasiatisches Museum). The **Bode-Museum** (with Egyptian and Graeco-Roman sculpture and Byzantine collections), is in a splendidly restored building next to the Spree. The refurbished **New Museum** (Neues Museum) – which actually dates from 1855 – reopened in 2009 and once again houses the collections of the **Egyptian Museum**, of which the star attraction is the bust of the ancient Egyptian queen Nefertiti.

The **Old National Gallery** (Alte Nationalgalerie) was the first building on Museum Island to be reopened after extensive renovation and is now one of the most beautiful and most visited museums in Berlin. The gallery houses important paintings and sculptures from the 18th–20th centuries.

Just south of Museum Island is **Berlin Cathedral** ⓮ (Berliner Dom), built in 1894 as "the chief church of Protestantism". In Oranienburger Strasse, the **Neue Synagoge** ⓮, constructed in 1866, was rebuilt after World War II bombing and now houses the Centrum Judaicum Museum. It once served the largest Jewish community in Europe. This neighbourhood, around Hackescher Markt, has again become one of the liveliest areas of the city, with a thriving art scene and bustling cafés, restaurants and clothes shops.

Charlottenburg

West of the city centre is the impressive Baroque **Charlottenburg Palace** ⓯ (Schloss Charlottenburg; daily). Built in 1695 as a country house for Sophie Charlotte, grandmother of Frederick the Great, it was elaborated in the 18th century. Across from the beautiful palace grounds are the **Museum Berggruen** (Tue–Sun), a gallery with an exemplary collection of modern art, and the **Bröhan Museum** (Tue–Sun), which houses art and design objects from the late 19th and early 20th centuries. ❏

BELOW:
Charlottenburg palace.

The Berlin Wall

For a quarter-century (1963–89), the Berlin Wall was the city's grimly defining feature. Today, virtually nothing of it is still standing. Visitors who want to see what little remains can visit important stretches along Niederkirchnerstrasse, between Potsdamer Platz and Checkpoint Charlie; along Spree-side Mühlenstrasse, at the East Side Gallery, in the Friedrichshain district; and along Bernauer Strasse, in Mitte. None of these gives the complete picture of the Wall, with its death-strip, watchtowers and surprising depth, but they do afford a small insight into what it was like. Elsewhere, there are some odd bits and pieces here and there, and a line of double cobblestones running through the city, in some places supplemented by memorial plaques, shows where the once formidable barrier stood.

AROUND GERMANY

From the sparkling vineyards of the Rhine to the fairy-tale castles of the Romantic Road, Europe's leading industrial nation has a rich variety of historic sites

Berlin ●

ermany, with its cosmopolitan cities, ever-changing landscapes and wealth of cultural attractions, is one of the classic tourist destinations. Its rich and turbulent history is ever-present. Visitors to **Berlin ❶** (*see pages 183–7*) should also take in **Potsdam ❷** and **Sanssouci** (Tue–Sun), the grand palace that Frederick the Great designed in 1744. Here he patronised the arts and entertained his famous guest, the French philosopher Voltaire. Today tourists flock to Sanssouci, which has 12 gloriously decorated rococo rooms and an adjacent 290-hectare (717-acre) park. Left of the main alley the gold of the **Chinese Tea House** reflects the sunlight. At the end of the long path is the **New Palace** (Neues Palais), the home of Frederick the Great's household and guests towards the end of his reign. Within the park there is also a Sicilian Garden, with subtropical plants; the Renaissance-style **Orangery**; and the **Picture Gallery**, with paintings by Caravaggio, Rubens and Van Dyck. **Cecilienhof Palace** (Tue–Sun), venue for the 1945 Potsdam Conference, is nearby.

Through the Harz

The journey from Berlin through Sachsen-Anhalt to Leipzig is a series of contrasts. In the Harz Mountains, the picture-book landscape is one of half-timbered houses and fine Romanesque buildings. The industrial present takes over in Halle, while Leipzig is a busy cultural and commercial centre. **Brandenburg ❸**, straddling the River Havel, flourished in the 14th and 15th centuries as a centre for trade and the manufacture of cloth, but its importance declined with the rise of Berlin. Today, the town is dominated by the steel industry, but some gems remain, such as the cathedral. Transformed into a Gothic basilica in the 14th century, it retains some stained-glass windows from its medieval origins.

Magdeburg ❹, on the River Elbe, is the capital of Saxony-Anhalt and

Main attractions
POTSDAM
LEIPZIG
DRESDEN
NUREMBERG
ROMANTIC ROAD
ROTHENBURG OB DER TAUBER
AUGSBURG
NEUSCHWANSTEIN CASTLE
MUNICH
STUTTGART
HEIDELBERG
COLOGNE
HAMBURG

LEFT: Heidelberg.
BELOW: Sanssouci Palace.

Decorative plaster-work in the Church of St Nicholas in Leipzig.

BELOW: Bauhaus Building in Dessau.

easily the biggest inland port in eastern Germany. The city suffered extensive damage during World War II, but many Romanesque buildings survive, including the **Monastery of Our Lady** (Unser Lieben Frauen Kloster; 1064–1160), which now serves, among other cultural roles, as a concert hall.

Approaching **Lutherstadt Wittenberg ❺** from the west, the first impression is of the **Schlosskirche**, whose dome looks like a well-fitting crown. It was to the door of this church, on 31 October 1517, that Martin Luther posted his 95 Theses against the Catholic practice of indulgences, which eventually led to the Reformation.

The Bauhaus School

Dessau ❻, on the main route between Berlin and Leipzig, was home to the Bauhaus School of Architecture from 1925 until it moved to Berlin in 1932; in 1977 the town reopened the **Bauhaus Building** as a museum (daily). It is on the Unesco World Heritage list. Other examples of Bauhaus architecture around the town include the old labour exchange on August-Bel-Platz

designed by Gropius, the Bauhaus housing estate with the Cooperative Building in the Törten district, and the Meisterhäuser in Ebertallee.

Dessau's heyday was the era of Prince Leopold Friedrich Franz von Anhalt-Dessau (1740–1817), who surrounded himself with artists, poets and architects and established a country park at **Schloss Wörlitz** (Apr–Nov Tue–Sun). Over 800 varieties of trees grow among winding paths, canals and lakes. The art collection here includes works by Rubens and Canaletto. The grounds are dotted with imitation buildings, such as an Italian farmstead, a Greek temple, a Gothic folly and a palm house.

With the founding of its university in 1409, **Leipzig ❼**, already an important trading centre, also became a cultural enclave, attracting such influential students as Leibnitz, Nietzsche and Goethe, who named Leipzig "Little Paris". In 1930 the population was around 700,000, but the division of Germany hit the city hard. Today the streets are fast returning to their former elegance. The exquisite interior of the **Church of St Nicholas**, begun

in the 12th century, is testament to the city's former wealth. The **Church of St Thomas**, home of the Thomaner Choir, was founded in around 1212 and assumed its late Gothic form in the 15th century. At first the choir consisted of only 12 boys who sang at Mass, but soon they went on to sing at Church and state ceremonies. Johann Sebastian Bach (1685–1750) became choirmaster and organist in 1723 and wrote most of his motets for this choir. More can be learnt about his life in the **Bach Museum** (daily), where the Bach Archive is kept. The Bach Festival is held annually in spring or early summer (www.bach-leipzig.de for dates).

The palaces of Dresden

Dresden ❽ will for ever be associated with the devastating bombing raid of 14 February 1945, when almost the entire city centre was destroyed. A great deal of rebuilding has been done since then, however, to restore the city's epithet of "most beautiful city in Germany". A key symbol of the city's rebirth was the reconsecration in 2005, after 13 years of rebuilding, of the **Church of Our Lady** (Frauenkirche), a Baroque masterpiece from 1743.

Six buildings comprise the Dresden State Art Collections. They include the stunning **Dresden Royal Palace**, to which has now returned the **Green Vault** (Grünes Gewölbe; Wed–Mon), with jewellery, precious stones and paintings belonging to the Saxon princes. The **Zwinger Palace**, a masterpiece of German Baroque (1710–32) was based on the Orangery at Versailles, but the complex of pavilions, galleries and gardens grew to take up a vast area. It contains the **Old Masters' Gallery** (Gemäldegalerie Alte Meister; Tue–Sun), holding 2,000 works of art, including the *Sistine Madonna* by Raphael and Rembrandt's *Self-Portrait with Saskia*, plus works by Titian, Ribera and Murillo.

The **Albertinum** (closed for renovations until 2010) nearby was built as an armoury but is now home to the **Modern Art Gallery** (Galerie Neuer Meister), with a large collection of works by the German Romantics and Expressionists. The **Jägerhof** (Tue–Sun) houses a fascinating Museum of Saxon Folk Art. The **Garrison Church**, the only non-denominational church in Europe, houses the Puppet Theatre Collection. Finally, in the environs of Dresden is the **Pillnitz Palace** (May–Oct daily), the opulent summer residence of Augustus the Strong (1670–1733). With its sweeping pagoda-like roofs, it is an important example of the Chinese style so fashionable at the time. A large collection of camellias imported from Japan in 1770 provides a riot of blossom in spring. The palace also houses a Museum of Decorative Arts.

The mountain range bordering the Czech Republic to the southwest of Dresden is known as the Erzgebirge (Ore Mountains), where minerals such as lead, tin, silver and iron ore have been extracted since the 12th century. The silver-mining town of **Freiberg** ❾ was the richest town in Saxony until the 15th century, dwarfing even Dresden and Leipzig, and some of the town's old buildings, such as the 15th-

WHERE

To get a feel for the city of Dresden, take a trip on the Elbe in one of the excursion boats (Sächsische Dampfschiffahrt, Terrassenufer 2; tel: 0351-866090).

BELOW: the Zwinger Palace in Dresden.

Goethe and Schiller still dominate the cultural landscape of Weimar.

century town hall and cathedral, still display its former wealth.

In the footsteps of Goethe

Further west is **Weimar** ⑩, the natural starting point for any journey across the Thuringian Forest. From the mid-18th century Weimar was the hub of German cultural life. Goethe (1749–1832) became privy councillor of the duchy of Saxony-Weimar-Eisenach in 1775, and later served as education minister and director of the Weimar Theatre, where he came into contact with playwright and poet Friedrich Schiller (1759–1805), with whom he shared a close friendship.

An ensemble of 16 historic monuments known as Classical Weimar are now under Unesco protection. They include **Goethe's House** (Tue–Sun), containing his 6,500-volume library, as well as his **Gartenhaus** (summer house; daily) and the **Schillerhaus** (Apr–Sept daily, Oct–Mar Tue–Sun), each effectively portraying the daily lives and work of these great men of literature. The **Weimar Art Collections** (Kunstsammlungen zu Weimar;

Tue–Sun) are housed in the castle (Stadtschloss) and include paintings by Lucas Cranach the Elder, Tintoretto and Caspar David Friedrich (for more details, visit www.weimar-klassik.de).

Undulating, thickly forested hills, narrow river valleys and rounded mountain tops combine to form the unique quality of the **Thuringian Forest**. Goethe himself enjoyed the natural surroundings of this region, and today's hikers will be in good company if they follow the **Rennsteig** – a famous 168km (105-mile) ridge path that crosses the area. The route also passes the Grosser Inselsberg (916 metres/3,000ft), only the fourth-highest mountain in the region but the one offering the best views.

Bavaria

South of Weimar, the attractive and ancient town of **Arnstadt** was the home from 1620 of the Bach family. The most famous of them, Johann Sebastian, was the organist from 1703–7 in the church that today bears his name. Further south still, the town of **Bayreuth** ⑪ in Bavaria is associated

with another composer – Richard Wagner, who built an opera house here in 1876. Every year it is the setting for the Bayreuth Festival, from late July to late August, devoted to Wagner's operas.

The city of **Nuremberg** ⑫ (Nürnberg) was devastated by bombs during World War II but has been faithfully restored, so that much of its old charm remains. From the 12th–16th centuries it was regarded as the unofficial capital of the Holy Roman Empire of the German Nation. The River Pegnitz divided the **Old City** into the Sebalderstadt in the north and the Lorenzerstadt in the south, both surrounded by a sturdy 13th-century defensive wall with 46 fortified towers – the landmarks of the city.

The oldest parts of the enormous **Imperial Castle** (Kaiserburg; daily), built on sandstone crags high above the Old City, date from the 11th and 12th centuries. Between the 15th and 17th centuries, the city attracted artists and scientists such as Albrecht Dürer, Adam Krafft and Veit Stoss. The **Albrecht Dürer House** (Tue–Sun), near the castle, is now a museum. The **Hauptmarkt** (main market) is the site

of Nuremberg's famous annual **Christmas Market** (Christkindlesmarkt); while at the Kornmarkt the **Germanisches Nationalmuseum** (Tue–Sun) was founded in 1852 and has a huge collection of artefacts devoted to German arts and culture, some dating back to prehistory. A less celebrated chapter in Nuremberg's history was written by the Nazis, who held rallies here between 1933 and 1938.

The Romantic Road

The **Romantic Road** (Romantische Strasse), the name given to the route from **Würzburg** ⓐ in the north to Füssen near the Austrian border, attracts many visitors. Despite massive Allied bombing of Würzburg in March 1945, a painstaking rebuilding programme restored every major structure in the city. Start your tour at the **Residenz** (daily), built in 1720–44 by Balthasar Neumann and ranked as one of the finest Baroque palaces in Europe. The impressive stairwell is crowned by a single concave vault 30 metres (100ft) long by 18 metres (59ft) wide. More renowned than the vault itself is the

WHERE

Take a steamer along the Main to Veitshöchheim (7km/4 miles), where you can visit the Baroque palace with its beautiful Rococo gardens, once the summer residence of the Würzburg bishops. The steamers leave Würzburg at the landing stage located close to the Alter Kranen.

BELOW: Würzburg is a majestic town.

Würzburg's Residenz, a splendid Baroque palace and Unesco World Heritage site.

ceiling fresco painted by Giambattista Tiepolo, who was summoned to Würzburg in 1750 to create the largest painting in the world. Tiepolo depicted the gods of Olympus and allegories of the four continents known at the time. Leave time to stroll in the **Hofgarten** behind the Residenz, with its fine wrought-iron gates and beautiful Baroque group of figures.

From the Residenz follow Hofstrasse to Kiliansplatz and the Romanesque **Cathedral**, which was rebuilt after its destruction in 1945. The **Schönborn Chapel**, one of Balthasar Neumann's most important works, contains the shrine of the prince-bishops of Schönborn. Cross the River Main by the Alte Mainbrücke (Old Main Bridge) and follow the steep path up to the **Festung Marienberg** (mid-Mar–Oct Tue–Sun). Founded in 1201, the massive rectangular fortress encloses a courtyard and 13th-century keep as well as the Renaissance fountain and the Church of St Mary. After 1631, when the city was taken by Gustav Adolf of Sweden during the Thirty Years War, the fortress was extended and began to take the

BELOW: Marienberg Fortress, Wurzburg.

form of the building seen today, with its Baroque facades and the Fürstengarten (Princes' Garden).

One of the main attractions of the fortress is the **Mainfränkisches Museum** (Tue–Sun), whose exhibits include a remarkable collection of statuary by the woodcarver and sculptor Tilman Riemenschneider (1460–1531), who came to Würzburg from his home in the Harz Mountains in 1483 and rapidly rose to fame in Franconia.

The Romantic Road passes through **Tauberbischofsheim** ❷ (Home of the Bishop), where St Boniface founded a convent in 725, and **Lauda-Königshofen** ❸, which for centuries has been the hub of a wine-producing region. A 16th-century house at Rathausstrasse 25 has a **museum** dedicated to wine and local history (Apr–Oct Sun pm). What is often regarded as Riemenschneider's greatest achievement can be admired in **Creglingen** ❹ – the **Church of our Lord** (Herrgottskirche), where his carved altarpiece is dedicated to the Virgin.

One of the best-preserved medieval towns in Germany is **Rothenburg ob**

...ler Tauber **Ⓔ**, whose special status as a free imperial city from 1274 provided the basis for its prosperity. Its streets converge like the spokes of a wheel from the city walls to the central marketplace and the **Rathaus** (town hall) which, with its Renaissance archway and Baroque arcades, is a rich mix of architectural styles. Its 55-metre (180ft) Gothic tower affords the best view of the town's maze of red-tiled roofs. The medieval churches are rich in ecclesiastical art, the pride of the town being the **Altar of the Holy Blood** (Heilig-Blut-Altar) in the **Church of St James** (St-Jakobs-Kirche), commissioned from Riemenschneider in 1501–5. The **Plön-ein** area in the centre is the prettiest part of Rothenburg.

South to Augsburg

The Romanesque cloisters of the Stifts-kirche in **Feuchtwangen Ⓕ** serve as a stage for excellent open-air theatre in summer. **Dinkelsbühl Ⓖ**, a little further south, can only be entered through one of its four main gates. Here, each July, the **Kinderzeche** play and a colourful parade commemorate

the Thirty Years War (1618–48), when the town was under siege by Swedish forces. From the tower of St George's Church in **Nördlingen Ⓗ** there is a panoramic view of the 99 villages of the **Rieskrater**, a crater formed 15 million years ago when a meteorite struck the earth's surface at a speed of around 70,000km (40,000 miles) per hour. The impact created a wall-like formation of rock and earth about 13km (8 miles) in diameter. The modern **Rieskrater-museum** (Tue–Sun) has a multimedia show which explains the very specific geological history of the crater. Continue on through **Harburg Ⓘ**, the setting for one of Germany's oldest castles, and **Donauwörth Ⓙ**, home of the Käthe Kruse dolls, which have been made here since 1910. The **Museum of Dolls** (Käthe-Kruse Puppenmuseum; Apr–Oct Tue–Sun pm, Nov–Mar Wed, Sat–Sun pm) is worth a detour if you or your children like dolls.

The Fuggerei

The medieval trading city of **Augsburg Ⓚ** grew to a commercial centre, a place noted for its goldsmiths and

WHERE

Don't miss the Museum of the 3rd Dimension (Alte Stadtmühle; Jan–Mar and Nov–Dec Sat–Sun 11am–4pm, Apr–Sept daily 10am–6pm) in Dinkelsbühl's Old Mill. Here holograms, three-dimensional art and other illusionary features will startle your eyes and stun your mind.

BELOW LEFT: medieval Rothenburg. **BELOW:** the Golden Hall in Augsburg's town hall.

Mechanical figures draw crowds as they dance in the tower of Munich's town hall.

silversmiths, and an episcopal seat at the crossroads of the important routes linking Italy and the centre of Franco-Carolingian power. By about 1500 it was among the largest cities in the German-speaking world. The wealthy Fuggers banking family was responsible for the extraordinary social housing settlement of the **Fuggerei** (1516), where poor Catholic senior citizens could live for a peppercorn rent; the same applies today.

The town has a wealth of artistic treasures, including the Renaissance **city hall** (Rathaus), with onion-domed towers and magnificent **Golden Hall** (Goldener Saal; daily). The Romanesque-Gothic **Cathedral** (Dom) is the home of precious works of art, including valuable altar pictures and the oldest stained-glass windows in Germany (dating from around 1130).

Neuschwanstein Castle (daily) near **Füssen** ❶ was built by Ludwig II in 1869–86 and was a total anachronism even then. Its sole *raison d'être* was that of a glorified stage set. In the **Sänger-saal**, the "Minstrels' Hall" that forms the centrepiece of the fairy-tale castle,

Ludwig staged performances of scenes from the opera *Tannhäuser*.

The 2,000-year-old city of **Regensburg** ⑬, at the northernmost point of the River Danube, was largely undamaged during World War II. There is a fine view from the **Stone Bridge** (Steinerne Brücke), a masterpiece of medieval engineering, 310 metres (1,017ft) in length. The river is lined by stately mansions, over whose roofs tower the spires of St Peter's Cathedral, the most impressive Gothic structure in Bavaria. To the north, the landscape of the heavily wooded Bavarian Forest extends as far as the Czech border and is a great place to get away from it all.

Capital of Bavaria

Duke Henry the Lion performed a historic function 800 years ago when he put a new bridge across the River Isar to transport salt from the mines in Bad Reichenhall to Augsburg. **Munich** ⑭ (München), the town that grew up around the bridge, took its name from the occupants of a nearby monastery and was originally called Mönchen (Little Monk). Its symbol

s still a childlike monk, the *Münchner Kindl* (Munich Child). It was not until the 19th century that the city, during the reigns of Ludwig I and Ludwig II, acquired a reputation as a centre for the arts and sciences, due to ambitious and flamboyant architectural projects and the city's power to attract leading scientists, artists and writers.

Munich's true centre begins near the **main railway station** (Hauptbahnhof) at busy **Karlsplatz**. Through the imposing gate, the 14th-century **Karlstor**, you reach a pedestrian zone, passing **Michaelskirche**, one of the best-known Renaissance churches in Germany, where Ludwig II of Bavaria is buried. The **Church of Our Lady** (Frauenkirche), one of the largest hall churches in southern Germany, is a late Gothic edifice of red brick, with two distinctive onion-domed towers. Central **Marienplatz** throbs with life throughout the year. In winter the Christmas Market takes over, the stalls clustering around the statue of Munich's patron, the Virgin Mary. One side of the square is taken up by the neo-Gothic **New Town Hall** or Neues

Rathaus (1867–1908), with a world-famous **Glockenspiel** in its tower. The mechanical figures perform three times a day in summer (11am, noon and 5pm) and at 11am and noon in winter. South of the square is bustling **Viktualienmarkt**, where you can buy sausages, herbs, fruit, French wines and home-brewed beer. Most visitors find their way (east of the Rathaus) to the famous **Hofbräuhaus** (the former court brewery's beer halls) for true Bavarian atmosphere, beer and food.

The historic rooms of the **Royal Palace** (Residenz; daily) are worth a tour. They include the **Antiquarium**, an impressive Renaissance hall now used for state receptions, the ornate **Treasury** (Schatzkammer), and the Rococo **Cuvilliés Theatre**, which is still in use. To the east, beyond the **Isartor**, another of the old city gates, lies the scientific and technological **Deutsches Museum** (daily). It includes a replica of a coal mine and a planetarium, and numerous exhibits from the worlds of engineering, seafaring and flight.

The Neoclassical **Königsplatz** (northwest of the centre) is probably

Frauenkirche is one of the largest and most impressive hall churches in southern Germany.

BELOW LEFT: the Hofbräuhaus in Munich.

Munich's Beer Gardens

By five o'clock on a hot summer's afternoon, you can find most of Munich's population sitting out under the chestnut trees in one of the city's beer gardens, hoisting a *mass* (a litre mug) of beer, polishing off a *hendl* (roast chicken) and lingering until late into the night, when lights festooned in the branches light up the area like a stage set.

Class barriers are unknown here. A group of rowdy teens may be seated between a group of middle-aged men in *tracht* (national costume) and three elegantly coiffed ladies in Jil Sander ensembles, at a single table. Self-service is the rule, and standing in line is part of the beer garden experience. Not that you have to buy all your food: many families come with picnic baskets loaded with radishes, cheese, cold cuts, bread and even a checked tablecloth, just picking up beer to complete the meal.

In Munich, beer gardens come in all shapes and sizes. While the classic brass band still oom-pahs away from the Chinese Tower in the English Garden, jazz sets the tone at the popular Waldwirtschaft in Grosshesselohe, south of Munich. And while little Max Emanuel Brauerei in Schwabing still concentrates on traditional specialities like spare ribs, Mangostin, in the south of town, offers a range of Asian dishes along with the beer and *wurst*.

Heidelberg's castle complex, with its fortifications, domestic quarters and palaces, took 400 years to complete, so the building styles evolved all the way from 14th-century Gothic to Baroque.

the most impressive square in Munich. Here you will find the **Museum of Antiquities** (Antikensammlung; Tue–Sun), with renowned Greek vases, and Roman and Etruscan statues, and the **Glyptothek** (open Tue–Sun), devoted to Greek and Roman sculpture. Not far away, the **Alte Pinakothek** (Tue–Sun) exhibits works of 14th–18th-century European masters; its collection of Rubens's paintings is perhaps the finest in the world. Works in the adjacent **Neue Pinakothek** (Wed–Mon) range from Impressionism to Art Nouveau and Symbolism.

Outside Munich

The Theresienwiese, southwest of the centre, is the site of the world-famous 14-day **Oktoberfest**, which has been held in the city since 1810 and draws more than 6 million visitors every year. The ultra-modern headquarters and **museum** of the **Bavarian Motor Works** (BMW; Tue–Sun), shaped like a car cylinder, lie to the north of the ring road around the city.

Also outside the city centre is **Schloss Nymphenburg** (daily), the summer residence of the Bavarian princes and kings, which now houses a porcelain factory and the famous **Gallery of Beauty** (Schönheitsgalerie), with paintings of women including the dancer Lola Montez, the beautiful mistress of Ludwig I. The park is laid out in the French style and includes the **Amalienburg** hunting lodge, considered a masterpiece of European Rococo.

Stuttgart and the Black Forest

The whole length of road from the ancient university town of **Freiburg** to Stuttgart ⓑ winds along narrow river valleys through an area of outstanding natural beauty. Tourists have been coming to the **Black Forest** (Schwarzwald) since the 18th century, attracted by the contrast of the Rhine Plain and the mountains rising some 1,200 metres (4,000ft) above it. The forested slopes above the picture-postcard valleys are great for walking. Grouse and pheasant, buzzards and hawks, deer, foxes and badgers populate more remote areas.

Stuttgart, surrounded by forested hills and speckled with parks, has one of the highest per capita incomes of any city in Germany, due in part to its manufacture of Mercedes cars. Opulence was displayed differently by the rich and powerful in earlier times, as evidenced by the striking central ensemble of the 16th-century **Old Palace** (Altes Schloss; Tue–Sun) and 18th-century **New Palace** (Neues Schloss; open for specially arranged tours) on Schillerplatz. Well worth a visit outside the city centre are the **Daimler-Benz Museum** (Tue–Sun) in the district of Untertürkheim, and the **Porsche Museum** (open Tue–Sun) in Stuttgart-Zuffenhausen.

Down the valley to Heidelberg

Although the spa tradition of **Baden-Baden** goes back to Roman times, it was not revived until 1838, when Jacques Bénazet opened his **Casino**, a luxurious fun palace, in the Kurhaus

At that point it suddenly became fashionable again to visit Baden-Baden. The existence of **Karlsruhe** 🔟, further north, is entirely due to the palace that Margrave Karl Wilhelm of Baden-Durlach had built around 1715. Most of its attractions are found around the palace, which houses the **Baden State Museum** (Badisches Landesmuseum; Tue–Sun). The **State Majolica Museum** (Tue–Sun), with a display of faïence pottery; the **State Art Gallery** (Staatliche Kunsthalle; Tue–Sun), containing one of the best displays of European painting in southern Germany; and the **Botanical Gardens** (Sun–Fri) are all nearby.

Heidelberg 🔟 lies on the edge of the Odenwald Forest, where the Neckar reaches the Rhine Plain, and is regarded as the epitome of German Romanticism. High above the picturesque lanes, the ruins of the **castle** (daily; guided tours) rise majestically. To the left of the massive gate tower, the simple **Gothic House** is the oldest part of the complex. In the cellar is the famous **Heidelberg Tun**, one of the largest wine vats in the world. The

most interesting part of the castle is the Otto-Heinrich Wing, which houses the **German Apothecary Museum** (Deutsches Apothekenmuseum; daily), a collection of furniture, books, medical instruments and medicine bottles of all shapes and sizes. Beneath the castle, the six arches of the **Old Bridge** (Alte Brücke) span the river. Its 13th-century gate is topped by Baroque spires and leads to **Philosopher's Way** (Philosophenweg), a hillside promenade along **Heiligenberg**. In the attractive Old City, near the Kornmarkt, you will find two of Heidelberg's most famous student taverns, and the mighty, late Gothic **Church of the Holy Ghost** (Heiliggeistkirche).

Frankfurt

Germany's financial centre on the River Main is **Frankfurt** 🔟, which has developed into a pulsating metropolis thanks to its location at the intersection of road, rail and air traffic routes. The skyscrapers housing international banks and financial corporations create a dramatic skyline which epitomises the power of this bustling city.

Ornate decorations adorn many of the buildings in Heidelberg.

BELOW: a view of Heidelberg from the castle high above.

The idyllic Moselle Valley is the best known of Germany's wine-producing areas. Winningen, Zell, Bernkastel-Kues and Piesport are typically picturesque towns and villages along the route.

BELOW: the colossal bulk of the Porta Nigra. **BELOW RIGHT:** Frankfurt's financial district.

Reflected in the glass of soaring modern buildings is the Gothic tower of Frankfurt's cathedral, and apple-wine pubs stand at cobblestone-street level in **Sachsenhausen**. An impressive collection is on show at the **Museum of Modern Art** (Museum für Moderne Kunst; Tue–Sun); and nine museums line the south bank of the Main, in a district known as the **Museumsufer**. The **Städel Museum** (Tue–Sun) displays paintings from the 14th century to the present, while the **Liebighaus** (Tue–Sun) exhibits sculptures from antiquity to the Baroque period. The **Deutsches Filmmuseum** (Tue–Sun) documents the German film industry, and films are shown here. Others include the **Deutsches Architekturmuseum** (Tue–Sun), the **Museum of Applied Arts** (Museum für Angewandte Kunst; Tue–Sun) and the **Ethnological Museum** (Museum der Weltkulturen; Tue–Sun).

In the city centre, the **town hall** (Römer; daily), is a collection of three neo-Gothic buildings and includes the church where the Holy Roman Emperors were crowned. The nearby **Goethe-**haus (Grosser Hirschgraben 23–25; daily) is where Johann Wolfgang von Goethe, Germany's greatest man of letters, was born in 1749.

The Rhine and Moselle

The River Main slices through Frankfurt on its way to join the Rhine. Not far from their confluence lies the ancient city of **Mainz** ⑲, founded in 38 BC. In AD 747 St Boniface made it the seat of an archbishop, and the centre of Germanic Christendom. Johannes Gutenberg (*c.*1397–1468), the inventor of printing, is Mainz's most famous son. Two of his 42-page Latin Bibles can be seen in the **Gutenberg Museum** (Tue–Sun), along with old printing apparatus and a replica of the master's workshop.

Almost due west, in the heart of the Moselle valley, is **Trier** ⑳, the oldest city in Germany, founded in 16 BC by the Roman Emperor Augustus. Dominated by the well-preserved **Porta Nigra**, the huge Roman gate, the city is a treasure chest of ruins and relics, and many residents dabble in archaeology. It is said that, to store potatoes safe from

the winter frost, the people simply dig down to the Roman mosaics. The **Rhineland Museum** (Rheinisches Landesmuseum; Tue–Sun) has a wealth of Roman treasures, including mosaics, sculpture, glass and coins. The fortress-like, Romanesque **St Peter's Cathedral** is one of Germany's oldest churches.

At **Koblenz** ㉑, the Mosel, perhaps Germany's loveliest river, joins the Rhine. Where the two great rivers meet stands an impressive monument known as the **German Corner** (Deutsches Eck). On the opposite side of the river, high on the edge of a ridge, lies **Ehrenbreitstein** (daily; guided tours), a 13th-century fortress that once controlled this key area and changed hands several times between the French and Germans. Above the Pfaffendorf Bridge, with the Moselle on the left and the Rhine on the right, is the famous **Wine Village**, built in 1925 as a replica of a wine-producing village, complete with authentic vineyards and typical half-timbered houses from the most celebrated German wine-growing regions.

The route to Cologne

With the fall of the Berlin Wall, the city of **Bonn** ㉒ returned the function of German capital to Berlin. Before it was chosen as the seat of the Federal Government in 1949, the major claim to fame of this sleepy city was as the birthplace of Ludwig van Beethoven (1770–1827). But, thanks to its **Museum Mile**, Bonn still has a lot to offer, including the **Art and Exhibition Hall** (Kunst-und Ausstellungshalle), the **Museum of Art** (Kunstmuseum) and the **Zoological Museum** (Alexander Koenig Museum; all museums open Tue–Sun). Exhibits at the **Beethoven-Haus** (Tue–Sun) include the piano made specially for the composer in Vienna.

Cologne ㉓ (Köln) is a lively city with a population of about 1 million. It is famous for its twin-spired cathedral, exuberant Carnival celebrations and religious processions, and the determination with which it was rebuilt

after being reduced to rubble during World War II. The spirit of Cologne is embodied in its mighty **Cathedral** (Dom) and the **Severin Bridge** (Severinsbrücke), named after a 4th-century bishop of Cologne, a unique construction across the Rhine, supported by only one off-centre pillar. The cathedral, considered the greatest Gothic church in Christendom, contains what are said to be the remains of the Wise Men of the East, the paintings of Stephan Lochner (*c*.1445) and a feeling of immense space and lofty aspirations that have an awesome effect on the visitor. Begun in 1248, its twin spires, each 157 metres (515ft) high, were not built until 1842–80, a time when heady ideas and monuments were in vogue.

The city also has some excellent museums. The outstanding **Romano-Germanic Museum** (Römisch-Germanisches Museum; Tue–Sun) contains priceless treasures and offers an insight into the city's Roman past. It was built over the world-famous **Dionysus Mosaic**, which was discovered during construction work on an air-raid shelter. The 2nd-century masterpiece

Cologne is highly acclaimed for its theatre and music. Carnival here in April is celebrated with gay abandon and plenty of local Kölsch beer.

BELOW: cyclists on the bridge outside Cologne railway station.

In the Dortmund Brewery Museum you will learn all you ever wanted to know about brewing beer.

BELOW: Lübeck's town hall and marketplace.

covers an area of 70 sq metres (84 sq yds) and consists of more than 1 million ceramic and glass components. Next door is a museum complex that includes the **Ludwig Museum** (Tue–Sun), with a fabulous collection of 20th-century art.

If you have time, take a detour to **Aachen**, one of Germany's oldest cities and the favourite residence of Charlemagne, who is buried in the **Cathedral** (Dom) there, before visiting **Düsseldorf** ㉔, 40km (25 miles) to the north of Cologne. Düsseldorf's trademarks, the **Schlossturm** tower and the **Church of St Lambert**, with its characteristic slightly crooked spire, stand directly by the Rhine. Take a stroll along the Uferpromenade, the pedestrianised space between the river and the bustling Old Town – a square mile packed with pubs and restaurants. The city has a reputation as a centre for the arts; the **State Art Collection** (Kunstsammlung Nordrhein-Westfalen; Tue–Sun) on Grabbeplatz has 20th-century works by artists ranging from Picasso to Lichtenstein, and a comprehensive collection of works by Klee.

Dortmund ㉕, on the eastern edge of the industrial Ruhr district, in which many old factories, warehouses and mines now host tourist attractions, is at the top of the German brewing league. Indeed, more brewing goes on here than in any other city in Europe, including its rival to the south, Munich. All is explained in the **Brewery Museum** (Brauerei Museum; Tue, Thur, Sat).

On the trail of the Brothers Grimm

The picturesque Weser Valley, further east, picks up the trail of the **Fairy-Tale Road** (Märchenstrasse), which leads from **Hanau**, birthplace of Jacob and Wilhelm Grimm, to Bremen. Riverside meadows, spruced-up towns, castle ruins and Renaissance palaces make it seem as if time has stood still here. In **Hamelin** (Hameln), midway along the route, the **Rattenfängerhaus** recalls the story of the *Pied Piper of Hamelin*, and every Sunday in summer a play depicting the legend is performed in front of the **Wedding House** (Hochzeitshaus, 1617).

The old Hanseatic town of Bremen **26** is the oldest German maritime city, although its modern deep-sea port of **Bremerhaven**, 57km (35 miles) further north, was founded in the 19th century. *The Bremen Town Musicians*, a dog, a donkey, a cat and a cockerel, from the story by the Brothers Grimm, stand near the **town hall** (Rathaus). The cavernous cellar beneath this building is famous for its Gothic vaults, and houses a restaurant serving all the wines of Germany.

Maritime Hamburg

Hamburg **27** is Germany's second-largest city (population 1.8 million), and a major port, although it is 110km (66 miles) from the sea. Cargo ships reach it by sailing up the River Elbe, and one of the most attractive areas is the **Speicherstadt**, the old warehouse district, which can be explored on a narrow-boat cruise.

Hamburg's red-light district, the **Reeperbahn** and adjacent **Grosse Freiheit** and **Herbertstrasse**, may be one of Europe's raunchiest, but the area is well policed. A more elegant side of

town can be seen by strolling from the railway station into the centre. To the north of the station is the **Art Gallery** (Kunsthalle; Tue–Sun), with a magnificent collection of paintings and sculpture from the 13th–20th centuries. On the other side of the station is one of the world's best Jugendstil (Art Nouveau) collections, in the **Arts and Crafts Museum** (Museum für Kunst und Gewerbe; Tue–Sun). Surprisingly, Hamburg's most popular visitor attraction is **Miniatur Wunderland** (daily), a vast model-railway complex in an old harbour warehouse.

Lübeck 28, on the Baltic Sea, was the commercial metropolis of the Holy Roman Empire for 250 years, and by 1356 was the most powerful of the Hanseatic towns. It is now a prime port for ferries to Scandinavia. The **Holstentor** (Holsten Gate), one of the few remaining sections of the city wall, leads to the Old Town, and Lübeck's five Gothic brick churches with their combined Seven Towers, a trademark image of the city. **Travemünde** in Lübeck Bay has been Lübeck's beach resort since the 19th century. ❑

Relaxing in Travemünde, the beach resort just a few kilometres from Lübeck.

BELOW LEFT: Hamburg has a fine seafaring tradition.
BELOW: Lübeck's Holsten Gate.

DESIGN ICONS OF EUROPE

Over the course of the 20th century, industrialism, ingenuity and a drive towards aesthetic appeal came together to create classic designs

In the early days of industrialisation objects were made in the only way they could be, with form dictated by function. But improved processes of production and increased competition encouraged manufacturers to engage artists to give products a deliberate style. And so was born the notion of design.

It could be said that we live in an age of design, and that Europe in the 20th century was the crucible in which many of the ideas we now take for granted were born. But it wasn't always like that.

For a long time, design was the humblest of the arts, a marriage between jobbing creativity and the mundane commercial world in which the object was to get consumers to part with their money for desirable products. Then, with the emergence of pop culture, design came into its own, and gradually the notion spread that you do not have to look in an art gallery for artefacts to admire: they are there, too, on the breakfast table or parked in the street outside.

Design is very much an evolutionary force, with the weak, unpopular idea passing quickly out of sight and the strong becoming so familiar to us that it is hard to imagine a world without it. The objects on these two pages have all, by general agreement of the critics, attained the status of design classic through longevity, functionality and good looks.

ABOVE: adult wristwatches were sombre and serious affairs until Swatch came along in the 1980s with thin plastic watches cast in colourful and fun designs, often sold at affordable prices.

TOP: AEG fan designed by Peter Behrens, 1911.
LEFT: Gerrit Rietveld's red-and-blue chair (Netherlands, 1917). Its simplicity made it suitable for mass production.

ABOVE: road signs can be stylish as well as functional.

ART NOUVEAU

At the end of the 19th century a "new style" spread across Europe, partly as a reaction to the academic, rule-bound art that preceded it, partly as a response to the new materials available and the techniques of mass production, and partly because modern communications allowed the rapid international diffusion of its ideas.

Usually known as "Art Nouveau", after a trend-setting shop of that name which opened in Paris in 1895, the style developed simultaneously in different countries under a variety of names: Jungendstil in Germany, Secession in Austria, Modernismo in Spain.

Each of these has its distinguishing features, but all Art Nouveau shares the same delight in ornament, drawing inspiration particularly from organic forms, as seen in its emblematic sensuous curve.

After 1900 the influence of Art Nouveau waned, but it has never really gone out of fashion. The objects it created – genuine or reproduction – have always been in demand, and the style has served as an inspiration for many subsequent schools of art and design.

ABOVE: a lithographed poster by Czech artist Alphonse Mucha (1897) illustrates late 19th-century fusion between what had been hitherto the preserve of high art, and the needs of commerce.

RIGHT: this clay-and-bronze Liberty vase demonstrates Art Nouveau's ability to push technique beyond its previous limits.

ABOVE: the Italian Vespa motor-scooter was created by a former aircraft designer in 1946. Beloved by European youth for its streamlined sense of freedom, it has passed effortlessly from contemporary cool, when it was first launched, to being today's retro chic.

BELOW: few cars have won such affection as the Volkswagen Beetle, originally conceived as a "people's car" in 1930s Germany. It saw massive sales in the post-war years, and although it went out of production in 2003, the New Beetle has replaced it as a design icon.

SWITZERLAND

Landlocked at the heart of Europe, the
country's most treasured possession
is its breathtaking Alpine landscape

Switzerland's country code, CH, stands for Confoederatio Helvetica. The Helvetii were a Celtic tribe who occupied most of the Swiss plateau before they were crushed by Julius Caesar. The source of the word Switzerland comes from Schwyz, one of the three cantons which formed the original union at Rütli in 1291. Today there are 26 members of the confederation, and the cantons are divided into those that speak French, German or Italian.

Switzerland is small country, about the same size as the Netherlands but with half the population. About 21 percent of its 7.7 million inhabitants are foreigners. The country is famed for its banking, neutrality, watches and outstanding scenery, and it works hard to maintain its independence: all able-bodied male citizens spend time training each

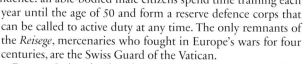

year until the age of 50 and form a reserve defence corps that can be called to active duty at any time. The only remnants of the *Reisege*, mercenaries who fought in Europe's wars for four centuries, are the Swiss Guard of the Vatican.

Eastern Switzerland and the lowlands are best in spring. Summer visitors head for the lakes. Autumn can be enjoyed in the vineyards of the Valais or the Vaud, in the larch forests of the Engadine and the southern valleys of Graubünden, or in the Ticino, where even in October the days seem to be longer and certainly warmer than in much of the rest of Switzerland. Finally, winter provides endless possibilities through the entire Alpine region, for skiing, or simply enjoying the beautiful snow scenes.

The climate of the country ranges from subtropical warmth to Arctic cold in the Alpine peaks. The range of climates results in an equal variety of vegetation – from fertile plains in the lowlands to mountain pastures and vineyards.

In contrast to tourists of the past, who were compelled to explore the still undiscovered Alpine country of Switzerland on foot, on the backs of mules, or in coaches, today's travellers have an astonishingly comprehensive public transport system at their disposal, known as the Swiss Travel System. ❏

PRECEDING PAGES: looking down on Lucerne; Carnival masks. **LEFT:** Verbier ski resort. **ABOVE:** Switzerland is famous for dairy farming; castle on Lake Thun.

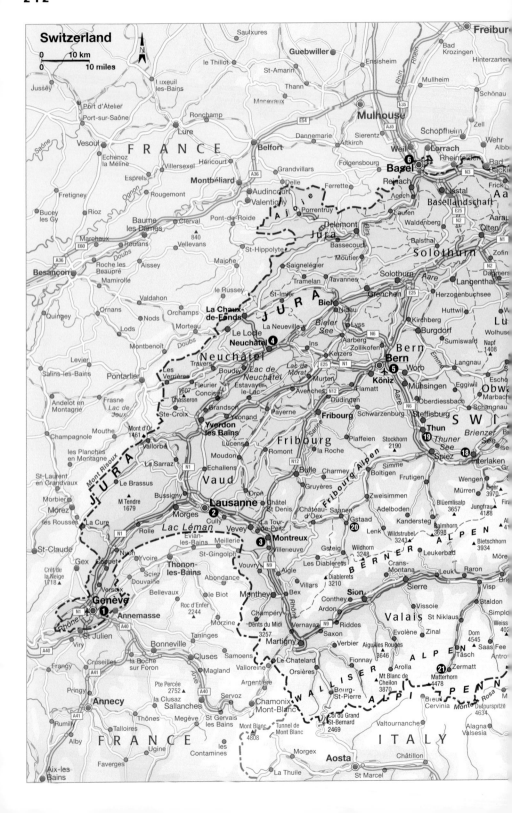

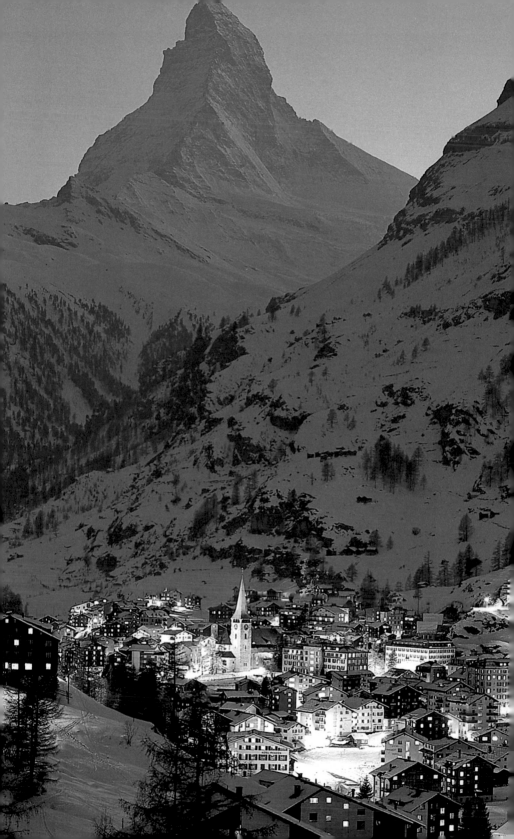

AROUND SWITZERLAND

Despite its small size, Switzerland has an extraordinary variety of landscapes and traditions and some of the most culturally rich cities in Europe

Bern

The first tourists were British, and connections between Britain and Switzerland are everywhere. Lord Byron's *The Prisoner of Chillon* was set in a castle on the shores of Lake Geneva (Lac Léman), and Sir Arthur Conan Doyle's fictional creation Sherlock Holmes was to end his successful career at Reichenbach Falls in the **Bernese Oberland** at the hands of the infamous Professor Moriarty, the "Napoleon of Evil". Sir Arthur also wrote about skiing in Switzerland and started an influx of British skiers that continues up to this day.

The earliest package tours to the continent were arranged by Thomas Cook's of London, the world's oldest travel agency. The first one, in 1863, set off from London bound for Lake Geneva and the Bernese Oberland. The group travelled by train and channel boat to Paris, where they changed trains for the 17-hour journey to Geneva. From there they went up the **Rhône** to **Sion** and then to **Interlaken** and the region around **Lake Luzern**.

Victorian restraints were thrown to the winds. The gentlemen dared to wear knickerbockers with their tailcoats and top hats, and a snowball fight erupted in one of the passes. Giggling ladies protected themselves with their parasols and one gentleman lost his glass eye in the snow. The group also travelled by boat, stagecoach and mule.

Let the train take the strain

Modern means of transportation and the Alpine rail and road tunnels make access to Switzerland much easier. Once there, most visitors use the world's best public transport system to get around. Many of the most scenic places can be reached only by mountain railway or cable car, so it makes sense to buy one of the range of Swiss Travel System passes *(see page 435)* and enjoy the landscape without having to concentrate on driving. Many of the narrow-gauge railways that serve the

Main attractions
LAKE GENEVA
GRUYÈRES
NEUCHÂTEL
BERN
BASEL
ZÜRICH
LUZERN
LAKE CONSTANCE
GRAUBÜNDEN ALPS
BERNESE OBERLAND
VALAIS

LEFT: Zermatt and the Matterhorn.
BELOW: Matterhorn skiers.

You will often come across small local festivals, complete with brass bands.

BELOW RIGHT: Reformation Monument in the Parc des Bastions, Geneva.

more mountainous and remote areas have trains designed for tourists with panoramic windows, open cars for photographers and sometimes a multilingual commentary.

For travellers with time, the national PostBus system reaches the remotest of valleys, and buses connect seamlessly with the train timetable. As punctual as the trains, these regularly scheduled modern buses, run by the postal service (PTT), provide a good way of seeing rural Switzerland. Route Express Lines operate largely for tourists over some of the highest mountain passes, twisting up and down endless hairpin bends. Some of the routes are operated by double-deck coaches to give even better views from the upper level.

Although Switzerland has a good motorway network, the centres of many Swiss cities are pedestrianised, and so well served by trams or buses that a car is a pointless encumbrance. Mountain roads require total concentration and, in bad weather, some skill. Most Alpine passes are closed all winter; those that aren't can be crossed only by cars equipped with snow chains or tyres.

Mountain trains and cable cars take skiers and sightseers up the **Kleines Matterhorn**, **Jungfrau**, **Corvatsch** and hundreds of other peaks. Among the best known is Europe's highest railway, to Jungfraujoch, and the Alps' longest aerial cableway. The world's highest underground funicular railway, the Metro-Alpin, 3,456 metres (11,339ft) up in **Saas Fee** in the canton of Valais, makes year-round skiing possible. Among the various means of transportation, railways and funiculars stay on the ground at all heights. Cable cars and chairlifts do not. Those lacking a head for heights should ask about routes before journeying into the mountains.

Around Lake Geneva

Geneva ❶ (Genève) is at the westernmost tip of **Lake Geneva** (Lac Léman), the second-largest freshwater lake in Europe, which is fed by the River Rhône. This is the westernmost point of Switzerland; the city is surrounded by France on three sides. It has a panorama of water, mountains, parks and flower beds, and its elegant villas lining the

Languages and Lifestyles

Travelling through Switzerland clearly reveals how the linguistic and cultural background, predominantly German, French or Italian, influences everything, especially food, architecture and lifestyle.

About two-thirds of the Swiss are German-speaking. They speak *Schwyzerdütsch*, a German-Swiss dialect that is used at all social levels. Even fluent German-speakers have difficulty understanding this heritage from Alemannic tribes, and its regional and local variations. French has worked its way into Swiss-German, too, so that people say *merci vielmals* for "thank you very much". Menus may use a mix of German, French and *Schwyzerdütsch*. The languages in the French and Italian areas of the country are almost identical to those spoken in France and Italy.

The German area extends from the French-speaking west all the way east to the border with the pocket Principality of Liechtenstein and with Austria. Language divisions do not always follow the borders of the cantons. Basel, Zürich and St Gallen in the north, and Bern, Luzern, Zermatt and Davos are all part of the German-speaking region. The Italian Swiss are found primarily around lakes Maggiore and Lugano and in parts of Graubünden where Romansch, the fourth official language, can be heard. Calvin's strict Protestant ethic forbade the wearing of jewellery, which resulted in Geneva's jewellers turning to clockmaking instead.

lakeshore and coloured sails out on the water create a delightful setting for Switzerland's most cosmopolitan city.

Many of the well-known sights are found right where the River Rhône leaves Geneva. The **Water Fountain** (Jet d'Eau) out in the harbour can send a dazzling plume of white foam 145 metres (476ft) into the air. The first bridge to span the Rhône is the **Pont du Mont-Blanc**. From here and from the **Quai du Mont-Blanc**, on the right bank, one can enjoy (on clear days) an unobstructed view of **Mont Blanc**, the highest peak in Europe at 4,810 metres (15,781ft).

The **English Garden** (Jardin Anglais) and Flower Clock (decorated with over 6,300 plants) are here (on the left bank), while a little further on is **Ile Rousseau**, a place for literary pilgrims. The French philosopher Jean-Jacques Rousseau (1712–78) was born in the city and the island, which can be reached by a footbridge from the **Pont des Bergues**, was named after him when a statue of him was erected in 1834.

Behind the English Garden, crossing the Rue de Rhône (one of Geneva's main shopping streets) are numerous steep, narrow lanes leading to the **Old Town** (*vieille ville*), with its picturesque streets and squares. Don't miss the **Place du Bourg-de-Four** and the **Cathédrale St-Pierre**. Geneva was the birthplace of Swiss watchmaking. The **Patek Philippe Museum** (Tue–Sat) displays timepieces, enamelled watches and music boxes dating from the 16th century.

Protestant work ethic

Next to the cathedral is the **International Museum of the Reformation** (Musée International de la Réforme; Tue–Sun), which explores the roots and development of this religious movement against the Church of Rome. Down from the far side of the Old Town is the Parc des Bastions, where the **Reformation Wall** commemorates some of the key figures of Protestantism, including John Calvin, John Knox, Oliver Cromwell and the Pilgrim Fathers. As the city of Calvin (1509–64), Geneva figures prominently in the history of the Protestant Reformation. He inspired the city to take up the

Geneva's clock tower is one of the city's best-known sights.

BELOW: the SS *Savoie* sets off from Geneva.

The Palace of Nations in Geneva is the European headquarters of the United Nations.

BELOW: Rivaz nestles on the shores of Lake Geneva.

cause in 1536, and made it the "Protestant Rome", promulgating his doctrine of rigid morality, the sovereignty of God and predestination. He closed the theatres, banned dancing and the wearing of jewellery, and considered food and drink to be necessities and not sources of enjoyment.

Calvin's influence was not entirely negative. It can be argued that it was he who made it such an international city. Protestant refugees flocked in from England, France and Italy, giving Geneva a cosmopolitan air. Calvin also made the city a centre of French learning, founding an academy that evolved into the university. And since there were no recreational activities, the people of Geneva had no choice but to work and accumulate wealth.

As the city of Jean-Jacques Rousseau, Geneva was the wellspring of many of the ideas that led to the French Revolution of 1789. Rousseau's social theory of the equality of man caused the whole Western world to rethink the notion of aristocratic government. He not only laid the groundwork for the French Revolution, but also sparked

the Romantic movement in literature and the arts. The city and locality of Geneva became a place of ideas largely because of him. The French philosopher Voltaire was also a Genevan by adoption, and Romantic writers such as Lord Byron and Shelley were drawn to the area.

Geneva is important today because of its role as the headquarters for many international organisations. The **Palace of Nations** was built between 1929 and 1936 for the League of Nations, the predecessor to the UN, and is now its European headquarters. Several other UN subsidiary organisations, including the International Labour Organization (ILO) and the World Health Organization (WHO), are based in Geneva, as is the Red Cross.

The city has a small population of 186,000 – less than Switzerland's other main city, Zürich. Yet Geneva is linked in the public mind with the struggle for peace and brotherhood. It is from this that it derives its own unique stature.

The lakeshore

Lake Geneva is shared between France to the south and Switzerland to the north. The Swiss side is known as the **Vaud Riviera**, and the name is appropriate. The mountains protect the area from north and east winds, giving it a mild climate with 2,000 hours of sunshine a year. There is little rain, and the temperature rarely falls below 5°C (40°F), even on winter nights. The lakeside towns and villages are lined with well-tended flower beds and trees. Behind them, neat vineyards grow on terraces that date from the 11th century; the Lavaux Vineyard Terraces are a World Heritage site. A ferry service – extensive in summer – links the towns around the lake, including Evian and Yvoire on the French side.

A string of pretty towns and villages lines the lakeshore between Geneva and the eastern end of the lake, just beyond Montreux. **Coppet**, with its picturesque main street and small château

– the **Villa of Madame de Staël** – is the first of these. Exiled from Paris by Napoleon for her liberal ideas, Madame de Staël continued to entertain the literary figures of the day, including Byron, at her salons in Coppet. Further along, **Nyon**, founded by the Romans, clings to a steep hillside. This attractive town, with its lakeside castle, winding streets and tree-lined lakeside promenade, makes for a good place to stop. The **Château de Prangins**, 2km (1 mile) east of Nyon, is a beautiful 18th-century building housing the **Swiss National Museum** (Tue–Sun) for the French-speaking part of the country. The extensive collection details Switzerland's 18th- and 19th-century history. In the grounds, the pretty kitchen garden has been faithfully recreated.

Lausanne ❷, the "second city" of French Switzerland, midway between Geneva and Montreux, enjoys a sheltered, sunny spot on the southern slopes of steep terraces and gorges. The city is the capital of Vaud. The old quarter goes by the name of **La Cité** and is the location of the medieval

Cathedral, which has the most impressive exterior in Switzerland. The International Olympic Committee has its headquarters in the city, and an Olympic Museum down on the quayside at **Ouchy**. In summer, this lakeside area attracts a cosmopolitan crowd for boating and other water sports. Opposite Lausanne on the French side of Lake Geneva is **Evian-les-Bains**, a fashionable spa famous for its mineral springs.

Tsars and festivals

The region of **Montreux-Vevey** lies along the lakeside near the southeastern end of Lake Geneva. While on a visit, the mother of Tsar Alexander II wrote: "I am in the most beautiful country in the world."

The tsars are long gone, and **Montreux ❸** is now seeking to attract a different kind of international clientele. Only 72km (45 miles) away from Geneva International Airport, the city has built a conference and exhibition centre and mounts international festivals such as the Montreux Jazz Festival and the Montreux Classical Festival. With adjacent Vevey, the town spreads

Rural processions are often colourful affairs.

BELOW: the Palais de Rumine in Lausanne.

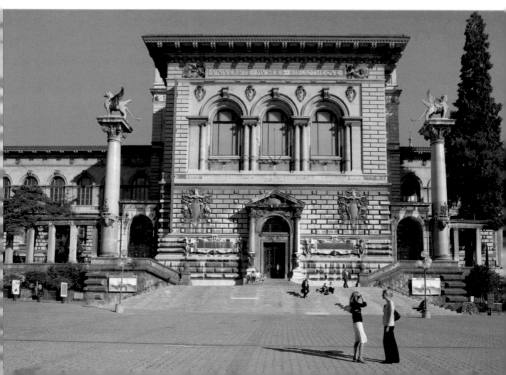

The symbol of Bern. Legend says that Duke Bechtold of Zähringen hunted down a bear in the area shortly after establishing the town in 1191.

BELOW: Gruyères Castle, dating from the 11th century.

along 6.5km (4 miles) of lakeshore, making it the biggest resort on Lake Geneva. The pre-World War I glitter may have faded, but the beautiful natural setting remains. The lush green hills still slope down to the lake, with the mountain peaks in the background. Flowers bloom easily in the unusually mild climate.

The literary set of the 18th and 19th centuries could not stay away. Rousseau set his 1761 novel, *La Nouvelle Héloïse*, in the village of **Clarens**, now part of Montreux. Voltaire arrived, followed shortly by Lord Byron, who put Montreux on the itinerary of British tourists for the next 150 years. Charles Dickens, Leo Tolstoy, Hans Christian Andersen and Fyodor Dostoevsky are some of the other literati who came. The best-known resident of nearby **Vevey** was Charlie Chaplin, who is buried here. His statue stands in the main square.

Just 1.6km (1 mile) east of Montreux is the **Château de Zermatt** (daily). It was built by one of the dukes of Savoy in the 9th or 10th century and expanded in the 13th century to its present appearance. The building has large dungeons into which critics and plotters against the dukes were tossed.

Home of Gruyère

The Montreux-Vevey area provides a starting point for several excursions, such as the one to the cheese-making town of **Gruyères**, home of the light yellow, very rich Gruyère cheese. A model dairy farm shows the cheese-making process (samples provided), and there is a short film.

The Gruyères district is idyllic. In addition to the famous cheese, it produces country ham, cream, strawberries and chocolate (there is a Nestlé plant in nearby Broc). Both cheese and chocolate factories can be visited by the Swiss Chocolate Train from Montreux, using Belle Epoque Pullman and panoramic cars. The medieval town of Gruyères has only one main thoroughfare – a wide cobblestone area from which cars have been banned and which is lined with traditional buildings. This street, which leads up the hill to a **castle**, is liberally planted with flowers.

At the foot of the Jura mountains

Historians would like to know more about the Raurici, the ancient warriors who once populated the forests and valleys of the Jura. Despite a lot of archaeological finds, no one actually knows how large an area they covered. The **Haut Jura Neuchâtelois**, part of a mighty system of mountains 780km (500 miles) in length, can be reached from **Neuchâtel ❹** itself, at the eastern end of the largest lake lying wholly in Swiss territory. Founded in the 11th century under the counts of Neuchâtel, the city has expanded on land reclaimed from the lake. There are also some fine museums here, in particular the **Museum of Art and History** (Musée d'Art et d'Histoire; Tue–Sun), which has a large collection of old clocks and watches and other antiquities.

Bern ❺ is the national capital of the Swiss Federation and also known

as the town of bears, which is translated as *Bearn* in the local dialect. There are automated metal bears on the glockenspiel at the **Zeitglockenturm** and bears in the zoo. The Old City is located on a peninsula, a sharp bend in the **River Aare**, with bridges heading off to the "mainland" in three directions. After a disastrous fire in 1405, the town was rebuilt with locally quarried sandstone, and the result is so impressive that it is a World Heritage site. Gothic sandstone buildings, with elaborate bay windows, overhanging gables and red geraniums in window boxes, are ubiquitous, as are squares with flower-decked fountains. There are more arcades (6km/4 miles of them) than in any other city in Europe. The Florentine **Parliament Building** and a number of banking houses face each other on the same square. Notable among Bern's many museums is the **Paul Klee Centre** (Tue–Sun), in a striking building designed by Renzo Piano, which houses the world's largest collection of the painter's work.

Where three countries meet

Switzerland's second-biggest economic centre after Zürich is **Basel ❻**, which is one of the largest ports on the Rhine and an important centre of the chemical industry. It is home to the **Zolli** (Basel Zoo; daily), Switzerland's largest zoo, and plays a leading role in the international arts and antiques trade.

Nearly all the sights of the city are in what local people call Grossbasel, the **Old Town**, which rises steeply from the Rhine's right bank. Among the striking Gothic buildings are the impressive **town hall** (Rathaus) and the 12th-century cathedral. Basel has no fewer than 35 museums, catering for every taste. Auguste Rodin's *Les Bourgeois de Calais* welcomes visitors to the most prestigious of these at the **Fine Arts Museum** (Kunstmuseum; Tue–Sun), which has an outstanding selection of 19th- and 20th-century art, including works by Gauguin, Van Gogh, Picasso, Chagall, Klee, Max Ernst

and Kandinsky. Hans Holbein the Younger and Arnold Böcklin, a native of the city, are also well represented. To the north of the Old Town, The **Three Country Corner** (Dreiländereck) is something of a novelty. By walking around a marker there, you are able to pass in a matter of seconds through Switzerland, France and Germany – all without having to show a passport.

Zürich

Tucked in between high hills at the north end of Lake Zürich is the country's largest city, **Zürich ❼**, also one of the world's key financial centres. The region here is not yet part of the Alps but part of the Mittelland (Midland), a wide strip of land that cuts across Switzerland from the northeast to the southwest. The River Limmat divides the **Old Town** (Altstadt) between the **Main Station** (Hauptbahnhof) on the west side and **Limmatquai**, a riverside promenade, on the east. **Bahnhofstrasse**, one of Europe's most elegant shopping streets, runs south from the Hauptbahnhof parallel to the river. Price tags, if there are any, suggest a city

Byron visited the Château de Chillon in 1816 with Shelley. The Prisoner of Chillon was published in the same year and describes the incarceration of prior François Bonivard between 1530 and 1536.

BELOW:
a Zürich tram, with the towers of the Grossmünster in the background.

The road from Luzern to Bern passes through the valley of the River Emmo, home of Emmental cheese.

of millionaires – which is what many of the city's population are.

The city has some architectural gems, notably the Romanesque-Gothic **Grossmünster**, with twin towers, cut down to size somewhat after an 18th-century fire. At the nearby **Kunsthaus** (Tue–Sun) on **Heimplatz** you can race through two millennia of European art history at one of Switzerland's largest galleries. The labyrinthine **Swiss National Museum** (Schweizerisches Landesmuseum; Tue–Sun) just north of Hauptbahnhof has Roman relics, cultural artefacts from the Middle Ages, heraldic shields and rooms furnished in the styles of the 15th to 18th centuries. On the west bank of the Limmat is the Rococo **Zur Meisen Guildhall** (Zunfthaus zur Meisen; Tue–Sun), a jewel-box of a building, alongside the slim Gothic grandeur of the **Fraumünster**, and also **St Peter's** church, with the largest church clockface in Europe.

Luzern

The French name, Lucerne, leaves the visitor totally unprepared for the very German character of this city. It's far

better to use the same name as the locals: **Luzern 8**. The covered **Chapel Bridge** (Kapellbrücke), built in 1333 and reconstructed after a serious fire in 1993, is Luzern's best-known landmark. It has a distinctive red-tile roof and its interior is lined with gabled paintings which glorify the martyrs and heroes of the region. A few hundred yards further downstream a second medieval bridge with a small chapel crosses the **River Reuss**, which drains **Lake Luzern** (Vierwaldstätter See). **Spreuer Bridge** (Spreuerbrücke) is made of wood and has a gable roof. The gable ends are decorated with paintings of Caspar Meglinger's *Totentanz* ("Dance of Death").

Luzern's medieval ambience is enhanced by its breathtaking surroundings: the large lake, criss-crossed by majestic paddle steamers, is flanked on either side by the two mountain giants of the **Rigi** and **Pilatus**. The crystal-blue waters meeting the mountain faces are reminiscent of Norwegian fjords, the perfect setting for a romantic evening dinner cruise with live jazz. Boat cruises stop at various

BELOW: picturesque bridge and water tower on Lake Luzern.

points from where cable cars stretch up to the surrounding peaks. You can walk up from the village of **Vitznau** to the peak of the Rigi in about four hours, or take the cog-wheel train. The Alpine panorama is splendid, stretching 300km (nearly 200 miles) in every direction. The cog-wheel railway (closed Dec–Apr) on Pilatus, with a 1 in 2 gradient, is one of the world's steepest. Yodelling, flag-throwing and alphorn concerts are kept alive for tourists.

Luzern is also known as the place where German composer Richard Wagner wrote *Die Meistersinger, Siegfried* and *Götterdämmerung* – three of his major works. He lived in Luzern between 1866 and 1872, in a mansion on the Tribschen peninsula which is now the **Richard Wagner Museum** (mid-Mar–end Nov Tue–Sun). This was where Wagner had his illicit rendezvous with Cosima von Bülow, the daughter of Franz Liszt. When Cosima's husband learnt about the trysts he divorced her, whereupon she became Wagner's wife.

Each year in August and September, Luzern is host to the **Lucerne Festival**, a month-long celebration of classical music. A popular feature of the music festivals are outdoor serenades at the **Löwenplatz**. The acoustics of the water and rock, and the soft illumination of the colossal lion carved from a cliff, combine to provide an enchanting nocturnal experience.

The town of **Schwyz ❾**, on the other side of Lake Luzern, gave its name to the country. Switzerland's most important document – the Swiss Charter of 1291 – is housed in the **Museum of the Swiss Charters of the Confederation** (Bundesbriefmuseum; Tue–Sun) here. Close to the centre, the wonderfully preserved 17th-century mansion, **Ital Reding Estate** (Ital Reding-Hofstatt; Tue–Sun), tells the story of the rich families who supplied foreign courts and countries with the town's most famous export – mercenaries – in the 17th and 18th centuries.

Lake Constance

Eastern Switzerland is still relatively unexplored, but the area around the broad expanse of **Lake Constance** (Bodensee) ❿, with vine-covered slopes,

It was at Altdorf, above Lake Luzern, in 1291 that William Tell, the country's national hero, was forced to shoot an apple off his own son's head. Needless to say, the arrow was true and the boy was spared.

BELOW LEFT: the Rococo library in St Gallen abbey.

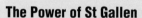

The Power of St Gallen

The Baroque monastery area of St Gallen bears magnificent witness to the final flourishing of one of Europe's most important abbeys, its history stretching back more than 12 centuries. In AD 612, an Irish itinerant monk named Gall built a wooden chapel and a cell in which to live and sleep, here in the Steinach Valley, which at that time was still thickly overgrown with forest. In 747 a Benedictine monastery was erected on the site, but this was replaced in the 9th century by an abbey complex which subsequently became a great centre of ecclesiastical power.

In the 15th century it developed into a self-contained state ruled by prince-abbots. Their reign continued until 1798, when the monastery was disbanded by the French, but in 1847 its minster was elevated as the Cathedral of the newly formed diocese of St Gallen.

The abbey seen today was freely modelled on Caspar Mosbrugger's plan of 1721, now kept in the Rococo abbey library. The library, nave and rotunda were built in 1755–67 by Peter Thumb, and the new choir with the twin-towered facade was added in 1761. The abbey houses an important collection of rare manuscripts, including the *Folchart* and *Golden Psalters*, from AD 864–72, and the *Evangelium Longum* from around AD 900.

The Matterhorn has become a symbol of Switzerland.

BELOW: wooden huts huddle on the Alpine slopes.

orchards, meadows and historic towns and villages, is a scenic oasis scarcely equalled anywhere else in Switzerland. The city of **St Gallen** ⓫, the largest in eastern Switzerland, can be reached from Zürich. It originally developed from a monastery precinct now dominated by the Baroque **Cathedral** (daily). The city also contains a series of exceptionally successful Baroque facades, particularly the **Zum Greif** house (Gallusstrasse 22) and the **Haus zum Pelikan** (Schmiedgasse 15).

In a quiet corner on the Swiss-Austrian border, next to the cantons of St Gallen and Grisons, lies **Liechtenstein** ⓬ *(see also Microstates, page 358).* This independent *Fürstentum* (principality), left over from the Holy Roman Empire and occupying only 162 sq km (62 sq miles) between the River Rhine and the Vorarlberg mountains, offers fabulous scenery.

The Graubünden Alps

Chur ⓭, the capital of Graubünden, is the oldest town in Switzerland, having been settled by the Celts 5,000 years ago. The old part of town is exceptionally beautiful when snow lies on the mighty roofs of the Gothic **town hall**, the **Bishop's Palace** and the Romanesque **Cathedral**, which contains a magnificent late Gothic carved High Altar.

Anyone who wants to cross the passes in Graubünden has to take the route through the narrow gap formed by the Bündner Herrschaft and Chur via either **Lenzerheide** and **Tiefencastel** or **Landquart** and **Klosters**, to **Davos** ⓮. Davos's fame lies in hosting the World Economic Forum, but for skiers its attraction is the **Parsenn** – which provides 200km (125 miles) of its total of 320km (200 miles) of piste leading into the valley below. The story of rival **St Moritz** ⓯ began in 1864, when Johannes Badrutt, who built St Moritz's Kulm Hotel, invited some English summer guests to spend the winter here. In 1880 Europe's first curling tournament took place here, and in 1884 the first toboggan run was built.

To escape the bustle and crowds of the town and lake, take the route down the north side of the valley down to **Maloja**, which leads across wooded sheltered slopes through an idyllic landscape with wonderful views of Lake Silvaplana below; continue past the foot of the **Corvatsch**, considered by many to be the best mountain for skiing in the world.

The Ticino

In the **Ticino** it is still possible to find seemingly endless and wonderfully quiet valleys filled with sunshine and sub-Alpine vegetation, although they may be just a few kilometres from noisy motorways and railways. Predominantly mountainous, the region has two great lakes at the foot of the Alps where the Ticino borders Italy which are part Swiss part Italian: **Lago Maggiore** and **Lago di Lugano**.

Lugano ⓰ has a modern banking quarter, but the developers spared a few arcaded alleyways; the **Cathedral of San Lorenzo**, on the steep slope

between the railway station and the lower part of town, has also survived. Its facade is a masterpiece of Lombardy Renaissance. The **Museo Cantonale d'Arte** (Tue–Sun) is housed in the Villa Malpensata and has a good collection of works by Swiss artists.

Locarno ⑰ and the numerous small villages on the banks of Lago Maggiore can claim to enjoy the mildest climate in the Ticino. This has encouraged tourism to the extent that the perpetual traffic around the lake area can sometimes be unbearable. The 14th-century **Castello Visconteo** (Apr–Oct Tue–Sun) now houses the **Archaeological Museum** (Museo Archeologico; Apr–Oct Tue–Sun), which has a good collection of Bronze Age and Roman artefacts. **Ascona** is one of the most ancient settlements on the lake, and the houses along the promenade are now colourful cafés and restaurants overlooking the small harbour, still used by fishing boats. Boat services on the lake call at 36 piers, most of them in Italy. The most notable Swiss port of call is the island of Brissago for its villa and botanic garden.

The Bernese Oberland

There are 51 mountains over 4,000 metres (13,000ft) high in the chain formed by the Valaisan and Bernese Alps, which lie between the Rhône Glacier and Lake Geneva. The town of **Interlaken** ⑱, full of splendid hotel buildings, serves as a reminder of the health spa-oriented lifestyle of the upper classes of 19th-century Europe. **Thun** ⑲, considered the gateway to the Oberland, is dominated by its castle, perched on a steep hill above the town. The 12th-century keep, with its four corner towers, is reminiscent of a Norman castle.

The route to Montreux passes through the mountain resort of **Gstaad** ⑳, where high society from all over the world meets up in the winter months. Further south in the **Valais** region, **Zermatt** ㉑, the skiing and mountaineering mecca, lies at the foot of the majestic Matterhorn. The finest easily reached view of the famous mountain is from Gornergrat, summit of a cogwheel railway from Zermatt and the highest open-air station in Europe, at 3,092 metres (10,145ft). ❑

South of Interlaken are the classic valleys and peaks of the Jungfrau region – the ultimate destination of those first tourists on Thomas Cook's original excursion.

BELOW: a stunning view from Thun.

AUSTRIA

Combining Alpine scenery with Mozart
and Strauss, the country is hard to
beat when it comes to romance

The opening words of Austria's national anthem are "Land of mountains…", and that is exactly what this 84,000 sq km (32,000 sq mile) country is. For centuries these uplands were a bugbear, making life hard for the farmer. John Gunther, a traveller in the 1930s, remarked: "The chief crop of provincial Austria is the scenery." That scenery is now the country's highest earner, and the year-round tourist industry accounts for the largest slice of the national economy.

Nestled among the wild Alpine scenery are hundreds of mountain lakes and idyllic watercourses which are especially attractive in summer. The gentle charms of the Salzkammergut and the Carinthian Lake District are underlined by the majestic backdrop of mountains. To the east, the foothills of the Alps gradually peter out in the Vienna woods, reaching right up to the suburbs of the capital. Vienna, once the seat of the Babenberg dynasty, was for 600 years the centre of one of Europe's superpowers, the Austro-Hungarian Empire. It is a beautiful city today, and it houses a wealth of treasures. Salzburg, on the north side of the Alps and largely associated with *The Sound of Music*, is equally romantic, and has become almost a theme park for its most esteemed inhabitant, Wolfgang Amadeus Mozart.

Every period of European cultural development is reflected in Austria. Romanesque, Gothic, Renaissance and Baroque buildings are scattered across the land. Statues, frescoes, ceiling and wall paintings document more than 1,000 years of often turbulent history.

Austrians are known for their courtesy and hospitality, but they have their regional differences. The inhabitants of the eastern provinces reveal a mixture of German and Slavic characteristics. In Salzburg and the Tyrol the people have more affinity with Bavarians. The natives of Vorarlberg in the west are of Alemannic and Rhaetian descent, and are related to the inhabitants of the Engadine and Upper Rhine. Half of Austria's borders lie against Eastern European countries – the Czech and Slovak republics, Hungary and Slovenia – which make it feel at the centre of the changing new world. For the visitor, however, it still looks very much like the old world.   ❑

PRECEDING PAGES: stunning Tyrolean scenery; wooden balconies on houses in the Salzkammergut region. **LEFT:** tower in the grounds of 12th-century Gurk Cathedral. **ABOVE:** "waterfall hat" in the National Park.

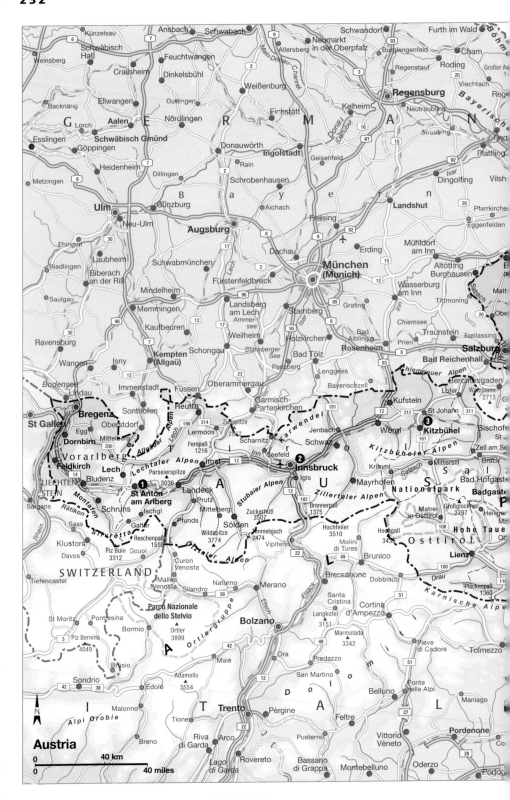

Künzelsau
Schwäbisch Hall
Weinsberg
Backnang
Lorch
G E Aalen
Esslingen
Göppingen
Schwäbisch Gmünd
Heidenheim
Metzingen
Ulm
Neu-Ulm
Ehingen
Riedlingen
Laubheim
Biberach an der Riß
Saulgau
Ravensburg
Wangen
Isny
Bodensee
Lindau
St Gallen
Bregenz
Egg
Dornbirn
Feldkirch
LIECHTEN-
STEIN
Saas
Klosters
Davos
SWITZERLAND
Tiefencastel
St Moritz
Piz Bernina
4049
Sondrio
I
Malonno
Breno
Austria

Ansbach
Schwabach
Feuchtwangen
Crailsheim
Dinkelsbühl
Ellwangen
Oettingen
Nördlingen
R
Donauwörth
Dillingen
Günzburg
Schwabmünchen
Mindelheim
Memmingen
Kaufbeuren
Schongau
Kempten (Allgäu)
Immenstadt
Füssen
Sonthofen
Reutte
Oberstdorf
Mittelberg
Lermoos
Fernpaß 1216
Imst
Lech
Parseierspitze
St Anton am Arlberg
3036
Landeck
Schruns
Ischgl
Galtür
Pfunds
Reschenpaß 1510
Piz Buin 3312
Scuol
Curon Venosta
Malles Venosta
Silandro
Pontresina
Bormio
Ortler 3899
Brusio
Edolo 3554
Malé
Riva di Garda
Arco
Lago di Garda

Schwandorf
Neumarkt in der Oberpfalz
Allersberg
Weißenburg
Eichstätt
Kelheim
Ingolstadt
Rain
Schrobenhausen
Aichach
Freising
Dachau
Fürstenfeldbruck
Landsberg am Lech
Ammersee
Weilheim
Starnberger See
Penzberg
Oberammergau
Garmisch-Partenkirchen
Zugspitze 2962
Scharnitz
Seefeld
Innsbruck
Igls
Stubaier Alpen
Zuckerhütl 3507
Wildspitze 3774
Sölden
Timmelsjoch 2474
Vipiteno
Molini di Tures
Naturno
Merano
Bolzano
Ora
Predazzo
San Martino
Trento
Pèrgine
Tione
Rovereto
Bassano di Grappa

Furth im Wald
Cham
Burglengenfeld
Regenstauf
Roding
Großer A
Viechtach
Regensburg
Reg
Neutraubling
Straubing
Plattling
Geisenfeld
Isar
Dingolfing
Vilsh
Landshut
Pfarrkirche
Eggenfelden
München (Munich)
Erding
Mühldorf am Inn
Altötting
Burghausen
Wasserburg am Inn
Matt
Grafing
Tittmoning
Obe
Chiemsee
Bad Aibling
Traunstein
Freilassing
Holzkirchen
Prien
Salzburg
Bad Tölz
Rosenheim
Bad Reichenhall
Lenggries
Berchtesgaden
Bayerischzell
Chiemgauer Alpen
2713
Kufstein
Lofer
Watzmann
St Johann
Wörgl
Kitzbühel
Bischof
Jenbach
St J
Schwaz
Kitzbüheler Alpen
Zell am S
Mittersill
Bruck
Krimml
Mayrhofen
Zillertaler Alpen
Nationalpark
Badgast
Brennerpaß 1375
Matrei in Osttirol
Großglockner 3797
Heiliger
Hochfeiler 3510
Hochgall 3436
Hohe Taue
Osttirol
Ob
Brunico
Lienz
Bressanone
Dobbiaco
Drau
Plöckenpaß 1360
Santa Cristina
Cortina d'Ampezzo
Karnische Alpe
Langkofel 3151
Marmolada 3342
Pieve di Cadore
Tolmezzo
Ponte nelle Alpi
Belluno
Maniago
Feltre
Pordenone
Vittorio Vèneto
Co
Montebelluno
Oderzo
Porto

Mein-Donau-Channel
Donau (Danube)
Bayerisch
Bayern
Lech
Isar
Inn
Salzach
Karwendel
Allgäuer Alpen
Lechtaler Alpen
Ötztaler Alpen
Vorarlberg
Montafon
Rätikon
Silvretta
Rhein
Ortlergruppe
Parco Nazionale dello Stelvio
Alpi Orobie
A U S T R I A
D O L O M I T E S
I T A L Y

0   40 km
0   40 miles

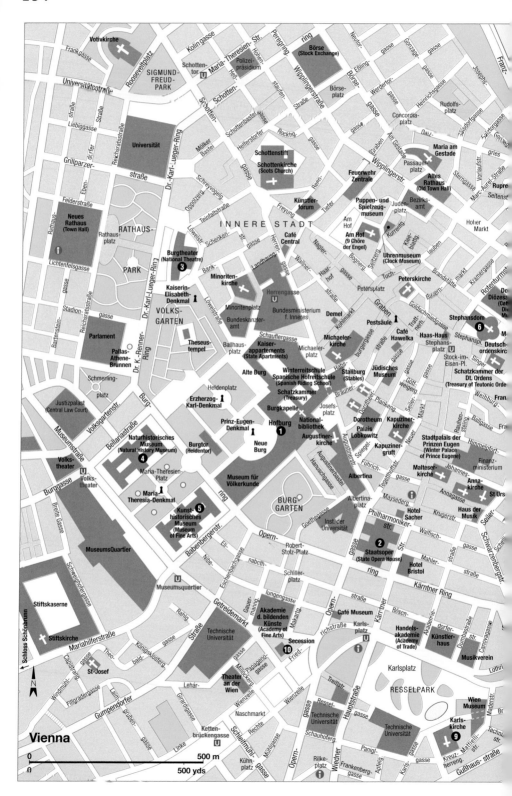

Vienna

0 _____ 500 m
0 _____ 500 yds

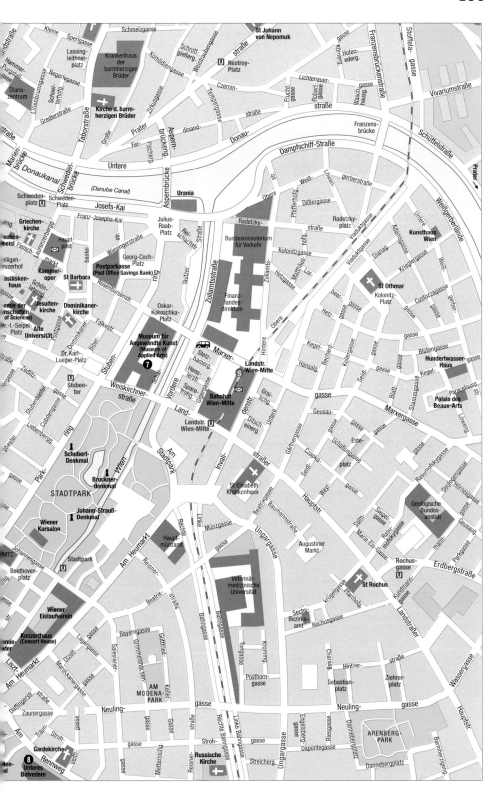

VIENNA

The capital of the former Habsburg Empire gave the world the waltz, and has been home to some of the world's great composers

Vienna is an easy city to get to know, not because nobody ever gets lost in its maze of streets and passages (they do), but because the Viennese themselves have a reputation for being courteous and helpful. The diversity of people here can be traced directly to the far-flung Habsburg Empire; Vienna was the seat of the ruling family for almost 650 years. Situated in the Danube Valley, it was first settled by the Celts around 400 BC, and known as Vindobona.

Austria's capital of 1.6 million people lies on the eastern edge of the country where East meets West and has always been something of a bulwark. It was recognised by Europe as the saviour of Christendom when it finally repelled the Turks in 1683. For centuries, all manner of ideas fomented and flourished among the city's cultural palaces and cafés. Art and music, theatre, medicine and psychology found the ideal climate in which to grow. Vienna has been home to some of the great composers, from Haydn to Beethoven to Schoenberg, and to some equally great architects, from the historicist Heinrich von Ferstel to Otto Wagner, founder of the Viennese Art Nouveau (Jugendstil) movement. Today Vienna serves as a neutral meeting ground for diplomats of all political persuasions. It is the seat of OPEC (Organization of Petroleum-Exporting Countries) and the third seat of the United Nations (after New York City and Geneva).

Building for glory

The Habsburgs were great builders. At the heart of the Old Town they erected the **Imperial Palace ❶** (Hofburg), a town itself within the city, which was "always being built but never finished". Construction began about 1220, but it was enlarged and renovated right into the 20th century. The **Neue Burg** (Wed–Mon) wing was completed just 10 years before the collapse of the Habsburg Empire; it houses collections of ancient musical instruments, armour and weapons, the **Ephesus**

Main attractions

IMPERIAL PALACE
IMPERIAL COURT CHAPEL
SPANISH RIDING SCHOOL
THE RING
OPERA HOUSE
MUSEUM OF FINE ARTS
BURGTHEATER
ST STEPHEN'S CATHEDRAL
BELVEDERE
SCHÖNBRUNN PALACE

LEFT: ice-skating in front of the city hall. **BELOW:** the Imperial Palace.

Tickets for Spanish Riding School performances can be obtained from the visitor centre in Michaelerplatz (Tue–Sun), or at the box office in Josefsplatz (Tue–Sat), when the horses' morning exercise takes place.

Archaeological Museum and the Museum of Ethnology.

The oldest part of the Hofburg is the Swiss Court (Schweizerhof). The Imperial Court Chapel was added next, then the stables (Stallburg), now a Lippizaner museum. The Imperial Apartments (Amalienburg) were built next, followed by the Chancellery, the Spanish Riding School, the Albertina (originally not part of the Hofburg complex) and the Neue Burg, of which the National Library is part, all of which open onto lovely courts and gardens.

Notable collections housed in the Imperial Palace include the Imperial Silver Collection (daily) and the Imperial Treasury (Wed–Mon). The treasury contains the bejewelled crown of the Holy Roman Empire, which was founded in 800 by Charlemagne and lasted until 1803, when it was broken up by Napoleon. The crown was carried from 1278 onwards by the Habsburg dynasty, a role which made them one of the most influential dynasties in Central Europe. Among other exhibitions from the time of the Habsburg emperors is the Albertina (daily), which has a remarkable collection of watercolours, prints and drawings, including works by Albrecht Dürer, Klimt and Rubens. The state apartments have been magnificently restored.

The all-white Baroque confection of the Spanish Riding School (Spanische Hofreitschule; Feb–June and Sept–Dec for performances) dates from the 17th century, when Emperor Karl VI introduced the Spanish court ceremonial in Vienna. The Lipizzaner horses, originally a Spanish breed, were first raised in Lipizza, Slovenia, and then in the Styrian town of Piber. It is a unique experience to watch the white stallions perform the delicate steps of the *haute école* of riding to the music of classical dances such as the gavotte, quadrille, polka and waltz.

The magnificent Ring

Vienna has hundreds of palaces, large and small, but the biggest building spree the city has ever seen was the Ring. This wide avenue, 57 metres (187ft) across, follows the line of fortifications which stood until Emperor Franz Joseph ordered the ramparts razed in 1857. Architectural competitions were launched, and the city received a brand-new face. Standing at the centre of the Ring, and the first of the buildings to be completed, in 1869, is the Opera House ❷ (Staatsoper). The Viennese ridiculed the Romantic-Historicist style as it was being built and, stung by the criticism, one of its architects hanged himself.

It remained for the prolific architect Heinrich von Ferstel to set the traditional tone of the Ring with the Votive Church (Votivkirche), built in gratitude for the failure of an assassination attempt against Franz Joseph in 1853. The church is Neo-Gothic down to the last detail, and later buildings in the vicinity were adjusted to fit the style.

Von Ferstel's other Ring building is the University, built in the Italian Renaissance style. The soaring archi-

Music until Dawn

Vienna loves music, and musicians of every kind thrive in Vienna. In the Imperial Court Chapel (Hofburgkapelle), members of the Vienna Boys' Choir and the Vienna State Opera form the Court Music Orchestra (Hofmusikkapelle) and sing Mass at 9.15am on Sundays from January to June and from September to December.

Waltzes by Johann Strauss and Franz Lehár are especially popular at Carnival season, when the elegant balls continue until dawn. Then there are the great composers like Haydn, Schubert, Mozart, Mahler, Bruckner, Schoenberg and others. Traces of them can be found in many streets throughout Vienna.

Among the houses which have been turned into small museums or memorials are: the house where Haydn wrote his *Creation* (Haydngasse 19; Tue–Sun); the apartment where Mozart spent the happiest years of his life (Figaro House, Domgasse 5; daily); the places where Schubert was born (Nussdorferstrasse 54; Tue–Sun) and where he died (Kettenbrückengasse 6; Fri–Sun). Beethoven had more than 25 different addresses. In 1800, he moved to Heiligenstadt in the 19th district of Döbling. It was here at Probusgasse 6, today the Beethoven Museum (Tue–Sun), that he wrote his *Heiligenstädt Testament*, a moving document in which he revealed his feelings about his growing deafness.

tecture continues around the circle with the **city hall** (Rathaus), built in imitation Gothic, and **Parliament Building** in Hellenistic style. The **Burgtheater ❸**, just steps from the University, was built in the shape of a Greek lyre, but its acoustics were so poor that it had to be reconstructed 10 years later. The "House on the Ring" is justifiably considered the most significant theatrical stage in the German-speaking world. The convex arch of the central tract is particularly impressive, and the spreading wings on either side house the staircases leading to the boxes.

Museum Quarter

Both the **Natural History Museum ❹** (Naturhistorisches Museum; Wed–Mon), with a wide-ranging collection of dinosaur skeletons, human skulls, gemstones and Iron and Bronze Age items, and the **Museum of Fine Arts ❺** (Kunsthistorisches Museum; Tue–Sun) are also Italian Renaissance. They stand across the Ring from the Neue Burg and its parks. The Fine Arts Museum contains a vast collection of paintings, among them works by Dutch, Flemish, Italian and Spanish masters such as Rembrandt, Vermeer, van Eyck, Rubens, Titian, Bruegel and Velázquez. There are also fine collections of European sculpture and decorative art, as well as Greek, Roman, Oriental and Egyptian antiquities.

St Stephen's Cathedral

On the other side of the Hofburg complex lies **Stephansplatz**, Vienna's most famous square and also the city's bustling centre. The south tower of **St Stephen's Cathedral ❻** (Stephansdom; daily, guided tours available) gives a fabulous overview of the city: climb the 343 steps to the watchman's room and you are rewarded with a dramatic view of the heart of the city. As an alternative, an elevator ascends the unfinished north tower of the cathedral as far as *Pummerin* (Boomer), a copy of the giant bell that was destroyed

in World War II. The original *Pummerin* was cast in 1711 from cannons captured from the Turks. Habsburg marriages took place in St Stephen's cathedral (*Steffl* to the Viennese), in accordance with their habit of acquiring territory through marriage rather than war whenever possible.

In front of the asymmetrical *Steffl* is the smart shopping centre of Vienna, the pedestrian zone including the **Graben** and **Kärntnerstrasse**. The latter continues on the other side of the Ring as **Mariahilferstrasse**, where the large department stores can be found. The area behind St Stephen's is called **Old Vienna** because it best retains the air of the past, though it is not actually the oldest quarter. A jumble of building styles from the 16th and 17th centuries in the network of narrow lanes are well preserved. In **Bäckerstrasse** and **Schönlaterngasse**, in particular, there are many bars and restaurants which are often thronged with people until the early hours of the morning.

From here, stroll down Wollzeile to the Stubenring, and cross over to the

The highlight of the Vienna Ball season is the glamorous Opera Ball at the Staatsoper. The event attracts guests from all over the world. It is held every year on the Thursday before Ash Wednesday.

BELOW: the Café Central, famous for its history as well as its coffee and cakes.

The Upper Belvedere now houses some wonderful works of Austrian art.

BELOW: Johann Strauss plays on in the Stadtpark.
BELOW RIGHT: the Secession Building.

Museum of Applied Arts ❼ (Museum für Angewandte Kunst; Tue–Sun). This enormous building is the repository for fine Austrian furniture as well as porcelain, textiles, glass and jewellery from around the world.

Upmarket Belvedere

Between the Applied Arts Museum and the Belvedere Palace lies the **Stadtpark**, laid out in 1862 and the most extensive patch of green in the vicinity of the Ringstrasse. The ancient trees are reflected in the ponds and River Wien, which is flanked by a string of pavilions and a promenade adorned with statuary.

The **Belvedere ❽** (daily), a palace of sumptuous proportions, was built between 1714 and 1723 for Prince Eugene of Savoy, who routed the Turks in 1683. In fact, it is really two palaces, the Upper and Lower Belvedere, joined by terraced gardens. The former houses the **Austrian Gallery** (Österreichische Galerie), containing art from the Middle Ages to the present day, including a memorable Gustav Klimt collection; the Lower Belvedere houses the former living quarters and the Hall of Grotesques, while the Orangery next door displays regularly changing temporary exhibitions. The medieval art collection is split between the Upper Belvedere and the Palace Stables.

Going back in the direction of the city centre you'll come to Karlsplatz and the splendid Baroque **St Charles Church ❾** (Karlskirche; daily). Regarded as the finest ecclesiastical Baroque building in the city, it was pledged by Charles VI during an epidemic of plague in 1713, started by Johann Fischer von Erlach and completed by his son, Joseph Emanuel. Its unique design includes a magnificent green cupola, twin triumphal pillars with spiral reliefs, and exterior belfries.

Tucked in between the Karlskirche and the Opera House, at Friedrichstrasse 12, is the Jugendstil **Secession Building ❿** (Tue–Sun and public holidays). It was designed by Joseph Maria Olbrich as a showcase for the Secession movement's artists such as Schiele, Kokoschka and Klimt, whose *Beethoven Frieze* (1902) covers three interior walls of a room in the basement.

Excursions from the city

A map of Vienna shows that it is laid out in concentric circles. The **Inner City** (Innenstadt), known as I. Bezirk (first district), is enclosed by the Ring and the Danube Canal (Donaukanal). On the other side of the Ring is the **Vorstadt**, the part of the city that grew up outside the fortifications. It is surrounded by another ring road – the Gürtel. Outside the Gürtel come the suburbs, little villages such as Grinzing, Nussdorf, Gumpoldskirchen and Severing, and their wine taverns, called *Heurigen*.

The woods and meadows between the Danube and its canal to the east of the city enclose the **Prater** (daily), once a playground of emperors but opened to the public as a park in 1766 by Emperor Joseph II. Its landmark is the *Riesenrad* (daily), a giant Ferris wheel that arcs to a high point of nearly 65 metres (213ft). Notices above the cabin windows help to identify important landmarks in the city. There are also a Planetarium, miniature railway, and an old-fashioned amusement park plus adrenalin-pumping rides, bicycle-hire shops and a swimming pool in the park, as well as the 4.5km (3-mile) **Hauptallee** (main avenue), mainly populated with joggers and cyclists.

Exploring Vienna can be followed with a trip along the Danube, although its waters are disappointingly brown. Boats (www.ddsg-blue-danube.at) operate from April to mid-October and make various journeys including popular day trips to Bratislava, the capital of Slovakia, and daily cruises to Hungary's capital, Budapest. Or take a national park boat out into the Danube's water meadows (May–Oct). The city subsides into the **Vienna Woods**, where the Alps end – or begin – at the edge of the Hungarian Plains.

Serene residence

A short distance beyond the confines of the Ringstrasse and the inner city lies the **Schönbrunn Palace** (Schloss Schönbrunn; Apr–Oct daily), the imperial summer residence. The site of the palace is the Beautiful Fountains (Schöne Brunnen), the spacious grounds where Emperor Leopold I wished to build a palace to rival Versailles. Financial difficulties stalled his plans, and it was not until 1743 that Empress Maria Theresa (1717–80) employed Nikolaus Pacassi to build the fabulous palace and gardens we see today.

Schönbrunn contains 1,200 rooms, 45 of which are open to the public. Notable among these are a selection of private rooms used by Emperor Franz Joseph – who was born in the palace and died here in 1916 – and others used by Maria Theresa, including the Breakfast Room and Vieux-Lacque Room, and various ceremonial and state rooms. In the grounds are the Baroque Zoo, the English Botanic Garden and Palm House, and the Gloriette with its views over the whole complex. ❏

The manicured gardens of the 18th-century Schönbrunn Palace, the imperial summer residence.

BELOW: the Baroque splendour of Karlskirche.

AROUND AUSTRIA

With two-thirds of the country taken up by the Alps, Austria is the place for winter skiers and summer hikers. Salzburg and Innsbruck make good centres to stay

Austria is a land of valleys and peaks, high roads and mountain passes, ski slopes and Alpine meadows that fall away eastwards to the Hungarian Plains. The spectacular scenery, friendly people, good food and well-developed resorts have earned Austria a deservedly high reputation around the world. Where farmers once eked out a living during the short summers, well-established hotels and restaurants have sprung up. A vast network of lifts and cable cars lace the mountainsides, taking visitors, winter and summer, to the high playgrounds.

The birthplace of downhill skiing

The **Arlberg** mountain region, straddling the border of the Tyrol (Tirol) and Vorarlberg provinces, is considered the cradle of Alpine skiing. Here Austrian skiers refined the Scandinavian sport to suit their own steep slopes and founded a system of teaching. Hannes Schneider gave the first ski lessons to tourists in 1907 in **St Anton am Arlberg ❶**, a village that has grown into a first-class ski resort. Others include **Kitzbühel** and **Ischgl**, whose slopes lead into Switzerland, and **St Johann** and **Seefeld** in Tyrol – usually sleepy villages whose population is greatly outnumbered by winter visitors.

The **Tyrol** is the best known of the ski regions, but good skiing is by no means limited to that province. Next

to Vorarlberg is the **Montafon Valley**, gateway to the Silvretta High Alpine Road, with 3,312-metre (10,863ft) **Piz Buin** towering in the background. The Montafon was the site of Austria's first ski championships after World War II, and the story is told of the local official who wanted to provide good food for the participants in the event. He managed to acquire two cows, even though meat was severely rationed at the time. The people dined well, but the official spent six months in jail for his hospitality. Interestingly,

Main attractions

TYROL
INNSBRUCK
GROSSGLOCKNER HIGH
  ALPINE ROAD
VILLACH
GRAZ
SALZBURG
ABBEY OF MELK
WACHAU
KREMS AN DER DONAU

LEFT: Wilten Abbey Church. **BELOW:** National Games competitor.

Cows graze the green pastures in summer.

BELOW: Parish Cathedral of St James and mountain backdrop, near Innsbruck.

Montafoners are descended from the Rhaeto-Romansch civilisation, as their dialect and place names attest.

The Tyrol and the Vorarlberg reach like an arm between Germany to the north and Switzerland and Italy to the south; it is no wonder that the Montafon folk so closely resemble the Engadine Swiss, and the Tyroleans are hard to tell from their Bavarian cousins.

Innsbruck

Just as the Tyrol juts between countries, the province of **Salzburgerland** juts into the Tyrol and touches the Italian border, for practical purposes cutting the East Tyrol district off from its provincial capital, **Innsbruck ❷**. (The connecting section of country was chopped off and passed to Italian control in 1919.)

The city had its Golden Age as the residence of the House of Habsburg in the 15th and 16th centuries, and reached its prime under the reign of Emperor Maximilian I (1493–1516). Trade and manufacturing flourished, as well as architecture. Many of the city's landmarks hail from this period.

A tour of the Old Town

Innsbruck's Old Town (Altstadt) is oval-shaped and constitutes a precious assembly of medieval architecture. It is bordered by the **River Inn** and the streets of **Marktgraben, Burggraben** and **Herrengasse**. Almost every street offers a view of the peaks of "**The Two Thousand**" mountain ("die Zeitausender") nearby. The narrow lanes in the centre have been turned into a pedestrian precinct, allowing visitors to stroll without hindrance past the pergolas, oriel windows, painted facades and stucco ornaments. Another way of viewing these architectural treasures is by hiring one of the horse-drawn carriages that wait on Rennweg, in front of the **Tyrolean Provincial Theatre** (Tiroler Ländestheater).

Herzog-Friedrich-Strasse leads straight into the heart of the Old Town to **Golden Roof** (Goldenes Dachl), a magnificent mansion built around 1500 in the late Gothic style. It was added to the **New Palace** (Neuer Hof) in commemoration of the betrothal of Maximilian I and Maria Bianca Sforza, daughter of the Duke of Milan. The decorative balcony, adorned with 2,738 gilt copper shingles, served as a box for spectators watching tournaments and plays in the square below. It is Innsbruck's best-known landmark.

Herzog-Friedrich-Strasse is known for a string of medieval houses among which **Trautsonhaus**, built during the transition from the Gothic to the Renaissance period, and **Katzunghaus** with its unique reliefs on the balcony dating back to 1530, are especially noteworthy. Another landmark is the 56-metre (180ft) **City Tower** (Stadtturm) built in 1360 as a watchtower against fire. There is a 33-metre (110ft) gallery, which has a magnificent view of the whole town and the mountains. The sights include the **Ottoburg**, a residential tower on the embankment built in 1495, and the **Burgriesenhaus** in **Hofgasse**, which Duke Siegmund built in 1490 for his court favourite, Niklas Haidl, a 2.4-metre (7ft 10in) giant.

In the opposite direction through Pfarrgasse is Domplatz (at the rear of Golden Roof). It is the location of Innsbruck's **Parish Cathedral of St James** (Domkirche zu Jakob; daily), which, with its twin towers, represents a splendid example of Baroque architecture. A copy of *Mariahilf* (Our Lady of Succour) by Lukas Cranach the Elder adorns the high altar.

Renaissance building boom

No other place in Austria conveys such a vivid impression of 16th-century architecture as the eastern part of the Old Town. The 15th-century **Hofburg** (Imperial Palace; daily) was rebuilt from 1754 to 1773 in late Rococo style. One highlight of the guided tours is the Giant's Hall (Riesensaal), a two-storey stateroom with Rococo stucco-work and portraits of the imperial family. The **Imperial Church** (Hof-kirche) houses the **Mausoleum of Maximilian I**, although he was actually buried in Wiener Neustadt near Vienna. Twenty-eight of his forebears and contemporaries, all cast as larger-than-life bronze statues, stand guard around the grave.

To the east of the Imperial Church, in an old Franciscan monastery, is the **Folk Art Musuem** (Tiroler Volkskunst-museum; daily), which contains 20 rustic interiors from various periods, as well as costumes from different social classes and art illustrating the creativity of the Tyrolean people.

Leading to the south from Herzog-Friedrich-Strasse is Innsbruck's principal thoroughfare, Maria Theresien Strasse, where **St Anne's Column** (Anna Säule) commemorates 26 July 1703, St Anne's Day, when the Bavarian troops forced the inhabitants out of Innsbruck during the War of the Spanish Succession (1701–14). Leopoldstrasse, to the south, leads both to Wilten Abbey Church (Stift-skirche Wilten), founded in 1138 by the Premonstratensians, and to the **Wilten Basilica** (Basilika Wilten), built in 1755 on the foundations of a previous building. The abbey church as it stands today was completed in 1670. It is regarded as one of the loveliest churches of the early Baroque period in Austria, and the basilica ranks highly as an example of Rococo.

The former residence of Archduke Ferdinand, **Ambras Castle** (Schloss Ambras), lies 3.2km (2 miles) southeast of the city. Today the castle is a museum housing a substantial art and armour collection from the 16th century. In the age of chivalry, Innsbruck was a major jousting place, where the cream of Europe's knights used to gather for their tournaments to seek the favour of the young ladies of the castle.

Olympic legacy

In 1964 and 1976 Innsbruck hosted a different kind of games: the Winter Olympics. An imposing legacy of the games just outside the city in front of Bergisel is the stadium seating 28,000 spectators, while a new Zaha Hadid-designed **Olympic ski jump** has replaced the old one, its tower providing great views. Also remaining from the games is the bobsleigh

Innsbruck is the gateway to a variety of ski areas in the Tyrol region. The Stubai Alps, south-west of the city, are easily accessible; Neustift, at 1,000 metres (3,300ft) above sea level, is perhaps the best-known resort.

BELOW: the decorative balcony of Golden Roof.

Klagenfurt's Dragon Fountain has become the emblem of the city, now that the legendary creature no longer terrifies the local population.

BELOW: a street musician gets a young audience.

run at **Igls**, a popular holiday resort located a short distance outside the city. You can experience flying down the run with a professional driver from December to March.

The reputation of **Kitzbühel ❸** as a chic winter sports centre dates from the triple Olympic victory in 1956 of local boy Toni Sailer – the "Kitz Comet". The famous **Hahnenkamm** races, in the mountains to the west of the centre, and the **Kitzbüheler Horn** to the east, also ensure that the Kitzbühel skiing area attracts top enthusiasts from all over the world. In summer, the relatively tame Kitzbühel Alps afford an extensive range of mountain walks; for those who prefer it steeper, rockier and more challenging, there are the vast limestone peaks of the **Wilder Kaiser**. The best starting point for a mountain walk is **St Johann**, the resort town lying in the valley between the Kitzbüheler Horn and the Wilder Kaiser.

The East Tyrol and the provinces of Salzburgerland and Kärnten (Carinthia) converge at the **Grossglockner**, the highest point in Austria at 3,797 metres (12,460ft). At its foot glistens the **Pasterze Glacier**. The best view of both mountain and glacier is from **Franz-Josef-Höhe**, a spur at the end of one branch of **Grossglockner High Alpine Road**. The road (May–Oct) is one of the great Alpine highways beginning at **Bruck** and ending at the mountaineering town of **Heiligenblut** in Carinthia.

Klagenfurt and Lake Wörther

A faster scenic route linking north and south is the motorway, the **Tauernautobahn**, where two large tunnels cut the travel time between Salzburg and the Carinthian capital, **Klagenfurt ❹**. This is a region of lakes and rivers, majestic mountains, gently rolling meadows and secluded valleys. Legend tells of a winged dragon that once struck terror into the hearts of local inhabitants. Its statue, the Dragon Fountain, is immortalised as the emblem of Klagenfurt, in the middle of the Neuer Platz, where most of the lovely houses date from the 17th century.

The town has a number of important historical buildings; **the Golden Goose** (Zur Goldene Gans), listed in records of 1489, was planned as an imperial residence; the **Landhaus**, dating from the 16th century, displays 665 coats of arms, while the Palais Porcia (now a hotel) and town hall also date from the 16th century. There are also no fewer than 22 castles within a radius of a few miles. On the **Magdalensberg** lies the site of the largest archaeological excavations in Austria – a Celtic-Roman town, with an open-air museum (May–mid-Oct daily).

Lake Wörther, lying beside Klagenfurt, is the largest lakeside bathing area in Europe. In spite of its depth of 85 metres (275ft) in places, the water temperature can reach 28°C (83°F). Numerous resorts adorn the lakeshore including **Krumpendorf**, **Pörtschach**

Velden and **Maria Wörth**. A further attraction beside the lake is **Minimundus** (Apr–Oct daily), a miniature world on a grand scale, where there are more than 140 replicas of famous buildings, a miniature railway and a harbour with model ships. Carinthia has over 1,200 lakes, providing excellent beaches, sports facilities and amenities in idyllic surroundings to suit all tastes.

North of Klagenfurt is the pilgrimage town of **Gurk** ❺. Here, the 12th-century Cathedral is the finest example of Romanesque architecture in Austria; decorated with magnificent 13th-century frescoes, it shelters the shrine of Hemma, a beloved Austrian saint.

Villach ❻, a chic and historic town, lies at the centre of the Carinthian Lake District. The Romans built a fort and a bridge over the Drava here during the 1st century AD, constructing paved roads as they did so, and the town became the economic and cultural centre of Carinthia in the 16th century. Paracelsus spent his youth here and described the healing powers of the springs which were to move Napoleon to rapturous enthusiasm. Even

today, the warm waters offer relaxation and healing to guests from all over the world in the cure and bathing centres.

Styria

Further east is **Graz** ❼, the capital of Styria and the second-largest Austrian city, with a population of 250,000. The Italian influence on the architecture of the city is unmistakable, notably the town hall, the late Gothic Franciscan Church (1520) and the Renaissance-style Landhaus. Other architectural jewels include the Castle, Old University, Cathedral and numerous Baroque palaces. The **Armoury** (Landeszeughaus; Tue–Sun), on the south side of the Landhaus, is one of the finest in the world, with 15th-century suits of armour, two-handed swords, shields, muskets, guns and rifles all on view. The **Schlossberg**, the dolomite rock 470 metres (1,550ft) high, can be ascended by funicular, a glass lift or on foot. It is crowned by the **Uhrturm** (Clock Tower; 28 metres/90ft high and with a clock dating from 1712), which has become the city landmark and is visible for miles around.

*Some 40km (25 miles) west of Graz lies the **Piber Stud Farm**, where the Lipizzaner stallions for the Spanish Riding School in Vienna are bred (daily tours available Nov–Mar, Apr–Oct Tue–Sat).*

BELOW: Altausee, a beautiful setting for a popular Styrian ski resort.

The window boxes in Salzburg are usually decked with geraniums.

Austrians regard Styria as the "Green Province" of Austria. This second-largest Austrian province includes Alpine topographical forms – perpetual ice and deeply cut ravines – as well as extensive expanses of forest which slowly give way to gently rolling ranges of hills skirting the lower Hungarian Plains.

The town of **Eisenerz** ❽ lies in a wild, romantic basin at the mouth of the Krumpentala and Trofeng valleys. It is also the centre of an ore-mining region and has a well-developed infrastructure for tourists: campsites, climbing school, fitness circuit, footpaths and a lake for bathing. The **Erzberg** (1,465 metres/4,806ft) rises high above the valley floor and is still in use as an opencast iron ore mine. Eisenerz is the ideal starting point for tours up the Erzberg (guided tours May–Oct daily).

Salzburg

BELOW: the piano in Mozart's studio.
BELOW RIGHT: Salzburg, seen from Mönchsberg.

Many towns in Austria are blessed with splendid churches, squares and ornamental fountains; in none but **Salzburg** ❾, however, do they enjoy such a vibrant, cosmopolitan atmosphere and such magnificent surrounding scenery. The birthplace of Wolfgang Amadeus Mozart (1756–91), Salzburg is one of the most visited towns in Austria, especially during the annual festival in tribute to the composer in January. The annual summer Salzburg Festival (www.salzburgerfestspiele.at) also bears Mozart's indelible stamp. His birthplace at **Getreidegasse 9** is now a museum (Mozarts Geburtshaus; daily) with many mementoes of his life, including his violin.

Traditionally the summer festival of drama, operas and concerts opens with Hugo von Hofmannsthal's *Jedermann* (Everyman), a morality play performed in the **Cathedral Square** (Domplatz).

The **Mönchsberg** and the **Burgberg** – the two mountains within the city boundaries – still stand sentinel over the narrow alleys of the **Old Town**, with their tall, narrow merchants' houses, arcaded courtyards, Baroque-domed churches, palaces and spacious squares of the prince-bishops' quarter. Clinging to the side of Mönchsberg, and dominating the Old Town, is the

fortress **Festung Hohensalzburg** (daily), a symbol of the powerbase that shaped so many chapters in the city's history. Archbishop Gebhard began its construction in 1077, and the castle was continuously expanded until the 17th century. It includes staterooms, a torture chamber and an observation tower.

The countryside around Salzburg is worth exploring, especially the pretty village of **Hallstatt** and its lake, the **Hallstättersee** (12km/7 miles south of Bad Ischl). The lake is surrounded on all sides by dramatic mountain scenery and its clear, deep waters make it ideal for swimming and scuba diving.

The Wachau

The **Brucknerhaus**, which opened in 1974 in **Linz** ❿, is the location of the annual Bruckner Festival. Anton Bruckner (1824–96), "God's musician", as he was dubbed, is a great favourite among Austrian people. The Danube flows through the town, which boasts Austria's most modern port. It is an industrial city, but pretty in spite of that, especially around the **main square** (Hauptplatz). A white marble Trinity Column stands in the centre, and among the buildings surrounding the square are the **Old City Hall**, built in 1513, and the **Old Cathedral** (Jesuit Church) with its twin spires.

The River Danube meanders across the north of Austria, past woods and fields, through cities, in the shadow of churches and abbeys. The spectacular Benedictine **Abbey of Melk** ⓫ (Stift Melk; daily, in Nov–Mar guided tours only), its side facade some 340 metres (1,115ft) long, is poised in all its Baroque splendour on a promontory, and gives a fine view of the river and its valley. Apricot blossoms and Richard the Lionheart, the waves of the Danube, castles, fish and wine are all aspects of this charming river region known as the **Wachau**.

Dürnstein, in a beautiful setting, is probably the region's most popular village. At the end of the 12th century, Richard the Lionheart, King of England,

was captured on his return from a crusade and languished in the dungeons of Dürnstein castle. According to legend, Blondel, his faithful minstrel, set off to find him and eventually struck up the first bars of Richard's favourite song beneath the impregnable fortress. Soon afterwards Richard was released, following payment of a huge ransom by the English (the money was used to finance the building of Vienna's first city wall).

A few miles downstream is **Krems an der Donau** ⓬, the "Model City for Historical Preservation". The town lies nestled among terraced vineyards, clinging to the bank of the Danube. Every visitor to the Wachau should taste the region's fine wines and, in particular, its apricot brandy. The entire valley is filled with apricot trees, whose early springtime blossom turns the countryside into a spectacle of great beauty.

The river continues past the villages of the **Vienna Woods**, such as Heiligenkreuz, with its 12th-century Cistercian abbey, and Sooss, a classic wine-growing village. Further on from here, the Vienna High Road affords a magnificent view of the capital. ❑

Sunset reflected in the gleaming glass of the Brucknerhaus, where the Bruckner Festival is held each September.

BELOW: the Old Cathedral in Linz main square.

EUROPE'S BEST FESTIVALS

Noisy, colourful, passionate affairs, festivals in Europe often show few signs of their religious roots; many are well worth seeking out

From earthy fun to highbrow culture, Europe has a busy programme of recurring (usually annual) festivals. Several of them are internationally renowned and are worth going out of the way to see or even building a trip around.

Broadly, festivals divide into two kinds, the traditional and the contemporary. Traditional festivities are often religious in form, although even these may have pagan roots and usually derive from the customs and necessities of country life – giving thanks for fertility, a good harvest and the changing of the seasons. More recently created festivals invariably celebrate some particular performing art: opera, classical music, rock, pop, jazz, theatre, dance, film, etc. – or a mixture of all of these and more. Usually entrance to the main events in these kind of festivals is by ticket only, but there are likely to be other things going on in the streets for free.

Both kinds of festival are concentrated into the summer months when the weather is warm enough for things to happen outdoors, and several take place in spectacular locations against the backdrop of some ancient building or in the grounds of a château.

To get the best out of Europe's festivals you need to plan ahead. Note that the most popular events tend to get booked up well in advance, and the same goes for accommodation. By the same token, festival time is not the best time for sightseeing. Monuments and museums may well be closed, and the crowds can make a city difficult to negotiate your way around.

LEFT: Mark Ronson at the Montreux Festival in Switzerland, an annual lakeside event that draws top-line performers and large crowds.

ABOVE: the Oktoberfest in Munich has been running since 181͘ Huge amounts of beer are drunk and vast quantities of mea and sausages consumed over a period of 16 days in autumn.

CARNIVAL EXTRAVAGANZAS

Many countries across Western Europe, especially those with a significant Catholic population – including Spain, Portugal, Italy, Germany and Belgium – celebrate Carnival. This takes place on the days leading up to Shrove Tuesday (Mardi Gras), the start of the Christian fast of Lent, which falls sometime between early February and early March. The most famous European Carnival is in Venice. Other major ones include Cologne in Germany, Binche in Belgium *(pictured above)* and Cádiz in Spain.

Carnival developed as a time for ordinary people to buck the Church's authority before knuckling under for the fast. It involves dressing up, street parades, music and generally licentious behaviour. The word "Carnival" is often used for events at other times of year that have nothing to do with the traditional festival, except for sharing the same spirit of an anything-goes street party.

OVE: effigies are burnt in an ?rmous conflagration at Las as, in Valencia, a hugely popular nd fairly dangerous – festival in '-March that welcomes spring commemorates San José, ?on saint of carpenters.

ABOVE: the Palio, held in the Campo in Siena, is one of the wildest and most exciting horse races in the world.

LEFT: a very young and serious penitent taking part in a Semana Santa (Holy Week) procession in Madrid, a sombre and impressive ritual.

RIGHT: the statue of the Virgin Mary is carried in procession in Fátima, Portugal, where she is believed to have appeared to three shepherd children in 1917.

ITALY

Italian art and architecture draw the visitors, as do the stunning landscapes, pretty villages and the country's reputation for good food and wine

The Italian boot, which dips its toes into the middle of the Mediterranean, has the Apennine hills running up it and is divided between the more businesslike north and the Mezzogiorno, the poorer, agricultural south. It is said that a man's assets in the north are his shares and property. In the south a man's only asset is his honour: thus even a poor man can be rich. The two halves are divided by Rome, which is on roughly the same latitude as New York.

Every town has its Duomo and each region has its own architectural style, from the Byzantine buildings of Ravenna and the elegant Renaissance monuments of Tuscany to the lavish Baroque of Lecce. Every town has at least one piazza: in the south they are crowded with men smoking and playing cards; in the north, the men are still there, but so are the women and the tourists. In Italy the past is always present: a housing development rises above a crumbling Roman wall; ultra-modern museums display pre-Roman artefacts; old people in mountain villages preserve centuries-old customs, while the young embrace the latest styles of Armani and Versace.

There are few idle pastimes more rewarding than observing Italians going about their lives. They are past masters at showing off, at preserving *la bella figura*. Both their public and social life is intricate and intriguing. Governments lurch from one crisis to another and scandals regularly invade public lives.

This is the country that inspires imagination in the dull, passion in the cold-hearted, rebellion in the conventional. Whether you spend your time under a colourful beach umbrella on the Riviera, shopping in Milan or diligently examining churches and museums, you cannot be unchanged by the country. Whether you are struck by the beauty of a church facade rising from a perfectly proportioned piazza, the aroma of freshly carved *prosciutto*, or the sight of a stylish passer-by spied over the foam of your cappuccino, there is the same superb sensation: nowhere else on earth does just living seem so extraordinary. ❑

PRECEDING PAGES: Poggio, in Prato province; gondolas and pigeons in Venice.
LEFT: Basilica of Sant' Ambrogio, Milan. **ABOVE:** girls chatting in front of a Versace shop window; scooters were first designed in Italy.

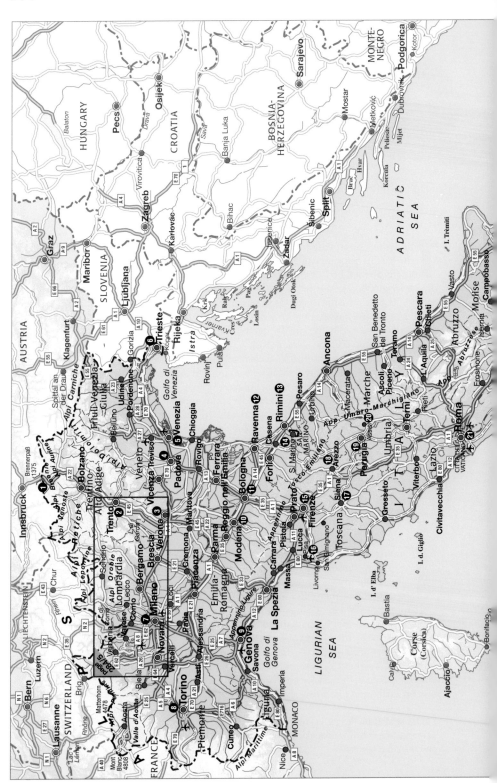

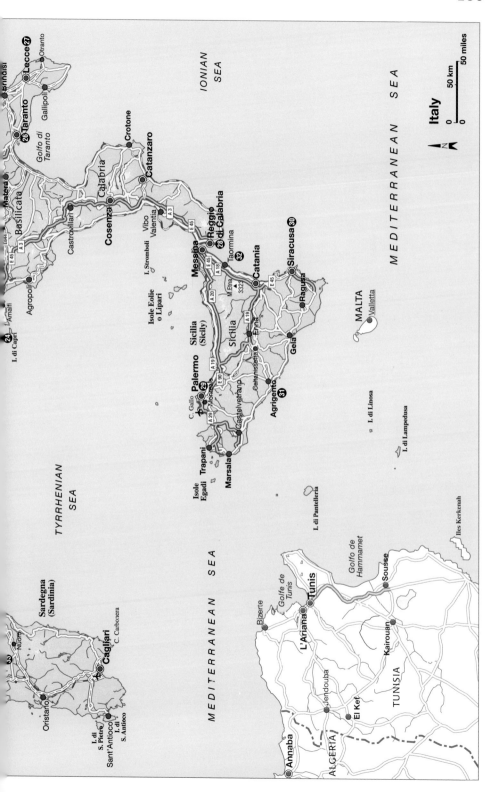

Italy

0 ——— 50 km
0 ——— 50 miles

Rome

0 ———————— 500 m
0 ———————— 500 yds

N

Villa Ruffo

P.za Cinque
Giornate

Via della Giuliana

Via S. Pellico

Viale Angelico

Via A. da Brescia

Via Flaminia

Viale delle Milizie

Via Michelangelo

M Lepanto

Flaminio

P.le Viale
Flaminio

MONTE

Via L. di Savoia

M

S. Maria
d. Popolo

Viale Giulio Cesare

Via M. Colonna

S. Vincenzo
d. Paoli

P.za del Popolo

PINICO

VILI
MED

P.le
degli Eroi

M
Ottaviano-
san Pietro

S. Gioacchino

Via in Augusta

Casa di
Goethe

Villa Me

Via Candia

Via Leone IV

Via Barletta

Via Vespasiano

Via Ottaviano

Via F. Massimo

Via Cola di Rienzo

Via Gracchi

PRATI

Boezio

Via del Corso

P.za di
S. Maria
d. Grazie

SS. Rosario

Via Crescenzio

Via Cicerone

Chiesa
Valdese

Ara
Pacis

Mausoleo
di Augusto

Scalinata della
Trinità dei Monti

13

Viale Vaticano

P.za del
Risorgimento

P.za
Cavour

Via V.
Colonna

Ponte
Cavour

Lgt. in Augusta

P.za
Spa

S. Carlo
al Corso

GIARDINI
CITTÀ DEL
VATICANO

Pinacoteca
Musei
Vaticani

Borgo Pio

Castel
Sant'Angelo

23

Ex Palazzo
di Giustizia

Mausoleo
di Adriano

P.za
Tribunali

Palazzo
Borghese

S. Lorenzo

Palazzo
Ruspoli

Prop

Lgt. Marzio

S. Antonio
d. Portoghesi

S. Sil

VATICANI

24

Cappella
Sistina

Palazzo
Giraud

S. Maria in
Traspontina

Via d. Conciliazione

Giovanni XXIII

Museo
Napoleonico

Palazzo
Montecitorio

Galler
Alber
Sordi

Basilica di
San Pietro

P.za
San Pietro

Ponte
S. Angelo

Lgt. Tor di Nona

S. Salvatore

P.za
Cinque
Lune

S. Agostino

P.za S. Agostino

Palazzo
Chigi

Colonna

Aula delle
Udienze Pontificie

Palazzo del
Sant'Uffizio

S. Spirito
in Sassia

Ponte Pr.
Amedeo

Palazzo
Taverna

Palazzo
Gov. Vecchio

11

S. Luigi d.
Francesi

S.
Ignazio

Via Aurelia

L.go di P.
Cavalleggeri

Via d. P.ta
Cavalleggeri

P.za
d. Rovere

S. Giovanni
d. Fiorentini

Palazzo
Sacchetti

Chiesa
Nuova

Corso V.

S. Agnese
in Agone

Navona

Palazzo Madama

10

Pantheon

S. Ivo

S. Maria
s. Minerva

Via del Corso

Divi
Gregorio VII

S. Maria
alle Fornaci

Via delle Fornaci

S. Onofrio

Lgt. Gianicolense

Emanuele II

Pal. d.
Cancelleria

Pal.
Braschi

S. Andrea
d. Valle

Galleria
Doria Pamphilj

Via Gregorio VII

Chiesa
dell' Annunziata

S. Eligio

Campo
de' Fiori

Museo
Barracco

Area
Sacra

Gesù

V. d. Plebiscito

Pal.
Venezia

Mon. Naz.a Vit
Eman

Via della Cava Aurelia

Palazzo
Corsini

(Galleria Nazionale
d'Arte Antica)

22

Villa
Farnesina

21

Palazzo
Farnese

Lgt. dei Tebaldi

Tevere (Tiber)

Palazzo
Spada

Palazzo
Cenci

Palazzo
Mattei

Teatro di
Marcello

Palazzo
Cenci

Via del Teatro di Marcello

C
Ca

VILLA
ABAMELEK

Villa
Lante

P.le
Garibaldi

Palazzo
Torlonia

P.za
Trilussa

Museo di
Roma in
Trastevere

Lgt. Sanzio

I. Tiberina

Lgt. dei Cenci

Pierleoni

4

S. Nic
in Ca

Porta
S. Pancrazio

Via
Garibaldi

S. Maria in
Trastevere

20

S. Cristogono

Palazzo d.
Congregaz.

Ponte
Garibaldi

S. Bartolomeo
all'Isola

Ponte
Rotto

Lgt. d. Anguillara

B
d. V

Via Aurelia Antica

Il Vascello

Viale delle Mura

P.le
Aurelio

Via
Garibaldi

Via L. Manara

Sidney
Sonnino

S. Cecilia in
Trastevere

Tempio
di Vesta

19

S. M
Cos

Villa Doria
Pamphili

P.za S.
Pancrazio

Gianicolensi

Villa
Sciarra

Via di Trastevere

TRASTEVERE

Via E.
Morosini

Palazzo
d. Esami

S. Francesco
a Ripa

Porto di Ripa Grande

RIP

Mo

Via Vitellia

Via G.
Induno

P.za Porta
Portese

S. Sabin

Via Pio Fra

Via Fontelana

Via Alessandro Poerio

S. Maria
Regina
Pacis

P.za Ippolito
Nievo

Via Portuense

Via Testaccio

Via
Giovanni Branca

S. Alessio

Priorato
di Malta

P.za
dell'Emporio

S. Anselmo

P.za
Donna
Olimpia

Via di Donna Olimpia

Via G. Gunizzelli

Via G. Cavalcanti

Viale di Trastevere

Via Portuense

TESTACCIO

Via Nicola Galvani

L.go Manlio
Gelsomini

P.za
S. P

P.za
Madona
della Saletta

Via G. Ghislieri

MACRO al
Mattatoio

Ponte
Testaccio

MONTE
TESTACCIO

Via B. Franklin

Via Marmorata

P.ta S. Paolo
Piramide di
Caio Cestio

Ost

Lgt. Aventino

Sta
S.

ROME

Follow in the footsteps of emperors and saints, discovering the monuments and churches that mark Rome as the capital of Italy and the ancient world

The best introduction to Rome is the **Palatine Hill ❶** (Palatino; daily; combined ticket with the Forum and Colosseum). It was here, the story goes, that Romulus and Remus were brought up by a wolf in a cave and, as if to show that there is more to myth than mere legend, archaeologists have discovered traces of Iron Age huts that date back to the 8th century BC.

Byron's description of the romantic pastoral ruins still rings true: *Cypress and ivy, weed and wallflower grown/ Matted and mass'd together, hillocks heap'd/ On what were chambers, arch crush'd, column strown/ In fragments, choked up vaults, and frescos steep'd/ In subterranean damps…* You can wander around the romantic ruins of imperial dwellings, see the frescoes in the newly opened **House of Augustus** (Domus Augusti) and trace the long history of the Palatine in the **Palatine Museum** (Museo Palatino; daily).

Heart of ancient Rome

Below the Palatine lies the **Roman Forum ❷** (Foro Romano; daily), ancient Rome's commercial and political centre. In the fading light, and with some imagination, the stark columns and ghostly white blocks of weather-beaten marble take on flesh and life. The Forum emerges for a few minutes again as the magnificent civic and religious heart and soul of the world. And if there are pieces missing, the blame must be placed squarely on successive popes and the noble families of Rome who, for more than a millennium, have used the Forum as a convenient quarry to provide stones for their palaces. The star attraction is the **Arch of Septimius Severus** (Arco di Settimio Severo), built in 203 after the emperor had conquered the Parthians and made Mesopotamia a new province of Rome.

Flanking the Forum are the **Imperial Forums** (Fori Imperiali), built by five successive emperors. The new

Main attractions
ROMAN FORUM
CAPITOLINE MUSEUMS
COLOSSEUM
PANTHEON
PIAZZA NAVONA
TREVI FOUNTAIN
GALLERIA BORGHESE
VATICAN CITY

LEFT: houses in Piazza della Rotonda.
BELOW: the ruins of the Forum.

Entertainment in Piazza Venezia.

BELOW: fragments of a colossal statue of Emperor Constantine in the Capitoline Museum.

Museum of the Imperial Forums (Museo dei Fori Imperiali; Tue–Sun) gives access to the best preserved of the five, **Trajan's Forum** (also called Markets of Trajan), dominated by the soaring **Trajan's Column**. The museum helps the visitor understand the evolution of the Forum, from administrative centre of Rome to noble residence, military fortress, prestigious convent and barracks. With the completion of recent restoration work, the architectural changes from these different eras are all visible.

The Capitoline Hill and the Ghetto

Overlooking the Forum, the **Capitoline Hill ❸** (Capitolino) is home to the **Capitoline Museums** (Musei Capi-

tolini; Tue–Sun; www.museicapitolini.org), housed in two palaces – Palazzo Nuovo and Palazzo dei Conservatori – on opposite sides of Michelangelo's **Piazza di Campidoglio**. The collection comprises priceless treasures from ancient Rome, along with works of art by Italian 16th- and 17th-century masters such as Veronese, Titian, Caravaggio and Tintoretto. The equestrian state of Marcus Aurelius on the piazza is a replica – the original is given pride of place in the museum's new glassed-over hall.

On the western side of the hill lies the old Ghetto, near the ruins of the **Theatre of Marcellus ❹**. Although Jews first came to Rome as slaves, their skills were quickly appreciated, but in the 16th century the pope ordered them to live inside a high-walled enclosure. You will still find kosher food here, and the impressive synagogue on Lungotevere dates from the 1870s.

The main streets of modern Rome meet at **Piazza Venezia ❺**, dominated by **Palazzo Venezia**. This palatial Renaissance building served as the headquarters of Benito Mussolini, Italy's dictator from 1922 to 1945; the central

balcony is where Il Duce would stand to address the crowds in the 1930s. Built in 1455 for a Venetian cardinal who later became Pope Paul II, it now houses a collection of art within the **Museo del Palazzo di Venezia** (Tue–Sun). Amongst the items on display are medieval and early Renaissance paintings, sculptures by Bernini, tapestries and armour.

Around the Colosseum

Standing as an awesome monument to Roman ambition (and bloodlust), the **Colosseum ❻** (Colosseo; daily) held up to 55,000 spectators in its heyday in the 1st and 2nd centuries AD. To create space for the building of the Colosseum, Vespasian had drained the lake of the **Golden House ❼** (Domus Aurea; Tue–Fri), a recently restored palace built by the tyrannical Emperor Nero after the fire in AD 64. The conflagration that destroyed much of the city was thought to have been ordered by Nero who, according to Tacitus, then "set up as the culprits and punished with the utmost refinement of cruelty a class hated for their abominations,

who are commonly called Christians." The Golden House was not discovered until the Renaissance, when artists such as Raphael and Michelangelo were excited by the finds that were revealed from the ruins; you can still see the vast rooms of the palace, some with frescoes still intact.

From the Colosseum, Via di San Giovanni in Laterano opens into the **Piazza di San Giovanni in Laterano ❽**, overlooked by the magnificent **Basilica San Giovanni in Laterano**, seat of the popes until the schism in 1309, when they moved to Avignon. It has an imposing facade by Alessandro Galilei and a breathtaking Baroque interior by Borromini. The nearby **Scala Santa** attracts the pious, who climb the stairs on bended knee to reach the Sancta Sanctorum, the private chapel of the pope.

Terme di Caracalla

From the piazza, Via Amba Aradam leads southwest towards the **Baths of Caracalla ❾** (Terme di Caracalla; Tue–Sun and Mon am). Many baths had been built by previous emperors,

TIP

The Domus Aurea has guided tours only, which are in English on Tue–Fri at 11.20am, 12.40pm, 2pm and 3.20pm. For visits and information, tel: 06-3996 7700 or visit www.ticketclic.it.

BELOW: the Colosseum is even more impressive at night.

Detail from the Trevi Fountain, which dates from 1762.

but Antoninus Caracalla was determined to relegate them all to history when construction began in AD 212 on the largest baths Rome had ever seen. Holding up to 1,500 bathers at a time, the baths continued to function until the Goths invaded two centuries later and vandalised the aqueducts that supplied them with water.

Roman baths were a place for social, physical and intellectual pursuits, with stories of less salubrious activities arising from the sessions of mixed bathing. Rich patrons came here with their slaves, but the poor masses were not excluded. The poet Shelley composed his great *Prometheus Unbound* (1820) on a visit to the ruins of the baths, and the cultural associations with the place are evoked each summer when operas are staged here.

The Pantheon

BELOW: the Pantheon.
BELOW RIGHT: Keats's tomb in the Protestant Cemetery.

The **Pantheon** ❿ (daily) was built as a temple in 27 BC, first restored by Emperor Domitian in AD 80 and by Hadrian in the 2nd century. The early Christian emperors kept it closed, along with other buildings that pro-

claimed their paganism, and it was finally converted into a church in the 7th century. The best preserved of all Rome's ancient buildings, its most extraordinary architectural feature is its massive dome, which has a single hole at the very centre of the coffered ceiling, providing the only light. The building of such a structure was an ambitious undertaking; a wooden framework was used to support the tons of masonry that were incorporated into the building, and the total weight was distributed among a set of supporting arches that are built into the walls. The geometrical proportions are such that the diameter is equal in size to the overall height. In 1520 the artist Raphael, in accordance with his own wishes, was buried inside the Pantheon. His restrainted monument contrasts with the huge marble and porphyry sarcophagi of Italian monarchs.

Piazza Navona and Trevi Fountain

The pedestrianised **Piazza Navona** ⓫, west of the Pantheon, lies at the heart of the city, and its pavement restaurants,

MAGRIPPA·L·F·COS·TERTIVM·FECIT

This Grave contains all that was Mortal, of a
YOUNG ENGLISH POET,
Who, on his Death Bed, in the Bitterness of his Heart, at the Malicious Power of his Enemies, Desired these Words to be engraven on his Tomb Stone
"Here lies One Whose Name was writ in Water"
Feb 24ᵗʰ 1821

cafés and *gelaterie* are a great place for people-watching and soaking up the atmosphere. The piazza's centrepiece is Bernini's monumental **Fountain of the Four Rivers.**

Northeast of the Pantheon, the extravagant Baroque **Trevi Fountain** ⓬ (Fontana di Trevi) is a popular rendezvous. Tourists come here to take snapshots and toss coins into the water, which, so the superstition goes, ensures their return to the Eternal City. Designed by Nicola Salvi and completed in 1762, the central figure is Neptune, flanked by two Tritons holding sea creatures.

Spanish Steps

An even more popular meeting place is the **Spanish Steps** ⓭ (Scalinata della Trinità dei Monti), which lead up from the **Piazza di Spagna** to the twin-towered church of the **Trinità dei Monte**, where Mendelssohn listened to the famous choir of nuns who could be heard but not seen. The steps take their name from the residence of the Spanish Ambassador in the square. Everyone gathers here to watch the

world go by, as they have done for centuries. The **Keats-Shelley House** (Mon–Sat) is the place where the poet John Keats died in 1827; Henry James stayed at the Hotel Inghilterra; Goethe lived nearby at No. 18 Via del Corso, where there is a museum devoted to his travels in Italy.

Via Veneto and Villa Borghese

Via Veneto, Rome's Hollywood Boulevard, became synonymous with *La Dolce Vita* (the sweet life) after Federico Fellini's film of that name.

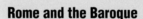

Most visitors spend some time sitting on the Spanish Steps, just watching the world go by.

BELOW LEFT: the ever-popular Trevi Fountain.

Rome and the Baroque

The Baroque movement (1600–1750) was born in Rome, and nurtured by a papal campaign to make the city one of unparalleled beauty "for the greater glory of God and the Church". One artist to answer the call was Caravaggio (1573–1610), whose early secular portraits of sybaritic youths revealed him to be a painfully realistic artist. His later monumental religious painting entitled *The Calling of St Matthew*, in San Luigi dei Francesci, shocked the city by setting a holy act in a contemporary tavern.

The decoration of the interior of St Peter's by Gianlorenzo Bernini (1598–1680) was more acceptable to the Romans: a bronze tabernacle with spiralling columns at the main altar; a magnificent throne with angels clustered around a burst of sacred light at the end of the church; and, for the exterior, the classically simple colonnade embracing the piazza (1657).

Bernini's rival was Francesco Borromini (1599–1667), whose eccentric designs were the opposite of Bernini's classics. Many of Borromini's most famous designs hinge on a complex interplay of concave and convex surfaces, which can be seen in the undulating facades of San Carlo alle Quattro Fontane, Sant'Ivo, and Sant'Agnese in Piazza Navona (1653–63).

Close-up of Bernini's Fontana dei Fiumi in Piazza Navona.

The pavement cafés are still there, along with white-aproned waiters, but film stars nowadays are few and far between and the café tables overlook bumper-to-bumper traffic.

Stretching north from the Via Veneto is the **Villa Borghese**, whose gardens provide respite from the heat and hassle of the city. Here you'll find an artificial lake, fountains and follies, a zoo and various museums and galleries, but the cultural highlight is the **Galleria Borghese** ⓴ (Tue–Sun; reservations compulsory; www.galleria borghese.it; tel: 06-841 3979) within the Baroque Villa Borghese. The exquisite art collection of Cardinal Scipione Borghese includes works by Raphael, Titian, Caravaggio, Bernini – and Canova's famous marble sculpture of Napoleon's sister, Pauline, depicted as a topless, reclining Venus.

The masterwork of Gianlorenzo Bernini

Sant' Andrea al Quirinale ⓯, on Via del Quirinale, is reckoned by many to be the finest example of the work of Bernini (1598–1680), the Baroque genius who, more than any other architect, has left his mark on Rome. The interior decoration of this church is supreme justification for the high esteem in which Bernini is held; every inch is covered with gilt and marble, and *putti* ascend the walls as if in a cloud of smoke. The church was built for the Jesuits, but there is nothing spartan about the rooms of St Stanislas Kostka, a Polish saint who is celebrated in rich marble by Pierre Legros.

Bernini was one of a handful of leading architects who built the Baroque **Palazzo Barberini** to the north of Via del Quirinale, and his work also features inside in its **National Gallery of Ancient Art** ⓰ (Galleria Nazionale d'Arte Antica; Tue–Sun), a priceless collection of medieval, Renaissance and Baroque art.

Northeast of Palazzo Barberini, the church of **Santa Maria della Vittoria** ⓱ is home to one of Bernini's most ambitious undertakings, the *Ecstasy of St Theresa*. This depiction of the 17th-century Spanish mystic evokes for many visitors a sense of sensual ecstasy rather than the physical pain that

might seem more appropriate. Bear in mind, however, St Theresa's own description of her feelings when God sent an angel down to pierce her with an arrow: "The pain was so sharp that I cried aloud but at the same time I experienced such delight that I wished it would last for ever."

The tomb of Bernini lies in the church of **Santa Maria Maggiore** ⑱ to the south, reached by Via Torino. This great basilica manages to combine a variety of architectural styles more successfully than any other church in the city. The basilica was built in the 5th century, the marble floor and the belltower are medieval, the ceiling is unmistakably a product of the Renaissance, while the twin domes and imposing front and rear facades are pure Baroque. Inside the church there are stunning mosaics dating from the 5th century in the nave and on the triumphal arch, and medieval mosaics in the loggia and apse.

Across the Tiber

Trastevere, from *trans Tiberim* ("over the Tiber"), was a working-class, bohemian neighbourhood, which has developed into a trendy and colourful tourist quarter, with atmospheric restaurants and bars. It is also popular for the Porta Portese flea market which bursts into life every Sunday morning. You can buy anything here from fake icons to fashion items; and it's always worth bargaining. There are two churches of note in Trastevere. **Santa Cecilia** ⑲ (daily, with lunchtime closure) is dedicated to the patron saint of music, who was martyred in AD 230; the church was founded on the site of her execution. The artistic highlight is a fresco of *The Last Judgement* by Pietro Cavallini (*c.*1290) in the adjoining gallery.

Santa Maria in Trastevere ⑳ (daily; free) is one of the oldest churches in Rome, and its foundation is credited to Pope Callixtus I in the 3rd century, when Christianity was still a minority cult. The chief attractions are the 12th- and 13th-century mosaics, especially those by Cavallini depicting the life of the Virgin Mary.

A little way north, close to the Tiber, is the Renaissance **Villa Farnesina** ㉑ (Mon–Sat am), built for a wealthy papal

TIP

An excellent source of information is the Rome Call Centre, www.060608.it, tel: 060608 (add 00 39 if calling from abroad), with English-speaking operators. You can call daily from 9am–9pm to reserve tickets for museums, shows and events, book hotels or find out information on local transport. Tickets can be paid for by credit card and picked up at the venue.

BELOW: the Castel Sant'Angelo, the setting for the last act of Puccini's *Tosca.*

TIP

Sightseers who are using public transport should consider purchasing the 3-day Roma Pass (see page 414).

banker who commissioned Raphael and his pupils to decorate the interior. Some of the works still survive.

Across the road, the late Baroque **Palazzo Corsini** houses part of the collection of the **National Gallery of Ancient Art ㉒** (Galleria Nazionale d'Arte Antica; Tue–Sun), which includes works by Rubens, Van Dyck, Caravaggio, Tintoretto, Poussin and Guido Reni.

Castel Sant'Angelo

Dominating the Tiber to the north are the mighty brick walls of **Castel Sant'Angelo ㉓** (Tue–Sun), linked to the city by the ancient Ponte Sant'Angelo. The castle started life as a mausoleum for Emperor Hadrian in AD 139 and was later adapted as a fortress, a prison and a hideout for popes (a secret passageway links it to the Vatican). Over 50 rooms charter its remarkably chequered history, from its dark prison cells to the lavish Renaissance papal apartments. If time is short, seek out the frescoes by Perin del Vaga and Pellegrino Tibaldi that play little tricks with the eye in

BELOW:
an overview of
St Peter's Square.

the style of a 16th-century Magritte, and admire the views from the terrace which provided the scene for the last act of Puccini's *Tosca*.

St Peter's Square

From Castel Sant' Angelo, Via della Conciliazione leads to the **Vatican City ㉔** (Città del Vaticano; *see opposite; see also Microstates, page 358*). **St Peter's Square** (Piazza San Pietro) is packed when the pope appears on the balcony to address and bless the vast crowds (This happens on most Sundays at noon and, provided the weather is fine, also on Wednesdays at 10.30am; tel: 06-6988 4947). When the square was begun by Bernini in 1656, the effect he intended for his grand colonnades, which sweep into an embrace (some say a claw) of **St Peter's** was quite different from what is experienced today. His idea was to surprise the pilgrim visitor with a sudden view of the basilica, but when the Via della Conciliazione was built in the 1930s it provided a distant view of the church and so now acts as the monumental approach to St Peter's. ❑

The Vatican

The Vatican is an anomaly, a sovereign city within a city. A place of pilgrimage for devout Catholics, it is on every visitor's itinerary

Rome and the Vatican have lived for more than one and a half millennia in symbiosis, not always perfect, not always happy, but always mutually rewarding. Rome is where the Church gained its martyrs, where Emperor Constantine had made Christianity the predominant religion by the time of his death in AD 337. In return, the Vatican eventually gave Rome another empire, a spiritual and a political one, at times almost as powerful as the worldly one lost to the barbarians.

Vatican is the name given to a hill on the right bank of the Tiber. There Emperor Nero completed a circus which Gaius (Caligula) had built and adorned with an obelisk brought from Egypt (the one which now rises in the middle of St Peter's Square). Early Christians were tortured here, and Emperor Constantine gave the land to the church where, over the grave of St Peter, who had been martyred in the Neronian persecutions of AD 64, a place of worship was built that developed into the vast complex to be seen today. St Peter's Church is the largest in Christendom, and some 700 million Catholics are governed from this walled-in hill known as the Vatican City.

There is plenty to see and do, beginning perhaps with the purchase of some Vatican stamps and the posting of a card from the Vatican post office or a climb up the 244 stairs to the top of St Peter's Dome. As you enter St Peter's, on the right, Michelangelo's *Pietà* still enthrals, as it first did in 1499 when the artist finished it at the age of 25. Since being vandalised in 1972, the marble sculpture has been enclosed by glass. Further up the nave is the bronze statue of St Peter, its toe worn away by the countless kisses of pious pilgrims. A highly ornate Baroque canopy by Bernini dominates the nave above the Papal Altar where only the pope may conduct Mass.

The **Vatican Museums** (Mon–Sat 8.30am–6pm, last Sun of the month 9am–1.45pm, closed Catholic holidays) comprise eight museums, five galleries and the Borgia Apartments, with tours culminating in the star attractions: the Stanze di Raffaello (Raphael Rooms) and Michelangelo's **Cappella Sistina** (Sistine Chapel). The walls of this famous chapel are covered in frescoes by Botticelli (*Temptations of Christ*, with the devil disguised in a monk's habit, and *Punishment of the Rebels*), Ghirlandaio *(Calling of St Peter and St Andrew)* and Perugino (Handing over the Keys to St Peter); the celebrated ceiling was painted by Michelangelo between 1508 and 1512.

Michelangelo worked alone on the ceiling from a specially designed scaffold, and the controversial restoration work of the 1980s has allowed a new generation of visitors to appreciate some of the skill and passion that went into the work. The only subject matter that is not from the Bible's Old Testament is the classical Sibyls, and they only get a nose in because of the highly suspect story that they prophesied the birth of Christ.

"All the world hastened to behold this marvel and was overwhelmed, speechless with astonishment," the 15th-century art historian Vasari wrote of Michelangelo's handiwork. The validity of his judgement may help sustain you as the queue to enter the chapel slowly makes its way forward.   ❑

ABOVE: crowds waiting to see the Pope at St Peter's.
RIGHT: a nun crosses St Peter's Square.

FLORENCE

One of the world's great artistic centres, packed with aesthetic masterpieces, the city is the essential destination for students of Renaissance art and architecture

lorence and the Renaissance are almost synonymous. No city in Italy has produced such an avalanche of genius: Leonardo da Vinci, Michelangelo, Dante, Brunelleschi, Donatello, Machiavelli, Botticelli, Raphael, Fra Angelico, Fra Filippo Lippi, Ghirlandaio, Giotto, Ghiberti, Uccello. No city has so reshaped modern thought and art, nor gathered within its walls such a treasure of local art and architecture. Florentines ushered in the Renaissance and took the arts to heights not even the Greeks had attained.

Magnificent cupola

The beautiful black and white **Cathedral ❶** (Duomo; Mon–Sun) lies at the heart of Florence. Its dome (Mon–Sat), a free-hanging cupola designed by Brunelleschi, has astonished architects and builders for centuries. Florentines refer to it as *Il Cupolone*, the dome of domes. A seemingly endless stairway leads to the lantern gallery where Brunelleschi's building secret is revealed: there are two mutually supporting domes, one shell inside the other. Giotto's free-standing **Campanile** entails another long climb (414 steps), but rewards you with intimate views of the cathedral dome and roofline. Close by, the octagonal Romanesque **Baptistery ❷** (Battistero) is the oldest building in Florence, celebrated for its bronze doors by Ghiberti and inside (daily) wonderful ceiling mosaics.

To see other cathedral treasures, visit the **Museo dell'Opera del Duomo ❸** (Mon–Sun) on the east side of Piazza del Duomo. The Cathedral's museum is full of outstanding sculptures, from Donatello's haggard *Mary Magdalene*, carved in wood in the 1460s, to Michelangelo's unfinished *Pietà*, begun around 1545 .

Michelangelo Buonarroti (1475–1564) was the man who perhaps best symbolises both the greatness and the parochialism of this city. He was, like many Florentines of his time, thrifty and

Main attractions
CATHEDRAL
BAPTISTERY
PIAZZA DELLA SIGNORIA
UFFIZI
BARGELLO
PONTE VECCHIO
ACCADEMIA GALLERY

LEFT: the Uffizi gallery at night.
BELOW: the bronze Baptistery door.

A detail from Botticelli's St John and the Angels *in the Uffizi.*

endowed with a dose of insolence. A firm republican, Michelangelo mourned the public burning in 1498 of the Florentine Dominican friar Girolamo Savonarola, who ruled Florence from 1494 to 1497. Savonarola denounced the sins of the pope and corruption in the Church and, during the Lent Carnival of 1497, organised the "Bonfire of the Vanities", a massive conflagration of books and works of art deemed indecent or frivolous. On the orders of the pope, he was arrested, tortured, hanged and burnt. On the **Piazza della Signoria** ❹ a plaque on the spot pays tribute to this popular orator.

After midnight, it is said, when the city is asleep, a ghostly spectacle appears in this piazza. "The Great White Man", Ammanati's imposing Neptune, climbs from his fountain, walks across the piazza and talks to his friends. Florentines believe he is really the river god Arno, famous for spurning the love of women.

Florentines have believed for centuries that spirits are imprisoned in their marble statues. They believe that the spirits begin to move and talk as soon as the **Uffizi** ❺ (Tue–Sun), one

of the world's greatest art galleries closes down at night. The galleries were built as offices (*uffizi*) alongside the **town hall** (Palazzo Vecchio), and the collection is arranged chronologically so you can trace the development of Florentine art from 13th-century formal Gothic to the Mannerist period of the 16th century. From here it is a short step to the **Bargello** ❻ (Tue–Sat and some Sun and Mon), an outstanding sculpture museum where you can see works by Donatello, Michelangelo, Cellini and Giambologna.

From the Uffizi you can walk across the **Ponte Vecchio** ❼, the historic bridge across the River Arno which dates in its present form from 1345. Some of Italy's finest silver jewellery is made and sold in kiosks lining the bridge and there is always a throng jostling to see it. In boutiques in the Old City, a tradition of leather goods and textiles still flourishes.

Home of the Medicis

On the other side of the bridge, the forbidding-looking **Palazzo Pitti** ❽ home of the Medici Grand Dukes in

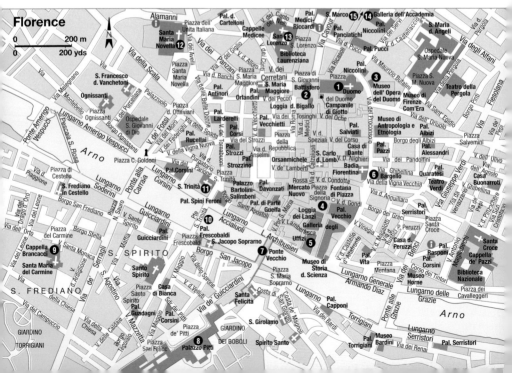

the middle of the 16th century, now houses a number of museums containing art treasures. If you visit only one, make it the **Palatine Gallery** (Galleria Palatina; Tue–Sun), where you can admire masterpieces by Raphael, Titian and Rubens. On the same side of the Arno the **Brancacci Chapel** ❾ (Mon, Wed–Sun), within the church of Santa Maria del Carmine, contains Masaccio's restored fresco cycle of *The Life of St Peter* and *The Expulsion from Paradise*, one of the great works of the early Renaissance.

Back by the River Arno, the **Ponte Santa Trinità** ❿ had a miraculous rebirth after being blown up by retreating Nazis in 1944. After World War II the city launched a frenetic search for the missing head of "Spring", a vital member of the Four Seasons quartet guarding each end of the bridge. It was found at the bottom of the River Arno and, in a noisy procession, taken back to the bridge.

The bridge is named after the nearby church of **Santa Trinità** ⓫, famous for its frescoes by Ghirlandaio, depicting the life of St Francis against a recognisably Florentine background. The church of **Santa Maria Novella** ⓬ to the north is home to Masaccio's celebrated *Trinity* and in its **museum** (Mon–Thur, Sat and Sun) is Paolo Uccello's *Universal Deluge*, a painting that itself fell victim to heavy floods in 1966 but which was not damaged beyond recognition.

To the east, the church of **San Lorenzo** ⓭ (daily) was the Medici family church and contains the tombs of various members of the great dynasty within both the Old Sacristy by Brunelleschi and the New Sacristy by Michelangelo. Affordable and colourful market stalls fill the streets around the church. Find time for a visit to the northeast of this area, where one of the most famous works of world art, Michelangelo's sculpture *David*, is on display in the **Accademia Gallery** ⓮ (Galleria dell'Accademia; Tue–Sun). Worth considering, if your patience is challenged by the length of the queue, is a visit instead to the nearby convent of **San Marco** ⓯ (daily), where the heavenly paintings and frescoes of Fra Angelico are on view. ❏

The Florentines introduced perspective and painted the first nudes of the Renaissance. The original humanist, Petrarch, was born in Florence, and Tuscan scholar Boccaccio initiated literary criticism and wrote the first modern love story.

BELOW: the Ponte Vecchio spans the River Arno.

VENICE

For a millennium the Republic of Venice repelled unwelcome invaders. Now the city built on water embraces a tidal wave of tourists – on its own terms

Map on page 278

I
n the early morning, when the mist still lingers over the lagoon, and the palaces seem to float on water, you may be forgiven for thinking that Venice is only an illusion. Nothing in Venice is ever quite what it seems. The placid lagoon is gnawing at the foundations, having already gobbled up all but 30 of the 490 islands that existed 1,000 years ago. Yesterday's Venetians defended their city for 986 years with bluff, bluster, cunning and masterly diplomacy – and then let it fall without a blow. The city itself, once the bazaar of the world and the centre of cosmopolitan life, today has a fast-declining population and an infrastructure which is threatened by the 20 million tourists that descend here annually, as well as by the high tides which frequently flood its streets and squares.

The republic reached its peak in 1203 with an act of treachery as wicked as it proved expedient. In exchange for allowing the Crusaders to use his port, the blind Doge Enrico Dandolo persuaded the flotilla of 500 ships to ransack Constantinople, capital of Byzantium, the Eastern Roman Empire that had been founded after the sack of Rome. It had become the richest city in the world, and its power and seafaring influence had long been a thorn in the side of Venice.

In 1204, the pious Crusaders sacked Constantinople, murdering the city's inhabitants. As booty, Venice was awarded the legendary "quarter and a half of a quarter" of the Eastern Roman Empire. The priceless monuments and relics looted from Constantinople, and now in St Mark's Basilica, include the Quadriga from the emperor's box at the Hippodrome and the Madonna Nicopeia, a sacred icon which served as the Byzantine battle standard. Venice became the greatest repository of Byzantine art.

Piazza San Marco

Heart of the Venetian Republic, St Mark's Square ❶ (Piazza San Marco)

Main attractions
ST MARK'S BASILICA
PALAZZO DUCALE
GRAND CANAL
ACCADEMIA GALLERY
RIALTO MARKETS
SCUOLA GRANDE DI SAN ROCCO

LEFT: Venetian Carnival mask.
BELOW: Piazza San Marco.

Venice

0   200 m
0   200 yds

is still the city's great showpiece and home to some of its finest monuments. The square teems with tourists and pigeons, while café orchestras play on, determined to see the Grand Old Lady dance to her grave. When Napoleon first set eyes on the gossiping multitudes and lavish decor, he called it "the finest drawing room in Europe". Byron, Dickens, Proust and Wagner all sat at the famous Caffè Florian, which still serves the best (and most expensive) coffee on the piazza; Thomas Mann brooded here in the early 20th century and wrote *Death in Venice*; and Ernest Hemingway drank six bottles of wine a night here while he wrote some of his best prose.

Despite the queues, be sure to visit **St Mark's Basilica ❷** (Basilica di San Marco; Mon–Sun) to see the gold-backed mosaics, carved galleries, jewel-encrusted altar screen (Pala d'Oro) and the original four bronze horses which used to adorn the facade (the Quadriga outside are replicas). A striking feature of the square is the soaring **Campanile**, a replica of the original tower that collapsed in 1902. Inside, a lift (daily) ascends 100 metres (330ft) for a sweeping panorama of the city. The piazza's other tower is the **Clock Tower** (Torre dell'Orologio; pre-booked guided tours only, tel: 041-520 9070), designed in 1496.

Adjoining the piazza and extending to the waterfront is the **Piazzetta San Marco**. On the right as you face the lagoon stands the 16th-century **Libreria Sansoviniana ❸** (daily), also known as the Biblioteca Marciana. Palladio, Italy's greatest 16th-century architect, considered this structure, with its finely sculpted arcades and detailed figures, one of the most beautiful buildings ever constructed. It houses the National Library of St Mark, the Venetian Old Library and the **Archaeological Museum** (daily). Access is via the **Museo Correr** (daily; charge), a notable but often over-looked civic museum devoted to Venetian history and art. Overlooking the lagoon stands the sumptuous, oriental

Palazzo Ducale ❹ (Doge's Palace; daily; charge), residence of the doges, seat of government and home to the law courts and prisons. Behind the palace is the **Bridge of Sighs** (Ponte dei Sospiri), where prisoners from the palace who crossed to the dungeons drew their last breath of free air.

The lagoon end of the square is dominated by two columns bearing St Theodorus and the Lion of Venice. From the wharf where pleasure boats set out for trips around the lagoon, merchant ships used to ride at anchor. *Vaporetti* (water buses) and speedboat taxis stop here, with the remaining gondolas from the flotilla that was once 10,000 strong. The black-lacquered gondolas, half rowed, half punted with a single oar, were multicoloured until 1562, when the City Council decreed that they all had to be black – the proper colour for the vehicles of a serious city.

Along the Grand Canal

The **Grand Canal** (Canal Grande) is the Champs Elysées of Venice; along its winding 3.5km (2-mile) route stand 200 palaces and seven churches.

TIP

The best way to see the Palazzo Ducale without the queues and the crowds is to book a place on Secret Itineraries (Itinerari Segreti), a fascinating behind-the-scenes tour which also gives you (unguided) access to the rest of the palace. Tours take place daily in English at 9.55am, 10.45am and 11.35am, and bookings can be made at the museum information desk the day before the visit or on the same day, depending on availability.

BELOW:
the Palazzo Ducale, once the residence of the doges.

*In January 1996
La Fenice, the historic
opera house where
Verdi's* La Traviata
*was first performed,
was razed to the
ground. It finally rose
from the ashes, with
the plush interior
recreated, and in
November 2004
the first opera to
be performed in
the "new" Fenice
was – fittingly –*
La Traviata.

BELOW: the Rialto
Bridge, thronged
with visitors.

At times this unique waterway is as congested as an urban road. Polished mahogany speedboats jostle for space with the *vaporetti*. Dodging in and out between them are the freight barges, the postman's barge, the milkman, the debt collector, the tourist gondolas and the *traghetti* that ferry pedestrians across the canal.

Venice was one of Europe's largest ports until the 16th century, when the Portuguese navigator Vasco da Gama found a new sea route to the East Indies around the Cape of Good Hope. The discovery ruined the overland spice traffic that had filled Venetian treasuries with revenue far greater than the income of the papacy or the empires of the time.

The all-pervading church of **Santa Maria della Salute ❺** guards the Grand Canal entrance at the San Marco end. The church was built in the 17th century by the city's fathers in gratitude for the deliverance of Venice from the plague. On the same side of the canal, the squat **Palazzo Venier dei Leoni ❻** (Wed–Mon) houses the Guggenheim Collection

of modern art. Classical Venetian art – Bellini, Giorgione, Titian, Tintoretto – is housed further along in the **Galleria dell'Accademia ❼** (Mon–Sun). A great admirer of Venetian painting, the poet Robert Browning (1812–89) died in the **Ca' Rezzonico ❽**, now the museum of 18th-century Venice (Mon–Wed).

Beyond the Volta, on the opposite side, the **Palazzo Corner Spinelli ❾** is a fine example of the early flowering of the Renaissance spirit in Venice; **Palazzo Grimani ❿**, a little further along, represents a final Renaissance flourish from the master Sanmicheli. Up ahead is one of the city's most famous sights, the **Ponte di Rialto ⓫**, built in the late 16th century to replace an original wooden structure that had collapsed. The area around the original bridge was known simply as the Rialto, and in its day it was the Wall Street of Europe. Venetians still go to the Rialto every day to shop in its popular stores and **markets**.

The Grand Canal's most famous palace, the Gothic **Golden Palace ⓬** (Ca' d'Oro; daily), stands at the first

landing stage beyond the Rialto. The pink, lace-like facade was once covered in gold, hence the name. Further up, on the same side, is the **Palazzo Vendramin-Calergi** ⓭, designed by Mauro Coducci – yet another superb Renaissance creation, now housing the city's casino. This is the last major building before the railway station, **Ferroviaria Santa Lucia** ⓮.

Venetian quarters

North of the Grand Canal, between the station and the Palazzo Vendramin-Calergi, is **Cannaregio,** home to the **Ghetto.** The name comes from an iron foundry (*getto*) that stood here, in an area where Jews were confined in the 16th century.

The area of **San Polo** that lies within the large bend of the Grand Canal is home to the **Scuola Grande di San Rocco** ⓯ (daily), visited for its works of art by Tintoretto (1518–94). They include *The Crucifixion*, which inspired Henry James to exclaim: "Surely no single picture in the world contains more human life, there is everything in it including the most exquisite beauty."

The eastern section of the city, **Castello**, has charm of its own, and a good place to begin a visit is the **Campo Santa Maria Formosa** ⓰, a congenial market square. The elegant church is worth visiting to admire Palma il Vecchio's *St Barbara and Saints*.

Further north is another fine square, **Campo Santi Giovanni e Paolo** ⓱, enlivened by an imposing statue the of the mercenary Bartolomeo Colleoni, and the great Gothic church of **Santi Giovanni e Paolo**, commonly called San Zanipolo and known as Venice's Pantheon as it contains the tombs of 25 doges. In the Baroque church of the **Gesuiti** ⓲ near the Fondamente Nuove, the prize work of art is Titian's *Martyrdom of St Lawrence*.

The islands

The Fondamente Nuove is the ferry departure point for the northern islands.

Across the water lies **San Michele**, the lagoon's cemetery island. Further north is **Murano**, the island of the glass blowers, which produces the fragile Murano glass that is known all over the world. The **Museo Vetrario** (Thur–Tue) houses a fine collection of antique pieces.

The Laguna Nord ferries carry on from here to the lively island of **Burano**, traditionally known for lacemaking and fishing, and with narrow streets lined with brightly painted houses. From here it's a short ferry hop to **Torcello**, an evocative and remote little island, where the Byzantine Cathedral is the sole evidence of its former glory. ❑

The island of San Giorgio Maggiore, with Palladio's church of the same name at its heart.

BELOW: take a gondola for the best views of the city.

AROUND ITALY

On a tour of Italy, the northern lakes and the rolling Tuscan landscape will soothe the spirits, while the Bay of Naples and the sun-drenched island of Sicily promise excitement

The majority of travellers crossing the Alps from Austria into Italy use the **Brenner Pass ❶**; its Alpine landscape of wooden chalets and onion-domed churches is more German than Italian. The people in this region of Italy are South Tyroleans and the majority speak German, while their cuisine is Austrian and their manners Teutonic. Fiercely independent, they have been granted a measure of autonomy by the Italian government. The Brenner Highway runs past castles, fortifications and independence monuments to medieval **Trento ❷**, which has a Romanesque **Cathedral** (Duomo; daily) and the **Castle of Good Counsel** (Castello del Buon Consiglio; Tue–Sun), with permanent and touring art exhibitions. The highway runs south from Trento and close to **Verona ❸**, where Romeo and Juliet are said to have lived and loved. **Juliet's House** (Tue–Sun), at Via Cappello 23, is a real medieval townhouse of the kind the fictional Juliet could have inhabited.

To the east of Verona, a highway leads to the lovely city of **Padua ❹** (Padova), the setting for Katherine's challenge to the male order in Shakespeare's The *Taming of the Shrew* and home to Giotto's beautifully preserved frescoes in the **Scrovegni Chapel** (daily; reservations compulsory; www.cappelladegliscrovegni.it).

From Padua it is a short hop further east along the highway to **Venice ❺**

(Venezia; *see pages 277–81*), and the Adriatic coast. The city of **Trieste ❻** has been subjected to constant ownership disputes, none of which bothered Irish writer James Joyce when he arrived in the city in 1905. He thought his stay would be a short one, but Trieste became his home for 10 years. Back at Verona, the A4 highway speeds westwards to **Milan ❼** (Milano), Italy's second-biggest city after Rome. Understandably, perhaps, Milan regards itself as the true capital of Italy. Not only is it the leading industrial and financial

Main attractions
CATHEDRAL, MILAN
ITALIAN LAKE DISTRICT
PISA
SIENA
POMPEII
CAPRI
AMALFI COAST ROAD
GREEK TEMPLES, SICILY
SARDINIA

LEFT: Sorrento's fishing harbour.
BELOW: on the roof of Milan Cathedral.

capital, but it has forged ahead to become the country's most dynamic and influential city. Since 1980 it has been the bastion of Italian fashion, drawing paparazzi and celebrities to its famous fashion fairs. It is also home to Leonardo da Vinci's *The Last Supper*, **La Scala Theatre** and Europe's largest and most sumptuous Gothic **Cathedral** (**Duomo**). Milan was chosen to stage EXPO 2015, and the city is currently gearing up to host an expected 30 million visitors at this world class fair.

Milan, **Turin** ❽ (Torino) and **Genoa** ❾ (Genova) form Italy's industrial triangle, the largest concentration of industry in the country. Turin, Italy's first capital, was the seat of the royal house of Savoy which, under Vittorio Emanuele II, became the Italian royal family. The city centre is graced with palatial Baroque residences and the **Cathedral** safeguards one of Italy's most famous relics, the much-contested **Holy Shroud**. Genoa, the ancient maritime republic on the Italian Riviera, is still the country's busiest port. The picturesque coast east of Genoa is known for the exclusive little resort of

Portofino and the lovely cliff-hanging villages called the **Cinque Terre.**

The Lakes

Italy's Lake District comprises five major lakes. The most westerly is **Lake Maggiore** Ⓐ (Lago Maggiore), with the *grande dame* resort of **Stresa** Ⓑ on its western shore. From here it's a quick ferry hop to the **Borromean Islands** Ⓒ (Apr–Oct daily) and a short drive or cable-car ride from Stresa Lido to the top of **Monte Mottarone,** which commands a wonderful panorama of the lakes and Alps.

On the far side of Monte Mottarone lies little **Lake Orta** Ⓓ (Lago di Orta), the setting of the perfectly preserved medieval village of **Orta San Giulio** with mesmerising views across the lake to **Isola San Giulio.**

The most visually stunning of the lakes is **Lake Como** Ⓔ (Lago di Como), almost 50km (30 miles) long and up to 5km (3 miles) wide. The Alps enclose the lake to the north and skiers enjoy unparalleled views as they whoosh down the glaciers. Ferry boats are the best way of seeing the lake

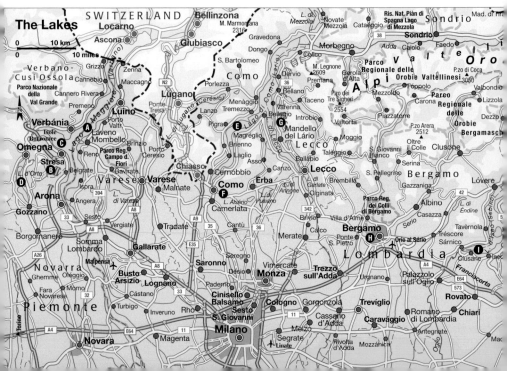

From the small town of **Como** ⑤ you can take a slow, scenic cruise north to **Bellagio** ⑥, "pearl of the lake", which enjoys sublime views of the mountains and lake. Grand old villas and luxuriant gardens line the lakeshores of Como, the most celebrated among them being **Villa Carlotta** at Tremezzo (Apr–Oct daily), across the water from Bellagio.

Southeast of Lake Como is **Bergamo** ⑦, which has one of Italy's most enchanting medieval centres, reached from its lower town by funicular. **Piazza Vecchia** is flanked by magnificent medieval and Renaissance monuments, and neighbouring Piazza Duomo is overlooked by the jewel-like **Colleoni Chapel** (daily). Down in the lower town, the **Accademia Carrara** (Tue–Sun) has a remarkably rich collection of Venetian masterpieces .

East of Bergamo is **Lake Iseo** ⑧ (Lago d'Iseo), where Monte Isola (Mountain Island) occupies the centre of the lake and dominates the view. The city of **Brescia** ⑨, southeast of the lake, is home to the **Santa Giulia Museo della Città** (Tue–Sun), one of the best archaeological and historical museum complexes in Italy. It incorporates the 8th-century Basilica of San Salvatore, the Romanesque oratory of Santa Maria in Solario, the Renaissance church and cloisters of Santa Giulia and the frescoed nuns' choir.

The largest of the Italian lakes, and the most popular, is **Lake Garda** ⑩ (Lago di Garda). Windsurfing and sailing draw in large numbers of watersports enthusiasts, and beaches in the southern section of the lake are popular with families. A reminder of an unhappy chapter in Italy's history is found in the resort town of **Gardone Riviera** ⑪, on the western shore. Gabriele d'Annunzio, the flamboyant poet, pilot and patriot who became an ardent supporter of Mussolini, was given a home here by the dictator. His eccentric residence, **Il Vittoriale** (Tue–Sun), is a shrine to dreams of Italian imperialism. Neighbouring **Salò** ⑫, an attractive lakeside resort, is synonymous with the notorious wartime Republic of Salò, where Mussolini made his last stand. On a peninsula jutting into the lake at its southern

BELOW: the western shore of Lake Garda.

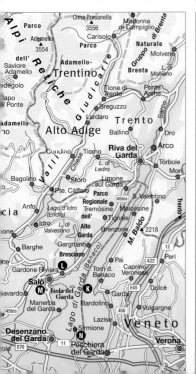

Fine mosaic in the Basilica di San Vitale in Ravenna.

end, the ancient town of **Sirmione** is a good place to while away an hour or two.

The Po Valley

South of Verona begins the great Italian plain in the Po Valley, cut by irrigation channels and shivering with ghostly poplar trees. This fertile region between Milan in the west and Rovigo in the east is Italy's larder as well as its fruit and vegetable garden. The Brenner Highway links up with the Sun Motorway (Autostrada del Sole) near **Modena** ⑩. This 1,200km (780-mile) artery, beginning at Milan, runs the length of the peninsula down to Reggio di Calabria on the Strait of Messina at Italy's toe. A far more ancient road, the Via Emilia, was built by the Romans, and it still runs through the centre of Modena with the city's most illustrious sight, the Romanesque **Cathedral** (Duomo),

sitting grandly alongside the road. The **Palazzo dei Musei** contains several galleries, including the Galleria Estense (Tue–Sun) and the Biblioteca Estense (Mon–Sat), the library of the d'Este family, dukes of Modena.

Part of the Via Emilia linked Modena with the historic city of **Bologna** ⑪, a prosperous town with a finely preserved historic centre and a well-deserved reputation for gastronomy. The city is centred around the grand **Piazza Maggiore** and **Piazza del Nettuno**. To the east are the two **Leaning Towers** (Torri Pendenti), built by two aristocratic families who competed to build the tallest tower in the city. One of the towers is now only 48 metres (157ft) high, having been shortened for safety reasons in the 14th century, but still leaning more than 3 metres (10ft). The other tower stands 97 metres (318ft), leans more than 1 metre (3ft) and has 500 steps up for a rooftop view. Bologna's university is the oldest in Europe and was attended by the great lyric poet Petrarch (1304–74). Its buildings are now dotted all around the city, but the official centre is the 16th-century

Palazzo Poggi northeast of the centre. Beyond the university, the **National Art Gallery** (Pinacoteca Nazionale; Tue–Sun) is mainly devoted to the Bolognese School, notably Carraci and Guido Reni.

If you are travelling down the east coast on the A14 Adriatic Highway don't overlook **Ravenna** ⑫, where the churches have dazzling Byzantine mosaics. The city acquired these art treasures when it was capital of the Western Roman Empire, and later under Emperor Justinian (482–565). The finest mosaics can be found in the 6th-century **Basilica of San Vitale** (daily) and the 5th-century **Mausoleum of Galla Placidia** (daily).

The Adriatic

Sandy beaches stretch southwards down the coast. **Rimini** ⑬ is the Adriatic's principal resort. Hedonistic pleasures apart, it has a cultural attraction: the Renaissance **Tempio Malatestiano** (daily), built c.1450 for Sigismondo Malatesta, an evil *condottiere* (mercenary). It was condemned by the pope as a "temple of devil worshippers".

Barely half an hour's drive inland from Rimini lies Europe's oldest and smallest republic – **San Marino** ⑭. (It was the smallest in the world until 1968, when Nauru gained independence.) It has just 29,000 inhabitants and is dramatically set on the rocky slopes of Monte Titano. Thanks to the setting it escaped most of Italy's invaders and to this day is an independent country *(see Microstates, page 358)*. In 1861 Abraham Lincoln accepted honorary citizenship of the republic, though this did not prevent the Americans from bombing it during World War II when German troops were in occupation. To the southwest of San Marino stands the hilltop fortress of San Leo, a conspicuous sight that attracts thousands of visitors annually.

Tuscany

Tuscany presents the quintessential Italian landscape: medieval hilltop towns, silvery olive groves, neat vineyards carpeting gently rolling hills, and old farms and villas watched over by sentinel cypress trees. The beauty of the landscape, the intensity and

Perhaps the most spectacular sight in Tuscany is the town of San Gimignano, bristling with medieval towers and such artistic treasures as the Wedding Scene frescoes in the Museo Civico and the richly decorated interior of the Collegiata.

BELOW LEFT: sunbathing in Rimini. **BELOW:** San Marino, Europe's smallest republic.

Gently undulating landscape around Pienza in the Val d'Orcia.

BELOW: the Leaning Tower of Pisa – still leaning, but still standing.

of Sicily, and its ships carried the First Crusade to the Holy Land, a journey that gave Pisa trading posts in the East. Pisa's links with Hohenstaufen Emperor Frederick Barbarossa gave it a leading position in Tuscany during the 12th century, which ended with the city's defeat by Genoa in 1284. In 1406 it was taken by Florence after a long siege. The Campo dei Miracoli is a theatrical architectural ensemble which, apart from the tower, is home to the **Baptistery** and **Cathedral**. It is the Islamic influence on the architecture of these two buildings that makes them so distinctive, a legacy of the Pisan merchants who established important trading links with North Africa and Moorish Spain.

dramatic changes of the light and the natural harmony were the inspiration of Renaissance artists and architects in its capital, **Florence ⓯** (Firenze; *see pages 273–5)*.

One of the main gateways to Tuscany is **Pisa ⓰**, west of Florence and famous for its **Torre Pendente** (Leaning Tower; *see box below*) in the **Campo dei Miracoli** (Field of Miracles). Pisa is also renowned as one of Italy's great cities of art. The old maritime republic, once a flourishing seaport on the River Arno's estuary, was an ally of the Normans during their conquest

South of Florence, **Siena ⓱** lies at the geographical heart of Tuscany – a perfect medieval town of narrow lanes and alleys. The fan-shaped Piazza del Campo in the centre is one of the finest squares in Italy, a great place to enjoy a drink at one of the many pavement cafés or, if you happen to be here on 2 July or 16 August, to watch the fantastic scene of horses and their

Saving Pisa's Leaning Tower

In December 2001, after more than a decade under wraps, the Leaning Tower of Pisa (Torre Pendente di Pisa; daily) reopened to the public. The dramatic tilt, caused by building on shallow foundations in unstable, silty soil, has now been staunched by an international team of engineers. The admission charge for the half-hour guided tour is steep, and visitor numbers are limited to 30. Queues develop quickly, so you should try to get there before opening time (8.30am in summer, 9am in mid-season, 10am in winter). To reserve a ticket, go to www.opapisa.it, between two and nine weeks in advance, or visit the ticket office. In the high summer season, be prepared to wait at least a couple of hours for a slot.

iders charging around the square in one of the wildest horse races in the world: the Palio. A colourful procession of pages, knights, flag-wavers and men-at-arms, all dressed in 15th-century costumes, opens the spectacle. Riding bareback, the participants risk life and limb.

The square slopes down to the graceful Gothic **town hall** (Palazzo Pubblico), with a crenellated facade and waving banners. This is now home to the **Museo Civico** (daily), housing outstanding early Renaissance art, including two great frescoes by Simone Martini and Ambrogio Lorenzetti's *Allegories of Good and Bad Government*. The strenuous climb up 500 steps to the top of the slender **Torre del Mangia** (Belltower; daily) is worth it for the panorama of the city. The facade of Siena's Gothic **Cathedral** (Duomo; daily) is a festival of green, pink and white marble, while the interior is decorated with a series of black-and-white geometric patterns. A crypt (daily; guided tours only) has been discovered below the Duomo, decorated with some stunning

Sienese School frescoes. In the **Cathedral Musuem** (Museo dell'Opera; daily), pride of place goes to Duccio's *Enthroned Madonna* (1308); other fine examples of Sienese art can be found in the **Pinacoteca Nazionale** (daily), in the Palazzo Buonsignori on Via San Pietro, south of the Campo.

The best introduction to the Tuscan hill country is a tour of **Chianti**. The SR222 from Siena leads through the Chianti Way with rolling hillsides of vineyards of the famous estates that produce this classic Italian wine.

East of Siena, the town of **Arezzo ⑱** offers worthy relief from the rigours of the highway. The chief attraction lies in Piero della Francesca's remarkable fresco cycle depicting *The Legend of the True Cross* in the **Basilica of San Francesco** (daily).

Umbria

To the east of Tuscany is the province of Umbria and its handsome, prosperous capital, **Perugia ⑲**. The city reflects the bellicose side of a region where the martial and the mystical are inextricably intertwined, where the harsh oak

Siena's Gothic Cathedral has a colourful facade.

BELOW: view of Siena's Piazza del Campo from the Torre del Mangia.

The local wine is usually the best.

and the gentle olive grow on the same hillside and where the shepherd cuts the sheep's gullet then plays the flute to mourn it. Perugia's churches were never completed in the same generation, since the citizens were too busy with wars, feuds, pillage and murder. In this barbed hill-top fortress Raphael studied under the great artist Pietro Perugino.

If you have only enough time for one site, make it the **Galleria Nazionale dell'Umbria** (Tue–Sun), which displays works by many of Umbria and Tuscany's most noted painters – Fra Angelico and Piero della Francesca are both well represented. The tradition of fresco painting was established by the Florentine Giotto at **Assisi ⑳** *(see box, below)*. This beautiful medieval town, with its famous frescoed basilica, is well worth an overnight stay.

BELOW RIGHT: fresco of St Francis in the Basilica of San Francesco, Arezzo.

The Bay of Naples

South of **Rome ㉑** (Roma; *see pages 263–71*), the Bay of Naples will draw you in, just as it has the Phoenicians, Greeks, Romans, Goths, Vandals, Saracens, Turks, Normans, Germans, Spaniards, French and British.

Founded by Greek colonists who named it "Neapolis" (the New City), **Naples ㉒** (Napoli) was once part of Magna Graecia, the ancient Greek colonies. It was captured by the Romans in 326 BC, and they enriched the settlement with temples, gymnasiums, aqueducts, hippodromes, arenas and numerous catacombs outside the city. It became the favourite residence of many of the emperors, and this is where the infamous Nero made his stage debut.

After the fall of the Roman Empire, Naples became a Byzantine dukedom, and early in the 12th century it fell to the feudal Norman Kingdom of Sicily. European monarchies then converted it into the flourishing capital of a kingdom, inhabited by a people who quickly learnt to adjust to the whims of their foreign rulers. They were sons of a city where politics and business were a blend of Machiavellian realism and Byzantine intrigue. In this atmosphere laws were never taken too

St Francis of Assisi

The picture-postcard town of Assisi in Umbria, flower-decked and wood-smoke-scented, draws tremendous crowds, who come to experience something of the spiritualism of the Franciscan order, founded by the town's most famous son, Francis of Assisi.

Born Giovanni Bernadone in 1181, Francis embraced asceticism at an early age, and by 1219 had a brotherhood of 5,000 monks. The main tenets of the original Franciscan order were poverty, chastity and obedience; in particular, Francis repudiated the decadence of the Catholic Church, posing a challenge to the worldliness of the papacy. On his return from preaching in the Holy Land, Francis is said to have received the marks of the stigmata, and was canonised in 1228, two years after his death.

Construction of the two-tiered Basilica of St Francis (Basilica di San Francesco; daily) began in the mid-13th century. The Lower Basilica (Basilica Inferiore; often closed) was built around the saint's crypt and commemorates Francis's modest life with frescoes by Simone Martini and Cimabue. The Basilica Superiore (Upper Basilica), contains Giotto's famous fresco cycle of *The Life of St Francis*. It has been faithfully restored after damage caused by the 1997 earthquake, although it will never be quite what it was.

seriously; after all, they were made by foreign bosses to benefit themselves and rob poor Neapolitans.

Despite its teeming streets, unemployment and widespread crime, Naples today continues to exert a fascination. It is a huge city (the third-largest in Italy), with remarkable vitality and theatricality. Tourism, however, has taken a recent downturn, with worldwide publicity over the piles of rubbish in the city and surrounds, and the increasing prevalence of the Camorra (Naples's mafia), who have made huge profits by illegal dumping.

Polluted it may be, but the city has a beautiful natural setting, and a wealth of sights. A good place to begin a tour of Naples is the **Castel Nuovo** (Mon–Sat), where a stupendous Triumphal Arch stands in commemoration of Alfonso I's 15th-century defeat of the French. From outside the castle the Via San Carlo leads to Italy's largest opera house, the **Teatro San Carlo** (regular tours; tel: 081-797 2331; www.teatrosancarlo.it). The **Duomo** of Naples is sandwiched between apartment blocks in the north of the historic centre.

In the right aisle of the museum of the Chapel of San Gennaro is a treasured relic: a phial containing the blood of San Gennaro, who was martyred in AD 305. The blood must liquefy three times a year – on the first Saturday in May, on 19 September and on 16 December – if Naples is to escape disaster. The Vatican has eliminated San Gennaro from the official list of saints, but liquefication ceremonies remain the highlights of the Neopolitan ecclesiastical year. The last great eruption of Vesuvius in 1944 and the earthquake northeast of Naples in 1980 occurred in the years when, apparently, the blood did not liquefy.

Among Naples's many churches are **Monteoliveto**, which contains a wealth of Renaissance monuments; the 16th-century **Gesù Nuovo**, perhaps the most harmonious example of the Neapolitan Baroque; the Gothic **Santa Chiara**, the largest in Naples,

where the cloister has been carefully restored and medieval frescoes rediscovered; and **San Pietro a Maiella**, which has one of the most famous ceilings in Italy, painted by Mattia Preti between 1656 and 1661.

Naples also has a wealth of splendid museums: the **National Archaeological Musuem** (Museo Archeologico Nazionale; Wed–Mon) is one of the greatest museums in the world, housing the most spectacular finds from Pompeii and Herculaneum and fine examples of Greek sculpture. Exhibits include wonderful mosaics on the mezzanine floor. Two other excellent museums are the **Museo di Capodimonte** (Mon–Sat), within the Palazzo di Capodimonte, which contains some of the best paintings in southern Italy; and the **Certosa di San Martino** (Thur–Tue), a beautifully restored Carthusian monastery with a history museum, and spectacular views over Naples and its bay.

Shiny and speedy, the favourite form of transport for young people in Naples, ideal for nipping in and out of traffic.

BELOW: Naples and its sweeping bay, with Vesuvius in the background.

Serving pasta in a neighbourhood restaurant.

Vesuvius, Pompeii and Herculaneum

The eyes of the people living on the Bay of Naples are imperceptibly drawn every day towards **Vesuvius**, the giant sentinel looming above them. The height of the cone is 1,280 metres (4,200ft), but it varies after each eruption. It last erupted in 1944, and the remnants are still scattered in a vast slag heap around the crater. The lava became the fertile Vesuvian soil where the finest vines and olive grow, the main reason why peasants for thousands of years have stubbornly clung to the precarious slopes.

The most famous explosion occurred in AD 79, when the volcano was assumed to be extinct, and woods inhabited by wild boar covered the summit. Spartacus and his rebellious slaves had withdrawn into these woods 150 years earlier to escape the first punitive expeditions of the Roman legions. The eruption, elaborately described by Pliny the Younger, buried the flourishing cities of **Pompeii** ㉓ and **Herculaneum** (both daily) under the mountains of ashes and brimstone.

The life and last drama of these cities preserved in volcanic ash, came to light when archaeologists dug them from their airtight tomb. The imprints and skeletons make this one of the most impressive ancient monuments in the world. Excavators found the bones of a rich man, his fingers still clutching the keys to the treasure chests his slaves carried behind him. A thief, one hand still on a stolen purse, is nailed against the wall with his victim. Wine stands on tables, bread lies in the oven. The skeleton of an aristocratic lady is found in the sleeping quarters of a gladiator. Graffiti proclaims love and engages in obscenities and political baiting.

The tour groups that congregate at Pompeii can prove dismaying at the height of the tourist season, and a visit to lesser-known Herculaneum is one way of dealing with the problem. Although the town was never animated by the commercial buzz that made Pompeii so lively and diverse a community in its heyday, there is still plenty to see. Well-preserved frescoes decorate the **Casa dell'Atrio Mosaico** (House of the Atrium Mosaic), the **Casa**

BELOW: wall mosaic in the House of Neptune and Amphitrite, Herculaneum.

del Mosaico di Nettuno ed Anfitrite (House of Neptune and Amphitrite) and the **Casa dei Cervi** (House of the Stags). Nestling just below the volcano, Herculaneum is also a convenient starting point for an early evening ascent of Mount Vesuvius. A regular bus service connects it with the city.

Capri and the Amalfi coast

The island of **Capri** ❷ is easily reached by ferry or hydrofoil from Naples or Sorrento. Tiberius chose the island as his retirement home in AD 27, and while he may or may not have organised rural orgies on the island, the story has certainly not diminished Capri's appeal. The ruins of his luxurious imperial Roman villa, **Villa Jovis** (daily), reached by bus from the town of Capri, have spectacular sea views. But the most popular island excursion is the **Grotta Azzurra** (Blue Grotto; tickets for boat trip available from Marina Grande). The sun shining through the water in this cave creates a strange blue light which has made it the most visited attraction in the region after Pompeii.

Opposite Capri lies **Sorrento** and the start of the attractive, twisting **Amalfi coast road**, which dips into pretty fishing villages such as **Positano** and **Amalfi** itself before reaching the beautiful cliff-top village of **Ravello**, which is famous for its splendid villas and gardens. The controversial American writer Gore Vidal had a home here for 30 years.

Apulia: the heel of the boot

From south of Naples you can drive to the Adriatic coast where Puglia forms the heel and spur of Italy's boot. **Bari** ❷, originally a Greek colony, is the main commercial centre of this corner of Italy, but there is a wonderful absence of modernity in the warren of narrow streets and dazzling white houses in the ancient half of the city. Two sites worth

A fresco from Pompeii, depicting Cleopatra entering the underworld, in the National Archaeological Museum, Naples.

BELOW: houses cluster around the bay on the island of Capri.

seeking out are the fine Romanesque Basilica of San Nicola, built to house the bones of St Nicholas which were brought back from Asia Minor in 1087 by local sailors; and the **Pinacoteca Provinciale** (Tue–Sun), devoted to Apulian art. Picturesque **Alberobello**, 50km (30 miles) southeast of Bari, is a major tourist attraction, consisting almost entirely of the distinctive *trulli* – single-storey, whitewashed shepherds' huts with conical slate roofs.

The coastal road from Bari continues to **Brindisi**, where a column marks the end of the Via Appia, the first and greatest of the ancient roads that lead to Rome. The town lacks the charm of Bari, and most visitors here are those arriving or departing at the airport or port – this is the main ferry port for Greece.

Taranto ㉖, on the instep of Italy's boot and founded by Spartan navigators in 706 BC, became the largest city in Magna Graecia, the Greek Empire in Italy. Its **Museo Archeologico** (daily) is the second-most important archaeological museum in southern Italy, after the one in Naples. In

a region of restrained Romanesque architecture, the sumptuous buildings of **Lecce** ㉗ to the east come as something of a pleasant surprise. The flamboyant style of its 17th-century churches and palazzi became known as "Lecce Baroque".

And so to the toe of the boot, and **Reggio di Calabria** ㉘, from where ferries to Sicily depart. The first Greek settlers made the sea journey from Sicily in the 8th century BC; the most celebrated evidence of this early contact between the two great ancient civilisations only came to light in 1972, when fishermen discovered two colossal Greek statues thought to have gone down with a ship. They are, deservedly, the chief exhibits in the **Museo Nazionale della Magna Graecia** (Tue–Sun).

Sicily and Sardinia

The fertile island of **Sicily** (Sicilia) has always been at the confluence of the Mediterranean world, serving as a springboard for ambitious conquerors. It is best seen by road, although the ever-smouldering Mount Etna provides the most dramatic single vantage point. Around the central town of Enna, the countryside is one rolling plain of golden cornstalks.

Palermo ㉙, Sicily's capital, is a turbulent place, known both for its Mafia connections and for some wonderful architecture. The **Palazzo dei Normanni**, originally a Norman palace, is now the seat of the Sicilian Parliament. It is home to the exquisite **Palatine Chapel** (Cappella Palatina, Mon–Fri). Within easy reach of Palermo is the glorious **Cathedral of Monreale** (daily), which has beautiful cloisters and some of the finest medieval mosaics in Europe. East of Palermo on the north coast is the pretty seaside town of **Cefalù**, with a 12th-century cathedral that is surprisingly impressive for a town of this size.

Syracuse ㉚ (Siracusa), one of the most important Greek colonies, is on the other side of Sicily. In the city'

sprawling Parco Archeologica della Neapolis (daily) the great **Greek Theatre** (Teatro Greco) holds up to 15,000 spectators. Here, in summer, high-quality classical performances are staged (call the tourist office for details, tel: 0931-65068). Even more spectacular is the **Valley of the Temples** at **Agrigento ③**. The Temple of Concord here is arguably the best-preserved Doric temple in the world.

Further up the coast, clinging to the cliffs, is pretty **Taormina ③**. This chic and internationally popular resort also has a **Teatro Greco** (daily), dramatically positioned above the village. Music and drama performances are staged (July–Sept; tel: 0942-23243).

Off Sicily's northeastern tip, the **Aeolian Islands** (Isole Eolie) are where the Greeks believed the god Aeolus imprisoned the winds. Now a holiday resort, the scattered volcanic islands include **Stromboli**, which spews lava into the night.

The island of **Sardinia ③** (Sardegna) may not have the sophistication or wealth of sights of Sicily or the mainland, but it would be hard to find a concentration of such enticing white beaches elsewhere in the Mediterranean. The interior is striking too, with wild gorges and valleys carved into it. The most distinctive of Sardinia's cultural attractions are the *nuraghi* – Bronze Age stone towers. Built as dwellings, fortifications and sanctuaries, these megaliths offer a tantalising glimpse of Sardinia's early civilisation. ❑

Cefalù's 12th-century cathedral in the town's main square.

BELOW: the old town of Cefalù comes right down to the water's edge.

GREECE

A heady mix of sun, sea and ancient sites bathed
in brilliant Aegean light, Greece has been
enchanting travellers for centuries

odern Greece, which emerged in the 19th century
from 400 years of Ottoman rule, covers scattered,
rocky peninsulas and islands at the south end of the
Balkans in the eastern Mediterranean, with a language evolved
directly from the ancient Greek of the philosophers and play-
wrights. There are several fertile plains, in central mainland
Thessaly and on the Peloponnese, the southwestern part of the
country beyond the Corinth Canal. But in general the country's rugged profile makes life hard. To the north, this 132,000-
sq-km (51,000-sq-mile) Balkan nation is bordered by Albania, the former
Yugoslav Republic of Macedonia, Bulgaria and, for a short distance, its
former master, Turkey, where Asia begins. Just inside Turkey is Istanbul –
formerly Constantinople, capital of Byzantium and centre of Orthodox
Christianity, of which the Greek Orthodox Church is a major faction.

Modern towns and regions of this often austere landscape echo the
familiar names of kingdoms and city-states which vied for supremacy in the

eastern Mediterranean two, three and more millennia ago: Corinth,
Sparta, Mycenae, Knossos, Athens. Here too are Delphi with its oracle, the Athenian Acropolis, the shrine and games venue at Olympia,
and Mount Olympus, still haunted by the ancient gods and uniquely
important in Western culture. However, this is not a country living in
the past: EU membership and Athens's hosting of the 2004 Olympic
Games have done much to accelerate modernisation.

It is easy to fall in love with Greece – its beauty is self-evident.
Travellers return time after time, for the mirror-smooth Aegean Sea
shimmering in the still of the morning, for the *kafenía* with their
marble-topped tables and wicker-bottomed chairs offering respite
from blistering afternoon heat, and for the silvery olive groves where
cicadas trill until dark. It is a land for connoisseurs and explorers, with
an ancient inheritance that remains relevant to this day.

Greece is not a hard place to get around. Try taking a boat from Athens's
port of Piraeus to explore just a few of the hundreds of islands the gods
tossed into the Aegean and Ionian seas; or, if time is short, take a flight to
a remote corner of the mainland or one of the border islands.   ❑

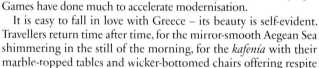

PRECEDING PAGES: Temple of Apollo, Corinth; view from the water towards Paros.
LEFT: peaceful Pórto Ráfti. **ABOVE:** scooting around Kos.

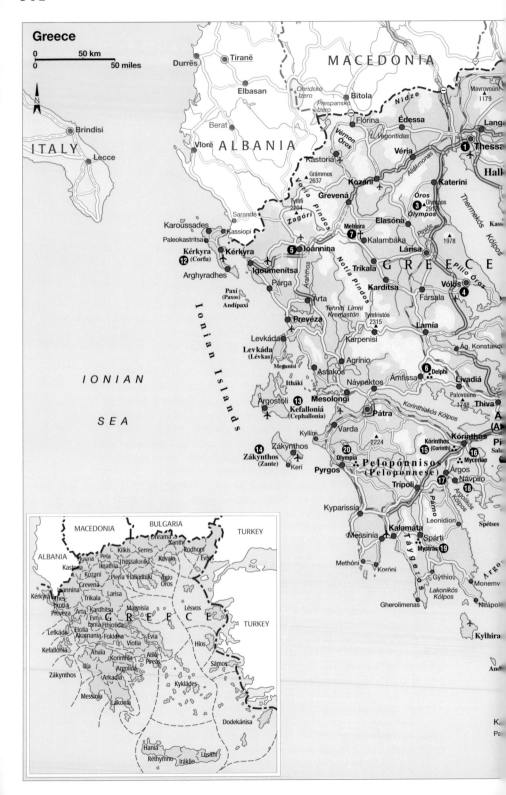

Greece

0 — 50 km
0 — 50 miles

N

ITALY
Brindisi
Lecce

Durrës
Tiranë
Elbasan
Ohridcko Izero
Prespansko Izero
Bitola

MACEDONIA

Mavrovoúni 1179

Berat
Vlorë
ALBANIA
Florína
Édessa
Langa

Vérnon Óros
L. Vegoritidas
Véria
1 Thessa

Kastoriá

Grámmos 2637
Kozáni
Kateríni
Hall

Tymfi 2204

Grevená
Óros Olympos 3 Olympos 2917

Sarandë
Zagóri
Metéora 7
Elasóna
Kass

Karoussades
Kassiopi
Kalambáka
Lárisa
1978

Paleokastritsa
Kérkyra 5 Ioánnina
G R E E C E

Kérkyra 12 (Corfu)
Kérkyra
Trikala
Pilio Óros

Arghyradhes
Igoumenitsa
Notia Pindos
Karditsa
Vólos 4

Párga
Aráthos
Fársala

Paxí (Paxos)
Ándípaxi
Árta
Tehnití Limni Kremastón
Tymfristós 2315
Lamía

Prevéza

Ionian Islands
Levkáda
Karpenísi
Ág. Konstandi

Levkáda (Lévkas)
Meganísi
Agrínio

IONIAN
Ithákî
Astakós
Ámfissa
6 Delphi
Livadiá

SEA
Argostóli 13 Mesolongi
Náypaktos
Palovoúna 1748
Thiva

Kefalloniá (Cephallonia)
Pátra
Korinthiakós Kólpos
A (A)

Kyllíni
Varda
Kórinthos
Pi

Zákynthos
2224
Kórinthos 15 (Corinth)
16 Mycénae
Sala

14 Zákynthos (Zante)
Kerí
20 Olympia
Pyrgos
Pelopónnisos (Peloponnese)
Árgos
Návplio
17 18

Kyparissía
Trípoli
Argolikós Kólpos

Messinía
Kalamáta
Spétses

Methóni
Koróni
Spárti
Mystrás 19

Gýthio
Monemv

Lakonikós Kólpos
Neápol

Gherolimenas
Kythira
And

K
Pa

Inset map

MACEDONIA
BULGARIA
TURKEY

ALBANIA
Drama
Xanthi
Kilkis
Serres
Rodhopi
Ilouna
Pela
Thessaloniki
Kavala
Evros
Kastoria
Imathia
Kozani
Pieria
Halkidhiki
Agio Oros

Grevena
Ioannina
Larisa
Trikala
Magnisia
Kérkyra
Thes-
Protia
Kardhitsa
Lésvos
Préveza
Arta
Evri
Iania Fthiotida
G R E E C E
TURKEY
Lefkáda
Etolia Akarnania
Fokidha
Évia
Híos
Kefalloniá
Ahaía
Korinthia
Atiki Pireás
Ília
Argolida
Sámos
Zákynthos
Arkadia
Kykládes
Messinía
Lakonia
Dodekánisa
Hania
Réthymne
Iráklio
Lasíthi

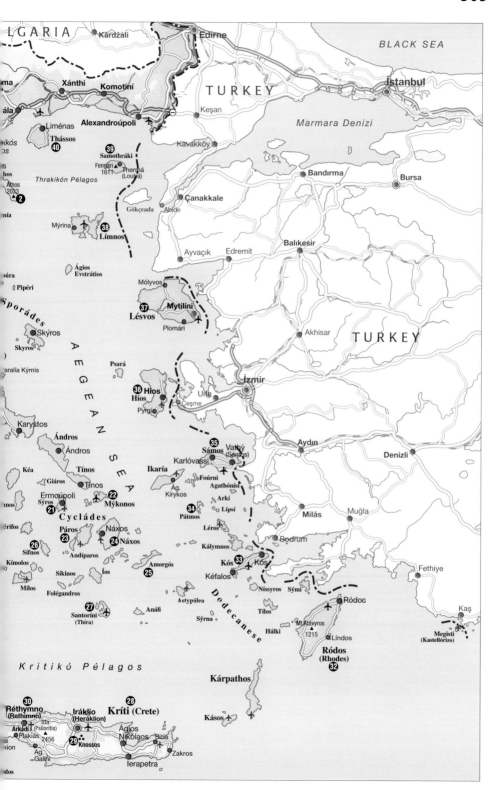

ATHENS

The power and beauty of the ancient Athenian empire breathe through this muddle of a modern city, overlooked on every street by the pinnacle of classical architecture: the Parthenon

he English novelist John Fowles described Athens as a mass of dice scattered across the Attic Plain. It certainly isn't the prettiest European capital: looking down from Mount Pendéli you'll appreciate the full extent of its architectural sprawl, with block after block of characterless cement buildings. Combine this visual chaos with hooting traffic and the *néfos* (air pollution) that envelops the centre and eats away at its monuments, and you might just be tempted to head straight for the islands.

But be patient with Athens: catch the Parthenon when the crowds are thinnest, visit one of the richly endowed art or archaeological museums, patronise an *ouzerí* until the small hours as the locals do, or barter over a pair of sandals in Pláka, and this muddle of a city will grow on you.

Acropolis

The **Acropolis ❶** (daily; entrance ticket also valid for all surrounding archaeological sites) rises over 60 metres (200ft) above the city. Viewed from the streets below, the "upper city" makes all else in Athens fade into insignificance. The best times to visit are early morning in summer or early afternoon in winter.

On top is the **Parthenon** (Virgin's Chamber). Fifteen years under construction, this temple to the goddess Athena was the crowning glory of Pericles' giant public works programme during the 440s BC. The spectacle it

presented then is hardly matched by the familiar ruin we know today.

There was colour everywhere, so much so that some observers found the overall effect quite offensive. "We are gilding and adorning our city like a wanton woman", was how Plutarch reported these complaints, "decking her with costly statues and offerings and 1,000-talent temples." But when you catch a glimpse of the temple's tawny marble columns you'll forgive Pericles his extravagance. In fact the columns incline slightly inwards and

Main attractions
ACROPOLIS
NEW ACROPOLIS MUSEUM
BYZANTINE AND
  CHRISTIAN MUSEUM
BENÁKI MUSEUM
NATIONAL ARCHAEOLOGICAL
  MUSEUM
PLÁKA
POSEIDON TEMPLE, SOÚNION

LEFT: the Parthenon crowns the Acropolis.
BELOW: the Peplos Kore in the New Acropolis Museum.

The Erechtheion, the site where Poseidon left his trident marks and where Athena's olive tree sprouted.

not a single structural line is straight, testament to the mathematical genius of its architect Iktinos.

Conservation and reconstruction work has made the Parthenon the most most attractive it has been in living memory, though this can be hard to see behind the necessary scaffolding and cranes. Hundreds of blocks of masonry have been remounted to replace rusting, 1920s-vintage iron clamps with non-corrosive titanium, and restorers have collected about 1,600 chunks of its marble scattered over the hilltop.

Beyond the Propylaia or "stepped entry" looms the **Erechtheion**, an elegant temple completed in 396 BC, over a generation after the Parthenon. The Caryatids – noble maidens in the service of the goddess Athena – now supporting the porch are copies, but five originals are displayed in the new Acropolis Museum. On what was once the citadel's southern bastion is the small, square temple of **Athena Nike**, completed in 421 BC and completely reconstructed since the millennium. According to legend, from this spot Theseus's father, King Aegeus, threw

himself to his death on seeing a black sailed ship approaching. Theseus had promised to hoist a white sail on his return if he succeeded in killing the Minotaur in Crete, but forgot to change the colour.

The sculptures and reliefs that Lord Elgin failed to loot (*see box, opposite*) can be viewed in the **New Acropolis Museum ❷** (Tue–Sun) which opened mid-2009 in a huge building overlooking the Acropolis. For an idea of the ancients' notions of beauty, take a close look at the *korai* also displayed there. you can still discern traces of make-up and earrings, and the patterns of their close-fitting dresses.

Below the Acropolis

On the south approach to the Acropolis lies the **Theatre of Dionysos ❸** (entrance on Leofóros Dionysíou Areopagítou; daily). The theatre's origins date back to the 6th century BC, when it was initially a simple, possibly rectangular, structure of wooden stands. Then an amphitheatre was dug out of the hillside. The marble seating tiers date from 320 BC and later, but the

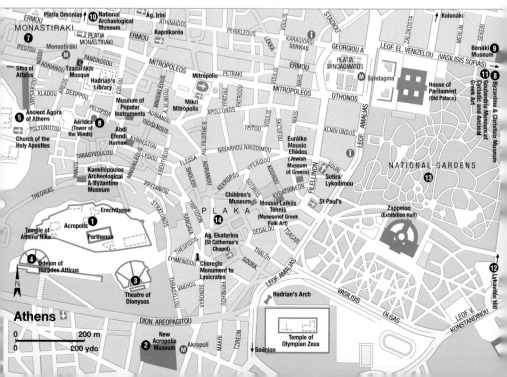

stage area hosted the plays of Aeschylus, Sophocles, Euripides and Aristophanes at the Festival of Dionysia during the 5th century BC – major annual events enjoyed by some 17,000 citizens. The theatre fell into disuse after the fall of Rome in the 5th century AD.

Just west, up Dionysíou Areopagítou, the smaller **Odeion of Herodes Atticus** ❹ was built in the 2nd century AD by a prominent Athenian. Here, from its steep, semicircular rows of seats, you can have a summertime taste of the atmosphere and occasion of the ancient Greek plays, when Herodes Atticus hosted most of the musical and theatrical performances of the Hellenic Festival.

On the other side of the Acropolis, extending northeastwards, lies the large, sprawling site of the **Ancient Agora** ❺ (daily), marketplace and centre of Periclean public life. This was where much of the city's trade and administration was carried out. Its focal point is the **Stoa of Attalos**, an impressive two-aisled colonnade 122 metres (400ft) long, restored during the 1950s and now housing a small museum.

Further east stands the **Tower of the Winds** (Aérides) ❻, built in the 1st century BC as a water-driven clock, compass and weathervane; it predates the surrounding **Roman Agora**, part of the building programme undertaken 200 years later by philhellene Roman Emperor Hadrian.

Modern Athens

Athens's heart lies within an almost equilateral triangle defined by Omónia Square (Platía Omónias) in the north, Monastiráki on the south and Sýndagma Square (Platía Syndágmatos), or Constitution Square, to the southeast. Cars are restricted to just a handful of main arteries. Ermoú, once a traffic-clogged mess, is now pedestrianised with reinvigorated shops, enlivened by buskers and the exquisite Byzantine church of Kapnikaréa about halfway along.

Sýndagma is ringed by luxury hotels, travel agencies, fast-food outlets and a few cafés. The square itself has been attractively re-landscaped since the opening of its strategic metro station. Less than a mile northeast lies

BELOW LEFT: exhibits in the New Acropolis Museum.

The Elgin Marbles

During the 18th and early 19th centuries, Greece attracted Grand Tourists intent on mega-souvenir-hunting in the form of archaeological pillaging. None has acquired more notoriety than Lord Elgin, who while ambassador to the Ottomans in the early 1800s secured permission from the sultan to excavate on the Parthenon and study stones with inscriptions. He interpreted this as a licence to remove most of the pediment friezes with their rich bas-reliefs, as well as one of the six Caryatids, all sold to the British Museum. Elgin's actions were controversial even then – Lord Byron deplored them in his poetry – and in recent decades have sparked a major dispute between Greece and the UK. The Greeks, who studiously use the term "Parthenon friezes" and regard Elgin as a vandal, have since the 1980s been demanding their return. The top floor of the new Acropolis Museum is pointedly designed for their eventual accommodation, with a mock-up of the pediment orientated exactly like the original structure, visible just uphill through glass windows. Defenders of British retention point out that Elgin's behaviour was normal for the time and probably saved the friezes from local lime kilns, and returning them would set a precedent that could strip many First World museums of their treasures. So despite a vociferous philhellene lobby in Britain advocating restitution, these treasures are unlikely to come back to Athens soon.

A stylised sculpture from the Museum of Cycladic Art.

BELOW: Tzisdarákis Mosque in Monastiráki Square.
BELOW RIGHT: mosaic in the Byzantine and Christian Museum.

Omónia, considerably less glamorous with its noisy (and thus cheaper) businessmen's hotels, swirling traffic and jobless immigrants.

Linking these two squares are the main, parallel streets of Stadíou and Panepistimíou, with neat shopping arcades between them, the Attica department store (modelled on London's Selfridges), various shops and cinemas. Heading uphill from Panepistimíou, the streets get smarter as they blend with **Kolonáki**, Ground Zero for the boutiques favoured by trendy, well-heeled Athenians. Contrastingly downmarket is **Monastiráki ❼**, with everything from tools, beads, army surplus items and religious paraphernelia, to gawdy, mass-produced tourist tat, used records, and handmade leatherware. After much wrangling, the plaza in front of the eponymous metro station here has been redesigned and pedestrianised according to plan. The famous **Flea Market** occupies Platía Avyssinías, where weekend mornings see browsers of genuine (and expensive) portable antiques and furniture.

Top museums

Athens is well endowed with museums. The revamped **Byzantine and Christian Museum ❽** (Tue–Sun) houses a brilliant array of icons, frescoes and other religious art from pagan times to the 18th century; the **Benáki Museum ❾** (Wed–Sun) is an eclectic collection of Greek treasures from all periods, including jewellery, costumes, engravings, and two icons attributed to El Greco.

The **National Archaeological Museum ❿**, reorganised around the millennium, is a fantastic storehouse of ancient Greek art (daily). Here reside the so-called Agamemnon's mask, found by the famous German archaeologist Heinrich Schliemann at Mycenae; a lifelike equestrian statue of Emperor Augustus; the bronze of Poseidon poised to throw his (now vanished) trident; the Antikythera mechanism, a geared astronomical computer a millennium ahead of its time; plus Minoan frescoes from Akrotíri.

The permanent highlight of the **Goulandrís Museum of Cycladic and Ancient Greek Art ⓫** (Mon, Wed–Sat)

is a unique collection of slim, stylised Cycladic figurines in marble, originally painted but now white. Dating from 3200–2000 BC, they have fascinated such artists as Picasso, Modigliani and Henry Moore. The museum also hosts frequent temporary art and photographic exhibitions with distinctly unarchaeological themes.

Escapes near and far

A saving grace of Athens is the variety of easy – and visible – ways out of the urban din. Take the funicular railway up **Lykavitós Hill** ⑫ for spectacular views (every 20 minutes in summer, 9am–3am) from the top of Ploutárhou Street, near Platía Kolonáki. In mythology, Lykavitós Hill resulted from a fit of pique on the part of the goddess Athena, who hurled a large rock at the daughters of King Kekrops, and missed; the missile, on landing, became the ridge.

A jungly haven for birds and cats, criss-crossed by irrigation rivulets, the **National Gardens** ⑬ are a stone's throw from the Byzantine and Benáki museums (*see opposite*).

Not particularly green, but certainly an oasis, is **Pláka** ⑭, the original 19th-century quarter clustered at the foot of the Acropolis. In amongst protected domestic architecture and part-pedestrianised streets are several minor museums, a handful of Byzantine churches, a Turkish bath and a mosque. Pláka ends and more raucous Monastiráki begins at **Hadrian's Library** (currently being excavated) and another mosque, the Tzisdarákis, now home to a ceramics museum.

The one "must" excursion out of Athens is to **Cape Soúnion**. On this sea-lashed promontory towers the **Temple of Poseidon** (Tue–Sun 9.30am–sunset), probably Greece's most evocative ancient temple and, with 16 out of 34 columns remaining, one of the best preserved. On the column nearest to the entrance, Romantic poet Lord Byron scratched his name in 1810; because of subsequent imitation, the temple precincts are now off-limits. In clear conditions, especially near sunset, you can see various Cyclades islands to the southeast and the Peloponnese to the west. ❑

TIP

If you stay at one of the campsites on the beach, you can enjoy the Temple of Poseidon in Byronic solitude. You will need to book ahead, though.

BELOW LEFT: eating out in Pláka.
BELOW: a view of modern Athens.

AROUND GREECE

Greece's ancient monuments reflect an expansive culture that, at its height, stretched from Iberia to India. The islands also offer paradise – and beaches galore

Greece's second-largest city, capital of the north mainland, is **Thessaloníki ❶**. Founded in 315 BC by Macedonian king Kassander, the town later rose to prominence thanks to its position on the Via Egnatia between Rome and Byzantium. A dozen Byzantine churches survive here, many being clear adaptations of colonnaded Roman basilicas, in turn descended from Greek temples. The town's **Museum of Byzantine Culture** (daily) features superb wall paintings rescued from locally excavated early Christian tombs. Macedonian, Hellenistic and Roman finds from the region grace the **Archaeological Museum** (daily), including many gold, silver and ivory treasures from the Vergina tombs of the Macedonian dynasty.

The furthest east of the three peninsulas extending east of Thessaloníki into the Aegean Sea is **Mount Áthos ❷**, one of the Balkan's most stunning monastic realms. There are 20 surviving monasteries, the first founded by St Athanasios in AD 963 and the most spectacular being **Símonos Pétra**, with vertiginous drops on three sides. Women are still banned from the peninsula, with only a limited number of non-Orthodox pilgrims admitted. South from Thessaloníki, where Macedonia blends into Thessaly, **Mount Olympus** (Ólympos) ❸, home of the ancient gods, rises to 2,917 metres (9,750ft), the highest point in Greece.

From here, Zeus let fly with his thunderbolts; this close to the sea, the weather is still fickle, and climbers or trekkers should take care.

South to Thessaly, west to Epirus

Further south, mostly modern **Vólos ❹** is the major port of Thessaly, but not without charm and a lively nightlife; it's the major gateway to the Sporádes *(see page 313)*. Directly above rises **Mount Pílio**, with exquisite traditional villages, secluded beaches and

Main attractions
METÉORA
DELPHI
KÉRKYRA TOWN
MYCENAE
MYSTRÁS
OLYMPIA
KNOSSOS
RHODES WALLED CITY
ST JOHN MONASTERY, PÁTMOS
MASTIC VILLAGES, HÍOS

LEFT: Skiáthos street scene...
BELOW: and Skiáthos smile.

The ruins of the Temple of Apollo at Delphi date from the 4th century BC.

BELOW: Metéora, built on sandstone.

dense forests in which the mythical centaurs were said to dwell.

Píndos Mountains

Just beyond the Metéora loom the **Píndos Mountains**, the spine of mainland Greece, separating Thessaly from **Epirus**, the country's remotest region (though the new Vía Egnatía expressway has eased its isolation). Both this and the old highway cross the mountains to the scenic upland containing the lakeside city of **Ioánnina ❺**, with a citadel, mosques and inhabited islet with frescoed monasteries. Immediately north lies **Zagóri**, the most scenic

stretch of the Píndos, fissured by the deep **Víkos Gorge** and speckled with 47 villages built from the same grey limestone as the mountains.

Delphi: world navel

Nestled in a natural stone amphitheatre on the southern slope of **Mount Parnassós**, the terraced sanctuary of **Delphi ❻** was for centuries antiquity's most revered oracle. The ancient Greeks believed that here, where Zeus's two released eagles met, was the "navel of the earth".

The site closest to the road is the **Castalian Spring**; across the road is the **Gymnasium** area, with its mysterious round **Tholos**. The main **Sanctuary of Apollo** (daily; charge includes a rich **museum**) has ruins spanning all eras from the Classical Greek to the Roman. The meandering **Sacred Way** ascends among temples, statue bases, stoas and treasuries protecting the votive offerings of various devoutly grateful city-states. Only the Doric **Athenian Treasury** is intact, rebuilt in 1904–6 with the marble of the original structure dating from 490 BC.

The Metéora

At the western edge of the Thessalian Plain, on molar-like rock pinnacles, eroded from prehistoric seabed, perch the **Metéora monasteries ❼**, worthy rivals to the Áthos group, but visitable (variable hours) by all. As on Mount Áthos, religious hermits appeared here in the 10th century, but only in 1344 was the first proper monastery built, and by the 1500s 24 religious communities adorned the monoliths. From this zenith, decline set in, until only six foundations survive today. Historically the only way up was by winched rope-basket, until stairs were fashioned in the early 1900s. **Megálou Meteórou** – the highest and largest – took nearly three centuries to complete, but **Ágios Nikólaos Anapafsá** and **Roussánou** have better frescoes from the 16th-century heyday.

The present **Temple of Apollo** was the third built on the site, during the 4th century BC. The god Apollo, son of Zeus and Leto, was associated with music, art, philosophy, law, medicine, archery – though prophecy was his main function here. The small **theatre** just above, dedicated to Dionysos, seats 5,000 people, has marvellous acoustics and a wonderful view. Near the top of the sanctuary, the **Stadium**, 178 metres (600ft) long, hosted the Pythian Games in honour of Apollo, and its tiers of Roman seats accommodated up to 7,000 spectators.

The Sporádes and Saronic Gulf islands

Scattered across the three Greek seas – the Aegean, Mediterranean and Ionian – are more than 1,400 islands, though fewer than 100 are permanently inhabited. A popular target east of Vólos are the strikingly green Sporádes, the closest being **Skiáthos** ❽, which has more than 60 good beaches. Nightlife is lively on this island, especially in the busy main town (known as Skiáthos town). With a scooter or a car, you can explore more tranquil bays and remote monasteries. **Skópelos** ❾, next island out and now famous as filming location for *Mamma Mia!* is prettier, better wooded and boasts one of the handsomest port towns in Greece. **Alónissos** is for nature-lovers and hikers, while **Skýros**, accessed from eastern Évia, has a spectacular *hóra* (capital) and a lively carnival.

Southwest of Athens lie the several islands of the **Saronic Gulf.** Closest is **Aegina** (Égina) ❿, a 45-minute hydrofoil ride from Piraeus. Its most interesting monument, on a pine-tufted northeasterly hilltop, is the well-preserved Doric **temple** of the nymph **Aphaea.** The elegant port-town, facing vivid sunsets, was briefly the first capital of modern Greece.

Mountainous **Hydra** (Ýdra) ⓫, about 90 minutes out of Piraeus, has just one exquisite town. It is virtually car-free, and mules still haul most of the cargo. The slopes above are forested, with several monasteries to which you can climb; the few beaches must be reached on foot or by boat, there being few roads.

TIP

The three domestically operating airways (Olympic, Aegean, Athens Airlines) are largely web-based, and tickets bought from walk-in agents are heavily surcharged. Get online early enough, however, and fares from Athens to the islands can be the same as or less than a ferry cabin berth.

BELOW: dining alfresco in Skiáthos town.

Citrus fruit was not grown in Greece until after World War II, but is now a valuable crop.

BELOW: the bay of Paleokastritsa, Corfu.

The Ionian islands

Several islands in the Ionian Sea off Greece's west coast are often rainy and thus green, unlike the Aegean's arid, relatively bare outcrops. Best known (thanks to English novelist Lawrence Durrell) is **Corfu** (Kérkyra) **⑫**, just off the mainland but closer to Italy than Athens. The Venetian-influenced capital town of **Kérkyra** is a gem, comparing well to Dubrovnik further up the Adriatic. Although its beach resorts often prove overcrowded, Corfu is big enough to preserve quiet spots, especially in the inland villages on the slopes of northerly Mount Pandokrátor, and the exclusive resorts of the northeast coast. If it all gets too much, escape to the tiny, olive-cloaked satellite islet of **Paxí**.

Kefalloniá ⑬, of late inextricably linked to Captain Corelli and his mandolin, is the largest and most mountainous Ionian island, culminating in 1,628-metre (5,340ft) **Mount Énos**, covered in *Abies cephalonica* firs. But Kefalloniá's main business – especially after a 1954 earthquake destroyed its rich architectural heritage – is beaches and the traffic in and out of its little ports. The peninsula beyond westerly Lixoúri, the coast around southeastern Skála, and the photogenic bay of **Mýrtos** on the west coast near **Ássos** and its castle are all sandy, while the northerly port **Fiskárdo** survived the earthquake unscathed.

Directly east stretches **Ithaca** (Itháki) island, Odysseus' legendary homeland: quieter, with few beaches but three fine harbour villages sympathetically rebuilt after the quake.

Zákynthos ⑭ offers more green mountains and plains, stunning beaches and both good and awful tourist developments. Villages in the mountainous west largely escaped earthquake damage; not so the busy main town. Unfortunately, the resorts of **Laganás Bay** in the south have of late become notorious for the lewd public behaviour of young British visitors, yet just a sandy cove east at

unspoilt **Gérakas** on the Vassilikós peninsula, sea turtles lay their eggs.

The Peloponnese

The little isthmus joining the **Peloponnese** (Pelopónnisos) to the mainland is cleft by the deep, narrow **Corinth Canal**; blink and you'll miss it. **Ancient Corinth** ⑮, just beyond its modern namesake, prospered from trans-isthmian haulage in pre-canal days. The Hellenistic city was razed in 146 BC by the Romans but refounded a century later. What remains is the most complete Roman imperial town in Greece (daily summer 8am–7.30pm, winter 8am–5pm; charge).

The new motorway towards Kalamáta forges southwest from here, while the old highway enters the Argolid Plain at modern **Mykínes**, behind which stands the ancient fortified palace complex of **Mycenae** ⑯ (daily). Heinrich Schliemann excavated here 1874–6, relying on little other than intuition and the literal accuracy of Homer's epics. Greek archaeologists had already revealed the citadel's imposing **Lion Gate**,

but Schliemann's tomb finds, which are now in the National Archaeological Museum of Athens (*see page 308*), amply corroborated Mycenae's Homeric epithet "rich in gold".

Near modern **Árgos**, further into the Argolid, stands **ancient Argos** ⑰, among the oldest Greek settlements; notable are the huge, steeply raked classical **Theatre** (Tue–Sun), and the Frankish castle atop nearby Lárissa hill, the ancient acropolis. The upmarket resort of **Návplio** ⑱ is overawed by **Akronávplia** just overhead, plus the sprawling, early 18th-century **Palamídi**, comprising three self-contained Venetian fortresses. Almost 900 steps

Photogenic Kefalloniá is the most mountainous of the Ionian islands.

BELOW: a shepherd tends his flock in the Máni, a wild region in the southern Peloponnese.

TIP

You can travel the mainland (but not the islands) pleasantly in winter. Good hotels are heated, the Metéora or Pílio under snow is a treat, and many mountain villages double as ski resorts. Watch out for weekends, though, when Athenians flood them and a high-season ethic (and pricing) prevails.

BELOW: the rooftops of Santoríni, bathed in mellow light.

lead up from the Old Town to the summit and sweeping views.

The best route southwest takes in **Spárti**, successor to ancient Sparta, and the nearby Byzantine strongholds of **Mystrás** ⓳, with exquisite ruined palaces and frescoed monasteries. Atmospheric, walled **Monemvasiá**, a mini-Gibraltar southeast of Spárti, was the port of Mystrás and later an important Venetian stronghold. A drive west over the mountains from Spárti leads to **Kalamáta**, of little intrinsic interest but the gateway to **Messinía** with its balmy climate, fine beaches, more Venetian castles at **Koróni** and **Methóni** and (unsurprisingly) a huge expat population.

Proceeding north along the coast brings you to **ancient Olympia** ⓴ (daily). For almost two millennia, the religious sanctuary here hosted that most prestigious of pan-Hellenic athletic competions associated with shrines, the Olympic Games. The most salient monuments are the **Palaestra**, the Archaic **Hera Temple**, the enormous **Zeus Temple**, and the **Stadium** with its vaulted entrance.

The Cyclades

Adorning the central Aegean, the 24 inhabited **Cyclades** are the original island-hopping archipelago; in summer, inter-island boats (and flights from Athens) make connections easy. On **Sýros** ㉑, the elegant, Unesco-listed town of Ermoúpoli is capital of the group; **Mýkonos** ㉒ just across a strait and veteran of around half a century of concentrated tourism, offers the quintessential Cycladic profile of marshmallow windmills and churches, plus sybaritic beaches. **Páros** ㉓ is a marginally calmer place for beginners, with a bit of everything in a more expansive landscape. Just east lies **Náxos** ㉔, largest of the Cyclades, with high ridges, fertile farmland, great (if sometimes windy) beaches and labyrinthine Naxos Town, with Venetian fortifications and mansions. Beyond, the last of the Cyclades before Crete and the Dodecanese, **Amorgós** ㉕ is long, narrow and steep-sided, with a cult following for its excellent walking on cobbled trails and 11th-century monastery of Hozoviótissa, clinging limpet-like to a sheer cliff.

A separate ferry line threads through the westerly islands of Sérifos, Sífnos, Kímolos and Mílos; **Sífnos ㉖**, with its multiple villages and white monasteries and culinary tradition, is the busiest. Boats continue to **Síkinos** and **Folégandros**, once (like Amorgós) used to exile political dissidents but now celebrated for their unspoilt architecture and way of life. Transport converges on **Santoríni** (Thíra) **㉗**, most famous (and visited) of the group, aside from Mýkonos. About 3,500 years ago this volcano-island erupted cataclysmically, leaving only a submerged caldera and high, banded cliffs of a remnant isle behind, as well as the inspiration for Atlantis, the utopia-city lost beneath the waves. Myth perhaps meets fact at **Akrotíri** on Santoríni's south cape, a Minoan town preserved Pompeii-like under volcanic ash until excavated.

Crete

Crete (Kríti) **㉘**, Greece's largest island, could probably just survive as an independent country (certainly the proud Cretans think so). It has a vibrant folk culture, a strong regional cuisine nurtured by a long growing season, atmospheric Ottoman-Venetian harbour towns on the north coast, and sheltered beach resorts mostly on the south shore. Crete also produces – as the British writer Saki (H.H. Munro) noted wryly – "more history than can be consumed locally", from the Minoan culture of the 2nd millennium BC to one of the fiercest battles of World War II. Start at the reconstructed Minoan palace complex of **Knossos ㉙** (daily) just outside the the the capital Iráklio, a monument as much to the personal whims of excavator Sir Arthur Evans (including an unlikely colour scheme painted throughout) as to this vanished people. To appreciate it fully, pay a visit to Iráklio's outstanding, revamped **Archaeological Museum** when it reopens in 2010, with choice finds from all over the island.

Iráklio, except for its medieval centre, is not the most alluring of Cretan towns; for those head instead west to **Réthymno ㉚** and **Haniá ㉛**, each with postcard-perfect old harbour districts lined with Venetian buildings, fortifications and graceful Ottoman mosques. Inland, the countryside is dotted with dozens of monasteries – the most celebrated being **Arkádi** near Réthymno – and hundreds of little frescoed Byzantine and post-Byzantine churches. Nature-lovers will find beaches in all sizes and consistencies – the busiest resorts on the south coast are **Plakiás**, **Agía Galíni** and **Paleóchora** – and challenging hiking in the **White Mountains** (Lefká Óri) above Haniá. You can traverse the 18km (11-mile) **Gorge of Samariá** – the longest and deepest in Europe – for just a taste of a day in the life of a Cretan shepherd or World War II resistance fighter.

The Dodecanese

In the southeast Aegean off the Turkish coast lie the **Dodecanese**, although this group has, in fact, 17 inhabited islands, not 12 as the name implies. **Rhodes** (Ródos) **㉜** is the largest, most populated and most crowded, because

Iráklio's Archaeological Museum (reopening 2010) has the most magnificent collection of Minoan art; here is the Phaistos Disc, dating from the 2nd millennium BC.

BELOW: the Palace of Knossos, Crete.

A fisherman untangles his nets in the sun.

BELOW: the barren caldera at Níssyros.

of its Unesco-listed walled city, vast beaches along the southeast coast, and acropolis-castle at **Líndos**. Rhodes is a palimpsest legacy of ancient Greeks, crusading Knights of St John, Ottoman overlords and Italian colonialists. Although the **fortified Old Town** contains a clutch of worthwhile museums, the showcase Street of the Knights and a few prominent mosques whose minarets pierce the skyline, more rewarding are random wanderings along pebble-paved lanes, past medieval houses and under flying buttresses. Smaller, but still impressive, islands lie just a day trip (or longer) away: **Hálki** and **Sými** with their stage-set port towns built from sponge-diving wealth, and **Kárpathos** with its natural grandeur and tenaciously retained traditional life.

On the second-largest Dodecanese, **Kós** ㉝, a 1933 earthquake devastated most of **Kós Town** but allowed Italian archaeologists comprehensively to excavate the ancient city. Thus, much

of the town centre is an archaeological park, with the **Roman Agora** (the eastern excavation) lapping up to the 18th-century **Loggia Mosque**, the millennial **Plane Tree of Hippocrates** and the **Nerantziás** castle.

In the western excavation stand the *cardo* (main colonnaded street), and some excellent mosaics. The most scenic and sheltered beaches line the coast facing southeast towards the volcano-island of **Níssyros**, a popular day-trip destination with its dormant caldera and photogenic villages.

Northwest from Kós are smaller islands that are governed from rambunctious **Kálymnos**, all with prominent castles and distinctive vernacular architecture. **Astypálea**, close to Amorgós, seems more like a Cycladic island, as does **Pátmos** ㉞, at the fringes of the group, with its volcanic scenery and fine beaches. But Pátmos is best known for its sumptuous *hóra* (Old Town) clustered around the massive walls of the summit monastery of **St John the Theologian** (daily), which is among the most revered sites in the Orthodox world.

Northeast Aegean Islands

Beyond Pátmos, **Sámos** ⑮ boasts two high mountains, hill villages amidst wine terraces, emerald waters and a superb **Archaeological Museum** (Tue–Sun 8.30am–2.30pm; charge) showcasing items from the Archaic Sanctuary of Hera near the airport. **Híos** ⑯ exhibits outstanding domestic architecture in its fortified mastic villages of the south, designed by the Genoese to protect the precious resin extracted from the mastic bush. There are more preserved medieval villages facing the west coast, culminating in **Vólissos** with its castle overlooking the island's best beaches.

Lésvos ⑰ is one of the country's main olive-producing centres, but it also draws visitors with its thermal springs, and resorts like **Mólyvos**, **Plomári** and **Skála Eressoú**, the last a mecca for lesbians on account of Sappho having been born there. The capital Mytilíni's **Archaeological Museum** (Tue–Sun 8.30am–3pm; charge) houses some of the finest Roman mosaics in the country. Languorous **Límnos** ⑱ has the best

beaches in the group, exceptional food and wine, and a Byzantine-Genoese castle dominating the basalt-built port-capital, **Mýrina**.

Samothráki ⑲ to the northeast has an ominous, legend-cloaked mountain to climb, and the mysterious **Sanctuary of the Kabiri** (daily summer 8am–7.30pm, winter 8.30am–3pm; charge) at its base. **Thássos** ⑳, which, like Samothráki, is most reliably accessed from the north mainland – offers beaches and characterful hill villages, although not much pine forest since a series of devastating fires.   ❏

Island-hopping is easy to do in the Dodecanese.

BELOW: the resort of Mólyvos, on Lésvos.

WILDLIFE OF EUROPE

The animals and plants of Western Europe are surprisingly varied, and some regions extremely wild, despite the best efforts of generations of inhabitants to tame the continent

Centuries of development have cut vast swathes through the natural habitats of Western Europe, but the area still retains remarkably diverse wildlife. Remote mountainous or infertile corners hold rich pockets of virtually pristine biodiversity, but agricultural and even urban areas can turn up real surprises.

The best parts of the Mediterranean Sea and the wilder Atlantic coasts still harbour whales, dolphins and sharks. Inland, the desiccated regions of Spain, Italy and Greece are a few degrees short of being deserts, and have fauna to match: trumpeter finches, sandgrouse, scorpions and vultures. Centuries of grazing and browsing have created the *maquis* and *garrigue* scrublands of the Mediterranean, teeming with insects, orchids and reptiles.

There are still deep, dark forests in Western Europe. None could be called truly natural, but some corners remain undisturbed enough for brown bears to subsist in small numbers.

Where farming is of low intensity, ancient hedgerows, pastures and meadows exist alongside woodland, wetlands and open waters to provide a microcosm of the natural habitats that were once present across the continent. Though the larger fauna have long gone, such places can provide engrossing interest for the visiting naturalist.

And to cap it all, Europe's mountains are vast regions with a great many endemic species – plants and insects in particular – that have developed in geographical isolation.

ABOVE: a spectacle reminiscent of Afric[ ] Rift Valley: at least 10,000 greater flamingos breed on the salt pans of the[ ] Camargue in France.

LEFT: a larger, more colourful version o[ ] domestic relative, the wild hamster is n[ ] a protected species.

BELOW: sea turtles are quite widespree[ ] in the eastern Mediterranean, but decreasing as tourists take over the beaches where they lay their eggs.

LEFT: Eurasian griffon vultures are numerous in the Cévennes in France, where there has been a very successful reintroduction programme.

RESERVED FOR NATURE

Western Europe is now peppered with national parks, nature reserves and other protected areas, although the conservation of its natural heritage only became widespread in the last 20 years. While each country has its own laws, powerful EU legislation now spotlights the most significant habitats and species, and huge areas of member states are being designated.

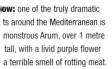

Doñana National Park in southern Spain is among the natural showpieces of Europe. Its 40 pardel lynx comprise almost a fifth of the world's most endangered feline. An estimated 8 million birds breed, migrate through, or winter on the site annually.

Few mountain parks can better the magnificent Pyrenees National Park for spectacular vistas, populated by bearded vultures and dozens of rare plants.

Abruzzo National Park in Italy's Apennines was a refuge for Western Europe's persecuted wolves. With protection, their fortunes have reversed and the wolf's howl can today be heard in central and eastern France.

OW: one of the truly dramatic ts around the Mediterranean is monstrous Arum, over 1 metre tall, with a livid purple flower a terrible smell of rotting meat.

ABOVE: of Western Europe's many orchid species, Lady's Slipper orchid is one of the most distinctive. It is generally rare in the lowlands but more common in mountain woodlands.

LEFT: although on the increase in mountain areas, the wolf's nocturnal habits and huge territories mean It Is rarely seen. It is prone to taking livestock, which inevitably leads to conflicts with farmers.

RIGHT: there are many chameleon species in Africa and Asia, but just one has a toehold in Europe. It inhabits sand dunes and trees along the southern Iberian coast, and has also been introduced to a few other sites elsewhere in the Mediterranean.

SPAIN

A relaxed atmosphere, plenty of sun, and
towns with a medieval flavour all help
give Spain its inimitable appeal

Continental Spain covers about four-fifths of the Iberian peninsula, Europe's southwest corner lying on the sunny side of the Pyrenees. The other fifth belongs to Portugal, and a few square miles at its extreme tip is Gibraltar, which belongs, somewhat contentiously, to the United Kingdom. Spain is divided into 50 provinces, grouped into 17 semi-autonomous regions, one of which is the Balearic Islands in the Mediterranean, and another two the Canary Islands in the Atlantic (not featured in this book). Some of the regions, especially the Basque Country and Catalonia, have very distinct identities and use their own languages. With an area of 505,000 sq km (195,000 sq miles), the country is Europe's second-largest after France.

From the wet Atlantic coast in the north, which has often been compared to Scotland, to the desert of Almería province in the southeast corner, Spain is a country of great contrasts. It is the most mountainous country in Europe after Switzerland, and much of its landscape is breathtakingly vast. It is a land of illusion: in the clear, bright air the windmills on the horizon seem close enough to touch, and nearly every journey is longer than it appears on the map. It has thousands of romantic castles and a number of splendid cities where old town quarters seem locked in the Middle Ages.

At the heart of the central plateau, or *meseta*, which covers 40 percent of the country, is Madrid. Established as the capital in the 16th century because of its geographical location, it is as far inland as you can get. Its great rival, Barcelona, Spain's second city, is the largest metropolis on the Mediterranean. Other cities that should be on any itinerary are Valencia, Seville, Granada, Córdoba, Salamanca and the pilgrimage shrine of Santiago de Compostela. But for most visitors, cities and scenery come second to Spain's greatest natural asset: the beaches along its famous coastlines, especially the Costa del Sol, Costa Blanca and Costa Brava. ❑

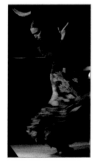

PRECEDING PAGES: bullfighter in Marbella; *mirador* on Mallorca's west coast.
LEFT: hillside village near Valence. **ABOVE:** ornate balconies in Palma de Mallorca's main square; flamenco flourishes in the south of Spain.

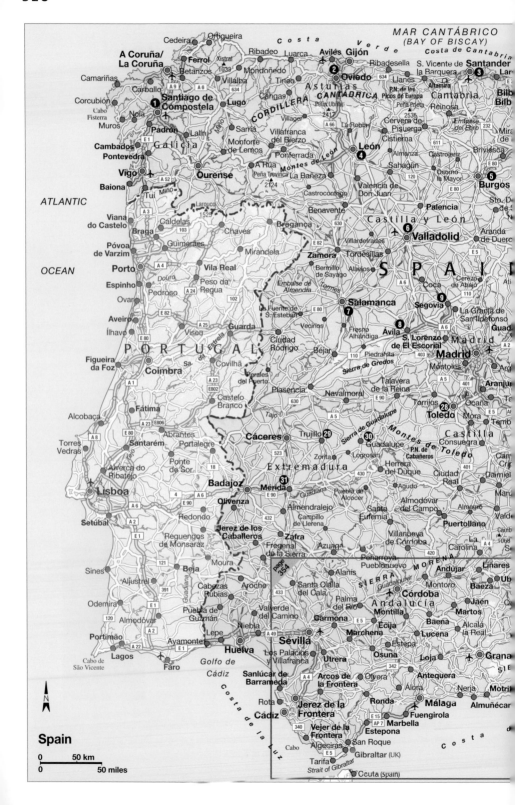

Spain

0   50 km

0   50 miles

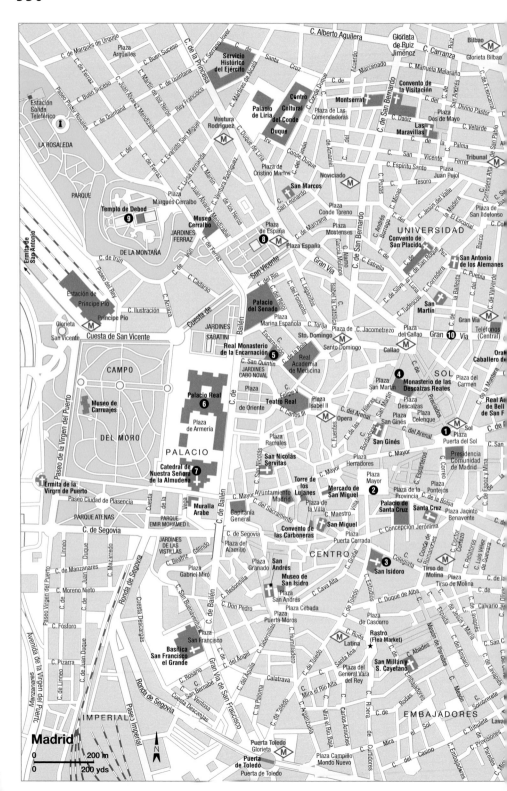

Madrid

0 ———— 200 m
0 ———— 200 yds

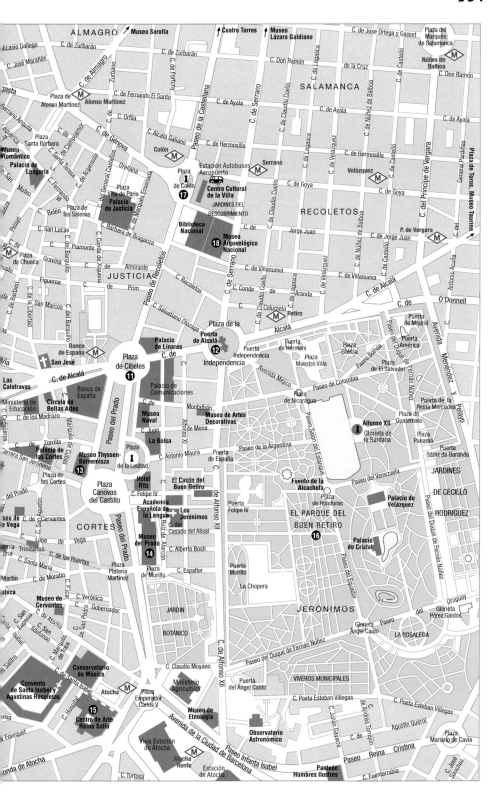

MADRID

Europe's loftiest capital has some splendid monuments from its regal past, and a lively population who like to stay out late

Madrid is the geographical centre of mainland Spain. At 655 metres (2,150ft) above sea level, it is the highest capital in Europe, with a population of 3.2 million. Situated on the central plateau surrounded by mountains, it has not only been climatically sheltered from maritime influences, but culturally and socially insulated as well.

In the 10th century the future capital of Spain was a Moorish fortress named Majerit which, a century later, was captured by Alfonso VI, King of Castile. In 1561, during Spain's Golden Age of empire, Philip II moved his residence here from nearby Toledo and proclaimed Madrid his new capital. Except for the brief period between 1601 and 1607 when Philip III moved to Valadolid, it has remained the capital ever since. In 1808, the French invaded Spain and installed Joseph Bonaparte, Napoleon's brother, on the Spanish throne. The city rose in rebellion. In his paintings *Dos de Mayo, 1808* and *Tres de Mayo, 1808*, in the Prado Museum, Goya chronicles the gruesome street battles and reprisals that cost more than 1,000 lives. The resulting Peninsular War, known in Spain as the War of Independence, brought British troops under the command of the Duke of Wellington to Spain's side and the conflict dragged on until 1814, when the French were finally defeated.

The city was again besieged in November 1936, three months after General Franco's Nationalist uprising against the Republican government. The central post office sustained 155 direct hits from Nationalist artillery fire but the city did not succumb until 28 March 1939. Franco remained in power until his death in 1975, when the monarchy was restored under King Juan Carlos.

Echoes of empire

Most of Madrid's sightseeing attractions are intimately linked with its history as a royal residence and the centre

Main attractions
PUERTA DEL SOL
PLAZA MAYOR
PALACIO REAL
MUSEO THYSSEN-BORNEMISZA
MUSEO DEL PRADO
CENTRO DE ARTE REINA SOFÍA
EL ESCORIAL

LEFT: Edificio Metropolis, Madrid.
BELOW: Cervantes memorial, Plaza de España.

*Metro sign in the busy
Puerta del Sol, the
heart of the city.*

BELOW: selling old
photos in the street.

of a vanished empire. The oldest part of the city is the area between the Palacio Real (Royal Palace) and the Paseo del Prado. It embraces the Plaza Mayor, the Puerta del Sol and the districts of La Latina and Lavapiés. The chaotic arrangement of narrow streets and small irregular squares has changed little since the 17th century.

Heart of the city

The centre of this area, of Madrid, and in a sense of the whole of Spain (as all road distances are measured from here), is the **Puerta del Sol ❶**, the site of a city gate which disappeared in the 16th century. Today it is Madrid's Times Square, where metro and bus lines, as well as major roads, converge. On New Year's Eve Madrid revellers gather here to tick off the final seconds of the old year and usher in the new with the tradition of *las uvas,* the grapes. The idea is to swallow one with each stroke of the midnight clock.

In its younger days the **Plaza Mayor ❷**, a square just to the west surrounded by 17th-century townhouses, saw tournaments and bullfights, politi-

cal gatherings, book burnings, and an occasional hanging or *auto da fé*. With the passing of time it has become the scene of coin and stamp fairs on a Sunday morning, theatrical productions in summer, and fiesta celebrations. In the centre of the square stands a statue of Philip III.

Not far south of the Plaza Mayor is the gloomy 17th-century former cathedral of **San Isidoro ❸**, where the bones of Madrid's patron saint lie. Keep going in the same direction and you come to the site of the **Rastro,** Madrid's animated Sunday flea market. If you're hoping to find a bargain, arrive before 11am, and watch out for pickpockets.

Heading north from the Plaza Mayor across Calle Mayor and Calle del Arenal you come to the **Monasterio de las Descalzas Reales ❹** (Tue–Sun), a royal convent, still functioning as a religious house, with an impressive collection of art treasures. Also worth seeing is the **Real Monasterio de la Encarnación ❺** (open Tue–Sun), which has a renowned reliquary.

Across the Plaza del Oriente from here is the **Palacio Real ❻** (daily). Built between 1738 and 1764 by Italian architects in an imitation French style, the palace is not much to look at from the outside, but inside it is overwhelming. Sumptuous and elegant it is without doubt one of the most splendid palaces in Europe. Though it has more than 2,000 rooms, only some are open to the public. The highlights are the apartments of Charles III, the Salas Gasparini, the throne room and the dining room. King Juan Carlos and Queen Sofía do not live here, but they frequently use the palace for receptions and gala banquets. The inner courtyard has statues of the Roman emperors Trajan, Hadrian, Theodosius and Honorius, all born in Spain.

On the south side of the palace is the **Catedral de Nuestra Señora de la Almudena ❼**, Madrid's Cathedral consecrated by Pope John Paul II in 1995, 110 years after it was begun.

From the Plaza de España to Cibeles

The focal point of the west end of Madrid is the **Plaza de España** ❽, where larger-than-life statues of Don Quixote and his faithful servant Sancho Panza ride into the sunset. A short walk from here leads into the Parque de la Montaña, in which stands the graceful 4th-century BC **Templo de Debod** ❾ (Tue–Sun), a gift to Spain from the Egyptian government.

The Plaza de España marks one end of Madrid's principal street, the **Gran Vía** ❿, which has some magnificent buildings on it, particularly near its junction with the Calle de Alcalá. This in turn leads to the city's emblematic roundabout, the **Plaza de Cibeles** ⓫, at the top of the Paseo del Prado. The main post office dominates the square, and in the middle is a fountain of the goddess Cybele in a chariot harnassed to lions. A short way up the continuation of the Calle de Alcalá is another of Madrid's landmarks, the **Puerta de Alcalá** ⓬, an 18th-century monumental gateway. The streets north of here are laid out in a grid plan and comprise the fashionable shopping and dining district of **Salamanca**.

Art treasures

Madrid's greatest attractions for visitors are its three major museums of art, all within a short stroll of each other. Heading down the Paseo del Prado from the Plaza de Cibeles, you soon come to the first great art gallery, the **Museo Thyssen-Bornemisza** ⓭ (Tue–Sun) in the Palacio Villahermosa. The collection, bought from Baron Thyssen-Bornemisza in the 1990s for £230 million (US$372 million) is notable for its 17th-century Dutch Old Masters, 19th-century North American paintings and 20th-century Russian and German Constructivist paintings.

Across the Plaza Cánovas del Castillo is the internationally renowned **Museo del Prado** ⓮ (Tue–Sun), which holds

The new wing of the Prado, designed by Rafael Moneo, has been described as "quietly heroic".

BELOW:
the Palacio Real.

The Infanta Margarita in Velázquez's Las Meninas.

BELOW RIGHT: the magnificent library in El Escorial.

more than 6,000 paintings, including nearly all the collections of Spain's former royal families. If time allows for only one brief visit, it should include Francisco de Goya (1746–1828). His work is represented in its full range and shines at its brilliant best on its home turf. No one who has seen the Prado's Goyas can fail to feel that he or she has been privy, however briefly, to the most intimate musings of the Spanish soul. A first visit should also include the works of Spain's other celebrated artists, Diego Velázquez (1746–1828) and El Greco (1541–1614), although El Greco is seen to better advantage in his adopted home town of Toledo *(see page 352)*. Among the works of Velázquez not to be missed are *Las Meninas* (The Maids of Honour), *Las Handeras* (The Spinners) and *Los Borrachos* (The Drunkards). Entry to the Prado includes a visit to the museum's annexe, the **Casón del Buen Retiro**, which houses 19th-century work.

To get to the last of the trio of art galleries, continue down the Paseo del Prado. The **Centro de Arte Reina Sofía** ⑮ (Wed–Mon) is a showcase of modern art. It houses Picasso's *Guernica*, a depiction of the obliteration of a village in northern Spain by Nazi war planes during Spain's civil war. Formerly the city hospital, the building has been dramatically renovated to house works by 20th-century Spanish masters Dalí and Miró, as well as Picasso. It also has a lively programme of contemporary exhibitions.

If you want a respite from sightseeing, Madrid's main park, **El Retiro** ⑯, is conveniently located a few streets behind the Prado. In the middle of it is an ornamental boating lake, Two pavilions in the park, the Palacio de Velázquez and the Palacio de Cristal, are used for exhibitons and other cultural events.

Paseo de la Castellana

Modern Madrid could be said to start at the **Plaza de Colón** ⑰, north of the Plaza de Cibeles. Its main artery is the broad and busy Paseo de la Castellana which is lined with prestigious buildings and culminates in the city's latest four skyscrapers, the stunning **Cuatro**

Antique Bars

Madrid has a prodigious variety of bars to choose from, and while the trend is towards contemporary and cutting-edge design, of perennial popularity are the city's old-fashioned taverns *(tabernas)*, dating from the 19th century or early 20th century. Before the days of television, *tabernas* provided homes from home for *madrileños* to congregate and hold intellectual, political and artistic debates.

Around 100 original *tabernas* survive, mostly in the old part of the city. Some of them have beautiful tilework outside and dim, atmospheric interiors with old chairs and tables and shining zinc countertops. Classic examples include **Taberna de Antonio Sánchez** (Calle del Mesón de Paredes 13), **Bodega de Angel Sierra** (Plaza de Chueca), **La Dolores** (Plaza de Jesús), **Casa Labra** (Calle Tetuán 12) and **El Abuelo** (Calle Victoria 12). Most *tabernas* serve food – tapas at least – as well as wines and other drinks, but a few have become renowned restaurants in their own right, notably **El Botín** (Calle de los Cuchilleros 17, behind the Plaza Mayor) and **La Bola** (Calle Bola 5), which specialises in Madrid's traditional warming winter stew, *cocido madrileño*.

Recently, new *tabernas* have been created in the spirit of the real thing, and you may be hard put to tell the difference between the authentically old and the modern re-creation.

Torres, which can be viewed from Chamartín railway station.

Some of Madrid's most interesting museums are just off the Paseo de la Castellana. Behind the Plaza de Colón is Spain's national antiquities museum, the **Museo Arqueológico Nacional** ⑱ (Tue–Sun). While major renovation work is going on, only a selection of the collection is on display, but even this is worth seeing. Its prize exhibits include the Iberian statue of the *Dama de Elche* (Lady of Elche).

Madrid's quaintest museum is the **Museo Lázaro Galdiano** (Wed–Mon), up Calle de Serrano from the Archaeology Museum. An eclectic private collection displayed in the owners' mansion includes paintings, furniture, enamels, ivories, armour and jewellery.

Just across the Paseo de la Castellana from here is the **Museo Sorolla** (Tue–Sun), former home and studio of Spain's best known Impressionist painter, Joaquín Sorolla. A pleasant free-standing villa almost engulfed by modern apartment blocks, it is a good spot to escape from the noise and rush of the city.

Days out

Two of Madrid's most popular sights require a day trip from the city, one to the south, one to the north.

The royal summer retreat, the **Real Palacio de Aranjuez** (Tue–Sun; guided tours only), made famous by Rodriguez's Guitar Concerto, is 45km (27 miles) south of the capital. Stuffed with portraits and porcelain, its attraction lies in its setting in 300 hectares (740 acres) of gardens.

San Lorenzo de El Escorial (Tue–Sun), 50km (30 miles) northwest of Madrid, is the monstrously grandiose fantasy of Philip II, built between 1563 and 1584. Part palace, part monastery, part church and part pantheon, the king had it built in honour of San Lorenzo, on whose feast day (10 August) in 1557 the Spanish won an important victory over the French at St-Quentin. The Museum of Art houses a very fine collection of Flemish, Italian and Spanish paintings. In a country that has always built its cathedrals and monuments in a competely overwhelming style, El Escorial remains in a class of its own.   ❏

TIP

Real Madrid's home stadium – Estadio Santiago Bernabeu – can be visited by guided tour (daily but not during the six hours before a match; tel: 902-311 709 to reserve a place). The tour includes the changing rooms, tunnel, presidential box and trophy room.

BELOW: El Retiro, Madrid's main park.

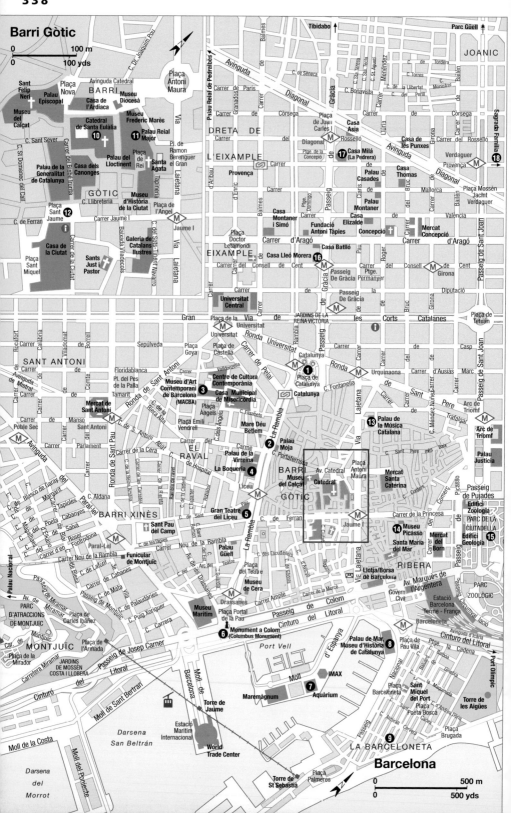

Barri Gòtic

0 ————————— 100 m
0 ————————— 100 yds

BARRI

Plaça Nova

Sant Felip Neri

Museu del Calçat

Palau Episcopal

Casa de l'Ardiaca

Museu Diocesà

Plaça Antoni Maura

Catedral de Santa Eulàlia **10**

Museu Frederic Marès

Palau Reial Major **11**

C. Sant Sever

Casa dels Canonges

Palau del Lloctinent

Pl. de Ramon Berenguer el Gran

Plaça del Rei

Santa Àgata

GÒTIC

Palau de la Generalitat de Catalunya

C. Llibreteria

Museu d'Història de la Ciutat

Plaça de l'Àngel

Plaça Sant Jaume **12**

C. de Ferran

Casa de la Ciutat

Carrer Jaume I

Galeria de Catalans Illustres

Jaume I

Plaça Sant Miquel

Sants Just i Pastor

DRETA DE L'EIXAMPLE

Avinguda Catedral

Avinguda Diagonal

Carrer de Paris

Carrer Còrsega

Plaça de Joan Carles I

Casa Àsia

Diagonal

Rosselló

Casa de les Punxes

Casa de Rosselló

Verdaguer **18**

Ptge. de la Concepció

Casa Milà (La Pedrera) **17**

Provença

Casa Thomas

Provença

L'EIXAMPLE

Carrer d'Aragó

Mallorca

Plaça Mossèn Jacint Verdaguer

València

Palau Casades

Palau Montaner

Casa Montaner i Simó

Casa Elizalde

Fundació Antoni Tàpies

Concepció

Mercat Concepció

d'Aragó

Casa Lleó Morera **16**

Casa Batlló

Passeig De Gràcia

Girona

EIXAMPLE

Carrer del Consell de Cent

Consell de Cent

Ptge. Permanyer

Diputació

Universitat Central

Gran Via de les Corts Catalanes

JARDINS DE LA REINA VICTORIA

Plaça de Tetuán

Plaça de la Universitat

Universitat

Ronda Universitat

Ronda

Casp

SANT ANTONI

Sepúlveda

Plaça Goya

Plaça de Castella

Carrer de Pelai

Plaça de Catalunya **1**

Urquinaona

Carrer d'Ausiàs Marc

Floridablanca

Pl. del Pes de la Palla

Museu d'Art Contemporani de Barcelona (MACBA) **3**

Centre de Cultura Contemporània **3**

Casa Municipal de Misericòrdia

Catalunya

C. Fontanella

Arc de Triomf

Tamarit

Plaça Àngels

Plaça Emili Vendrell

Mare Déu Betlem

Carme

Palau Moja **2**

Palau de la Música Catalana **13**

Arc de Triomf

Mercat de Sant Antoni

Sant Antoni

Manso

Parlament

EL RAVAL

Palau de la Virreina

La Boqueria **4**

Liceu

BARRI GÒTIC

Museu del Calçat

Catedral

Plaça Antoni Maura

Mercat Santa Caterina

Palau Justícia

BARRI XINÈS

Sant Pau del Camp

Gran Teatre del Liceu **5**

C. de Ferran

Jaume I

Museu Picasso **14**

Santa Maria del Mar

Mercat del Born

PARC DE LA CIUTADELLA

Edifici Zoologia

Edifici Geologia **15**

Funicular de Montjuïc

Palau Güell

Plaça del Teatre

RIBERA

Llotja/Borsa de Barcelona

PARC ZOOLÒGIC

Museu de Cera

Drassanes

Museu Marítim

Plaça Portal de la Pau

Passeig de Colom

Av. Marquès de l'Argentera

Govern Civil

Estació Barcelona Terme - França

Barceloneta

Plaça de Pau Vila

Palau Nacional

PARC D'ATRACCIONS DE MONTJUÏC

Av. de Miramar

Plaça de Carles Ibáñez

Monument a Colom (Columbus Monument) **6**

Port Vell

Palau de Mar Museu d'Història de Catalunya **8**

MONTJUÏC

Plaça de la Mirador

JARDINS DE MOSSÈN COSTA I LLOBERA

IMAX

Aquàrium **7**

Plaça Barceloneta

Sant Miquel del Port

Torre de les Aigües

Cinturó

Torre de Jaume I

Maremàgnum

LA BARCELONETA

Plaça Brugada

Darsena San Beltrán

Estació Marítim Internacional

World Trade Center

Torre de St Sebastià

Plaça Palmeres

Barcelona

0 ————————— 500 m
0 ————————— 500 yds

Darsena del Morrot

BARCELONA

Almost half the population of Catalonia lives in Barcelona, Spain's second city and one of the most vivacious and stimulating places in Europe

Spain's principal Mediterranean port is a lively, cosmopolitan city. Although it is somewhat smaller than Madrid, it rivals the capital in its commercial and cultural energy and is known for its own brand of Art Nouveau, Modernisme, and in particular, the strikingly original architectural creations of Anton Gaudí (1852–1926).

The heart of Barcelona is **Plaça de Catalunya ❶**, an open space just beyond the inland medieval wall that was knocked down to build the Eixample (expansion) in the 1850s. Seven thoroughfares converge on the square, which hides a main metro station. The square is the centre of political demonstrations, particularly on National Day, 11 September, and the latest statue is to Francesc Maciá, the brief president of the Catalan Republic of 1931.

The Rambla

The Plaça de Catalunya connects the elegant 19th-century Rambla de Catalunya with **La Rambla ❷**, Barcelona's most famous street, which heads 1.2km (¾ mile) down to the port and was originally a seasonal riverbed. The Rambla is in five parts. The Rambla Canaletes is named after a drinking fountain where Barça football supporters meet. Next comes the Rambla dels Estudis, known as the Rambla dels Ocells (Rambla of the Birds). Canaries, parakeets and other exotic birds, as well as chinchillas, iguanas and terrapins, are on sale here, despite threats of closure from

the authorities. Behind the Rambla dels Estudis in the working-class Raval district is the shockingly modern **Museu d'Art Contemporani de Barcelona ❸** (MACBA; Wed–Mon), designed by the American architect Richard Meier. Its changing exhibitions of sculptures and installations seem secondary in attraction to the building itself.

From the Rambla dels Estudis the twitter of birds gives way to the kaleidoscope of flowers in the Rambla de Sant Josep or Rambla de les Flors, overlooked by the imposing **Palau de la**

BELOW:
the chimneys on Gaudí's Casa Milà.

*Santa Eulàlia
Cathedral in the
Barri Gòtic.*

BELOW: the
Rambla is busy
night and day.

Virreina (1778). Built for the Viceroy of Peru, it is now the property of the city, which has installed a bookshop and gallery spaces.

Just beyond is **La Boqueria** ❹, or the Mercat de Sant Josep, a food emporium of iron and stained glass built in 1835 and containing all the best food of the season Catalonia has to offer, from mushrooms and truffles to bright fruits, neat piles of vegetables and shimmering fish. Shop before 10am for the best bargains, and try the small bars, such as La Garduña, at the market's edge. Outside the market, coloured pavings by Joan Miró in the middle of the Rambla mark the Plaça Boqueria, a former place of execution just outside the city gates.

The **Gran Teatre del Liceu** ❺ on the Rambla dels Caputxins is one of Europe's great opera houses, which has risen from the ashes of a devastating fire in 1994. Opposite is the Cafè de l'Òpera, a delightful period café, said to have been a haunt of Casanova.

Beside the opera, Carrer Nou de la Rambla leads to **Palau Güell** , gloomiest of Gaudí's buildings, bristling with dark metalwork. Ten years earlier, in 1878, Gaudí designed the lamp-posts in **Plaça Reial**, opposite Carrer Nou. With classical, arcaded facades, restaurants, palm trees and a central fountain, this is one of the most exciting squares in the city.

The Rambla Santa Mònica is the last wide stretch of promenade before the sea. At weekends craft stalls give this traditionally low-life end of the Rambla an innocent air. The Rambla terminates in front of the 50-metre (160ft) **Columbus Monument** ❻ (Monument a Colom; daily), built in 1888 by Gaietà Buigas and sitting on a traffic island. A lift takes visitors to the top for a grand view over the city and waterfront. Barcelona's seafaring activities can be appreciated with a visit to the **Museu Marítim** (daily), housed in the impressive 13th-century Reials Drassanes (Royal Shipyards) close by.

At the end of his first American voyage, Columbus came ashore on the steps in front of his statue, where the *Golondrinas* (pleasure boats) now give trips round the harbour and to the Olympic port. The port authority building lies beside the steps. The jetty over to the right is the Moll de Barcelona, site of the World Trade Centre and the terminal for cruise liners.

After this brief interruption, the Rambla continues as the Rambla del Mar, a walkway out over the harbour to shops and restaurants, IMAX cinema and the **Aquàrium** ❼ (daily), where visitors walk through glass tunnels to see creatures of the deep. The only remaining industrial building on the north side of the port is the warehouse designed by the Modernist architect Elies Rogent and now turned into the Palau de Mar, where the **Museu d'Història de Catalunya** ❽ (Tue–Sun) tells the story of the region. Behind it is the fishermen's quarter of **La Barceloneta** ❾, a nighttime haunt of good small bars and fish restaurants. Barceloneta is the start of the city's 6km (4-mile) beach, which leads past Nova Icària, the former Olympic Village, to the **Port Olímpic**, dominated by twin towers and lined with popular restaurants.

The Barri Gòtic and royal city

The Gothic Quarter is Barcelona's Old City, begun by the Romans and still darkly medieval, with thick-walled buildings, narrow lanes and heavy doorways. The **Catedral de Santa Eulàlia** ❿ is built near the high point of Mons Taber, selected by the Romans for their settlement. To the right of the main entrance of the cathedral is the Romanesque Capella de Santa Llúcia, dating from 1268. Inside, to the left of the main entrance, a tablet commemorates the baptism here of the natives Columbus brought back with him from America. The cloisters are not to be missed; this shady quadrangle surrounds a garden of ferns, tropical plants and a family of geese which has lorded it here for centuries.

Behind the Cathedral and cloisters is a network of alleys and courtyards. Carrer Condes, on the left, leads to the **Museu Frederic Marès** (Tue–Sun), an eccentric museum in part of the former

Palau Reial Major ⓫ (Tue–Sun), palace of the count-kings of Barcelona-Aragon. The palace faces onto the **Plaça del Rei**, the heart of royal Barcelona looked down on by the tall rectangular watchtower of Martí I (the Humanist), last of the 500-year dynasty of counts of Barcelona. On the outer side of this intimate square is the 15th-century Palau Clariana Padellàs, entrance to the **Museu d'Història de la Ciutat** (Tue–Sun). The main reason for visiting the city museum is to see the layout of extensive Roman streets and walls uncovered beneath the Plaça Real.

Beyond the museum, a flight of steps leads to a reception hall and the 36-metre (120ft) **Saló de Tinell**, built in 1370. Used as a throne room, and by the Inquisition, this impressive space is where Ferdinand and Isabella greeted Columbus on his return from America. To the right of the hall is the 14th-century royal **Chapel of Santa Àgata**, which has a fine altarpiece by Jaume Huguet (1414–92).

Between the Cathedral and Plaça del Rei is **Plaça Sant Jaume** ⓬, the city's political hub, with the **Palau de**

In 1926 the great Modernist architect Antoni Gaudí i Cornet, was run down by a tram A reclusive and dishevelled figure, he was mistaken for a tramp and put in the local hospital's "paupers' ward", where he died five days later. By contrast, the streets of Barcelona were lined with mourners at his funeral.

la Generalitat de Catalunya, the seat of Catalonia's government, on one side and the **Casa de la Ciutat**, home of the city council, on the other. The Palau de la Generalitat opens up on St George's Day, 23 April, the patron saint of the city. Behind the Generalitat building was the medieval **Jewish Quarter** or Call, which occupied the streets between Carrer del Call and Carrer Banys Nous. A Hebrew inscription on the wall of No. 1 Carrer Martlet dates from 692. The Jews were forced from the city in 1424.

La Ribera and the Picasso Museum

La Ribera lies on the far side of Via Laietana, the 19th-century thoroughfare. Towards the top on the right is **Palau de la Música Catalana ⓭**, a fine Modernist concert hall designed by Domènech i Montaner (1850–1923) in 1908. It has a magnificent tiled facade and its interior is equally impressive. La Ribera is penetrated by Carrer Princesa and its noblest street is Carrer Montcada. Palau Berenguer d'Aguilar, built in the 15th century

by Marc Safont, is one of a string of elegant mansions that crowd this narrow lane, and it has become the home, with the adjoining Palau Castallet, of the **Museu Picasso ⓮** (Tue–Sun). The museum has a collection of around 3,000 of Picasso's works, including some ceramics. Many are from his early years when he was a student in the city, and they show what a competent and precocious draughtsman he was. Pride of place goes to *Las Meninas*, 58 paintings based on Velázquez's originals in the Prado in Madrid.

Carrer Montcada leads into Passeig de Born, and **Santa María del Mar**, the finest church in the city, built in one harmonious hit, between 1329 and 1384.

Beyond La Ribera lies the 34-hectare (85-acre) **Parc de la Ciutadella ⓯**. The Catalan Parliament sits here in the former arsenal. The 30-hectare (75-acre) city **zoo** (daily) covers the south side of the park, and beside it is a fountain with *Dama del Paraigues*, a captivating sculpture of a young woman beneath an umbrella, by Roig i Soler.

The Modernist city

Catalonia's distinctive Art Nouveau, called Modernisme, flowered among Ildefons Cerdà's 19th-century Eixample. It was his grid plan, in which the corners of the squares were clipped off, that provided the platform for the city's newly enriched industrialists to show off. The best examples lie within the Quadrat d'Or, the Golden Square, centred on the fashionable **Passeig de Gràcia**, which leads up from the Plaça de Catalunya. **Casa Lleó Morera ⓰** at No. 35 is by Domènech i Montaner, perhaps the purist of the Modernist practitioners, and from here you can obtain a ticket to visit the main Modernist sites.

No. 41 is **Casa Amatller**, a beautiful, eclectic building by Josep Puig i Cadafalch (1867–1967), beside the more excessive work of its neighbour, **Casa Batlló** (daily), by Antoni Gaudí i Cornet (1852–1926), a glazed and undulating building typical of the movement's greatest exponent. The three buildings

BELOW: the Palau de la Música Catalana.

are known as the Mançana de Discòrdia, the "block of discord".

Further up the Passeig de Gràcia, on the right, is Gaudí's best-known civic work, **Casa Milà ⑰** cultural centre (daily), known as La Pedrera (the Stone Quarry), an eight-storey apartment block devoid of straight lines and topped with sinister chimneys nicknamed *espantabruixes*, "witch scarers".

After he finished La Pedrera, Gaudí devoted himself exclusively to his most famous work, the **Sagrada Família ⑱** (daily), reached along Carrer de Provença, which runs beside La Pedrera. He finished only the crypt and the Nativity facade with three doorways to Faith, Hope and Charity. Work continues to complete the ambitious project, which will eventually be 27 metres (87ft) longer than Barcelona's old Cathedral and twice the height. Gaudí spent his last 10 years living, unpaid, in a hut on the site, abandoning the house he had lived in at **Park Güell**. This stunning pleasure garden, originally designed as a housing project, is 15 minutes' walk from Lesseps metro station on the outskirts of the Collserola hills and has good views of the city.

Pedralbes

Count Eusebi Güell, Gaudí's industrialist patron, had a country estate at Pedralbes, and, in 1919, a year after his death, his manor house was turned into a palace for visiting royalty. **The Palau Reial de Pedralbes** houses the **Museu Ceràmica** (Tue–Sun), an excellent collection of pottery and kitchenware going back to the 8th century. On the inland side of the estate is the exquisite **Museu Monestir de Pedralbes** (Tue–Sun), one of the jewels of the city. This collection of buildings includes the monastery church where its founder, Queen Elisenda, wife of Jaume II, is buried. Inside, the Santa Maria convent looks much as the nuns left it. Their dormitory is now given over to the **Thyssen-Bornemisza Collection** of some 70 religious paintings, mostly from Italy.

Montjuïc and Tibidabo: hilltop playgrounds

Montjuïc, the hill overlooking the port, has been the city's playground since it was laid out for the International Exhibition of 1929. The austere **Palau Nacional** houses the **Museu Nacional d'Art de Catalunya** (MNAC; Tue–Sun). This is an exemplary collection, particularly of Catalan Romanesque art taken from remote churches in the Pyrenees.

Housed in a stylish white building is the **Fundació Joan Miró** (Tue–Sun am), built by the painter's friend Josep Lluís Sert in 1975. The most ambitious project for the 1929 Exhibition was the **Poble Espanyol** (daily) a "village" comprising buildings that display the architectural differences of the various regions of Spain. This is a popular place to visit: its nightlife of bars, cafés and restaurants makes the place lively until dawn.

The city's other hilltop playground is **Tibidabo**, also offering great views. The last word in heights, however, must go to Norman Foster's nearby tower, the **Torre de Collserola**, a vertiginous needle with a glass viewing panel 115 metres (337ft) above the ground. ❏

BELOW: the view from Torre de Collserola.

AROUND SPAIN

Most visitors head for Spain's beaches, but inland the country has a rich heritage to explore, including Roman and Moorish monuments, historic towns and cities and wild nature reserves

Madrid

The northwest of the country, which juts out into the Atlantic beneath the Bay of Biscay, is "Green Spain", where Atlantic winds are driven onto the mountainous coast and rainfall averages up to 250cm (100in) a year. This area was the least touched by the Moorish incursion, and from its inhospitable mountains the reconquest of the peninsula, under the ancient dynasties of Asturias and Navarre, began. This is also where one of the world's first "tourist" destinations is to be found.

Santiago de Compostela

Santiago de Compostela ❶ has been drawing pilgrims since the apparent discovery of the tomb of St James, patron of Spain, in AD 812. The city's present cathedral dates from 1075 and remains the goal of pilgrims. Consecrated in 1211, the handsome Romanesque building faces onto Praza do Obradoro, where the grand Hostal de los Reyes Católicos, begun in 1501 under the order of Ferdinand and Isabella as an inn and hospital for pilgrims, is now an elegant hotel.

Pilgrims from England sometimes reached Santiago by sailing to **La Coruña** (A Coruña), Galicia's principal city and port in the northwest corner of the country, where white buildings with characteristic enclosed glass balconies (*miradores*) line the seafront. The city's showpiece is the Torre de Hércules, a Roman lighthouse. Southwest of La Coruña, the coast of Spain intrudes into the wild waters of the Atlantic as the headland of Cabo Fisterra, "Land's End", which in medieval times was thought to be literally the limit of the world. The most accessible and attractive stretch of Galicia's coast is the Rias Baixas, stretching roughly from Padrón to Baiona. Pontevedra and Vigo, home to the largest fishing fleet in Europe, are the main towns, but the prettiest spots include Combarro, with its numerous *horreos* (stone granaries on stilts), Cambados and the island of A Toxa, joined

Main attractions
SANTIAGO DE COMPOSTELA
PICOS DE EUROPA
SALAMANCA
MUSEO GUGGENHEIM, BILBAO
GIRONA AND THE COSTA BRAVA
VALENCIA
TOLEDO
SEVILLE
CÓRDOBA AND THE MEZQUITA
GRANADA AND THE ALHAMBRA
COSTA DEL SOL
COSTA DE LA LUZ

LEFT: a human tower in Catalunya.
BELOW: Santiago de Compostela.

TIP

A novel way of seeing the north of Spain is to take the luxury Transcantábrico train from Bilbao to Ferrol in Galicia. See www. transcantabrico.com for times, prices and the full route.

to the mainland by a bridge. Anywhere on this coast you will eat fish and seafood without equal accompanied by the local dry white wines.

The Costa Verde

The **Cordillera Cantábrica** is a high range of mountains that cuts Asturias and Cantabria off from inland Spain. The coastal drive along the northern coast, the Costa Verde, winds over cliffs and through valleys, arriving at picturesque fishing ports such as **Luarca**. This is a land of cider, and the apple brew is poured from fizzy heights in the cider bars around the country. Inland, the capital, **Oviedo ❷**, is a treasure house of pre-Romanesque architecture, the finest in Spain. Part royal palace, part church, **Santa Maria del Naranco** dates from Ramiri I in the 9th century; adjacent is the delightful San Miguel de Lillo. San Julián de los Prados, in Oviedo's suburbs, should also not be missed. The first King of Asturias was Pelayo, who began the reconquest in 722 by defeating the Moors at **Covadonga** in what is now the **Parque Nacional de los Picos de Europa**, the

most spectacular mountain region of Spain. Entry points are at **Potes** and **Cangas de Onis**, and a cable car rises 800 metres (2,625ft) from **Fuente Dé**, giving heavenly views.

The Cantabrian coast has a variety of resorts. There are sandy beaches at **Laredo** and around **Santander ❸**, the principal city and port, which was ravaged by fire in 1941 but now sits serenely between the green hills and blue sea. **Santillana del Mar** is a picturesque medieval village; nearby at **Altamira** is the "Sistine chapel" of cave art, which dates from 13,000 BC. The bison, deer, boar and horses painted on the ceilings in ochres, manganese oxide, charcoal and iron carbonate are the largest known group of prehistoric polychrome figures in the world. Access to the cave is severely restricted, but a **museum** (Tue–Sun) contains a replica which gives a flavour of the finds.

Castilla y León

When the reconquest of the peninsula from the Moors began, the Christian Spaniards came down out of the hills of Asturias onto the inhospitable

BELOW: Picos de Europa.

depopulated *meseta*, where winters are cold and summers baking hot. Here they built fortified castles to push their frontier forward. The first two cities to be created in this new land of Castilla (Castile) were León and Burgos, both on the main route from the Pyrenees to Santiago de Compostela, and both given Gothic cathedrals.

León ❹, formerly politically connected to Galicia, has a particularly fine Cathedral, with 1,800 sq metres (20,000 sq ft) of wonderful stained-glass windows, yet its construction is fragile and no one is sure quite how it still manages to stay up. Even more impressive is the **Basilica de San Isidoro**, with its adjoining **Panteón Real**, where some 20 monarchs are entombed, and which has delightful ceiling frescoes of the seasons.

Burgos ❺ is the home of the great vanquisher of the Moors, Rodrigo Díaz de Vivar (1043–99), known as El Cid, whose tomb lies in the cathedral. But the great treasures of this town are to be found in the **Real Monasterio de las Huelgas** (Tue–Sun), founded in 1187 by Alfonso VIII and surprisingly

decorated with Moorish patterns, as are the clothes, still in fine repair, worn by the medieval monarchs and their families. Southeast of Burgos is the **Monasterio de Santo Domingo de Silos** (daily), famous for its cloisters and chanting Benedictine monks.

Much of the rest of Old Castile, between Madrid and the north coast provinces, is drab, remote from modern life and sparsely populated, but several great cities punctuate the plains and ranges of hills. **Valladolid** ❻, a rambling town with elaborate churches, has the **Museu Nacional de Escultura** (Tue–Sun), providing a crash course in Spanish Renaissance architecture. **Salamanca** ❼, on the other hand, is very much a part of cultural Spain. Its university was founded in 1218, though the Inquisition put paid to its reputation as a haven for new ideas and thinkers. The philosopher and novelist Miguel de Unanumo brought it brief glory before the Civil War, and it has again begun to take its place at the forefront of Spanish literary life.

The main square, **Plaza Major**, designed in the early 18th century by

If you have a head for heights, take the cable car from Fuente Dé for splendid views.

BELOW: the Casa de las Conchas in Salamanca.

*Gehry's Guggenheim
Museum, Bilbao, has
attracted many
visitors to the city.*

BELOW: the Roman
aqueduct in
Segovia can be
seen while you
have a drink at a
pavement café.

Alberto Churriguera, is magnificent both for architecture and ambience.

Ávila ❽, 113km (70 miles) northwest of Madrid, has been compared by poets to both a coffer and a crown. The highest city on the peninsula, it is sealed within perfectly preserved medieval walls 10 metres (33ft) high, with 88 round towers and nine fortified entrances.

Closer to Madrid is **Segovia ❾**, whose charms are evident at first sight. It fills up with *madrileños* every weekend who come to admire the Roman **Aqueduct** and fairytale *Alcázar*, and feast on the cuisine for which the province is famous. The *Alcázar* (daily) is a child's dream of a castle. The most interesting rooms are the Sala de Reyes, containing woodcarvings of early kings, and Sala del Cordón, decorated with a frieze of the Franciscan cord. The arduous climb up to the Torre de Juan II is rewarded by sweeping views of the Segovian countryside.

Rioja – Spain's wine region

To the east of Burgos lies **Rioja**, Spain's best-known wine country. Its reputation was made in the 19th century by the Marqués de Riscal and the Marqués de Murrieta, who returned from exile in Bordeaux to emulate methods they had encountered in France, using oak barrels to age the wines. Their wineries still operate, in **Elciego** and **Logroño ❿** respectively, and there are now 350 wine houses in the 500-sq km (200-sq mile) region. The main wine town, **Haro**, holds the bacchanalian Batalla del Vino on 29 June, when everyone is drenched with wine.

The Basque Country and Aragón

Rioja's northern neighbour is the Basque Country, home of a singular people with ancient roots who speak a language (Euskera) of uncertain origin. Its capital is **Vitoria-Gasteiz ⓫**, built on a high point. The *miradores* on the old houses around its main square, **Plaza de la Virgen Blanca**, are typical of the northern coast. The main port of the Basque country is **Bilbao ⓬** (Bilbo), a grey city squeezed into the lower valley of the Nervión, which has reinvented itself after the decline of the steel industry around the **Museo Guggenheim** (Tue–Sun), a shining "metallic flower" designed by the Californian architect Frank O. Gehry. Shockingly modern, it is set by the river and has changing exhibitions, though most people come to see the building itself.

Basque food is one of the wonders of Spain, and there are many places along the coast where the seafood is fresh and delicious. **San Sebastián ⓭** (Donostia) is queen of the resorts, with great restaurants and an old quarter that is great for bar-hopping.

Heading eastwards takes you to Navarra in the foothills of the Pyrenees. **Pamplona ⓮** (Iruña), former capital of the kingdom of Navarre, was made famous beyond Spain by Ernest Hemingway, who came to see the running of the bulls which he wrote about in *The Sun Also Rises* (1926). The event still takes place each year with a wild, week-long festival starting on the eve of San Fermín (6 July) and culminating

in the *encierro*, when bulls run through the streets to the bullring. There are often serious accidents among the daredevil participants.

The **Monasterio de Leyre**, southeast of Pamplona, was Navarre's 11th-century spiritual centre and pantheon for its kings. It is a beautiful Romanesque building with a fine vaulted crypt, consecrated in 1057. Recently restored by Benedictines, whose chants can be heard, it now includes a hotel. Further east, in the landlocked region of Aragón, is **San Juan de la Peña** (daily), wedged between enormous boulders under a sheer rock cliff. It was built for Sancho Ramírez (1063–94) and contains tombs of early Aragonese kings. Just to the north is **Jaca** ⓯, a good centre for exploring the lovely valleys in the central Pyrenees.

The regional capital of Aragón is **Zaragoza** ⓰, a Roman town (its name derives from "Caesaraugusta") which was knocked about in the Napoleonic Wars. It has two cathedrals: **Nuestra Señora del Pilar** has 11 distinctive domes and a cupola painted by Goya, a native of Aragón. More impressive is the **Aljafería**, built in the 11th century by the ruling Moorish king.

Catalonia

Aragón was united with the royal house of Barcelona in the 12th century, but the seafaring Catalans fiercely guarded their independence, their rights and their language. A variant of their language is Aranese, spoken in the **Vall d'Aran**. Cut off every winter until 1948, when a tunnel was built through the mountains, the lovely valley around the town of **Vielha** ⓱ supports rare butterfly life and is a popular ski centre, notably at **Baqueira-Beret**, a haunt of the royal family. Catalan is the official language, too, of **Andorra** ⓲, the anomalous 468-sq km (180-sq mile) principality *(see Microstates, page 358)*. The upper reaches of the principality are pleasing and remote, but the roads leading to Andorra la Vella can be hell during holidays, weekends and in August. **La Seu d'Urgell**, on the other hand, is a sleepy old mountain town with a 12th-century Cathedral, 13th-century cloister and an excellent collection of Romanesque art in its Episcopal Museum.

Catalonia was Spain's most important centre for Romanesque painting, which shows the Byzantine influence. Its ritualistic figures are almost expressionless, even when they undergo horrifying martyrdoms.

BELOW: view over Aiguablava on the Costa Brava.

Girona Cathedral dominates the steep cobbled streets of the historic town.

BELOW: the Dalí Museum in Figueres is great fun and always busy.

Catalonia's Pyrenean valleys are notable for their stunning Romanesque churches with tall belltowers, such as Sant Climent de Taüll in the Boí Valley, just south of the **Parc Nacional de Aigüestortes**. A masterpiece of Romanesque carvings can be seen on the facade of the former monastery of Santa Maria in **Ripoll** ⓳, a sheep town with an excellent Folk Museum. Ripoll Monastery was founded in 888 by Guifré el Pilós, first Count of Barcelona, and the town has been called "the cradle of Catalonia". At the nearby monastery of **Sant Joan de les Abadesses**, where Guifré's daughter was abbess, there is an exquisite Romanesque Calvary in the church.

The Costa Brava and Dalí

Brava means wild or rugged, and this coast, running some 90km (60 miles) from the French border to **Blanes**, just short of Barcelona, twists and turns around coves and over cliffs in one of the most celebrated shores of the Mediterranean. This was where the Romans first arrived on the peninsula, to subjugate the people. They made a base at **Empúries** in the Bay of Roses, where the Greeks already had a trading settlement with the indigenous Iberians. The site includes the remains of the Greek harbour wall. On the north side of the bay is Cap de Creu and Spain's easternmost mainland town, **Cadaqués** ⓴. This is the St-Tropez of the coast, with galleries and boutiques in steep cobbled streets. The painter Salvador Dalí lived at **Port-Lligat**, just to the north, and **Casa-Museu Salvador Dalí** (mid-Mar–Dec Tues–Sun, July–Aug daily), the two fishermen's houses he famously made his home, are now visitable. It is a strangely enchanting place. A Dalí route takes in the castle he bought inland at Puból, and the town of **Figueres**, where the **Teatre-Museu Dalí** (June–Sept daily, Oct–May Tue–Sun) is one of the most popular museums in Spain.

There is an old-fashioned, family air to many of the resorts on the coast, particularly the more intimate coves and beaches such as **Aiguablava**, **Tamariu**, **Calella de Palafrugell** and even **Tossa de Mar**. The larger resorts of **Roses**, **Platja d'Aro**, **Lloret de Mar** and **Blanes**

have spread along sandy beaches and are brighter and brasher, catering for a younger, trendier, night-owl crowd.

The main town for the Costa Brava is **Girona ㉑**, some 20km (12 miles) inland. It is attractively sited beside the River Onyar, where bridges lead to a Rambla and steep cobbled streets heading for a Cathedral with the widest nave in Christendom. An archaeological walk follows the old town walls, which were breached in a heroic siege in the Napoleonic Wars. At the heart of the Old Town a former Jewish quarter has been opened up.

Tarragona and the Costa Daurada

Sitges ㉒, 45 minutes on the train from Barcelona, is an eternally elegant resort, popular for Sunday lunch and also popular with gays, who dominate the outrageous pre-Lent carnival. The sandy beaches of the Costa Daurada continue past the wine town of **Vala-franca del Penedès** to **Tarragona ㉓**, the major provincial town of Roman Tarraconensis, where an amphitheatre, beneath the Balcó de Europa at the end of the Rambla, overlooks the sea. Its Roman walls have massive stones, and there is a museum of archaeological finds. Its cathedral is built on the site of a Roman temple and Arab mosque. Inland is the **Monestir de Poblet**, grandest of the "Cistercian Triangle" of monasteries. Founded in 1151 and several times despoiled, it contains royal tombs from the 12th to 14th centuries.

Near the resort of Salou, south of Tarragona, is **Port Aventura**, one of the biggest theme parks in Europe (Apr–Oct daily, Nov–Dec weekends and public holidays). The Costa Daurada ends at the rice-growing delta of the Ebro (Ebre), Spain's largest river, which fans out into the sea to create an important habitat for flamingos and other birdlife. There is an information centre in **Deltebre**.

Valencia and its coastline

Valencia ㉔ lies in the most fertile farmlands of Spain. The country's third-largest city is known for its oranges, paella and the sensational conflagration that ends the city's Las Fallas fiesta on 19 March. Ceramics are also a

Valencia's port was transformed to host the 2007 America's Cup and is now graced with a harbourside Formula 1 circuit. The city is one of the most modern and vibrant in Spain, with a stunning City of Arts and Sciences complex designed by Santiago Calatrava.

BELOW: Tossa de Mar looks romantic at night.

Santiago Calatrava's L'Hemisfèric in the City of Arts and Sciences, Valencia.

BELOW RIGHT: one of the Casas Colgadas (Hanging Houses) in Cuenca.

speciality, and there is some lovely tile-work to be seen in the city, as well as at the **Museo Nacional de Cerámica** (Mon–Sat). One of the city's most handsome buildings, the 15th-century commodities exchange, La Lonja, is now a concert and exhibition venue, and a modern vibrancy is reflected in galleries of contemporary art.

Many resorts on the varied coasts north (Costa del Azahar) and south (Costa Blanca) of Valencia, such as **Dénia** and **Altea**, have attractive old towns; **Peñiscola** is a memorable "tail" of land with a fortified community at its tip, surrounded by the sea. But it is **Benidorm**, with a fine sandy beach and acres of high-rise hotels, that has given the area its package-holiday reputation. **Alicante** ㉕ (Alacant) is the Costa Blanca's main city, with a port and airport, and it has a fine, palm-lined esplanade. In the town hall is a metal disc, which is the marker for all measurements above sea level around Spain. Near Alicante is the extraordinary plantation at **Elche** (Elx) of more than a quarter of a million palms, said to have been planted by the Phoenicians. A 5th-century BC stone

bust of a priestess, La Dame de Elche, found here, is one of the nation's great treasures; it is now in Madrid. Away from the coast, both Valencia and Murcia provinces are mountainous. One of the most picturesque upland areas is **El Maestrazgo** (Maestrat), where crags and flat-topped summits form a backdrop to stout medieval towns such as **Morella** ㉖, where significant Roman remains have also been found.

Toledo and Castilla-La Mancha

The saffron which colours Valencia's paellas comes from the inland region of **La Mancha**. On the edge of the plains – the stamping ground of Don Quixote – is **Cuenca** ㉗, one of Spain's most dramatically sited towns. Here, the Casas Colgadas (Hanging Houses) teeter on the edge of a cliff over the River Huéscar. One of them contains the **Museo de Arte Abstracto** (Tue–Sun), with works by the Catalan Antoni Tapiès and the Basque Eduardo Chillado.

Far across the plains is **Toledo** ㉘, the former capital of Spain and still its spiritual heart, which stands on a

The Quixote Trail

A tour of central La Mancha is an opportunity for fans of *Don Quixote* to trace key points in various chapters from Miguel Cervantes's novel – the world's first bestseller, published in 1615. El Toboso, on the N-301 between Albacete and Ocaña, was the village of Dulcinea, Don Quixote's fantasised true love for whom he was so quick to risk all. Casa de Dulcinea (Tue–Sun), thought to be the house of the woman on whom Cervantes modelled his damsel, has been restored to its 16th-century appearance. Puerto Lápiz, 20km (12 miles) southeast of Consuegra, matches Cervantes's description of the inn where Don Quixote was sworn in as a knight errant. The line of windmills nearby at Campo de Criptana look as if they might be the ones Quixote mistook for giants, their flailing sails "attacking" the deluded knight tilting at them. The Cueva de Montesinos near San Pedro lake in the Lagunas de Ruidera Valley is the cave where our hero was treated to elegiac visions of other bewitched knights and of his beloved Dulcinea. The town of Argamasilla de Alba, meanwhile, is a firm candidate for the place where it began: *"En un lugar de La Mancha…"* – In a place in La Mancha…

bend on the River Tajo (Tagus) 70km (45 miles) south of Madrid. The city has many claims to fame: damascene metalwork, El Greco and an Old Town that is listed as a Unesco World Heritage site. The city's Cathedral has a venerable history, and was a centre of Christianity before the Moors arrived. Richly embellished, it has a good picture collection in the sacristy. But the town's other worshippers are well represented: Visigothic crown jewels can be seen in the **Iglesia de San Román**; and there are two synagogues, one of which contains a Sefardic museum. El Greco lived in the Jewish Quarter from his arrival in the city in 1517 until his death in 1614. Toledo is dominated by the **Alcázar**, a mainly 16th-century fortress but dating back to the time of El Cid. It was the object of a protracted siege in the 1936–9 Civil War and today contains an Army Museum.

Extremadura, land of the conquistadores

West of Madrid is **Extremadura**, one of the least visited parts of Spain, which provided many adventurers for the New World. Francisco Pizarro, conqueror of Peru, was born in **Trujillo ㉙**, where his statue adorns the Plaza Mayor. His brother Hernando built the **Palacio del Marqués de la Conquista** opposite the statue. The facade has a bust of Francisco Pizarro and his wife, Inés Yupanqui, sister of the Inca emperor Atahualpa.

Many Catholics make their way to the **Real Monasterio de Guadalupe ㉚** (daily) to see the Guadalupe Virgin, who exercises her influence not just in Spain but also in the Americas, where more than 100 cities are named after her.

Southwest of Guadalupe is **Mérida ㉛**, capital of Lusitania, the Roman's western Iberian province. Roman history is scattered all over the town; the impressive theatre is still used for summer drama festivals, and the **Museo Nacional de Arte Roman** (Tue–Sun), designed in 1988 by Rafael Moneo, has the largest collection of Roman artefacts outside Italy.

The sultry south

Named al-Andalus by its Arabic conquerors, Andalucía, the province of

WHERE

South of Toledo is the Parque Nacional de Cabañeros, reached via the C-401 and C-403. You can take a guided tour of the park in a four-wheel-drive vehicle, during which you may well see wild boar, stag and imperial eagles.

BELOW: the Roman amphitheatre in Mérida is still used for drama festivals.

Taking a leisurely ride through the streets of Seville.

the south, is the soul of Spain. Warm, sleepy, proud, vibrant, it is the country's most populated region. Under Moorish dominion in the Middle Ages, it had one of the most highly developed civilisations in Europe. Until the reconquest of Granada by the Catholic monarchs Fernando and Isabel in 1492, Andalucía had rarely been united under one ruler. Internecine strife among *emirs* and *taífas* of Córdoba, Jaén, Granada and Seville undermined Moorish domination until the increasing pressure of Spain's northern Christian kingdoms ultimately vanquished it. Today its coast is the most cosmopolitan in Europe.

Seville and Córdoba

Seville Ⓐ (Sevilla), capital of Andalucía and the country's fourth-largest city, is the dazzling setting of Bizet's *Carmen*, Rossini's barber and the adventures of Don Juan. The city's two finest buildings face each other across the Plaza del Triunfo in the central Santa Cruz district. On the north side is the **Cathedral** (daily), Europe's largest, where Christopher Columbus has a highly figurative tomb. The adjoining Moorish belltower is known as the **Giralda**, after the weathervane (*giraldillo*) at the top, and from here there are good views of the city. God and Muhammad have been worshipped on the same sites; the Cathedral was built on an earlier mosque – Muslim worshippers would wash their hands and feet in the fountain of the **Patio de los Naranjos**, the orange orchard cloisters.

On the south side of the square is the **Real Alcázar**, the Royal Palace (Tue-Sun). Like the cathedral, it has excellent Mudéjar designs, in particular its patios and beautiful Ambassadors' Hall, which are fantasies in filigree. The former palace of the Almohads was redesigned by Pedro I in 1344 after the city's conquest. From here Isabella sent Columbus and other navigators to the New World, their ships sailing down the River Guadalquivir. The dockyards were to the south, in El Arenal district, where the fine 18th-century bullring can be found.

Spring is Seville's busiest time, with the exuberant processions of Easter Week immediately followed by the

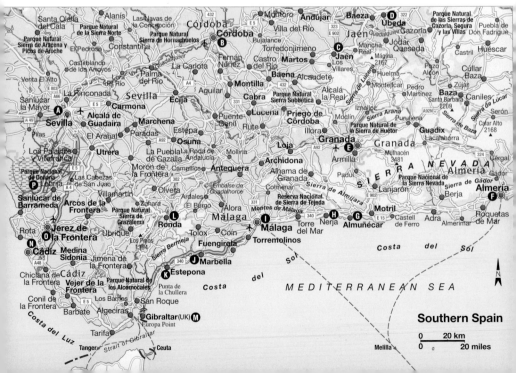

Southern Spain

brilliant April Feria. Held in the fairground across the river from the city centre, this is when everyone dresses up to the nines and lets down their hair in a confluence of Andalucian stereotypes: wine, bulls, horses and flamenco.

Córdoba Ⓑ, smaller and less flamboyant than Seville, was the city of a brilliant Caliphate, and its Great Mosque, the **Mezquita** (daily), dating from Abd al Rahman in the 8th century, is one of the splendours of Moorish Spain. Take a walk in the Jewish Quarter beside the mosque for an idea of how the medieval city must have been; the area includes the remains of a 14th-century synagogue.

Jaén province

On the eastern side of Andalucía is Jaén province, an undulating expanse of 150 million olive trees. Its capital, **Jaén Ⓒ**, perched above the western plain with its back to the sierras, has a massive Cathedral, fine Arab baths and hilltop Moorish castle. The towns of **Úbeda Ⓓ** and **Baeza**, on adjacent hilltops between Jaén city, are superb compilations of Renaissance buildings; the historic cores of both towns are Unesco World Heritage sites. The nature reserve of Cazorla y Segura is the biggest in Spain.

Granada

The jewel of Moorish Spain is the **Alhambra** (daily; advance reservation advised) in **Granada Ⓔ**, the last stronghold of the longest-running kingdom of the Moors, and the home of Spain's great poet and playwright Federico García Lorca (1898–1936). No amount of description can prepare the visitor for the Alhambra's exquisite architecture, which is the epitome of Moorish imagination and artistry. The royal residence is highlighted by the **Patio de los Arrayanes** (Patio of the Myrtles) and **Patio de los Leones** (Patio of the Lions). The **Alcazaba** (castle), at the western end of Alhambra Hill, is a 9th-century Moorish citadel with grand views over the city. The adjoining **Generalife**, dating from 1250, was the summer palace of the sultans – cool and green and full of restful pools and murmuring fountains. In summer an International Festival of Music and

BELOW: the Patio de los Leones in the Alhambra, Granada.

One of the pueblos blancos *(white villages) in the hills near Ronda.*

Dance is held in the grounds. The conquerors of the Moors, Ferdinand and Isabella, share a mausoleum in the Royal Chapel next to the Cathedral in the city centre below the Alhambra.

Costa del Sol

Spain's southern coast stretches from **Almería ⒡**, an arid province which has specialised in early fruit, vegetables and flowers grown in vast plastic greenhouses, in the east to Tarifa in the west and, although it is mainly known for its package-holiday resorts, it has great variety along its length and even some unfrequented beaches.

The strip of coast due south of Granada around **Salobreña** and **Almuñécar ⒢** has a microclimate suitable for the cultivation of exotic fruits, and hence is known as the Costa Tropical. To the west, the Costa del Sol starts at **Nerja ⒣**, standing on cliffs above sandy coves. A series of prehistoric caves were discovered here in 1957 and summer concerts are held in the largest one.

Málaga ⒤ is the capital of the Costa del Sol, a bustling town visited by cruise liners. This was the port of the city of Granada, and its Moorish castle, the 11th-century **Alcazaba** (Tue–Sun) was built inside the extensive Roman fort beside an amphitheatre. Phoenician, Roman and Moorish artefacts are displayed in the **Museo Arqueológico** inside. Picasso spent his early childhood in the town, and the **Museo Picasso** (Tue–Sun), situated in the Palacio de Buenavista in Calle San Agustín, shows some of his works. Some of his early sketches are in the **Museo de Bellas Artes** (Tue–Sun), which also has paintings by Murillo and Zubarán. By the train station in Calle Alemania is the **Centro de Arte Contemporáneo de Málaga** (Tue–Sun). Housed in the former wholesale market, CAC Málaga is a cultural initiative whose aim is to promote 20th- and 21st-century art.

The Costa del Sol has its densest population between Málaga and Marbella, and reaches a downmarket low at **Torremolinos**, which was a poor fishing village until it was "discovered" in the 1960s. It is now grotesquely overgrown and packed with tourists. Coastal traffic is heavy in summer all along the coast through **Fuengirola**, where high-rise

buildings pack the water's edge all the way to **Marbella** ❶. Between Marbella and the flashy marina **Puerto Banús** is the playground of celebrities, sheikhs, millionaires, royalty and bullfighters, though Marbella's Old Town remains attractive. **Estepona** ❶, the most westerly of the Costa's swollen fishing villages, has avoided too many high-rises.

Inland the contrast is stark. The countryside grows wilder towards **Ronda** ❶ and the "white villages", with dazzling communities such as **Grazalema, Ubrique, Zahara** and **Jimena de la Frontera**. Ronda is a bustling town on a rocky bluff with sheer walls falling dramatically away on three sides and one of the oldest bullrings in Spain.

Gibraltar and the Costa de la Luz

Gibraltar ❶, Britain's enclave in Spain, can be freely entered. With pubs and policemen, its 7 sq km (3 sq miles) are a strange placewarp. Its rock, looking out across the narrow strait, joins the Mediterranean to the Atlantic. The industrial town of **Algeciras** next door is the boarding point for ferries to Tan-ger (Tangier) and the Spanish North African enclave of Ceuta.

West of Gibraltar the tidal Atlantic washes the **Costa de la Luz**. The wind and waves make the whole coast, particularly around **Tarifa**, a popular spot for kitesurfing. After the discovery of the Americas, **Cádiz** ❶ became the wealthiest port in Europe. The town has a safe harbour and is known for its seafood, as well as for flamenco artists. Its grand Cathedral contains the tomb of the native composer Manuel de Falla, and the Oratorio de la Santa Cueva has scenes from the New Testament painted by Goya. Inland from Cádiz is the rolling landscape of the sherry triangle, centred on **Jerez de la Frontera** ❶.

Sanlúcar de la Barrameda, north of Cádiz, is known for its light, dry sherries. It looks across the mouth of the Guadalquivir to the dunes and marshlands of the **Parque Nacional de Doñana** ❶, one of the country's principal nature reserves. The imperial eagle and Spanish lynx are among its rarer inhabitants. Organised tours in four-wheel-drive vehicles start from **El Acebuche** (book ahead). ❑

WHERE

While in Marbella, make a point of visiting the 17th-century Iglesia Santa María de la Encarnación, the town's main church, from where a signpost leads to the Museo del Grabado, devoted to contemporary art.

BELOW LEFT: graceful architecture in the centre of Palma de Mallorca.

The Balearics

Spain's Mediterranean archipelago consists of four main islands: Mallorca, Menorca, Ibiza and Formentera. At their closest point the Balearics are only 85km (53 miles) offshore and are easily reached by domestic flight or by ferry from Barcelona, Valencia, Denia or Alicante. Their local language is *mallorquín*, a variant of Catalan.

The Balearics are best known abroad for their high-rise package-holiday resorts and extravagant nightlife, but the islands have much more to offer than beaches, raves and clubs.

Mallorca is the largest and most varied of the islands, with mountains reaching over 1,445 metres (4,740ft) and a dramatic series of caves near its east coast. Palma, the capital, has a Gothic Cathedral and many other historic buildings. The tiny offshore island of Cabrera is a national park.

Menorca, furthest away from the mainland, is littered with prehistoric megalithic monuments and has a famous June festival in which horses prance in crowded streets. Ibiza (properly called Eivissa) also has surprises if you drag yourself away from the bars and beaches. The main town, with the same name as the island, has a pristine old quarter and in its countryside are pretty, brightly whitewashed villages to explore. Formentera, the smallest of the main islands, is visited from Ibiza and, being mainly flat, is best explored by bicycle.

MICROSTATES

Squeezed between their larger neighbours are a handful of tiny countries, each with its own idiosyncratic national identity

We tend to think of Europe in terms of its most conspicuous political chunks: the major nation states that coalesced behind established borders in the 19th century. There are, however, a few much smaller entities that usually slip under the radar. These are the microstates, diminutive areas of sovereign territory inhabited by correspondingly small populations that are counted in their thousands rather than millions.

The microstates – Andorra, Liechtenstein, Luxembourg, Malta, Monaco, San Marino and the Vatican – are in almost all aspects fully functioning countries, with their own constitutions, passports, currencies and symbols of national identity. They are recognised by international organisations such as the EU and UN, even if their prestige and influence are small. But it would be a mistake to think of them as existing independently of their gigantic neighbours on whom they inevitably depend for an inflow of revenue and, tacitly, for such means as only size can bring, especially defence capability.

Some people dismiss the microstates as quaint anachronisms in the modern world; anomalies that only survive by economic specialisation, such as offering duty-free shopping, gambling or confidential banking, or by peddling themselves as mini-geopolitical theme parks for the curiosity of tourists. For others, the microstates represent a bastion against globalisation: proof that diversity and idiosyncrasy can exist despite the trend towards international homogenisation.

What is true is that each microstate is a unique oddity in how it came to be and how it functions today; and each is a curiosity worth visiting in its own right.

ABOVE: the 12th-century Vaduz Castle dominates the capital of Liechtenstein, a tiny constitutional monarchy with 35,000 inhabitants.

RIGHT: the cross of the Knights of St John carved on the wall of Valletta cathedral. The order ruled the independent island state of Malta from 1530 to 1789.

LEFT: the flag of the Principality of Andorra. Sandwiched between Spain and France in the Pyrenees, it has a population of just 84,500, but the highest life expectancy in the world.

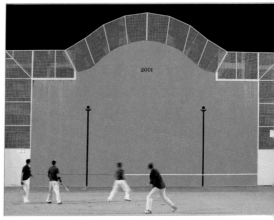

WOULD-BE NATIONS

Several Western European countries have regions within them that aspire to nationhood in their own right, and there is often an uneasy tug of war between capital and province. These would-be countries-within-a-country base their claim for greater or full autonomy on a shared language and culture that is not the same as that of the existing nation state of which they form a part.

In Spain, the Catalans and the Basques enjoy great autonomy under what is largely a federal constitution, but extremists in both places claim even more. France also has Catalans and Basques, although they are far less vociferous than the Corsicans who rail against control of their island emanating from Paris.

One controversial vision for the European Union is that it should allow such regions to enjoy statehood under the umbrella of a federalised EU that provides internationalised services, such as foreign policy and defence.

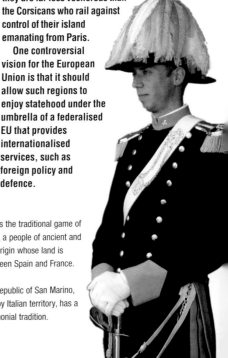

ABOVE: the Vatican in Rome is the smallest independent state in the world, with just 450 official citizens, half of whom do not live there. It is an absolute monarchy under the auspices of the pope.

LEFT: the Grand Duchy of Luxembourg is a polyglot state, bordered by France, Germany and Belgium. It has an economy that larger countries can only dream of, and has found a modern role as home to several European institutions, including the European Commission.

TOP: *pelota* is the traditional game of the Basques, a people of ancient and mysterious origin whose land is divided between Spain and France.

RIGHT: the Republic of San Marino, surrounded by Italian territory, has a strong ceremonial tradition.

PORTUGAL

Europe's most westerly country is best known for the beach resorts of the Algarve, but its rugged interior and ancient cities are also worth exploring

Tucked in the corner of the continent, nobody passes through Portugal because, really, there is nowhere else to go. It is a land on the edge, "where land ends and sea begins" as the 16th-century epic poet Luís Vaz de Camões put it. At the western periphery of Europe, the country appears suspended between a culture of traditional living – fishing and farming – and the technology that has made the world smaller, more integrated, more complex. However, it is increasingly attracting tourists, who come for the unspoilt landscape and lifestyle, as well as delightful villages, family-geared beach resorts, and the proud historic towns and cities.

Although in many ways Portugal has a Mediterranean feel, its light is more limpid and its shores are washed clean by the Atlantic tides. The cosmopolitan nature of the country is evident everywhere: nearly 2 million returned from former colonies when they were granted independence in the mid-1970s. Many headed for the countryside rather than towns, and Lisbon, the capital, has a comparatively small population of 1 million – out of a total population for the country of well over 10 million.

This is a country that is easy to explore, thanks to an ever-improving network of motorways and secondary roads. Covering some 92,100 sq km (35,550 sq miles), its land borders Spain, of which it was part until the 12th century: their languages, as well as the overall character of the people, are surprisingly different. Portugal benefits from Spain's gift of three important rivers. In the north are the Minho and the Douro, while Lisbon lies on the Tejo (Tagus), south of which is the Alentejo and the popular Algarve coast. The cities have a distinct flavour, and the people savour their differences. "Coimbra sings, Braga plays, Lisbon shows off and Porto works," is one way the Portuguese people sum them up.

One very positive aspect that travellers will appreciate while visiting is the price tag: Portugal is one of the least expensive countries in Western Europe. ❏

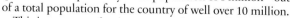

PRECEDING PAGES: Castelo de Vide, Alentejo; the Gloria funicular, Lisbon.
LEFT: the Portuguese day starts with coffee and newspapers.
ABOVE: typical Portuguese tiles; tourists flock to the Algarve beaches.

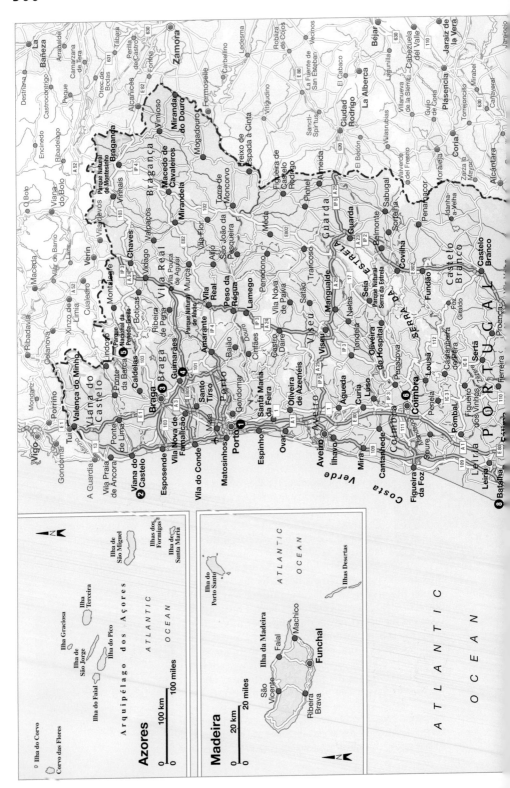

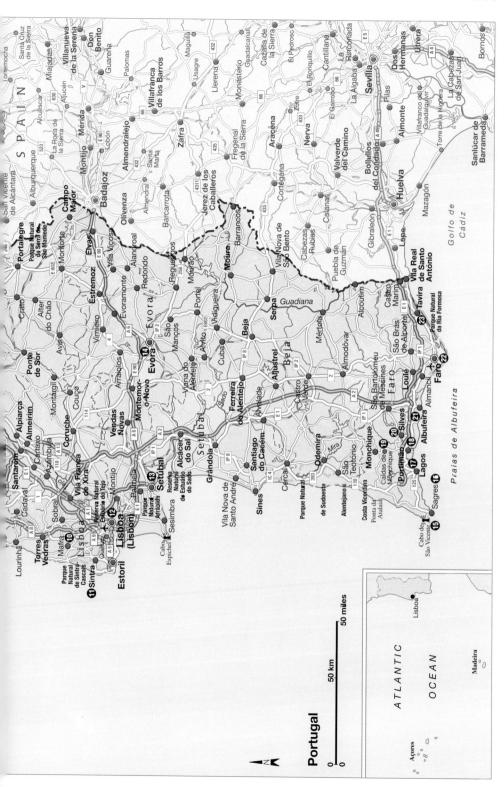

Portugal

0

0

50 km

50 miles

ATLANTIC OCEAN

Açores

Madeira

Lisboa

Golfo de Cádiz

Praias de Albufeira

LISBON

With a population of just 1 million inhabitants, Lisbon feels more like a large town than a major city; nevertheless, it is a vibrant and cosmopolitan capital

L isbon is one of Europe's smallest capitals, but bristles with the evidence of former empires from Brazil to Macao. The town is set on the right bank of the River Tagus (Tejo), facing south, and is spread over seven hills, which have a number of *miradouros* – terraces and viewing points which look down over the city's rooftops. One such is the **Castelo de São Jorge ❶**. Originally Roman, this was where the Moorish governor had his residence until 1147 when the Moors were driven out and it became the Portuguese royal palace, occupied and embellished by Dinis I (1279–1325) and Manuel I (1495–1521). When the palace moved down to the river, it became a fortress, then a barracks. Ten towers and sturdy walls remain, surrounded by a moat, and there is an audiovisual show of the city's history.

The area around the castle, the **Alfama**, is the oldest part of the city, where lanes and tram lines meander up and down hill and some of the alleys are so narrow two people can barely pass. One such is Rua de São Pedro, where fisherwomen sell the daily catch or eat fresh fish in the tiny front rooms. The **Sé ❷** (Cathedral) is in this part of town, a solid structure fronted by two crenelated towers and a fine rose window. Inside is the font where St Anthony of Padua, the city's unofficial patron saint, was christened in 1195. The relics of St Vincent, the city's official patron saint, are displayed in the treasury. Opposite

is **Sant Antonio de Sé**, a small church which was built over the room where St Anthony was born.

Regal square

The royal residence was transferred from the castle to the waterside at what is now the **Praça do Comércio ❸**. The palace was just one of the casualties of the 1755 earthquake that reduced most of the city to rubble. The massive rebuilding in the aftermath was undertaken by the Marquês de Pombal, the autocratic prime minister who didn't bother to wait for

Main attractions
CASTELO DE SÃO JORGE
SÉ
SOLAR DE INSTITUTO DO
   VINHO DO PORTO
FUNDAÇÃO CALOUSTE
   GULBENKIAN
MUSEO NACIONAL DO AZULEJO
MOSTEIRO DOS JERÓNIMOS
MUSEO DO DESIGN E DO MODA

LEFT: the colossal archway in the Praça do Comércio.
BELOW: on Vasco da Gama bridge.

The walls of the Cervejaria de Trinidade in the Chiado shopping centre are covered with painted tiles.

the rubble to be cleared away, but just rebuilt the new city on top. The Neo-classical pink arcades of this square are typical "Pombaline Lisbon". On 1 February 1908, in the northwest corner, Carlos I and his heir Luís Felipe were assassinated in an open landau.

Two years later a republic was declared from the balcony of the 19th-century **town hall** in the nearby Praça do Municipio. At its centre is a twisted column with a banded sphere, a typical Manueline architectural device and the symbol of the city. The central archway, on the northside of Praça do Comércio, leads through to the **Baixa**, the downtown shopping district, a lively few blocks of old shops, modern boutiques, cafés and restaurants. Its Rua do Ouro and Rua da Plata, Gold and Silver streets, give a flavour of the times when precious metals arrived from the New World.

Up on the west side of the Baixa is the **Bairro Alto**, reached via steep lanes by the Santa Justa lift, a whimsical iron structure designed by the French engineer Gustave Eiffel.

The 18th-century earthquake demolished the monastery of **Carmo ❹**, and

left its church roofless; today it is an archaeological museum. The quake also brought down the facade of the pretty little church of **São Roque**.

The Bairro Alto is full of restaurants and nightspots, and *fado*, the famous Portuguese song, can be heard here. The city's Italianate opera house, **Teatro de São Carlos**, built in 1792, is also here, as is the smart shopping district, **Chaido**. An evening out may well start at the **Solar de Instituto do Vinho do Porto ❺**, the Port Wine Institute in Rua São Pedro de Alcântara, a bar with a club-like atmosphere which serves a large selection of ports. The *miradoura* opposite has a grand view across the Baixa to the castle. The Gloria funicular leads back down to the Praça de Restauradores and the neo-Manueline Rossio station, where suburban trains run to Benfica and Sintra. **Rossio** was once the city's main square, where bullfights, carnivals and *autos da fé* took place. Today, entertainment is confined to the **National Theatre ❻** (Teatro Nacional), built in 1840. The two large fountains in the square were brought from Paris in 1890.

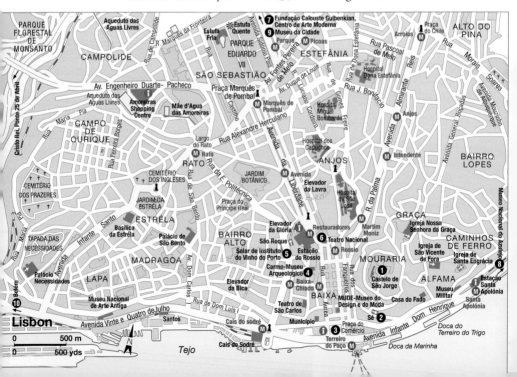

Lisbon

0   500 m

0   500 yds

Beyond Restauradores is the Avenida da Liberdade, where airline offices and banks line the city's grand avenue. At the top, in a square named after him, is a statue of the Marquês de Pombal, looking down on all he created.

Millionaire's museums

Lisbon's other benefactor was Calouste Gulbenkian, the Armenian oil magnate. His gift to the city is the **Fundação Calouste Gulbenkian** ❼, the city's principal culture centre, with a large general art collection and a Museum of Modern Art. This is above the Pombal statue beside Parque Eduardo VII, where there are two fine botanical houses.

To the east of the city, just beyond the Alfama, is the **Museo Nacional do Azulejo** ❽ (Tue–Sun), a museum dedicated, as its name indicates, to Portugal's principal native art, the striking highly coloured glazed tiles. The museum is housed in the splendid Madre de Deus church. The **Museu da Cidade** ❾, the City Museum, is in the Palacio Pimenta at Campo Grande, a fine manor built during the reign of King João V (1706–50).

Although **Belém** ❿ is 5km (3 miles) west of the centre, no visit to the city should exclude it. This is the Lisbon of the navigators, the visionaries and the soldiers of fortune. On the flat land beside the river is the **Torre de Belém**, the city's enduring landmark. Built in 1521 to defend the harbour called Restello that used to be here, this was the navigators' point of departure.

In 1497, at the start of his epic voyage to India, Vasco da Gama prayed in a small chapel beside the Restello, built by Henry the Navigator. The chapel was levelled shortly afterwards, and in its place arose the spectacular **Mosteiro dos Jerónimos** and its church of **Santa María**. It is a perfect symbol of the extravagant Age of Discovery, built in traditional Manueline style.

Beyond Belém the river widens as it enters the ocean. On the same bank are the smart resorts of **Cascais** and **Estoril**, 30 to 45 minutes from Cais do Sodré station on Lisbon's waterfront. This is the former "Coast of Kings", which several of the 20th century's deposed European monarchs chose as their place of exile. ❏

BELOW: the Monument to the Discoveries by the River Tagus in Belém.

Design and Fashion Museum

Lisbon's former Design Museum closed its doors in August 2006 and reopened in August 2009 with an exciting new look – and name: **Museo do Design e do Moda** (Design and Fashion Museum; Tue–Sun). Touted as one of the world's top museums for 20th-century design, it includes Portuguese businessman Francisco Capelo's fashion collection, comprising some 1,200 couture pieces, including the famous Jean Desses gown worn by Renee Zellweger to the 2001 Oscars. Other top designers represented include Philippe Starck, Charles Eames, Arne Jacobsen, Paul Henningsen, Masanori Umeda and Tom Dixon.

Visit www.mude.pt for information about the museum's exhibitions.

AROUND PORTUGAL

This is the land of sad songs called *fados*, and the place from which two great navigators, Vasco da Gama and Ferdinand Magellan, set sail to discover new worlds

Lisbon

Portugal takes its name from its second city, **Porto** ❶ (Oporto), which has become synonymous with its fortified dessert wine. Majestically sited on rocky cliffs overlooking the River Douro, it was originally two cities each side of the river's mouth: Portus on the right bank, Cale on the left. And, when Alfonso Henriques united the country in the 12th century, he called his new kingdom Portucalia. Oporto is a stern and sober city of granite church towers and narrow streets, and its Baroque treasures must be hunted out. The **Church of São Francisco** in Praça do Infante Dom Henrique should be seen for its Baroque splendour, while the **Salon de Arabe** in the Palacio da Bolsa is a remarkably opulent neo-Moorish reception hall. Up the hill from the stock exchange, wines can be tasted at the **Solar do Vinho do Porto** or at any of the 60 or so port-wine lodges in **Vila Nova de Gaia** on the south side of the Dom Luís I Bridge. The **Cais de Ribera** on the riverbank is the liveliest part of the city, where small shops and restaurants are built into the old city wall.

Night-times are quiet, and young people tend to head for the Foz de Douro suburb, older people to the coastal resort of Espinho, where there is a casino and nightclub. When festivities are on the calendar, however, the town livens up. At the **Alameda das Fontainhas**, a square overlooking the Dom Luís I Bridge, people sing and dance round bonfires, drink *vinho verde*, the refreshing, slightly sparkling local wine, and feast on roast kid and sardines.

The Green Coast

The green wine lands of the Duoro and Minho rivers colour the whole coast, giving it its name, the **Costa Verde**. The main resort town north of Oporto is **Viana do Castelo** ❷, where the splendid Basilica of Santa Luzia looks over the sweep of sandy beaches.

LEFT: the pretty streets of Óbidos.
BELOW: Dom Luis I bridge in Porto.

*Flowers add splashes
of colour to Coimbra's
whitewashed walls.*

BELOW: the Church
of Bom Jesús do
Monte is a place of
pilgrimage.

Minho's capital, **Braga** ❸, is the former seat of powerful bishops. Its Baroque **Sé** (Cathedral) was built in the 12th century by Henri of Burgundy and his wife Dona Teresa, whose tombs you can find in one of the richly decorated chapels. A famous church in the vicinity is the **Bom Jesús do Monte** (5km/3 miles from Braga), an important place of pilgrimage.

Just to the south is **Guimarães** ❹, the first capital of Portugal, with a 10th-century castle (Tue–Sun) and the Church of Our Lady of the Olive Tree, which has a Romanesque cloister and an interesting museum. The massive granite Paço do Duques, the Palace of the Dukes of Bragança, can also be visited.

In the far northwest is the remote **Trás-os-Montes**, where life was so harsh in post-war years that many people emigrated to become peasant farmers in what were then the Portuguese colonies in Africa. On its edges is the 70,000-hectare (173,000-acre) **Peneda-Gerês National Park** ❺, which is crossed by several rivers, has a series of lakes and is superb for water sports.

Seat of learning

To the south of Oporto, perched on a hill overlooking the River Mondego, is the university town of **Coimbra** ❻. The tangle of narrow streets at the heart of the Old Town leads to the Pátio das Escolas, which is reached through the 17th-century Porta Férrea. Behind the statue of João III, who gave his palace to the university, is a magnificent view of the river below, and in the far corner, one of the most beautiful libraries in the world, with magnificent ceiling frescoes. Luís de Camões (1524–80), Portugal's greatest poet, was a student here. University graduates have something of a monopoly on the local *fado*, which is more serious and intellectual than the *fado* sung in Lisbon, and to show their approval the people in the audience are not supposed to clap but merely to clear their throats.

One of the country's greatest traditions is the pilgrimage at **Fátima** ❼, situated between Coimbra and Lisbon. On 13 May 1917 three shepherd girls had a vision of the Virgin, who appeared in a glow of light over an oak tree. She asked them to pray for the peace of the world and promised to return on the 13th day of each month until October. Those are the days which have been celebrated since, when thousands come to visit the basilica that has been built beside a colonnaded square, where up to 1 million people have congregated during visits by the pope.

Tomar, east of Fátima, is a delightful town with a castle, the former headquarters of the Knights Templar in Portugal, and the splendid **Convento do Cristo**, a Unesco World Heritage site. **Batalha** ❽, 20km (12 miles) west of Fátima, has a beautiful Gothic abbey, in the Santa Maria da Vitória Monastery. The ornate facade hides a simple, elegant interior. The cloister is built in Portugal's elaborate Manueline style, named after the monarch who benefited most from South American riches. Its typical flourishes include nautical fantasy and, the symbol of Portuguese knowledge and power,

the armillary sphere. Most striking of all are the **Capelas Imperfeitas**, the Unfinished Chapels, which suffered when the royal coffers ran low.

At **Alcobaça**, just to the south, is Portugal's largest church in a Cistercian Abbey, another Unesco World Heritage site. Fine medieval stone carvings tell the tale of Pedro I, who exhumed his skeletal queen, crowned her and made his nobles kiss her hand. On the coast is **Nazaré** ❾, a timeless fishing village where fishermen wear stocking caps, and the colourful boats are hauled up the beach by oxen. On the road to Lisbon, stop off at **Óbidos**, a picturesque gem of a town perched on a hill, with narrow cobbled streets lined with whitewashed, bougainvillea-draped houses.

Around Lisbon

Near Lisbon is **Mafra** ❿, which started life as a Capuchin monastery and was expanded into something more palatial by João V. A craft school was established, and among the teachers was Joaquim Machado de Castro *(see margin, right)*. The resultant limestone facade is 220 metres (720ft) long, and

behind it is a church which shows off Portugal's wonderful marble, as well as six statues of saints from Italy in Carrara marble. But the high spot of the building is its beautiful Baroque library of 35,000 books, including the first editions of Camões's *Os Lusíadas* and the earliest edition of Homer in Greek.

Mafra is a good place to visit from Lisbon, but **Sintra** ⓫, 25km (15 miles) northwest of the city, is a must. It has captivated everyone who has been there. The **Royal Palace** (daily), used by Portugal's monarchs for 600 years, was built by King João I at the end of the 14th century. It was extended by Manuel I in the 16th century and has Portugal's finest *azulejos* (tiles), which cover its Arab and Swan halls and the chapel. Beautifully situated, the palace is floodlit at night and there is often a *son et lumière* performance in summer.

Another royal residence is at **Queluz**, an 18th-century small-scale Versailles in a rather dull town 14km (9 miles) west of Lisbon. Among the interior's gilt and glass is a magnificent throne room, used for a season of concerts. A ferry ride across the Tagus from the

Born in Coimbra, Joachim Machado de Castro (1731–1822) was one of Portugal's foremost sculptors; his most famous work is the equestrian statue of King José I in Lisbon.

BELOW: the flamboyant Royal Palace at Sintra.

city of **Lisbon** ⓬ (Lisboa) leads to the industrial heartland of **Setúbal** ⓭, which is worth negotiating for the Church of Jesus. This was an early work of Boytec, master of the Jerónimos Monastery. There are some good primitive paintings in the museum.

Alentejo is the "land beyond the Tejo" – in other words, south of the River Tagus. This is the flattest part of the country, one-third of it covered by parched plains of oak woods and olive groves. Its main town is **Evora** ⓮, an ancient city which had its time of brilliance as a favoured residence of the kings of Burgundy and Avis dynasty; its sites, from a Roman Temple of Diana to the Cathedral and university, are worth a day's excursion.

The Algarve

The south-facing 150km (95-mile) southern coastal strip of Portugal is very different from the rest of the country. Its architecture is Moorish, its vegetation is almost subtropical and the sea temperature in winter rarely falls below 15°C (59°F). In the 1970s it began to take off as a tourist desti-

BELOW: strange rock formation at Praia da Rocha.

nation, served by the increasingly busy airport at Faro. Time-share villas and apartments and second homes began surrounding the towns and springing up as isolated "property resorts". But there are still unspoilt villages and beaches to go with the infrastructure of golf courses, casinos, water sports and other tourist necessities.

Algarve is from the Arabic *el gharb*, meaning "the west". Its western extremity is **Cabo de São Vicente** ⓯ described as *o fim do mundo*, "the end of the world". It is a wild corner, where the wind has bent almond trees double. Europe's second-most powerful lighthouse, which can be visited, has 3,000-watt bulbs and can be seen 96km (56 miles) away. Along this coast the red earth rises in cliffs of impressive height, reaching 150 metres (500ft) at **Tôrre de Asp**.

Five km (3 miles) east of Cape St Vincent at the lobster-fishing port of **Sagres** ⓰, Henry the Navigator (the Infante Dom Henrique, 1394–1460) established a school of navigation, where Vasco da Gama, Christopher Columbus and many other explorers acquired their skills. The school was housed in the Forteleza, the huge, severe-looking fortress, rebuilt in the 17th century, and the 39-metre (130ft) compass rose Henry used to make his calculations is laid out in stone. Henry's interest in Sagres helped open up an area cut off from the rest of the country. The **Caldeirão** and **Monchique** mountain ranges stretching behind it had seen to that, while in the east the River Guadiana provided a border with Spain.

In the exciting whirl of adventure in the 15th century, as riches were being brought back from the east, the port of **Lagos** ⓱ was filled with caravels, and it was here that the first slave market was established in Europe. The town has a good natural harbour which the Romans used, and in Moorish times it was a trade centre with Africa. An especially delightful church is the Igreja de Santo António. Its rich, gilt Baroque

interior has earned it the name of the "Golden Chapel". Near the town are a number of grottoes which can be explored by boat.

Game-fishing centre

From Silves (*see below*), the River Arade slips down to the sea at **Praia da Rocha**, the best-known and longest-established resort on the coast. The wide sandy beach is backed by a cliff-top promenade lined with villas and hotels. The resort was started at the beginning of the 20th century by the wealthy people of **Portimão ⓲**, an attractive old fishing port 3km (2 miles) up the estuary which has become the busiest and biggest city on this western stretch of the coast. *Carinhas*, horse-drawn coaches, take tourists between the two places.

Portimão is a good shopping centre, and the tuna and sardine catches can be sampled in its many restaurants, such as the Lanterna, where smoked swordfish is a speciality and its fish soup is claimed to be the best on the coast. *Caldeirada*, a fish chowder, is often on restaurant menus, as is *cataplana*, a dish of clams and meat. Game-fishing cruisers can be hired at Portimão, or visitors can just go along to watch. This is said to be the last part of Europe where game fishing is still possible. The reefs where the sharks hunt are 20km (12 miles) offshore, about two hours out. Blue and copper sharks lie in wait, as does the tasty mako – the sharp-nosed mackerel shark. **Ferragudo** on the eastern side of the River Arade, with a fine fort overlooking the estuary, is a centre of windsurfing and surfboarding.

Caldas de Monchique ⓳, a spa town in the hills behind the coast, makes a change from the cosmopolitan resorts. The water is supposed to have healing properties, but people also come to buy bottles of *Medronho*, a spirit distilled from the strawberry tree, *Arbutus uneda*, which blossoms all around the spa. In the town of **Monchique** the Franciscan convent has good views over the coast.

In between is **Silves ⓴**, which as *Chelib* was the Moorish capital of the region. Then it was on a navigable part of the River Arade. Chelib was a centre for arts and learning, and at its height it had a population of 30,000. It fell to

Straw hats are often locally made and offer good protection from the heat of the sun.

BELOW: an olive grove in the rolling Alentejo landscape.

TIP

Portugal's weekly
English-language
newspaper, *The News,*
is a great guide to
what's on. It's also
available on the web
at www.the-news.net.

BELOW: clear
green waters at
Praia da Coelha,
near Albufeira.
RIGHT: enjoying the
Alentejo sunshine.

Sancho I of Portugal in 1189 after a six-week siege, and from then on the monarchs took the title of "King of Portugal and the Algarve". Silves has a 13th-century Cathedral with part of a Moorish mosque behind the altar, and its huge castle, a walled fortress with solid square Albarra towers, is one of the best Moorish buildings in Portugal. The earthquake of 1755 reduced most of the town to rubble, and today the population has settled at 20,000. The **Cross of Portugal** is a 16th-century stone lacework cross on the Silves–Messines road just outside the town. Beside the main Estrada Nacional 125, 5km (3 miles) east of Lagos near **Porches**, a town famous for its decorated pottery, is an artisans' village where local wines can be tasted.

The morning fish market is one of the attractions of **Albufeira ㉑**, a small fishing port with steep narrow streets and a tumble of whitewashed houses, topped with Moorish cupolas. But it has been overwhelmed by the biggest resort on the Algarve coast: it is now turned over entirely to tourism, with a number of fish restaurants around the fish market, and souvenir shops spilling out onto the main shopping street. The beach is crowded in high summer, but there are quieter beaches, such as **São Rafael** and **Olhos d'Água**, nearby.

Regional capital

Albufeira is 36km (22 miles) west of **Faro ㉒**, the finest town on the coast and the regional capital since the 18th century. The 1755 earthquake put paid to earlier buildings, but many fine Baroque flourishes remain. The Old Town is inside what remains of its old walls and is approached through the 18th-century Arco da Vila. Built on the site of a Moorish mosque, the **Sé** (Cathedral) has a fine interior with a Renaissance misericordia and a lacquered organ. Among other notable churches are São Francisco, with a gilded interior, São Pedro, with good *azulejos*, and the curious Igreja do Carmo, which has a chapel decorated with human bones. The Archaeological Museum in a 16th-century convent has a good Roman collection, some of which comes from the ruins of Milreu in **Estói** 11km (7 miles) north. The yacht basin in the centre of town shows how much Faro is linked to leisure and tourism. Some explore the islands and sandbars just off the coast which make up the **Parque Natural da Ria Formosa**, and from Faro spits continue towards the Spanish border.

The prettiest resort on the coast is the surprisingly unspoilt fishing village of **Tavira ㉓**, 32km (20 miles) east of Faro. The River Asseca on which it stands, crossed by a seven-arch Roman bridge, has long been silted up. Sparkling white with a castle, several churches, Moorish cupolas and lovely little gardens, it is the epitome of an Algarve town.

The country east of Tavira is little visited. The drive up to the hilltop castle at Castro Marim beside the River Guadiana gives a feeling of remoteness. The salt marshes to the south are busy breeding grounds for storks and noisy black-winged stilts.   ❑

⚡INSIGHT GUIDE   TRAVEL TIPS

WESTERN EUROPE

Overview

GENERAL TIPS ON TRAVELLING IN WESTERN EUROPE

Accommodation

Reservations

If your itinerary is more or less concrete, it's a good idea to reserve accommodation in advance, especially when travelling in the peak season (June–Sept). This can be done on the internet, through a travel agent or, if you're flying, through the airline's hotel reservations department. The various national tourist offices can book your lodgings or provide you with a listing from which you can book directly.

Although a bit inflexible (deposits can be forfeited or room prices still charged if reservations are cancelled without notice), advance bookings save time and energy and prevent chaos when you first arrive at your destination. For the traveller without advance reservations, it's wise to check if there is any major event coming up which could make accommodation hard to find. Local tourist information offices in major train stations and airports usually have hotel reservation services which, for a small fee, can book you a room on the spot.

Youth Hostels

These are widespread in Europe and provide one of the cheapest ways of keeping a roof over your head while travelling. You usually need a valid membership card, which can be purchased at home before departure or on the spot. In most instances, addresses of youth hostels can also be acquired from the local tourist offices, or see www.hihostels.com.

Climate and When to Go

It is difficult to generalise about the weather across a continent, but using the Alps as a rough dividing line helps. North of the Alps you can count on cold, damp winters, usually with grey skies. Summers are warm but can be rainy. The maritime climate in the west has moderate temperatures all year round. The North Atlantic Drift, a continuation of the Gulf Stream, keeps coastal areas mild. In parts of northwestern Spain, for example, the winter/

summer variation might be no more than 10–18°C (18–32°F). Rainfall is fairly even throughout the year. The climate becomes more continental further to the east, with increasing summer warmth. Temperatures fall well below freezing in midwinter in parts of Germany and Austria.

South of the Alps, it is a different story. The Mediterranean region has

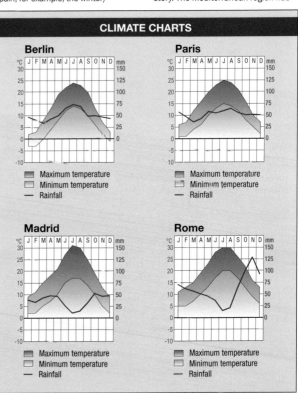

CLIMATE CHARTS

Berlin
Maximum temperature
Minimum temperature
— Rainfall

Paris
Maximum temperature
Minimum temperature
— Rainfall

Madrid
Maximum temperature
Minimum temperature
— Rainfall

Rome
Maximum temperature
Minimum temperature
— Rainfall

AUSTRIA

BELGIUM

FRANCE

GERMANY

GREECE

ITALY

NETHERLANDS

PORTUGAL

SPAIN

SWITZERLAND

dry, hot summers and mild, rainy winters – although rainy days are interspersed with days of brilliant sunshine. Much of spring and late autumn can be quite fickle in these southern regions. Alpine and other highland regions are, of course, cooler throughout the year, while central Spain has noticeably cooler winters than other Mediterranean areas. Southern Spain and mainland Greece are usually the hottest places in Europe in the summer months.

Most people prefer to visit Europe in the warmer months, between May and September. In the southern Mediterranean regions, the heat in July and August can be unbearable, and cities are crowded with tourists. Obviously the best time to visit will depend on what you are doing.

What to Wear

Two cardinal rules for travellers: travel light and dress comfortably. Don't bring things you'll only wear once or clothes you wouldn't be comfortable in for up to 24 hours (sometimes it can be a long time between stops). In summer, cotton clothes with a light jacket or jumper will suffice. In winter, sturdy waterproof shoes, a warm overcoat and several layers will keep you cosy. An umbrella or a lightweight raincoat is always a good thing to carry along, and comfortable walking shoes are very important.

Throughout Europe, dress is informal except for an occasional evening out at the opera, theatre or a smart restaurant. Women should also remember to dress respectfully when visiting churches or cathedrals, especially in Italy, where those wearing shorts or bare-backed dresses will be refused entry. You may be asked to cover bare arms as well.

Crime and Safety

The main problem for tourists is petty crime – pickpocketing, bag-snatching, theft from cars; it is wise to have insurance against this and to take basic, sensible precautions against theft. The usual traveller's precautions are recommended:
• Don't keep all money, credit cards or travellers' cheques in one wallet or purse; disperse them so one theft won't leave you totally penniless.
• Hold bags close and keep them fastened. Never leave them unattended.
• Make use of the hotel safe.
• Always lock your car and never leave luggage, cameras or other valuables inside. This applies

ABOVE: many Northern European tourists head south in search of the sun.

particularly in major cities.
• If walking, especially at night, in the centre of a city, avoid wearing flashy jewellery and try to blend in.
• Have some form of identification in your wallet, because sometimes the thief will deposit your stolen wallet (minus the money, of course) where someone might recover it. Immediately notify the local police station and your nearest consulate or embassy and see if it turns up. If you're in town long enough, check periodically at the main post office. If you are the victim of a crime (or suffer a loss) and wish to claim against your insurance, it is essential to make a report at the nearest police station and get documentation to support your claim. Refer to the Travel Tips for each individual country for emergency numbers.

Customs

Precise customs formalities vary from country to country, but as a general rule, if you are visiting from within the EU there are no restrictions on what you bring in for your personal consumption. In other words, customs barriers do not exist between the following countries, which are all European Union members: Austria, Belgium, Bulgaria, Cyprus, Czech Republic, Denmark, Estonia, Finland, France, Germany, Greece, Hungary, Ireland, Italy, Latvia, Lithuania, Luxembourg, Malta, the Netherlands, Poland, Portugal, Romania, Slovakia, Slovenia, Spain, Sweden, and the United Kingdom.

Non-European travellers coming to the countries in this book may import the following items duty-free:

All articles intended for personal use (clothing, luggage, toiletries, photographic equipment and amateur cine cameras with film, camping and

sports equipment, personal jewellery, etc.) on the condition that they are re-exported and not intended for sale; food provisions required in transit; souvenirs, gifts and personal purchases whose total value does not exceed the limitations of the individual countries; 200 cigarettes or 100 small cigars (cigarillos) or 50 cigars or 250g of tobacco. Some countries apply the lower limit on tobacco products: 40 cigarettes or 20 cigarillos or 10 cigars or 50g of tobacco. All travellers are allowed 1 litre of spirits containing more than 22 percent alcohol or 2 litres of sparkling or liqueur wine or any other beverage containing less than 22 percent alcohol, and 4 litres of still wine; 16 litres of beer and other goods, including perfume, up to a value of €300 per traveller (or €430 if travelling by air and sea) are also allowed.

If you are in doubt about what you can bring back, check with your local customs office.

Embassies and Consulates

Foreign embassies and consulates are usually located in the national capitals, but many foreign governments, especially those of the larger countries, maintain additional consulates or missions in other major European cities and tourist regions. These are invaluable if you lose your passport or encounter any other problems while travelling.

Electricity

Most of Europe runs on 220 volts. Visitors from the US will need a transformer for shavers, hairdryers and other equipment; visitors from the UK just need an adaptor plug.

Only in extreme cases, if you are without money, travellers' cheques or transport because of loss, theft or other damages, can they arrange for your passage home, and they will sometimes hold your passport as security on the loan.

Embassies and consulates are often listed in the literature distributed by the various tourist offices. If not, consult the telephone directory or refer to the A–Z section of the relevant country in this guide.

Health and Medical Care

Vaccinations

Inoculation certificates are only required of passengers coming from certain officially declared infected areas (normally selected African countries), or those who have been in these areas for over five days.

Within Europe, vaccinations are not normally necessary. North of the Alps is almost always free from diseases requiring vaccination, but Southern Europe has had occasional instances of cholera, typhoid and hepatitis. If you want vaccinations against any of these, you need to arrange them with your doctor at least eight weeks before departure. If you have recently been to an area affected by yellow fever, you will need to acquire a vaccination certificate before you arrive in Western Europe.

Food and Drink

Generally speaking, drinking and eating in the Northern European countries is quite safe. In the Mediterranean countries, however, some precaution is necessary. When in doubt, drink bottled water or tea and be careful to wash your hands whenever possible before handling food.

Hospital Treatment

It is always prudent to buy health and travel insurance with medical cover prior to a trip – especially since reimbursement for medical expenses involves mounds of paperwork. Nationals of the United Kingdom can receive free or partially free, state-provided medical care through the reciprocal scheme of the European Union (EU). You will need a European Health Insurance Card (EHIC) to receive healthcare, but this doesn't cover repatriation. Application forms are available online from www.dh.gov. uk. To apply by phone, call 0845-606 2030. You will need to give the following information: name, date of birth and National Insurance (NI) number.

Lost Property

If you lose your passport or have it stolen, report it to the police and then to the nearest embassy or consulate. They will issue you with a new passport or some emergency papers for immigration purposes. They will usually take a week or two to come through and will probably only have limited validity (extendable when you get home). Make sure you have your document number or, better still, a photocopy of it (kept in a separate place) and extra passport photos, as this will speed up the process considerably.

Emergencies

In emergencies, if you require an English-speaking doctor, dentist or pharmacist, a list is supplied by the American or British consulate and, sometimes, the local tourist office. At night, on Sunday or holidays, your hotel receptionist or the police can obtain this information for you. In several of the countries listed in this guide, pharmacies operate on a rota system for Sunday and night duty.

All countries maintain 24-hour emergency numbers for the police, fire brigade and ambulance services which can be found in phone directories and are listed under each individual country in this book.

Travel Insurance

Taking out a comprehensive travel insurance policy to cover yourself and your property for the entire time you are away from home is strongly recommended. Such policies can include medical costs, loss or damage to baggage or property – including travellers' cheques and money – personal accident, third-party liability and cancellation and curtailment fees which can result in substantial additional costs should you alter your plans. Make sure you have the kind of policy that provides you with instant money to get replacement clothing, luggage or camera, without having to wait months for a reimbursement.

Language

In Southern Europe, the Romance group of languages predominates, being found in France, southern Belgium, Spain, Portugal and Italy.

The Germanic group of languages predominates in Germany, Austria, Switzerland, the Netherlands and northern Belgium.

Greece has a Hellenic language. Some old languages linger on among small groups. Bretons in northwestern France speak a variety of Celtic, while Basque and Catalan are spoken on the Spanish-French border.

In France, three separate regional languages are spoken: Breton in Brittany, Basque in the southwest and Catalan in Roussillon (Eastern Pyrenees). A form of German is also spoken in Alsace. The first foreign language taught in schools is English, but few people speak it outside of the tourist centres. As with much of Europe, even rudimentary attempts at the language will often break the ice for a continued conversation in English.

Money

Customs

You may enter or leave many of the countries mentioned in this book with up to €10,000 in cash without declaring it, although some countries apply cash controls to those travelling between EU countries. It is advisable to declare large amounts of incoming currency at customs if the same amount is to be exported. In the euro zone (see *Changing Money, opposite*) unlimited amounts of local currency can be brought in and out; in the remaining countries there are certain limitations on import and export. As all of this information is subject to alteration, it is a good idea to check with your travel agent or bank before you depart.

Travellers' Cheques

Travellers' cheques have the advantage of being fairly quickly reimbursed if lost or stolen. You are responsible for any cheques fraudulently cashed between the time of loss or theft and the time of notification, so it is important that you report any loss or theft immediately to the issuing office or to a representative agent abroad. Keep a record of the serial numbers separate from the cheques themselves and cross off each one as you use it. Fastidious record-keeping will expedite your reimbursement. In terms of easy cashing and refundability, American Express US$ travellers' cheques are your best bet; other currencies you could consider buying travellers' cheques in are British sterling, euros or Swiss francs, all of which are usually easily negotiable for cash throughout Europe. Australian dollar

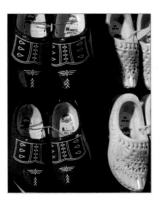

Above: take home some clogs.

travellers' cheques are not easily convertible in Europe.

Credit Cards and ATMs

Credit and debit cards are the easiest way of obtaining money while travelling. Credit cards are generally cashable at all banks and accepted in most large hotels and business establishments.

ATMs (cash machines) operate in all banks, dispensing the local currency in a variety of languages. Check before travelling whether your bank will charge you for using ATMs. Your ordinary credit or debit card and PIN should work: check with your bank before leaving home.

Changing Money

Since January 2002, the euro zone includes the following European Union countries: Austria, Belgium, Cyprus, Finland, France, Germany, Greece, Ireland, Italy, Luxembourg, Malta, the Netherlands, Portugal, Slovakia, Slovenia and Spain. This makes life easier for the traveller in Europe, as the only currency you need for travelling through all these countries is the euro. The only EU member states in Western Europe not participating are Denmark, Sweden and the UK. Although not part of the EU, Andorra, Monaco, San Marino and Vatican City have adopted the euro.

Throughout Europe, foreign currency and travellers' cheques can

Pets

An EU pet passport is needed if you live within the EU and wish your pet (dog or cat) to travel with you between EU countries. Pets entering the EU from non-EU countries need a Third Country Official Veterinary Certificate.

be exchanged at banks and exchange agencies during normal working hours. Outside these hours, and sometimes round the clock, currency can be exchanged at most major train stations, airports, seaports and frontier crossings. Currency can also be exchanged on board international trains and in some post offices with foreign-currency departments. Money can be changed at major hotels (four- and five-star), travel agencies and some stores, usually at a much less favourable rate. When entering or leaving the euro zone, try to use up coins before reaching the frontier, as they not usually exchangeable.

Religious Services

Most tourist offices can supply you with a list of English-speaking religious services. The Catholic countries of the south hold Mass in English in the larger towns and resorts. For Protestant churches in Europe, visit Intercontinental Church Society, www.ics-uk.org, and click on "Find a Church".

Shopping

Prices

In the majority of European countries, fixed prices are normal. You should bargain only at stalls in flea markets and bazaars.

In some countries a consumer does not have the legal right to an exchange, so verify this before buying. In larger shops and department stores exchange is a common practice.

VAT

Value Added Tax or sales tax is included in the price you pay when you purchase goods in an EU country. However, the actual level of tax varies between countries.

Tax-Free Shopping

Many of the larger shops and department stores in Europe display the "tax-free" sign, which means that travellers from non-European Union countries can receive a refund of the Value Added Tax or sales tax levied on the more substantial purchases intended for export outside the EU. By filling out a tax form available at the place of purchase, you can receive a refund, amounting to as much as 25 percent of the purchase price, either upon leaving the country or by mail at your home address: see www.globalrefund.com.

Tax-free shopping at airports and aboard ships, available to those

leaving the country or in transit, takes on a different form: the tax is excluded from the purchase price, eliminating the need for refunds. However this does not apply when travelling between EU countries, as the entire EU is one single market.

European Sizes

The clothing chart is a general guide when shopping in Europe, but it's best to try on items in the store. Most stores in Europe will have salespeople who speak English to provide assistance. As there are no rules or agreements within the clothing sector; every manufacturer is free in the use of sizes.

Clothing Chart

Women's Clothing

Europe	US	UK
34	6	8
36	8	10
38	10	12
40	12	14
42	14	16
44	16	18

Women's Shoes

Europe	US	UK
36	4½	3
37	5½	4
38	6½	5
39	7½	6
40	8½	7
41	9½	8
42	10½	9

Men's Suits

Europe	US	UK
44	34	34
46	36	36
48	38	38
50	40	40
52	42	42
54	44	44
56	46	46

Men's Shirts

Europe	US	UK
36	14	14
37	14½	14½
38	15	15
39	15½	15½
40	16	16
41	16½	16½
42	17	17

Men's Shoes

Europe	US	UK
39	6½	6
40	7½	7
41	8½	8
42	9½	9
43	10½	10
44	11½	11

AUSTRIA

BELGIUM

FRANCE

GERMANY

GREECE

ITALY

NETHERLANDS

PORTUGAL

SPAIN

SWITZERLAND

Telecommunications

Phone boxes
Public phone boxes and booths can be found at airports, railway stations and on the street. They are coin- or card-operated, and are a much cheaper option than calling from a hotel. Prepaid phone cards can be bought from newsstands, post offices and tobacconists, come in different denominations, and are available for both local and international calls.

Mobile Phones
European mobile (cell) phones work on the GSM standard, and their systems are constantly being revised and updated. Many US cell providers use a different system, and their phones cannot be used in Europe. You can buy or rent a cellphone that works in Europe and a SIM card for the country you are going to, and calls are relatively inexpensive. If you are on a GSM system in the US that allows roaming, calls will be expensive, but still handy if only to be used in an emergency.

Internet and Wi-fi
Most large hotels have internet connections, often in the bedrooms, and Wi-fi can usually be picked up here or in central coffee shops and public areas, such as stations and airports.

Tourist Information

All of the countries listed in this guide have intensive tourist information services. Their national tourist organisations, widely represented at home and overseas, provide information before you go and once you're there. The more popular destinations are usually supplemented with a city or a regional tourist office, which dispenses more detailed information about that specific area. They are the best places to obtain city and road maps, informative brochures, schedules of cultural programmes, sightseeing guides, hotel listings and weekly magazines, all of which are available in English. Addresses of these organisations are listed under individual countries later in this guide.

Transport

Getting There
By Air
Most visitors travel to Europe by air, either via London or direct to one of the continent's major international gateways, which include Amsterdam, Brussels, Frankfurt, Luxembourg, Paris, Rome and Zürich. Continental Europe has air links worldwide and is served by a wide choice of international carriers which run scheduled and charter flights.

If you fly from London, Heathrow and Gatwick airports provide daily connections to all major continental cities. Gatwick and other UK airports have regular budget flights to many continental destinations.

The major international airport in most European countries is located in the capital city. Exceptions to this rule include Germany, where the main gateway is Frankfurt, and Switzerland, where travellers generally fly to Zürich or Geneva.

By Rail
Continental Europe can be reached from the Far East by the Trans-Siberian Railway via Moscow, with onward connections to Berlin, Paris and other cities. Trains and buses link Istanbul and the continent, travelling via Bulgaria and former Yugoslavia. Motorists can use the frontier crossings of Algeciras, Spain (from Morocco), the Channel Tunnel from London to Paris and Brussels, or the cities of Belgrade and Vienna (from points east).

By Sea
Passenger ferry services depart from the British ports of Dover, Harwich, Hull, Newhaven and Portsmouth to the Hook of Holland and Rotterdam in the Netherlands; Ostend and Zeebrugge in Belgium; Boulogne, Caen, Calais, Cherbourg, Dieppe, Le Havre and St-Malo in France; and Santander and Bilbao in Spain. Cunard's *Queen Mary 2* makes regular 7- and 8-day crossings from the USA to Britain, France and Germany.

Getting Around
Public Transport
By Air
Europe has such a dense network of airways interlinking all the countries in the continent that flying from country to country has long become a matter of ease and convenience. Airlines, both domestic and international, servicing these routes are innumerable. For more specific information, refer to information on individual countries.

By Rail
To move about in Europe, travellers have the choice of many types of trains – the high-speed TGV, the inter-city, border-crossing EuroCity, the modern Intercities, AVE, Talgo or Corail trains. The EuroCity trains are faster than the Intercity trains and travel through two or more countries. Those with more time to spare can use the regular trains that take a less direct, but usually more picturesque route. Almost all of the major routes run night trains.

The Eurail Global Pass Youth and Eurail Global Pass offer unlimited travel by the national carriers of 21 European countries, for 10 days to three months. These are among the most economical ways of getting around in Europe, providing unlimited travel on all national railways and many private rail lines, steamers and ferry crossings. The Eurail pass entitles its holder to unlimited first-class travel within the validity period (from 15 days to 3 months). The Eurail Pass Youth, available to travellers under 26 years of age, allows unlimited second-class travel. Both must be purchased before leaving home through a travel agent or from one of the issuing offices in your country. The InterRail Global Pass allows travel in up to 30 countries, valid for a certain number of days or weeks. For more information, contact **Eurail**, www.eurail.com; **Rail Europe**, www.raileurope.co.uk (www.raileurope.com in the US); and **InterRail**, www.internationalrail.com. All of these offer deals.

Rules of the Road

• Drive on the right, pass on the left (passing on the right is strictly forbidden).
• The wearing of safety belts by the driver and the front-seat passenger is compulsory, as is the use of crash helmets by both the driver and the passenger on a motorcycle.
• Children under 12 years can sit in the front seat only if no other seats are available.
• As a rough guide, speed limits in built-up areas are 50–60kph (31–37mph) or as posted. On motorways they are 100–130kph (62–80mph) and 40–70kph (25–43mph) on dual carriage-ways (divided highways) – with the exception of Germany, where there is no maximum speed limit on some *Autobahnen* (motorways) and very disciplined driving is therefore essential. Speed limits on all other roads are 80–100kph (49–62mph).

AUSTRIA

BELGIUM

FRANCE

GERMANY

GREECE

ITALY

NETHERLANDS

PORTUGAL

SPAIN

SWITZERLAND

Time Zones

Almost all of Western Europe lies in the Central European Time Zone, which is Greenwich Mean Time (GMT) plus one hour, and US Eastern Standard Time (EST) plus six hours. Greece is an exception, being two hours ahead of GMT and seven hours ahead of EST, as is Portugal, which lies in the GMT zone, five hours ahead of EST. All countries observe Daylight Saving Time, setting their clocks one hour forward in the last weekend in March and one hour back in the last weekend in October.

In the UK you can also visit **Rail Europe Travel Centre**, 1 Regent Street, London SW1 (nearest tube Piccadilly Circus; Mon–Fri 10am–6pm, Sat 10am–4pm), tel: 08448-484 070.

To find the optimum train route within several countries in Europe, try The Man in Seat 61, www.seat61.com.

By Taxi

Taxis are abundant in the larger cities and can be hailed in the streets, booked by telephone, or obtained at taxi ranks, usually at railway stations, airports and near major hotels or shopping centres. Fares differ from place to place, but in general they are significantly lower (and taxis scarcer) in the small towns. All official taxis are equipped with meters – beware of those that aren't; the taxi *pirati* in Rome, for example, charge two or three times the normal taxi rates for rides in their private cars. Supplements are charged for luggage, extra passengers and often for trips outside the city limits (the airport,

BELOW: Greek passport control post.

for example). A tip of 10 percent or rounding up the fare is customary.

Private Transport
Car Rental

You can book a car from major international car-rental companies in offices all over Europe in all large towns and at airports and train stations. Most of them have one-way rental policies – rent it here, leave it there. If you want to rent a car for just a day or two, the cheapest deals are offered by the smaller local car-rental firms, which advertise in local papers or can be found in the telephone directory (under *Autonoleggio* in Italy, *Location des Voitures* in France, and *Autovermietung* in Germany). The local tourist office can also supply the addresses of car-rental firms. If you fly to Europe and want to pick up a car at the other end immediately, ask a travel agent about inclusive Fly-Drive offers, where the price of the air ticket includes car hire, usually for one week.

Motorways

The whole of Western Europe is intricately laced with an extensive network of main and secondary roads. European "E" Routes, easily distinguishable by the "E" preceding the road number, make up the motorway system and provide links between all major cities and some of the lesser-known towns en route. Major motorways are lined with rest stops open 24 hours a day, providing maps, information and necessary facilities, as well as intermittent emergency telephones for breakdown services. Most countries have motorway tolls: Germany and Belgium are notable exceptions.

Motoring Advice

No customs documents are required for the temporary import of a motor vehicle for personal use. Foreign driving licences and car registration papers issued abroad are recognised in many countries, although the motorist planning extensive travel in Europe should get an international driving licence. This can be done by applying to your local motoring organisation. Third-party insurance is mandatory throughout Europe. Motorists who don't have this insurance will be obliged to take out a temporary policy at the border of each country entered. (This does not apply to rented cars.) International signs and symbols mark all roads and motorways, and traffic regulations are fairly standardised.

Driving while under the influence of alcohol carries stiff penalties in Europe, and motorists with a blood-alcohol content of 0.8 percent or more are considered intoxicated. In some countries, *any* use of alcohol before or while driving is illegal and punishable by a fine.

Each country has at least one motoring club which usually operates breakdown services and which should be contacted for further information (consult a telephone directory or refer to relevant sections in this guide).

Visas and Passports

Visa requirements vary between nationalities and change from time to time, so it is wise to check with your embassy or travel agent about current regulations. A valid passport is required by all Europe-bound travellers, with the exception of citizens of several European countries who only require a national identity card. Citizens of Canada, the United Kingdom, the Republic of Ireland, the United States, Australia, New Zealand and Japan do not require a visa for a stay of up to 90 days in any of the countries featured in this book.

All children are now required to hold their own passport when travelling abroad. This includes new-born babies and children up to the age of 16. Visitors requiring a visa should consult the relevant embassy or consulate in their homeland. Passports should be kept in a safe, handy place as they are needed when crossing borders, checking into hotels or changing money. It is a good idea to keep a photocopy of your passport on you at all times.

Weights and Measures

Western Europe uses the metric system. Some useful conversion rates include:

Metric to imperial
1 gram (g) = 0.04 ounces (oz)
1 kilogram (kg) = 2.2 pounds (lb)
1 litre (l) = 1.76 UK pints (pt)
1 litre (l) = 2.11 US pints (pt)
10 centimetres (cm) = 4 inches (in)
1 metre (m) = 3.28 feet (ft)
1 kilometre (km) = 0.62 miles
8 kilometres = 5 miles

Imperial to metric
1 ounce (oz) = 28 grams (g)
1 pound (lb) = 454 grams (g)
1 US pint (pt) = 0.47 litres (l)
1 UK pint (pt) = 0.55 litres (l)
1 inch (in) = 2.54 centimetres (cm)
1 foot (ft) = 30 centimetres (cm)
1 mile = 1.6 kilometres (km)

A USTRIA

Essential Travel Tips to Help You Get There and Get Around

Transport

Getting to Austria

By Air

Austrian Airlines (www.aua.com) has
daily services from most European
capitals to Schwechat Airport (Vienna
International; www.viennaairport.com),
less frequently to Salzburg, Graz, Linz,
Klagenfurt and Innsbruck.
UK: Tel: 0870-124 2625
US: Tel: 1-800-843 0002 (toll free)
Canada: Tel: 1-888-450 0088
(toll free)
Most European airlines fly between
Vienna and national capitals.
**Vienna International Airport
information counter:** tel: 22-233.

By Rail

There are two main stations in Vienna:
the Westbahnhof serves Germany,
France, Belgium, Switzerland and the

Netherlands, while the Südbahnhof
serves Slovenia, Slovakia, Italy,
Hungary and the Czech Republic.
From London St Pancras there are two
routes: via Paris and Munich, and via
Brussels, Cologne and Frankfurt. For
information and to book, visit www.
raileurope.co.uk. The Cologne–Vienna
sleeper (from London connect via
Brussels on Eurostar) takes about
13 hours; the entire trip, London to
Vienna, takes about 20 hours. Book
online at www.bahn.de/citynightline.

By Road

As there are no direct bus services
from Northern Europe, would-be bus
travellers are advised to travel to
Munich and from there change to the
rail network.
Vienna is about 1300km (800
miles) from Calais's car-ferry port,
with its frequent sailings to and from
Dover. The French terminal of the
Channel Tunnel with its car-shuttle
service is also at Calais. The best
route to Vienna is via Belgium and
Germany to take advantage of the
toll-free motorway network. Beware
of entering Austria via the less busy
Alpine passes, which can be closed
at night and in the winter. You could
put your car on the train for part of the
journey, as Austrian Federal Railways
(www.oebb.at) operates car-trains
between Vienna and Bischofshofen,
Feldkirch, Linz, Villach, and (during the
ski season) Innsbruck and Salzburg.

Getting around Austria

By Air

There are direct flights from Vienna to
Graz, Klagenfurt, Linz, Salzburg and
Innsbruck. For details consult airline
schedules. Schwechat Airport (Vienna

International) is 15km (9 miles) to
the east of the city. Information desks
are located in the arrivals hall. The
Vienna Airport Line express bus links
the airport with Vienna's two main
railway stations every 20 minutes
between 6am–8pm, and every 30
minutes between 8pm–midnight, and
to the U-Bahn (underground) station
Schwedenplatz/Morzinplatz in the
city centre every 30 minutes between
6.20am–12.20am.
The quickest connection (16 mins)
is by the CAT (City Airport Train), which
runs half-hourly to and from the City
Air Terminal at Wien Mitte station
from 6.05am–11.35pm. A cheaper
and slightly slower (24 minutes)
connection is provided by S-Bahn
(Schnellbahn or rapid transit train)
every 30 minutes from the airport to
Wien Mitte station from 4.54am–
12.18am. Airport Service Wien is a
private shuttle service that takes you
to your exact address (tel: 676-351
6420; www.airportservice.at).
Destinations in southern Carinthia
are an hour's drive from Slovenia's
Ljubljana and Maribor international
airports. Zürich's airport is convenient
for Bregenz and Vorarlberg. Northern
Tyrol can be reached from Munich's
international airport.

By Rail

Given the reliable services
operated by ÖBB (Österreichische
Bundesbahnen, the Austrian State
Railway; www.oebb.at) and a small
number of private companies, rail
is the preferred method of travel
within Austria. The almost completely
electrified network is comprehensive,
leaving only remote villages to be
served by bus. The fast Eurocity (EC)
and InterCity (IC) trains link the main

centres. The Greater Vienna area is served by an extensive S-bahn (suburban rail) network, with trains running at 15- or 30-minute intervals.

An Interrail Austria Pass giving unlimited travel for three non-consecutive days within a 15-day period costs around €110, and similar passes are available for four, six and eight days.

By Road

Postbus and Bundesbuses are operated by the post office and the rail network. For more bus information, call 0222-711 01 within Austria; www.postbus.at.

Motoring advice: (See also page 387.) To drive your own car in Austria you need a driving licence, vehicle insurance certificate, registration document, national identity sticker and red breakdown triangle. Motorists have to carry a reflective safety vest in their car, and have a toll sticker displayed on their windscreen if travelling on motorways and highways. These can be purchased from Austrian Automobile Clubs, car-hire companies and post offices. A 10-day sticker for cars costs €7.70.

Parking may be free of charge in town centres, but time-limited, in which case a parking disc must be obtained and set (available from tobacconists). Elsewhere, on-street parking is controlled by vouchers or meters.

The alcohol limit is set at 0.05 percent, meaning that you are at risk after a single drink. The police must be called to the scene of all car accidents in which anyone is injured. ÖAMTC (Austrian Automobile Club; www.oeamtc.at) and ARBÖ (Austrian Drivers' Association; www.arboe.at) maintain breakdown services along main roads.

ARBÖ breakdown service: tel: 123.
ÖAMTC breakdown service: tel: 120.

Waterways

From April until mid-October boats operate on regular schedules along the Danube, as well as on a regular basis on all larger lakes in Austria.

DDSG **Blue Danube Schiffahrt** (Handelskai 265, A-1020 Vienna; tel: 0222-588 80; www.ddsg-blue-danube.at) operates a number of services: daily one-way and round-trip cruises of Vienna and the World Heritage-listed Wachau Valley; cruises from Vienna to Dürnstein, and Donau-Auen National Park; catamarans to Bratislava (daily in summer) and hydrofoils to Budapest (daily May–Sept). Different timetables operate in winter.

Getting around Vienna

A car is superfluous in Vienna, and may even be a liability, as the city has excellent urban and regional transport systems. The **Vienna Card**, which provides unlimited travel by underground, bus and tram over a three-day period for €18.50, is available from the **Vienna Transport Authority** (Wiener Linien; tel: 7909-100) information booths at Stephansplatz, Westbahnhof and Landstrasse/Wien Mitte.

Trams (Strassenbahn): these cover some 35 routes, and on most of them the driver serves as the conductor. If you have a ticket, enter by the door marked *Entwerter* and have it stamped; otherwise board at the front and buy your ticket from the vending machine.

Underground (U-Bahn): five lines cover the main parts of the city. Purchase tickets from vending machines or ticket offices.

Buses: tickets can be bought from a conductor or a machine. The main city-centre routes are 1a (from Schottentor to Stephansplatz), 2a (from Burgring to Graben) and 3a (from Schottenring to Schwarzenbergplatz).

Trains (Schnellbahn/S-Bahn): rapid transit suburban trains depart from the Südbahnhof, Wien Nord and Wien Mitte stations for outlying districts. A single ticket for a journey by tram, bus and underground costs €1.70. Travel passes are available for 24 hours (€5.70), 48 hours (€10) and 72 hours (€13.60). Children under six travel free.

Cycling: The Ringstrasse makes a perfect circular route for sightseeing, and the Wienerwald on the city outskirts has 230km (144 miles) of cycle paths. Rent bicycles from main-line railway stations or from Pedal Power (www.pedalpower.at), which organises guided tours (advance booking required).

AUSTRIA A–Z

Accommodation

The Vienna Tourist Board (www.wien.info) publishes a list of hotels, *Pensionen* (guest houses) and *Saison-Hotels* (student hostels used as hotels from July to September). Or call Wien Hotels (tel: 1-24555) for assistance. Alternatives to hotels include staying on a farm (Ferien im Bauernhof; www.farmholidays.com),

renting an apartment, dossing down in a mountain hut or using campsites and youth hostels.

Arts and Activities

What's On

The Vienna Tourist Board has event listings at offices and online (www.wien.info). A Vienna Card also provides discounts on 210 attractions, theatres, concerts, restaurants and *Heurigen* (wine taverns). Pick one up from the tourist information centre on Albertinaplatz (daily 9am–7pm); it's valid for four days.

Classical music, opera and theatre are major attractions in Vienna. The two main opera venues are the **Staatsoper** (tel: 514-44 2250; www.staatsoper.at) and the **Volksoper** (tel: 514-44 3670; www.volksoper.at). The Vienna Philharmonic Orchestra performs at the **Musikverein** (www.musikverein.at). At **Schönbrunn Palace** (tel: 812-50 040), the Palace Orchestra performs Mozart and Strauss concerts. Tickets sell out early, so don't leave it until the last minute.

Jazz, gospel, ethnic, pop and classical music can be heard at the **Konzerthaus** (tel: 242 002; www.konzerthaus.at).

The **Vienna Boys' Choir** (Wiener Sangerknaben) is an institution dating back to 1498. The choir sings every Sunday at 9.15am (Jan–June and Sept–Dec) in the Hofburg's Burgkapelle (Court Chapel). Tickets for seats must be booked in advance; tel: 1-533 99 27; www.wsk.at.

Budgeting for Your Trip

The following price guide, correct in 2009, is only approximate. From the airport, the city airport train to the city centre costs €8 single. A single ticket on the S-bahn is €4.50. Children under 15 travel free on Sundays, public holidays and during the Viennese school holidays (ID essential). Taxi meters start at around €2, then add €1 per kilometre. Car rental (advance booking from abroad) is from €70 per day.

Allow €18–25 per person for a standard meal with a glass of wine. Museum entrance fees vary, with concessions for holders of the Vienna Card, schoolchildren (passport required) and students (international student identity card required). You should allow €30 for a short *fiaker* tour, €8 for a visit to the cinema, €40 for a nightclub and €5 for entrance to a disco.

Children

With numerous attractions, children up to 15 years travelling free on the U-bahn and buses on Sundays and school holidays, and some hotels offering special rates for family rooms, travelling in Austria with children is remarkably hassle-free. In Vienna, the Lainz Game Preserve has public feedings of wild boar, nature trails and playgrounds; the Diana Pool water playground has a 125-metre (410ft) slide, inflatable tyres to navigate the rapids and a wave machine, and Cobenzl Estate has a children's farm.

Climate

Spring is Vienna's most pleasant season, with chestnut trees in bloom for the city's music festival. In July and August the Viennese leave the city relatively free for visitors, and in autumn, the Wienerwald is in splendid colour for the Heuriger wine gardens (Mar–Oct), and the opera and theatre season kicks off. Even in winter Austria is worth the trip for a white Christmas. Take light cottons for the hot summer afternoons, your warmest woollens for the bitter winter, and a jumper and raincoat for the occasional cool summer evening. Austrians dress up for the theatre, concerts and opera, but a dark suit or cocktail dress is nearly always appropriate.

Disabled Travellers

Vienna is becoming more welcoming to travellers with disabilities, with improved access to public transport, sights and hotels. The Airport Transfer Service at Vienna International Airport has specially designed minibuses for disabled people (tel: 1-7007 359 10). The City Airport Train is accessible, and the U-Bahn has lifts and restrooms to accommodate wheelchairs at many stations. However, older trams and buses are less accessible due to their steps. For a variety of tours aimed at disabled or visually impaired travellers, contact the Vienna Tourist Board (tel: 1-24555).

Eating Out

Remember that Vienna was once the centre of the old Habsburg Empire, so Bohemian dumplings, Hungarian goulash, Polish stuffed cabbage and Serbian schaschlik all feature. Three Austrian staples are the Wienerschnitzel (thinly sliced veal sautéed in a coating of egg

and seasoned breadcrumbs), the Backhendl (roast chicken prepared in the same way) and dumplings (knödel). Try the Apfelstrudel, a flaky pastry filled with apples, raisins and cinnamon, and the Sachertorte, one of the world's most famous chocolate cakes. Viennese sausage stands are popular, the most famous being Hoher Markt on Marc Aurel Strasse.

Wine in Austria is almost always white, the best known being the Gumpoldskirchner. Of the reds, the Vöslauer and the Kalterersee are recommended. The local Gösser beer is a fine alternative to the imported Pilsner Urquell. Try the Hungarian Barack (apricot) and Serbian Slivovitz (plum) brandies. The Viennese Kaffeehaus dates back to the 17th century, and the varieties of coffee are virtually endless.

Embassies and Consulates

Australia: Mattiellistrasse 2–4, 1040 Vienna, tel: 506 740; www.australianembassy.at.
Canada: Laurenzerberg 2, 3rd floor, 1010 Vienna, tel: 531-383 000; www.canadainternational.gc.ca.
South Africa: Sandgasse 33, 1190 Vienna, tel: 320-6493; www.saembvie.at.
UK: Jauresgasse 12, 1030 Vienna, tel: 716 130; www.britishembassy.at.
US: American Citizen Services Section (ACS), Parkring 12a, A-1010 Vienna; tel: 31339-7535; www.usembassy.at.

Emergency Numbers

Fire brigade: 122
Police: 133
Ambulance: 144
Doctors' hotline for visitors (24-hour): 513 9595
Dentist emergency service (at night and at weekends): 1-512 2078
International chemist: 1, Kärntner Ring 17, tel: 1-512 2825

Festivals

January: Mozart Week music festival in Salzburg.
March/April: Vienna Osterklang (Sounds of Easter) music festival.
May: Gauderfest beer festival in Zell im Zillertal.
May/June: Wiener Festwochen (Vienna Festival Weeks) featuring music, dance, drama and film.
June/July: Innsbruck Tanzsommer festival of dance. Lower Austrian Danube festival of all the arts, various locations.

July–August: Bregenz Festival of music and opera with performances on a floating stage on Lake Constance. Innsbruck Festival of Ancient Music in Schloss Ambras. Jazz Fest Wien. Mörbisch Lakeside Festival of operetta on the Neusiedlersee. Salzburg International Festival of opera, music and drama.
August/September: Spittal an der Drau drama festival in the courtyard of Schloss Porcia.
September: Haydn Festival in Schloss Esterhazy in Eisenstadt.
September/October: Linz International Bruckner festival.
October: Vienna Viennale film festival. Zell am Ziller Alpabtrieb celebrations to mark the return of cattle from the Alpine pastures.

Gay and Lesbian Travellers

The capital has plenty of gay-friendly bars and other establishments, and in June stages an annual gay festival, Wien Andersrum ("Vienna the Other Way Round"), which ends with a Rainbow Parade along the Ringstrasse. The Life Ball in May was founded as an AIDS awareness event. A "Vienna Queer Guide" is available from the city's tourism website: www.vienna.info. Smaller-scale gay scenes exist in Linz, Innsbruck, Salzburg and Graz. In the countryside, while overt hostility is unlikely, attitudes are much more conservative. The age of consent for gay men is 18. Contact Rosa Lila Villa (6, Linke Wienzeile 102, tel: 586 8150; www.villa.at) for information.

Health and Medical Care

Austria is generally a very safe country with excellent medical services. Emergency medical care is free for EU citizens (make sure you have a European Health Card), though you may have to pay for medicines (see page 384). Citizens of non-EU countries should ensure they are covered by a private health insurance policy. EU citizens need insurance to cover longer-term problems and repatriation if necessary. Visit a pharmacy (apotheke) for minor health problems.

Chemists operate a rota system for night and Sunday duty, and display the address of the nearest shop on duty. Dial 1550 to find an on-duty pharmacist, or call the toll-free hotline 0800-633 4246 for a free first consultation for medical problems. In case of accident or serious illness, call the ambulance service on 144.

Nightlife

Vienna has more than 6,000 bars, nightclubs, discos and cabarets. The area around Ruprechtsplatz, Seitenstettengasse and Rabensteig forms the previously hot Bermudadreieck (Bermuda Triangle). Apart from the excellent First Floor bar (Seitenstettengasse 5), this area is now passé, and much of the action has moved on to the Naschmarkt and Bäckerstrasse districts, and the railway arches along the Hernalser Gürtel. The tacky nightclubs around Kärntnerstrasse cater largely to the tourist trade. Flex is one of Vienna's best-known clubs (www.flex.at), while along the Gürtel the scene revolves around chic bars, such as Chelsea (www.chelsea.co.at) and Q[kju:] (www.kju-bar.at). Consult the weekly listings magazine, *Falter*, for the latest information.

Opening Hours

Banks: Monday to Friday 8am–3pm (sometimes until 5.30pm on Thursday). Most branches close 12.30–1.30pm.
Shops: Monday to Friday 9am–6pm. Small shops close at lunchtime while major department stores are open 8am–6pm, and in some cases 8pm. Most shops close on Saturday afternoon (though some remain open until 5pm) and all day Sunday. Shops in railway stations are open daily 7am–10.30pm.
Pharmacies: Monday to Friday 8am–noon and 2–6pm, Saturday 8am–noon.
Museums: Most open at 9am or 10am and close at 5pm or 6pm; there may be late opening on one day a week. Many are closed Monday.

Postal Services

Post offices are generally open 8am–noon and 2–6pm. A few open on Saturday from 8–10am. Post offices at the Westbahnhof and Südbahnhof railway stations in Vienna, the Central Post Office (Fleischmarkt 19) and Central Telegraph Office (Börseplatz 1) offer a 24-hour service for registered, air and express mail. Letterboxes and post office signs are yellow. Stamps can also be bought at tobacconists *(Tabaktrafik)*.

Public Holidays

Banks, museums, official services and many restaurants are closed on public holidays. On Good Friday, a holiday for Protestants only, shops remain open.
January: 1 New Year's Day, 6 Epiphany; **March/April**: variable Easter Monday; **May**: 1 Labour Day; **May/June**: variable Ascension Day, Whit Monday, Corpus Christi; **August**: 15 Assumption Day; **October**: 26 National Holiday; **November**: 1 All Saints' Day; **December**: 8 Immaculate Conception, 25 Christmas Day, 26 St Stephen's Day.

Shopping

Austria has an abundance of high-quality, valuable and handmade articles, including glassware, jewellery, china ware and winter-sports gear.

Vienna

The most elegant and expensive shops, as well as art galleries and antique shops, are in the inner city area along Kohlmarkt, Graben and Karntner Strasse. Mariahilferstrasse and the university district also provide good shopping opportunities. Almost every city district has an open-air market, the most famous of these being the Naschmarkt, held along the Wienzeile near Kettenbrückengasse and open daily. Other traditional markets include:

All Saints' Market (Allerheiligen-markt) in front of gates 1–3 of the Central Cemetery (early November).
Christmas Market (Christkindlmarkt) in front of the City Hall in Rathausplatz (December).
Lenten Market (Fastenmarkt), 17 Kalvarienberggasse (February–March).

Telecommunications

Telephone calls may be made from post offices and telephone kiosks. Some public telephones require a telephone card, which is obtainable from post offices. GSM mobiles can be used in Austria, but check with your network provider beforehand that your phone is activated for international roaming. Directory enquiries: 118 899. The international code for Austria is 43, and the regional code for Vienna 1.

Tipping

Tipping is traditionally expected in restaurants, in taxis, at hairdressers and at service stations. Usually 5–10 percent is adequate.

Tourist Information

Austrian National Tourist Office, Margaretenstrasse 1, A-1040, Vienna, tel: (from abroad) (+43-1) 588 660, (in Austria) 0810-101 818; www.austria.info.
Vienna Tourist Board, Albertinaplatz 1 (behind Vienna State Opera), tel: (+43-1) 24555; e-mail: info@wien.info; www.wien.info.
The nine federal provinces all maintain their own tourist boards, whose local offices can provide detailed information.

Tourist Offices Abroad

Australia: tel: 02-9299 3621; e-mail: info@antosyd.org.au
Canada: tel: 416-967 3381; e-mail as US
Ireland: tel: 189-093 0118; e-mail as UK
UK: tel: 0845-101 1818; e-mail: holiday@austria.info
US: tel: 212-944 6880; email: travel@austria.info

What to Read

Insight Guide: Austria is a companion volume to this book. The *Salzburg Smart Guide* packs information into an easily portable format arranged in handy A–Z sections with comprehensive listings.

BELOW: Austria is famous for its cakes and pastries.

B ELGIUM

ESSENTIAL TRAVEL TIPS TO HELP YOU GET THERE AND GET AROUND

FACT FILE

Area: 30,520 sq km
(11,780 sq miles)
Capital: Brussels
Population: 10.7 million
Languages: Flemish (Dutch), French
and German
Highest point: Signal de Botrange
694 metres (2,277ft)
Religion: Roman Catholic
(±50 percent), plus Protestant,
Muslim, Hindu, Sikh, Buddhist and
others
Time zone: Central European Time
Currency: The euro (€)
Electricity: AC 230 volts,
two-pin plugs
International dialling code: 32

TRANSPORT

Getting to Belgium

By Air

The main gateway to Belgium is Brussels Airport (tel: 0900-70000 from inside Belgium, 02-753 7753 from outside; www.brusselsairport.be) at Zaventem. Among the international airlines that fly to Brussels Airport are: Aer Lingus (tel: 070-359 901; www.aerlingus.com), Air Canada (tel: 070-220 100; www.aircanada.com), British Airways (tel: 02-717 3217; www.britishairways.com), Brussels Airlines (tel: 0902-51600; www.brusselsairlines.com), Delta (tel: 02-788 3344; www.delta.com), US Airways (tel: 078-150 026; www.usairways.com), United Airlines (tel: 02-713 3600; www.ual.be).

By Rail

The majority of destinations in Belgium can be reached easily from other parts of the continent by train, and many international lines run through Belgium. International trains stop at the three main railway stations in Brussels: Brussels-North, Brussels-Central and Brussels-South. These stations are linked to each other by rail and provide connections to further destinations in Belgium. For information contact: Belgian Railways (SNCB/NMBS), tel: 02-528 2828; www.b-rail.be.

By Channel Tunnel: The direct rail service from London St Pancras station to Brussels South through the Channel Tunnel is operated by Eurostar (tel: 08705-186 186 in the UK; www.eurostar.com). The journey time is about 2 hours.

By Road

Bordered by the Netherlands to the north, France to the south, and Germany and Luxembourg to the east, Belgium can be reached by a number of European "E" routes, namely: E40, which links Ostend and Cologne, via Brussels; E19, which passes through Antwerp and Brussels from Amsterdam or Paris; and E411/E25, which runs from Brussels to Luxembourg.

By Sea

Passenger and car ferries link the Belgian ports of Ostend and Zeebrugge year-round with various points in Britain. In connection with most crossings, there are direct train services to the main Belgian cities. P&O Ferries go from Hull to Zeebrugge, tel: 0871-664 5645 (070-707 771 in Belgium); www.poferries.com. Norfolkline go from Rosyth (Edinburgh) to Zeebrugge, tel: 0844-499 0007 (+44 208-127 8303 from Belgium); www.norfolkline.com. Transeuropa Ferries go from Ramsgate to Ostend, tel: 01843-595 522 (059-340 260 in Belgium); www.transeuropaferries.com.

Getting around Belgium

Belgium is small enough and the transport infrastructure good enough to make getting around the country pretty straightforward. The train is generally the best way to go by public transport, with the bus service being useful for short distances and for places not served by train. Excellent motorways and other fast roads criss-cross the country.

To and from the Airport

Located 11km (7 miles) from the city centre, Brussels Airport is linked by rail to Brussels Central (Centrale/Centraal), North (Nord/Noord) and South (Midi/Zuid) stations. Up to four trains depart every hour from the airport and from the three Brussels stations 5am–11pm. See www.brusselsairport.be. For flight information, tel: 0900-70000. In addition, there are taxi and express bus services to the city centre.

By Air

Since the longest distance across the country from southeast to northwest is only 314km (212 miles), there is little need for domestic air services.

By Rail

Belgium has extremely good trains that cover practically the whole country. In addition, many international express

AUSTRIA

BELGIUM

FRANCE

GERMANY

GREECE

ITALY

NETHERLANDS

PORTUGAL

SPAIN

SWITZERLAND

services link the country with Paris, Amsterdam and numerous German cities. A Belgian Railways Rail Pass is valid for 10 journeys between Belgian cities and lasts for one year. It costs €73 for second class and €112 for first class. Train information may be obtained from: SNCB, tel: 02-528 2828; www.b-rail.be.

By Road

Distances are relatively short, and motorways serve most of the country with the exception of the hilly regions of the Ardennes. Access to all roads is free: there are no toll roads in Belgium.

Motoring advice: In the northern part of the country, road signs appear in Flemish – in the southern part, in French. Several towns and villages have two names, one in each of the official languages, but it is important to note that road signs only show place names in the language of that particular region. Winter tyres are recommended, especially for the Ardennes, but are not compulsory. In case of accident, call the emergency number 100 to request help.

Getting around Brussels

The excellent public transport network of metro, trams and buses, operated by STIB, is easy to use and tightly integrated. The Brussels Card can be purchased from tourist offices in Brussels, online from the tourist office website, and from some participating museums. It can save you money by offering free use of public transport, free or reduced admission to many city museums, and discounts in some restaurants, bars, entertainment venues and shops.

Metro: The fast and modern metro service consists of four main lines, connecting the eastern and western parts of the city. The underground network is supplemented by two premetro lines, which are trams that run partly underground.

Transport Advice

The following organisations are good sources of information:
• Royal Automobile Club of Belgium (RACB), 53 Rue d'Arlon, 1040 Bruxelles, tel: 02-287 0911; www.racb.be
• Touring Club de Belgique (TCB), 44 Rue de la Loi, 1040 Brussels, tel: 02-233 2468, breakdown 070-344 777; www.touring.be

Public Transport Tickets

Cards for single journeys, for five and 10 journeys, and for one and three days of unlimited travel, are available either from drivers or from STIB sales points and rail stations. Cards must be inserted into machines on metro station platforms, or on board trams and buses, which automatically authorise the journey and cancel the fare. Single- and multiple-journey cards permit unlimited transfers within a one-hour period, provided the card is inserted after each vehicle change.

Buses/trams: Buses can be reduced to near-immobility in rush hour. For short distances, the tram is usually the fastest way to travel.
Trains: The suburban above-ground train service is also good, but is not so useful for tourists within the city limits.
Cars: Travelling by car in the city is not recommended. All the usual international car-hire companies, plus some local ones, have offices in Brussels. Trams and buses always have traffic priority, as, usually, do vehicles coming from the right, unless the road is posted with orange diamond signs.
Cycling: Brussels is striving to become a cycle-friendly city, and cycle routes are increasing. See www.bicycle.irisnet.be for information and maps. For bike tours and hire contact ProVelo, tel: 02-217 0158 (English spoken); www.provelo.org.

BELGIUM A–Z

Accommodation

The city's hotels run the gamut from ultra expensive to cheap. Due to the presence of the European Union institutions and many international diplomatic and business organisations, there's a prevalence of business-orientated hotels. The city's official hotel guide is available at the tourist offices at 61 Rue du Marché aux Herbes, in the town hall, and at Rue Royale 2–4. You can also book accommodation here.

Arts and Activities

The Brussels Card can give you free or reduced entry to many city museums. All information concerning this and cultural activities in Belgium can be

obtained from the various branches of the Brussels International Tourist Office, tel: 02-513 8940. World-class institutions like the Théâtre Royal de la Monnaie for opera and dance, and the Musées Royaux des Beaux-Arts, are complemented by a large range of local museums, galleries and performance venues. Highlights include the Musée Horta for Brussels's Art Nouveau heritage, and the Centre Belge de la Bande Dessinée, which caters to the city's obsession with comic-strip art.

Budgeting for Your Trip

Prices of comparable hotels vary considerably, and those of restaurants, clubs and museums to a lesser extent, from place to place around Belgium. Brussels and Antwerp tend to be the most expensive among the major cities, followed by Bruges, Ghent and Liège. A taxi from Brussels Airport to the centre of Brussels costs about €35. Brussels has a paid-for tourist card valid for 1, 2 or 3 days, and Bruges a free card for budget travellers; both offer discounts for museums, attractions and nightlife venues, and the Brussels Card affords free use of public transport.

The starting rate for a double room is €50; for a decent mid-range hotel in most cities, expect to pay €100–200; above €300 is starting to get into de luxe territory. Brussels is more expensive for accommodation than Antwerp, Bruges, Ghent and Liège. Dining costs are €10–25 for a 2–3-course meal at a decent local restaurant, €25–60 at a fine restaurant, and €100 and beyond for Michelin-level cuisine. A glass of beer can cost as little as €2 and a glass of house wine €4.

Children

There are many places of interest for children in Belgium. The coast, the Kempen district and the Ardennes are especially rich in theme parks and other attractions with activities suitable for children of all ages. The country's only regular zoo is the superb Antwerp Zoo, Koningin Astridplein 26, tel: 03-202 4540; www.zooantwerpen.be. In Brussels, a fascinating attraction is Mini-Europe, Bruparck, tel: 02-478 0550; www.minieurope.com. Bruges scores high with the dolphins and other marine creatures at the Boudewijn Seapark, Alfons De Baeckestraat 12, tel: 050-383 838; www.dolfinarium.be.

Climate

Belgium's climate is temperate and much influenced by its proximity to the sea, an influence that diminishes the further inland you go until, in the low mountains along the German border in the east, the climate becomes sub-Alpine. The finest weather is between April and October. July and August can be quite hot, but rain is probable even then. Winters range from mild to severe, with snowfalls common in the Ardennes, though temperatures rarely fall below freezing for long.

Disabled Travellers

Trains, trams and metro trains are the easiest from the point of view of accessibility; the newest buses on some routes have access ramps. Contact:
Croix Rouge de Belgique
Rue de Stalle 96
Tel: 02-371 3111
Email: info@redcross-fr.be
www.redcross.be

Eating Out

Belgium has plenty of regional cuisine and specialities, from the *jambon d'Ardenne* (smoked Ardennes ham) and *salade liégoise* (Liège bacon salad) of the French-speaking areas, to the *waterzooï op Gentse wijze* (a fish or chicken stew from Ghent) and *paling in 't groen* (eel in a green sauce) of Flanders, and the *moules/ mosselen* (mussels) and *steak-frites* (steak with French fries) that are popular everywhere. Vegetarian food is becoming ever more popular, both by way of dedicated restaurants and vegetarian options on the menus of general restaurants. Belgians like to linger over lunch and dinner in a restaurant.

Embassies and Consulates

Belgian Embassies
Australia: 19 Arkana Street, Yarralumla – ACT 2600, Canberra, tel: 02-6273 3392; www.diplomatie.be/ canberra.
Canada: 360 Albert Street, Suite 820, Ottawa, ONT, K1R 7X7, tel: 613-236 7267; www.diplomatie.be/ ottawa.
Ireland: 2 Shrewsbury Road, Ballsbridge, Dublin 4, tel: 01-205 7100; www.diplomatie.be/dublin.
South Africa: Leyds Street 625, Muckleneuk, 0002 Pretoria, tel: 012-440 3201; www.diplomatie.be/pretoria.

UK: 17 Grosvenor Crescent, London, SW1X 7EE, tel: 020-7470 3700; www. diplomatie.be/london.
US: 3330 Garfield Street NW Washington, DC 20008, tel: 202-333 6900; www.diplobel.us.

In Belgium
Australia: Rue Guimard 6–8, tel: 02-286 0500; www.austemb.be.
Canada: Avenue de Tervuren 2, tel: 02-741 0611; www.dfait-maeci.gc.ca/ missions/belgium-belgique/menu-eng.asp.
Ireland: 50 Rue Wiertz, 1050 Brussels, tel: 02-235 6676; www. embassiesabroad.com/embassies-of/ Ireland#4204.
New Zealand: Square de Meeûs 1, tel: 02-512 1040; www.nzembassy.com/ home.cfm?c=24.
South Africa: Rue Montoyer 17–19, tel: 02-285 4400; www.southafrica.be.
UK: Rue d'Arlon 85, tel: 02-287 6211; www.britain.be.
US: Boulevard du Régent 25–27, tel: 02-508 2111; http://belgium. usembassy.gov.

Festivals

March/April: Carnival, Binche, Sunday to Shrove/Pancake Tuesday (the day before Ash Wednesday). Belgium's most colourful pre-Lenten Carnival culminates in the parade of the fabulously costumed Gilles de Binche.
April/May: Heilig-Bloedprocessie (Procession of the Holy Blood), Bruges, Ascension Day (fifth Thursday after Easter). The bishop of Bruges leads a costumed procession bearing the Relic of the Holy Blood from the basilica in the Burg through the city streets.
July: Ommegang, Brussels, first Tuesday and Thursday in July. A spectacular costumed pageant in the Grand'Place re-enacts the "Joyful

Emergency Numbers

Police: 101
Accident and fire brigade: 100
Doctor (Brussels): 24 hours, 02-479 1818 or 02-513 0202
Dentist (Brussels): Mon–Sat 9am–7pm, 02-426 1026
SOS **Youth**: 02-512 9020
SOS **Solitude**: tel: 02-548 9808

Lost credit cards:
American Express, tel: 02-676 2121
Diners Club, tel: 02-206 9800
Eurocard, MasterCard, Visa, tel: 070-344 344

Entry" of Habsburg emperor Charles V into Brussels.
Gentse Feesten (Ghent Festivities). Ten days of street parties, music and cultural performances in July.

Gay and Lesbian Travellers

For information on Brussels and Wallonia, contact the gay and lesbian community centre, Telsquels, Rue du Marché-au-Charbon 81, Brussels, tel: 02-512 4587. In Flanders, contact the Holebifederatie, Kammerstraat 22, Ghent, tel: 09-223 6929. The age of consent for gay men is 16.

Health and Medical Care

Pharmacies close on Saturday afternoon and all day Sunday. However, in emergencies, consult the weekend editions of the local papers for the duty rotas of pharmacies, doctors, dentists and vets. Pharmacy rotas are also displayed in pharmacy windows, or call 0900-10500. To find the nearest on-duty doctor or dentist (whole of Belgium), tel: 100.

Language

Three official languages are spoken in Belgium: Flemish, a variation of Dutch, in the north; French in the south; and German in the east, by a small minority. English is widely spoken in hotels, restaurants, shops and places of business, and is more welcome than French in Flanders (the northern, Flemish-speaking area).

Nightlife

Brussels International publishes *Bru XXL*, a free bimonthly guide to entertainment in the city. Information about scheduled events in Brussels and around Belgium is contained in the weekly English-language magazine *The Bulletin*.
Brussels and Antwerp are Belgium's nightlife hotspots, followed by Ghent and Liège. Bruges is not noted for its nightlife – which doesn't mean there isn't any, only that it takes third place to culture and dining.

Opening Hours

Shops usually open Mon–Sat 9am–6pm, although some of them close on Monday. There are a few late-night shops in the city centre, and the neighbourhood corner store may stay open until 9pm. It's best to ask around as to the best after-hours shops and chemists. Banks are open 9am–4pm or 5pm. On Friday, some larger stores and supermarkets stay open until around 9pm.

Postal Services

Post offices open Mon–Fri 9am–6pm, Sat 9am–noon. Smaller branches may close for lunch noon–2pm, close by 4 or 5pm and on Saturdays. Mail boxes are red.

Brussels

Normal post office hours are Mon–Fri 9am–5pm. Some offices are open longer, including the office at Centre Monnaie, Place de la Monnaie, open Mon–Fri 8am–6pm, Sat 10.30am–4.30pm, tel: 022-012 345; and the office at South station, open Mon–Fri 7am–8pm, Sat 10.30am–4.30pm, tel: 022-012 345.

Public Holidays

January: 1 New Year's Day; **March/April**: variable Easter Monday; **May**: 1 Labour Day; **May/June**: variable Ascension Day, Whit Monday; **July**: 11 Flemish Community Holiday, 21 Independence Day; **August**: 15 Assumption Day; **September**: 27 French Community Holiday; **November**: 1 All Saints' Day, 11 Armistice Day, 15 German Community Holiday; **December**: 25 Christmas Day, 26 St Stephen's Day.

Shopping

Belgium is noted for hand-beaten copperware from Dinant; crystal from Val-Saint-Lambert of Liège; diamonds from Antwerp; handmade lace from Bruges, Brussels, Binche and Mechelen; tapestries from Mechelen, Sint-Niklaas, Brussels and Ghent, and sporting guns from Herstal, for which Liège is world-famous. Credit cards are accepted everywhere, and many shops offer tourists special terms exclusive of VAT on certain goods.

Brussels

There are numerous areas in Brussels where you can shop to your heart's content. In the Lower City go to Place de Brouckère, Place de la Monnaie, along Boulevard Anspach (predominantly fashion and books), and Rue Neuve, including the City 2 shopping complex.

Rue du Beurre is good for food and gift shops. Rue du Midi is another well-known shopping beat, where there are quite a few art-supply shops

and music stores. One of the best places for window-shopping is the glass-roofed arcades of the famous Galeries Royales Saint-Hubert, which opened in 1847, the first covered shopping mall in Europe. Rue Antoine Dansaert is the place to find ultra-fashionable and expensive boutiques.

Fancy shops with internationally recognised designer names are concentrated in the Upper City. Streets to look out for include Avenue Louise, Chaussée d'Ixelles, Boulevard de Waterloo and Avenue de la Toison d'Or. The most chic arcades are also located here. You'll find Galerie Espace Louise and Galerie Louise at Place Louise; Galeries de la Toison d'Or and the Galerie d'Ixelles are at Porte de Namur.

Department stores generally open Mon–Sat 9am–6pm and stay open until 8pm on Friday.

The city has many markets. **Antique market**: Grand Sablon, Sat 9am–6pm, Sun 9am–2pm. **Flower market**: Grand'Place, Mar–Oct Tue–Wed and Fri–Sun 8am–6pm. **Flea market**: Place du Jeu de Balle, daily 7am–2pm. **Food and textile market**: Place Bara (South station), Sun 5am–1pm.

Telecommunications

Most public telephones are operated by phone cards, which are available from post offices, kiosks and newsagents. Apart from the old coin-operated phones, all can be used for international calls.

BELOW: an old-style post box.

Tipping

Taxis, most restaurants, hairdressers, etc. very considerately include your tip in the bill, in the certainty that you couldn't fail to be impressed by the service. Toilet attendants will make your visit a misery if you pass their saucer without leaving a few coins.

Dialling Codes

To call other countries, first dial the international access code 00, then the country code: Australia 61; Ireland 353; New Zealand 64; South Africa 27; US and Canada 1; UK 44. The code for Belgium is 32.

Tourist Information

Tourist Offices Abroad

Canada: 43 Rue de Buade, Bureau 525, Québec G1R 4A2, tel: 418-692 4939; email: ndroulans@belnet.ca; www.belgique-tourisme.qc.ca.

UK: Belgian Tourist Office Brussels & Wallonia, 217 Marsh Wall, London E14 9JF, tel: 020-7537 1132; email: info@belgiumtheplaceto.be; www.belgiumtheplaceto.be. Tourism Flanders-Brussels, 1a Cavendish Square, London W1G 0LD, tel: 020-7307 7738; email: info@visitflanders.co.uk; www.visitflanders.co.uk.

US: 220 East 42nd Street, Suite 3402, New York, NY 10017, tel: 212-758 8130; email: info@visitbelgium.com.

In Belgium

Brussels International – Tourism & Congress, Brussels Town Hall, Grand'Place, 1000 Brussels, tel: 02-513 8940; email: tourism@brussels international.be; www.brusselsinternational.be. Open summer daily 9am–6pm; winter Mon–Sat 9am–6pm, Sun 10am–2pm; closed Sun January to Easter.

OPT (Office de Promotion du Tourisme de Wallonie et de Bruxelles), Rue Saint-Bernard 30, 1060 Brussels, tel: 070-221 021; www.opt.be.

Toerisme Vlaanderen, Rue du Marché aux Herbes 61, 1000 Brussels, tel: 02-504 0300; www.toerismevlaanderen.be.

What to Read

Insight Guide: Belgium is a companion volume to this book. The *Smart Guides to Bruges* and *Brussels* pack information into an easily portable and convenient format arranged in handy A–Z sections.

F RANCE

ESSENTIAL TRAVEL TIPS TO HELP YOU GET THERE AND GET AROUND

FACT FILE

Area: 547,030 sq km (210,026 sq miles)
Capital: Paris
Population: Around 63.8 million
Languages: Everyone in France speaks French, but regional languages exist in Brittany (Breton), Alsace (Alsatian), the western Pyrenees (Basque), across southern France (Occitan) and the eastern Pyrenees (Catalan).
Highest mountain: Mont Blanc 4,808 metres (15,775ft)
Religion: Roman Catholic (51%)
Time zone: Central European Time
Currency: The euro (€)
Electricity: AC 220 volts, two-pin plugs
Direct Dialling: 33

TRANSPORT

Getting to France

By Air

Air France, based in Paris, is the national carrier, and has flights to the major French cities. British Airways flies from UK destinations to Bordeaux, Lyon, Montpellier, Nice, Paris and Toulouse. Budget airlines such as bmibaby, easyJet and Ryanair fly to considerably more destinations.

Travellers from North America and elsewhere can get direct flights to Paris and major cities such as Nice and Lyon, via Air France and most national airlines. American Airlines, United Airlines and Delta also fly to France.

Air France
Canada: Montreal: 15th Floor, 2000 Rue Mansfield, Montreal, tel: 514-847 1106 or 1-800-667 2747. Toronto: 151 Bloor Street West, Suite 810, Ontario M5S 1S4.
France: 119 Champs-Elysées, 75384 Paris Cedex 08, Mon–Sat 9.30am–6.30pm; Central Reservations, tel: 3654.
Ireland: Dublin Airport, tel: 01-605 0383.
UK: 10 Warwick St, London W1 5RA, tel: 0871-663 377.
US: Toll-free reservations, tel: 800-237 2747. Chicago: Suite 3214, John Hancock Center, 875 North Michigan Avenue, Chicago, IL 60611. Los Angeles: Suite 3250, Ernst & Young LLP, 725 South Figueroa Street, Los Angeles, CA 90017-5432. New York: 120 West 56th Street, NY 10019.

Other Airlines
British Airways
Tel: 0844-493 0787
www.britishairways.com
bmibaby
Tel: 0905-828 2828
www.bmibaby.com
easyJet
Tel: 0871-244 2366

Paris Airports

Paris has two airports:
• **Paris-Charles de Gaulle**, 23km (15 miles) north of the city via the A1 or RN2, tel: 01-48 62 22 80; www.paris-cdg.com or www.adp.fr.
• **Paris-Orly**, 14km (9 miles) south of the centre via the A6 or RN7, tel: 01-49 75 15 15; www.paris-orly. com or www.adp.fr. Handles mostly domestic and charter flights.

www.easyjet.com
Ryanair
Tel: 0871-246 0000
www.ryanair.com

By Sea

There are several ferry services operating from the UK, the Republic of Ireland and the Channel Islands to the northern ports of France. All of them carry cars as well as foot passengers. The shortest crossing is between Dover and Calais, but cross-Channel services have been greatly undermined since the advent of much quicker Eurostar passenger trains and Eurotunnel vehicle trains, and competitively priced no-frills air carriers.

Getting around France

By Rail

France has a fast, efficient rail network operated by the SNCF (Société Nationale des Chemins de Fer). Its much-praised TGV programme offers comfortable express services via Paris and Lille to many destinations. For visitors travelling from Paris, the train is a comfortable way to reach any major destination in France, with most express services offering refreshments (and even play areas for young children). There are five main stations serving the provinces from Paris, so check which one you need before setting out. Car and bicycle hire is available at most main stations – as a package with your rail ticket if you prefer (details from SNCF; see below for contact numbers).

Tickets and Information
The easiest way to reserve a train ticket is in person at any large

railway station. Alternatively you can do it online at www.voyages-sncf.com or by phone, tel: 36 35 (within France). Outside France, tickets and information can be obtained from Rail Europe:

UK: Rail Europe Travel Centre, 1 Lower Regent Street, London SW1, tel: 08448-484 064; www.raileurope.co.uk.

US and Canada: Rail Europe Inc, 44 South Broadway, White Plains, NY 10601, tel: 1-800-622 8600 in the US or 1-800-361 RAIL (7245) in Canada; www.raileurope.com.

Rail Passes

UK residents can buy an InterRail pass specifically for France valid for 3, 4, 6 or 8 days, or a global InterRail pass covering 30 countries including France valid for 5, 10, 22 days or a month.

Residents of other countries including the US can choose from a variety of passes. The France Pass is valid for 3, 4, 5, 6, 7, 8 or 9 days. A Eurail Select Pass covers France and its immediate neighbours. A Eurail Global Pass covers all the major European countries for 15 or 21 days, 1 month, 2 months or 3 months.

There are reductions for children and for young people (12–25 years old). Most adult tickets can be either first or second class.

Motorail

Motorail takes much of the strain out of driving long distances to your holiday destination while allowing you the freedom of being able to drive your own car once you have arrived. Services operate May–Sept only, from Calais to Brive, Toulouse and Narbonne, and Calais to Avignon and Nice. Tickets can be booked to include cross-channel ferries. In the UK, tel: 08448-484 050.

By Bus

Eurolines is a consortium of almost 30 coach companies, operating in France and throughout Europe. They operate services from London (Victoria) to many major French destinations. Some (such as Paris) are daily, others are seasonal and some have services several times a week throughout the year.

This is one of the cheapest ways of reaching France, and there are discounts available for young people and senior citizens. The ticket includes the ferry crossing (via Dover). National Express coaches have connections from most major towns in the UK that link up with the London departures.

For details contact Eurolines UK, Ensign Court, 4 Vicarage Road, Edgbaston, Birmingham B15 3ES, tel: 08717-818 181; or in France at 28 Avenue du Général de Gaulle, 93541 Bagnolet, tel: 08-92 89 90 91; www.eurolines.com.

By Car

Most motorways *(autoroutes)* in France are privately owned and subject to tolls. These can be paid in cash or by credit card. Some motorways, however, are toll-free public roads, although there may be a fee to pay for using a bridge or tunnel en route. The trip from the northern ports to the south of France costs around €80 in tolls one-way. The benefits of paying for the use of the motorway can be seen in the high standards of maintenance of the roads and the frequent rest areas, picnic sites and catering facilities.

Free motorway maps are often available at motorway service stations/cafeterias and are useful as they mark the position and facilities of all the rest areas on the route (usually called *Aire de* and then the name of the place).

If speed is not of the essence and you intend to make the drive part of your holiday, follow the green holiday route signs BIS to your destination – these form part of a national network

The Channel Tunnel

The Channel Tunnel offers fast, frequent rail services between Britain and France.

The **Eurostar** service offers high-speed connections between London (St Pancras) or Ashford and Lille (1 hour 30 minutes) or Paris (Gare du Nord – 2 hours 15 minutes). Eurostar also operates high-speed trains direct from London and Ashford to Disneyland Paris.

For Eurostar passenger services, tel: 08705-186 186; www.eurostar.com.

Eurotunnel is the name of the train service that takes cars and their passengers from Folkestone to Calais on a simple drive-on-drive-off system. The journey time through the tunnel is about 25 minutes. Reservations are not needed – you just turn up and take the next service, but during holiday periods there can be a long wait. Eurotunnel runs 24 hours a day, all year round, with a service at least once an hour through the night.

For Eurotunnel car services, tel: 08705-353 535; www.eurotunnel.com.

of *bison futé* routes to avoid traffic congestion at peak periods. You will discover parts of France you never knew existed and are more likely to arrive relaxed. The first and last *(la rentrée)* weekend in August and the public holiday on 15 August are usually the worst times to travel, so avoid them if you can.

Getting to Paris

By Air

From Paris–Charles de Gaulle Airport
Train: The quickest and most reliable way to get to central Paris is by RER train, Line B. Trains run every 15 minutes from 5am to 11.45pm to metro Gare du Nord or Châtelet.

Motoring Advice

- All motorists must carry a red warning triangle, a fluorescent jacket and spare bulbs for headlights.
- After dark, motorists have the choice of using dipped headlights or parking lights, even in rainy weather.
- In some areas, horns may be sounded only in dire need.

BELOW: the ferry from Nice to Corsica.

ABOVE: Art Deco Paris metro sign.

The average journey time is 30–45 minutes to Châtelet.
Bus: Air France coach line 4 runs to Gare de Lyon then Gare Montparnasse (every 30 minutes, 5.45am–11pm). You can also take coach line 2 to Porte Maillot and Place de l'Etoile (7am–9.30pm); tickets can be bought on the bus (tel: 08-92 35 08 20). The Roissybus service runs between the airport and the Place de l'Opéra, taking about 45 minutes (every 15 minutes, 6am–11pm).
Taxi: It can take 30 minutes to over an hour, depending on traffic. The cost appears on the meter, but a supplement is charged for each large piece of luggage, pushchair and animal.

From Orly Airport
Train: Take the shuttle from gate H at Orly Sud or arrivals gate F at Orly Ouest to the Orly train station. The RER stops at Austerlitz, Pont St-Michel and the Quai d'Orsay. It runs every 15 minutes between 5.50am–10.50pm and takes about 30 minutes to Austerlitz.
The Orlyval automatic train is a shuttle to Antony (the nearest RER to Orly). It runs every 5–8 minutes from 6.30am–9.15pm Mon–Sat and

Public Transport

Details of routes and timetables are generally available free of charge either from bus stations (*gare routière*), which are often situated close to rail stations, or from tourist offices. They will also give details of coach tours and sightseeing excursions which are widely available.

7am–10.55pm Sun, and takes 30 minutes.
Bus: Air France coach line 1 runs to Gare Montparnasse then Invalides Terminal (every 15 minutes, 6am–11.30pm). The Orlybus can take you to Denfert-Rochereau metro station in the south of Paris (every 15 minutes, 6am–11pm).
Taxis: A taxi takes 30–40 minutes (much longer in the rush hour).

By Rail
The main train stations in Paris are Gare du Nord (for British connections), Gare de l'Est, Gare d'Austerlitz, Gare Saint-Lazare and Gare de Lyon (for links with the Riviera, Spain and Italy).

Getting around Paris

Orientation
Paris is one of the most densely populated urban centres in the world. Divided into 20 arrondissements (districts), Greater Paris is home to 11½ million people. Paris is traversed by the River Seine, dividing the city into two – the Right Bank and the Left Bank. The larger Right Bank is the home of Paris commerce and government, and is where most of the historic monuments, the great boulevards and museums can be found. The Left Bank is the stronghold of the intellectual community. Although the city is now ringed by high-rise suburbs, its essential character has been preserved.

Public Transport
Metro: Operates 5.30am–12.45am; the lines are identified by number and the names of their terminals. It operates in conjunction with the RER, suburban regional express trains which operate on four lines, identified as A–D. Flat-rate tickets can be bought from metro stations and some newsagents. For metro details, tel: 3246; www.ratp.info.
The Paris Visite card allows unlimited travel for 1, 2, 3 or 5 consecutive days on the metro, buses (including the Orlybus and Roissybus and the Noctambus night buses), RER trains, the Montmartre Funicular, the Tramway and all trains of the SNCF Ile de France network. There is a choice of zones: zones 1–3 cover central Paris; zones 1–6 include Disney, Versailles and the airports. This tourist-aimed card also gives discounted entry to various museums and sites of interest. Available from metro, RER and SNCF stations, Paris airports and many tour operators abroad.

The Mobilis is a 1-day card allowing unlimited travel within the chosen zones (1–5).
Buses: City buses, which operate 5.30am–8.30pm, are efficient and punctual. They are numbered and all stops have clear maps giving directions. Metro tickets are valid on the buses; one or at most two tickets are required, depending on the zones travelled. You can also buy tickets from the driver.
Maps: For maps and clear information in English on all public transport see www.ratp.fr. The information includes facilities for passengers with special needs, including an accompaniment service (Les Compagnons du Voyage, tel: 01-58 76 08 33; www.compagnons.com).

FRANCE A–Z

Accommodation

France has a wide choice of accommodation, as any tourist information office will tell you. Every town of any size has at least one small hotel, although its facilities might only be basic. Many such hotels are grouped under the Logis banner (www.logis-de-france.fr).
If you just want somewhere cheap to break a long drive and lay your head for the night, you might find that a no-frills, chain hotel such as a Formule 1 (www.hotelformule1.com) or the more classy Campanile (www.campanile. fr) suits your purpose. These are often beside ring roads or on industrial estates, so they're not the place to go if you intend to hang around sightseeing.
Top of the range, meanwhile, are the luxury hotels which may be in a château or other historic monument. See for instance www.relaisetchateaux. com or, for the Loire Valley, www. bienvenueauchateau.com.
If you want to get to know the locals, your best option is to look for a bed and breakfast, *chambre d'hôte*, and if you intend to stay in one place for a while it will be most economical to rent a self-catering house or apartment. For either of these options, you can ask at any tourist information office or book through Gîtes de France (www. gitesdefrance.fr) or Clévances (www. clevacances.fr).
France is extremely well equipped with campsites – you can find information about them at www. campingfrance.com.

Paris

Branches of the Paris Office du Tourisme et des Congrès can supply a list of hotel accommodation in every price range, or they can book you a room for a nominal fee, tel: 08-92 68 30 00. For bed and breakfasts, try www.bed-and-breakfast-in-paris.com.

Arts and Activities

France is extremely committed to supporting the arts, and not just in the large cities. Paris, of course, has its great museums and theatres, but plenty goes on in rural areas, often with the support of the local council. Ask the tourist information office and you might be lucky enough to stumble on some itinerant performing theatre troupe, exhibition in a château or outdoor concert.

Paris

Consult *Pariscope* or *L'Officiel des Spectacles* for a guide to events in Paris. Both weekly guides are sold at newsstands. They list the current exhibitions in museums, art galleries and exhibition halls, as well as theatre events and current films. There are also sections on night entertainment and where to eat. The tourist office's monthly *Paris Selection* also gives a choice of what's on in town. For more ideas and information visit www.thecatseyes.com and www.whatsonwhen.com.

Budgeting for Your Trip

Paris is generally more expensive to survive in than rural France, and what you spend will vary according to how lavishly you live, but as a rough guide you'll need to allow for the following:
Double room per night (including breakfast) in an average hotel: €60–120, depending on the season.
Modest à la carte or *menu du jour* lunch: €13–20 per person.
Three-course dinner with wine: €20–30 per person.
Admission charges: €10–15 per person per day.
Miscellaneous (drinks, snacks, tips, etc.): €20 per person per day.

Paris

The Paris Pass offers free entry to over 60 of the top tourist attractions, including the Arc de Triomphe and the Louvre, as well as free metro travel and public transport within Paris and other discounts. You can buy online and check prices at www.paris-pass.com, or from tourist offices.

Children

France is a great place for a family holiday, although you might have to adjust your itinerary to include fewer highbrow museums and Renaissance châteaux and more child-centred attractions. In Paris, the Eiffel Tower and Disneyland will be highlights of any child's stay. Elsewhere in the country there are other theme parks, and you'll never be far from a wildlife attraction or activity centre – you only have to ask at the local tourist office. The coasts offer beaches galore, although the northern coastline and Mediterranean Sea are more suitable for young children than the Atlantic coast, which has big waves and a strong undertow in places. Another idea may be a waterborne holiday on a canal. Hotels and restaurants everywhere are well used to catering for the needs of kids of all ages.

Climate

The French climate is varied and seasonal. In the north, it is similar to that of southern England, and springtime is often suggested as the best time to see the capital. However, be prepared for showers. In the autumn, mornings can be quite sharp, but by midday the skies are usually clear and bright.
In the southeast, summers are dry and temperatures can frequently rise to over 30°C (86°F). However, watch out for heavy thunder and hailstorms. Winters are mild (the temperature rarely falling below 10°C/50°F on the Mediterranean coast) and often wet; spring is even wetter.
Many areas of France have quite distinct microclimates, and the weather can change rapidly. The Midi has its own particular *bête noire*, the fierce wind known as the Mistral, which blows from the northwest, mainly in winter and spring, leaving clear blue skies in its wake.

Disabled Travellers

Initiatives in France to improve provision for handicapped people include a series of special signs for specific disabilities, such as impaired mobility, mental disability, blindness and deafness, which direct people and carers to help points.
Parking: The international blue scheme applies. Ensure you have all the documentation with you.
Reduced tolls: People with vehicles adapted for the disabled pay reduced toll prices on motorways.

Festivals

A programme listing all major festivals and *fêtes* throughout the country is published annually. The programme is available from French Government Tourist Offices around the world. Note that theatre and opera seasons generally run from September to June, with many theatres and concert halls closed in July and August, when cultural activity turns to the prestigious summer arts festivals in the regions.
Son et lumière (sound and light) displays still exist at some châteaux and historic monuments but are now in decline because they are very expensive to present. Performances normally begin at around 9 or 10pm, and there are often several shows a night in July and August.
For information and reservations contact the local tourist offices. A national guide of historical shows is published annually and is available from the Fédération Nationale des Fêtes et Spectacles Historiques, Hôtel de Ville, 60000 Beauvais, tel: 03-44 79 40 00.

Accommodation: The French Tourist Office publishes a list of hotels with facilities for the disabled. However, you should always check directly for specific facilities.
The Association des Paralysés de France, 13 Place de Rungis, 75013 Paris, tel: 01-53 80 92 97; www.apf.asso.fr publishes a guide called *Handiguide* listing accommodation suitable for disabled travellers.

Eating Out

Eating out is one of the quintessential pleasures of a stay in France, and in the summer it's never hard to find a shady outdoor terrace for lunch. Most restaurants offer a range of set menus, starting with the economical three-course *menu du jour* which usually offers little or no choice and includes wine but not coffee. There may also be a *plat du jour* menu, in which you can get the set main course and either a starter or a dessert, but in this case drinks will probably be extra. Your meal will be more expensive if you order items from the menu, and for anywhere with gourmet pretensions – particularly Michelin-starred restaurants – there is virtually no upper limit to the bill.

AUSTRIA

BELGIUM

FRANCE

GERMANY

GREECE

ITALY

NETHERLANDS

PORTUGAL

SPAIN

SWITZERLAND

Embassies and Consulates

In Paris

Australia: 4 Rue Jean Rey, 75724 Paris, tel: 01-40 59 33 00; www.france. ombassy.gov.gu.

Canada: 35 Avenue Montaigne 75008 Paris, tel: 01-44 43 29 00; www.international.gc.ca.

Ireland: 12 Avenue Foch, 75116 Paris, tel: 01-44 17 67 00; www.embassy ofireland.fr.

New Zealand: 7ter Rue Léonard de Vinci, 75116 Paris, tel: 01-45 01 43 43; www.nzembassy.com.

South Africa: 59 Quai d'Orsay, 75343 Paris, tel: 01-53 59 23 23; www. afriquesud.net.

UK: 35 Rue du Faubourg St-Honoré, 75383 Paris, tel: 01-44 51 31 00; http://ukinfrance.fco.gov.uk/en.

US: 2 Avenue Gabriel, 75382 Paris, tel: 01-43 12 22 22; http://france.us embassy.gov.

In UK and Ireland

French Consulate
England: 21 Cromwell Road, London SW7 2EN; tel: 020-7073 1250; www.consulfrance-londres.org.
Visa section: 6a Cromwell Place, London SW7 2EW.

In US

French Embassy/Consulate
www.ambafrance-us.org
Consulate General: 4101 Reservoir Road, NW, Washington DC 20007, tel: 202-944 6000.

Gay and Lesbian Travellers

France claims to be the first country in the world to legislate against discrimination on the basis of sexual preference, and it is generally an easy-going, gay-friendly place, although you might feel more at ease in one of the great cities or Mediterranean resorts than in a small village where life is more traditional and everyone knows everyone else's business. Paris in particular prides itself on its innumerable gay and lesbian bars, clubs, cabarets and shops. Le Marais is renowned as the centre of the city's gay life. Two good sites to go to for information are www. paris-gay.com and www.tetu.com.

Health and Medical Care

Emergency Medical Services

Pharmacies (designated by a green cross) are open Mon–Sat 9am–noon and 2–7pm. Sunday and evening rotas are posted in all chemists' windows. The duty chemist is officially

Emergency Numbers

Police: 17
Ambulance: 15
Fire brigade: 18
Emergencies: 112

on call at night – you will find a bell (*sonnette de nuit*) by his door. Doctors also have night and weekend rotas. They, and chemists, are listed in local papers under Pharmaciens de Garde and Médecins de Garde.

Paris

Pharmacies with green crosses are helpful with minor ailments or finding a nurse if you need injections or special care. The Pharmacie Dhéry, 84 Avenue des Champs-Elysées, tel: 01-45 62 02 41, is open 24 hours (metro: George V). Two private hospitals serve the Anglo-American community: American Hospital of Paris, 63 Bld Victor-Hugo, 92202 Neuilly, tel: 01-46 41 25 25; and the French-British Hospital of Paris, 48 Rue de Villiers, Levallois-Perret, tel: 01-46 39 22 22.
Doctor (SOS Médecins): Tel: 01-43 37 77 77 or 01-47 07 77 77.

Nightlife

Inevitably, the best French nightlife is mainly confined to the big cities, and if you are demanding you might not want to stray out of Paris. But provincial cities have their share of nightspots, and there is usually something going on in coastal resorts during the summer. Wherever you are, it is worth asking around, as almost every town and village stages an annual *fête* which usually includes a disco or a performance by a live group, sometimes outdoors. The chances are there is something within reach of wherever you are; if you're lucky and the weather's good, you might get a night out on a balmy summer's evening for free.

Paris

The action starts in Paris as soon as the sun goes down. Bars and clubs are all over the city, but particularly in the central areas around the Louvre, the Grands Boulevards, Marais, Bastille, Montmartre, Pigalle and the Latin Quarter. They are no longer called *boîtes* or *discos*, however; most people refer to *soirées* or *clubs*. Check the listings magazine *Pariscope* to find out more, or log on to: www. lemonsound.com and www.novaplanet.com. For national information try www.cityvox. com, www.citegay.fr or www.flyersweb.com.

Opening Hours

Hours of business vary from place to place and across the country, but as a rule shops open 8 or 9am to 7pm. Depending on the type of shop and where it is located, it may close for lunch, typically between midday and 2pm, although some shops including small supermarkets may close 1pm to 3.30 or 4pm. Large shops in cities and many out-of-town hypermarkets and chain stores do not close for lunch, and may stay open later in the evening, although each operates its own policy. In some towns all the shops are closed on Monday. All but a few shops are closed on Sundays. Paris is the exception. Fewer shops in the capital close for lunch and more stay open late and open on Sundays.

Postal Services

Provincial post offices – *Bureaux de Poste* – are generally open Mon–Fri 9am–noon and 2–5pm, Sat 9am–noon (opening hours are posted outside); in Paris and other large cities they are generally open continuously 8am–6.30pm. Exceptionally, the main post office in Paris is open almost 24 hours every day, at 52 Rue du Louvre, 75001 Paris.

Stamps may be purchased in post offices, cafés and newsagents. Post boxes are yellow, but at large post offices there are separate boxes for domestic and foreign mail. You may receive or send money through the post office (www.laposte.fr and http:// monbureaudeposte.laposte.fr).

Public Holidays

January: 1 New Year's Day; **March/ April**: variable Easter Sun/Mon; **May**: 1 Labour Day, 8 VE Day; **May/June**: variable Ascension Day, Whit Sun/ Mon; **July**: 14 Bastille Day; **August**: 15 Assumption Day; **November**: 1 All Saints' Day, 11 Armistice Day; **December**: 25 Christmas Day.

Shopping

In many ways France is a shopper's paradise, with many small, local shops clinging on to loyal customers in small towns. The personal service you get in such places is an attraction in itself.

The best places to hunt for bargains are local markets. Most towns hold one on an advertised day each week. Although the emphasis is always on food and drink, there are usually other items for sale too.

Almost everywhere you go in France there are local craftsworkers who open their studios to the public and sell their products direct.

At the other end of the scale are the great hypermarkets to be found on the outskirts of every French city and large town. They stay open later than smaller shops and don't close at midday.

Paris

Elegant department stores such as Galeries Lafayette and Au Printemps are on the Right Bank, as are the expensive shops of the Champs-Elysées. For younger (and cheaper) fashions try the Left Bank, particularly around St-Michel and St-Germain boulevards.

The flea market (Marché aux Puces) opens Sat, Sun and Mon (metro: Porte de Clignancourt). For flowers and plants: Ile de la Cité (Quai de la Corse), Mon–Sat 8am–7.30pm (metro: Cité). Other street markets are at Rue Mouffetard and Rue Poncelet (metros: Censier-Daubenton and Ternes respectively). Daily 9am–1pm and 4–7pm except Mon and Sun morning.

Telecommunications

All phone numbers have 10 digits. Paris and Ile-de-France numbers begin with 01; the rest of France is divided into four zones (northwest 02, northeast 03, southeast and Corsica 04, southwest 05). Freephone numbers begin 08 00; 08 36 numbers are charged at premium rates; 06 numbers are mobile phones.

For most phone boxes in Paris from which you can make local and international calls you will need a phone card (télécarte). A télécarte can be bought from kiosks, tabacs and post offices. Insert the card and follow the instructions on the screen: you can also dial from all post offices,

which have both coin- and card-operated phones. Cafés and tabacs often have public phones next to the toilets. They use coins or jetons, coin-like discs bought at the bar.

Remember that you get 50 percent more call-time for your money if you ring 10.30pm–8am on weekdays and from 2pm at weekends.

Like the rest of Europe, France operates a GSM mobile phone network, and any compatible phone registered abroad should work as normal as long as roaming is activated, although you will pay international charges for using it. An alternative is to buy and install a French SIM card in a foreign phone, giving pay-as-you-go access to the network at the same call charge as local users. Top-ups for the major networks in France (including Orange, SFR and Bouygues) are widely available. If you don't want to bring your mobile with you, or if it is not GSM compatible, it is possible to rent a mobile for the duration of your stay.

Contacts: www.orange.fr; www.sfr.fr; www.bouyguestelecom.fr.

Dialling Codes

To call other countries from France, first dial the international access code (00), then the country code: Australia 61, UK 44, US and Canada 1. The code for France is 33.

Tipping

The practice of adding 12–15 percent service charge to bills is common in restaurants, hotels and cafés all over France, so there is no obligation to leave anything additional, although most people either round up the change or leave around €1 extra, depending on the size of the bill. Tip room service almost everywhere, and wine waiters if they are helpful; taxi drivers usually get 15 percent.

Tourist Information

Paris

The city's main tourist information office is at the bottom of the Champs-Elysées at 25 Rue des Pyramides (metro: Pyramides), www.parisinfo.com (en.parisinfo.com), tel: 09-92 68 30 00. The Ile-de-France has a tourist office nearby at Carrousel du Louvre, Place de la Pyramide Inversée, 99 Rue de Rivoli (metro: Palais Royal-Musée du Louvre), www.nouveau-paris-ile-de-france.fr. There are also tourist information offices at the main stations: the Gare de l'Est, Gare de Lyon and Gare du Nord, and at Porte de Versailles and in Montmartre. The city council's official website is www.paris.fr.

Tourist Offices Abroad

Canada: Montreal: 1800 Avenue McGill Collège, Suite 1010, Montreal PQ, H3A 2W9, tel: 514-288 2026; www.ca-en.franceguide.com.
UK: Lincoln House, 300 High Holborn, London WC1V 7JH, tel: 09068-244 123; www.uk.franceguide.com.
US: New York: Maison de la France, 825 Third Avenue, 29th Floor, New York, NY 100022, tel: 514-288 1904, www.us.franceguide.com.
Chicago: Consulate General of France, 205 North Michigan Avenue, Suite 3770, IL 60601, tel: 312-327 0209.
Los Angeles: Suite 715, 9454 Wilshire Bld, 90212 Beverly Hills, CA, tel: 310-271 6665.

Monaco

Direction du Tourisme et des Congrès de la Principauté de Monaco, 2a Boulevard des Moulins, Monte-Carlo, MC 98030, Monaco, tel: (+377) 92 16 61 10, www.visitmonaco.com
UK: 7 Upper Grosvenor Street, Mayfair, London W1K 2LX, tel: 020-7491 4264.
US: Monaco Government Tourist Office, 565 Fifth Avenue, New York, NY 10017, tel: 800-753 9696 or 212-286 3330

What to Read

Other books in the Insight Guide series highlighting destinations in this region include: Insight Guides France and Southwest France; Insight Regional Guides: French Riviera and Provence, and Insight City Guide: Paris. The Paris Smart Guide packs information into an easily portable and convenient format arranged in handy A–Z sections. Paris Step by Step highlights the best walks and tours the city has to offer, with itineraries for all tastes.

BELOW: local lavender for sale in the Saleya market, Nice.

G ERMANY

ESSENTIAL TRAVEL TIPS TO HELP YOU GET THERE AND GET AROUND

FACT FILE

Area: 357,000 sq km
(138,000 sq miles)
Capital: Berlin
Population: 82 million
Languages: German, plus small
minorities speaking Frisian, Danish
and Sorbian. There is also a wide
range of regional dialects
Highest mountain: Zugspitze
2,962 metres (9,718ft)
Religion: About one-third Protestant,
one-third Roman Catholic, one-third
other religions or agnostic/atheist.
Time zone: Central European Time
Currency: The euro (€)
Electricity: AC 230 volts, two-pin
plugs
International dialling code: 49

TRANSPORT

Getting to Germany

By Air
Lufthansa, the national airline, is
Europe's largest airline in terms of
passenger numbers, and it has offices
in most capital cities: www.lufthansa.com.
Lufthansa serves most of the world
and has a domestic service.
Low-cost **Air Berlin** is Germany's
second-largest carrier and flies to
many destinations around Europe:
www.airberlin.com. Most air routes into
Germany lead to Frankfurt Airport (tel:
069 6900; www.frankfurt-airport.com).
Among Germany's other international
airports are: Berlin, Bremen,
Düsseldorf, Hamburg, Hanover,
Cologne, Munich, Nuremberg,

Saabrücken, Münster/Osnabrück,
Dresden and Stuttgart.
    Frankfurt Airport can be reached
by train, so the centre of Frankfurt is
only 15 minutes away. This is where
you can join the main German Inter-
City rail network. A reliable public
transport system, usually a shuttle
service, links all German airports with
the nearest city centre(s).

By Sea
There are no direct ferry services
from Britain to Germany; there are,
however, ferries to ports in Denmark
(Esbjerg), Holland (IJmuiden),
Rotterdam, Hook of Holland), Belgium
(Zeebrugge, Ostend), and France's
Channel coast, for onward travel
to Germany by road and rail. In
addition, there are ferries to several
of Germany's Baltic Sea ports (Kiel,
Lübeck/Travemünde, Rostock) from
Norway, Denmark, Sweden, Finland,
Russia, Latvia and Lithuania.

By Rail
You can travel through the **Channel
Tunnel** on the Eurostar high-speed
train service from London's St
Pancras station to Paris and Brussels.
Several German cities can be reached
by Thalys, TGV and ICE high-speed
trains from Paris and Brussels.
    For more details, contact:
Deutsche Bahn UK
Tel: 08718 80 80 66; www.bahn.co.uk.

By Road
Bordered by Denmark to the
north, the Netherlands, Belgium,
Luxembourg and France to the west,
Switzerland and Austria to the south
and Poland, the Czech Republic and
Slovakia to the east, Germany can be
reached by numerous motorways.

Getting around Germany

By Air
The main domestic airports are
interconnected by regular services
from local carriers. **Eurowings** (www.
eurowings.com) is Lufthansa's local
airline, in partnership with other
carriers, with hubs at Frankfurt and
Munich. Other local carriers are **Air
Berlin** (www.airberlin.com) and **Cirrus
Airlines** (www.cirrusairlines.de).

From the Airport
Berlin Schönefeld: There are S-Bahn
and train services to the centre of
Berlin, and express bus services to
the U-Bahn station closest to the
airport.
Berlin Tegel: Express buses connect
the airport with the city centre.
Frankfurt Airport: There is a
15-minute S-Bahn service to the
city's main transport interchange, the
Hauptwache, where the suburban
railway (S-Bahn) and the subway
(U-Bahn) meet.
Munich: There are S-Bahn and
express bus services from the airport
to the city centre.

By Rail
Deutsche Bahn operates tens of
thousands of passenger trains daily
over a huge domestic network, as
well as many international services.
The ICE (InterCity Express) high-speed
train network now covers most large
cities and is still being extended.
    The ICE and slower IC (InterCity)
trains do not run at night – for this
you travel by City Night Line trains,
which have sleeper, couchette and
ordinary-seating cars.
    Interregio (IR) trains run at about
two-hourly intervals from city to city,

stopping at stations along the way. EuroCity (EC) trains connect major European towns and cities.

It is possible to take your own bicycle on many trains for a small extra charge.

By Road

Germany is renowned for its 13,000km (8,100 miles) of motorways, the *Autobahnen*, *which* are marked with an "A" on blue signs; regional roads are marked with a "B" on yellow signs.

The ADAC motoring organisation (www.adac.de) provides road assistance.

Waterways

Regular, scheduled boat services operate on some rivers, lakes and coastal waters, including the Danube, Main, Moselle, Rhine and the Elbe and Weser with their estuaries, lakes Ammersee, Chiemsee, Königssee and Constance; also on Kiel Fjord and from the mainland to Helgoland and the East and North Frisian islands. Special excursions are conducted on practically all navigable waters.

By Bus

National Buses: Buses are a primary means of transport in cities and connect the smaller villages in the countryside.

There is no national coach network in Germany. The overland buses are a substitute for the railway system: wherever there are no railways, however remote, there will be a bus. You can pick up information on regional buses at railway stations and tourist information centres.

The so-called Europabusse are a cheap way of travelling between cities, many departing from main railway stations. Bahnbusse (buses owned by the German railway) operate services that link towns with smaller villages in the country. In remote parts of the country this is usually the only form of public transport.

The **Berlin Linien Bus** links Berlin with many cities and popular tourist areas in both Germany and the rest of Europe (www.berlinlinienbus.de).

City buses: A widespread network of public transport systems is available in every large city. Those cities with a population of 100,000 or more offer an efficient bus system that runs frequently and usually very punctually. You can buy the bus tickets from the driver or at machines in the bus or at the bus stop. In large cities like Berlin, Hamburg, Cologne, Munich, Frankfurt and Stuttgart, the bus lines

ABOVE: Velotaxis nip around Berlin.

are integrated with the underground (U-Bahn), the tram and the over-ground (S-Bahn) into one large public transport system. The same ticket may be used for all four means of transport.

By Tram

Trams (Strassenbahn) run on rails throughout the cities. The speed at which they travel allows for sightseeing, although there is the danger of getting into a traffic jam. Look out for yellow signs with a green "H" at bus and tram stops: they list the schedules.

By Underground

Underground (U-Bahn) stations are usually identified by a sign showing a white "U" on a blue background. Every station has detailed route maps displayed on the wall. The S-Bahn will transport you at about the same speed as the U-Bahn.

By Bicycle

In general, Germany is a very bicycle-friendly country, but it is still far from perfect. Many country areas have separate bicycle paths and special routes marked out for scenic bicycle tours. The north is fairly flat, which often makes for less arduous cycling; the Alps and other mountainous areas, understandably, can be extremely hard going, a fact that is likely to negate the natural beauty of many of these regions for cyclists who are not in good physical condition. Cycling along the banks of lakes, rivers and canals is a good way to travel, as it allows you to enjoy pleasant scenery without any overly strenuous contours. Travelling by bike in urban areas ranges from tolerable in some university towns to life-threatening in many parts of the big cities.

Getting around Berlin

Public Transport

The main station is Berlin Hauptbahnhof, which opened in 2006. **Berlin Transportation Services** (BVG) operate underground trains (U-Bahn), fast-trains (*S-Bahn*), bus lines, tramlines in the eastern part of the city, a well-organised network of buses running throughout the night, as well as boat connections crossing the River Havel between Wannsee and Kladow. A Berlin Welcome Card gives unlimited travel for 48 or 72 hours or five days on all public transport, and discounts on city tours, walking tours, boat trips, museums, theatres, sites and attractions.

Further information is available around the clock by calling BVG information: tel: 030-19449.

By Road

With more than a million cars cruising the streets of Berlin, finding a parking place in the city is a real challenge. If you still want to drive into the city, it is best to park at one of the Park-and-Ride areas and hop on a bus or take the underground.

Throughout the city no-parking and no-stopping zones are strictly patrolled, as well as the time-limited parking zones. At those zones you have either to set a parking disc or – more often – to pay for a ticket at a machine (coins only, no change) for a specified time in advance.

Parking offenders can expect to pay a hefty fine to retrieve their car should it be towed away. If this should happen to you, contact either the nearest police station, or call the central towaway service, tel: 030-4664 987800.

By Bike

Callbikes: On almost every major junction throughout the city, from March to December, bicycles are waiting to be hired for €0.06 per minute (about £3 per hour). Simply rent and return it by calling with a credit card; tel: 0700-0522 5522 or see www.callabike.de. To transport a bike on the underground or city trains you have to purchase an extra single fare

Motoring Advice

If your car breaks down on the motorway, use the orange telephones at the roadside. Black triangles on roadside posts indicate the direction of the next telephone.

AUSTRIA BELGIUM FRANCE GERMANY GREECE ITALY NETHERLANDS PORTUGAL SPAIN SWITZERLAND

or day ticket (free for Welcome Card holders, *see page 403*).
Velotaxis: Pedal-powered rickshaw-style taxis are available to hire at the main tourist junctions.

ABOVE: a welcoming hostelry in Oberwesel, the Rhineland.

GERMANY A–Z

Accommodation

Travellers should have no problem finding accommodation anywhere. In the peak season (June–Aug) it is advisable to book in advance if you are visiting a popular place; the German tourism website has sponsored hotel listings: www. cometogermany.com.

Local tourist offices are your first port of call if you arrive in a town without having a reservation in place. In rural areas, many castles and fortresses have been converted into luxurious hotels; at the other end of the scale, holidays on working farms are an entertaining and economical way of getting a taste of day-to-day life in the country.

Arts and Activities

Most larger towns and resorts publish a "What's On" type of booklet which can be obtained from tourist offices, bookstalls and hotels whenever they are available. Berlin and Munich have English-language magazines with detailed listings of what's on when and where.

Berlin

The best way to get a feel for what is going on in Berlin is to take a look in either of the city magazines, *Tip* or *Zitty*, where you'll find current events and performances listed.

BELOW: eat, drink and be merry.

Information, tickets and brochures for various festival events and performances are also available at **Berlin Tourismus Marketing** – *see Tourist Information, page 407.*

Budgeting for Your Trip

Accommodation: Hotels (double room per night): 5-star €300–500, 4-star €200–300, 3-star €100–200, 2- and 1-star €100 or less. Similar accommodation in a *Gasthof* (pension) or *Fremdenzimmer* (B&B) costs €50–75. Rates may double during a trade fair.
Car hire: A small car will cost around €50 per day, €300 per week.
Meals: A decent two-course meal ordered from the set menu could cost as little as €12, while a gourmet meal with wine at a sophisticated restaurant will cost upwards of €60.
Sightseeing: Entry to museums and similar establishments averages around €6. Most museums grant free admission or reduced prices on certain days, and there are reductions for children and students.
Taxis: A minimum fee of around €2.50 is usually charged, plus a charge per kilometre of about €1.50. A taxi from Berlin's Tegel Airport to the city centre costs about €16.

Children

You only need to observe the generous provision in cities of playgrounds and other facilities for children to realise that children are as well catered for in Germany as anywhere. And traffic-free town centres and good footpath and cycle networks also help to make the urban environment relatively child-friendly. Children from countries where trams are a novelty may enjoy riding round town aboard a Strassenbahn. With an abundance of lakes and rivers, and mountains with chairlifts, cable cars, and, at the Brocken (Harz Mountains), a steam railway, there's usually plenty to do in the German countryside, to say nothing of the North Sea and Baltic Sea coasts and islands, with all their attractions and activities.

Museums

Museums will help keep children occupied and entertained, particularly those with plenty of interactive exhibits like Munich's Deutsches Museum (*see page 197*), or those with huge model railways like Nuremberg's Transport Museum. The Chocolate Museum in Cologne is also a sure winner. Many museums have special programmes for children, though some German is usually required. A surprising fact is that the single most popular visitor attraction in Hamburg is Miniatur Wunderland, a vast model-railway exhibit (*see page 203*).

Zoos

There are several world-class zoos in Germany, among them Hellabrunn in Munich, Hagenbeck in Hamberg and Berlin's Zoo Berlin (*see page 184*), along with "safari parks" in many country areas. The Zoo am Meer in Bremerhaven focuses on sea creatures and animals from the Arctic.

Climate

Germany has a continental climate tempered by Atlantic influences. This gives warm, rather than extremely hot summers, and cool, rather than icy winters. The northwest tends to have cooler summers and milder winters than the rest of the country. Rainfall occurs throughout the year, rising somewhat in the summer months, particularly in the south.

The Alps are the wettest region and also experience the most snowfall, with ski slopes generally functioning between mid-December and March. Snowfall in other upland areas is less constant. Winds are strongest on the North Sea coast, while the warm, dry wind known as the Föhn blowing north from the Alps can create exceptionally clear conditions, as well as causing headaches and even depression among those exposed to it.

The best time to come to Germany is from May to September, though city visits can be made at any time. Popular tourist areas like the Rhine Gorge can get very crowded at the height of summer. Sea-water temperatures rarely rise above 18°C (64°F).

Disabled Travellers

Germany has installed many facilities to make public areas, public transport and events more accessible to disabled people, but, of course, older hotels cannot always be redesigned to accommodate wheelchairs. Many websites have a section called *Barrierefrei* (barrier-free), which explains facilities available for people with disabilities.

Travel tips for disabled people and information about facilities in hotels, campsites, youth hostels and specialised tour operators can be obtained through the following organisation:
Bundesarbeitsgemeinschaft der Clubs Behinderter und ihrer Freunde e.V. (BAG cbf)
Langenmarckweg 21,
51465 Bergisch Gladbach
Tel: 02202-989 9811
Email: info@bagcbf.de
www.bagcbf.de

Eating Out

Traditional German cuisine is unfussy, prepared from a limited range of good ingredients, with an emphasis on nourishing soups and quantities of meat, potatoes, dumplings and various kinds of cabbage. It is satisfying, if unsubtle. More recently, *Neue deutsche Küche* – new German cooking – has extended the range, lightened the preparation and reduced quantities. In addition, foreign cuisines have been enthusiastically adopted, making eating out in Germany an enjoyable, varied and often inexpensive experience.

To accompany the meal, there is, of course, beer, Germany being one of the world's great brewing nations. The country's numerous breweries turn out distinctive products, often with a strongly regional character. But this is also a wine country, producing mainly white wines, but with a number of palatable reds, as well as Sekt, the local equivalent of champagne.

Useful Tips

By and large, Germany follows the North European pattern of mealtimes, except that, as many Germans start work early, breakfast may be available in hotels, restaurants and bakers from about 7am onwards. Otherwise, lunch is taken in the middle of the day, and dinner from about 6–7pm. Vegetarian food is increasingly available, but still takes a distant second place to meat dishes. Ethnic restaurants are often a good source of vegetarian food. A tip is always welcome, but since service is included in the bill, a modest amount is acceptable.

Embassies

Australia: Wallstrasse 76–9, 10179 Berlin, tel: 030-880 0880; www. germany.embassy.gov.au.

Festivals

Music Festivals

These are held in nearly every city – from small chamber music events to the internationally acclaimed Bayreuther Festspiele.
Bayreuth: The Bayreuth opera festival (July/August) was founded by Richard Wagner and has been devoted to Wagner operas ever since. Bayreuth's theatre is famous for its acoustics and unpadded wooden seats, which seem to grow harder in the course of a five-hour work like *Parsifal* (www.bayreuther-festspiele.de).
Berlin/Dresden: Berlin's Staatsoper has started up a festival in spring (www.staatsoper-berlin.de), Dresden's Semper Oper too (www.semperoper.de).
Brandenburg: Brandenburgische Sommerkonzerte take place every weekend in a village church or castle within the state of Brandenburg, round Berlin (www.brandenburgische-sommerkonzerte.de).
Munich: Some of the world's top soloists perform at the Münchner Opernfestspiele in July (www. muenchner-opern-festspiele.de).
Rheinsberg: The Kammeroper Schloss Rheinsberg (in July and August) is well known as a

springboard for young talent (www.kammeroper-schloss-rheinsberg.de).
Schleswig-Holstein: The sprawling festival of Schleswig-Holstein, scattered through a number of towns in Germany's northernmost state, presents a wide range of orchestras, soloists and chamber groups. It has long been headed by popular pianist Justus Frantz (www.shmf.de).

In addition, many spa towns present festival concerts in their attractive *Kurhäuser*.
Schwetzingen: Another beautiful festival is held every spring in the Rococo palace of Schwetzingen, summer residence of the Electors of Mannheim, where audiences stroll in the Baroque formal gardens during the intermission (www.mozart gesellschaft-schwetzingen.de).
Würzburg: The Mozart Festival with its torchlit concerts in the formal gardens of the Residenz is a magnificent occasion (www.mozartfest-wuerzburg.de).

Other Festivals

Berlin stages the International Film Festival in February; the biennial MaerzMusic festival in March; the

German Theatertreffen in May (the latest productions from the German-speaking world); the Berliner Festwochen (Sept–Oct), with a wide range of concerts and performing arts; and the JazzFest in November, to which famous international artists are invited.
Hamburg: The Reeperbahn Festival showcases edgy new bands (Sept).
Munich: The Munich Biennale is devoted to new music theatre. The Oktoberfest attracts over 7 million visitors every year. A massive jamboree, it actually takes place mainly in September, ending early October, and is a thronging fête with processions, folk music, rides, circus, bands and much beer-drinking. The opening ceremony, with horse-drawn carriages leading a gigantic procession to the beat of brass bands, takes place on the first Saturday. A week later the brass bands hold a concert. Book rooms well in advance.

For information and tickets, contact the organisers:
Festleitung
Tel: 089-233 3091
www.oktoberfest.de

Emergency Numbers

Police: 110
Fire brigade: 112
Ambulance: 112
Emergency medical service
(Ärztliche Notdienst): 310031
All accidents resulting in injury
must be reported to the local
police station.

Canada: Leipziger Platz 17, 10117
Berlin, tel: 030-203 120; www.
international.gc.ca.
Ireland: Friedrichstrasse 200, 10117
Berlin, tel: 030-220 720;
www.embassyofireland.de.
New Zealand: Friedrichstrasse 60,
10117 Berlin, tel: 030-206 210;
www.nzembassy.com.
South Africa: Tiergartenstrasse 18,
10785 Berlin; www.suedafrika.org.
UK: Wilhemstrasse 70, 10117 Berlin,
tel: 030-204 570; http://ukingermany.fco.
gov.uk/de.
US: Pariser Platz 2, 10117 Berlin,
tel: 030-83050; http://germany.
usembassy.gov.

German Embassies Abroad

Australia: 119 Empire Circuit,
Yarralumla, ACT 2600, tel: 02-6270
1911; www.canberra.diplo.de.
Canada: 1 Waverley Street, Ottawa,
Ontario K2P OT8, tel: 613-232 1101;
www.ottawa.diplo.de.
Ireland: 31 Trimleston Avenue,
Booterstown, Blackrock, Co. Dublin,
tel: 01 269 3011; www.dublin.diplo.de.
New Zealand: 90–92 Hobson Street,
Thorndon, 6011 Wellington, tel:
04-473 6063; www.wellington.diplo.de.
South Africa: 180 Blackwood Street,
Arcadia, Pretoria 0083, tel: 012-427
8900; www.pretoria.diplo.de.
UK: 23 Belgrave Square, London
SW1X 8PZ, tel: 020-7824 1300;
www.london.diplo.de.
US: 4645 Reservoir Road NW,
Washington DC 20007-1998, tel:
202-298 4249; www.washington.diplo.de.

Gay and Lesbian Travellers

Germany is one of the more tolerant
countries for gays, though there are
striking contrasts between acceptable
behaviour in big cities and rural areas.
Strongly conservative attitudes in the
countryside mean that overt gayness
is frowned on. At the other end of
the spectrum, Berlin has a claim to
rival Amsterdam as the gay capital
of Europe, with traditions going back
to the Weimar era as depicted in the
novels of Christopher Isherwood. The
"scene" is vibrant, with numerous

welcoming cafés, bars and clubs,
and high-profile events like the Gay-
Lesbian City-Festival in late June.
Lesbenberatung, Kulmer Strasse
20a, tel: 030-215 2000; www.
lesbenberatung-berlin.de.
Mann-O-Meter, Bulowstrasse 106,
tel: 030-216 3336; www.maneo.de.

Health and Medical Care

Pharmacies

Pharmacies *(Apotheken)*, which
are open 8am–6.30pm, carry a list
of neighbouring outlets open for
emergencies during the night and at
weekends.

Medical Services (Berlin)

There are free emergency phones
in front of larger post offices and
elsewhere; emergency telephones
are common in suburbs. To call an
ambulance, dial 112; for emergency
medical services, call 310031.
All accidents resulting in injury must
be reported to the local police station.
Hospital
DRK Kliniken Berlin Mitte,
Drontheimer Strasse 39–40, tel: 030-
3035 6001; www.drk-kliniken-berlin.de.

Nightlife

The larger the city, the more choices
you have for entertainment at night.
Although in many areas early-closing
laws hamper night owls, anyone
who wants an evening on the town
should not have any problem in cities
like Munich, Hamburg, Cologne or
Frankfurt. In Berlin, closing restrictions
are minimal. There are numerous
concert halls and theatres, and
classical music-lovers will be spoilt
for choice. But there are also variety
shows, cabaret and late-night revues.

BELOW: an inviting offer.

The main cities have English-
language magazines/information
sheets highlighting what's on and
where, for example in Berlin, *Berlin
Magazin*; in Munich, *Munich Found*; in
Hamburg, *Hamburg Magazin*.

Berlin

Because Berlin is pretty much open
24 hours a day, going from a drink at
a bar or two right into the thick of city
nightlife is relatively effortless.
Hotspots are in Charlottenburg
around Savigny-Platz, Wilmersdorf
(south of Ku'damm), Schöneberg
(near Winterfeldtplatz) and
Goltzstrasse. Kreuzberg has
two main meeting points:
around Bergmannstrasse and
Marheinekeplatz or in Oranienstrasse
near Mariannenplatz. The social
scene in Prenzlauer Berg around
Kollwitzplatz is more relaxed and
diverse – you'll find students, artists,
tourists and locals all having fun.

Opening Hours

Most shops are open 9.30am–6
or 6.30pm. Small shops such as
bakeries, fruit and vegetable shops
and butcher's shops open as early as
7am, close for 2 hours midday, and
reopen around 3–6.30pm. Shops
in railway stations and airports are
usually open until late, some until
midnight. Business hours are usually
8am–5.30pm. Government offices
are open to the public 8am–noon.

Postal Services

Post offices are generally open Mon–
Fri 8am–6pm and Sat 8am–noon.
Station and airport post offices in
larger cities open until late on weekday
evenings, and some are open 24 hours
a day. Post boxes are yellow.

Public Holidays

January: 1 New Year's Day; **March/
April**: variable Good Friday, Easter
Mon; **May**: 1 Labour Day; **May/June**:
variable Ascension Day, Whit Mon;
June: 17 National Holiday; **August**:
15 Assumption Day; **October**: 3
Unification Day; **November**: 1 All
Saints' Day, 11 Armistice Day;
December: 25 Christmas Day, 26 St
Stephen's Day.
In some Catholic regions, the
following are also considered public
holidays: **January**: 6 Epiphany; **June**:
variable Corpus Christi. In Protestant
regions, Repentance Day, which
usually falls on the last Wednesday in
November, is also celebrated.

Shopping

Germany, being a popular tourist destination, offers lots of souvenirs. The shop to look out for is the *Andenkenladen*, which has anything from valuable souvenirs to all sorts of knick-knacks. Antiques enthusiasts will find many elegant, well-stocked shops, and numerous flea markets. If you can't afford to take home a Porsche or a Mercedes, or some other example of Germany's engineering skills, look for locally made products like beer (and beer steins) and wine; porcelain from Meissen; handmade Christmas decorations from the Erzgebirge; and cuckoo clocks from the Black Forest.

Among the country's top shopping streets are Kurfürstendamm ("Ku'damm") and Friedrichstrasse in Berlin, Maximilianstrasse in Munich, Königsallee ("Kö") in Düsseldorf, and the shopping arcades near Jungfernstieg and Neuer Wall in Hamburg. In practically every town you will find a *Fussgängerzone* (pedestrian zone) with all kinds of shops – big department stores and small specialised shops. Cigarettes, cigars and tobacco may be bought in newspaper shops, which also stock postcards, writing supplies, magazines and newspapers.

Berlin

There's only one rule that applies to shopping in Berlin: there's nothing that you can't buy. The free guide *Shopping in Berlin* is available from tourist offices.

Telecommunications

Most public telephones require telephone cards, which are sold at post offices, newspaper stands and some other shops. There are only a few kiosks left that take coins, and they are useful for making short local calls only.

Numbers starting with 0800 are free of charge. For national telephone information, tel: 11833; international telephone information, tel: 11834; national directory enquiries (in English), tel: 11837.

Dialling Codes

Area codes for some of the best-known cities are: Berlin, tel: 030; Bremen, tel: 0421; Cologne, tel: 0221; Dresden, tel: 0351; Frankfurt, tel: 069; Hamburg, tel: 040; Leipzig, tel: 0341; Munich, tel: 089; Nurmberg, tel: 0911. The code for Germany is 49.

ABOVE: some souvenirs tend to emphasise national stereotypes.

Tipping

Generally, service charges and taxes are included in hotel and restaurant bills. However, satisfied customers usually leave an additional tip or at least the small change. It is also customary to tip taxi drivers and hairdressers 10 percent, and cloakroom attendants a few coins.

Tourist Information

Tourist information offices, marked with an "i", can be found in the most visited towns. The national tourist office website, in multiple languages, is www.cometogermany.com.

Berlin

All kinds of information is available from the **Berlin Tourismus Marketing**, Am Karlsbad 11, 10785 Berlin, tel: 030-264 7480; www.berlin-tourist-information.de.

The largest tourist information centre is at Berlin Hauptbahnhof (main railway station), Europaplatz 1. The telephone number for this tourist office and those listed below is the same: tel: 030-250 025.

Other tourist information offices (BERLIN infostores) are: **Brandenburger Tor** (south wing), Pariser Platz; Berlin Pavilion (Reichstag), Scheidemannstrasse; Alexa Shopping Center, Grunerstrasse 20; Neues Kranzler Eck Passage, Kurfürstendamm 21.

Tourist Offices Abroad

The German National Tourist Office has very helpful tourist bureaux in the following cities:

Australia: c/o Ink Publicity, Suite 502, Level 5, 5 Hunter Street, Sydney, NSW 2000
Tel: 02-9236 8982
Email: germanytourism@smink.com.au
www.cometogermany.com
Canada: 480 University Avenue, Suite 1500, Toronto, ON M5G 1V2
Tel: 416-968 1685
Email: info@gnto.ca
www.cometogermany.com
UK: PO Box 2695, London W1A 2TN
Tel: 020-7317 0908
Email: gntolon@d-z-t.com
www.germany-tourism.co.uk
US: Chicago: PO Box 59594, Chicago, IL 60659-9594
Tel: 773-539 6303
Email: info@gntoch.com
Los Angeles: 1334 Parkview Ave, Suite 300, Manhattan Beach, CA 90266
Tel: 310-545 1350
Email: info@gntolax.com
New York: 122 East 42nd Street, Suite 2000, New York, NY 10168-0072
Tel: 212-661 7200
Email: info@gntonyc.com
www.cometogermany.com

What to Read

Insight Guide: Germany is a companion volume to this book, from Apa Publications' award-winning series. The *Berlin Smart Guide* packs information into an easily portable and convenient format arranged in handy A–Z sections with comprehensive listings. *Berlin Step by Step* highlights the best walks and tours the city has to offer, with itineraries for all tastes.

GREECE

ESSENTIAL TRAVEL TIPS TO HELP YOU GET THERE AND GET AROUND

FACT FILE

Area: 131,950 sq km (50,950 sq miles), including around 25,050 sq km (9,670 sq miles) of islands.
Capital: Athens
Population: About 11 million, 10 percent of this foreign-born. Greater Athens and Piraeús have a population of 4 million. Thessaloníki, the second-largest city, has 1 million residents, and the most populated island is Crete, with just over half a million inhabitants
Language: Modern Greek
Religion: Predominantly Greek Orthodox Christianity, with small minorities of Muslims, Catholics, Protestant sects and Jews
Time zones: Two hours ahead of Greenwich Mean Time
Currency: The euro (€)
Electricity: AC 220 volts, two-pin plugs
International dialling code: 30

TRANSPORT

Getting to Greece

By Air

Almost 50 international airlines, large and small, serve Athens from Eurasia, the Far East and North America. Elefthérios Venizélos International Airport is at Spáta, around 25km (15 miles) east of central Athens. Direct scheduled flights from Europe also go to Macedonia Airport in Thessaloníki, as well Rhodes, Corfu and Iráklio on Crete. An expressway called the Attikí Odós links Athens

Airport with Elefsína via the northern suburbs. The metro runs half-hourly from the airport to the town centre (€6 for one person, discounts for two or more), while express buses prefixed "X" serve a variety of points around Athens every quarter of an hour (€3.20) and remain popular. All services run around the clock (less frequently 11pm–5am).

By Rail

Trains link Thessaloníki and Athens with many major cities throughout Europe, though you will almost always have to change. The all-overland route goes via Vienna, Budapest, Belgrade and either Sofia or Skopje; otherwise you transit via France and Italy, doing the last leg by ferry. Allow three days' travel from Great Britain.

By Road

Bordered by Albania, the Former Yugoslav Republic of Macedonia and Bulgaria to the north and Turkey to the east, Greece is accessible by a number of major European arteries. Roads out of Albania and former Yugoslavia are pretty bad; the main E75 trunk route through Bulgaria is being steadily improved with EU money, but still has its dangerous patches. Major frontier crossing-points are open 24 hours.

By Sea

An extensive year-round network of ferries links Italy with Greece. Venice, Ancona, Brindisi and Bari are the Italian ports, with Corfu, Igoumenítsa and Pátra at the Greek end. The shortest routes are from Brindisi to Corfu (6–7hrs) and Pátras (16hrs); the latter has easy bus and train connections to Athens.

Getting around Greece

With so much of its territory as islands, inevitably travelling around Greece involves extensive use of seagoing transport and flying. Bus services on the mainland (and largest islands) are adequate, though the rail network (mainland only) is rudimentary. Many visitors imitate the car-mad Greeks by renting their own vehicle.

By Air

Domestic air services, mostly out of Athens but also some useful peripheral routes, are provided by several internal carriers. Olympic Airlines (www.olympicairlines.com) has the most extensive network, but you'll generally have better service from Aegean Air (www.aegeanair.com) or Athens Airways (www.athensairways. com). Crete-based Sky Express (www. skyexpress.gr) offers expensive links between Iráklio and a number of island and mainland destinations. Route networks and flight frequencies vary radically between summer and winter.

By Ferry, Catamaran, Hydrofoil

Seagoing transport schedules are famously erratic from year to year, and best obtained online from each company's website; www.gtp. gr, updated regularly, attempts to be comprehensive and unbiased. Major tourist information offices and the Athens News supply weekly schedules, which should not, however, be trusted implicitly. The most authoritative information source on each port's sailings is the Port Police (limenarhío), which maintain offices at Piraeús and near the harbours of all fair-sized islands. They post complete timetables and are the final arbiters of whether a ship will sail or not in stormy weather conditions.

Hydrofoils, nicknamed *delfínia* or "dolphins", connect Piraeús with most of the Argo-Saronic region, and many of the Dodecanese between Kós and Sámos. In Piraeús the embarkation booths are on Aktí Miaoúli. Hydrofoils tend not to sail in conditions above Force 6.

Catamarans or *tahyplóa* (high-speed boats) are newer, purpose-built craft which would have seen off slower conventional ferries were it not for their very high running costs (though fares are often little more). Unlike hydrofoils, they carry cars and are permitted to sail in weather conditions of up to Force 7. The bad news: often there are no cabins (if they finish their runs before midnight), food service is abysmal, and there are no exterior decks. The aeroplane-style seating salons are ruthlessly air-conditioned and subject to a steady, unavoidable barrage of Greek TV on overhead monitors.

By Rail

Greek train travel is generally slow, if relatively cheap and often scenic. The main route north from Athens (Lárissa station) reaches Thessaloníki, where it splits. One line goes to the former Yugoslavia, another to Bulgaria and the third to Istanbul. Another rail system operates from Athens (Peloponnese station) to the Peloponnese via Corinth. All trains are run by **Hellenic Railways/OSE**; information on tel: 1110 and www.ose.gr.

By Bus

The pan-Hellenic syndicate of bus companies, known as KTEL, offers relatively cheap and generally punctual service between all major towns (though increasingly rarely to depopulated villages). Additional bus services along major routes are provided by OSE, the state railway organisation. KTEL buses on the most rural routes are often idiosyncratically decorated by their proud drivers. Larger towns will often have different bus stations for different destinations – for example, Iráklio on Crete has three, Thessaloníki still has two (one for Halkidikí, one for everywhere else), and Athens also has two: Terminal A at Kifissoú 100 and Terminal B at 260 Liossíon 260.

By Car

Non-EU/EEA licences are not valid; motorists not in possession of an EU/EEA licence must obtain an International Driving Permit before departure. Insurance Green Cards are no longer required, but vehicles must carry a first-aid kit, warning triangle and a fire extinguisher. Front seatbelt use is mandatory, on pain of a €175 fine. Greece has the highest accident rate in EU Europe after Portugal, so drive defensively – speeding, aberrant overtaking and ignoring stop signs are common habits.

Tolls are charged on the two main motorways: Athens–Thessaloníki and Athens–Pátras. Petrol stations off the main highways generally close by 8pm, but automated pumps operated by banknotes or credit cards are becoming common.

The Automobile and Touring Club of Greece (ELPA; www.elpa.gr) has an emergency road service (tel: 10400) available on a reciprocal basis to some overseas club members (eg AAA). Other analogous organisations, used by car-rental firms, include Express Service (tel: 1154) and Hellas Service (tel: 1057).

Car rental is easily arranged, either on the spot or in advance through the usual websites. All the major international chains are present, but you will always get a better deal through smaller, equally reputable local chains. Even in high season you shouldn't pay more than €200 per week inclusive.

Getting around Athens

The ever-expanding metro system, a tramway, a fleet of modernised buses and taxis do the lion's share of getting locals and visitors around what is by Mediterranean standards a huge city. Suburban rail systems and (for the stout-hearted) driving yourself are more esoteric choices. The centre, however, is compact enough that you'll often choose to walk to and between attractions.

By Metro and Light Rail

The Athens metro (www.ametro.gr) has three intersecting lines operating from just after 5am until just after midnight. Line 1 (green-coded) is the older ISAP (electric train line) running mostly above ground between Kifissía and Piraeús (for ferries and hydrofoils). Lines 2 (red) and 3 (blue), inaugurated in 2000, are still being extended, with new stations set to open through to 2012. The three city-centre interchange stations are Monastiráki, Omónia and Sýntagma.

There is also a suburban rail service from the airport to Nerantziótissa on line 1, and on to OSE's Lárissa station; of more interest to most visitors is the tramway, with separate lines from Sýntagma to the beach suburbs of Néo Fáliron and Glyfáda, as well as a link line between the last two.

Tickets are purchased from counters and automatic machines (coins only) in the stations or tram platforms and are now valid for all mass transport in the city, for 90 minutes from validation in the stamping machines just beyond. If you're caught by plain-clothes inspectors with no ticket or an expired one, you get an on-the-spot fine of 60 times the standard fare. The best strategy is to buy a daily or weekly pass (*see Tip, page 307*).

The tram is circuitous and slowish (though it runs until late), but the metro is pretty much an unalloyed success: sleek, modern, with adverts kept to a minimum and (unlike the London Underground) rarely prone to malfunction. The most central stations display archaeological artefacts and even entire sections of street or water mains uncovered during the excavation of the tunnels.

By Bus

With an influx of new, air-conditioned vehicles since the Olympics, travelling by the regular Athens blue-and-white buses is less of an ordeal than it used to be, and the schedule is more regular and frequent. Tickets are sold individually or in bundles of 10, from designated kiosks and metro stations.

The most useful suburban services for tourists are the orange-and-white KTEL Attikís buses going from 14 Mavromateon Street, Pédio toú Áreos Park, to Rafína or Lávrio (alternative ferry ports for the Cycládes) and Soúnio (for the famous Poseidon temple there).

Trolley buses running on overhead pantographs have also been upgraded and their routes can be easier to fathom; number 1 links the centre of the city with the main railway station, number 15 calls at the taverna-rich central district of Petrálona, numbers 5 and 9 pass the Archaeological Museum, and number 7 does a triangular circuit of the central districts.

By Taxi

If a taxi flashes its headlights it wants your custom. If you decide to take it, ensure that the meter is switched on and registering 1, rather than 2 which is the rate from midnight–5am. Don't be worried if you find yourself

AUSTRIA

BELGIUM

FRANCE

GERMANY

GREECE

ITALY

NETHERLANDS

PORTUGAL

SPAIN

SWITZERLAND

joined, en route, by a cross-section of Athenian society going roughly your way. It is perfectly legal for drivers to pick up as many as four passengers, and charge them all individually for the distance they cover, plus the current minimum fare. Tariff rules are posted on dashboard cards in all taxis. There is a surcharge from airports, seaports, railway stations and bus terminals; passengers will also be charged a small fee for luggage.

Radio taxis will pick you up within a short time of your call to a central booking number. You pay more, but this is well worth it if you need a car at a busy time or if you're luggage-laden. **Íkaros**, tel: 210-51 52 800; www. athens-taxi.gr, is one established firm. Otherwise your hotel will be happy to arrange a pick-up for you.

By Car

Drive at your peril in Athens during the rush hour. Traffic jams and pollution reached such heights in the capital that a 1980s law was introduced: on even days of the month only cars with even-numbered licence plates are allowed in the centre; on odd days only those with odd-numbered plates. The law is seldom enforced now – certainly not for rental cars – and only the metro has really made a dent in traffic.

GREECE A–Z

Accommodation

Lodging in Greece comprises high-standard urban hotels, some worthwhile restored boutique accommodation in the provinces, standard Mediterranean self-catering villas, and that old warhorse of the more touristed islands, *enikiazómena domátia* (rented rooms). Hotels run the gamut from de luxe to the all-but-extinct D-class (five stars down to one in the new categorisation), and some are very fancy – and expensive – indeed, especially after pre-2004 Olympics facelifts. Best prices are typically had through generic websites if not the hotels' own pages. Island and coastal hotels, with some local variations, tend to be open from April to October, perhaps a bit into November on southerly Crete. By contrast, mainland hotels and inns can be busy in winter if near a ski resort and charge high-season prices because of heating costs. Local travel agents sometimes handle villas, but these are best booked through specialist companies in the

UK like Sunvil, Greek Islands Club and Cachet. Proprietors of rented rooms still often meet arriving ferries armed with glossy photos of their offerings, and they are the budget set's mainstay given the almost complete absence of youth hostels as understood elsewhere. In less commercial provincial locales, a rented room or hotel room can be found for under €80 even in peak season, but in big-name resorts like Zagóri, Pílio, Rhodes or Santoríni the sky is literally the limit.

Arts and Activities

The weekly (Friday) English-language paper *Athens News* has selected events and television listings for Athens and to a limited extent Thessaloníki, as does the daily English edition of *Kathimeriní* (www.ekathimerini. com). If you can puzzle out the Greek script, the only comprehensive suriviving listings magazine for Athens is *Athinórama* (every Thursday).

Athens and Epidaúros Festival

This runs, with slight annual variations, from late May to late August/early September, featuring ballet, opera, jazz and modern music, and modern and classical plays from world-class artists. The main Athens venues are the Iródio (Herod Atticus Odeion), Pireós Avenue 260, and the Mégaro Mousikís; the Epidaúros amphitheatre is used during July and August. Top performances are popular, so book tickets on the internet (www.greekfestival.gr), or as soon as you arrive in Greece. Information and tickets can be obtained from the main festival box office in the arcade at Panepistimíou 39 (tel: 210-32 72 000), or, for events at the Iródio only, its very own box office on the day of performance. Bring cushions and binoculars for the cheap seats – they're hard marble and quite far from the stage.

Budgeting for Your Trip

Especially since the advent of the euro, Greece is no longer by any stretch of the imagination an inexpensive country. Travelling as one of a couple, allow a minimum of €30 for a share of accommodation (€40–50 each minimum in Athens or Thessaloníki), €14–25 for your half of a meal with modest intake of beer or cheap wine, €4–12 each for site admission, and €15–18 for your share of the cheapest small rental car – before petrol costs, which are

typically less than in France or Italy but more than in Spain.

Children

Children are adored in Greece, and many families are still highly superstitious about their welfare – toddlers may have blue-bead amulets pinned to their clothes to ward off the evil eye. So expect your own kids to be the centre of attention. Children, especially boys, are treated very indulgently, though at the same time are not allowed to determine adults' schedules – they are very early on inculcated into the stay-up-late routine, including being taken to taverna meals. Resort hotels are slowly introducing dedicated kids' activities.

Climate

The Greece of tourist posters is a perennially warm and sunny place – and it is, by European standards. But this picture does not reflect the considerable climatic variety. The north and inland regions have a modified continental climate, so winters are quite cold and summers extremely hot. In Ioánnina, Trípoli and Kastoriá, for example, snow and freezing temperatures are not uncommon. In mountainous regions, winters are even more severe, with a score of ski centres operating above elevations of 2,000 metres (6,500ft).

The southern islands, the coastal Peloponnese and the Attic peninsula conform more to the traditional Mediterranean image: a long, warm season of rainless, sunny days extending roughly from late May to mid-October. But here too the winters can be cool, with rain falling in unpredictable spells between November and early May.

In general, spring (late April–June) and autumn (September–October) are the best times to visit. During these periods, you will find mild to warm temperatures, sunny days and fewer tourists. Throughout July and August, Greece is at its hottest and stickiest, and most crowded.

Disabled Travellers

Despite nudging from the EU, Greece has some way to go before becoming fully compliant with regulations on facilities for disabled people.

Athens, with lifts in the metro, "kneeling" buses on many routes, recorded announcements of upcoming stops on the metro plus

Emergency Numbers

Police emergency: 100
Tourist Police (Athens only): 171
Ambulance: 166
Coastguard patrol: 108
Fire: 199
Forest fire: 191

some buses, and ramps (when not blocked by illegally parked cars) at kerbside, is furthest ahead.

Elsewhere, amenities can be poor – there are few or no sound pips for the sight-impaired at pedestrian crossings, and it is common to see the wheelchair-bound tooling down the middle of the asphalt rather than risk the obstacle course of a pedestrian pavement.

Few hotels in the provinces are disabled-friendly, though things are improving, with some preparing a few rooms with wide doors and safety handles in the bath – ask when booking.

Eating Out

Eating out in Greece is a social affair, although the ritual of families and friends patronising tavernas twice a week is less observed now owing to hard economic times. Greeks have had to learn to be careful with money – it is still considered an honour to snaffle the bill, but this tends to be a less extravagant gesture these days. A meal with bulk wine or local beer will cost at least €13 per person: €16–20 is a more typical figure. If you order fish or bottled wine, then it's €25 minimum, more realistically €35. Check bills carefully – variance from the cited menu price is far from unknown.

Cuisine has improved in recent decades, with the dousing of everything in superfluous quantities of oil somewhat reined in, and "slow food", or rather its local equivalent, catching on. Estiatória or magería specialise in the more elaborate, home-style casserole dishes known as magireftá; psistariés are grillhouses featuring only meat platters plus a few salads and mezédes (starters); while tavernas try (with varying degrees of success) to do all these things. Psárotavernas specialise in fish, with some exceptions as expensive as anywhere in the Mediterranean.

Booking at all but the poshest eateries is not required. Greeks eat late by Northern European standards: 1.30–4pm for lunch, 9pm–midnight

(later at weekends) for dinner. Sunday night and part of Monday are the typical days of closure outside the more tourist areas.

Kalamári-and-chips or *moussakás* may be the resort stereotypes, but the best-value main dishes (and what Greeks themselves tend to eat) include *frikasé* (any meat stew with celery), *spetzofáï* (sausage and pepper hotpot), *papoutsákia* (eggplant "shoes" stuffed with ground meat) and *kounélli stifádo* (stewed rabbit). Vegetarians – and the impecunious – will do better assembling a meal from various *mezédes*, and indeed a whole class of eatery – the *ouzerí* – specialises in this. Favourite starters include *plevrótous* (oyster mushrooms), *bourekákia* (various stuffed turnovers), *revythokeftédes* (chickpea/garbanzo croquettes), *sykotákia* (chicken livers) and *hórta* (any wild or cultivated green, often of the chicory family). Seafood that doesn't cost an arm and a leg includes seasonally fresh *sardélles* (sardines), *gávros* (anchovy), *xifías* (swordfish) and of course octopus *(khtapódi)* either grilled or stewed in wine. For desserts you'll have to go to an ice cream-and-cake parlour (Dodóni is a decent nationwide chain) – most tavernas merely offer a plate of seasonal fruit or perhaps some semolina *halvás* at the end of the meal.

Embassies and Consulates

All embassies are in Athens and open Mon–Fri, usually 8am–2pm.
Australia: Corner Kifissías and Alexándras avenues, Level 6, Thon Building, 115 23 Ambolókipi, tel: 210-87 04 000, consulate 210-87 04 055, www.ausemb.gr.
Canada: 4 Gennadíou Street, 115 21 Athens, tel: 210-72 73 400.
Ireland: 7 Vassiléos Konstandínou Avenue, 106 74 Athens, tel: 210-72 32 771/2; www.dfa.ie/embassies.
New Zealand General Consulate: 76 Kifissías Avenue, 115 26 Ambelókipi, tel: 210-69 24 136.
South Africa: 60 Kifissías Avenue, 151 25 Maroúsi, tel: 210-61 06 645.
UK: 1 Ploutárhou Street, 106 75 Athens, tel: 210-72 72 600; http://ukingreece.fco.gov.uk/en.
US: 91 Vassilísis Sofías Avenue, 115 21 Athens, tel: 210-72 12 951; http://athens.usembassy.gov.

Festivals

Carnival/Apokriátika – three weeks up to the seventh weekend before Easter. Pátras with its elaborate floats

and gay participation is the liveliest, but the very pagan "goat dance" on Skýros and the *boúles* revels at Náoussa in Macedonia are also well attended.
Easter weekend (variable April/May) – sombre, moving procession of the *Epitáfios* or Christ's funeral bier in all major towns Good Friday evening, with brass band accompaniment; each parish competes for the most elaborate floral bier. Saturday midnight sees (and hears) the Anástasi or Resurrection church service, with deafening fireworks and the best chanting into the small hours.
Firewalking by *anastenarídes* cult members – at Agía Eléni (near Sérres) and Langadás (near Thessaloníki) on 21 May. This observance, which comemorates the rescue of precious icons from a medieval church fire, was brought to northern Greece by refugees from what is now Bulgarian Thrace (where identical rites still occur).
Dormition of the Virgin (15 August) – major festivals on Kárpathos, Agiássos and Tínos, where the icon is carried over the unwell kneeling on the street. But almost every island and mainland county has a bash of some sort; the second-most important festival after Easter.

Gay and Lesbian Travellers

Overt gay behaviour is not a feature of Greek society. The age of consent is 17, and bisexual activity fairly common among younger men, but few couples (male or female) are openly gay. Mýkonos is famous as a gay mecca, and Skála Fressoú on Lésvos (birthplace of poetess Sappho) is essentially a lesbian resort. Elsewhere in Greece single-sex couples are liable to be regarded as odd, but are usually as welcome as any other tourists. If discreet, you will attract no attention asking for a double room and will find most people tolerant.

Health and Medical Care

EU nationals are entitled to free basic healthcare at state clinics or hospitals upon presentation of your European Health Insurance Card *(see page 384)*, though you will have to pay full price for medication and specialist tests. Public hospitals vary widely in reputation (some acceptable ones for Athens are listed below), so it's best to have travel insurance, including private healthcare. If you do fall ill in Athens, your hotel may provide the name of a reputable private doctor.

The British and American embassies keep a list of GPs and specialists, including dentists upon request.

Pharmacies

Chemists/pharmacies are open during normal morning shop hours, but some stay open day and night. Duty rotas are displayed on chemists' windows, or tel: 1434 for information (in Greek). Pharmaceuticals are produced to international standards, and, being subsidised, are often much cheaper than in Northern Europe. Most pharmacists speak English, and are often very helpful in assisting visitors with treating minor ailments such as diarrhoea, colds, insect or jellyfish stings and sunburn.

Hospitals (Athens)

Most hospitals line Vassilís Sofías and its continuation into the northeastern suburbs.
Evangelismós, Ypsilándou 45, Kolonáki, tel: 210-72 01 000. Good general hospital, with nearby namesake metro station.
KAT, Níkis 2, Kifissiá, tel: 210-62 80 000. Designated casualty ward; has its own metro station.
Children's hospitals: Agía Sofia, Thivón and Mikrás Asiás streets, Goudí, tel: 210-77 71 811; Aglaía Kyriakoú, Thivón and Levadías streets, Goudí, tel: 210-77 26 000. Open 24 hours, alternate days.

Opening Hours

Banks are open Mon–Thur 8.30am–2.30pm, closing at 2pm on Friday. In heavily visited areas like Rhodes, however, you may find banks open additional late-afternoon hours and on Saturday mornings.

Business hours vary. The main thing to remember is that businesses generally open at 8.30am and close for the rest of the day on Monday, Wednesday and Saturday at 2.30pm. On Tuesday, Thursday and Friday most businesses close at 2pm and reopen in the afternoon from 5.30–9pm. An increasing number of business and shops, especially in Athens, are working continual shifts of 9am–6pm or even later. Supermarkets are typically open Mon–Fri 8.30am–9am, closing Saturday at 8am. Some branches of the Carrefour Marinópoulos chain open on Sundays.

Postal Services

Most local post offices are open weekdays from 7.30am until 2pm.

The main post office in central Athens on Sýntagma Square at the corner of Mitropóleos Street, however, is open Mon–Fri 7.30am–8pm, Sat 7.30am–2pm and Sun 9am–1pm. There are also long hours post offices in Thessaloníki, Ioánnina and Rhodes.

Public Holidays

January: 1 New Year's Day, 6 Epiphany; **February/March**: variable Orthodox Shrove Monday; **March**: 25 Independence Day; **March/April**: variable Orthodox Good Friday/Easter Mon; **May**: 1 Labour Day; **May/June**: variable Orthodox Whit Mon; **August**: 15 Assumption Day; **October**: 28 Ochi Day; **December**: 25 Christmas Day, 26 Boxing Day.

Shopping

Handcrafted jewellery and durable-but-crude leather goods are favourite purchases. Worry beads, Greek coffee pots (*bríkia*), colourful tin retsina-measuring cups and olive-oil soap will remind you of your visit. Foodstuffs (with an eye to baggage/customs regulations at your destination) are also popular: pickled capers, honey, pistachio nuts, olives and olive oil, pickled wild bulbs, ouzo, or dried figs make ideal souvenirs or gifts.

Telecommunications

For local or intercity calls, purchase an OTE (Greek Telecoms) telephone card from a kiosk and use (invariably noisy) street-corner phone booths. If you need to make international calls, there are two economical ways: buying a prepaid card (typically €5 for brands like Face) with a 12-digit scratch code and a free access number prefixed 807, or carrying a laptop loaded with some VOIP software like Skype. Prepaid cards will work from most fixed phones and phone booths but not some of the more antiquated hotel phone circuitry. With the growing prevalence of Wi-fi zones, using VOIP is generally feasible from your hotel. Don't make anything other than the briefest of local calls direct from a hotel room – surcharges on the basic local telecoms rates are typically quadruple.

Foreign mobile phone users can roam on any of the three local networks, but charges are ruinous. If you're going to stay for more than a week, it makes sense to buy a local pay-as-you-go SIM for €20 or under – with most providers the number is

valid for a year, so you can use it on your next visit. North American visitors should have a triband apparatus.

Dialling Codes

All telephone numbers within Greece, whether fixed or mobile, have 10 digits. Land lines start with 2, mobiles with 6. The prefix for Athens and Piraeús numbers is now 210, for Thessaloníki 2310. The code for Greece is 30.

Tipping

Restaurant prices notionally include "service", but an extra 5–10 percent depending on the size of the party is expected as coins on the table. Round up the charge on the taxi meter. Around Christmas and Easter, all taxis (and a few restaurants) add a *filodórima* (holiday gratuity) to the bill. At the end of your stay a few large euro coins for your hotel chambermaid are much appreciated.

Tourist Information

The Greek National Tourism Organisation (GNTO, or EOT in Greek; www.gnto.gr) has information desks at: Amalías 26 (tel: 210-33 10 392; daily, Sat–Sun closes 4pm) and in the airport arrivals hall (tel: 210-35 30 445; daily, Sat–Sun closes 4pm).

These stock reasonable plans of Athens and basic touring maps of the country, but the best detailed commercial regional maps of Greece, including topographic products suitable for mountaineering, are produced by two rival companies: Road Editions and Anávasi. These are much cheaper within Greece and fairly widely sold.

GNTO Offices in English-Speaking Countries
Australia: 37–49 Pitt Street, Sydney NSW 2000, tel: 9241 1663; email: hto@tpg.com.au.
Canada: 1500 Don Mills Road, Suite 102, Toronto ON M3B 3K4, tel: 416-968 2220, email: grnto.tor@on.aibn.com.
UK: 4 Conduit Street, London W1R 0DJ, tel: 020-7495 4300; www.gnto.co.uk.
US: 645 Fifth Avenue, New York, NY 10022, tel: 212-421 5777; www.greektourism.com.

What to Read

Other books in the *Insight Guide* series highlighting destinations in this region include *Insight Guides Greece* and *The Greek Islands*.

TALY

ESSENTIAL TRAVEL TIPS TO HELP YOU GET THERE AND GET AROUND

FACT FILE

Area: 301,245 sq km
(116,280 sq miles)
Capital: Rome
Population: 59.8 million
Language: Italian
Highest mountain: Gran Paradiso
4061 metres (13,323ft); Mont Blanc
on French/Italian border 4,810
metres (15,781ft).
Religion: Roman Catholic
Time zone: Central European Time
Currency: The euro (€)
Electricity: AC 220 volts, two-pin plugs
International dialling code: 39

TRANSPORT

Getting to Italy

By Air

Rome and Milan are the main
gateways to Italy, and both have
excellent services from many
European capitals, including
London. There are also direct flights
from British airports to another
24 Italian destinations, including
Venice, Verona, Florence, Pisa,
Naples, Sardinia and Sicily. The
main scheduled airlines are the flag
carrier Alitalia (now merged with Air
One, Italy's No. 2 airline) and British
Airways. Low-cost carrier Ryanair
operates services from Stansted to 22
Italian destinations; easyJet also has
a good choice of services. From the
US and Canada there are direct flights
to Milan and Rome.
British Airways: tel: 0844-493 0787;
www.ba.com.

Alitalia: tel: 0871-424 1424;
www.alitalia.com.
easyJet: tel: 0905-821 0905;
www.easyjet.com.
Ryanair: tel: 0871-246 0000;
www.ryanair.com.

By Rail

Frequent and fast train services link
Italy with neighbouring countries
and major European cities. For
information on trail travel to Italy,
including InterRail passes, contact
Rail Europe at www.raileurope.co.uk or, for
non-European residents, www.raileurope.
com. Italian State Railways (Ferrovie
dello Stato; www.trenitalia.it) can also
help plan an itinerary.

By Road

Bordered in the north by France,
Switzerland, Austria and the former
Yugoslavia, Italy can be reached by
a number of European routes and
motorways.
    When calculating the cost of
travelling to Italy by car, allow for
motorway tolls and Swiss motorway
tax as well as accommodation en
route and petrol. Visit the ViaMichelin
website (www.viamichelin.com) for route
planning and details of the extra
costs.
    The cost of travelling to Italy from
the UK by scheduled coach can work
out more expensive than travelling by
air. **National Express Eurolines** (www.
nationalexpress.com) run from London
Victoria, via Paris and Mont Blanc, to
Aosta, Turin, Genoa, Milan, Venice,
Bologna, Florence and Rome.

By Sea

Ferries link Venice with Greece,
Slovenia, Croatia and Albania; Genoa,
Livorno and Civitavecchia with

Barcelona; and Brindisi and Bari with
Greece. There are regular car-ferry
or hydrofoil connections to the main
islands – see www.italiantourism.co.uk
for a list of inter-island ferry operators.

Getting around Italy

By Air

From Milan and Rome there are
regular scheduled flights to some 30
destinations within Italy, including
Sicily and Sardinia. The main Italian-
based airlines are Alitalia/Air One and
Meridiana/Eurofly.
Alitalia: tel: (within Italy) 06-2222 or
toll-free 0800-650 055; from the UK:
0870-225 5000; from other parts of
the world: +39 06-2222; www.alitalia.
com.
Meridiana: tel: (within Italy) 892 928;
from the UK: 0871-222 9319; from
other parts of the world: +39 0789-
52682; www.meridiana.it.

By Rail

The cheapest, fastest and most
convenient way to travel is by train.
The state-owned Ferrovie dello Stato
(FS) extends over the entire country. A
new high-speed network, connecting
Turin to Naples, is almost complete,
significantly reducing travel time
between major Italian cities. The price
of a journey depends on the type of
train. The faster ETR 500 and other
high-speed premier trains which
link Italy's main cities and towns are
usually worth the extra cost for time
saved and comfort. Reservations
are normally required on these
faster trains, and a fee for this is
charged on top of the supplement.
The less comfortable Diretto (D),
InterRegionale (IR) and R (REG) are
slower and cheaper trains, used on

more peripheral routes and stopping at local stations. Tickets must be validated in the yellow machines located on station platforms prior to boarding. For timetables and booking online, visit the Ferrovia dello Stato website at www.tronitalia.it.

By Bus

While trains are usually the best form of transport, buses can be a better bet in some areas, particularly mountainous regions, where they are generally cheaper and faster than trains. Each province has its own intercity bus companies and each company has its own fares and lines.

By Road

Autostrade (motorways) are excellent and numerous, but are mostly subject to tolls. Speed limits are 50kph (30mph) in towns, 90kph (55mph) on main roads and 130kph (80mph) on motorways. Driving is on the right, overtaking on the left. Police can impose on-the-spot fines for speeding, driving under the influence of alcohol and other offences.

Getting around Rome

From the Airports

Rome is served by two airports: Leonardo da Vinci, commonly referred to as Fiumicino, located 30km (18 miles) southwest of the city, and Ciampino, located 16km (10 miles) southeast. Fiumicino mainly handles scheduled air traffic, while Ciampino is used by most charter companies.

From Fiumicino, an express rail service operates every 30

BELOW: tram in Piazza Porta Maggiore.

minutes to Rome Termini (central station). Journey time is 30 minutes. It's a short taxi ride to most hotels from Termini. Trains for Trastevere, Ostiense, Tuscolana and Tiburtina stations leave Fiumicino approximately every 15 minutes. A taxi from the airport to the centre will cost around €42.

From Ciampino, expect to pay about €35 for a taxi into the centre. Bus connections between the airport and Roma Termini station are operated by Atral, Cotral, Sit and Terravision. Buses depart from opposite International Departures (single fare €5–8). The Terravision bus (www.terravision/eu) is only for passengers on Ryanair or other low-cost carriers.

For flight information, at Fiumicino tel: 06-65951; for Ciampino tel: 06-794 941; website for both airports: www.adr.it.

By Rail

Most international trains arrive at Termini station, which is connected to other parts of the city by both the A and B lines of the subway.

The official taxi stand is in front of the station. Do not be tempted by the offers of "taxi" from unofficial cab drivers loitering about the station. Taxis can be ordered by calling the "Radiotaxi", tel: 06-3570. The station and the area are pretty seedy at night.

General Information

Train enquiries, tel: 892021. Train information office open daily 7am–9pm.
Tourist office, platform 24, open daily 8am–9pm.
Lost property, tel: 06-4730 6682 , by platform 24. Open daily 7am–11pm.
Station police, Polizia: platform 1, Carabinieri: platform 20.
Left luggage, platform 24. Charged per piece, set price for 5 hours, then charged per hour thereafter. Open 6am–midnight.

Cycling

Rome has a 35km (22-mile) rarely used network of cycle paths. To encourage cyclists the city has introduced a trial bike-sharing scheme whereby you leave a deposit at one of several PIT tourist offices, and pick up a swipecard to unlock a bike. The first half-hour is free; every 30 minutes is charged thereafter. For a map of cycle paths and points to locate the bike stations, visit www. roma-n-bike.com. For bike rental try Top Bike at Via dei Quattro Canti 40, tel: 06-488 2893; www.topbikerental.com.

Motoring Advice

The **Automobile Club d'Italia** (ACI) has offices at all main frontier posts, offering emergency breakdown services. Throughout Italy 24 hours a day, you can call 803 116 for breakdown services (English-speaking service available). Members of other European automobile associations can get help from the ACI, Via Marsala 8, I-00185, Rome, tel: 49981; www.aci.it.

By Road

Driving in the traffic-logged streets of Rome is best avoided. The city is completely encircled by a motorway, the Grande Raccordo Anulare (GRA), intersected by various roads leading from other Italian cities. The A1 links Rome to Milan and Florence in the north, and to Naples in the south.

Public Transport

Rome has two underground lines (*metropolitana* or metro), line A and line B, which pass most of Rome's popular tourist sights and intersect at Termini railway station. A third line, C, is currently under construction, and will link the Colosseum to Largo Argentina. A big red letter M marks the entrance to the underground, and tickets are sold at each station. A complete network of buses and trams covers the whole city, providing frequent service until midnight and a special night service (*servizio notturno*).

The same ticket is valid for metro, bus or tram lines. Tickets can be purchased from major metro stations, vending machines at stations and bus stops, tourist offices, some bars and newsstands. Tickets should normally be validated before boarding, though on some of the newer buses you can buy a ticket on board. A ticket is valid for 85 minutes; there are also passes for 1, 3 and 7 days. Public transport is included in the Roma Pass (*see page 270*).

ITALY A–Z

Accommodation

Italy has a wonderful variety of accommodation, from luxury villas and palatial apartments to small, family-run hotels, rustic retreats and an increasing number of B&Bs. For the last, try www.caffeletto.it or www.bbitalia.it.

AUSTRIA

BELGIUM

FRANCE

GERMANY

GREECE

ITALY

NETHERLANDS

PORTUGAL

SPAIN

SWITZERLAND

Rome

Tourist offices can provide a comprehensive list of hotels with details, but cannot make reservations. However, the Hotel Reservation Service (tel: 06-699 1000; www.hotelreservation.it), with desks at both airports and at Termini station, will book a hotel for you free of charge.

Arts and Activities

What's On

The Italian State Tourist Board, with offices abroad (see below), gives details of major events, exhibitions and festivals in Italy on its website (www.italiantourism.com). More specific information, including "What's On" brochures and a current list of opening hours, can be picked up at the local APT (Azienda di Promozione Turistica) office in Italy. Bear in mind that many museums and other sites in Italy are closed on Mondays. In cities like Rome and Venice listings can be found in the local press. Your hotel should be able to organise tickets for the most popular events – or for museums and galleries requiring advance reservations. A small fee is normally charged for this service.

Rome

The free Museums of Rome booklet, with listings and opening hours, and Evento, with a cultural programme for the month, can be picked up from any of the Rome tourist offices.

You can also find comprehensive listings of what's on in Roma C'è (www.romace.it), the weekly booklet, with an abbreviated section in English, that comes out on Wednesdays.

The English-language bi-weekly Wanted in Rome is out every other Wednesday and has information about events throughout Italy; www.wantedinrome.com. The Thursday edition of La Repubblica also has a listing insert, Trova Roma. All are available from newsstands.

English-speaking guides and interpreters can be hired from the main APT office, hotels or travel agencies. For multilingual guided bus and walking tours in Rome see www.wheninrometours.com or www.tourome.com. Taking a guided tour of the Vatican is a good way of bypassing the invariably long queues.

Budgeting for Your Trip

Taxi to central Rome from Fiumicino Airport: €42, from Ciampino: €35.

Hotel: Double room with breakfast in high season, inclusive of tax: inexpensive, under €130, moderate €130–250, expensive/de luxe €300–400.
Museums and attractions in Rome: €5–14. (Free entry to some museums for EU citizens who are under 18 or over 65.)
Restaurants: Full meal at inexpensive restaurant €20–30, moderate €30–45, expensive €45–60 plus; light lunch €10–20.
Drinks: Beer €3–5, glass of house wine €2–4, coffee and soft drinks €1.50–3.50
Romapass (3-day tourist card): €23
Rome metro/bus/tram: €1 per journey, €11 for 3-day pass.

Children

Italians love children and take them everywhere. They are welcomed in restaurants in the evening as well as lunchtime (but note many restaurants do not open until 7.30pm), and the vast majority of hotels are happy to accept them. An extra bed or cot in a guest room costs around 30 percent extra. Nappies and baby foods are widely available and sold in all pharmacies. On trains children under 4 ride free, 4–12-year-olds are half price. Many museums and sites have free entrance for children under 6, and discounts for 6–18-year-olds.

Climate

In the Alpine region, winters are long and cold, but often sunny, while summers are short and pleasantly cool. The northern lakes and Po Valley see cold and foggy winters and warm, sunny summers. The rest of the country, even the northern Ligurian coast, has mild weather in winter. Summers are dry and hot to scorching, depending on how far south you go, but sea breezes often compensate for the searing heat.

The best time for a visit to the Ligurian and Adriatic coasts is from May/June to September. Before or after this period it can be rather chilly and rainy, with most hotels closed and beaches practically deserted. The best time to visit the cities of Italy is in spring or autumn between April and June and again in September and October – when the weather is most pleasant. However, the streets can be just as crowded. To check the weather on the web, try: www.wunderground.com, with five-day forecasts for Italian cities.

Disabled Travellers

Many of Italy's older cities are not easily navigable by disabled travellers: cobblestones, narrow pavements and cramped lifts can make getting around tricky. The Rome-based company CO.IN offers information on disabled facilities in restaurants, museums, shops and stations; tel: 800-271 027 (toll-free, Italy only); www.coinsociale.it (website in Italian only). CO.IN can also organise guided tours with transport equipped for disabled passengers; tel: 06-7128 9676. Roma Per Tutti is a useful information line for disabled travellers to Rome; tel: 06-5717 7094; www.romapertutti.it.

Transport in Italy's larger cities is gradually becoming more accessible, with increasing numbers of buses and trams now wheelchair-accessible. For train travel check the Trenitalia website, www.trenitalia.it; the wheelchair symbol denotes accessible trains. Call the relevant station to arrange assistance 24 hours prior to departure.

Accessible Italy is a non-profit organisation which organises accommodation and tours for people with disabilities; tel: 39-378-941111; www.accessibleitaly.com.

Eating Out

Italian **breakfast** (colazione) is usually a light affair, consisting of a cappuccino and brioche (pastry), biscuits or crispbreads, or simply a caffè (black, strong espresso).

Lunch (pranzo) is traditionally the main meal of the day, but this is gradually changing as Italy comes more into line with Northern Europe, particularly in the north of Italy and in the industrialised cities. A traditional lunch is increasingly the preserve of the south or the leisured classes. However, when Italians have the time to indulge in such lunches, then an ideal one might run as follows: after

Emergency Numbers

Police: 113, or 112 for the armed police (Carabinieri)
Ambulance: 116
Fire: 115
Public emergency assistance: 113
These numbers and their services operate on a 24-hour basis, and the number 113, in the principal cities, will answer in the main foreign languages.

Festivals

The Italians' attachment to regional customs and religious festivals has dwindled in the 20th century, but many continue for the tourist trade. Here is a far from exhaustive list of some of the main processions and festivities around the country.

January: Piana degli Albanesi (near Palermo): a colourful Byzantine ritual for Epiphany.

February: Venice: historical Carnival, masked balls and processions in magnificent costumes. Viareggio: more contemporary Carnival with parade of floats. Agrigento: Almond Blossom Festival in Sicily.

April: Rome: Pope's Easter Sunday blessing.

May: Assisi: Calendimaggio Christian and pagan festival. Naples: Miracle of San Gennaro (liquefaction of the saint's blood, also on first Sunday in May, 19 September and 16 December). Camogli (Riviera): Fish Festival, communal fish-fry in giant pan. Gubbio: Wooden candle race, crossbow competition. Orvieto: Pentecost feast of the Palombella (Holy Ghost). Florence: Maggio Musicale (May–June), musical performances in various venues throughout the city.

June: Pisa: San Ranieri, jousting and torchlit regatta on River Arno. Florence: medieval football game in costume. Spoleto: Festival dei Due Mondi (June–July), international theatre, prose, music and dance performances by leading artists from Europe and the Americas.

July: Siena: First Palio (2 July, *see page 251*). Sardinia: "Sa Ardia" – more dangerous than Il Palio (6–7 July). Palermo: festival of patron Santa Rosalia. Venice: Redentore regatta. Rimini: Festival of the Sea. Rome: Noantri street festival in Trastevere. Perugia and other Umbrian cities: Umbria Jazz, one of the most important jazz festivals in Europe.

August: Siena: Second Palio (16 August). Venice: (late August, early September) Venice International Film Festival held at the Lido.

September: Naples: Piedigrotta, Neapolitan music and cuisine and the 19 September feast day of San Gennaro. Venice: historical Regatta.

October: Assisi: Feast of St Francis. Perugia: Franciscan Mysteries.

December: Rome: Christmas food and toy market on Piazza Navona. Assisi and Naples: Nativity scenes in streets.

---

an *antipasto* (hors d'oeuvre), there follows a *primo* (pasta, rice or soup) and a *secondo* (meat or fish with a vegetable known as a *contorno*) or just a salad. The meal ends with a *dolce* (dessert), typically *gelato* (ice cream), almond tart or tiramisu. Italians usually drink an espresso *(but never a* cappuccino*)* after a meal and sometimes a liqueur, such as *grappa*, *amaro* or *sambuca*. Traditionally, **dinner** (*cena*) is similar to lunch, but lighter. However, where it has become more normal to eat less at lunchtime, dinner is the main meal of the day.

Every region in Italy has its own typical dishes: Piedmont specialises in pheasant, hare, truffles and *zabaglione* (a hot dessert made with whipped egg yolks, sugar and Marsala wine). Lombardy is known for *risotto alla Milanese* (with saffron, onions and beef marrow), minestrone, veal and *panettone* (a sweet Christmas cake made with sultanas and candied fruits). Trentino-Alto Adige is the place for dumplings and thick, hearty soups to keep out the cold; Umbria is best for roast pork and black truffles, and Tuscany is good for wild boar, chestnuts, steak and game. Naples is the home of mozzarella cheese and pizza and is good for seafood, and Sicily is the place to enjoy delectable sweets.

Italy still claims the best ice cream in the world, as well as the Sicilian speciality *granita* (crushed ice with fruit juice or coffee).

Opening times are generally 12/12.30pm–2/3pm for lunch, 7.30/8–10pm for dinner. In main towns and resorts restaurants may stay open later – this is often the case with pizzerias. Restaurant bills will often include a €1–4 bread and cover charge, per person. Italy lags behind the UK in its choice of vegetarian dishes, but there are an increasing number of places offering at least one meat- and fish-free dish. In other restaurants you can always opt for a vegetable-based antipasto or pasta, provided of course the stock is meat-free.

Embassies and Consulates

All embassies are in Rome, but many countries also maintain consulates in other Italian cities.

Australia: Via Antonio Bosio 5, tel: 06-852 721; www.italy.embassy. gov.au.

Canada: Via Zara 30, tel: 06-697 9121; www.canada.it.

Ireland: Piazza Campitelli 3, tel: 06-697 9121; www.ambasciata-irlanda.it.

New Zealand: Via Clitunno 44, tel: 06-853 7501; www.nzembassy.com.

South Africa: Via Tanaro 14, tel: 06-852 541; www.sudafrica.it.

UK: Via XX Settembre 80a, tel: 06-4220 0001; www.ukinitaly.fco.gov.uk.

US: Via Vittorio Veneto 119A, tel: 06-46741; www.rome.usembassy.gov.

Gay and Lesbian Travellers

Arci-gay, the national gay rights organisation, is a great source for finding bars, hotels, beaches and other gay-friendly localities. More than 15 cities have an Arci-gay office. Contact Arci-gay, Via Don Minzoni 18, 40121 Bologna, tel: 051-649 3055; www.arcigay.it. A magazine widely available is *Spartacus International Gay Guide*; www.spartacusworld.com/ gayguide.

Health and Medical Care

Medical Services

For minor complaints, seek out a *farmacia*, identified by a green cross. Trained pharmacists give advice and prescribe drugs, including antibiotics. Normal opening hours are 9am–1pm and 4–7pm, but outside these hours the address of the nearest *farmacia* on emergency duty will be posted in the window.

Rome

The Italian *farmacia* is open during shopping hours and at least one operates at night and weekends in each district of Rome. The schedule of pharmacists on duty is posted on every pharmacy door and in the local papers. Next to Termini station there is a 24-hour *farmacia* at Piazza dei Cinquecento 51.

Nightlife

Rome and Milan are the hotspots, but other large cities, especially university ones, have plenty of nightlife, particularly on Friday and Saturday nights. Out of the cities, most of the action takes place in midsummer in the open-air clubs of coastal resorts. Rimini is the liveliest resort, with a whole strong of open-air clubs and bars along the coast. Listings for nightlife in towns and resorts are available from tourist offices, newsstands and in local newspapers.

Rome

Rome's nightlife has livened up in recent years, with an increasing number of nightclubs, live bands and international DJs. The liveliest and trendiest areas, particularly popular with the young, are the up-and-coming quarters of Testaccio (notably around Monte Testaccio) and Ostiense. Trastevere has more or less lost its reputation as an arty hangout, but attracts many tourists for its friendly bars and small outdoor restaurants. Not all the city's discotheques charge entrance fees, but they're usually very crowded and drinks are never cheap. A few larger establishments have dance floors and cabarets.

There's an outdoor opera almost every evening at the ruined Baths of Caracalla (Terme di Caracalla), an easy bus or taxi ride from the city centre. Equally popular sound and light performances are at the Forum and outside Rome in Tivoli. People-watching at the Trevi Fountain, Piazza Navona and the Spanish Steps also lasts well into the night during the summer months.

Opening Hours

Banks are generally open Mon–Fri 8am–1.30pm and 2.30–4pm. Museums and galleries have varied openings, but are typically from 9am or 9.30am–4pm, or later in the

BELOW: Italian chic.

larger cities. Closing day is generally Monday.

Shops are usually open Mon–Sat 8.30 or 9am–1pm and 3.30 or 4–7.30 or 8pm, with some variations in the north where the lunch break tends to be shorter or non-existent and shops therefore close earlier. In areas serving tourists, hours are usually longer. Shops often close on Monday (or Monday morning). An increasing number of stores in cities and main resorts are open all day on Sundays.

Postal Services

Post office hours are usually 8am–1.30pm, but every town has a main post office open all day Mon–Fri and Sat am. The post office can also provide such services as *raccomandata* (registered), *prioritaria* or *postacelere* to speed up delivery of letters. Stamps *(francobolli)* may also be purchased from tobacconists.

Rome's main post office at Piazza San Silvestro, open Mon–Sat 8.25am–7pm, is in a splendid Renaissance palazzo.

The Vatican runs its own postal service, reputed to be faster than the Italian service. It does not always live up to this, but when visiting St Peter's, buy Vatican-issued stamps for your postcards and post them immediately: they are only valid in the Vatican City's blue post boxes. The postmark may interest your correspondents.

Public Holidays

January: 1 New Year's Day, 6 Epiphany; **March/April**: variable Easter Mon; **April**: 25 Liberation Day; **May**: 1 Labour Day; **May/June**: variable Corpus Christi; **June**: 2 Anniversary of the Republic; **August**: 15 Assumption Day; **November**: 1 All Saints' Day; **December**: 8 Immaculate Conception, 25 Christmas Day, 26 St Stephen's Day.

Shopping

The Italians' design sense has turned their country into an emporium of style and elegance. The luxury goods of Milan, Venice, Rome and Florence – jewellery, clothes, accessories, especially shoes, but also luggage and household goods and items of interior design – are second to none in the world. Not inexpensive, but then the bargain here is not in the price, it's in the centuries-old tradition of workmanship.

There is an abundance of gourmet delicacies that make the perfect gift. Consider the cheeses, salamis, Parma ham, Milanese sweet *panettone brioche*, Ligurian olive oil; Siena's cakes and famous *panforte*, a spicy fruit-and-nut concoction; and the small-production Chianti and Orvieto wines that you may not find back home. If you've fallen in love with Italian coffee, why not buy a compact version of the espresso machine or packaged roasted beans? Italian kitchenware is in general styled with a great sense of colour and line. The flea markets and street stalls in Florence are a bargain-hunter's paradise, where particularly good buys on leather goods, scarves and clothes are available. Other major cities have similar markets.

Popular souvenirs include blown glass from Venice, decorative and beautifully produced paper from Florence, high fashion from Milan and Italian shoes and handbags anywhere.

Rome

Via del Corso, Piazza di Spagna and Via del Babuino mark the boundaries of the classic window-shopping area. Here you can find everything from designer jeans to handcrafted jewellery and antique furniture. Nearby Via della Croce and Via del Corso offer fashion at more accessible prices.

Streets around Piazza Navona, the Pantheon and Campo de' Fiori offer unusual handcrafted goods and a range of smaller boutiques. The Campo de' Fiori, scene of a colourful morning market, is an interesting quarter to amble around and is still home to craftsmen, art restorers and market traders. This is a traditional working-class mix with a genuine feel that is fast dying out in trendy Trastevere.

Via del Babuino, Via Margutta, Via Giulia, Via dei Coronari and Via del Pellegrino are the main streets for antiques, *objets d'art* and paintings.

Via Nazionale is an undistinguished but relatively inexpensive shopping street, with a wide range of basic clothes.

Via Cola di Rienzo, the thoroughfare linking the Vatican with the Tiber (and Piazza del Popolo on the other bank) is lined with small boutiques and elegant shops selling a wide range of goods.

Via della Conciliazione, the street linking the Vatican with Castel Sant'Angelo, offers a wide range of religious artefacts. These include

Vatican coins, statues, stamps, religious books and souvenirs. Similar objects are on sale on the streets around the Vatican itself and on Via dei Cestari, which runs between the Pantheon and Largo Argentina.

Via del Governo Vecchio is one of the best streets for stylish second-hand clothes, as are the markets at Porta Portese and Via Sannio.

Telecommunications

Italy has plenty of public phone boxes, and many bars have payphones. Most public telephones now only take phone cards (carta telefonica), available from tobacconists, post offices or some newsstands. Some phones also accept credit cards. Phone cards can be used for international calls, but there are better-value prepaid international cards which come with a PIN number and can be used from any phone, including hotels. British mobiles function in Italy; American ones will only work if they are multiband and the service provider uses the world-standard GSM network. The cost of using a foreign mobile is expensive; if you are staying some time you could might consider buying a new SIM card or renting a mobile. Most rental contracts require a deposit. Phones can be rented from mobile retail outlets and some internet cafés.

For directory enquiries, tel: 12; international enquiries, tel: 176; reverse-charge calls, tel: 170.

Dialling Codes

The area code which starts with a 0 must be used whether you are calling from within or outside the area, eg if calling Rome dial the full city code (06) when calling within the city or

from abroad. The area codes of main cities are: Rome (06), Milan (02), Florence (055), Pisa (050), Venice (041), Turin (011), Naples (081), Como (031), Palermo (091). The code for Italy is 39.

Tipping

Tipping is not taken for granted in Italy, though a bit extra will always be appreciated.

A service charge of 10–15 percent may be added to restaurant bills, if not 10 percent is ample. Taxi drivers do not expect a tip, but will appreciate it if you round up the fare. Custodians of sights and museums also expect a tip, particularly if they have opened something especially for you.

Tourist Information

General tourist information is available from the Italian Tourist Board, which has offices abroad:
Australia: Level 4, 46 Market Street, NSW 2000, Sydney, tel: 02-9262 1666; e-mail: italia@italiantourism.com.au.
Canada: 175 Bloor Street East, Suite 907, South Tower, Toronto, Ontario, M4W3R8, tel: 416-925 4882.
UK: 1 Princes Street, London W1B 2AY, tel: 020-7408 1254; www.italiantouristboard.co.uk.
US: New York City: 630 Fifth Avenue, Suite 1565, NY 10111, tel: 212-245 5618. Los Angeles: 12400 Wilshire Blvd, Suite 550, CA 90025, tel: 310-820 1898; Chicago: 500 North Michigan Avenue – 2240, IL 60611, tel: 312-644 0996.
Website for Canada and US offices: www.italiantourism.com.

Within Italy look for the local APT (Azienda di Promozione Turistica), often marked with an "i" or "Turismo".

Main towns in Italy have a **Touring Club Italiano** (TCI; www.touringclub.it) office, which provides free information about points of interest. The club also produces some of the best maps and food-and-wine guides.

Provincial Tourist Offices

Offices are usually open seven days a week in season, sometimes closing at lunchtime.
Milan: Piazza Duomo 19/A, tel: 02-7740 4343; Stazione Centrale, tel: 02-7740 4318/4319; www.provincia.milano.it/turismo.
Florence: Via Manzoni 16, tel: 055-23320; www.firenzeturismo.it.
Venice: Venice Pavilion, Ex Giardini Reali, San Marco, tel: 041-529 8711; www.turismovenezia.it.

Rome

ENIT head office is at Via Marghera 2, tel: 06-49711; www.enit.it.
APT (Azienda di Promozione Turistica), Via Parigi 11, tel: 488 991.
There are also 10 tourist information points called PITs (Punto Informative Turistico) throughout the centre. Addresses and opening hours of the PITs are given on the Rome tourist information website, www.romaturismo.it.

You can reserve tickets for museums and shows and book hotels through the Rome Call Center, www.060608.it, tel: 06-0608.

The 3-day Roma Pass (www.romapass.it) is a multifunctional card giving full access to public transport and entry to two participating museums or archaeological sites, plus reductions on other museums and major events. The pass costs €23 and can be bought online, at sites, or from the call centre, tel: 06-0608.

Fiumicino Airport: tourist information point at Arrivals, Terminal C, open daily 9am–6.30pm.
Ciampino Airport: tourist information point at Baggage Claim, International Arrivals, open 9am–6.30pm.

What to Read

Other books in the Insight Guide series that highlight destinations in this region are: Insight Guides Italy, Rome, Tuscany, Florence, Venice, Northern Italy, Italian Lakes, Sardinia and Sicily. The Smart Guides covering Rome and Venice pack information into an easily portable and convenient format arranged in A–Z sections. The Step by Step Guides to Florence, Italian Lakes, Rome and Venice highlight the best walks and tours, with itineraries for all tastes.

BELOW: Italians drink their coffee on the run, standing up at the bar.

AUSTRIA

BELGIUM

FRANCE

THE NETHERLANDS

ESSENTIAL TRAVEL TIPS TO HELP YOU GET THERE AND GET AROUND

GERMANY

FACT FILE

Area: 41,500 sq km (16,000 sq miles), of which 18.4 percent is water
Area below sea level: one-fifth
Capital: Amsterdam
Seat of government: The Hague
Population: 16.5 million
Language: Dutch
Religion: Roman Catholic (27 percent), Protestant (16 percent), Muslim (6 percent), unaffiliated (51 percent)
Time zone: Central European Time
Currency: The euro (€)
Electricity: AC 230 volts, two-pin plugs
International dialling code: 31

TRANSPORT

Getting to the Netherlands

By Air
Most visitors from America or from other parts of Europe fly into Schiphol Airport, 14km (9 miles) southwest of Amsterdam. The airport is connected with 262 cities in more than 100 countries. Frequent flights link Schiphol with all major European airports, and there are several flights a day from the USA, Canada and Australia. KLM is the national airline. KLM information in the UK, tel: 0871-222 7740; in North America, tel: 1-800-225 2525; www.klm.com.

By Rail
There are good rail connections to all parts of the country from the main ferry ports of arrival, and frequent

services to the Netherlands from Brussels, Paris, Antwerp, Cologne and Berlin.
By Channel Tunnel: The Eurostar train (tel: 08705-186 186) links London to Brussels in about 2 hours, from where there are fast connections to destinations in Holland.

By Road
The Netherlands has an excellent network of roads, and signposting is good. From the ferry port at Hoek van Holland to Amsterdam, travel time is roughly 1 hour 30 minutes.
Eurotunnel: The Channel Tunnel service taking cars and their passengers from Folkstone to Calais on a drive-on-drive-off system takes 25 minutes to Calais, from where there are motorway connections to the Netherlands. Amsterdam is 370km (230 miles) from Calais.

By Sea
From the UK, **Stena Line** (tel: 08705-707 070; www.stenaline.com) has a day and a night sailing from Harwich to Hoek van Holland, taking around 6 hours. **P&O Ferries** (tel: 0871-664 5645; www.poferries.com) sails from Hull to Rotterdam, taking 10 hours. **DFDS Seaways** sails from Newcastle to IJmuiden, west of Amsterdam, taking 15 hours (tel: 0871-522 9955; www.dfdsseaways.co.uk).

Getting around the Netherlands

By Air
Schiphol, near **Amsterdam**, is the Netherlands' principal airport (tel: 0900-0141; +31-20-794 0800 from outside Holland; www.schiphol.nl). Schiphol railway station is located

below the arrivals hall. Trains leave for the principal Dutch cities every 5–15 minutes or so between 5.25am and 0.15am, and every 60 minutes or so during the remaining period.
Rotterdam has a small airport served by scheduled flights from London City Airport, Manchester, Hamburg and others, located 15 minutes from the city centre. A regular local bus service runs between the airport and the city.
Eindhoven, Groningen, Enschede and **Maastricht** have airports that are principally for domestic and charter flights.

By Rail
Netherlands Railways (Nederlandse Spoorwegen) has a network of express trains linking major cities. Trains every 5–15 minutes link Schiphol Airport and Amsterdam. There is an hourly night service between Utrecht, Amsterdam, Schiphol, The Hague and Rotterdam. Frequently stopping trains serve smaller places. There are at least half-hourly services on most lines and 4–8 per hour on busier routes. It is not possible to reserve seats on domestic services. For further information about public transport and tickets:
Amsterdam: Stationsplein 1, Centraal Station, tel: 0900-9292 (Mon–Fri 8am–10pm, Sat and Sun 9am–10pm).
Nationwide: Tel: 0900-9292.
For information on international trains, tel: 0900-9296. Information on train travel in the Netherlands can be found at www.gvb.nl.

By Road
The Netherlands has a dense and modern toll-free road system.

GREECE

ITALY

NETHERLANDS

PORTUGAL

SPAIN

SWITZERLAND

The smaller country roads are in excellent condition. There are around 80–170km (50–105 miles) of tourist routes, some of which continue into neighbouring countries.

There are ferry services on secondary roads crossing rivers and canals. Most ferries are equipped to carry cars, and in general the fares are not high. You may also be required to pay nominal fees for the use of tunnels, bridges and dams which appear throughout the country.
Motoring Advice: To drive in the Netherlands, you must carry a current driving licence (an international licence is not necessary), vehicle registration document, Green Card insurance policy, and a warning triangle for use in the event of an accident or breakdown.

Waterways

There are a few scheduled boat and hydrofoil services in and around major cities, and boat tours, excursions and trips operating on the various bodies of water in the Netherlands.
Boat charter: Around the IJsselmeer and in the northern provinces of Groningen and Friesland, boat-rental agencies offer a range of craft, some of which have living accommodation. Another area popular with those who enjoy boating is Zeeland province.
Canal tours: A popular way to get to know Amsterdam is by taking a canal tour; numerous companies operate from the canal basin opposite Centraal Station and other points around the city. Tours take an hour or more; candlelit dinner cruises are also available.
Canal buses: Amsterdam's canal bus system is essentially geared to visitors. Modern glass-topped launches will pick you up at various points of the city and take you through some of the loveliest parts of Amsterdam. Day tickets with unlimited use are available. Be prepared to queue in summer.
The Museum Quarter line: This stops at nine docks in easy reach of multiple museums at 75-minute intervals – worth considering if you intend doing a lot of sightseeing.

Public Transport

From 2010, to travel anywhere in the Netherlands on buses, trams, the metro and the train between certain stations, travellers need an electronic stored-value card called the *OV-chipkaart*, which replaces the old *nationale strippenkaart* (national strip card). You can buy the cards at offices of local public transport companies,

like the GVB in Amsterdam, and from metro stations; the fare for the trip is automatically deducted by electronic readers as you travel. There are various versions of this card and different prices for each one. The main distinctions are between "personal" cards (which require the user's photograph), "anonymous" cards and "throwaway" cards. In most cases, for short-stay visitors, the anonymous and throwaway cards are likely to be the most useful; the former can function as a day and multi-day card, and the latter is most useful for single journeys.

Getting Around Amsterdam

Orientation

Amsterdam, capital of the Netherlands and its most populous city with 755,000 inhabitants, stands on the River Amstel. Much of the city stands below sea level on reclaimed land known as polders and is supported by stilts, some driven 18 metres (59ft) into the marshy ground below, enabling parts of the city to spring up where there were once only waterways. Built on a design of expanding horseshoe canals that fit one within the other, the city contains some 4,000 17th-century merchants' houses and warehouses and over 1,000 bridges.

Financial and economic centre of the Netherlands, Amsterdam is part of the so-called Randstad (Rim City), which mainly comprises the provinces of North and South Holland and contains the country's major industries and largest cities (Rotterdam and The Hague).

From the Airport

Trains leave Schiphol Airport every 5–15 minutes for Amsterdam Centraal station during the day, and once an hour at night. Travel time is under 20 minutes. Trains also run to the RAI station and to Amsterdam Zuid for the World Trade Centre. Connexxion operates a hotel-shuttle coach service to the city every half an hour, but it's over twice the price of the train. A much cheaper public bus service links the airport to the city.

By Road

Driving in the city centre is best avoided. If you do take a car, be prepared for parking problems, mad cyclists, narrow canal streets (often blocked by delivery vans), the complexity of one-way systems and trams that always have right of way.

If you arrive by car, the best thing to do is leave it in a car park and go the rest of the way by public transport. The multi-storey Europarking at Marnixstraat 250 usually has space and is within walking distance of the city centre.

Amsterdam makes a good base for day trips. Distances to Dutch towns of interest are short: The Hague 52km (33 miles), Utrecht 43km (27 miles), Delft 62km (39 miles).
Cycling: Bikes may be hired for €10–15 (this includes insurance but not the deposit). Mike's Bike Tours, Kerkstraat 134, tel: 020-622 7970; www.mikesbiketoursamsterdam.com. Damstraat Rent-a-Bike, Damstraat 20–22, tel: 020-625 5029; www.bikes. nl. Holland Rent a Bike, Damrak 247, tel: 020-622 3207.

By Rail

A wide and very efficient network of rail services operates throughout the country. Fast electric trains link Amsterdam with most Dutch towns on an hourly or half-hourly basis. It is well worth finding out about excursion fares, which include entrance fees to museums and other attractions, as well as the return rail fare. The GVB office outside Centraal station can give you all the information you need.

Public Transport

Unless you are travelling out of the centre you are unlikely to need the buses or metro. Within the city the prominent blue-and-grey trams are easily the best means of getting around and are not expensive.

The GVB office outside Centraal station provides information in English and free transport route maps. See Getting Around *(above)* for details of the new *OV-chipkaart* public transport cards.

THE NETHERLANDS A–Z

Accommodation

It is wise to book in advance in the summer and the holiday season and, in the case of North Holland, during the bulb season (April–May). This is especially true of Amsterdam, where the central hotels are usually booked up from June to August.

If you haven't booked, however, it is worth telephoning hotels at short notice in case they have cancellations. You can book directly with the hotel – staff on the reservations desk will invariably speak English.

ABOVE: dining in De Bazar restaurant, in Amsterdam.

Arts and Activities

There are more than 600 museums in the Netherlands, with 440 of them listed in the *Attractions* booklet from VVV offices. The entry price varies; some museums are free. A Museum Year Card gives free admission to all of them.

At VVV offices bearing the *i* – *Nederland* sign, visitors can, in addition, obtain information on cultural activities and order tickets for concerts and theatre productions.

Brown café noticeboards are another good source of information on local events.

Amsterdam

VVV Amsterdam, the city's tourist office (www.iamsterdamtourist.com), publishes a monthly magazine, *Amsterdam Day by Day*, which has details of current cultural attractions. The AUB Ticketshop, Leidseplein 26 (tel: 0900-0191; www.uitburo. nl) provides advance bookings for theatres, operas, ballets and concerts. It is open Mon–Sat 10am–7.30pm and Sunday from noon to 7.30pm. Another useful source of cultural information is the monthly magazine *Amsterdam Times*, available at hotels and tourist offices; www.amsterdamtimes.com.

After dark, entertainment focuses on three main areas: Leidseplein, popular with tourists and with locals for restaurants, lively dance clubs and nightclubs; Rembrandtsplein for clubs, cabarets and strip shows pandering to slightly older tastes; and the Red Light District, notorious for scantily dressed women sitting in windows and for noticeboards saying "room to hire".

Strip shows, porn videos and sex shops centre on the canals of Oudezijds Voorburgwal and Oudezijds Achterburgwal. The smaller, sleazier streets leading off these two canals are best avoided, and you are advised never to take photographs.

On an entirely different note, you could spend the evening on a candle-lit canal cruise, with wine and cheese or full dinner provided.

In any case, try out one of the numerous brown cafés, a classic grand café with a reading table and more of a modern ambience, or, alternatively, one of the new-wave bars, with cool, whitewashed and mirrored walls, an abundance of greenery and a long list of cocktails. Some cafés and bars have live music, often jazz or blues.

Budgeting for Your Trip

The Netherlands is not the most expensive European country: you will find that accommodation costs in particular can be a drain on your budget – especially in the centre of Amsterdam – but this is often outweighed by reasonably priced restaurants and good-value public transport. A taxi from Schiphol Airport to the centre of Amsterdam costs about €40.

Although it's not difficult to stick to as little as $33 a day per person if you cycle everywhere, picnic on supermarket-bought food and sleep under canvas, you should reckon on a more realistic budget of around $100–130 a day per person for two decent meals, public transport to get around, the odd admission fee and a modest hotel. Add on roughly another 20–30 percent if you're staying in Amsterdam.

Prices of comparable hotels vary considerably, and those of restaurants, clubs and museums to a lesser extent, from place to place around Holland. Amsterdam, The Hague and Rotterdam are the most expensive among the major cities, followed by Utrecht, Eindhoven and Maastricht. Amsterdam has a paid-for tourist card, the **I amsterdam Card**, valid for 1, 2 or 3 days, which offers discounts for museums, attractions and nightlife venues, and free use of public transport.

The starting rate for a double room is €50; for a decent mid-range hotel in most cities, expect to pay €100–200; above €300 is starting to get into de luxe territory. Dining costs are €10–25 for a 2–3-course meal at a modest local restaurant, €25–60 at a

fine restaurant, and €100 and beyond for Michelin-level cuisine. A glass of beer can cost as little as €2.50 and a glass of house wine €5.

Children

Children are welcome in restaurants and cafés, many of which serve a *kindermenu* (children's menu). It is easy to hire bicycles fitted with children's seats for getting about town or for excursions into the country.

Ask at the VVV for details of special activities for children. Several cities now have *kinderboerderijen*, or children's farms; in Amsterdam, for example, there are city farms within the zoo complex and at the Amstelpark (near the Rai Exhibition Centre in the southern suburbs).

The towns of the Netherlands, with their harbours, bridges, canals, parks and windmills, naturally appeal to children. Specific top children's attractions include, in Amsterdam: Artis Zoo, Plantage Kerklaan 38–40, tel: 0900-278 4796; www.artis.nl; Science Center NEMO, Oosterdok 2, tel: 020-531 3233; www.e-nemo.nl; and Madame Tussauds, Dam 20, tel: 020-523 0623; www.madametussauds. nl. In Enkhuizen: Zuiderzeemuseum, Wierdijk 12–22, tel: 0228-351 111; www.zuiderzeemuseum.nl. In Arnhem: Burgers' Zoo, Antoon van Hooffplein 1, tel: 026-442 4534; www.burgerszoo. nl. In The Hague: Madurodam miniature town, George Maduroplein 1, tel: 070-416 2400; www.madurodam. nl. In Rotterdam: Zoo (Diergaarde Blijdorp), Blijdorplaan 8, tel: 010-443 1495; www.rotterdamzoo.nl. In Tilburg: De Efteling family leisure park, Europalaan 1, Kaatsheuvel, tel: 0900-0161; www.efteling.nl.

Climate

Amsterdam has a mild, maritime climate, but is wet and cool in winter. Summers are generally warm, but you can expect rain at any time of year. Spring is the driest time of the year and a favourite time for tulip enthusiasts. The advantages of a visit in winter are the cut-price package deals and the fact that museums and galleries are pleasantly uncrowded.

Disabled Travellers

Many train stations have lifts, which are marked clearly at arrival points. Buses and trams are increasingly being made easier to access. But older hotels have very steep staircases and no lifts. Most of the 4-

AUSTRIA
BELGIUM
FRANCE
GERMANY
GREECE
ITALY
NETHERLANDS
PORTUGAL
SPAIN
SWITZERLAND

and 5-star hotel chains have wheelchair access and lifts. For assistance in the Netherlands, contact:

Leefwijzer
Postbus 169
3500 AD Utrecht
Tel: 030-291 6600
Email: bureau@cg-raad.nl
www.leefwijzer.nl

Eating Out

When it comes to dining out in the Netherlands, you can choose from the simplest fare in an *eetcafé* or the more costly, formal environs of a top-level restaurant. In between, you can select from one of the many ethnic restaurants, which are especially predominant in larger cities like Amsterdam, Utrecht, Rotterdam, Maastricht and The Hague.

Eetcafés are a kind of informal local eatery, offering a daily changing menu with a choice of fish, meat or vegetarian main course. They are popular because they are reasonably priced; but don't dine too late or the menu will be sold out.

Broodjes, filled sandwiches with cheese, meat or fish, are the fare when it comes to lunch, and generally you need to consume a couple of them to fill you up. Soups and salads also predominate on café menus.

Amsterdam

Dutch national cuisine has a limited range of dishes, falling into the meat and potatoes and hearty stews and soups categories, yet eating out in Amsterdam can be one of the highlights of the trip. This is because the wide range of nationalities that inhabit the city have brought their own unique culinary delights to its restaurants. You could stay in Amsterdam for over a month and not eat the same style of food twice. This

Emergency Numbers

Police/fire/ambulance: 112

Amsterdam
SOS doctor/dentist/chemist: 020-592 3434
Lost property: 0900-8011
City police : 0900-8844

The Hague
Doctor/dentist: 070-346 9669
Lost property: 0900-8011

Rotterdam
Doctor/dentist: 010-433 9866
Lost property: 0900-8011

offers boundless opportunities to try something new, and means you'll never get tired of eating out.

Amsterdam is a café society, and restaurants and bars form a lively part of the social scene. Restaurants range from the very formal to the informal, with prices to match. There is a range of vegetarian restaurants, and general restaurants often offer a few vegetarian dishes.

Embassies and Consulates

Embassies in The Hague

Australia: Carnegielaan 4, 2517 KH Den Haag, tel: 070-310 8200; www.australian-embassy.nl.
Canada: Sophialaan 7, 2514 JP Den Haag, tel: 070-311 1600; www.international.gc.ca.
Ireland: Dr Kuyperstraat 9, 2514 BA Den Haag, tel: 070-363 0993; www.irishembassy.nl.
New Zealand: Eisenhowerlaan 77N, 2517 KK Den Haag, tel: 070-346 9324; www.nzembassy.com.
South Africa: Wassenaarseweg 40, 2596 CJ Den Haag, tel: 070-392 4501; www.southafrica.nl.
UK: Lange Voorhout 10, 2514 ED Den Haag, tel: 070-427 0427; www.britain.nl.
US: Lange Voorhout 102, 2514 EJ Den Haag, tel: 070-310 2209; http://thehague.usembassy.gov.

Consulates in Amsterdam

UK: Koningslaan 44, Amsterdam, tel: 020-676 4343.
US: Museumplein 19, Amsterdam, tel: 020-575 5309.

Festivals

Carnival, Maastricht, four days preceding Ash Wednesday. In the "capital" of the Catholic south of the Netherlands, the pre-Lenten Carnival is a major spectacle.
Koninginnedag (Queen's Day), 30 April. Amsterdam is the best place to celebrate the queen's official birthday, with a staggering number of street parties and open markets.
Vlaggetjesdag, Scheveningen, Saturday in mid-June. Celebrations surround the return of the year's first barrel of herring at this North Sea fishing port.
North Sea Jazz Festival, Rotterdam, three days in mid-July. Holland's top jazz festival sets feet tapping at the Ahoy concert venue.
Grachten Festival, five days in mid-July, Amsterdam. A feast of classical music centred on the city's canals and ending with the Prinsengracht concert.

Gay and Lesbian Travellers

The Netherlands, and Amsterdam in particular, has plenty to offer gay and lesbian visitors. The capital rightly considers itself to be Europe's gay capital, boasting a considerable infrastructure of clubs, bars, restaurants, hotels, festivals and events, and considerable local acceptance. The Amsterdam Gay Pride festival, on the first weekend in August, is a particularly good time to be in town. In recent years, however, there has been a disturbing growth in violence against gay people.

Health and Medical Care

Medical Services

The standard of medical and dental services in the Netherlands is extremely high, and most major cities have an emergency doctor and dental service. Enquire at your hotel or a tourist information centre, or consult the introductory pages to local telephone directories. For non-emergency medical care and dental treatment in Amsterdam, tel: 020-592 3434.

Amsterdam

The most central hospital is the **Onze-Lieve-Vrouwe Gasthuis**, Oosterpark 9, tel: 020-599 9111.

The main hospital is the **Academisch Medisch Centrum**, Meibergdreef 9, tel: 020-566 9111. Both hospitals have an outpatients and casualty ward.

Pharmacies/chemists *(Apotheek)* are normally open Mon–Fri 9am–5.30pm or 6pm. Late-night and Sunday chemists operate on a rotating basis; rotas are also posted in pharmacy windows.

Nightlife

Of all the Dutch cities, Amsterdam is the king, or queen, of Holland's nightlife, with the largest number of cultural options, including music, dance, theatre and cinema, along with numerous bars and clubs. But its position is by no means undisputed. The Hague poses the strongest challenge for the highbrow crown, Rotterdam for its high-energy scene, and Utrecht makes its own contribution.

The great thing is that all these cities lie within easy reach of each other by public transport or car – roughly within the distance that encompasses European metropolises like London and Paris – so it's

Tourist Information

Tourist information offices (Vereniging voor Vreemdelingenverkeer – or VVV for short) are clearly marked and often located just outside the railway station in every main town and city, or in the centre of town. Here the multilingual staff will answer all your questions, provide maps and brochures, handle your accommodation bookings and reserve tickets for the theatre. There is a charge for most of these services. It is useful to carry passport-sized photographs for various identity cards you may want to purchase.

In Amsterdam, the address of the head office is:
VVV Amsterdam Tourist Office PO Box 3901, 1001 AS Amsterdam, tel: 020-551 2525 or 0900-400 4040; www.iamsterdam.nl. To visit in person, go to: Stationsplein 10 (the white building across the road to the left outside Centraal Station). Open daily 8am–9pm.

There are also VVV offices inside Centraal station (Mon–Wed 9am–8pm, Thur–Sat 8am–8pm, Sun 9am–6pm), and on Stadhouderskade at Leidseplein, Amsterdam (daily 9am–5pm).

The main website for the Netherlands is www.holland.com. This has the addresses of all the local tourist offices (VVV).

Tourist Offices Abroad

UK and Ireland: PO Box 30783, London WC2B 6DH, tel: 020-7539 7950.

US and Canada: 355 Lexington Avenue, 19th Floor, New York, NY 10017, tel: 212-370 7360.

possible to mix and match, and even consider taking in something at nearby Haarlem, Delft or Leiden. Beyond the Randstad towns and cities, Maastricht in the far south, Groningen in the far north, and Eindhoven roughly in between, all have nightlife scenes worth exploring.

Nightlife in Amsterdam

Amsterdam scores so highly thanks to venues like the Concertgebouw for classical music, and the Muziektheater for opera and dance. Among the local outfits that perform in these and other venues around town are the Royal Concertgebouw Orchestra, the Netherlands Philharmonic Orchestra, the Netherlands Chamber Orchestra, the Netherlands Opera, the National Ballet and the Netherlands Chamber Choir. From time to time, visitors arriving from elsewhere include the Residence Orchestra and the Netherlands Dance Theatre from The Hague, and the Rotterdam Philharmonic Orchestra.

Theatrical works in Dutch are something of an acquired taste – especially if you don't speak Dutch – but there are occasional performances in English. Most films are shown in original language (which most often means English), with Dutch subtitles; children's films are generally an exception to this rule.

To get information about what's on, pick up a copy of the English-language monthly magazine *Amsterdam Day by Day* from the VVV (there is a charge for this).

Opening Hours

Normal shopping hours are 8.30 or 9am–6 or 6.30pm. Late-night shopping is usually Thursday. Food stores close at 4pm on Saturday. Some shops in the cities open on Sunday. Many shops close for one half-day a week, often Monday morning. Most museums open Tue–Sun 10am–5 or 6pm.

Postal Services

Main post offices open Mon–Fri 8.30am–6pm, Sat 9am–noon. Stamps are available from post offices, tobacconists, newsstands and machines attached to the red-and-grey post boxes.

Poste restante facilities are available at the main post office. You need a passport to collect your mail.

Amsterdam

The main office is at Singel 250. Open: Mon–Fri 7.30am–6pm, Sat 9am–noon. Stamps are available from post offices, tobacconists, newsstands and stamp machines attached to the orange post boxes.

Public Holidays

January: 1 New Year's Day; **March/April**: variable Good Fri/Easter Sun/Mon; **April**: 30 Queen's Birthday; **May:** 1 Labour Day, 5 Liberation Day; **May/June**: variable Ascension Day, Whit Monday (Pentecost) Day, **December**: 25 Christmas Day. 26 St Stephen's Day.

Shopping

The VVV tourist office provides a series of useful shopping guides and maps.

Amsterdam

Bargains are a rarity but browsing is fun, particularly in the markets and the small specialist shops, such as those selling antiques and Delftware. For general shopping the main streets are Kalverstraat and Nieuwendijk, for exclusive boutiques try P.C. Hooftstraat, and for the more offbeat shops you should head to the Jordaan, northwest of the centre, where many of the local artists live. Two unusual shopping centres are also worth a visit: Magna Plaza opposite the Royal Palace and Kalvertoren on Kalverstraat.

Telecommunications

Telephone boxes are mainly green, but are also recognisable in more compact and contemporary styles. Most take phone cards and/or coins. You find them at railway stations, large stores, cafés and in some streets. Beware of hole-in-the-wall shops offering so-called cheap long-distance telephone services, as many are actually overpriced.

The code for dialling the Netherlands from abroad is 00 31. Most telephone numbers have 10 digits (the initial "0" of the area code is omitted when calling from abroad). To make an international call from the Netherlands, dial 00 followed by the country code: Australia 61, Ireland 353, New Zealand 64, South Africa 27, the UK 44, and the US and Canada 1.

Tipping

Service charges and value-added tax are included in restaurant and bar bills. An extra tip of 5–10 percent can be left for extra attention or service, but this is by no means compulsory. Taxi meters also include the service charge, though it is customary to give an extra tip. A lavatory attendant is usually given a small tip.

What to Read

Insight Guides Amsterdam and *The Netherlands* are companions to this book, providing a more in-depth look at the city and country. *Smart Guide Amsterdam* packs information into an easily portable and convenient format arranged in A–Z sections.

P ORTUGAL

ESSENTIAL TRAVEL TIPS TO HELP YOU GET THERE AND GET AROUND

FACT FILE

Area: 92,072 sq km (33,549 sq miles), including Madeira and the Azores
Capital: Lisbon
Population: 10.6 million
Language: Portuguese
Highest mountain: Serra da Estrela 1,993 metres (6,539ft)
Religion: Roman Catholic (94 percent)
Time zone: GMT (summer time Mar–Oct GMT +1); the Azores are 1 hour behind continental Portugal
Currency: The euro (€)
Electricity: AC 220 volts, two-pin plugs
International dialling code: 351

TRANSPORT

Getting to Portugal

By Air

TAP Air Portugal is Portugal's national airline and has wide international links. Many major airlines make non-stop direct flights to Lisbon Oporto and Faro (on the Algarve) from capital cities in Europe and to Lisbon from other continents. The UK has excellent connections with several no-frills carriers flying to various destinations in Portugal, including easyJet (to Lisbon and Faro), Ryanair (to Oporto and Faro), Thomson Fly (to Lisbon and Faro) and Monarch Airways (to Faro). From the US, there are several flights a week to Lisbon from New York, Los Angeles and Boston via TAP and Continental.

The main domestic carrier is Portugália Airlines.
TAP: (UK) 0845-601 0932, (US) 973-344 8267; www.flytap.com
Thomson Airways: www.thomsonfly.com

By Rail

There are international services to Lisbon from both Paris and Madrid. The TGV-Atlantique leaves Paris (Montparnasse) at 3.50pm each day and connects with the Sud-Express at Irún, arriving in Lisbon late morning the next day. The Lusitania Hotel train leaves Madrid at 10.45pm and arrives in Lisbon the next morning.
    For information about train services contact **Comboios de Portugal** (Portuguese Railways), Lisbon, tel: 21-21 102 1221 or 808-208 208; www.cp.pt.

By Road

Good roads link Portugal with Spain at numerous border points. Main east–west routes to Lisbon are from Seville via Beja; Badajos via Elvas; Salamanca via Viseu.

Getting around Portugal

Portugal has a modern network of excellent highways, and even secondary roads are, overall, of a high standard. Bus routes are comprehensive although operated by a baffling number of bus companies. Train travel is generally more expensive and slower.

By Air

TAP Air Portugal has a daily service between Lisbon, Porto, Faro, Madeira and the Azores (www.flytap.com). The airline Portugália also operates a busy domestic and international service.

The ticket counter is located at Lisbon Airport (departures), tel: 21-8425 560/1/2/3; www.pga.pt.

By Rail

Once in Portugal, you have a good, fast north–south route (Porto–Lisbon–Faro) as well as slow, scenic rides, especially in the north. The main categories of train in Portugal are: Regional "R" (slow); Inter-Regional "IR" (fast); Intercidades (Intercity) "IC"; Rapido and Alfa express (very fast). Generally, the most efficient routes are the Lisbon–Coimbra–Porto and the Lisbon–Algarve lines. Trains from across Europe arrive at Santa Apolónia station.
Special passes: A variety of rail discount cards are available, including group tickets, senior citizens' cards, InterRail cards, Rail-Europe Senior tickets, tourist tickets, family cards, and International Youth tickets. No discounts are available on the express service.
    For more information on train services, tel: 808-208 208; www.cp.pt.

By Road

There are numerous private bus lines which tend to specialise in particular routes or areas of the country. Many travel agencies can book bus tickets.
Algarve: Eva Transporte, tel: 289-899 740; wwww.eva-bus.net.
Lisbon: Carris; www.carris.pt/en/home. TST Transportes Sul Do Tejo: www.tsuldotejo.pt.
Porto: STCP, tel: 808-200 166 or 22-507 1000; www.stcp.pt.

Public Transport

Lisbon and Oporto both have metro systems, and Lisbon still has a few trams running, including the scenic number 28 that runs from Praça da Figueira to the atmospheric narrow streets of the Alfama. In cities, passengers either pay the driver a flat fare or buy prepaid modules from Carris kiosks, and validate the number required by the length of the journey. You can pick up an excellent local transport map at the tourist office (see page 427).

Getting around Lisbon

Lisbon is a relatively straightforward city to navigate. The compact centre is small enough for strolling, and the bus, tram and metro services are efficient and frequent, and offer a comprehensive service to the outer regions of the city. A LisboaCard, sold at the Lisbon tourist offices and Carris kiosks, provides free travel on the metro, buses and trams, plus the train to Belém.

To and from the Airport

The AeroBus departs from outside Arrivals every 20 minutes from 7.45am to 9pm, with several central destinations in Lisbon.

Taxis are also available and should cost around €12 to the city centre.

By Rail

There are four railway stations in Lisbon: Santa Apolónia, Rossio, Cais do Sodre and Oriente, plus Barreiro on the south side of the River Tejo. Santa Apolónia is the main train station for national and international rail travel.

The Rossio station serves such places as Queluz and Sintra. From Cais do Sodré, on the waterfront, electric trains make the run to and from Cascais.

Metro: There are four lines (blue, yellow, green and red). First train 6.30am, last train 1am. Check www. metrolisboa.pt for more information.

Funicular railways: Known locally as elevadores, these ancient trains and the panoramic views from the hilltop stations are a major tourist attraction.

Motoring Advice

There are numerous car hire companies at Lisbon airport and in the city. Avis, for example, has an office conveniently located in the garage of the Hotel Tivoli in the Avenida da Liberdade. Rental prices are cheaper than in most European countries. Petrol, however, is comparatively high.

The elevadores of Gloria and Lavra are located on either side of Praça dos Restauradores. The Elevador da Bica climbs up the hill from Rua de São Paulo (near Cais do Sodré station) to Bairro Alto.

By Road

Excellent service is provided cheaply by the numerous black-and-green cabs of Lisbon. A meter operates within the city, but it is switched off at Lisbon's city limits.

Bus/tram: Lisbon can be packed with traffic, but the buses and trams go everywhere at surprising speed – except during rush hours (avoid them). Open-top bus tours are available, and an antique tram makes daily 2-hour tours in summer from the Praça do Comércio.

Lisbon buses:
Scotturb, tel: 21-469 9100; www. scotturb.com
Carris, tel: 21-361 3054; www.carris. pt/en/home/

Waterways

To cross the Tejo, you can take the Vasco da Gama Bridge or a Transtejo ferry. Check the website (www.transtejo. pt) for more information.

PORTUGAL A–Z

Accommodation

The Portugal Hotel Guide, at www. maisturismo.pt, is a useful website for hotels and other services throughout the country. Posadas – hotels located in historic state-owned buildings – are an interesting alternative (tel: 218-442 001; email: guest@pousadas.pt; www.pousadas.pt).

Arts and Activities

Portugal has acquired global recognition for its melancholy fado music. A fashionable exponent of fado today is Marissa, with her bold, contemporary image. Also unique to Portugal is Manueline architecture, named after King Manuel I (1495–1521). which has a Gaudí-style appeal with its elaborate columns and flamboyant ornamentation. The tilework is similarly stunning and distinctive in Portugal, seemingly covering every surface. Throughout Portugal many museums are free on Sunday mornings. In addition to free travel, a LisboaCard provides free entry to many museums and sights, including several in nearby Sintra.

The card is sold at the Lisbon tourist offices and Carris kiosks.

Lisbon

The best place to listen to authentic fado is in the Alfama region, although choose carefully, as some fado houses are unabashedly geared to tourists. There are some fabulous examples of Manueline architecture, including the soaring extravaganza of Lisbon's Mosteiro dos Jerónimos. For the best tilework head for the Museu Nacional do Azulejo (see page 370).

Budgeting for Your Trip

Portugal remains one of the cheapest countries in Western Europe, particularly if you travel out of season, when many hotels dramatically reduce their rates. Approximate costs: A beer/coffee €1/0.80c; glass of house wine €1; main course at a budget/moderate/expensive restaurant €5/€8/€12; cheap/ moderate/de luxe hotel double room €35/€50–65/€80 upwards; museum entry €2.50.

The **LisboaCard** gives free access on all public transport and free entrance to museums and monuments. Available in three tariffs (children half-price): 24 hours €17; 48 hours €27; or 1 week €33.50.

Children

The most popular destination for children is likely to be the beach.

The beaches of the Algarve, with long, sandy, gently shelving beaches for small children and small rocky coves ideal for older children to explore, are perfect for family holidays. Pay attention to the beach warning flags, however. Green means the sea is calm and a lifeguard is on duty; green plus a checked flag means that no lifeguard is on duty; yellow stipulates no swimming; red means danger and warns bathers to stay ashore.

The top attraction in Lisbon for children is the Parque das Nações with its splendid aquarium (Oceanário de Lisboa), playgrounds, fountains, paddleboats and aerial cable cars.

Portugal dos Pequeninos, in Coimbra (see page 374), is a theme park of miniatures of Portugal's famous buildings, while the Monumento Natural das Pegadas dos Dinossáurios near Fátima will thrill the children with its dinosaur footprints.

The Algarve has a number of theme parks, zoos and water parks, including Aquashow near

AUSTRIA
BELGIUM
FRANCE
GERMANY
GREECE
ITALY
NETHERLANDS
PORTUGAL
SPAIN
SWITZERLAND

Emergency Numbers

All emergencies: 112
Fire: 213 422 222
Ambulance (Red Cross): 219 421 111

Quarteira Semino Slide & Splash, near Lagoa, and Aqualand – The Big One near Alcantarilha, reputedly Europe's largest. Another attraction is Zoomarine, a theme park with performing dolphins and sea lions, a parrot show, fairground rides and swimming pools.

Climate

Portugal's climate is kind, especially in the exceptionally sunny Algarve, where summers are warm and winters mild. Lisbon and the Alentejo, especially, can be uncomfortably hot in summer. Further north the weather can be cold in winter, especially in the mountains.

Disabled Travellers

Portugal is not the best when it comes to facilities for the disabled, although most museums and popular sights will have wheelchair ramps and disabled toilets and the airports and main train stations are similarly equipped. Special parking spaces are also increasing in city and town centres. Useful associations here include ACAPO (Association for the Blind and Partially Sighted), Rua de San José 86, 1st floor, Lisbon, tel: 21-342 2001; (www.portuguese alliance.com).

Eating Out

Portuguese cuisine is true to its origins, the food of fishermen and farmers. Traditional dishes are found in both expensive restaurants and the simplest of cafés. But the Portuguese can also be very inventive; you're likely to sample combinations like clams and pork, sole and bananas, or pork and figs.

Seafood fans are in luck in Portugal, with a surfeit of freshly caught fish and shellfish. The humble but noble Portuguese sardine is an inexpensive standard, especially down south, and with a hunk of local rustic bread and a bottle of house wine, you can still feast well on a small budget. Note that it's not a good idea to order a seafood or fish dish on a Monday as, traditionally, Portuguese fishing fleets have a day

off on Sundays, so your "catch-of-the-day", is more likely to be a couple of days old.

Portions in Portuguese restaurants tend to be rather large. You can also ask for a half-portion *(uma meia dose)* which is usually charged at around two-thirds of the full price.

Some of the best dishes are regional stews – the *ensopadas* of the Alentejo, *caldeiradas* of the Algarve and *açordas* of Estremadura. These dishes are found in restaurants all over the country. Also don't miss the sweet treats – in particular, the delicious custard tarts *(pastéis de nata)*.

Many restaurants and cafés offer an *ementa turística* – tourist menu. The term does not, however, imply a poor-grade international tourist meal. Rather, it is an economically priced set meal – typically bread, butter, soup, main course and dessert. Another inexpensive option at many restaurants and cafés is the *prato do dia* (dish of the day). Be wary of the *couvert* (cover) which is brought to the table at the beginning of a meal and usually comprises cream cheese, fish paste, olives and bread. This is not free and will generally cost from between €2 to a hefty €4 per person; you can send it back if you like.

Embassies and Consulates

Lisbon
Australia: Avenida da Liberdade 198–200, 2nd Floor 1–4, tel: 21-310 1500.
Ireland: Rua da Imprensa a Estrela 1–4, tel: 21-3929 440.
Canada: Avenida da Liberdade 198–200, 3rd Floor, tel: 21-316 400.
South Africa: Avenida Luis Bivar 10, Lisbon, tel: 21-319 2200.

BELOW: Lisbon's trams wind their way around the steep, narrow streets.

UK: Rua de São Bernardo, 33, tel: 21-392 4000.
US: Avenida das Forças Armadas, 16, tel: 21-727 3300.

All embassies are listed in the Lisbon phone book under the word *Embaixada*, or consult Ministério dos Negócios Estrangeiros, Palácio das Necessidades, tel: 21-394 6000.

Festivals

February–March: Funchal, Loulé, Nazaré, Ovar, Torres Vedras: biggest carnivals (Mardi Gras), but there are processions and fireworks everywhere with superb flamboyant costumes. Lisbon: Fado Festival at various sites at Carnival time.
March–April: Braga: Pilgrimage to Bom Jesus is the largest of many Holy Week processions.
May: Barcelos: Feast of the Crosses music concerts and a spectacular display of fireworks on the River Cávado (first weekend). Algarve: International Music Festival throughout month at various sites.
June–July: Lisbon: Festival of music, dance and theatre all month, with lots of live music and special arts activities. Fairs and festivities for the People's Saints, honouring St Anthony (13 June), St John (24 June) and St Peter (29 June). Vila do Conde: Festa do Corpo de Deus procession in the Old Town's streets strewn with flowers. Vila Franca de Xira: running of bulls in the streets (first two Sundays of July).
July–August: Estoril/Cascais: Estoril International Music Festival.
August: Guimarães: "Festas Gualterianas", three-day festival dating from the 15th century, with religious torchlight processions, bands, folk dance groups and colourful medieval parade (4–6 August). Viana do Castelo: Festa da Nossa Senhora da Agonia (Our Lady of Agony Festivities), famous religious festival with traditional costumes (weekend nearest to the 20th).
September: Lamego: festivities honouring Nossa Senhora dos Remédios, annual pilgrimage to Baroque shrine, with torchlight procession, folklore festival, fairs and fireworks, ending with triumphal procession (6–9 September). Nazaré: Nossa Senhora da Nazaré (Our Lady of Nazaré): fishermen carry an image of the town's patron saint in processions; also bullfights, fairs, concerts, folk dancing and singing (second week September).
October: Fátima: last pilgrimage of year (12–13 October). Vila Franca de Xira: lively October Fair that

Nightlife

Nightlife in Portugal means different things to different people. In Lisbon, try the Bairro Alto and Alfama quarters for *fado* (Portuguese folk music), although authentic *fado* can also be heard in the Alcântara district near the river. Tickets for concerts and sports events can be had at the ABEP kiosk, Praça dos Restauradores.

For a list of just about everything going on in the cities and larger towns consult the *Agenda Cultural Lisboa* website (www.agendalx.pt)

includes bull-running and bullfights (first two weeks).
December: Lisbon: Bolsa de Natal Christmas markets throughout the city.

Gay and Lesbian Travellers

In a country heavily influenced by the Catholic Church, attitudes towards gays are not as tolerant as elsewhere in Europe. Lisbon is the most important city in Portugal's gay scene and offers a number of bars and clubs catering to a gay crowd. In certain enclaves of the Algarve, such as "the Strip" in Albufeira, gay visitors will find accommodating bars and restaurants. The website, www.portugalgay.pt, contains a travel guide for gays and lesbians, with information in English and other languages.

Health and Medical Care

Medical Services

In Lisbon, a rota of emergency, night service and Sunday schedules are posted on the door of all pharmacies. If you can't find one, dial 118 for the *Farmácias de serviço*. Hospitals are mostly big and chronically overfull. Some visitors head for the **British Hospital**, 49 Rua Saraiva de Carvalho, tel: 21-394 3100, which also offers dental care. When you need the police, an ambulance or the fire brigade, tel: 112.

Opening Hours

Most stores open for business Mon–Fri 9am–1pm and about 3–7pm. Stores are open Sat 9am–1pm, and closed Sun and holidays. Major banks open Mon–Fri 8.30am–3pm and are closed Sat, Sun and holidays.

Lisbon

Most shops open Mon–Fri 9am–1pm and 3–7pm, Sat mornings only.

Offices often start later and finish earlier. Major banks open Mon–Fri 8.30am–3pm.

Postal Services

Most post offices (called CCT) are open Mon–Fri 9am–6pm; smaller branches close for lunch 12.30–2.30pm. In larger cities, the main branch may be open at weekends.

Lisbon

Most post offices are open Mon–Fri 8.30am–6pm. The central post office at Praça dos Restauradores is open 8am–midnight, and offers the best service to tourists.

Public Holidays

January: 1 New Year's Day; **February/March**: variable Mardi Gras; **March/April**: variable Good Friday/Easter Sun/Mon; **April**: 25 Freedom Day; **May**: 1 Labour Day; **May/June**: variable Corpus Christi; **June**: 10 Portugal Day, 24 St John's Day; **August**: 15 Assumption Day; **October**: 5 Republic Day; **November**: 1 All Saints' Day; **December**: 1 Restoration Day, 8 Immaculate Conception, 25 Christmas Day, 26 St Stephen's Day.

Shopping

Portuguese handicrafts range from wicker furniture to blankets and rugs to hand-carved toothpicks. The most famous Portuguese handicrafts include ceramic tiles *(azulejos)* and pottery, Arraiolos rugs and embroidery and lace work. In Lisbon, the Baixa quarter is good for shopping and, of course, the Vila Nova de Gaia is the place to visit for the port wine lodges, where you can taste the port and pick up a bottle. *Fado* music is also a good buy here, and easy to find in most music shops.

Telecommunications

Mobile phone usage is extensive, and you can pick up a prepaid SIM card from the major operators (Vodafone, TMN and Optimus), which you can insert into a GSM mobile phone. If you are planning to use public phone boxes, invest in a telephone card (€5) which has an access and key-in number. You can also make calls – international and local – from post offices. In Lisbon, there is also a phone office in Rossio, open every day 9am–11pm; in Oporto, there is one in Praça da Liberdade.

To reach an English-speaking international operator, tel: 098 (international service) or 099 (European service).

There are hotspots for wireless broadband in the major centres. Internet cafés are also fairly common and typically charge around €2–2.50 an hour. The tourist office can provide you with a list.

Dialling Codes

The international access code is 00. After this, dial the country code: Australia 61; UK 44; US/Canada 1.

To call Portugal from overseas, get an international line then tel: 351, followed by 21 for Lisbon. Inside Portugal, Lisbon's code is 021.

Tipping

A tip of between 5–10 percent is normal for service in restaurants and for taxi drivers.

Tourist Information

For general information, visit www.visitportugal.com.
Lisbon Airport tourism service, tel: 218-450 660.

Lisbon

Turismo de Lisboa: Tel: info line 21-346 3314, brochure line: 21-031 2810; email: info@atlx.pt; www.askmelisboa.com.
Lisboa Welcome Centre, Praça do Comércio, tel: 210-312810; 9am–8pm.
Palacio Foz, Praça dos Restauradores, tel: 213-463 314; 9am–8pm.
Airport (Arrivals), tel: 218-450 660; 7am–midnight.
Santa Apolónia railway station, tel: 218-821 606; Wed–Sat 8am–1pm.

Tourist Offices Abroad

Canada: Suite 1005, 60 Bloor Street West, Toronto, Ontario M4W 3B8, tel: 416-921 7376.
Ireland: 54 Dawson Street, Dublin, tel: 353-1670 9133.
South Africa: Mercantile Lisbon House, 142 West Street, Sandown 2196, Johannesburg, tel: 2711-302 0444.
UK: Portuguese Embassy, 11 Belgrave Square, London SW1X 8PP, tel: 020-7201 6666, 0845-355 1212.
US: 590 Fifth Ave, 4th Floor, New York, NY 10036, tel: 212-764 6137.

What to Read

Insight Guide Portugal is a companion volume to this book.

S PAIN

ESSENTIAL TRAVEL TIPS TO HELP YOU GET THERE AND GET AROUND

FACT FILE

Area: 505,955 sq km
(194,885 sq miles)
Capital: Madrid
Population: 46 million
Languages: Spanish (Castilian), plus
Catalan, Basque and Galician
Highest mountain: Mulhacén in
the Sierra Nevada 3,478 metres
(11,413 ft)
Religion: Roman Catholic
Time zone: Central European Time
Currency: The euro (€)
Electricity: AC 220 volts, two-pin
plugs
International dialling code: 34

TRANSPORT

Getting to Spain

By Air

The national carrier, **Iberia** (tel: UK
0870-609 0500, US 1-800-722
4642, Spain 902-400 500; www.iberia.
es), and many foreign airlines maintain
regular flights to more than 30
international airports in Spain. There
are also numerous foreign charter
companies that arrange periodic
flights to the country.
Iberia is allied with American
Airlines, Qantas, Avianca and British
Airways, and has a stake in the
Barcelona-based low-cost airline,
Clickair.
As one of Europe's most popular
and longest-established holiday
destinations, Spain is served by a
large number of European budget
airlines.

By Rail

There are train services linking
Spain to France, Italy, Portugal and
Switzerland. The national train
company is RENFE, tel: 902-240
202; international queries, tel:
902-243 402. In partnership with
other national railways, RENFE runs
Trenhotel, sleepers using the Talgo
high-speed trains named after
famous Spaniards. The Francisco
de Goya goes from Paris to Madrid,
Joan Miró from Paris to Barcelona,
Pau Casals from Zurich to Barcelona
and Salvador Dalí from Milan to
Barcelona.

By Road

Bordered by France and the
Principality of Andorra to the north
and Portugal to the west, Spain is
accessible via a number of European
motorways and other main roads.
Regular ferry services allow drivers to
enter the southern tip of Spain from
Morocco and the north at Santander
if coming from Great Britain. The main
motorways are: N-I (Madrid–Irun); N-II
(Madrid–Barcelona); N-III (Madrid–
Valencia); N-IV (Madrid–Andalucía);
N-V (Madrid–Extremadura); and N-VI
(Madrid–La Coruña).
By bus: The Estación del Sur de
Autobuses at Calle Méndez Alvaro
83 is Madrid's main bus station, and
most of the major bus companies
covering the long-distance routes
use this terminal.

By Sea

Various foreign shipping companies,
operating more than 50 scheduled
lines, bring passengers to Spain. **P&O
Ferries** from Portsmouth to Bilbao
takes around 36 hours, tel: 08716-
645 645; www.poferries.com.

Getting around Spain

By Air

Iberia operates a wide network of
routes within Spain, linking all the
main cities. **Iberia**'s main offices
are at Calle Velázquez 130, 28006
Madrid. For flight information and
reservations: Serviberia, tel: 902-400
500. You can buy an air ticket at any
travel agency.
Two domestic airlines based in
Mallorca are **Spanair**, a subsidiary
of SAS (tel: 902-131 415; www.spanair.
com), and **Air Europa**, (tel: 902-401
501; www.aireuropa.com).

By Rail

The Spanish national railway service
(Red Nacional de los Ferrocarriles
Españoles or RENFE) provides
extensive local service within the
country, with various types of trains:
Talgo, Inter-city, ELT (electric unit
expresses), TER (diesel rail cars), AVE
high-speed trains and ordinary semi-
fast and local trains. Supplementary
fares are levied on all express trains.
On expresses you must either have
a reserved seat or a ticket endorsed
at the station before getting on. For
travel information from RENFE, tel:
902-240 202; www.renfe.es.
Unlike the national services, the
regional trains between cities tend
to be slow. However, the Costa del
Sol between Málaga and Fuengirola
is served by an efficient commuter
service, every 20 minutes.

Public Transport

Spain has an excellent bus network,
cheaper and more frequent than
trains. On major routes and at holiday
times it is advisable to buy your ticket
a day or two in advance.

ABOVE: the beautifully renovated Estació de França in Barcelona.

By Road

The cities, towns and regions of Spain are linked with nearly 144,000km (90,000 miles) of roads and highways. If you take the minor roads, expect bad surfaces and large potholes. The number of toll roads is increasing, particularly in the north and east and around Madrid.

International car-hire chains have airport offices and offer collect and deliver services. Local companies are cheaper and will arrange to meet you on arrival if you book.

The following addresses and telephone numbers may be useful:
Real Automóvil Club de España, Alcalá 195, Madrid, tel: 902-404 545; www.race.es.
Real Automóvil Club de Catalunya, Avinguda Diagonal 687, tel: 902-414 143; www.racc.es.

Getting to Madrid

By Air

Most international airlines have flights to Madrid; the airport (Barajas) is 16km (10 miles) from the city centre. To get into the city from the airport, there is a bus service which runs regularly to the underground bus terminal at Avenida de América. For information about timetables, contact the Empresa Municipal de Transportes, tel: 902-507 850; www.emtmadrid.es.

If you are taking a taxi from the airport into Madrid, you should avoid unofficial cab drivers. Official Madrid taxis are white with red stripes painted transversally across the doors. An additional fee will be added to the fare as an airport surcharge, and each large piece of luggage will also be charged for. On Sunday, holidays and after 11pm, there is a further surcharge.

By Rail

The main train stations in Madrid are Chamartín station, Príncipe Pio (Norte) station and Atocha station. RENFE train information and reservations, tel: 902-240 202.

Known as Talgo Night, "hotel trains" leave Paris at 7.37pm and arrive in Madrid at 8.58am. There is a choice of premier-class private cabins, first-class private cabins and 4-bed standard-class cabins. Tel: 902-240 202 for details.

By Bus

The two main bus stations in Madrid are Estación Sur de Autobuses, tel: 914-684 200; www.estacionautobusesmadrid.com, and Auto Res, tel: 920-020 052.

By Car

The car journey from London and Northern Europe takes a minimum of 24 hours (in a fast car, without an overnight break). Allow 6 hours from the Spanish border at Irún to Madrid. Burgos is a good stop-off to visit the magnificent cathedral and eat well. You need a Green Card, log book and bail bond, and it's advisable to carry an International Driving Licence.

Motoring Advice

The roadside SOS telephones are connected to the nearest police station, which sends out a breakdown van with first-aid equipment. There is a small charge for work done and spare parts used. The automobile clubs of Spain are the Real Automóvil Club de España (RACE) and the Touring Club de España (TCE). See contact details above.

For information on road conditions, tel: 900-123 505 or 917-421 213; www.dgt.es.

Getting around Madrid

Public Transport

Metro: The quickest way of moving around the city, the metro runs 6am–1.30am. The 10 lines (120 stations) are labelled by number, colour and final destination. Bulk-buying tickets for 10 journeys saves up to 50 percent. You can get a metro map at the ticket booth.

For information, tel: 902-444 403; www.metromadrid.es.

Bus: More than 150 routes are covered by red-and-yellow air-conditioned buses, which run 6am–11.30pm. Tickets for both are a flat price. A reduced-price ticket for 10 journeys can be bought in an *estanco* (tobacconist/newspaper kiosk). Night services leave on the hour from Plaza de Cibeles. Buses for out-of-town trips, belonging to various private companies, go mainly from the Estación Sur de Autobuses in Calle Méndez Alvaro. For information, tel: 914-684 200.

For municipal bus information, tel: 902-507 850.

By Taxi

Taxis can be hailed with relative ease in main thoroughfares, found at a *Parada de Taxi* (taxi stand, indicated by a large white "T" against a dark-blue background) or requested by phone. For taxis, call Radio Teléfono Taxi, tel: 902-478 200; www.radiotelefono-taxi.com or Tele Taxi, tel: 902-501 130; www.tele-taxi.es.

SPAIN A–Z

Accommodation

Hotels in Spain are officially classified in five categories marked by stars, but this system tells you more about the amount of facilities an establishment has than its quality, atmosphere or charm. *Hostales* (one to three stars) and *pensiones* (one to two stars) are supposedly less comfortable and cheaper than hotels, but there are many exceptions to the rule, and it is not uncommon to find an exquisite, well-run *pensión* offering better-maintained facilities and more of a welcome than a 3-star hotel.

Note that when a major fiesta is on such as Seville's April Fair you will be lucky to find a room at short notice,

What's On

The most complete listings magazine for **Madrid** and other major cities is the *Guía del Ocio*, published every Friday or fortnightly. **Seville** has a useful entertainment guide, *El Giraldillo* (www.elgiraldillo.es). **Barcelona** also has a weekly *Guía del Ocio* (www.guiadelociobcn. es) and *Metropolitan* (www.barcelona-metropolitan.com), a free monthly magazine published in English with listings. It can be found in the Palau de la Virreina (La Rambla, 99), the city council's cultural information centre, also the best place to see what's on and purchase tickets.

and if you do, the cost of a room will be considerably more than at any other time of the year.

In general, there is a much better choice of hotel in the country than the big cities. Spain has undergone a "green tourism" revolution in the last 20 years, leaving it with a supply of charming rural or small-town hotels.

In a class of their own are the *Paradores*, a state-run chain of uniformly luxurious hotels often occupying historic buildings like converted castles and monasteries. Special deals out of season can make them surprisingly affordable, although the best get booked up well ahead.

For a complete list of hotels in Spain, pick up a copy of the current *Guía Oficial de Hoteles* from bookshops and newsstands.

Arts and Activities

Information on cultural activities can be obtained at national, local and city tourist offices. Among the great venues for concerts and opera are Barcelona's Gran Teatre del Liceu, Madrid's Teatro Real, Sevilla's Teatro de la Maestranza and Valencia's Palau de les Arts. *Zarzuela* theatre, a uniquely Spanish form of operetta incorporating music, dance, singing and dialogue, is also popular, particularly at its spiritual home of the Teatro de la Zarzuela in Madrid.

For concerts, Madrid's Auditorio Nacional de Música is home to the Spanish National Orchestra. Check with local tourist offices for details of concerts and recitals elsewhere. They often take place in historic surroundings, especially during the summer months.

Madrid

A **Madrid Card** gives entry to 40 museums from the Prado to the Wax Museum, plus a tour of the Bernabéu Stadium, the cable car, the nature theme park, IMAX, the Madrid Visión tourist bus, with discounts in over 100 establishments involved in various activities, such as eating, shopping and leisure (www.madridcard.com).

Tickets for plays, concerts, films, bullfights and football matches can be bought at Taquilla Último Minuto, Plaza del Carmen 1, tel: 902-876 426. Tickets for bullfights and football games only are sold at the small stores and booths set up along Calle Victoria, a small street off the Puerta del Sol.

Concerts, dance and recitals can be enjoyed throughout the year in the capital. The main venues are the **Teatro Real** (Pl. de Oriente s/n, tel: 91-516 0660; www.teatro-real. com), the **Auditorio Nacional de Música** (Príncipe de Vergara 146, tel: 91-337 0100; www.auditorionacional. mcu.es) and the **Teatro de la Zarzuela** (Jovellanos 4, tel: 91-524 5400; www. teatrodelazarzuela.mcu.es).

The exquisite small central **Teatro Español** (Príncipe 25, tel: 91-360 1484; www.esmadrid.com/teatroespanol) and its new second venue, **El Matadero** (Paseo de la Chopera 12, tel: 91-177 309; www.mataderomadrid. com), offer excellent world theatre. *Zarzuela* (light opera) is a Spanish genre which you can see in the Auditorio Nacional and the Teatro de la Zarzuela, and other Madrid theatres (check press for details).

You can purchase tickets at the venues themselves (check local press for opening hours of individual box offices, as they may vary), in the FNAC building (Preciados 28, tel: 91-595 6100) or by phone from Tel-Entradas (tel: 902-101 212; www.telentradas.com).

Barcelona

Barcelona has a full agenda of cultural activities throughout the year, though it dwindles slightly in August when most locals escape the city.

The opera house, **Gran Teatre del Liceu** (La Rambla 51–59, tel: 93-485 9913; bookings are made through Servicaixa, tel: 902-533 353; www.liceubarcelona.com) rose from the ashes of a devastating fire as a fully modernised theatre on a par with the best European opera houses, offering more productions including recitals, ballet and opera for children.

The two key venues for classical music are **L'Auditori**, which offers a broad programme including family

concerts (Plaça de les Arts; www. auditori.com) and the magnificent *modernista* **Palau de la Música Catalana** (Palau de la Música 4–6, tel: 902 442 882; www.palaumusica.org).

The main venues are the **Teatre Nacional**, a vast Neoclassical building near L'Auditori (Plaça de les Arts; www. tnc.es) and the **Teatre Lliure** (Plaça Margarida Xirgu; www.teatrelliure.com) for more avant-garde productions, as well as several small alternative spaces where there is more chance of catching an international production. **The Mercat de les Flors** (Lleida 59; www.mercatflors.org) is a vibrant centre for dance and movement which always has an interesting programme.

Budgeting for Your Trip

Allow €50 upwards per day for two persons for the least expensive accommodation, which will generally be in an *hostal*; €35 per person per day upwards for basic meals or tapas. Wine or spirits will obviously push this up. Public transport is generally inexpensive in Spain: allow around €10 for local bus and train and (where applicable) metro travel.

Children

Long, sunny days and soft, safe, sandy beaches mean that coastal Spain is a favourite family destination. Many hotels have special features for junior guests, ranging from organised poolside games and outings to babysitting facilities. When sea water and sandcastles start to wear thin, you can try some of the following: **Make a splash**. Water parks are a highly popular alternative. While kids shoot down waterslides and ride the machine-made waves, parents can top off their tans in landscaped gardens. Additional attractions often include bowling and mini-golf.

Go-karting. A favourite with the children (not to mention their parents), go-kart tracks are common along the Costas and in the islands.

A night out. The Spanish take their children out at night, so why not do likewise? Older children will probably enjoy a colourful flamenco show, and there are no restrictions on children accompanying adults into bars, restaurants or cafés, as long as they are well behaved.

Fiesta. Older children will love the firework displays and music, while the younger ones watch wide-eyed as dancers and giant papier-mâché figures perform. Carnival is always a colourful event, where the local children usually wear the best and most innovative costumes. Larger fiestas often have special entertainment for children.

Fair rides. Most big cities or resorts have a *parque de atracciones* where the rides range from the old-fashioned carousel and big wheel to high-tech thrills. Barcelona's funfair at Tibidabo, accessible by funicular railway, deserves a special mention for its old-fashioned rides and tremendous views.

Theme parks. Spain's biggest theme parks are Port Aventura on the Costa Dorada, Terra Mítica near Benidorm, Isla Mágica in Seville and Warner Brothers Movie World outside Madrid, but there are many more, and transport to them is often laid on from resort hotels.

Climate

As a general rule, late spring to early summer and late summer to early autumn are the best times for visiting most parts of Spain. This avoids the most oppressive heat, not to mention the crowds and high-season hotel rates. In winter, temperatures plummet in the high central plains.

Summer temperatures in the north are ideal for swimming and sunbathing, but expect rain any time in the northwest. At the height of summer (July–August) even the locals try to escape the dry, merciless heat of Madrid and the central plains; the southern and eastern coast areas can be uncomfortably humid.

For winter sun, the south coast and parts of the central and southeastern coast are pleasantly mild all year, but swimming is not really an option in winter. Of course, winter is the season for skiing in the Pyrenees and Andalucía's Sierra Nevada.

Disabled Travellers

Overall, facilities for disabled visitors are limited, although public transport is increasingly wheelchair-friendly, and major sights are required by law to provide wheelchair access. Restaurants are gradually introducing toilets that are disabled-friendly. Organisations that can provide more information include:

Mobility Abroad, UK tel: 0871-288 0888; www.mobilityabroad.com provides support and hire of wheelchairs and disabled-friendly vehicles throughout the Costa del Sol, Costa Blanca and Mallorca areas.

Once, tel: 915-068 888; www.once.es is the Spanish association for the blind.

ECOM, tel: 934-515 550; www.ecom. es is a federation of private Spanish organisations that provide services.

Eating Out

The Spanish take their food very seriously, and you will rarely be disappointed by the variety and flavour of the hearty portions served in local *restaurantes* throughout Spain. Each region has its own distinctive culinary strengths, from the seafood creations of the north to the rice platters of the east, from the roasts of the central area to the succulent hams and fried fish of the south. And for every dish, there is usually a locally grown wine to match.

Venta, posada, mesón, casa de comidas and *fonda* are all synonyms for restaurant. Many bars also double as restaurants, serving both tapas and full meals. The menu will be displayed outside or at the door, giving an idea of what you can expect to pay.

Most restaurants offer a good-value *menú del día* (daily special).

Emergency Numbers

National Police: 091
Municipal Police: 092
Emergencies: Call 112 and ask for *una ambulancia* (ambulance) or *los bomberos* (the fire department)

This is normally a three-course meal, including house wine, at a reasonable set price, although it may only be available at lunchtime.

The prices on the menu include a service charge and taxes, but it is customary to leave a tip of 5 to 10 percent if you have been served efficiently. Bars and cafés, like restaurants, usually include a service charge, but additional small tips of a few coins are customary. Prices are slightly lower if you stand or sit at the bar rather than occupy a table.

Two notes of caution: the prices of tapas, those tasty bar snacks, are not always indicated and can be surprisingly expensive: it is not unusual for the cost of several tapas to equate to or exceed the price of the *menú del día*. Also, ask how much your meal will cost when ordering fish or seafood that is priced by the 100g weight. The price is based on the uncooked weight and can be more than you expected.

Mealtimes are generally later in Spain than in most parts of Europe. Peak hours are 2–3.30pm for lunch and 9–11pm for dinner. However, in tourist areas or big cities, you can get a meal at most places just about any time of day.

Embassies and Consulates

Madrid

Australia: Torre Espacio, Paseo de la Castellana, tel: 913-536 600.
Canada: Núñez de Balboa 35, tel: 914-233 250.
Ireland: Paseo de la Castellana 46, tel: 914-364 093.
New Zealand: Pinar 7, tel: 915 230 226.
South Africa: Claudio Coello 91, tel: 914-363 780.
UK: Torre Espacio, Paseo de la Castellana, tel: 917-146 300.
US: Calle Serrano 75, tel: 915-872 200.

Festivals

The best way to experience Spanish customs is to watch a fiesta (festival), held in honour of the local patron saint and offering locals the chance to dress up in costume, dance through the night, let off firecrackers or run

BELOW: tapas originated in the south but are now popular in bars all over Spain.

with bulls. Every community, whatever its size, has its own fiesta – with the larger towns and cities often celebrating more than one. Check with the tourist office for details of local celebrations during your stay. Here's a selection of the very best from around the country:

February/March: Carnival before the beginning of Lent. Processions in Santa Cruz de Tenerife, Cádiz, Sitges and many other places.

March/April: Las Fallas Festival in Valencia, with the setting alight of hundreds of papier-mâché figures. Semana Santa (Holy Week). Processions of hooded penitents in all major cities from Palm Sunday until Easter Sunday, with the most famous in Seville.

April: Seville's famous Feria (Spring Fair) with colourful costume parades, plenty of *sevillana* music and bullfights. In Alcoi on the Costa Blanca people stage mock battles between "Moors and Christians".

May: Festival of the Patios in Córdoba and International Horse Fair in Jerez de la Frontera.

May/June: Fiesta de San Isidro: bullfighting, concerts and funfairs in Madrid. Corpus Christi: festivities everywhere, especially in Granada, Toledo, Sitges and the Canary Islands. El Rocío pilgrimage in Andalucía.

July: Fiesta de San Fermín: bull runs, bullfights and festivities in Pamplona. Festival of the Virgen del Carmen, patroness of fishermen. Festival of St James, Santiago de Compostela, with firework displays and bonfires.

August: Assumption: national holiday on 15 August with numerous towns holding festivals.

September: Logroño Wine Harvest: wine festival in Jerez de la Frontera. Mercè Festival: music and folklore in Barcelona.

October: Pilar Festival: processions, bullfights and folklore in Zaragoza.

Gay and Lesbian Travellers

There are plenty of gay- and lesbian-friendly hotels, clubs and bars, as well as resorts, such as Torremolinos (Costa del Sol) and Sitges (Costa Brava), that cater specifically for a gay clientele. There are several gay internet sites relating to Spain, including www.universogay.com and www.gayinspain.com.

Health and Medical Care

Medical Services

Spain has countless chemist shops or *farmacias*, each identifiable by

ABOVE: Spanish nightlife usually starts in a bar before it's time for a late dinner.

a big, white sign with a flashing green cross. They are open Mon–Fri 9.30am–1.30pm and 5–8pm, Sat 9am–1.30pm.

Madrid

A green or red cross identifies a chemist *(farmacia)*. Outside shop hours, go to a *farmacia de guardia*, listed in chemists' windows and in newspapers.

If you need emergency medical treatment you will be taken to the *Urgencias* (casualty) at a large hospital or the local *Ambulatorios*, which are open 24 hours a day (addresses can be found in the windows of pharmacies and in the newspapers).

The Unidad Médica **Anglo-American (Anglo-American Medical Unit)**, Calle Conde de Aranda 1, tel: 914-351 823; www.unidadmedica.com gives bilingual attention 9am–8pm Monday to Friday and 10am–1pm Saturday.

Language

The national language of Spain, Castilian Spanish *(castellano)*, is spoken throughout the country. But it is estimated that two out of every five Spaniards speak another language primarily, and by preference, and this trend has been especially marked since the decentralisation of a great many political powers to the regions. The inhabitants of the Basque Country, Galicia, Catalonia and the Valencia region and the Balearic Islands speak Euskara, Gallego, Catalan and variants of Catalan, respectively.

English is widely spoken in the resort towns, though it is polite to learn at least a few basic phrases of Spanish.

Nightlife

Since Spaniards don't start thinking about their dinner until 9 or 10pm, Spanish nightlife tends to begin later and keep going far later than in other countries. The most popular first stop is a "pub" or *bar de copas* – a bar playing loud music with few places to sit down. Only around 2am do people decide to move on to a club. Barcelona is one of the most fashionable nightspots in Europe. Madrid is the city that never sleeps, and Ibiza is the leader of Europe's clubbing scene.

Opening Hours

Shops are open 9.30am or 10am–1.30 or 2pm and then reopen again in the afternoon from 4.30 or 5pm–8pm, or a little later in summer. Most are closed on Saturday afternoons and all day Sunday. However, major department stores are open without interruption six days a week 10am–9pm, and frequently on Sunday.

Banking: Hours vary slightly from one bank to another. Most open Mon–Fri 8.30 or 9am–2pm and Sat 9am–12.30 or 1pm. All are closed Sunday and holidays. Several banks keep major branches in the business districts open until 6pm.

Madrid

Shops are open Mon–Fri 9.30 or 10am–1.30 or 2pm and then reopen again in the afternoon from 4.30 or 5–8pm, or a little later in summer. Most are closed on Saturday afternoon and Sunday. However, the major department stores like El Corte Inglés and Galerías Preciados are open without interruption six days a week, 10am–9pm, and frequently on Sunday, despite the protests of small shopkeepers.

Postal Services

The few existing district post offices are only open Mon–Fri 9am–2pm, Sat 9am–1pm and are closed Sunday. Principal post offices are open 9am–2pm and 4–7pm for general services. Post boxes are painted yellow and in two parts – one marked *ciudad* (for local mail) and the other marked *provincias y extranjero* (for the rest of the country and abroad). Stamps are sold at post offices and at the *estancos*, or tobacconist shops.

Madrid

Post offices (*correos*) open Mon–Fri 9am–2pm and Sat until 1pm. You can buy stamps in an *estanco* and use either a yellow or red (express) post box. The ornate central Palacio de Comunicaciones, in Calle Alcalá opposite Cibeles fountain (Mon–Fri 8am–midnight), is much faster than other post offices. Most hotels have a fax service and Wi-fi internet connection. For more information, contact the Spanish postal service website, www.correos.es.

Public Holidays

January: 1 New Year's Day, 6 Epiphany; **March**: 19 St Joseph's Day (San José); **March/April**: variable Maundy Thursday/Good Friday; **May**: 1 Labour Day; **May/June**: variable Corpus Christi; **July**: 25 St James's Day (San Diego); **August**: 15 Assumption Day; **October**: 12 National Day; **November**: 1 All Saints' Day; **December**: 8 Immaculate Conception, 25 Christmas Day. Each autonomous community has its own public holiday on a particular day.

Shopping

Well-known Spanish souvenirs include *damasquino* jewellery, knives and swords from Toledo; ceramics from Toledo, Valencia, Granada and Seville; filigree silver from Córdoba; *botas* (wineskin), castanets, Spanish dolls and bullfighting posters.

Madrid

Madrid offers visitors every shopping possibility from all the regions of Spain. For craftwork, leather goods, footware and furniture, try the state-run Artespaña shop (Hermosilla 14) and the craft and ceramic shops around Calle Mayor. Department stores and tourist shops are in the centre between Puerta del Sol and Plaza Callao, and along the Gran

Vía. Select shops and international boutiques line Calle Serrano and its adjoining streets in the Salamanca area. Designer shops are in Calle Almirante, just off Paseo de Recoletos. The streets directly to the west of Almirante lead into one of Madrid's crime zones.

Telecommunications

There are coin- and card-operated telephone booths (*cabinas*) throughout cities and larger towns and usually on the main square of smaller towns and villages. Wait for the tone, deposit the necessary coins and dial the number. For long-distance calls you may need to insert several coins before dialling.

You can also purchase a phone card in various denominations at any *estanco*. This is by far the easiest option for calling internationally, although you will have to put up with street noise. You might be better looking for a Telefónica (the Spanish telephone company) office, or a privately run telephone shop (*locutorio*) where you talk in a private booth first and pay later. If you call from your hotel room, you will be charged considerably more than you would on a public phone.

To make a direct overseas call, first dial 00 and then wait for another dial tone before dialling the country and city codes. It is cheaper to call before 8am and after 10pm. There are no additional discounts at weekends.

If you need information, operator assistance or wish to reverse the charges, tel: 1408.

You can use a mobile phone in Spain as long as it conforms to GSM technology – which might rule out phones from the USA – and has roaming enabled

All major cities have at least one internet café, but these are gradually disappearing in favour of Wi-fi hotspots where you can use your own laptop. Several hotels now offer free Wi-fi internet access.

Tipping

As a guideline, tipping is frequent in bars, *cafeterías* and restaurants (8–10 percent), taxis (5 percent), for cinema and theatre ushers, and bellboys (according to services rendered).

Tourist Information

The official tourist office website is www.spain.info.

Madrid

Plaza Mayor 3, tel: 913-665 477. Chamartín railway station, tel: 913-159 976.

Barajas Airport has several information counters throughout the four terminals. There are also tourist information counters in terminals 1 and 2.

The city tourist office website is www.esmadrid.com.

Tourist Offices Abroad

Canada: 2 Bloor Street West, Suite 3402 Toronto, Ontario M4W 3E2, tel: 416-961 3131.

UK: 2nd Floor, New Cavendish Street, London W1W 6XB, tel: 020-7317 2010.

US: 665 Fifth Avenue, New York City, NY 10103, tel: 212-265 8822; 845 N. Michigan Avenue, Suite 915, Chicago, IL 60611, tel: 312-642 1992; 8383 Wilshire Boulevard, Suite 960, 90211 Beverly Hills, CA, tel: 323-658 7195.

What to Read

Other books in the *Insight Guide* series highlighting destinations in this region include *Insight Guide: Spain* and *Northern Spain*, *Insight Regional Guide: Southern Spain* and *Insight City Guides: Madrid* and *Barcelona*.

The *Insight Smart Guide Barcelona* packs information into an easily portable and convenient format arranged in handy A–Z sections. *Insight Step by Step Barcelona* highlights the best walks and tours the city has to offer, with itineraries for all tastes.

BELOW: innovative footwear.

S WITZERLAND

ESSENTIAL TRAVEL TIPS TO HELP YOU GET THERE AND GET AROUND

FACT FILE

Area: 41,285 sq km
(15,935 sq miles)
Capital: Bern (pop. 126,000)
Population: 7.7 million (with 21
percent foreigners)
Languages: Swiss-German (62.7
percent), French (20.4 percent),
Italian (6.5 percent), Romansch (0.5
percent), other languages (9 percent)
Highest mountain: Not the
Mattherhorn 4,478 metres (14,692ft)
but the Dufourspitze/Monte Rosa
4,634 metres (15,202 ft)
Religion: Catholic (42 percent),
Protestant (35 percent), Muslim
(4 percent)
Time zone: Central European Time
Currency: Swiss franc (SFr)
Electricity: AC 230 volts, two-pin
plugs
International dialling code: 41

TRANSPORT

Getting to Switzerland

By Air

The five international airports in
Switzerland are: Zürich, Geneva,
Basel, Lugano and Bern. Swiss
International Air Lines connects
Switzerland with 90 cities in 42
countries. The airports in Zürich and
Geneva have their own train stations
which are part of the national fast-
train network; frequent trains each
hour run between the airport stations
and the main railway station and
other destinations. Basel-Mulhouse
Airport is situated in France; the

journey by bus from here to the Swiss
train station in Basel SBB takes
about 25 minutes. There are regular
connections between the Zürich,
Basel and Geneva international
airports. Other airports with regular
and/or charter airlines as well as
local air-taxi services include Berne-
Belp, Lugano-Agno, Gstaad-Saanen,
Sion and Samedan-St Moritz airfields.

The national carrier is **Swiss
International Air Lines** (www.swiss.
com). Its offices abroad include:
UK: tel: 0845-601 0956 (no walk-in
office); www.swiss.com/uk.

Fly-Rail Services

With "Fly-Rail Baggage", train
passengers don't have to lug
their baggage around the airport
any more. Instead, it is unloaded
from planes arriving at Zürich and
Geneva and forwarded by train
directly to its destination point
(in 76 train stations, mostly in
cities and the larger holiday resort
areas). The same service applies
for the return trip: you can send
your baggage – up to 24 hours in
advance – directly through to your
hometown airport from the town
where you've been staying.

Travellers may also check in at
over 50 train stations (including
Basel, Berne, Geneva, Lausanne,
Lugano, Luzern, Neuchâtel, St
Gallen and Zürich) and obtain a
boarding pass up to 24 hours prior
to departure.

The service is offered from
any airport around the world, no
matter which airline you fly. Further
information from SBB, www.mct.sbb.
ch/mct/en.

US: JFK International Airport Terminal
4, tel: 1-877-FLY-SWISS,
1-877-359-7947 (24 hours);
www.swiss.com/usa.

By Rail

Intercity and some high-speed trains
connect Switzerland with large cities
in surrounding countries. Intercity,
fast and regional trains link the cities
and towns with all cities and most
holiday resort areas; the few that are
not on the railway, such as Adelboden
and Saas Fee, have frequent bus
connections. For further information
contact **Switzerland Tourism
offices**. In London the **Switzerland
Travel Centre** sells rail and PostBus
tickets and passes: 30 Bedford
Street, London WC2E 9ED, tel: 020-
7420 4908; email: sales@stc.ch; www.
swisstravelsystem.com.

By Road

Although not a member of the EU,
Switzerland is part of the Schengen
area, so travellers can enter
Switzerland by car and train from all
neighbouring countries without the
formality of border controls.
Motoring advice: Motor vehicles
weighing up to 3.5 tonnes (including
trailers and caravans) are charged
SFr40 per year for what is commonly
referred to as the *motorway
vignette* (a sticker you place on your
windscreen that permits you to drive
on Swiss motorways). This is valid
from 1 December to 31 January (14
months). They can be purchased at
borders, post offices, petrol stations
and garages in Switzerland and in
other countries from automobile
associations, Switzerland Tourism
offices and online at www.myswitzerland.
com. The sticker should be fixed to

the left edge of the vehicle's front windscreen. Hire cars come with a valid vignette. A caravan requires an extra vignette.

Getting around Switzerland

Public Transport

There are many scenic boat and train rides, and transport is coordinated by **the Swiss Travel System**, www. swisstravelsystem.ch. The most flexible of a range of passes is the **Swiss Pass**, which offers 4, 8, 15 and 22 days or one month's unlimited travel over the Swiss Travel System's rail, bus and boat network; and discounts are offered on the few mountain railways and cable cars that it does not cover. The **Swiss Flex Pass** confers 3, 4, 5 or 6 days' unlimited travel within a month and half-price travel on other days. The Swiss Pass also confers free entry to more than 400 museums.

By Air

Generally speaking, people don't take internal flights in Switzerland, the businessman travelling by helicopter being the exception. The train service is so good and the main cities so close timewise that there's no advantage in flying.

However, if you want to experience the beauty and majesty of the Alps from above, the ideal way to travel, being "green" and peaceful, is by balloon. Balloon flights from Château d'Oex are organised by SkyEvent Ballons (tel: 26-924 2220; www.ballon chateaudoex.ch) or from Gstaad (tel: 26-924 3452; www.alpine-ballooning.com).

By Rail

More than 5,780km (3,400 miles) of dense, electrified railways open up the remotest sections of the country with trains every hour on most lines and every half-hour on the busiest. More than 100 trains call at Zürich Airport each day. For further information contact one of the Switzerland Tourism offices, located in many European countries and overseas.

Swiss Federal Railways is referred to by its initials, which vary between the official languages: SBB (German), CFF (French) and FFS (Italian). Over 100 trains have dining or bistro cars, and all long-distance trains have buffets or trolley refreshments in operation every day. If you plan to travel in a large party or during mealtimes, you'd be wise to reserve a table in advance when buying your tickets or passes.

By Road

Switzerland has a dense network of main and subsidiary roads covering over 64,600km (40,000 miles). Twenty-five major roads running through Alpine tunnels or over the passes form one of the main attractions for visitors; depending on the snow, they are open from May or June to late autumn. Special rail facilities are provided for motorists wishing to transport their cars through the tunnels.

More road information can be obtained from the Swiss National Tourist Office or one of the two Swiss Automobile clubs: **Automobile-Club der Schweiz** (ACS), Wasserwerkgasse 39, CH-3000 Berne 13, tel: 031-328 3111; www. acs.ch. **Swiss Touring Club** (TCS), Chemin de Blandonnet 4, CH-1214 Genève-Vernier, tel: 022-417 2424; www.tcs.ch.

Waterways

Regularly scheduled boats cruise all the big Swiss lakes. There are steam-driven paddlesteamers to put you in a nostalgic mood on Lake Geneva, Lake Zürich, Lake Brienz and Lake Luzern. It's also possible to take a trip along the Rhine, Rhône, Aare and Doubs rivers. Details from tourist offices.

By Coach

The Alpine PostBus (PTT) network takes travellers over the principal mountain roads and covers 9,800km (6,090 miles). The buses are all modern and comfortable. Conducted tours by rail, PostBus or private bus are regularly organised in many towns and resorts. The local tourist office can supply all necessary details.

SWITZERLAND A–Z

Accommodation

There are around 5,000 hotels, motels, pensions, youth hostels, mountain sanatoria and health resorts in Switzerland. Holiday apartments and bed-and-breakfast establishments have grown in popularity. For more information and brochures, contact **Switzerland Tourism**, Tödistrasse 7, 8027 Zürich, tel: 044-288 1111; www.myswitzerland. com, or one of the Switzerland Tourism offices abroad.

The *Swiss Hotel Guide*, published online by the Swiss Hotel Association (www.swisshotels.com) is another useful source of information. Further details can be found in the free regional and local hotel listings, available from regional tourist associations.

Arts and Activities

Switzerland Tourism publishes an annual calendar of events including complete details on music festivals, art exhibitions, sightseeing, as well as a listing of more than 100 museums and art collections open to the public.

Museum Pass

The Swiss Museum Pass (adults SFr 144) enables visitors to have free entry to more than 420 museums throughout Switzerland. The pass is valid for a year, and is obtainable, along with a planner/ museum directory, from participating museums. Note that unfortunately some of the main galleries (eg, in Zürich and Basel) are not included in the pass. Information is available at tourist offices, www.swisspasses.com or tel: 01-389 8456.

Concerts

All larger cities maintain at least one theatre and a symphony orchestra. There are performances by internationally acclaimed artists, and even the smaller outlying communities put on dramatic and musical events. In the concert scene, the leading venue currently is Luzern's spectacular Kultur and Kongress-zentrum (KKL) designed by France's Jean Nouvel. Zürich's Opera has an international reputation, and the late 19th-century building also hosts ballet. In general, the theatre and concert season begins in September and ends in June. In summer, highly acclaimed festivals take place in which distinguished musicians and conductors entertain music-lovers the world over. The best known of these take place at Lausanne, Zürich, Thun, Braunwald, Sion, Gstaad, Interlaken, Luzern, Ascona and Vevey.

Budgeting for Your Trip

It is a myth that Switzerland is expensive. Of course there are plenty of expensive hotels, restaurants and shops, but it is easy to find ways of saving money: choosing cheaper resorts or accommodation away from urban centres, eating at self-service buffets in chains such as Migros or the Coop, buying food to take up mountains (where the high overheads inevitably make Alpine restaurants expensive). A beer or glass of wine may cost around SFr 5.50, a main

AUSTRIA BELGIUM FRANCE GERMANY GREECE ITALY NETHERLANDS PORTUGAL SPAIN SWITZERLAND course SFr 20–50, a double room SFr 70–500, a taxi journey from Zürich Airport to the centre about SFr 50, and entry to a major museum about SFr 10–15.

Children

Switzerland is well geared up for young visitors, from family-friendly hotels and accommodation (www. kidshotels.ch and www.reka.ch) to special experiences, such as sleeping on straw in an Alpine cowshed (www. holiday-farms.ch), an igloo (wwww.iglu-dorf. ch) or a yurt (www.goldenpass.ch and click on Rochers-de-Naye). There are adventure playgrounds for all ages, railed toboggan runs (the longest in the world is at Churwalden, www. pradaschier.ch), scooters and monster bikes on which to freewheel down mountains on traffic-free paths, and major zoos at Basel, Bern, Langnau and Zürich. Children under 16 with their parents can use the Swiss Travel System for free.

Climate

Located in the centre of Europe, the Swiss climate is influenced by maritime and continental air masses. Summers are mostly warm at lower altitudes, although they can be quite wet with frequent thunderstorms. Winters are generally cold with plenty of cloud, snow and fog.

The high mountains mean great differences can occur within just a short distance – one valley can be sunny and dry while the next is shrouded in mist. The Ticino area bordering the Italian lakes is markedly warmer and sunnier than the rest of the country throughout the year.

Don't forget to bring along a warm fleece, raincoat, waterproof boots and an umbrella, even in the height of summer, and likewise, sunglasses and suntan lotion even in the depths of winter.

Disabled Travellers

Contact **Mobility International Schweiz** at Froburgstrasse 4, 4600 Olten, tel: 062-206 8835; www. mis-ch.ch. They provide a list of easy-access accommodation and a hiking brochure for those with mobility difficulties.

You can get information on special services on public transport for travellers with disabilities at most railway stations. In the UK, **Tourism For All** provides practical advice, support and information for disabled

travellers and their families; visit www.tourismforall.org.uk or tel: 0845-124 9971 for information.

Nautilus Reisen, Froburgstrasse 4, 4601 Olten, tel: 062-206 8830; www.nautilus.ch organises its own tours and arranges holiday bookings for the disabled.

A list of ski schools with professional assistance for the disabled is available at **Schweizerischer Zentralverein für das Blindenwesen**, Schützengasse 4, 9000 St Gallen, tel: 071-223 3636; www.szb.ch.

Eating Out

The French, German and Italian influences make for great variety in the three areas. Though the origins of the country's staple dishes are rustic, there is nothing basic about Swiss cuisine at its best; the country has more Michelin-starred restaurants per capita than any other country in Europe. But really good food needs seeking out, as there are plenty of restaurants that serve sustaining rather than refined dishes.

Best-known dishes include *fondue*, made with melted cheese and wine, into which speared bread is dipped; *rösti* – grated fried potatoes; *raclette* – hot cheese dribbled over potatoes and served with gherkins and pickled onions; in Ticino, saffron risotto and polenta made of cornmeal; and the now universal breakfast, muesli.

Lunch is served from 11.30am and dinner from 6–9pm, though in the larger cities there are restaurants taking orders into the small hours.

Embassies and Consulates

Australia: Embassy/consulate, Chemin de Fins 2, 1211 Geneva 19, tel: 022-799 9100.
Canada: Embassy/consulate, Kirchenfeldstrasse 88, 3005 Berne 6, tel: 031-357 3200; email: bern@dfait-maeci.gc.ca.
Consulate, Rue de l'Ariane 5, 1202 Geneva, tel. 022-919 9200.
UK: Embassy, Thunstrasse 50, 3005 Bern, tel: 031-359 7700.
Consular Section, tel: 031-359 7741; email: info@britishembassy.ch; www.britishembassy.ch.
British Consulate General, Avenue Louis Casal 58, Case Postale 6, 1216 Cointrin-Geneva, tel: 022-918 2400.
Vice-consulates: Zürich, temporarily closed, tel: 031-359 7700; Basel, tel: 061-483 0977; Montreux/Vevey, tel: 021-943 3263.
US: Embassy, Sulgeneckstrasse 19, CH-3007 Bern, tel: 031-357 7011;

Emergency (24 hours) 031-357 7011; www.bern.usembassy.gov; American Citizen Services, tel: 031-357 7234.

Festivals

There are numerous festivals throughout the year. For information and tickets contact Switzerland Tourism, tel: 00800-100 200 30 (from Switzerland and abroad) or visit www. myswitzerland.com or Swiss Ticket Corner, tel: 0900-800 800, www.ticketcorner.ch. Another good website is www.events.ch.

Jazz and folk music festivals are organised in Basel, Bern, Lugano, Nyon, Montreux, Willisau and Zürich. There are also regular rendezvous points for film and TV industries: the competition for the Rose d'Or in Luzern, international film festivals in Locarno, Nyon and Les Diablerets, and film and literature days in Solothurn. Among the biggest traditional festivals is Fasnacht in Basel, a 3-day Carnival that starts on the Monday after Ash Wednesday.

Gay and Lesbian Travellers

Attitudes among the Swiss towards homosexuality are open-minded and progressive. All cities have gay communities and areas where there are gay bars and entertainment venues. The age of consent for gay sex is 16, the same as for heterosexuals. A new law recognising same-sex unions came into effect in 2007. Switzerland's de facto gay capital is Zürich, which has a Gay Pride parade every July. There's a similar annual event in Geneva.

Health and Medical Care

All chemists have duty rota lists on their doors. Many doctors speak English and many hotels have house physicians. Doctor's fees and hospital costs are high. All hospitals have emergency wards with doctors on 24-hour duty. Every city and the larger villages have a number for an emergency doctor. This can be found in local newspapers or on the general information number 111, which can also give you the addresses and phone numbers of the nearest 24-hour pharmacies.

Language

Switzerland has four national languages. German is spoken in central and eastern Switzerland; French in the west; Italian in the southern part of the country; and

0.5 percent of the population speaks Romansch in southeastern Switzerland. People who work with visitors usually speak several languages, including English.

Nightlife

Disregard the rumour that nightlife in Switzerland is pretty provincial; in larger cities you'll find a wide variety of stylish bars and nightclubs. There is a rich musical life in Switzerland, with quite small places hosting internationally renowned soloists.

Opening Hours

Offices are open weekdays 8am–noon and 2–6pm, closed on Saturday. Shops are usually open 8am–12.30pm and 1.30–4pm. In larger cities they are also open during lunchtime. Shops are often closed Monday mornings, but they stay open until 9pm on Wednesday or Thursday. Bear in mind there are also local and regional differences.

In large cities, banks and bureaux de change open Mon–Fri 8.30am–4.30pm, closed Sat. In the countryside these hours are Mon–Fri 8.30am–noon and 2–4.30 or 5.30pm, closed Sat.

Postal Services

Post offices in large cities open Mon–Fri 7.30am–noon and 1.45–6.30pm, Sat until 11am. Stamps can be purchased at post offices, postcard kiosks and stamp machines. Post boxes are yellow and are often set into walls.

Public Holidays

January: 1 New Year's Day, 2 Berchtold's Day; **March/April**: variable Good Friday/Easter Monday; **May/June**: variable Ascension, Whit Monday; **August**: 1 National Day; **December**: 25 Christmas Day, 26 Boxing Day.

Shopping

If you're searching for something typical and of good quality, try one of the Schweizer Heimatwerk (Swiss Handicraft) shops, located in Zürich, Basel and Geneva.

Chocolates: Synonymous with Switzerland, chocolate has been made here since the early 19th century, the first factory opening in 1819. Relying on the milk that comes from mountain-pastured cows, the industry is dominated by Nestlé, Cailler, Lindt, Suchard and Tobler.

Cheese: Swiss cheeses are best known for their use in cooking, especially Gruyère and Emmental, but there are hundreds of small mountain producers making a variety of cheeses and charcuterie. Visits to them can often be arranged by local tourist offices.

Sausages: The sausage known as the *cervelat* (pronounced "servella") is the most common. It is made of beef, pork, ice water, salt, onions and spices and packed into the intestines of a zebu (a kind of ox) before being smoked and boiled.

Wines: Swiss wines are little known outside the country because production levels barely meet domestic demand. Most of the wines are produced in the Valais, Vaud and Ticino, some from the highest vineyards in Europe. Fruit schnapps are drunk as a *digestif*.

Telecommunications

Most telephones take phone cards, which are on sale in various denominations at post offices, newsagents and railway stations. For directory assistance, dial 113; international calls 114 or 191;

Emergency Numbers

Ambulance: 144
Police: 117
Fire brigade: 118
Breakdown service: 140

information (in English) 111. For calls made at hotels, substantial service charges are levied.

Dialling Codes

Bern 31; Basel 61; Geneva 22; Lausanne 21; Zürich 1. The code for Switzerland is 41.

Tipping

Officially in Switzerland all services are included in the price, but it is widespread practice to honour good service by tipping. In restaurants, the bill is normally rounded up for snacks, and 2 or 3 francs extra are usually added to the bill for a meal.

Tourist Information

Switzerland Tourism has offices and agencies abroad *(see below)*. Detailed tourist information in Switzerland may be obtained from the head office in Zürich (Tödistrasse 7, 8002 Zürich, tel: 044-288 1111; email: info.uk@ myswitzerland.com; www.myswitzerland.com).

For the addresses of local tourist offices throughout the country, tel: 120.

Tourist Offices Abroad

Swiss Tourist Office official website: www.myswitzerland.com. Order brochures online.
Australia: Switzerland Tourism, PO Box 695, CH-8027 Zürich, tel: 0041 43 210 5627; email: info@myswitzerland.com.
Canada: Switzerland Tourism, 926 The East Mall, CA-Toronto, Ontario M9B 6K1 (not open to public), tel: 800-794 7795 (free-phone); email: info.caen@myswitzerland.com.
UK: Switzerland Tourism, 30 Bedford Street, London WC2E 9ED, tel: 0800-1002 0030 (free-phone) or 020-7420 4900; email: info.uk@myswitzerland.com.
US: Switzerland Tourism, Swiss Center, 608 Fifth Avenue, New York, NY 10020, tel: international toll-free 011800-100-200-30; or US only 1-877-SWITZERLAND (1-877-794 8037); email: info.usa@myswitzerland.com.

What to Read

Insight Guide: Switzerland is a companion to this book, from Apa Publications' award-winning series.

BELOW: Swiss francs; Switzerland is the only country in this guide not to use euros.

ART AND PHOTO CREDITS

Alamy 75
akg-Images 35
A.P. Interpress 53
Art Archive 28B, 29T&BR, 30R, 33, 36, 37
AWL Images 8T, 11BR, 86/87, 88/89, 96/97, 123, 137, 195R, 200L, 206/207, 210, 222, 288&T, 291, 295T, 379
Bildarchiv Preussischer Kulturbesitz 51
Neil Buchan-Grant/APA 65L, 70R, 80L, 252/253, 285, 291T, 413, 417
Cité de l'Espace 127T
Corbis 9TR, 12B, 14/15, 31T, 55, 56, 74, 81, 94/95, 98, 114, 116, 124L, 128, 192R, 322/323, 332, 337, 347, 348&T, 350
Kevin Cummins/APA 18/19, 21, 91L
Nikos Daniilidis/Acropolis Museum 307
Jerry Dennis/APA 150
Jurjen Drenth/Images of Holland 172R
Annabel Elston/APA 106R, 107L, 108T, 109T, 148, 152T, 244T, 340T
Eye Ubiquitous/Rex Features 335
Fotolia 130T, 236, 356, 426
fotoLibra 6BL, 11T, 13B, 84/85, 90, 122, 125, 217, 218, 279, 281, 315T, 347T, 351
Ann Frank Stichting 166T
French Tourist Office 26/27
Guglielmo Galvin/APA 172T, 377T
G. Galvin & G. Taylor/APA 290T
Glyn Genin/APA 6CR, 7CL&BL, 12CL&R, 71L, 76, 78, 142, 143L&R, 151, 152, 153, 174/175, 176/177, 178, 185&T, 186L, 190, 192T, 195L, 197&T, 198, 199&T, 200T, 201, 202&T, 203R, 256, 283, 292T, 294, 295, 300, 333, 382, 395, 402, 404&T, 407
Getty Images 4T, 25, 57, 214, 344
Greg Gladman/APA 7CR, 11C, 22, 70L, 72, 154/155, 156/157, 158, 159, 162, 163, 166, 167, 171&T, 324/325, 327L&R, 341L, 342, 343, 357, 385, 419, 421, 428, 429, 432, 433
Frances Gransden/APA 268T, 274
Heidelberg Tourist Office/Loosen Foto 188
Images of Holland 172L, 173
iStockphoto.com 4B, 6/7T, 7BR, 8CRT, 9CL, 10C, 12T, 13T&C, 22B, 28R, 29BL, 30C, 31B, 36B, 43B, 48B, 91TR, 117, 118, 119L&R, 121, 126T, 129, 137T, 169, 170, 193, 194&T, 196, 208/209, 211L&R, 217T, 238, 254/255, 265, 266L, 276, 277, 281T, 286, 287L&R, 289,

292, 293&T, 312, 326, 334T, 352L, 360/361, 365L&R, 424, 437
Wadey James/APA 9CR
Britta Jaschinski/APA 3B, 5, 7TR, 8CRB, 9TL&BR, 10TR, 11BL, 16/17, 20, 62/63, 67, 68, 73L&R, 80R, 226/227, 228/229, 230, 231, 237, 239, 240(all), 241&T, 244, 245, 246&T, 249&T, 257L&R, 262, 263, 264&T, 266R&T, 267T, 268L&R, 269, 270, 271L&R, 273, 275, 289T, 298/299, 301, 310, 311, 313, 317&T, 318&T, 319&T, 380, 388, 391, 408, 414, 418
Jochen Keute/GNTO 200R
Robin Laurence/APA 203L&T
Julian Love/APA 69, 146, 392
Museu Nacional de Arte Atiga 40
Museum of Cycladic Art 32
Magnum Photos 54
Ilpo Musto/APA 6C, 10CL, 65R, 68B, 99L&R, 104, 105, 106L, 107R&T, 108, 109, 110, 111&T, 112, 113, 396, 398
Daniella Nowitz/APA 296/297, 305, 308R, 309L&R
Richard Nowitz/APA 24, 91BR, 304, 308L, 312T, 387
Christine Osborne 168
PA Images 60/61
Parc du Futuroscope 122T
Alexander Van Phillips/APA 121T, 147
Photo Bibiotheque Nationale 45, 119T
Photolibrary 355
Pictures Colour Library 2/3, 8CL&B, 10B, 23, 66, 115, 124R, 125T, 126, 127, 131, 140/141, 165, 215, 216, 224, 225, 267, 272, 280, 282, 286T, 336, 352R&T, 353, 371, 372, 373, 374, 375, 376, 377, 378
Andrea Pistolesi 335T, 362/363, 364, 368
Sylvaine Poitau/APA 77, 129T, 133&T, 134, 135, 136T, 383, 397, 401
Prof saxx 123T
Mark Read/APA 190T, 191, 192L, 354, 356T, 374T
Salzburg Tourist Office 248L
Jon Santa Cruz/APA 64, 179L&R, 182, 183, 186R&T, 187, 189, 334, 403, 406
Scala Archives 28T, 34, 41, 44, 46, 47
Jeroen Snijders/APA 118T, 349
Jon Spall/APA 243, 247, 248T
Superstock 6BR
Swissimage 219&T, 220, 221, 434
Jochen Tack/Images of Holland 170T

George Taylor/APA 135T, 136
Topfoto 39L&R, 50
The Travel Library/Rex Features 346
Bill Wassman 216T, 242
Bill Wassman/APA 131T, 132&T, 134T, 218T, 220T, 223, 224T, 306, 308T, 345
Roger Williams 341R, 350T
Phil Wood/APA 196T, 314, 370
Gregory Wrona/APA 79, 316, 339, 340, 431

PHOTO FEATURES

58/59: Kevin Cummins/APA 59TR; fotoLibra 59BR; iStockphoto.com 58CR&BR, 59CL; Ilpo Musto/APA 58BL; Richard Nowitz/APA 58TL; Photolibrary 58/59

82/83: AISA 82BL; Glyn Genin/APA 83BR; Orient Express 83C; Photolibrary 82CR; RhB 82/83, 82BR; TIPS 83BL; VFE 83TR

138/139: akg-images 138BL; Kevin Cummins/APA 139BL; Glyn Genin/APA 139BR; FMGB Guggenheim Bilbao Museoa 139CL; Photolibrary 138/139; Rijksmuseum 138BR; Jon Santa Cruz/APA 139TR

204/205: Alamy 204TL; Neil Buchan-Grant/APA 204/205; iStockphoto.com 204BR; Keystone/Photopress 204CR; Scala Archives 204BL, 205TR&BR; Volkswagen AG 205BL

250/251: Corbis 250/251, 251TR; Getty Images 250BR, 251BL, C&BR; Elma Okic/Rex Features 250BL

320/321: Alamy 321BL; FLPA 320C&BL, 321C; NPL 321BR; Still Pictures 320/321, 320BR, 321TR

358/359: Alamy 358BR, 359TR; Fotolia 358BL; Getty Images 359BR; Britta Jaschinski/APA 359CL; Sylvaine Poitau/APA 358CR; Still Pictures 358/359

Map Production:
Keith Brook and Mike Adams

© 2010 Apa Publications GmbH & Co.
Verlag KG (Singapore branch)

Production: Linton Donaldson

INDEX

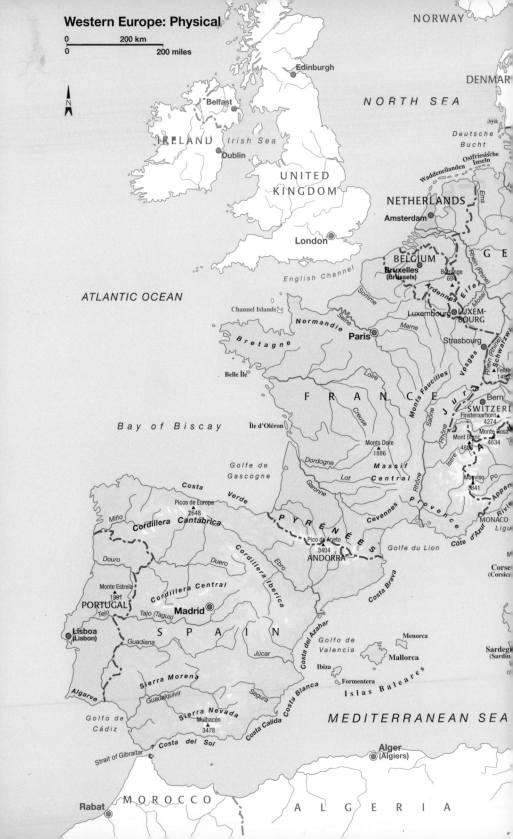

Western Europe: Physical

0   200 km
0   200 miles

N

NORWAY

DENMAR

NORTH SEA

Deutsche
Bucht

3ylt

Edinburgh

Belfast

IRELAND   Irish Sea

Dublin

UNITED
KINGDOM

NETHERLANDS

Amsterdam

Ostfriesische
Inseln

Waddeneilanden

Ems

G E

BELGIUM

Bruxelles
(Brussels)

Botrange
694

Ardennes

Eifel

Rhein (Rhine)

LUXEM-
BOURG

Luxembourg

Mosel

ATLANTIC OCEAN

English Channel

Channel Islands

Normandie

Bretagne

Seine

Somme

Paris

Marne

Strasbourg

Monts Faucilles

Vosges

Rhein (Rhine)

Schwarzw

Feldb
1493

Belle Île

F R A N C E

Loire

Creuse

Monts Dore
1886

Saône

Rhône

Jura

Isère

Bern

SWITZERL

Finsteraarhorn
4274

Monte Rosa
4634

Mont Blanc
4808

Bay of Biscay

Île d'Oléron

Dordogne

Golfe de
Gascogne

Garonne

Lot

M a s s i f

C e n t r a l

Rhône

Provence

Côte d'Azur

MONACO

Monviso
3841

Appen

Rivi

Ligu

Costa
Verde

Picos de Europa
2648

Cordillera Cantábrica

Miño

Cordillera

P Y R É N É E S

Pico de Aneto
3404

ANDORRA

Cevennes

Golfe du Lion

Costa Brava

Corse
(Corsica

Douro

Duero

Ebro

Cordillera Ibérica

Monte Estrela
1991

Cordillera Central

PORTUGAL

Tejo

Tajo (Tagus)

Madrid

Lisboa
(Lisbon)

S   P   A   I   N

Guadiana

Júcar

Costa del Azahar

Golfo de
Valencia

Menorca

Mallorca

Sardeg
(Sardi

Ibiza

Formentera

Islas Baleares

Algarve

Sierra Morena

Guadalquivir

Segura

Sierra Nevada

Mulhacén
3478

Costa Calida

Costa Blanca

MEDITERRANEAN SEA

Golfo de
Cádiz

Costa del Sol

Strait of Gibraltar

Alger
(Algiers)

Rabat

M O R O C C O

A L G E R I A